Georgia

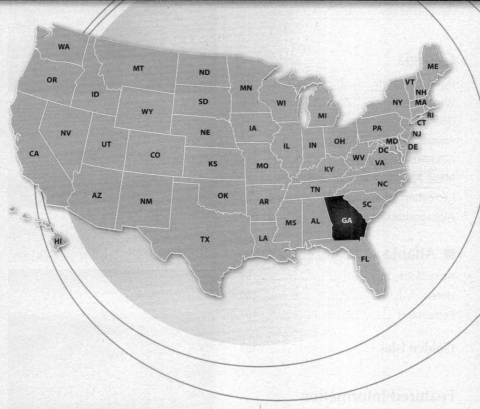

Published by AAA Publishing
1000 AAA Drive, Heathrow, FL 32746-5063
Copyright AAA 2016, All rights reserved

The publisher has made every effort to provide accurate, up-to-date information but accepts no responsibility for loss or injury sustained by any person using this book. TourBook® guides are published for the exclusive use of AAA members. Not for sale.

Advertising Rate and Circulation Information: (407) 444-8280

Printed in the USA by Quad/Graphics

This book is printed on paper certified by third-party standards for sustainably managed forestry and production.

Printed on recyclable paper.
Please recycle whenever possible.

Stock #4666

CONTENTS

Attractions, hotels, restaurants and other travel experience information are all grouped under the alphabetical listing of the city in which those experiences are physically located—or the nearest recognized city.

Georgia

■ Atlanta 43-135

Golden Isles 187

Featured Information

To view these helpful tools, visit tdr.aaa.com/tb/4666/

- Using Your Guide & Just For Members
- Metric Equivalents Chart
- Driving Distances Map
- Points of Interest Index

Dream.
Plan.
Go.

Picture yourself …
- At your ideal destination
- In a comfortable hotel
- Eating your favorite meals
- Exploring the sights

Turn your dreams into reality
with **TripTik® Travel Planner**.

Online: AAA.com/ttp | On the go: AAA or CAA Mobile app

explore

The card that gets you there™

Get the credit card that lets you earn **3x points** on qualifying AAA and travel purchases, **2x points** on gas, grocery store and drugstore purchases, and **1 point** per **$1** on all other purchases.*

Planning to explore the new world, or just visit your old stomping grounds? It's easier than ever to get there with a AAA Member Rewards Visa® credit card.

To apply for an account, visit a participating AAA branch or AAA.com/creditcard.

Using Your Guide

AAA TourBook guides are packed with travel insight, maps and listings of AAA Approved places to play, stay and eat. To unpack the details, revisit this section as you plan and explore.

A to Z City Listings

Cities and places are listed alphabetically within each state or province. Attractions, hotels and restaurants are listed once — under the city in which they are physically located.

Cities that are considered part of a larger destination city or area have an expanded city header. The header identifies the larger region and cross-references pages that contain shared trip planning resources:

- Destination map – outline map of the cities that comprise a destination city or area
- Attraction spotting map – regional street map marked with attraction locations
- Hotel/restaurant spotting map and index – regional street map numbered with hotel and restaurant locations identified in an accompanying index

Cities that are not considered part of a larger destination city or area but have a significant number of listings may have these resources within the individual city section:

- Attraction spotting map
- Hotel/restaurant spotting map and index

Location Abbreviations

Directions are from the center of town unless otherwise specified, using these highway abbreviations:

Bus. Rte.=business route

CR=county road

FM=farm to market

FR=forest road

Hwy.=Canadian highway

I=interstate highway

LR=legislative route

R.R.=rural route

SR/PR=state or provincial route

US=federal highway

About Listed Establishments

AAA/CAA Approved hotels and restaurants are listed on the basis of merit alone after careful evaluation and approval by full-time, professionally trained AAA/CAA inspectors. An establishment's decision to advertise in the TourBook guide has no bearing on its evaluation or rating; nor does inclusion of advertising imply AAA endorsement of products and services.

Information in this guide was believed accurate at the time of publication. However, since changes inevitably occur between annual editions, please contact your AAA travel professional, visit AAA.com or download the free AAA mobile app to confirm prices and schedules.

Attraction Listing Icons

[SAVE] AAA Discounts & Rewards® member discount

[EV] Electric vehicle charging station on premises. Domestic station information provided by the U.S. Department of Energy. Canadian station information provided by Plug'n Drive Ontario.

[GT] Guided Tours available

[A] Camping facilities

[TT] Food on premises

[X] Recreational activities

[T] Pets on leash allowed

[A] Picnicking allowed

In select cities only:

[M] Mass transit station within 1 mile. Icon is followed by station name and AAA/CAA designated station number within listing.

[GEM] AAA/CAA travel experts may designate an attraction of exceptional interest and quality as a AAA GEM — a *Great Experience for Members®. See GEM Attraction Index (listed on CONTENTS page) for a complete list of locations.*

Consult the online travel guides at AAA.com or visit AAA Mobile for additional things to do if you have time.

Hotel Listing Icons

(May be preceded by CALL and/or SOME UNITS.)

[SAVE] Member rates: discounted standard room rate or lowest public rate available at time of booking for dates of stay.

[ECO] Eco-certified by government or private organization.

[EV] Electric vehicle charging station on premises. Domestic station information provided by the U.S. Department of

Energy. Canadian station information provided by Plug'n Drive Ontario.

[X] Smoke-free premises

In select cities only:

[⊞] Mass transit station within 1 mile. Icon is followed by station name and AAA/CAA designated station number within listing.

Services:

[✦] Airport transportation

[⊭] Pets allowed (Call property for restrictions.)

[S⊭] Pets allowed (Call property for restrictions and fees.)

[⫙] Restaurant on premises

[⫙→] Restaurant off premises

[⫚] Room service for 2 or more meals

[⊉] Full bar

[⫟] Child care

[BIZ] Business area

[&M] Accessible features (Call property for available services and amenities.)

Activities:

[⊛] Full-service casino

[⊐] Pool

[⊮] Health club on premises

In-Room Amenities:

[HS] High-speed Internet service

[sHS] High-speed Internet service (Call property for fees.)

[⊚] Wireless Internet service

[S⊚] Wireless Internet service (Call property for fees.)

[⊘] No wireless Internet service

[⊠] Pay movies

[◨] Refrigerator

[▣] Microwave

[▦] Coffee maker

[⊠] No air conditioning

[⊠] No TV

[⊠] No telephones

Restaurant Listing Icons

[SAVE] AAA Discounts & Rewards® member discount

[ECO] Eco-certified by government or private organization.

[⊞] Electric vehicle charging station on premises. Domestic station information provided by the U.S. Department of Energy. Canadian station information provided by Plug'n Drive Ontario.

[⊠] No air conditioning

[&M] Accessible features (Call property for available services and amenities.)

[◥] Designated smoking section

[B] Breakfast

[L] Lunch

[D] Dinner

[24] Open 24 hours

[LATE] Open after 11 p.m.

[⊭] Pet-friendly (Call property for restrictions.)

In select cities only:

[⊞] Mass transit station within 1 mile. Icon is followed by station name and AAA/CAA designated station number within listing.

Map Legend

For attraction and hotel/ restaurant spotting maps, refer to the legend below to identify symbols and color coding.

Roads/Highways

- Interchange
- Controlled access
- Controlled access toll
- Local toll
- Primary
- Secondary
- Local unpaved
- Under construction
- Tunnel
- Pedestrian only
- Auto ferry
- Passenger ferry
- Scenic byway

Areas of Interest

- Incorporated city
- ✈ Int'l/Regional airport
- Park
- Recreation sites
- Forest
- Natural lands
- Military
- Historic
- Native American
- Beach
- Marsh

Route Shields

	Primary	Secondary	
Interstate	95	95 Business	Trans-Canada
Federal	Primary 22	Secondary 22	Provincial Autoroute
State	1	1	Mexico
County	1	1	Historic

	Primary	Secondary
Trans-Canada	❂	❂
Provincial Autoroute	22	22
Mexico	1	1
Historic	66	

Boundaries

- International
- State
- ⊣ ⊣ ⊣ Time zone
- › › › › › › Continental Divide

Points of Interest

★	National capital	o	Town
✪	State/Prov capital	⋏	Campground
■	AAA/CAA club location	⚑	Winery
■	Feature of interest	⊛	Customs station
⬥	GEM attraction	■	Historic
⑫	Hotel listing	△	Mountain peak
③	Restaurant listing		Rapid transit
⬟	College/University	Stations	Metromover

Understanding the Diamond Ratings

Hotel and restaurant evaluations are unscheduled to ensure our professionally trained inspectors encounter the same experience members do.

- When an establishment is Diamond Rated, it means members can expect a good fit with their needs. The inspector assigns a rating that indicates the type of experience to expect.
- While establishments at high levels must offer increasingly complex personalized services, establishments at every level are subject to the same basic requirements for cleanliness, comfort and hospitality. Learn more at AAA.com/Diamonds.

Red Diamonds mark establishments that participate in the AAA/CAA logo licensing program for increased visibility to members.

Black Diamonds identify all other AAA/CAA Approved and Diamond Rated establishments.

Hotels	Restaurants
Budget-oriented, offering basic comfort and hospitality.	Simple, economical food, often quick-serve, in a functional environment.
Affordable, with modestly enhanced facilities, décor and amenities.	Familiar food, often cooked to order, served in casual surroundings.
Distinguished, multifaceted with enhanced physical attributes, amenities and guest comforts.	Trendy cuisine, skillfully prepared and served, with expanded beverage options, in an enhanced setting.

Refined, stylish with upscale physical attributes, extensive amenities and high degree of hospitality, service and attention to detail.	Distinctive fine-dining. Creative preparations, skillfully served, often with wine steward, amid upscale ambience.

Ultimate luxury, sophistication and comfort with extraordinary physical attributes, meticulous personalized service, extensive amenities and impeccable standards of excellence.	Leading-edge cuisine of the finest ingredients, uniquely prepared by an acclaimed chef, served by expert service staff led by maître d' in extraordinary surroundings.

Guest Safety

Inspectors view a sampling of rooms during evaluations and, therefore, AAA/CAA cannot guarantee the presence of working locks and operational fire safety equipment in every guest unit.

Contacting AAA/CAA About Approved Properties

If your visit to a AAA/CAA Approved attraction, hotel or restaurant doesn't meet your expectations, please tell us about it — **during your visit or within 30 days**. Be sure to save your receipts and other documentation for reference.

Use the easy online form at AAA.com/TourBookComments to send us the details.

Alternatively, you can email your comments to: memberrelations@national.aaa.com or submit them via postal mail to: AAA Member Comments, 1000 AAA Dr., Box 61, Heathrow, FL 32746.

View from Brasstown Bald

Georgia

Georgia is all about contrast. The 4,784-foot summit of Brasstown Bald and sandy, sea-level beaches. The fresh spray from a plunging waterfall and Cumberland Island National Seashore's salty tang. A stirring performance by the Atlanta Symphony Orchestra or a sunrise concert of warbling birds—and perhaps a bellowing gator—in an Okefenokee swamp.

A quartz representation of a spread-winged eagle near Eatonton, an estimated 2,000 to 4,000 years old, is one of the state's more mysterious Native American mounds, a New World version of Stonehenge. Within the gleaming chrome and glass buildings of Atlanta's CNN Center, meanwhile, breaking news and the twitterings of the celebrity blogosphere are cutting-edge 21st century.

Even American history trivia buffs might not know where the first U.S. gold rush took place. Hint: It's not California. The 1828 strike at Dahlonega was so great that 10

Cumberland Island

years later a federal mint was opened. Building materials from the region still contain traces of gold, and even today gold nuggets wash up in Atlanta water-treatment plants after very heavy rains.

A treasure trove awaits scholars of military history. Georgia provided troops for and was the site of battlefields during the Revolution and the Civil War. The most infamous is the prisoner-of-war camp at Andersonville, where thousands died of diseases resulting from overcrowding and malnutrition.

On a much lighter note, the civility and warm hospitality one expects in both the Old and the New South flourishes in the Peach State. "Sir" and "ma'am" make regular appearances in conversation, and merchants have been known not to ask for identification when cashing a check. Georgia is at once thoroughly sophisticated and as comfortable as an old shoe.

If reading the book or seeing the movie whets your appetite for grand, "Gone with the Wind"-style antebellum mansions built when cotton was king, you won't be disappointed. Many splendid old Georgia homes have been painstakingly restored, opulently refurnished and are open to the public.

Architectural Digest called Savannah's 1819, English Regency-style Owens-Thomas House "the most beautiful home in America." Among its delights is the pink drawing room, with a rectangular ceiling that nevertheless lends the impression of a circular room. Elegant mansions weren't the only buildings on cotton plantations, however. The overseer's house and slave cabins at Historic Square in Stone Mountain Park are reminders of how the other nine-tenths lived.

Sherman's Georgia

The distance between Atlanta and Savannah is some 250 miles and more than a century. Atlanta was still young when Gen. William Tecumseh Sherman's troops put the town to the torch toward the end of the War Between the States. Savannah had already accumulated more than 125 years of tradition, and was spared. The Union general's decision determined the futures of the state's two major cities.

Savannah continued along an already well-trodden path, and today the city's abundant charms are still displayed with a sense of grande dame decorum—even in "Midnight in the Garden of Good and Evil," based on a lurid true-crime story and featuring a number of eccentric local personalities. The book and subsequent movie adaptation boosted Savannah's profile and brought in a new wave of visitors.

Preservation of the past is big here; all but two of the stately squares laid out by city founder Gen. James E. Oglethorpe still survive, shaded by live oaks and lined with lovingly renovated town houses. Savannah's mix of old-fashioned tradition and contemporary verve is epitomized by restaurateur and celebrity chef perennial Paula Deen.

Atlanta, meanwhile, rebuilt from the ground up, becoming a financial and cultural mecca and eventually a late 20th-century symbol of the contemporary South. More than 5 million people live in the greater metropolitan area, and the city has three separate skylines: downtown, Midtown and Buckhead. Atlanta boasts a World Series-winning baseball team and a world-class aquarium, and its corporate headquarters include such worldwide enterprises as Coca-Cola and CNN.

Recreation

Many a golfing vacation that starts out in Florida and doglegs its way up the Eastern seaboard to Virginia putts out in Georgia. The rolling hills of the 18-hole course at Victoria Bryant State Park, just north of Franklin Springs, make it both challenging and aesthetically pleasing. Two stocked fishing ponds, a swimming pool and 8 miles of hiking and biking trails are other park diversions.

Georgia Veterans Memorial State Park, on US 280 near Cordele, woos non-golfers with boating, swimming, water skiing, an indoor and outdoor military museum, and fishing for bass, crappie, catfish and bream on 8,600-acre Lake Blackshear. Two hiking trails—the 1-mile Yucca Trace Trail and the half-mile Lake Shore Trail—offer leisurely walks with a backdrop of bald cypresses, loblolly pines and other native trees and plants, and provide opportunities to spot such resident wildlife as fox squirrels, beavers, great blue herons and the elusive American alligator.

A labyrinth of coastal channels and the surf off the beaches of the Sea Islands offer excellent saltwater fishing. Freshwater fishing enthusiasts will find plenty of bass, bream, shad and catfish in Georgia's rivers and marshlands. Or paddle a canoe amid quiet, scenic surroundings at the Chattahoochee River National Recreation Area or on the more untamed Chattooga National Wild and Scenic River, which winds through the Chattahoochee-Oconee National Forest along the Georgia/South Carolina border.

Atlanta skyline

Historic Timeline

1540	Hernando de Soto's expedition party of soldiers and priests explores what is now the southeastern United States.
1788	On Jan. 2, Georgia becomes the fourth state.
1838	Cherokee Native Americans are forced to leave their tribal lands and resettle in territorial Oklahoma via the "Trail of Tears."
1863	Gen. William Tecumseh Sherman's Union troops loot and burn Atlanta on their "March to the Sea."
1961	Georgia becomes the first state in the Deep South to integrate its public school system without major disruption.
1963	Atlanta native Martin Luther King Jr. delivers his "I Have a Dream" speech in Washington, D.C.
1972	Civil rights activist Andrew Young becomes the first state African-American elected to U.S. Congress since Reconstruction.
1980	CNN begins broadcasting in Atlanta.
1996	Atlanta hosts the Summer Olympic Games.
2002	Former President and Plains native Jimmy Carter receives the Nobel Peace Prize.
2003	George "Sonny" Perdue becomes Georgia's first Republican governor in 130 years.

What To Pack

Temperature Averages Maximum/Minimum	JANUARY	FEBRUARY	MARCH	APRIL	MAY	JUNE	JULY	AUGUST	SEPTEMBER	OCTOBER	NOVEMBER	DECEMBER
Albany	60 / 35	65 / 38	72 / 45	78 / 50	85 / 59	90 / 67	93 / 70	92 / 70	88 / 65	80 / 52	71 / 44	63 / 38
Atlanta	52 / 33	57 / 37	65 / 44	73 / 50	80 / 59	87 / 67	89 / 71	88 / 70	82 / 64	73 / 53	63 / 44	55 / 36
Augusta	56 / 33	61 / 36	69 / 43	77 / 48	84 / 57	90 / 65	92 / 70	90 / 68	85 / 62	76 / 50	68 / 41	59 / 35
Columbus	57 / 37	62 / 39	69 / 46	77 / 52	83 / 61	90 / 69	92 / 72	91 / 71	86 / 66	77 / 55	68 / 46	59 / 39
Savannah	60 / 38	64 / 41	71 / 47	78 / 53	84 / 61	90 / 68	92 / 72	90 / 71	86 / 67	78 / 56	71 / 47	63 / 40
Toccoa	51 / 31	56 / 33	64 / 40	72 / 47	79 / 55	85 / 63	88 / 68	87 / 67	82 / 62	72 / 50	63 / 42	54 / 34

From the records of The Weather Channel Interactive, Inc.

Good Facts To Know

ABOUT THE STATE

POPULATION: 9,687,653.

AREA: 59,425 square miles; ranks 24th.

CAPITAL: Atlanta.

HIGHEST POINT: 4,784 ft., Brasstown Bald.

LOWEST POINT: Sea level, Atlantic Ocean.

TIME ZONE(S): Eastern. DST.

REGULATIONS

TEEN DRIVING LAWS: No passengers (parent/guardian exempt) are permitted for the first six months. No more than one passenger under age 21 for the second six months. After the second six months, no more than three passengers under ages 21 (family members exempt). Driving is not permitted midnight-5 a.m. The minimum age for unrestricted driver's license is 18. Phone (678) 413-8400 for more information about Georgia driver's license regulations.

SEAT BELT/CHILD RESTRAINT LAWS: Seat belts are required for driver, front-seat passengers and children ages 8-17. Child restraints are required for children under age 8 and less than 57 inches tall; must sit in the rear seat if available. AAA recommends the use of seat belts and appropriate child restraints for the driver and all passengers.

CELLPHONE RESTRICTIONS: Text messaging is prohibited for all drivers. Instruction permit or Class D license holders under age 18 are prohibited from using any kind of wireless telecommunications device while driving. Handheld cellphone use by commercial drivers is also banned.

HELMETS FOR MOTORCYCLISTS: Required for all riders.

RADAR DETECTORS: Permitted. Prohibited for use by commercial vehicles.

MOVE OVER LAW: Driver is required to slow down and vacate the lane nearest stopped police, fire, rescue and tow truck/recovery vehicles using audible or flashing signals.

FIREARMS LAWS: Vary by state and/or county. Contact the State Attorney General's Office, 40 Capitol Sq., Atlanta, GA 30334-1300; phone (404) 656-3300.

HOLIDAYS

HOLIDAYS: Jan. 1 ▪ Martin Luther King Jr. Day, Jan. (third Mon.) ▪ State Holiday, Apr. 25 ▪ Memorial Day, May (last Mon.) ▪ July 4 ▪ Labor Day, Sept. (1st Mon.) ▪ Columbus Day, Oct. (2nd Mon.) ▪ Veterans Day, Nov. 11 ▪ State Holiday, Nov. 25 ▪ Thanksgiving ▪ Christmas, (observed Mon. Dec. 26) ▪ State Holiday, Dec. 27.

MONEY

TAXES: The statewide sales tax is 4 percent. Depending on local municipalities, the local tax rate can be as high as 8 percent.

VISITOR INFORMATION

INFORMATION CENTERS: State information centers are near Augusta, Columbus, Kingsland, Lavonia, Ringgold, Savannah, Tallapoosa, Valdosta and West Point. Open daily 8:30-5:30.

FURTHER INFORMATION FOR VISITORS:
Georgia Department of Economic Development—
Tourism Division
75 Fifth St. N.W., Suite 1200
Atlanta, GA 30308
(404) 962-4000
(800) 847-4842

NATIONAL FOREST INFORMATION:
U.S. Forest Service
Chattahoochee-Oconee National Forest
1755 Cleveland Hwy.
Gainesville, GA 30501
(770) 297-3000
(877) 444-6777 (reservations)

FISHING AND HUNTING REGULATIONS:
Department of Natural Resources
Wildlife Resources Division
2070 US 278 S.E.
Social Circle, GA 30025
(770) 918-6406 (fisheries)
(770) 918-6404 (game management)
(800) 366-2661

RECREATION INFORMATION:
Department of Natural Resources
Division of Parks, Recreation and Historic Sites
#2 Martin Luther King Jr. Dr., Suite 1252 East Tower
Atlanta, GA 30334
(770) 389-7270
(800) 864-7275 (reservations)

Get maps, travel information and road service with the AAA and CAA Mobile apps

Georgia Annual Events

Please call ahead to confirm event details.

JANUARY

- Martin Luther King Jr. Parade / Moultrie
  229-985-1974
- Atlanta Boat Show / Atlanta
  954-441-3220
- Augusta Futurity and Festival / Augusta
  706-823-3417

FEBRUARY

- Savannah Irish Festival
  Savannah
  912-665-2557
- Georgia National Junior Livestock Show and Georgia National Rodeo
  Perry
  478-987-3247
- Fireside Art and Craft Show
  Helen
  706-878-2201

MARCH

- Atlanta International Auto Show / Atlanta
  770-916-1741
- Savannah Tour of Homes and Gardens / Savannah
  912-234-8054
- St. Patrick's Day Celebration on the River
  Savannah
  912-234-0295

APRIL

- Rose Show and Festival
  Thomasville
  229-228-7977
- The Masters Tournament
  Augusta
  706-667-6000
- Dogwood Festival / Atlanta
  404-817-6642

MAY

- Savannah Scottish Games Festival / Savannah
  912-233-6017
- The Georgia Renaissance Festival / Fairburn
  770-964-8575
- Sweet Auburn Springfest
  Atlanta
  678-683-5647

JUNE

- Helen to the Atlantic Hot Air Balloon Race and Festival / Helen
  706-878-2271
- Georgia Blueberry Festival
  Alma
  912-310-7399
- AthFest / Athens
  404-881-8891

JULY

- Homespun Festival
  Rockmart
  770-684-8760
- 4th of July Celebration
  Dahlonega
  706-864-3711
- Georgia Mountain Fair
  Hiawassee
  706-896-4191

AUGUST

- Dillard Bluegrass and Barbeque Festival / Dillard
  706-746-9936
- Atlanta Underground Film Festival / Atlanta
  404-969-5217
- Folk Fest / Norcross
  770-532-1115

SEPTEMBER

- Labor Day Weekend Catfish Festival / Kingsland
  912-729-5999
- Yellow Daisy Festival
  Stone Mountain
  770-498-5690
- JapanFest / Duluth
  404-842-0736

OCTOBER

- Georgia National Fair
  Perry
  478-987-3247
- Stone Mountain Highland Games / Stone Mountain
  770-521-0228
- Oktoberfest / Helen
  706-878-1619

NOVEMBER

- Callaway's Fantasy in Lights
  Pine Mountain
  800-225-5292
- Indian Festival and Pow-Wow / Stone Mountain
  770-498-5690
- Lanier Islands Magical Nights of Lights / Buford
  678-318-2087

DECEMBER

- Victorian Christmas Festival / Thomasville
  229-227-7020
- Christmas in Roswell
  Roswell
  770-640-3253
- Marietta Pilgrimage Christmas Home Tour
  Marietta
  770-426-4982

Wild horse at Cumberland Island National Seashore

Savannah

Peaches

Jekyll Island Historic Landmark District Tour

Stone Mountain

Index: Great Experience for Members

AAA editor's picks of exceptional note

Fort Pulaski National
Monument

Martin Luther King Jr.
National Historic Site

Jekyll Island Historic
Landmark District
Tour

Stone Mountain

See Orientation map on p. 22 for corresponding grid coordinates, if applicable.
*Indicates the GEM is temporarily closed.

Turn your road trip dreams into reality

with the TripTik® Travel Planner

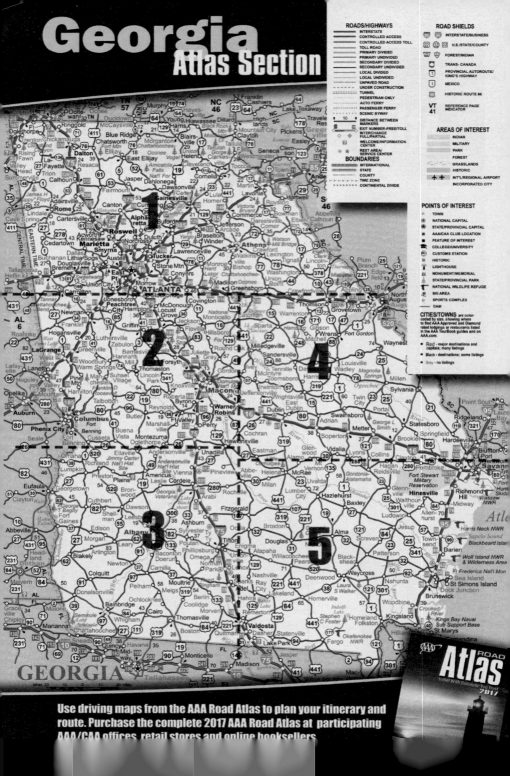

Georgia
Atlas Section

Use driving maps from the AAA Road Atlas to plan your itinerary and route. Purchase the complete 2017 AAA Road Atlas at participating AAA/CAA offices, retail stores and online booksellers.

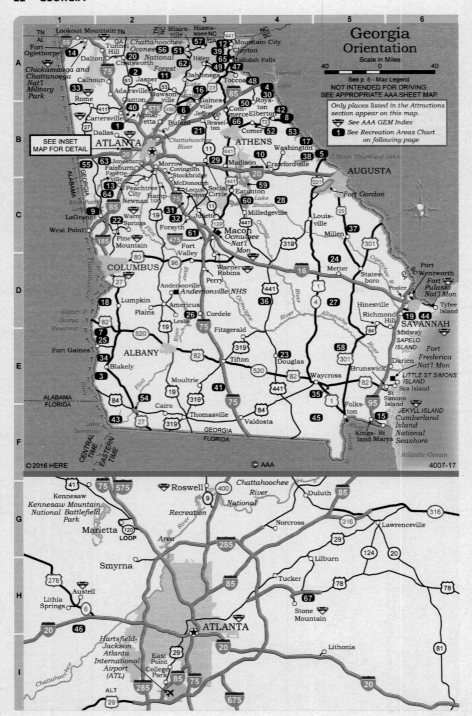

Georgia Orientation

Scale in Miles

See p. 6 - Map Legend
NOT INTENDED FOR DRIVING.
SEE APPROPRIATE AAA SHEET MAP.

Only places listed in the Attractions section appear on this map.

See AAA GEM Index

See Recreation Areas Chart on following page

©2016 HERE

© AAA

4007-17

Recreation Areas Chart

The map location numerals in column 2 show an
area's location on the preceding map.

	MAP LOCATION	CAMPING	PICNICKING	HIKING TRAILS	BOATING	BOAT RAMP	BOAT RENTAL	FISHING	SWIMMING	PETS ON LEASH	BICYCLE TRAILS	NATURE PROGS.	VISITOR CENTER	LODGE/CABINS	FOOD SERVICE
NATIONAL FORESTS *(See place listings.)*															
Chattahoochee and Oconee (A-2) 865,670 acres. Central and northern Georgia.		•	•	•	•	•	•	•	•	•	•		•		•
NATIONAL RECREATION AREA *(See place listings.)*															
Chattahoochee River (G-4) 7,587 acres n. of Atlanta.			•	•	•	•	•	•	•	•	•		•		•
NATIONAL SEASHORE *(See place listings.)*															
Cumberland Island (F-6) 36,415 acres 8 mi. e. of St. Marys. Bird-watching, wildlife viewing; bicycle rental.		•	•	•	•			•	•		•		•	•	•
ARMY CORPS OF ENGINEERS															
Allatoona Lake (B-2) 25,806 acres 6 mi. s.e. of Cartersville off I-75. Historic. Water skiing; playground.	❶	•	•	•	•	•	•	•	•	•	•		•		•
Carters Lake (A-2) 3,442 acres 34 mi. n. of Cartersville off US 411 to Old US 411. Water skiing; marina, playground.	❷	•	•	•	•	•	•	•	•	•	•		•		•
George W. Andrews Lake (E-2) 1,540 acres 1 mi. e. of Columbia, Ala., on the state line.	❸	•	•		•	•		•	•		•				
Hartwell Lake (A-4) 56,000 acres 6 mi. n. of Hartwell on US 29. Water skiing; bicycle trail.	❹	•	•	•	•	•	•	•	•	•	•		•		•
J. Strom Thurmond Lake (B-5) 70,000 acres 20 mi. n.w. of Augusta on SR 28.	❺	•	•	•	•	•	•	•	•	•	•		•		•
Lake Sidney Lanier (B-3) 39,000 acres. Geocaching, golf (18 holes), horseback riding, tennis, water skiing; amphitheater, beach, miniature golf, waterslide, wave pool.	❻	•	•	•	•	•	•	•	•	•	•	•	•	•	•
Lake Walter F. George (E-2) 46,000 acres 2 mi. n. of Fort Gaines off SR 39. Water skiing; playground.	❼	•	•	•	•	•	•	•	•	•			•		•
Richard B. Russell Lake (B-4) 26,500 acres 20 mi. e. of Elberton on SR 72.	❽	•	•	•	•	•	•	•	•	•	•		•		•
West Point Lake (C-1) 25,900 acres on the Alabama state line at West Point. Amphitheater, playground.	❾	•	•	•	•	•	•	•	•	•	•		•		•
STATE															
A.H. Stephens State Park (B-4) 1,177 acres at Crawfordville on US 278 and SR 22. Historic. Equestrian camping, geocaching, volleyball; bicycle, canoe and pedal boat rentals, equestrian trails, museum, playground. Electric boat motors only. *(See Crawfordville p. 168.)*	❿	•	•	•	•	•	•	•	•	•	•	•	•		•
Amicalola Falls (A-2) 829 acres 15 mi. w. of Dahlonega on SR 52 near jct. with SR 183. Scenic. Geocaching; playground, waterfalls. *(See Dawsonville p. 172.)*	⓫	•	•						•		•		•	•	•
Black Rock Mountain (A-3) 1,743 acres 3 mi. n. of Clayton via US 23/441. Scenic. Canoeing, geocaching, kayaking; playground.	⓬	•	•	•	•				•		•		•		
Chattahoochee Bend (C-2) 2,910 acres 17 mi. w. of Newnan off SR 34. Canoeing, geocaching, kayaking; observation tower, playground.	⓭	•	•	•	•	•		•		•			•	•	
Cloudland Canyon (A-1) 3,488 acres 25 mi. n.w. of La Fayette off SR 136. Scenic. Disc golf, geocaching, tennis; bicycle rental, observation tower, playground. Yurts available.	⓮	•	•	•						•	•	•	•	•	•
Crooked River (F-5) 500 acres 12 mi. e. of Kingsland via SR 40. Bird-watching, geocaching; bicycle rental, kayak trails, miniature golf, nature center.	⓯	•	•	•	•	•	•	•		•	•	•	•	•	•
Don Carter (A-3) 1,316 acres 11 mi. n.e. of Gainesville off US 129. Kayaking; beach, kayak rental, playground.	⓰	•	•	•	•	•	•	•	•	•	•	•	•	•	•
Elijah Clark (B-4) 447 acres 6 mi. n.e. of Lincolnton on US 378. Historic. Geocaching, water skiing; archery program, canoe rental, miniature golf, playground, shuffleboard.	⓱	•	•	•	•	•	•	•	•	•			•	•	•
Florence Marina (D-2) 173 acres 4 mi. s. of Omaha on SR 39C. Bird-watching, geocaching; miniature golf, playground.	⓲	•	•	•	•	•	•	•	•				•	•	•

Recreation Areas Chart

The map location numerals in column 2 show an area's location on the preceding map.

	MAP LOCATION	CAMPING	PICNICKING	HIKING TRAILS	BOATING	BOAT RAMP	BOAT RENTAL	FISHING	SWIMMING	PETS ON LEASH	BICYCLE TRAILS	NATURE PROGS.	VISITOR CENTER	LODGE/CABINS	FOOD SERVICE
Fort McAllister (D-6) 1,725 acres 10 mi. e. of I-95 on State Spur 144. Historic. Bird-watching, geocaching, water skiing; bicycle rental, birding trail, canoe and kayak rentals, playground. *(See Richmond Hill p. 238.)*	19	•	•	•	•	•	•	•	•		•	•	•	•	•
Fort Mountain (A-2) 3,712 acres 7 mi. e. of Chatsworth off SR 52. Historic. Scenic. Geocaching; beach, canoe, kayak and pedal boat rentals, miniature golf, playground.	20	•	•	•	•		•	•	•	•	•		•	•	
Fort Yargo (B-3) 1,816 acres 1 mi. s. of Winder on SR 81. Historic. Disc golf, geocaching, mountain biking, tennis; canoe and pedal boat rentals, miniature golf, playground. Yurts available.	21	•	•	•	•	•	•	•	•	•	•		•	•	
Franklin D. Roosevelt (C-2) 9,049 acres 5 mi. s.e. of Pine Mountain off US 27. Bird-watching, geocaching; canoe and kayak rentals, guided horseback rides, horse rental, playground, pool.	22	•	•	•			•	•	•	•		•		•	•
General Coffee (E-4) 1,511 acres 6 mi. e. of Douglas on SR 32. Equestrian camping, geocaching; amphitheater, bicycle rental, canoe and pedal boat rentals, farm, horse trails, playground. Electric boat motors only.	23	•	•	•	•	•	•	•	•	•	•		•	•	
George L. Smith (D-5) 1,634 acres 4 mi. s.e. of Twin City off SR 23. Bird-watching, geocaching; canoe/boat trail, canoe, kayak and pedal boat rentals, playground, self-guiding mill tours.	24	•	•	•	•	•	•	•	•	•	•		•	•	
George T. Bagby (E-2) 700 acres 3 mi. n. of Fort Gaines off SR 39. Bird-watching, geocaching, golf (18 holes), tennis, volleyball, water skiing; bicycle and canoe rentals, marina.	25		•	•	•	•	•	•	•	•			•	•	•
Georgia Veterans Memorial (D-3) 1,308 acres 9 mi. w. of Cordele on US 280. Historic. Bird-watching, disc golf, geocaching, golf (18 holes), water skiing; bicycle, canoe and kayak rentals, exhibits, model airplane flying field, pool. *(See Cordele p. 166.)*	26	•	•	•	•	•	•	•	•	•	•		•	•	•
Gordonia-Alatamaha (D-5) 662 acres on US 280 near Reidsville. Geocaching, golf (18 holes); miniature golf, pedal boats, playground. Electric boat motors only.	27	•	•	•	•		•	•		•			•	•	
Hamburg (C-4) 741 acres 6 mi. n.e. of Warthen via Hamburg Rd. on SR 102. Geocaching; gristmill, playground.	28	•	•	•	•	•		•		•			•		
Hard Labor Creek (B-3) 5,804 acres 2 mi. n. of Rutledge off I-20. Bird-watching, geocaching, golf (18 holes), horseback riding; beach, equestrian campsites, playground.	29	•	•	•	•		•	•	•	•			•	•	
Hart (A-4) 147 acres 3 mi. n.e. of Hartwell off US 29. Volleyball, water skiing; horseshoes, playground.	30	•	•		•	•		•		•					
High Falls (C-3) 1,050 acres 11 mi. n. of Forsyth just off I-75 at High Falls Rd. exit. Historic. Geocaching, swimming in pool only; canoe and kayak rentals, miniature golf, pedal boats, playground. Yurts available.	31	•	•	•	•	•	•	•	•	•			•	•	
Indian Springs (C-3) 528 acres 5 mi. s.e. of Jackson on SR 42. Historic. Geocaching; beach, miniature golf, playground.	32	•	•	•	•	•	•	•	•	•			•	•	
James H. "Sloppy" Floyd (A-1) 561 acres 3 mi. s.e. of Summerville off US 27. Geocaching; canoe, kayak and pedal boat rentals, playground.	33	•	•	•	•		•	•		•			•	•	
Kolomoki Mounds (E-2) 1,294 acres 6 mi. n. off US 27 in Blakely. Historic. Geocaching; beach, canoe, kayak and pedal boat rentals, miniature golf, museum, playground. *(See Blakely p. 144.)*	34	•	•	•	•		•	•	•	•			•	•	
Laura S. Walker (E-5) 626 acres 10 mi. s.e. of Waycross near US 82. Geocaching, golf (18 holes), water skiing, wildlife viewing; beach, kayak rental, playground.	35	•	•	•	•	•	•	•	•	•			•	•	•
Little Ocmulgee (D-4) 1,360 acres 2 mi. n. of McRae on US 441. Scenic. Geocaching, golf (18 holes), tennis, volleyball, water skiing; amphitheater, bicycle and canoe rentals, miniature golf, splash pad. Pool for lodge guests only.	36	•	•	•	•	•	•	•	•	•			•	•	•
Magnolia Springs (C-5) 1,070 acres 5 mi. n. of Millen on US 25. Geocaching; canoe rental, museum, playground, pool, springs. *(See Millen p. 225.)*	37	•	•	•	•	•	•	•	•	•			•	•	
Mistletoe (B-4) 1,920 acres 10 mi. n. of Appling off SR 150. Bird-watching, geocaching, wildlife viewing; canoe rental, playground.	38	•	•	•	•	•	•	•		•			•	•	

Recreation Areas Chart

The map location numerals in column 2 show an area's location on the preceding map.

	MAP LOCATION	CAMPING	PICNICKING	HIKING TRAILS	BOATING	BOAT RAMP	BOAT RENTAL	FISHING	SWIMMING	PETS ON LEASH	BICYCLE TRAILS	NATURE PROGS.	VISITOR CENTER	LODGE/CABINS	FOOD SERVICE
Moccasin Creek (A-3) 32 acres 16 mi. s.w. of Clayton on SR 197. Geocaching; canoe and kayak rentals, fish hatchery, observation tower, playground.	39	•	•	•	•	•	•	•	•	•					
Red Top Mountain (B-2) 1,776 acres 2 mi. e. of I-75 Red Top exit. Geocaching, tennis, water skiing; beach, kayak rental, marina, miniature golf, playground. Yurt available.	40	•	•	•	•	•	•	•	•	•	•	•	•	•	•
Reed Bingham (E-3) 1,613 acres 6 mi. w. of Adel off SR 37. Bird-watching, geocaching, water skiing; beach, bicycle rental, canoe and kayak rentals, miniature golf, playground, pontoon boat tours.	41	•	•	•	•	•	•	•	•	•	•	•	•		
Richard B. Russell (B-4) 2,508 acres 8 mi. n.e. of Elberton off SR 77 on Ruckersville Rd. Disc golf, geocaching, golf (18 holes), volleyball, water skiing; beach, bicycle, canoe and pontoon boat rentals, nature trails, playground.	42	•	•	•	•	•	•	•	•	•	•	•		•	
Seminole (F-2) 604 acres 16 mi. s. of Donalsonville off SR 39. Bird-watching, geocaching, water skiing; canoe and kayak rentals, miniature golf, playground, tree house campsites.	43	•	•	•	•	•	•	•	•	•		•		•	
Skidaway Island (D-6) 588 acres 6 mi. s.e. of Savannah; take I-16 to SR 21. Bird-watching, geocaching; bicycle rental, playground.	44	•	•	•						•	•	•	•		
Stephen C. Foster (F-5) 80 acres 18 mi. n.e. of Fargo on SR 177. Bird-watching, geocaching; bicycle rental, boat tours, canoe and kayak rentals, playground. **Note:** The park is open but the visitor center is temporarily closed; phone (912) 637-5274 for updates.	45	•	•	•	•	•	•	•		•	•	•		•	
Sweetwater Creek (H-1) 2,549 acres 15 mi. w. of Atlanta off I-20. Historic. Bird-watching, geocaching; canoe, kayak, paddleboard and pedal boat rentals, playground. Electric boat motors only. Yurts available. (See Lithia Springs p. 207.)	46		•	•	•	•	•	•	•	•		•	•	•	
Tallulah Gorge (A-3) 2,739 acres at Tallulah Falls. Geocaching, kayaking, tennis; archery range, beach, nature trails, playground, suspension bridge, waterfall. (See Tallulah Falls p. 288.)	47	•	•	•				•	•	•		•	•		
Tugaloo (A-4) 393 acres 6 mi. n. of Lavonia off SR 328. Geocaching, tennis, volleyball, water skiing; canoe and kayak rentals, horseshoes, miniature golf, playground. Yurts available.	48	•	•	•	•	•	•	•	•	•		•		•	
Unicoi (A-3) 1,050 acres 2 mi. n.e. of Helen via SR 356. Bird-watching, geocaching, tennis; canoe and kayak rentals, playground.	49	•	•	•	•	•	•	•	•		•		•	•	•
Victoria Bryant (B-4) 502 acres 4 mi. w. of Royston off US 29 and SR 327. Geocaching, golf (18 holes); archery range, playground, pool.	50	•	•	•					•	•		•	•		
Vogel (A-3) 233 acres 11 mi. s. of Blairsville on US 19/129. Geocaching; kayak and pedal boat rentals, miniature golf, playground. Non-motorized boats only. (See Blairsville p. 143.)	51	•	•	•	•		•	•	•	•		•		•	
Watson Mill Bridge (B-4) 1,118 acres 3 mi. s. on SR 22 in Comer. Historic. Scenic. Canoeing, equestrian camping, geocaching; canoe, kayak and pedal boat rentals, equestrian cabins and horse stalls, horse trails, playground. (See Comer p. 165.)	52	•	•	•	•		•	•	•	•		•		•	
OTHER															
Bobby Brown (B-4) 665 acres 21 mi. s.e. of Elberton off SR 72. Water skiing; playground, self-guiding navigation/compass course.	53	•	•	•	•	•	•		•	•		•	•		
Earl Maye Boat Basin and Park (E-2) 500 acres on W. Shotwell St. in Bainbridge. Water skiing; playground.	54	•	•	•	•	•		•	•	•				•	
John Tanner (B-1) 138 acres 6 mi. w. of Carrollton off SR 16. Volleyball; beach, horseshoes, miniature golf, pedal boat rental, playground. Electric boat motors only.	55	•	•	•	•	•	•	•	•			•	•		
Lake Blue Ridge (A-2) 3,290 acres 4 mi. e. of Blue Ridge via old US 76 and CR 23. Kayaking, water skiing; marina, pontoon boat rentals.	56	•	•	•	•	•	•	•		•					
Lake Chatuge (A-3) 6,950 acres 3 mi. s.w. of Hiawassee via US 76 and SR 288.	57	•	•	•	•	•	•	•	•			•	•		
Lake Lindsay Grace (E-5) 250 acres 8 mi. w. of Jesup on SR 203. Water skiing.	58		•		•	•		•	•						

Recreation Areas Chart

The map location numerals in column 2 show an area's location on the preceding map.

	MAP LOCATION	CAMPING	PICNICKING	HIKING TRAILS	BOATING	BOAT RAMP	BOAT RENTAL	FISHING	SWIMMING	PETS ON LEASH	BICYCLE TRAILS	NATURE PROGS.	VISITOR CENTER	LODGE/CABINS	FOOD SERVICE
Lake Oconee (C-4) 19,255 acres 7 mi. e. of Eatonton. Water skiing.	59	•	•	•	•	•	•	•	•	•				•	
Lake Sinclair (C-4) 15,330 acres n.e. of Milledgeville on SR 441. Water skiing; marinas.	60	•	•		•	•	•	•	•	•				•	
Lake Tobesofkee (C-3) 1,750 acres 12 mi. w. of Macon off I-475 at SR 74 and Thomaston Rd. Tennis, water skiing.	61	•	•		•	•	•	•	•	•				•	
Lake Winfield Scott (A-3) 18 acres 4 mi. e. of Suches on SR 180.	62	•	•	•	•			•	•	•					
Little Tallapoosa (B-2) 256 acres at 190 SR 113 N in Carrollton. Disc golf, geocaching; equestrian parking, nature trails.	63	•	•	•				•							
McIntosh Reserve (C-2) 527 acres US 27 from Carrollton, then 3 mi. w. on SR 5. Historic. Canoeing, horseback riding.	64	•	•	•				•			•	•			
Rabun Beach (A-3) 934 acres 13 mi. s. of Clayton via US 23, SR 15 and CR 10. Water skiing.	65	•	•	•	•	•		•	•	•	•				
Sandy Creek Park (B-3) 782 acres 2.5 mi. n. of Athens bypass off US 441. Disc golf, tennis; canoe and kayak rentals, dog park, horse trails, playground. Electric boat motors only.	66		•	•	•	•	•	•	•	•			•		
Stone Mountain Park (H-4) 3,200 acres about 18 mi. e. of Atlanta. Golf (36 holes), tennis; miniature golf, waterslides. Canoe rentals are for campers only. *(See Stone Mountain p. 284.)*	67	•	•	•	•	•	•	•	•	•			•	•	•

ACWORTH pop. 20,425
• Part of Atlanta area — see map p. 44

BEST WESTERN ACWORTH INN (770)974-0116

Motel
$80-$150

 Best Western.

AAA Benefit: Save 10% or more every day and earn 10% bonus points!

Address: 5155 Cowan Rd 30101 **Location:** I-75 exit 277, just w. **Facility:** 84 units. 2 stories (no elevator), exterior corridors. **Pool(s):** outdoor. **Activities:** exercise room. **Guest Services:** coin laundry. **Featured Amenity: full hot breakfast.**

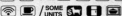

DAYS INN ACWORTH (770)975-9000

Motel
$70-$110

Address: 164 N Point Way 30101 **Location:** I-75 exit 277, just e. **Facility:** 38 units. 2 stories (no elevator), exterior corridors. **Terms:** 3 day cancellation notice. **Activities:** exercise room. **Guest Services:** coin laundry. **Featured Amenity: full hot breakfast.**

HOLIDAY INN EXPRESS 678/574-4222

Hotel
Rates not provided

Address: 200 N Point Way 30102 **Location:** I-75 exit 277, just e. **Facility:** 60 units. 3 stories, interior corridors. **Pool(s):** outdoor. **Activities:** exercise room. **Guest Services:** valet and coin laundry. **Featured Amenity: full hot breakfast.**

LA QUINTA INN ACWORTH (770)975-9920

Hotel
$67-$150

Address: 184 N Point Way 30102 **Location:** I-75 exit 277, just e. **Facility:** 44 units. 3 stories, interior/exterior corridors. **Pool(s):** outdoor. **Activities:** exercise room. **Guest Services:** valet laundry. **Featured Amenity: full hot breakfast.**

SUPER 8 (770)966-9700

Motel. $55-$75 **Address:** 4970 Cowan Rd 30101 **Location:** I-75 exit 277, just w. **Facility:** 49 units. 2-3 stories (no elevator), exterior corridors. **Parking:** on-site and valet. **Terms:** cancellation fee imposed. **Pool(s):** outdoor. **Guest Services:** coin laundry.

WHERE TO EAT

ART'S BAGELS & MORE 770/529-4567

Sandwiches. Quick Serve. $2-$7 **AAA Inspector Notes:** Roast beef, pastrami and whitefish salad piles high on this eatery's bagel sandwiches, and you can pile on plenty of good toppings, too. The pleasant staffers arrive daily at 3 am to bake each bagel, including whole wheat, rye and onion varieties. They also bake some mighty good cookies. **Address:** 3451 Cobb Pkwy, Suite 5 30101 **Location:** Jct US 41 (Cobb Pkwy) and Acworth Due West Rd; in Mars Hill Point Shopping Center.

BAR-B-CUTIE 770/917-8436

Barbecue. Quick Serve. $6-$20 **AAA Inspector Notes:** This family-friendly barbecue joint serves slow-cooked, hickory-smoked pork, beef brisket, ribs, sausage, chicken and turkey with tasty country-style side items. Enjoy good weather on the patio and an array of delicious desserts. **Address:** 3466 Cobb Pkwy NW 30101 **Location:** Jct Cobb Pkwy (US 41), 1 mi s.

CAPO'S 770/966-7770

Italian. Casual Dining. $6-$21 **AAA Inspector Notes:** Diners can create their own pasta dish here with many choices of noodles and sauces such as pesto, Alfredo, garlic and oil, pomodoro, clam and classic tomato. Baked ziti, lasagna and sausage and peppers are popular entrées. The Buffalo chicken, spicy Hawaiian, ultimate meat and Manhattan are great pizza options. Soups, salads, sandwiches and desserts round out the menu. **Features:** beer & wine, patio dining. **Address:** 3450 Cobb Pkwy 30101 **Location:** Jct US 41 (Cobb Pkwy) and SR 92, 1 mi s.

CENTER STREET TAVERN 770/917-0004

American. Casual Dining. $9-$21 **AAA Inspector Notes:** This local favorite is a good to place for a beer, local flavor and well prepared pub food. Try some jumbo chicken wings or oysters Rockefeller for starters and then delve into a grilled rib-eye, burger, specialty sandwich or smothered chicken. Cobb and chef salads also are available as are delicious desserts. **Features:** full bar, happy hour. **Address:** 4381 Senator Russell Ave 30101 **Location:** I-75 exit 278, 1 mi w; downtown.

DADDY'S COUNTRY KITCHEN 770/974-2281

Comfort Food. Casual Dining. $7-$10 **AAA Inspector Notes:** Three all-you-can-eat buffets a day are served at this home-style eatery. Some of the items available at lunch and dinner are fried chicken, boiled shrimp, baked fish, meatloaf, fried catfish and many vegetable offerings including mashed potatoes, collard greens, peas and beans. Salads and desserts also are available. **Address:** 4525 S Main St 30101 **Location:** I-75 exit 278, 1 mi w; downtown.

DOGWOOD TERRACE RESTAURANT 770/627-4069

Regional American. Fine Dining. $9-$27 **AAA Inspector Notes:** Creative small plates, main courses and pizza are served at this upscale downtown eatery which uses local resources for the décor and food. The asparagus soup, when available, is a do-not-miss. Many breakfast items are served at lunch as well as burgers, panini and Thai chicken salad. **Features:** full bar, patio dining, Sunday brunch. **Address:** 4975 N Main St 30101 **Location:** I-75 exit 277, 1 mi w; downtown.

FAST EDDIE'S SPORTS CAFE 770/529-5191

American. Casual Dining. $8-$21 **AAA Inspector Notes:** Pizza, wings, sandwiches, salads, championship chicken and mile-high burgers are some of the tasty items that this café serves up. The jumbo wings' sauces include the expected ones as well as inferno, lemonyaki and sweet red chili. French Quarter, buffalo, barbecue and Maui are but a sampling of the many pizza types. **Features:** full bar. **Address:** 3330 Cobb Pkwy N, Suite 1 30101 **Location:** Jct US 41 (Cobb Pkwy) and Acworth Due West Rd.

AAA Vacations® packages ... exciting itineraries and exclusive values

FISH THYME RESTAURANT & BAR 770/974-2323
▼▼▼ Seafood. Fine Dining. $10-$20 **AAA Inspector Notes:** Fresh seafood with many styles of preparation can be found at this eatery. Blackened Alaskan halibut, horseradish-encrusted grouper and stuffed salmon are just a few examples. Begin the meal with pass around items such as oyster shooters, Prince Edward Island mussels (the broth is sumptuous) and crab-stuffed mushrooms. For the landlubber there are Danish baby back ribs, pork schnitzel and chicken in Marsala as well as the steak of the day. **Features:** full bar, patio dining. **Address:** 3979 S Main St, Suite 100 30101 **Location:** I-75 exit 277, 1 mi s; in Main Street Exchange. [D] CALL [&M]

FUSCO'S VIA ROMA 770/974-1110
▼▼ Italian. Casual Dining. $8-$25 **AAA Inspector Notes:** A downtown jewel, this restaurant serves well-prepared Italian specialties such as lobster primavera, pork chop val 'dosta and calamari fritti as well as sea bass, ahi tuna and filet mignon. Pizza and desserts are available and the wine list features some good options to accompany the meal. **Features:** full bar, patio dining. **Reservations:** suggested. **Address:** 4815A S Main St NW 30101 **Location:** I-75 exit 278, 1 mi w; downtown. **Parking:** street only. [L] [D]

HENRY'S LOUISIANA GRILL 770/966-1515
▼▼ Cajun. Casual Dining. $8-$25 **AAA Inspector Notes:** It would not be surprising for diners to say 'Louisiana ooh la la' after diving into the dish of the same name. Other authentic preparations include jambalaya du jour, po'boys, hot chili gator, Louisiana shrimp and grits and succulent bread pudding. Chef Henry always makes the rounds to check on his customers and make them feel welcome. **Features:** full bar. **Address:** 4835 N Main St 30101 **Location:** I-75 exit 278, 1 mi w; downtown. **Parking:** street only. [L] [D]

HONG KONG STAR 770/917-0688
▼▼ Chinese. Casual Dining. $7-$23 **AAA Inspector Notes:** Upscale enough to attract couples on date night, yet casual enough to appeal to families, this eatery is a hot destination on the north-side dining scene due to its lively décor and delicious food that is a cut above what you typically see at a Chinese restaurant. Popular items include Chilean sea bass, dim sum, crispy boneless duck and a variety of noodle dishes. **Features:** beer & wine. **Address:** 3451 Cobb Pkwy, Suite 9 30101 **Location:** Jct US 41 (Cobb Pkwy) and Acworth Due West Rd. [L] [D]

J.D.'S BAR-B-QUE 770/974-8434
▼ Barbecue. Casual Dining. $6-$22 **AAA Inspector Notes:** This family restaurant prides itself on pit-cooked barbecue such as brisket, ribs and chicken. Choose from barbecue sandwiches in regular or jumbo sizes. The burgers are popular here and the big Dave sandwich is touted as eight layers of goodness. Other treats include loaded spuds, special wings and fried dill pickles. Cookies and milk are a great way to end the meal. **Features:** full bar. **Address:** 4424 S Main St 30101 **Location:** I-75 exit 277, 1.5 mi w to Main St, then just s. [L] [D] CALL [&M]

LA PARRILLA MEXICAN RESTAURANT 770/974-4600
▼▼ Tex-Mex. Casual Dining. $6-$16 **AAA Inspector Notes:** This festive and colorful restaurant bustles with activity from patrons eager to eat its Tex-Mex tacos, enchiladas, burritos and fajitas and to sip the yummy margaritas. Service is attentive. **Features:** full bar, patio dining. **Address:** 6110 Cedar Crest Rd 30101 **Location:** Jct US 41 (Cobb Pkwy). [L] [D] CALL [&M]

NEW THAI GINGER 678/494-0880
▼▼ Thai. Casual Dining. $7-$17 **AAA Inspector Notes:** The menu blends traditional curry and noodle dishes with more adventurous fare, such as the house specialty shellfish "hoe ra par". The tamarind duck and red snapper basil are two very delicious dinners. **Features:** beer & wine. **Address:** 5399 Bells Ferry Rd 30102 **Location:** Jct Bells Ferry Rd and SR 92, just s; in Market Center Shopping Center. [L] [D]

PACIFIC SPICE 770/529-8300
▼▼ Asian. Casual Dining. $6-$36 **AAA Inspector Notes:** This contemporary restaurant focuses on a wide variety of Chinese, Thai and Japanese fare, including sushi. Beijing duck, pineapple-flavor red snapper fillet and basil lamb are tempting entrées. Hibachi grill meals are available as well. **Features:** beer & wine. **Address:** 6110 Cedarcrest Rd NW, Suite 310 30101 **Location:** Jct Cobb Pkwy (US 41) and Cedarcrest Rd; in Governor's Towne Square. [L] [D] CALL [&M]

POBLANO'S MEXICAN GRILL 770/975-0993
▼▼ Tex-Mex. Casual Dining. $6-$15 **AAA Inspector Notes:** Sit back, relax and enjoy some good Tex Mex favorites while sipping a tasty margarita at this Mexican grill. Snack on some chips and fresh salsa while perusing the menu loaded with such offerings as tilapia and shrimp, tropical steak, salmon salad, pollo al mango and all manner of tacos, burritos, enchiladas, fajitas and nachos. **Features:** full bar, patio dining. **Address:** 3344 Cobb Pkwy NW 30101 **Location:** Jct Acworth Due West Rd, just s. [L] [D] CALL [&M]

RICO'S MEX MEX GRILL 770/917-9791
▼▼ Tex-Mex. Casual Dining. $4-$15 **AAA Inspector Notes:** For those looking for some great Tex-Mex food, this is the place. I had the huevos a la Mexicana and it was excellent. The portions are huge and the value is super. Standards include the obligatory tacos, enchiladas, burritos and fajitas (which get rave reviews). Flan or sopaipillas are good choices for dessert. **Features:** full bar, patio dining, happy hour. **Address:** 3770 Southside Dr 30101 **Location:** Jct Cowan Rd, 0.5 mi s. [L] [D]

THAI BASIL & SUSHI ZEN 770/975-8909
▼▼ Asian. Casual Dining. $7-$25 **AAA Inspector Notes:** Both Thai and Japanese dishes are served at this traditional restaurant, which employs friendly servers and has a sushi bar. The tom yum soup is excellent and specials, such as salmon pattaya, always are solid. **Features:** beer & wine. **Address:** 3330 Cobb Pkwy, Unit 15 30101 **Location:** Jct Cobb Pkwy (US 41) and Acworth Due West Rd; in Kroger Plaza. [L] [D] CALL [&M]

TOKYO JAPANESE STEAK HOUSE 770/975-1818
▼▼ Japanese. Casual Dining. $4-$25 **AAA Inspector Notes:** Hibachi and sushi are the main draws at this casual local eatery. The cooks work tableside and appreciate some encouragement to give a better show. A good variety of choices include red snapper, salmon, filet mignon, lobster, calamari, shrimp and scallops. **Features:** full bar. **Address:** 3450 Cobb Pkwy NE, Suite 210 30101 **Location:** Jct Cobb Pkwy (US 41) and SR 92, 1 mi s. [L] [D] CALL [&M]

ZEIGLER'S BBQ & CATERING 770/529-5227
▼ Barbecue. Quick Serve. $7-$17 **AAA Inspector Notes:** This hometown restaurant specializes in simple, filling and delicious barbecue. The dining room is small and many locals utilize the take-out or catering service. The brisket and macaroni and cheese is just like momma makes. Other options include slow-smoked ribs, chicken, pork and turkey as well as hot dogs and delicious country-style side items. **Address:** 3451 Cobb Pkwy 30101 **Location:** Jct US 41 (Cobb Pkwy) and Acworth Due West Rd; in Mars Hill Point Shopping Center. [L] [D]

ADAIRSVILLE (A-2) pop. 4,648, elev. 714'

BARNSLEY RESORT is at 597 Barnsley Gardens Rd. The 3,300-acre estate, built by Sir Godfrey Barnsley in the 1800s, features historic outbuildings, a cemetery, restored ruins of the original manor house and a museum containing Barnsley family memorabilia. The gardens have been restored to their 19th-century style; a variety of flowers and plants, more than 200 varieties of roses, water cascades and fountains are on view. A resort, spa and golf course are on the property. Hiking, bicycling, horseback riding, a hunting preserve and a sporting clays course with a covered shooting facility are available.

Hours: Garden open Sun.-Fri. dawn-dusk, Sat. dawn-2. Museum open Mon.-Fri. 9-5, Sat. 9-2, Sun. noon-5. The site may be closed for private events some Sat. afternoons; phone ahead to confirm schedule. **Cost:** (includes garden and museum) $10; $8 (ages 55+); $5 (ages 0-11). **Phone:** (770) 773-7480 or (877) 773-2447. 🍴 ✂ 🏠

HAMPTON INN & SUITES ADAIRSVILLE-CALHOUN
(770)773-3100

Hotel
$129-$169

AAA Benefit: Members save up to 10%!

Address: 101 Travelers Path 30103 **Location:** I-75 exit 306, just w. **Facility:** 79 units. 5 stories, interior corridors. **Terms:** 1-7 night minimum stay, cancellation fee imposed. **Pool:** heated indoor. **Activities:** exercise room. **Guest Services:** coin laundry. **Featured Amenity:** full hot breakfast.

MAGNUSON COUNTRYSIDE INN
770/773-3900

Hotel. Rates not provided. **Address:** 100 Georgia North Cir 30103 **Location:** I-75 exit 306, just w. **Facility:** 49 units. 2 stories (no elevator), interior corridors. **Pool(s):** outdoor.

QUALITY INN
(770)773-2886

Motel
$70-$169

Address: 107 Princeton Blvd 30103 **Location:** I-75 exit 306, just w. **Facility:** 50 units. 2 stories (no elevator), exterior corridors. **Pool(s):** outdoor. **Featured Amenity:** full hot breakfast.

RAMADA LIMITED
(770)769-9726

Motel. $60-$85 **Address:** 500 Georgia North Cir 30103 **Location:** I-75 exit 306, 0.3 mi w. **Facility:** 65 units. 2 stories (no elevator), exterior corridors. **Pool(s):** outdoor. **Guest Services:** coin laundry.

ADEL pop. 5,334

DAYS INN
(229)896-4574

Classic Motel. $50-$90 **Address:** 1204 W 4th St 31620 **Location:** I-75 exit 39, just sw. **Facility:** This basic accommodation features an expanded green space in the motel's courtyard. Guestrooms are comfortable with newly installed flat panel televisions for entertainment. 78 units. 2 stories (no elevator), exterior corridors. **Pool(s):** outdoor.

HAMPTON INN
(229)896-3099

Hotel. $89-$189 **Address:** 1500 W 4th St 31620 **Location:** I-75 exit 39, just nw. **Facility:** 74 units. 3 stories, interior corridors. **Terms:** 1-7 night minimum stay, cancellation fee imposed. **Pool(s):** outdoor. **Activities:** exercise room. **Guest Services:** coin laundry.

AAA Benefit: Members save up to 10%!

Visit AAA.com/searchfordiscounts to save on travel, shopping, dining and attractions

ALBANY (E-2) pop. 77,434, elev. 210'
• Hotels p. 30 • Restaurants p. 31

The site that eventually became Albany was bought in 1836 by a Connecticut man who hired surveyors to plat a town. Later that year Nelson Tift and a group of companions brought supplies up the Flint River from Apalachicola, Fla., and began to construct log buildings. The town took its name from the city in New York that also was at a river's head of navigation.

A bronze statue of Albany native Ray Charles playing his piano sits in Ray Charles Plaza on Front Street.

Albany Convention and Visitors Bureau: 112 N. Front St. Albany, GA 31701. **Phone:** (229) 317-4760 or (866) 750-0840. *(See ad p. 30.)*

ALBANY CIVIL RIGHTS INSTITUTE is at 326 Whitney Ave. Housed adjacent to the Old Mt. Zion Church, the museum commemorates the 1960s civil rights movement in southwest Georgia, emphasizing the role played by ordinary people in the struggle for civil rights. Exhibits, historic photographs and video footage recount the movement's history. Temporary exhibits also are on display.

Time: Allow 1 hour minimum. **Hours:** Tues.-Sat. 10-4. Closed Jan. 1, July 4, Thanksgiving, day after Thanksgiving, Christmas and day after Christmas. Phone ahead to confirm holiday closures. **Cost:** $6; $5 (ages 62+, 5th-12th-graders, college students and military with ID); $3 (1st-4th-graders); $2 (preschoolers); free (ages 0-4 with parent). Phone ahead to confirm rates. **Phone:** (229) 432-1698. GT

ALBANY MUSEUM OF ART, 311 Meadowlark Dr., features seven rotating galleries, a children's hands-on space and a collection of American, European and African art. Temporary exhibits also are available. Educational programs are offered throughout the year. **Hours:** Tues.-Sat. 10-5. Closed major holidays. **Cost:** Free. **Phone:** (229) 439-8400.

CHEHAW PARK is on Lake Chehaw on SR 91, 1.2 miles north of US 19/82/SR 50. The park offers a zoo with animals from all over the world in surroundings resembling their natural habitat. There also are nature trails, a children's playground, an 18-hole disc golf course, a mountain bike trail and a BMX racing track. **Hours:** Park daily 9-5. Zoo daily 9:30-5. **Cost:** Park only $3; $2 (ages 4-12, ages 62+ and military with ID). Zoo $7.85; $5.10 (ages 4-12 and military with ID). **Phone:** (229) 430-5275.

FLINT RIVERQUARIUM, at 101 Pine Ave., features a 175,000-gallon, blue-hole spring aquarium that is home to more than 120 varieties of aquatic life. The Flint River Gallery contains freshwater and saltwater tanks as well as a live fish hatchery. Discovery Caverns allows children to learn about nature through interactive exhibits.

The World of Water draws comparisons between rivers around the globe and Flint River. An aviary showcases birds and waterfowl native to the Flint

River watershed. RiverQuarium Imagination Theater shows nature and adventure films.

Time: Allow 1 hour minimum. **Hours:** Tues.-Sat. 10-5, Sun. 1-5. Theater open Fri.-Sun. 1-5. Theater shows at 1:15, 2:15, 3:15 and 4:15. Animal encounter programs are held Sat.-Sun. Closed Jan. 1, Thanksgiving, Christmas Eve and Christmas. **Cost:** $9; $8 (ages 62+); $6.50 (ages 4-12); $5.50 (college students with ID). Theater $6; $5.50 (college students with ID); $4.50 (ages 4-12). Combination ticket $14; $12.50 (ages 62+); $10 (ages 4-12 and college students with ID). **Phone:** (229) 639-2650, or (877) 463-5468 for the ticketing office.

THRONATEESKA HERITAGE CENTER AND WETHERBEE PLANETARIUM AND SCIENCE MUSEUM is at 100 W. Roosevelt Ave. The heritage center is housed on a historic plaza and includes a museum that recounts the history of southwest Georgia, a railroad exhibit, a planetarium and a science museum featuring hands-on exhibits. The South Georgia Archives features local history information and a research room. **Time:** Allow 1 hour minimum. **Hours:** Thurs.-Sat. 10-4. Planetarium show times 10:30, 11:30, 1, 2 and 3. Archives open Thurs.-Fri. 1-5 and by appointment. Closed most holidays; phone ahead. **Cost:** Heritage center and museum free. Planetarium show $3.50 (ages 4+). **Phone:** (229) 432-6955.

BAYMONT INN & SUITES ALBANY   (229)435-3737

Hotel
$59-$159

Address: 2720 Dawson Rd 31707 **Location:** 0.5 mi se of jct US 82 and SR 520. **Facility:** 62 units. 2 stories (no elevator), exterior corridors. **Pool(s):** outdoor. **Activities:** exercise room. **Featured Amenity:** continental breakfast.

FAIRFIELD INN & SUITES BY MARRIOTT (229)883-8288

Hotel
$96-$140

AAA Benefit: Members save 5% or more!

Address: 3011 Kensington Ct 31721 **Location:** Just se of jct Dawson Rd and US 82 W. **Facility:** 87 units. 1-3 stories, interior corridors. **Pool(s):** outdoor. **Activities:** exercise room. **Guest Services:** valet and coin laundry.

Request roadside assistance in a click — online or using the AAA or CAA apps

▼ See AAA listing p. 29 ▼

RELAX, HAVE FUN AND ENJOY

GENUINE
SOUTHERN CHARM.

FROM DELICIOUS LOCAL CUISINE, AWARD-WINNING MUSEUMS AND ATTRACTIONS TO PLENTY OF RECREATIONAL OPPORTUNITIES, YOU'LL FIND IT ALL IN ALBANY, GEORGIA.

discover Albany GA

WHERE history AND nature flow

VISITALBANYGA.COM

HAMPTON INN & SUITES ALBANY AT ALBANY MALL
(229)405-2000

▼▼▼ **Hotel.** $119-$184 **Address:** 2628 Dawson Rd 31707 **Location:** 0.5 mi se of jct Dawson Rd and US 82 W. **Facility:** 94 units. 1-5 stories, interior corridors. **Terms:** 1-7 night minimum stay, cancellation fee imposed. **Pool(s):** outdoor. **Activities:** exercise room. **Guest Services:** valet and coin laundry.

AAA Benefit:
Members save up to 10%!

[icons]

HILTON GARDEN INN ALBANY
(229)888-1590

▼▼▼ **Hotel.** $109-$189 **Address:** 101 S Front St 31701 **Location:** Between Oglethorpe Blvd and W Broad Ave. **Facility:** 122 units. 5 stories, interior corridors. **Terms:** 1-7 night minimum stay, cancellation fee imposed. **Pool(s):** outdoor. **Activities:** hot tub, exercise room. **Guest Services:** valet and coin laundry.

AAA Benefit:
Members save up to 10%!

[icons]

HOLIDAY INN EXPRESS & SUITES
229/405-2613

▼▼▼ **Hotel.** Rates not provided. **Address:** 2713 Pointe North Blvd 31707 **Location:** Just se of jct Dawson Rd and US 82 W. **Facility:** 80 units. 1-4 stories, interior corridors. **Pool(s):** heated indoor. **Activities:** exercise room. **Guest Services:** valet and coin laundry.

[icons]

PARK INN BY RADISSON ALBANY
229/446-2001

▼▼ **Hotel.** Rates not provided. **Address:** 2729 Pointe North Blvd 31721 **Location:** Just se of jct Dawson Rd and US 82 W. **Facility:** 61 units. 2 stories, interior corridors. **Pool(s):** outdoor. **Activities:** sauna, exercise room. **Guest Services:** valet and coin laundry. [icons]

QUALITY INN ALBANY MALL
(229)883-3300

▼▼ **Hotel.** $70-$134 **Address:** 806 N Westover Blvd 31707 **Location:** 7 mi w on Dawson Rd; 0.5 mi se of jct US 82 and SR 520. Adjacent to Albany Mall. **Facility:** 82 units. 2 stories, exterior corridors. **Pool(s):** outdoor. **Activities:** exercise room. **Guest Services:** valet laundry.

[icons] / SOME UNITS [icons]

WINGATE BY WYNDHAM
(229)883-9800

▼▼▼ **Hotel.** $104-$169 **Address:** 2735 Dawson Rd 31707 **Location:** Jct US 82 and SR 520, 0.4 mi se. **Facility:** 85 units. 3 stories, interior corridors. **Amenities:** safes. **Pool(s):** outdoor. **Activities:** hot tub, limited exercise equipment. **Guest Services:** valet laundry.

[icons]

WHERE TO EAT

CASA TAPATIA
229/903-8802

▼▼ Mexican. Casual Dining. $6-$15 **AAA Inspector Notes:** On the city's west side, the small, brightly colored cantina offers a good selection of Mexican favorites. Quesadillas and flautas with fresh pico de gallo are popular, but the menu is chock-full of options. **Features:** full bar, patio dining. **Address:** 108 N Slappey Blvd 31701 **Location:** Just n of E Oglethorpe Blvd. [L] [D]

THE CATCH SEAFOOD ROOM AND OYSTER BAR
229/446-2235

▼▼▼ Seafood. Casual Dining. $16-$35 **AAA Inspector Notes:** Fresh seafood is the star at this casual eatery featuring daily specials such as Alaskan halibut, diver scallops and stuffed grouper. Oysters are offered in a variety of preparations such as Rockefeller, baked and raw. Friendly staff are willing to assist with any questions in navigating the menu. **Features:** full bar. **Address:** 2332 Whispering Pines Rd 31707 **Location:** Jct US 82 W, 2.7 mi e, just e. [D] CALL [&M]

HARVEST MOON
229/439-7077

▼▼ American. Casual Dining. $5-$20 **AAA Inspector Notes:** Do not judge a book by its cover, this local hangout is a perfect example of this adage. The décor is basic and parking is limited but the food is delicious. Try the signature wings and pizza. You cannot go wrong with the roasted rooster, full moon or meat-eater pizza. The wings come in a variety of flavors and temperatures. **Features:** full bar. **Address:** 2347 Dawson Rd 31707 **Location:** Jct US 82 W, 2.7 mi e. **Parking:** street only. [L] [D] [LATE]

HENRY CAMPBELL'S STEAKHOUSE
229/594-9288

▼▼▼ Steak. Fine Dining. $22-$65 **AAA Inspector Notes:** This intimate dining room with exposed brick walls, plantation shutters, wood floors and flickering candlelight from various wall shelves offers a cozy, refined atmosphere. Try the Deep South egg roll made with collard greens, chicken and andouille sausage. **Features:** full bar. **Address:** 629 N Westover Blvd 31707 **Location:** Jct US 82 and SR 520, then just s; in Westover Crossings Shopping Center. [D] CALL [&M]

HONG KONG CAFE
229/888-2282

▼▼ Chinese. Casual Dining. $6-$13 **AAA Inspector Notes:** Situated in a plaza where the store fronts resemble Cape Cod-style homes, this intimate restaurant serves all of your favorites in a relaxed atmosphere. **Features:** beer & wine. **Address:** 2700 Dawson Rd, Suite 1 31707 **Location:** Jct US 82 and SR 520. [L] [D] CALL [&M]

MIKATA JAPANESE STEAKHOUSE & SUSHI BAR
229/435-3516

▼▼ Japanese Steak Sushi. Casual Dining. $8-$30 **AAA Inspector Notes:** When the hibachi grills fire up, savory aromas of teriyaki steak, chicken and seafood waft through this dining area. Skilled chefs wield knives with flair and entertain diners for the duration of their meal. An intimate dining area offers a quieter evening, with an expansive menu of sushi and sashimi options created with equally impressive style. **Features:** full bar. **Address:** 2610 Dawson Rd 31707 **Location:** 0.8 mi se of jct Dawson Rd and US 82 W. [D] CALL [&M]

SONNY'S REAL PIT BAR-B-Q
229/883-7427

▼▼ Barbecue. Casual Dining. $8-$17 **AAA Inspector Notes:** Bearing the name after its founder, Floyd "Sonny" Tillman, this barbecue restaurant first opened its doors circa 1968 in Gainesville, Florida and has since spawned over 150 more throughout the Southeast. The menu is steeped in finger lickin' favorites such as ribs, pulled pork, beef brisket, burgers, catfish, shrimp and chargrilled chicken. Let's not forget about the fried okra, which is the perfect starter dish, and their homemade baked beans. **Features:** beer only. **Address:** 1900 N Slappey Blvd 31701 **Location:** 3.3 mi nw on US 19 business route and 82. [L] [D]

VILLA GARGANO ITALIAN RESTAURANT
229/436-7265

▼▼ Italian. Casual Dining. $7-$20 **AAA Inspector Notes:** Established in 1968, this family-owned restaurant offers traditional favorites of Italian cuisine in an intimate setting. Wall murals depicting the Tuscan valley and artifacts embellish the ambience. Juicy chicken piccata, veal Marsala and spinach pizza are favorites. **Features:** beer & wine. **Address:** 1604 N Slappey Blvd 31701 **Location:** 3 mi nw on US 19 business route and 82. [L] [D]

ALMA   pop. 3,466

DAYS INN
(912)632-7000

▼▼ Motel. $63 **Address:** 930 S Pierce St 31510 **Location:** Jct SR 32 and US 1, 0.4 mi s on US 1. **Facility:** 36 units. 2 stories (no elevator), interior/exterior corridors. **Pool(s):** outdoor. **Guest Services:** coin laundry.

[icons] / SOME UNITS [icons]

ALPHARETTA (B-2) pop. 57,551, elev. 1,138'

• **Hotels p. 32** • **Restaurants p. 34**
• **Hotels & Restaurants map & index p. 82**
• **Part of Atlanta area — see map p. 44**

Alpharetta is home to the campus of DeVry University, as well as a campus of Georgia State University.

(See map & index p. 82.)

The 1910 Queen Anne-style Mansell House and Gardens is furnished in period; phone (770) 475-4663 Monday 11-2, Wednesday and Friday 10-2 and by appointment.

Alpharetta Welcome Center: 178 South Main St., Suite 200, Alpharetta, GA 30009. **Phone:** (678) 297-0102 or (800) 294-0923.

Shopping: The 130 establishments of North Point Mall, at 1000 North Point Cir. off SR 400 between Encore Parkway and Haynes Bridge Road, are anchored by Dillard's, Macy's, JCPenney, Sears and Von Maur. Avalon, 2200 Avalon Blvd. at jct. SR 400 and Old Milton Pkwy., offers shops, eateries and a movie theater.

ATLANTA MARRIOTT ALPHARETTA
(770)754-9600   **38**

Hotel
$85-$309

MARRIOTT

AAA Benefit: Members save 5% or more!

Address: 5750 Windward Pkwy 30005 **Location:** SR 400 exit 11, just e. **Facility:** 318 units. 8 stories, interior corridors. **Pool(s):** outdoor, heated indoor. **Activities:** hot tub, exercise room. **Guest Services:** valet and coin laundry, boarding pass kiosk, rental car service, area transportation. **Featured Amenity:** breakfast buffet.

COMFORT INN
(770)664-7997   **42**

Hotel. $79-$159 **Address:** 5455 Windward Pkwy 30004 **Location:** SR 400 exit 11, 0.4 mi w. **Facility:** 64 units. 4 stories, interior corridors. **Activities:** exercise room. **Guest Services:** valet laundry.

COMFORT SUITES
(770)645-6060   **55**

Hotel. $89-$159 **Address:** 3000 Mansell Rd 30022 **Location:** SR 400 exit 8, 0.7 mi e. **Facility:** 70 units, some efficiencies. 3 stories, interior corridors. **Pool(s):** outdoor. **Activities:** exercise room. **Guest Services:** valet and coin laundry, area transportation.

COURTYARD BY MARRIOTT ATLANTA ALPHARETTA
(678)366-3360   **39**

Hotel
$57-$230

COURTYARD Marriott
AAA Benefit: Members save 5% or more!

Address: 12655 Deerfield Pkwy 30004 **Location:** SR 400 exit 11, 0.5 mi w to Deerfield Pkwy, then just n. **Facility:** 154 units. 3 stories, interior corridors. **Pool(s):** outdoor. **Activities:** exercise room. **Guest Services:** valet and coin laundry, area transportation.

DOUBLETREE BY HILTON HOTEL ATLANTA-ALPHARETTA
(678)347-0022   **40**

Hotel. $89-$208 **Address:** 2925 Jordan Ct 30004 **Location:** SR 400 exit 11, 0.5 mi w. **Facility:** 79 units. 4 stories, interior corridors. **Bath:** shower only. **Terms:** 1-7 night minimum stay, cancellation fee imposed. **Pool(s):** outdoor. **Activities:** exercise room. **Guest Services:** valet laundry, area transportation.

AAA Benefit: Members save 5% or more!

EMBASSY SUITES HOTEL BY HILTON ALPHARETTA
(678)566-8800   **48**

Hotel. $99-$269 **Address:** 5955 North Point Pkwy 30022 **Location:** SR 400 exit 9, just e to North Point Pkwy, then just n. **Facility:** 150 units. 6 stories, interior corridors. **Terms:** 1-7 night minimum stay, cancellation fee imposed. **Amenities:** video games. **Pool(s):** heated indoor. **Activities:** hot tub, exercise room. **Guest Services:** valet and coin laundry, area transportation.

AAA Benefit: Members save 5% or more!

FAIRFIELD INN & SUITES BY MARRIOTT
(770)663-4000   **47**

Hotel
$65-$202

FAIRFIELD INN & SUITES Marriott
AAA Benefit: Members save 5% or more!

Address: 11385 Haynes Bridge Rd 30009 **Location:** SR 400 exit 9, just w. **Facility:** 88 units. 3 stories, interior corridors. **Pool(s):** outdoor. **Activities:** limited exercise equipment. **Guest Services:** valet and coin laundry, area transportation. **Featured Amenity:** breakfast buffet.

HAMPTON INN-ALPHARETTA/ROSWELL
(770)640-5511   **54**

Hotel. $84-$248 **Address:** 10740 Westside Pkwy 30004 **Location:** SR 400 exit 8, 0.6 mi w. **Facility:** 106 units. 5 stories, interior corridors. **Terms:** 1-7 night minimum stay, cancellation fee imposed. **Pool(s):** outdoor. **Activities:** exercise room. **Guest Services:** valet laundry, area transportation.

AAA Benefit: Members save up to 10%!

HILTON GARDEN INN ATLANTA/NORTH ALPHARETTA
(770)360-7766   **36**

Hotel. $79-$229 **Address:** 4025 Windward Plaza 30005 **Location:** SR 400 exit 11, 1.1 mi e to Windward Plaza, then just se. **Facility:** 164 units. 6 stories, interior corridors. **Terms:** 1-7 night minimum stay, cancellation fee imposed. **Pool(s):** heated indoor. **Activities:** exercise room. **Guest Services:** valet and coin laundry, area transportation.

AAA Benefit: Members save up to 10%!

HILTON GARDEN INN-ATLANTA NORTH POINT
(678)566-3900   **51**

Hotel. $99-$229 **Address:** 10975 Georgia Ln 30022 **Location:** SR 400 exit 9, 0.5 mi to Georgia Ln, then just n. **Facility:** 125 units. 5 stories, interior corridors. **Terms:** 1-7 night minimum stay, cancellation fee imposed. **Pool(s):** outdoor. **Activities:** hot tub, exercise room. **Guest Services:** valet and coin laundry, area transportation.

AAA Benefit: Members save up to 10%!

(See map & index p. 82.)

▼ See AAA listing this page ▼

HOLIDAY INN EXPRESS ALPHARETTA
770/552-0006 **56**

Hotel
Rates not provided

Address: 2950 Mansell Rd 30022 **Location:** SR 400 exit 8, 0.7 mi e. **Facility:** 67 units. 3 stories, interior corridors. **Pool(s):** heated indoor. **Activities:** hot tub, exercise room. **Guest Services:** valet and coin laundry, area transportation. **Featured Amenity:** full hot breakfast.

[SAVE] [†1→] CALL [&M] [🏊] [BIZ] [📶]
[✕] [🔌] [📷] [📋] / SOME UNITS [🅢] [🐾]

HOLIDAY INN EXPRESS & SUITES
678/339-0505 **41**

Hotel. Rates not provided. Address: 12505 Cingular Way 30004 **Location:** SR 400 exit 11, 0.5 mi w. **Facility:** 124 units. 6 stories, interior corridors. **Pool(s):** outdoor. **Activities:** exercise room. **Guest Services:** valet and coin laundry, area transportation.

[†1→] CALL [&M] [🏊] [BIZ] [HS] [📶] [✕] [🔌] [📋] [📋]

HOMEWOOD SUITES
(770)998-1622 **53**

Extended Stay Hotel.
$119-$259 **Address:** 10775 Davis Dr 30009 **Location:** SR 400 exit 8; northwest corner. **Facility:** 112 efficiencies, some two bedrooms. 6 stories, interior corridors. **Terms:** 1-7 night minimum stay, cancellation fee imposed. **Amenities:** video games. **Pool(s):** outdoor. **Activities:** exercise room. **Guest Services:** valet and coin laundry, area transportation.

AAA Benefit:
Members save up to 10%!

[†1→] CALL [&M] [🏊] [BIZ] [HS] [📶] [📷] [🔌] [📋] [📋]

HYATT PLACE ALPHARETTA/NORTH POINT MALL
(770)594-8788 **52**

Hotel
$79-$299

⁛HYATT PLACE®

AAA Benefit: Members save 10%!

Address: 7500 North Point Pkwy 30022 **Location:** SR 400 exit 8, just e to North Point Pkwy, then just n. **Facility:** 124 units. 6 stories, interior corridors. **Terms:** cancellation fee imposed. **Pool(s):** outdoor. **Activities:** exercise room. **Guest Services:** valet laundry, area transportation. **Featured Amenity:** full hot breakfast.

[SAVE] [†1] [🍸] CALL [&M] [🏊] [BIZ]
[📶] [✕] [📷] [🔌] [📋] / SOME UNITS [🅢]

HYATT PLACE ATLANTA/ALPHARETTA/WINDWARD PARKWAY
(770)343-9566 **43**

Hotel
$59-$219

⁛HYATT PLACE®

AAA Benefit: Members save 10%!

Address: 5595 Windward Pkwy 30004 **Location:** SR 400 exit 11, just w. **Facility:** 127 units. 6 stories, interior corridors. **Terms:** cancellation fee imposed. **Amenities:** video games. **Pool(s):** outdoor. **Activities:** exercise room. **Guest Services:** valet laundry, area transportation. **Featured Amenity:** full hot breakfast. *(See ad this page.)*

[SAVE] [†1] [🍸] CALL [&M] [🏊] [BIZ] [📶] [✕] [🐾] [🔌]
[📋] / SOME UNITS [🅢] [HS]

AAA.com/ TourBook Comments

Let Your Voice Be Heard

If your visit to a TourBook-listed property doesn't meet your expectations, tell us about it.

AAA.com/TourBookComments

(See map & index p. 82.)

LA QUINTA INN & SUITES ATLANTA ALPHARETTA
(770)754-7800 **49**

W W Hotel. $67-$202 Address: 1350 North Point Dr 30022 Location: SR 400 exit 9, 0.5 mi e. Facility: 131 units. 6 stories, interior corridors. Pool(s): outdoor. Activities: hot tub, exercise room. Guest Services: valet and coin laundry.

RESIDENCE INN BY MARRIOTT ATLANTA
ALPHARETTA NORTH POINT MALL   (770)587-1151 **50**

Extended Stay Hotel
$79-$250

Residence Inn® Marriott **AAA Benefit:** Members save 5% or more!

Address: 1325 North Point Dr 30022 Location: SR 400 exit 9, just e to North Point Dr, then just s. Facility: 120 units, some two bedrooms, efficiencies and kitchens. 3 stories, interior corridors. Pool(s): outdoor. Activities: hot tub, exercise room. Guest Services: valet and coin laundry, area transportation. Featured Amenity: full hot breakfast.

RESIDENCE INN BY MARRIOTT ATLANTA
ALPHARETTA/WINDWARD   (770)664-0664 **44**

Extended Stay Hotel
$90-$286

Residence Inn® Marriott **AAA Benefit:** Members save 5% or more!

Address: 5465 Windward Pkwy 30004 Location: SR 400 exit 11, 0.4 mi w. Facility: 103 units, some two bedrooms, efficiencies and kitchens. 2-3 stories, interior/exterior corridors. Pool(s): outdoor. Activities: exercise room. Guest Services: valet and coin laundry, area transportation. Featured Amenity: full hot breakfast.

SPRINGHILL SUITES BY MARRIOTT ATLANTA
ALPHARETTA   (770)751-6900 **37**

Hotel
$65-$275

SPRINGHILL SUITES MARRIOTT **AAA Benefit:** Members save 5% or more!

Address: 12730 Deerfield Pkwy 30004 Location: SR 400 exit 11, 0.5 mi w to Deerfield Pkwy, then just n. Facility: 82 units. 3 stories, interior corridors. Pool(s): outdoor. Activities: limited exercise equipment. Guest Services: valet and coin laundry, area transportation. Featured Amenity: breakfast buffet.

STAYBRIDGE SUITES   770/569-7200 **45**

W W W Extended Stay Hotel. Rates not provided. Address: 3980 North Point Pkwy 30005 Location: SR 400 exit 10, 0.5 mi e. Facility: 118 efficiencies, some two bedrooms. 3 stories, interior corridors. Pool(s): heated outdoor. Activities: exercise room. Guest Services: valet and coin laundry, area transportation.

TOWNEPLACE SUITES BY MARRIOTT ALPHARETTA
(770)664-1300 **46**

Extended Stay Hotel
$76-$212

TOWNEPLACE SUITES MARRIOTT **AAA Benefit:** Members save 5% or more!

Address: 7925 Westside Pkwy 30009 Location: SR 400 exit 9, 0.3 mi w. Facility: 88 kitchen units, some two bedrooms. 3 stories, interior corridors. Pool(s): outdoor. Activities: exercise room. Guest Services: valet and coin laundry, area transportation. Featured Amenity: breakfast buffet.

WINGATE BY WYNDHAM ALPHARETTA   (770)649-0955 **57**

W W Hotel. $74-$149 Address: 1005 Kingswood Pl 30004 Location: SR 400 exit 8, 0.7 mi w. Facility: 84 units. 4 stories, interior corridors. Amenities: safes. Activities: exercise room. Guest Services: valet and coin laundry, area transportation.

WHERE TO EAT

ATLANTIC SEAFOOD COMPANY   770/640-0488 **67**

W W W Seafood. Fine Dining. $16-$40 AAA Inspector Notes: Seafood lovers will rejoice with the selection of fresh options at this restaurant. The menu changes regularly, but you can expect to see items such as Atlantic salmon, Chilean sea bass, swordfish, African prawns and mountain trout. Oyster and sushi options are also available. Relax at the bar or on the patio while skilled chefs create mouthwatering dishes that celebrate the flavors of the ocean. Features: full bar, patio dining, early bird specials, happy hour. Address: 2345 Mansell Rd 30222 Location: SR 400 exit 8, just e. Parking: on-site and valet.

CABERNET   770/777-5955 **60**

W W W Steak. Fine Dining. $11-$44 AAA Inspector Notes: The rock salt-crusted rib-eye for two is renowned at this upscale steakhouse on the northern fringes of the metropolitan area. Prime steak options are the house specialty, but the seafood is nothing to sneeze at! The large, beautifully designed dining area and the intimate lounge make this an ideal location for an elegant dinner or night on the town. Features: full bar, patio dining, happy hour. Reservations: suggested. Address: 5575 Windward Pkwy 30004 Location: SR 400 exit 11, just w. Parking: valet only.

THE CHEESECAKE FACTORY   770/751-7011 **64**

W W W International. Casual Dining. $10-$30 AAA Inspector Notes: What started as a small bakery in Los Angeles in the 1970s has since blossomed into one of the most recognizable restaurant chains today. Known for their large portion sizes and seemingly never-ending menu, this restaurant features over 200 selections to choose from! The "SkinnyLicious" menu options may appeal to those counting calories. Features: full bar, patio dining, Sunday brunch. Address: 2075 North Point Cir 30022 Location: SR 400 exit 9, just e to North Point Dr, then just s; in North Point Mall.

(See map & index p. 82.)

DI PAOLO 770/587-1051 68

▼▼▼▼ Italian. Fine Dining. $7-$22 **AAA Inspector Notes:** A taste of Northern Italian cuisine with a touch of elegance can be found here. The chefs use fresh ingredients, delicious dishes and an extensive wine list to keep their customers coming back time after time. While the menu changes seasonally, popular options include lasagna with Bolognese sauce and spinach-flavored pasta, branzino flown in fresh daily and chocolate cremeux made by the house pastry chef. **Features:** full bar. **Reservations:** suggested. **Address:** 8560 Holcomb Bridge Rd 30022 **Location:** SR 400 exit 7, 4.5 mi se; in Rivermont Square Shopping Center. D

GROUCHY'S NEW YORK DELI & BAGELS
 770/667-6933 63

▼ Sandwiches. Quick Serve. $5-$9 **AAA Inspector Notes:** Enjoy the succulent and lean pastrami sandwich or choose from other New York style specialties such as panini, wraps, soups, salads and burgers. Finish off your meal with some three-layer chocolate cake or a freshly baked cookie. **Address:** 11525 Haynes Bridge Rd 30009 **Location:** SR 400 exit 9, 0.3 mi w. B L

IPPOLITO'S 678/624-1900 55

▼▼ Italian. Casual Dining. $8-$19 **AAA Inspector Notes:** Skillfully served pasta dishes, bathed in excellent homemade sauces, are highlights at this warm, family-oriented eatery where tasty pizza can be customized to suit your taste. Worth a splurge are the delicious homemade desserts, including spumoni served with a coconut macaroon. **Features:** full bar, patio dining. **Address:** 12850 State Hwy 9 N 30004 **Location:** SR 400 exit 11, 1.2 mi w; in Windward Commons. L D CALL M

J. CHRISTOPHER'S 770/740-8571 54

▼▼ Breakfast. Casual Dining. $5-$12 **AAA Inspector Notes:** Blueberry crunch cakes, strawberry waffles and eggs Christopher are some of the breakfast favorites found here along with such seasonal items as pumpkin pancakes. Many traditional breakfast standards also are available. Lunch favorites include the club house burger and the classic club sandwich. Waldorf salads and signature soups are popular. **Address:** 3070 Windward Plaza 30005 **Location:** SR 400 exit 11, 1.1 mi e; in Windward Plaza.

B L CALL M

NAHM FINE THAI CUISINE 678/762-1818 58

▼▼▼ Thai. Casual Dining. $8-$30 **AAA Inspector Notes:** This popular little eatery defines "relaxed elegance". The cheery atmosphere provides an escape from the hustle of the day while the delicious flavor transports you to far away lands. The menu features authentic cuisine focusing on curries, noodles and fresh seafood. My advice for first time visitors is to talk to your server about your spice tolerance levels. **Features:** full bar, patio dining. **Address:** 5310 Windward Pkwy, Suite C 30004 **Location:** SR 400 exit 11, 0.5 mi w; on north side. L D

PAPPADEAUX SEAFOOD KITCHEN 770/992-5566

▼▼ Cajun Seafood. Casual Dining. $11-$53 **AAA Inspector Notes:** A seafood lover's delight, the restaurant taps into a little bit of New Orleans with its Cajun dishes and elaborate menu selections. Patrons might start off with a creative choice of blackened oyster and shrimp fondeaux with crayfish and let the feast begin. While music plays in the background, patrons can dig into dirty rice or spicy gumbo loaded with seafood. Well-seasoned shrimp and fish are prepared in varied ways. **Features:** full bar, Sunday brunch, happy hour. **Address:** 10795 Davis Dr 30004 **Location:** SR 400 exit 8, just w. L D

P.F. CHANG'S CHINA BISTRO 770/992-3070 66

▼▼▼ Chinese. Fine Dining. $8-$25 **AAA Inspector Notes:** Trendy, upscale decor provides a pleasant backdrop for New Age Chinese dining. Appetizers, soups and salads are a meal by themselves. Vegetarian plates and sides, noodles, chow meins, chicken and meat dishes are created from exotic, fresh ingredients. **Features:** full bar, happy hour. **Address:** 7925 North Point Pkwy 30022 **Location:** SR 400 exit 8, just e. L D CALL M

RAY'S ON THE CREEK 770/649-0064 65

▼▼▼▼ American. Fine Dining. $10-$34 **AAA Inspector Notes:** Steak, chops and seafood are highlights at this popular eatery in the Northern Atlanta suburbs. Huge beams support the high ceiling of the innovatively-designed, upscale American outpost where diners can hear live music on certain evenings. Save room for the luscious desserts. **Features:** full bar, patio dining, Sunday brunch. **Address:** 1700 Mansell Rd 30004 **Location:** SR 400 exit 8, just w. L D CALL M

RISING ROLL 770/752-8082

▼ Sandwiches. Quick Serve. $7-$10 **AAA Inspector Notes:** As upscale as a self-serve delicatessen can be, this location can be busy during the lunch rush. Featuring a variety of in-house-made breads, the standards of sandwiches, soups and salads are given a few distinctive and creative twists. **Address:** 11417 Haynes Bridge Rd 30004 **Location:** SR 400 exit 9, just w. L CALL M

SRI KRISHNA VILAS 770/475-9195 56

▼▼ Indian. Casual Dining. $10-$18 **AAA Inspector Notes:** In a quiet strip mall, this eatery is a perfect spot to sample a wide selection of freshly prepared and well-spiced dishes. Vegetarians will find plentiful options among the traditional tandoori, dosa and uttapam (an Indian-style pancake). The setting is relaxed and comfortable and the service warm and personable. **Features:** full bar. **Address:** 5815 Windward Pkwy, Suite 100 30022 **Location:** SR 400 exit 11, just e; in Windward Crossing. L D

THAI THAI 770/777-1306 62

▼▼▼ Thai. Casual Dining. $8-$13 **AAA Inspector Notes:** This restaurant is noted for quick, efficient service and tasty Thai food that is easy on the purse. Lunch combination specials are popular and there are many other traditional Thai favorites to enjoy such as red snapper crispy basil, black garlic seafood, spicy catfish and a number of curries. **Features:** beer & wine. **Address:** 11525 Haynes Bridge Rd, Suite 150 30004 **Location:** SR 400 exit 9, 0.3 mi w. L D CALL M

TWISTED TACO 770/777-9199 57

▼▼ Tex-Mex. Casual Dining. $7-$16 **AAA Inspector Notes:** The fajita salad here is mouth-watering as are the tortillas with fresh salsa. There are a great variety of tempting tacos which include beef, chicken and fish—with such names as wild Alaskan, Greek and Buffalo Bill. Burgers and sandwiches also are available. They offer a good selection of premium tequilas. **Features:** full bar. **Address:** 5815 Windward Pkwy 30005 **Location:** SR 400, just e; in Windward Crossing. L D CALL M

THE VARSITY 770/777-4004

▼ Hot Dogs Burgers. Quick Serve. $2-$10 **AAA Inspector Notes:** This restaurant is part of a small chain of restaurants found only in Georgia. A popular post-game hangout, this place promises good, fast food in a quirky atmosphere. The cashier will greet you with a friendly "What'll you have?" (a catch phrase that is almost as famous as the chili dogs). Whether you choose the naked dog, heavy dog or glorified hamburger make sure you add the signature frosted orange drink. **Address:** 11556 Rainwater Dr 30009 **Location:** SR 400 exit 9, 0.3 mi w to Westside Pkwy, then just n. L D CALL M

VILLAGE TAVERN 770/777-6490 61

▼▼▼ American. Casual Dining. $9-$28 **AAA Inspector Notes:** Attentive, personable servers bring out fresh entrees of steak, seafood, chicken, wood-oven pizzas, sandwiches, soups, salads and some downright tasty made-in-house potato chips. The comprehensive offerings, including a children's menu, ensure there is something for everyone. **Features:** full bar, Sunday brunch. **Address:** 11555 Rainwater Dr 30004 **Location:** SR 400 exit 9, 0.3 mi w to Westside Pkwy, then just n. L D

VINNY'S ON WINDWARD 770/772-4644 59

▼▼▼ American. Fine Dining. $10-$30 **AAA Inspector Notes:** Contemporary, creative American cuisine flavored with Italian influences is served in an upscale, stylish atmosphere near business parks and lodgings in this tony northern Atlanta suburb. Try the fettuccine and seafood entrée, filled with mussels, sea bass, scallops, shrimp, onion and tomato. Don't forget the tiramisu! **Features:** full bar. **Reservations:** suggested. **Address:** 5355 Windward Pkwy 30004 **Location:** SR 400 exit 11, 0.5 mi w. **Parking:** valet only. L D CALL M

AMERICUS (D-2) pop. 17,041, elev. 360'

Americus-Sumter Tourism Council: 101 W. Lamar St., Americus, GA 31709. **Phone:** (229) 928-6059.

Self-guiding tours: A brochure detailing a driving tour past more than 40 antebellum, Greek Revival and Victorian homes in the historic district may be obtained from the Americus-Sumter Tourism Council.

HABITAT FOR HUMANITY INTERNATIONAL GLOBAL VILLAGE & DISCOVERY CENTER is at 721 W. Church St. The six-acre site includes the Welcome Center, the Living in Poverty Area and 15 replicas of Habitat homes from around the world. Traditional household items also are displayed. **Hours:** Mon.-Fri. 9-5 (also Sat. 10-2, Mar.-Nov.); phone for holiday schedule. **Cost:** Donations. **Phone:** (229) 924-6935, ext. 7937 or (800) 422-4828, ext. 7937.

BEST WESTERN PLUS WINDSOR HOTEL

(229)924-1555

Historic Hotel
$105-$255

| Best Western PLUS | **AAA Benefit:** Save 10% or more every day and earn 10% bonus points! |

Address: 125 W Lamar St 31709 **Location:** On US 280; downtown. Located in historic area. **Facility:** This historic hotel, circa 1892, displays charming castle-like architecture complete with turrets, and features an atrium lobby with rich oak wood and period décor of the Victorian-style era. 53 units. 5 stories, interior corridors. **Terms:** cancellation fee imposed. **Dining:** 2 restaurants. **Activities:** exercise room. **Guest Services:** valet laundry.

[SAVE] [↕] [♿] [⊤] [BIZ] [HS] [📶] [➊] [🖥] [💻]

HAMPTON INN

(229)924-3890

▼▼▼ **Hotel.** $99-$139 **Address:** 1609 E Lamar St 31709 **Location:** On US 280, 1.3 mi w of center. **Facility:** 55 units. 3 stories, interior corridors. **Terms:** check-in 4 pm, 1-7 night minimum stay, cancellation fee imposed. **Pool(s):** outdoor. **Activities:** exercise room. **Guest Services:** valet laundry.

AAA Benefit: Members save up to 10%!

[↕] [➔] [BIZ] [📶] [➊] [🖥] [💻]

QUALITY INN

(229)924-4431

▼▼ **Hotel.** $71-$100 **Address:** 1205 S Martin Luther King Jr Blvd 31709 **Location:** Jct US 280 and 19, just n on US 19; west of town. **Facility:** 96 units. 2 stories (no elevator), exterior corridors. **Pool(s):** outdoor. **Guest Services:** coin laundry.

[↕] [➔] [BIZ] [📶] [➊] [🖥] [💻] / SOME UNITS [S] [HS]

WHERE TO EAT

LITTLE BROTHER'S BISTRO & CAFE   229/924-6944

▼ Sandwiches. Quick Serve. $7-$10 **AAA Inspector Notes:** For a quick tasty lunch, this place really hits the spot. Hand-crafted sandwiches and a variety of specialty soups and salads are offered. Each is paired with a tasty muffin for just a hint of sweetness. Try a classic Reuben or the wicked Gouda filled with tasty roast beef and chipotle Gouda cheese. **Address:** 133 W Lamar St 31709 **Location:** On US 280; downtown. **Parking:** street only. [B] [L] CALL [♿M] [🛍]

THE STATION   229/931-5398

▼▼ American. Casual Dining. $6-$23 **AAA Inspector Notes:** Look for the storefront with the toy train display in the window and you have reached your destination. The menu here has a nice mix of meat, seafood, sandwiches and even pizza. Rotating daily specials add an extra option to the selection. Only dinner is served on Saturday. **Features:** full bar. **Address:** 222 W Lamar St 31709 **Location:** Between Cotton Ave and Jackson St; downtown. **Parking:** street only. [L] [D] CALL [♿M]

ANDERSONVILLE (D-3) pop. 255, elev. 394'

ANDERSONVILLE CIVIL WAR VILLAGE, .2 mi. e. on SR 49, is a restored village that once was the point of disembarkation for Civil War prisoners on their way to Andersonville, the Confederate prison. A self-guiding walking tour of the village begins at the welcome center located in the Drummer Boy Civil War Museum. Highlights include a pioneer farm and a 1927 log church. The museum displays Civil War uniforms and an Andersonville diorama.

Time: Allow 1 hour minimum. **Hours:** Welcome center and museum open daily 9-5. Closed major holidays. **Cost:** Civil War Village free. Drummer Boy Museum $5; $1 (ages 13-17); free (under 13 with adult). **Phone:** (229) 924-2558. [↑] [🅿]

ANDERSONVILLE NATIONAL HISTORIC SITE (D-3)

Andersonville National Historic Site is 10 miles northeast of Americus on SR 49. It encompasses the Andersonville National Cemetery, an active national cemetery and the final resting place of those who died at Camp Sumter, and The National Prisoner of War Museum *(see attraction listing)* as well as the grounds of what was probably the Civil War's most infamous prisoner-of-war camp.

Opened in February 1864, the Andersonville prison was an almost impenetrable stockade encompassing 26.5 acres. Inside this enclosure was a line—called the "deadline"—that prisoners were not permitted to cross under penalty of death. A creek was the main water supply and eventually, because of contamination, a prime source of illness and death among the prisoners.

Although built to accommodate 10,000 prisoners, Andersonville at one time confined more than 32,000. The impoverished Confederate government was unable to supply prisoners with the bare necessities, and the mortality rate soared. Although prison commander Capt. Henry Wirz was powerless to prevent the overcrowding, after the war he was convicted by a military tribunal and hanged for conspiring to murder Union war prisoners.

A July 1864 excerpt from the diary of Sgt. David Kennedy of the 9th Ohio Cavalry describes the conditions of the site and its inhabitants as a "hell on Earth, where it takes seven of its occupants to make a shadow."

Andersonville commemorates those who have been prisoners of war in defense of this nation. More than 18,000 veterans and their dependents are buried at the site. On the grounds is Providence

Spring, which reputedly gushed forth in answer to the prayers of thirsty prisoners. The remains of wells and escape tunnels still exist. One corner and the north gate of the prison stockade have been rebuilt. Picnicking is permitted in designated areas. An audio driving tour is available. Guided tours are available upon request. Site open daily 8-5. Museum daily 9-4:30. Audio and guided tours are available during museum hours. Closed Jan. 1, Thanksgiving and Christmas. Free. Phone (229) 924-0343.

THE NATIONAL PRISONER OF WAR MUSEUM, just e. of SR 49 adjacent to the prison, contains various types of exhibits about prisoners of war from the Revolutionary War to current conflicts. Letters and videos give first-hand historical accounts by prisoners; displays contain personal items belonging to those who were confined here. During the 14 months it existed from 1864-65, a total of 12,920 Union soldiers and civilians died at Andersonville. The museum stands as a memorial to all prisoners of war in American history. **Time:** Allow 1 hour minimum. **Hours:** Daily 9-4:30. Closed Jan. 1, Thanksgiving and Christmas. **Cost:** Free. **Phone:** (229) 924-0343.

ASHBURN pop. 4,152

BEST WESTERN ASHBURN INN	(229)567-0080

Classic Motel
$70-$90

Best Western. AAA Benefit: Save 10% or more every day and earn 10% bonus points!

Address: 820 Shoney's Dr 31714 **Location:** I-75 exit 82, just sw. **Facility:** Guest rooms at this modest property are comfortable and updated. The motel is conveniently located right off the highway. 53 units. 2 stories (no elevator), exterior corridors. **Pool(s):** outdoor. **Featured Amenity: continental breakfast.**

WHERE TO EAT

KEITH-A-QUE   229/567-0333
Barbecue. Quick Serve. $2-$12 **AAA Inspector Notes:** Smoking for more than 15 years, this local favorite is near hotels. The menu features buckets of fried chicken, smoked ribs, chicken, Boston butt, dogs, burgers, liver and gizzards. Portions are hearty and there is a wide selection of sides to go with each selection. Everything, even Keith's own bottled barbecue sauce, can be packaged to go. **Address:** 260 E Washington Ave 31714 **Location:** I-75 exit 82, 0.9 mi sw. L D

ATHENS (B-3) pop. 115,452, elev. 800'
• Hotels p. 40 • Restaurants p. 41

If Atlanta were able to produce a child, Athens would be its name. Venerable heritage spiced with a contemporary vibe? Check. Antebellum homes that epitomize the "Old South"? Check. Home to a beloved institution of higher learning? Check. A healthy interest in the arts? Check. A hip music scene? Definitely check.

But like all children, Athens also has its own distinctive identity. You could call it the prototypical "college town," since the University of Georgia (UGA) sets the tone for a lot of what happens here. UGA games are big social events, college kids hang out at downtown watering holes, and the city's musical rep is largely driven by the kids as well; in 2003 *Rolling Stone* anointed Athens the nation's No. 1 college music town.

Athens' actual birth goes back much further, though. It began as Cedar Shoals, a tiny trading settlement that arose where an old Cherokee trail crossed the Oconee River. In 1785 the Georgia General Assembly granted a charter for a state-supported college, paving the way for the University of Georgia. Classes began in 1801, 5 years before the city of Athens—named in honor of ancient Greece's center of higher learning—was incorporated.

As dignified Federal homes rose up around the new campus Athens assumed the mantle of intellectual center of Georgia, and its cultured social life led prominent families to relocate. It played only a small role as a supply center during the Civil War, but as a result escaped the ransacking that was wrought on Atlanta. But like many other Southern towns, Athens has a Confederate memorial; it's downtown on Broad Street near the University of Georgia Arch.

The arch, at the corner of Broad Street and College Avenue, was modeled after the arch on Georgia's state seal, and you'll see it depicted on everything from T-shirts to university staff business cards. The three columns represent wisdom, justice and moderation. School legend maintains that freshmen who walk under the arch will not graduate, a jinx attributed to one Daniel Redfearn (class of 1910), who vowed not to walk under the wrought-iron gateway marking the main entrance to the campus until he had a diploma in hand. The young man kept to his word, and the unofficial tradition has continued.

Of course UGA's football team, the Georgia Bulldogs, is the source of much hometown pride. On New Year's Day in 1981 the team, led by Heisman Trophy winner Herschel Walker, defeated Notre Dame in the Sugar Bowl, clinching the 1980 NCAA National Championship. "Uga," the university's bulldog mascot, is based on a long line of English bulldogs. Uga V even tasted fame; he made the cover of *Sports Illustrated* and appeared in the movie "Midnight in the Garden of Good and Evil."

Spend some time wandering around downtown and you'll see reminders of the past. Athens was the wartime home of the Cook and Brother Armory, which manufactured infantry rifles, artillery and the double-barreled cannon. This unusual Civil War relic was intended to maximize damage to the enemy by firing two balls joined by a chain. During the cannon's only firing the barrels failed to fire simultaneously, and it's said that a cow and a cabin were the unfortunate targets when the cannonballs went their separate ways. It stands on the grounds of City Hall,

301 College Ave. (you can't miss the building's distinctive green-scaled dome).

A real oddity is "The Tree That Owns Itself," in a residential neighborhood at the corner of Finley and Dearing streets (a block south of Broad Street). William H. Jackson, on whose property this white oak stood, deeded ownership of the land to the tree within 8 feet on all sides in order to protect it. Technically, however, it's the offspring of The Tree That Owns Itself, since the original tree was either felled by a violent windstorm in 1942 or succumbed to disease and finally toppled after a long period of decline (historical accounts differ). The current tree has grown from one of its parent's acorns and stands in the same spot. Unlike its neighbors, it doesn't have to pay property taxes.

Dogwoods, cherry blossoms and daffodils—there's nothing like spring in the rolling piedmont of northeastern Georgia, and it's Athens' loveliest season. The Piedmont Gardeners Garden Tour, sponsored by the Piedmont Gardeners garden club, visits several private city gardens on the third Saturday in April, rain or shine. Tickets are $15 in advance, $20 the day of the tour; for details phone (706) 357-4430. Everyone gets their groove on at the AthFest Music and Arts Festival in late June. Bands jam during the day on outdoor stages and at night in the clubs, and there also are film screenings, an artisans' market and activities for kids.

Gen. William Tecumseh Sherman's infamously destructive "March to the Sea" fortunately bypassed Athens, so many of the mansions built by antebellum-era Athenians still stand. The city is sprinkled with historic districts, and a good way to get in touch with this heritage is to take a tour. Pick up maps and ask about suggestions for self-guiding walks at the Athens Welcome Center, 280 E. Dougherty St. The center is an informative stop if you're a first-time visitor.

Greek Revival antiquity isn't what this city's all about, though; it has a major reputation for music, especially indie rock. The local scene got its start in the '70s, when bands began playing at house parties and the presence of the university guaranteed hip audiences. The B-52's, a self-described "tacky little dance band from Athens, GA," was the first to hit the big time, riding new wave's commercial popularity with quirky rave-ups like "Rock Lobster" and later "Love Shack," their biggest hit.

Athens' other big success story is R.E.M., whose members worked in Athens and attended UGA. They started out locally, but by the mid-'80s R.E.M. was one of the most popular college rock bands in the country, and their jangle pop sound—itself heavily influenced by '60s forebears the Byrds—has been extremely influential. Their success put Athens on the map and gave exposure to other local outfits like Pylon and Love Tractor. More recently, Athens bands like the Drive-By Truckers have added a dose of country rock to the musical mix.

Athens Convention and Visitors Bureau: 300 N. Thomas St., Athens, GA 30601. **Phone:** (706) 357-4430 or (800) 653-0603.

Self-guiding tours: Brochures and maps detailing a walking tour past historic homes are available at the Athens Convention and Visitors Bureau and at the Athens Welcome Center, 280 E. Dougherty St.; phone (706) 353-1820 or (866) 455-1820. The center is in the Church-Waddel-Brumby House Museum, a Federal-style house built in 1820. A driving tour brochure outlining the Antebellum Trail also is available. The trail covers seven communities along a 100-mile stretch from Athens to Macon.

Shopping: Downtown Athens offers an ideal environment for relaxed browsing: several compact, pedestrian-friendly blocks of tree-shaded streets lined with shops. Specialty retailers sell jewelry, fashion, gifts and books. The Native America Gallery (195 E. Clayton St.) has all kinds of interesting items, including jewelry with tiny preserved flowers set in silver. Wuxtry Records (197 E. Clayton St.) has tons of new and used CDs and records, and the staff really knows their stuff (this *is* Athens, after all).

And stop by The Clubhouse (157 College Ave.) for any and everything UGA and dawg-related.

Nightlife: The Globe (199 N. Lumpkin St. at Clayton Street) has been an Athens hangout for more than 2 decades. It has a big brass bar and a mural behind the bar that's something of a travelogue of the world's great beverages. Comfy sofas and rocking chairs will make you want to linger. The selection of beers, wines and single malts is extensive, and the kitchen whips up good soups, salads and sandwiches. This bar gets crowded on weekends.

Lots of people—many of them famous—have played the 40 Watt Club (285 W. Washington St.) since it opened in 1978, and this is still the best venue in town to see up-and-coming local bands as well as indie and alternative acts that tour the club circuit. The Georgia Theatre (215 N. Lumpkin St.) is the landmark of Athens' storied music scene and books all kinds of acts from bluegrass to country rock to quirky singer-songwriters; it's a good place to catch local and regional musicians. Its rooftop bar also offers live music. *Flagpole,* a free weekly available at many shops, restaurants and clubs, has all the music, arts and events information you need.

CLASSIC CITY TOURS, 280 E. Dougherty St., offers guided bus tours of the area. The Athens Heritage Tour is a 90-minute tour that visits the oldest houses in town, including some sites on the University of Georgia campus. Other tours also are available. **Hours:** Mon., Wed. and Fri. at 1, Sat.-Sun. at 2. Tours require a minimum of four people and are subject to availability. **Cost:** $15. Reservations are recommended. **Phone:** (706) 208-8687. GT

SANDY CREEK NATURE CENTER is at 205 Old Commerce Rd.; take the Athens Perimeter Loop to the US 441 exit (Commerce Rd.), then just n. This nature preserve has more than 4 miles of paved and dirt trails and a variety of themed nature walks and wildlife observation areas. The center itself has a very well put together collection of live animal displays (fish, reptiles) and interactive exhibits, including an exhibit for loggerhead sea turtles. An 1815 log house also is on the grounds. Educational programs, log house tours and planetarium sky shows are available by reservation.

Bicycles are permitted on paved surfaces only. The center is connected to the Oconee River Greenway. **Time:** Allow 1 hour minimum. **Hours:** Trails and recreational areas open daily dawn-dusk. Nature center open Tues.-Sat. 8:30-5:30; closed major holidays. **Cost:** Free. **Phone:** (706) 613-3615. GT ⚅

TAYLOR-GRADY HOUSE is at 634 Prince Ave. The restored Greek Revival mansion was built in the mid-1840s by Gen. Robert Taylor, a planter and cotton merchant. In 1863 it was purchased by the family of Henry W. Grady, a newspaper editor considered by many to be the spokesman of the New South. An impressive orator, Grady stressed the importance of reconciliation between the North and South after the Civil War.

Time: Allow 30 minutes minimum. **Hours:** Mon., Wed. and Fri. 9-3, Tues. and Thurs. noon-4. Closed holidays and during special events. Phone ahead to confirm schedule. **Cost:** $3. **Phone:** (706) 549-8688.

TERRAPIN BEER CO. is at 265 Newton Bridge Rd. Tour the brewery to learn about the making of craft beer, and visit the tasting room to enjoy the brews. Samples are limited to up to 36 ounces and can be enjoyed indoors or out. **Note:** Closed-toed shoes are required for guided tours. Safety glasses and earplugs are provided. Visitors may bring in blankets, chairs and food. Pets on leashes are permitted outdoors. Arrive early for tours on University of Georgia game nights as space and tours are limited and may not be reserved.

Hours: Wed.-Thurs. 5:30-7:30, Fri.-Sat. 1-7:30, Sun. 1:30-3:30. Last tasting 30 minutes before closing. **Cost:** Guided tour free. Tour with samples $12. **Phone:** (706) 549-3377. GT 🍴 ⚅

UNIVERSITY OF GEORGIA campus can be entered from Broad St. through a mid-19th-century arch that symbolizes the state seal of Georgia. Founded in 1785, it is said to be the nation's first state-chartered university. Visitors can stroll the 615-acre campus and view historic structures, many of which were built before 1850. The Collegiate Tennis Hall of Fame, at the Dan Magill Tennis Complex, pays tribute to collegiate tennis players and is open during tennis matches. Guided tours of the campus are offered Mon.-Sat. by reservation. **Cost:** Free. **Phone:** (706) 542-0842 for the visitor center and

tour reservations, or (706) 542-1231 for Georgia Bulldogs teams tickets. GT

Butts-Mehre Heritage Hall, at 1 Selig Cir. on the University of Georgia campus, is a modern athletic complex named for two former coaches of the Georgia Bulldogs, Wallace Butts and Harry Mehre. The Heritage Museum on the second, third and fourth floors contains exhibits honoring Georgia athletes. Displays include Heisman and National Championship trophies, the Circle of Honor and videos that replay great moments in the university's sports history.

Time: Allow 30 minutes minimum. **Hours:** Mon.-Fri. 8-5. Closed major holidays. **Cost:** Free. **Phone:** (706) 542-9036.

Founders Memorial Garden, 325 S. Lumpkin St. on the University of Georgia campus, honors the founders of the first garden club in America, begun in 1891. The 2.5-acre grounds, created 1939-1950, include a formal boxwood garden, a perennial garden, an arboretum, two courtyards and a terrace. This garden is listed on the National Register of Historic Places. **Time:** Allow 30 minutes minimum. **Hours:** Daily dawn-dusk. **Cost:** Free. **Phone:** (706) 542-1816.

The Georgia Museum of Art is at 90 Carlton St. on the East Campus of the University of Georgia. The museum was founded in 1945 when Alfred H. Holbrook donated his collection of 100 American paintings to the university.

Now the collection contains more than 8,000 works including 19th-century through contemporary American paintings, Italian Renaissance paintings and an extensive collection of prints and drawings by American, European and Oriental masters. An outdoor sculpture garden displays works created by women artists. Food is available Tues.-Fri. 10-2. **Time:** Allow 1 hour minimum. **Hours:** Tues.-Sat. 10-5 (also Thurs. 5-9), Sun. 1-5. Closed major holidays. **Cost:** Free. **Phone:** (706) 542-4662. 🍴

State Botanical Garden of Georgia is at 2450 S. Milledge Ave. just s.w. of the University of Georgia campus. The 313-acre botanical garden serves as a cultural, educational and recreational facility on the Middle Oconee River. Five miles of nature trails extend into the natural areas typical of the habitats and plant communities found in Georgia's Piedmont region. A number of theme gardens and special collections display species from around the world.

The Alice Hand Callaway Visitor Center and Conservatory contains a collection of tropical and semitropical plants that provide a backdrop for concerts, lectures and art exhibitions. **Note:** Pets are not permitted. **Time:** Allow 30 minutes minimum. **Hours:** Grounds open daily 8-8, Apr.-Sept.; 8-6, rest of year. Visitor center open Tues.-Sat. 9-4:30, Sun. 11:30-4:30. Closed major holidays. **Cost:** Free. **Phone:** (706) 542-1244. 🍴

BEST WESTERN ATHENS　　(706)546-7311

Motel
$80-$160

AAA Benefit: Save 10% or more every day and earn 10% bonus points!

Address: 170 N Milledge Ave 30601 **Location:** Jct US 78 business route (Broad St), 0.5 mi w on SR 15. **Facility:** 70 units. 2 stories (no elevator), exterior corridors. **Terms:** cancellation fee imposed. **Guest Services:** coin laundry. **Featured Amenity: full hot breakfast.**

CANDLEWOOD SUITES　　706/548-9663

Extended Stay Hotel. Rates not provided. **Address:** 156 Classic Rd 30606 **Location:** Jct SR 10 Loop and US 78 business route, 1.1 mi w on US 78 business route to Classic Rd, then just s. **Facility:** 97 efficiencies. 4 stories, interior corridors. **Activities:** exercise room. **Guest Services:** complimentary and valet laundry.

COMFORT INN & SUITES　　(706)227-9700

Hotel. $69-$499 **Address:** 3980 Atlanta Hwy 30622 **Location:** SR 10 Loop exit 18 (Atlanta Hwy), 0.7 mi w. **Facility:** 69 units, some kitchens. 4 stories, interior corridors. **Amenities:** safes. **Pool(s):** outdoor. **Activities:** exercise room. **Guest Services:** coin laundry.

COUNTRY INN & SUITES BY CARLSON - ATHENS
706/612-9100

Hotel. Rates not provided. **Address:** 236 Old Epps Bridge Rd 30606 **Location:** Oceanfront. Jct SR 10 Loop and US 78 business route (Broad St), 2.9 mi ne on US 78 business route (Broad St) to Old Epps Bridge Rd, just n. **Facility:** 81 units. 4 stories, interior corridors. **Pool(s):** heated indoor. **Activities:** hot tub, exercise room. **Guest Services:** coin laundry.

COURTYARD BY MARRIOTT DOWNTOWN ATHENS
(706)369-7000

Hotel
$98-$177

AAA Benefit: Members save 5% or more!

Address: 166 N Finley St 30601 **Location:** Corner of N Finley St and US 78 business route (Broad St). **Facility:** 105 units. 3 stories, interior/exterior corridors. **Terms:** check-in 4 pm. **Pool(s):** outdoor. **Activities:** exercise room. **Guest Services:** valet and coin laundry, boarding pass kiosk.

DAYS INN　　(706)543-6511

Motel. $137-$211 **Address:** 230 N Finley St 30601 **Location:** 0.3 mi w on US 78 business route (Broad St), just n. **Facility:** 76 units. 2 stories (no elevator), exterior corridors. **Pool(s):** outdoor.

GRADUATE ATHENS　　706/549-7020

Motel
Rates not provided

Address: 295 E Dougherty St 30601 **Location:** Jct Thomas and Dougherty sts; downtown. **Facility:** 122 units, some two bedrooms. 2 stories (no elevator), interior/exterior corridors. **Dining:** 2 restaurants. **Pool(s):** outdoor. **Activities:** exercise room, spa. **Guest Services:** valet laundry.

HAMPTON INN BY HILTON - ATHENS　　(706)548-9600

Hotel
$109-$279

AAA Benefit: Members save up to 10%!

Address: 2220 W Broad St 30606 **Location:** Jct SR 10 Loop and US 78 business route (Broad St), 3.1 mi ne on US 78 business route (Broad St). **Facility:** 112 units. 5 stories, interior corridors. **Terms:** 1-7 night minimum stay, cancellation fee imposed. **Pool(s):** outdoor. **Activities:** exercise room. **Guest Services:** valet laundry. **Featured Amenity: continental breakfast.**

HILTON GARDEN INN DOWNTOWN ATHENS　　(706)353-6800

Hotel. $119-$219 **Address:** 390 E Washington St 30601 **Location:** Jct N Thomas St; downtown. **Facility:** 185 units. 8 stories, interior corridors. **Parking:** on-site (fee). **Terms:** 1-7 night minimum stay, cancellation fee imposed. **Activities:** exercise room. **Guest Services:** valet and coin laundry.

AAA Benefit: Members save up to 10%!

HOLIDAY INN ATHENS　　(706)549-4433

Hotel. $79-$399 **Address:** 197 E Broad St 30603 **Location:** On US 78 business route (Broad St); jct N Hull St; center. **Facility:** 210 units. 2-7 stories, interior corridors. **Terms:** cancellation fee imposed. **Pool(s):** outdoor. **Activities:** exercise room. **Guest Services:** valet and coin laundry, area transportation.

HOLIDAY INN EXPRESS ATHENS　　706/546-8122

Hotel. Rates not provided. **Address:** 513 W Broad St 30601 **Location:** On US 78 business route (Broad St); center. **Facility:** 160 units. 5 stories, interior corridors. **Pool(s):** outdoor. **Activities:** exercise room. **Guest Services:** valet and coin laundry.

HOTEL INDIGO ATHENS DOWNTOWN/UNIV. AREA
706/546-0430

Contemporary Hotel. Rates not provided. **Address:** 500 College Ave 30601 **Location:** Just n of center. **Facility:** 130 units, some kitchens. 5 stories, interior corridors. **Parking:** on-site (fee) and street. **Activities:** exercise room. **Guest Services:** valet laundry.

QUALITY INN & SUITES   (706)549-1530

  Motel. $70-$300 **Address:** 2715 Atlanta Hwy 30606 **Location:** Jct Loop SR 10, 1.8 mi e. **Facility:** 45 units. 2 stories (no elevator), exterior corridors. **Activities:** limited exercise equipment.

SLEEP INN & SUITES   (706)850-1261

Hotel. $69-$399 **Address:** 109 Florence Dr 30622 **Location:** Jct SR 10 Loop and US 78 business route, 1.2 mi w on US 78 to Florence Dr, then just s. **Facility:** 65 units. 4 stories, interior corridors. **Pool(s):** heated indoor. **Activities:** exercise room. **Guest Services:** coin laundry.

SPRINGHILL SUITES BY MARRIOTT ATHENS   (706)353-8484

Contemporary Hotel. $69-$145 **Address:** 3500 Daniells Bridge Rd 30606 **Location:** Jct US 78/SR 8/10 Loop and US 29, just w on US 29 to Jennings Mill Rd, just s. **Facility:** 99 units. 5 stories, interior corridors. **Pool(s):** outdoor. **Activities:** exercise room. **Guest Services:** valet and coin laundry.

AAA Benefit: Members save 5% or more!

WINGATE BY WYNDHAM ATHENS NEAR DOWNTOWN   (706)995-4000

Hotel
$80-$240

Address: 255 North Ave 30601 **Location:** SR 10 Loop exit 11B (Dougherty St/North Ave); 1 mi n of downtown. **Facility:** 73 units. 4 stories, interior corridors. **Amenities:** safes. **Pool(s):** heated indoor. **Activities:** hot tub, exercise room. **Guest Services:** valet and coin laundry.

WHERE TO EAT

AGUA LINDA   706/543-1500

  Tex-Mex. Casual Dining. $6-$14 **AAA Inspector Notes:** This popular restaurant presents a menu of typical Tex-Mex dishes, as well as fish and barbecue selections. Three types of salsa are brought to the table along with tortilla chips to begin the meal and then guests can delve into a very good selection of tacos, burritos, fajitas, flautas, tostados and quesadillas. The locals love it. **Features:** full bar, patio dining. **Address:** 1376 Prince Ave 30606 **Location:** SR 10 Loop exit 7 (Prince Ave), 0.6 mi se.

BARBERITOS   706/549-9954

Southwestern. Quick Serve. $6-$10 **AAA Inspector Notes:** This regional chain features quick-serve, made-before-diners'-eyes Southwestern fare, most of which can be eaten without utensils. The menu appeals to people on the go, children eager to be creative, weight-watchers and the health-conscious. Guests choose burritos, tacos, salads, quesadillas, nachos, fajitas and munchies, each of will can be customized to suit the diner's tastes. **Bar:** beer only.

LOCATIONS:
Address: 1860 Barnett Shoals Rd 30605 **Location:** Jct US 78 and Barnett Shoals Rd, 1.5 mi sw; in Georgetown Square Shopping Center. **Phone:** 706/549-9954
Address: 259 E Clayton St 30601 **Location:** Downtown.
Phone: 706/549-9008

BAR-B-QUE SHACK   706/613-6752

Barbecue. Quick Serve. $7-$12 **AAA Inspector Notes:** Chicken, pork and stew are specialties of this rustic, well-known eatery where everything is smoked on site. Service is syrupy sweet and provided by a team of energetic young staffers who are eager to make sure you enjoy the simple fare. Those in a hurry can hit the drive-through window for ribs and banana pudding to go. **Address:** 4320 Lexington Rd 30605 **Location:** 4.2 mi e on US 78; jct US 129/SR 10 Loop/US 78, 2.6 mi se on US 78 (Lexington Rd).

BIG CITY BREAD CAFE   706/353-0029

Deli. Quick Serve. $7-$25 **AAA Inspector Notes:** In a former Salvation Army building and fire station, the restaurant prepares breakfast plates; salads and sandwiches for lunch; and dinner fare at night. Offering cafe food with a fresh, healthy flair. The pastries, cakes and breads available in the small market are simply delicious. The patio, where guests can dine under Chinese elms, opens seasonally. **Features:** beer & wine, patio dining, Sunday brunch. **Address:** 393 N Finley St, Studio A 30601 **Location:** Between Prince Ave and Broad St; downtown. **Parking:** on-site and street.

CLOCKED   706/548-9175

Sandwiches Burgers. Casual Dining. $5-$10 **AAA Inspector Notes:** This small, comfort-food eatery serves some of the best hamburgers and fries, chili and vegetarian food in town. All ingredients are free of pesticides, herbicides, growth hormones, ammonia, antibiotics and other additives and are organic whenever possible. For dessert, try one of the fountain creations. **Features:** beer & wine. **Address:** 259 W Washington St 30601 **Location:** Downtown. **Parking:** street only.

COPPER CREEK BREWING COMPANY   706/546-1102

American. Casual Dining. $9-$15 **AAA Inspector Notes:** The main feature of this dining room is the large copper brew barrels at the entrance. The house-brewed beers complement the eclectic menu offerings like the ground buffalo burger, falafel, Southern fish fry and Filipino egg rolls. **Features:** full bar, Sunday brunch. **Address:** 140 E Washington St 30601 **Location:** Downtown. **Parking:** street only.

DEPALMA'S ITALIAN CAFE   706/354-6966

Italian. Casual Dining. $6-$20 **AAA Inspector Notes:** This popular eatery is known for the number of delicious dishes on the menu, extensive wine and beer choices and the friendly service diners have come to expect. Located close to the University in historic downtown, this location caters to students and young professionals. **Features:** full bar, patio dining. **Address:** 401 E Broad St 30601 **Location:** Downtown. **Parking:** street only.

DEPALMA'S ITALIAN CAFE   706/369-0085

Italian. Casual Dining. $6-$20 **AAA Inspector Notes:** This strip mall storefront restaurant features a rustic décor accented by empty wine bottles to remind diners that other than great food they offer a huge selection of vintages, including by-the-glass selections which complement the menu. Offerings are rife with the chef's interpretation of Italian comfort food such as pasta DePalma (baked angel hair pasta with rosemary cream sauce), fettuccine di parma (fettuccine with Alfredo, peas, prosciutto and grilled chicken). **Features:** full bar, patio dining. **Address:** 1965 Barnett Shoals Rd 30605 **Location:** Jct US 78 and Barnett Shoals Rd, 1.5 mi sw; in Green Acres Center.

DEPALMA'S ITALIAN CAFE   706/552-1237

Italian. Casual Dining. $6-$20 **AAA Inspector Notes:** The empty wine bottles that make up part of the rustic decor remind diners of the impressive selection of vintages, including by-the-glass options. Menu options include patron-created pasta-and-sauce dishes, seafood entrées or classic Italian pasta dishes such as the chef's interpretations of pasta DePalma (baked angel hair pasta with rosemary cream sauce) or fettuccine di Parma (fettuccine with Alfredo, peas, prosciutto and grilled chicken). **Features:** full bar, patio dining, happy hour. **Address:** 2080 Timothy Rd 30606 **Location:** SR 8/10 Loop exit US 78 business route (Broad St), just e.

EAST WEST BISTRO   706/546-4240

▼▼▼▼ International. Fine Dining. $8-$28 **AAA Inspector Notes:** On the ground floor, the casual section of this restaurant serves fusion cuisine and tapas. Up the stairs on the second floor is a more upscale dining room in which Italian dishes tempt diners. The wine list is excellent. **Features:** full bar, patio dining, Sunday brunch, happy hour. **Reservations:** suggested, for upstairs dining. **Address:** 351 E Broad St 30605 **Location:** Downtown. **Parking:** street only.

[L] [D] [🐂]

FATZ   706/425-8780

▼▼▼ Regional American. Casual Dining. $7-$19 **AAA Inspector Notes:** Friendly staff and appealing country decor help set the tone for a relaxed and enjoyable dining experience. It's not unusual for guests to wait to be seated at the popular spot, which earns raves for its well-prepared variations on chicken, steak, ribs and pasta, as well as salads and sandwiches. The signature Southern-style peach cobbler served with vanilla ice cream and walnuts is scrumptious. **Features:** full bar. **Address:** 4115 Lexington Rd (US 78) 30605 **Location:** US 441 Loop exit 8, just e. [L] [D] CALL [✆M]

FIVE & TEN   706/546-7300

▼▼▼▼ New American. Fine Dining. $24-$36 **AAA Inspector Notes:** The converted home that this restaurant is located in provides an upscale, homey ambience which nicely complements the chef's cuisine. A multifaceted menu offers ever-popular Lowcountry frog-more stew and other Southern inspired options to blend and new. Dishes feature fresh seasonal ingredients and local and organic items when possible. Also find excellent wine and cheese selections. **Features:** full bar, early bird specials, Sunday brunch. **Reservations:** suggested. **Address:** 1073 S Milledge Ave 30605 **Location:** From US 78/10, 1 mi n on Milledgeville Rd, just e. [D]

THE GLOBE   706/353-4721

▼▼▼ American. Gastropub. $8-$17 **AAA Inspector Notes:** In business since 1989, this highly-touted pub serves pub food made with care. A wide selection of sandwiches and burgers as well as soups, salads and appetizers such as the famous Globe chips are offered. Try the fish and chips, New York style frites or a nightly special such as meatloaf with homemade mashed potatoes or a barbecue pulled-pork sandwich. An excellent choice of beer, wines and single malts are good thirst quenchers. Local art lends to the rustic feel with a Southern touch. **Features:** full bar, patio dining, Sunday brunch. **Address:** 199 N Lumpkin St 30601 **Location:** Jct US 78 business route (Broad St), just n. **Parking:** street only.

[L] [D] [LATE]

GOLDEN DRAGON   706/552-1688

▼▼ Mandarin. Casual Dining. $8-$20 **AAA Inspector Notes:** The restaurant prepares an excellent selection of Mandarin cuisine, soups and vegetarian dishes. Many enjoy the lunch buffet due to the friendly service, relaxed atmosphere and huge variety of options. The a la carte menu is also available all day. **Features:** beer & wine. **Address:** 126 Alps Rd 30606 **Location:** Jct US 78 business route (Broad St), just s; in North Alps Square Shopping Center.

[L] [D]

THE GRIT   706/543-6592

▼▼▼ Vegetarian. Casual Dining. $5-$12 **AAA Inspector Notes:** Housed in a charming historic building, this restaurant is a local favorite for hearty vegetarian and gluten-free cuisine since 1987. The food is delicious and varied with many international influences. Popular dishes include the vegetable plate, hot noodle bowl and the grit staple with pinto beans, brown rice and melted cheese. Save room for one of the many bakery items on display at the entrance. **Features:** beer & wine, patio dining, Sunday brunch. **Address:** 199 Prince Ave 30601 **Location:** Downtown. **Parking:** street only.

[B] [L] [D]

HILLTOP GRILLE   706/353-7667

▼▼▼ American. Casual Dining. $7-$31 **AAA Inspector Notes:** With original artwork and framed photos of University of Georgia legends, this country club-style restaurant offers a wide variety of well-prepared American standards. Lunch, blue-plate and early-bird specials are offered daily. Steaks, chops and seafood—with dishes such as crab au gratin and the signature Hilltop chops—dominate the selections in the evening. **Features:** full bar, patio dining, early bird specials, Sunday brunch. **Address:** 2310 W Broad St 30606 **Location:** Jct SR 10 Loop and US 78 business route (Broad St), 2.9 mi ne on US 78 business route (Broad St).

[L] [D] CALL [✆M] [🐂]

LAST RESORT GRILL   706/549-0810

▼▼▼ New American. Fine Dining. $7-$20 **AAA Inspector Notes:** This spot is an eclectic-style eatery with some very succulent and creative dishes such as the house-braised pork belly with an ancho glaze over sweet potato mash, sautéed greens and finished with grilled jalapeño-pineapple salsa and au jus. Farm fresh ingredients ensure delicious flavors and quality cuisine. This is a popular place and both patience and reservations are recommended. **Features:** full bar, Sunday brunch. **Reservations:** suggested. **Address:** 174-184 W Clayton St 30601 **Location:** Jct N Hull St, just e. **Parking:** street only. [L] [D]

LOCO'S GRILL & PUB   706/549-7700

▼▼ American. Casual Dining. $8-$15 **AAA Inspector Notes:** The popular chain started in Athens in 1988 and has since grown to more than 20 restaurants in three states. The 'grill & pub' moniker is a perfect fit since it's not just a popular place to eat but also a great place to hang out with friends. The menu is predominantly sandwiches and wraps with a few steak and seafood entrée offerings, but the diversity in those offerings leaves something for everyone. The kid-friendly atmosphere makes it a great and inexpensive option for family night out. **Features:** full bar. **Address:** 2020 Timothy Rd 30606 **Location:** SR 8/10 Loop exit US 78 business route (Broad St), just e, then just se. [L] [D] [LATE] CALL [✆M]

MARTI'S AT MIDDAY   706/543-3541

▼ Deli. Quick Serve. $5-$10 **AAA Inspector Notes:** In a seemingly out-of-place roadside house, this eclectic bistro offers a delightful selection of fresh, made-from-scratch soups, salads and gourmet sandwiches. Patrons shouldn't trifle with the huge sandwiches, and most are satisfied with a half-sandwich and cup of soup. Yummy grab-and-go confections make for a sweet trip back to work or school. Early risers get to enjoy freshly made muffins and Jittery Joe's coffee. **Features:** patio dining. **Address:** 1280 Prince Ave 30606 **Location:** SR 10 Loop exit 7 (Prince Ave), 0.7 mi se. [B] [L] [🐂]

THE NATIONAL   706/549-3450

▼▼▼ European. Fine Dining. $10-$26 **AAA Inspector Notes:** Local, seasonal and organic ingredients are used at this neighborhood eatery when possible. Diners can be wowed by frequently changing offerings of highly imaginative and creative cuisine such as crispy Springer Mountain chicken confit, grilled beef hanger steak, smoked trout chowder and boquerones (anchovies) with pickled chiles, caperberries and tomato-garlic toast. The espresso bar is open throughout the day. **Features:** full bar, patio dining. **Reservations:** suggested. **Address:** 232 W Hancock Ave 30601 **Location:** Just w of center; downtown. **Parking:** street only. [L] [D] [🐂]

PORTERHOUSE GRILL   706/369-0990

▼▼▼ Steak. Fine Dining. $9-$38 **AAA Inspector Notes:** Although this pizza is pegged as an American steakhouse—and the steaks are mouthwatering—its other choices are just as good. Among them are rainbow trout, crab cakes, duck, other fresh seafood and a few vegetarian dishes. **Features:** full bar, Sunday brunch. **Reservations:** suggested. **Address:** 459 E Broad St 30601 **Location:** Downtown. **Parking:** street only. [L] [D]

SONNY'S REAL PIT BAR-B-Q   706/546-0385

▼▼ Barbecue. Casual Dining. $8-$17 **AAA Inspector Notes:** Bearing the name after its founder, Floyd "Sonny" Tillman, this barbecue restaurant first opened its doors circa 1968 in Gainesville, Florida and has since spawned over 150 more throughout the Southeast. The menu is steeped in finger lickin' favorites such as ribs, pulled pork, beef brisket, burgers, catfish, shrimp and chargrilled chicken. Let's not forget about the fried okra, which is the perfect starter dish, and their homemade baked beans. **Features:** beer only. **Address:** 3755 Atlanta Hwy 30622 **Location:** Jct US 29/78, just w.

[L] [D]

THE VARSITY   706/548-6325

▼ Hot Dogs Burgers. Quick Serve. $2-$8 **AAA Inspector Notes:** "What'll you have?" is the question du jour at this absolute must for visitors to Athens. Employees shout the question from behind the long stainless steel counter, just as has been the tradition since 1928. The food here is not fussy—just burgers, dogs and a few other sandwiches with names such as the glorified burger or the heavy dog—but the experience is one not to be missed. The frozen orange drink is a real treat. **Features:** patio dining. **Address:** 1000 W Broad St 30601 **Location:** Jct US 78 business route (Broad St) and SR 15A. [L] [D] CALL [✆M]

Atlanta

Then & Now

Southern-fried California rockers Little Feat long to get back to city streets warmed by the Georgia sun. Gladys Knight, backed by the Pips, hops a late-night train to be with her man. Ludacris lays down slammin' beats about gangstas and all-night parties. Sometimes a song can tell you a lot about a city. And when you've got a lot going on, you're bound to end up being name-checked in song.

Atlanta—also known as Hotlanta, Mylanta and The Big Peach—has had a lot going on since 1837, when an army engineer surveyed routes for the Western and Atlantic Railroad that would connect Georgia with Chattanooga and provide a trade route to points west. A train depot was ~~~~~~~~~~~~ MARTA's Five Points station stands ~~~~~

Less than 30 years later the enterprising young city became a smoking ruin when Gen. William Tecumseh Sherman torched it on his infamous "March to the Sea" across central Georgia. But Atlanta rose phoenix-like from the ashes and prospered. A century later native son

Dr. Martin Luther King Jr. won the Nobel Peace Prize; 4 years after that prestigious honor his funeral and burial took place in the city.

Simultaneously extolled as a shining example of the "New South" and excoriated as a capital of crime, Atlanta's truth—as always—lies beyond the headlines. But if you judge the measure of success by an impressive vertical profile, it stands quite tall. At 1,039 feet, Bank of America Plaza (600 Peachtree St. N.E.) is one of a handful of buildings in the U.S. breaking the 1,000-foot barrier. In fact Atlanta has three separate skylines—downtown, Midtown and Buckhead. And more than 65 streets, avenues and drives in the metro region include "Peachtree" in their name, which has to be some sort of record.

Atlanta skyline

Looking beyond the statistics—and lacing up your walking shoes for a little exploring—will uncover the Southern grace and rich historical legacy that are integral components of the cityscape. That's certainly the case with the Margaret Mitchell House, which you might pass without even noticing (it's at the corner of Peachtree and 10th streets). During the 1920s the unobtrusive building was called the Crescent Apartments, and it was in apartment #1 that Mitchell wrote her Pulitzer Prize-winning novel "Gone With the Wind."

Nearby at 660 Peachtree St. N.E. is the Fox Theatre. The opulent interior of this Atlanta landmark is straight out of a Moorish/Egyptian fantasy. A checkered past includes moments of glory as well as an impending date with the wrecking

(Continued on p. 45.)

Destination Atlanta

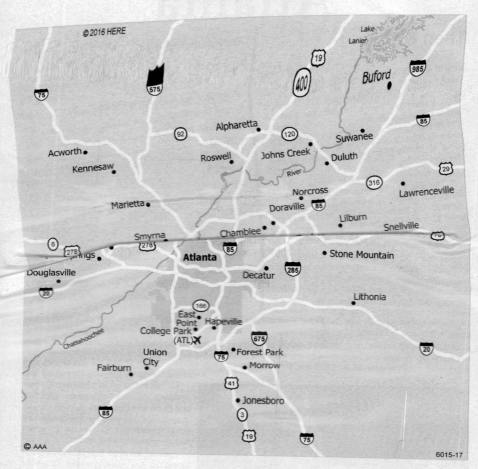

This map shows cities in the Atlanta vicinity where you will find attractions, hotels and restaurants. Cities are listed alphabetically in this book on the following pages.

Fast Facts

ABOUT THE CITY

POP: 420,003 ▪ **ELEV:** 1,050 ft.

MONEY

SALES TAX: The sales tax in the Atlanta metro area is 8 percent. An additional 7 percent is levied on hotel rooms, bringing the total tax on hotel stays to 15 percent.

WHOM TO CALL

EMERGENCY: 911

POLICE (non-emergency): (404) 614-6544

TIME AND TEMPERATURE: (770) 455-7141

HOSPITALS: Atlanta Medical Center, (404) 265-4000 ▪ Emory Saint Joseph's Hospital, (678) 843-7001 ▪ Emory University Hospital, (404) 712-2000 ▪ Grady Memorial Hospital, (404) 616-1000 ▪ Northside Hospital, (404) 851-8000 ▪ Piedmont Atlanta Hospital, (404) 605-5000.

WHERE TO LOOK AND LISTEN

NEWSPAPERS: Metro Atlanta's newspapers include the *Atlanta Journal-Constitution* and the weekly *Atlanta Business Chronicle*.

RADIO: WSB (750 AM and 95.5 FM) is a news/talk radio station ▪ WABE (90.1 FM) is a member of National Public Radio.

VISITOR INFORMATION

Atlanta Convention & Visitors Bureau: 233 Peachtree St. N.E., Suite 1400, Atlanta, GA 30303. **Phone:** (404) 521-6600 or (800) 285-2682.

TRANSPORTATION

AIR TRAVEL: Atlanta is served by Hartsfield-Jackson Atlanta International Airport (ATL), nine miles southwest of the business district via the Southwest Expressway and I-85. Rapid rail transportation to downtown Atlanta and the metropolitan area is provided by the Metropolitan Atlanta Rapid Transit Authority (MARTA). The fare is $2.50.

Taxi fare to downtown Atlanta averages $30 with a $2 charge for each additional person. A fuel surcharge may apply. Travel time to the business district is about 30 minutes.

RENTAL CARS: Hertz, with offices downtown and at the airport, offers discounts to AAA members; phone (404) 530-2925 or (800) 654-3131. For listings of other agencies check the telephone directory.

RAIL SERVICE: Amtrak train service is provided out of Southern Railway's Peachtree Station, known locally as Brookwood Station, at 1688 Peachtree St. N.W.; phone (800) 872-7245. Atlanta is a major stop on Amtrak's route known as "The Crescent," which connects New York City with New Orleans.

BUSES: Greyhound Lines Inc., 232 Forsyth St. S.W., is the major bus line serving Atlanta; phone (404) 584-1728 for recorded information or (800) 231-2222. There is a location at the airport at 6000 N. Terminal Dr.; phone (404) 765-9598.

TAXIS: Cab companies include Checker Cab, (404) 351-1111 ▪ and Yellow, (404) 521-0200. Taxis are metered. Base fare for Checker Cab and Yellow is $2.50, $2 for each additional mile and $2 for each additional passenger. A fuel surcharge may apply. Other taxi companies are listed in the telephone directory.

PUBLIC TRANSPORTATION: Atlanta's public transportation consists of the Metropolitan Atlanta Rapid Transit Authority's (MARTA) bus, rail and subway systems. *See Public Transportation for details.*
Note: Attraction listings often include the nearest MARTA Rapid Rail stop and, if applicable, the number of the connecting bus route.

(Continued from p. 43.)
ball in the 1970s—before the theater was spared from demolition thanks to committed citizens who organized a vigorous "Save the Fox" renovation campaign. This grand old palace remains just about the best place in town to see a show.

Atlanta doesn't lean entirely on past glories, though. Next to Centennial Olympic Park, the Center for Civil and Human Rights is a striking, LEED certified, sustainable building. Representing hands, two curved walls covered in differently hued panels cradle the center. The effect is one of angular sculpture conveying the strength, optimism and uplifting spirit of the center, while the panels represent how different individuals can come together to create social progress.

And yet some things are impervious to the passage of time. Historic Oakland Cemetery, founded in 1850, grew significantly in size when it came time to bury 7,000 Civil War soldiers. The final resting place of prominent Atlantans Margaret Mitchell, Maynard Jackson and Bobby Jones, the cemetery contains a fascinating assemblage of 19th-century mausoleums and headstones. Then head to The Varsity's original downtown location on North Avenue, which opened in 1928. In response to the genially barked question "What'll ya have?" order a "heavyweight," a "ring one" and a "frosted orange." Trust us; this beloved drive-in has fed hordes of hungry people—especially after Georgia Tech football games—for what seems like forever.

Must Do: AAA Editor's Picks

- Say hello to a whale shark and other denizens of the deep at the  **Georgia Aquarium** (225 Baker St. N.W.) where exhibits range from tropical coral reefs to freshwater rivers. Among the exotic inhabitants at this state-of-the-art facility are perpetually smiling beluga whales, bizarre-looking cuttlefish and dapper penguins.

- **Stone Mountain** (I-285 & US 78) is bowl-shaped rather than pointy, making the 1.3-mile hike to the summit easier than you might think; just follow the yellow-dotted line painted on the ground. If visibility is good you can see Atlanta's skyline and even the north Georgia mountains in the distance. Stick around at night to catch the Lasershow Spectacular.

- Ever taste Vegitabeta or Sparberry? Now is your chance. Try more than 100 beverages from around the globe—including Coca-Cola varieties—at the **World of Coca-Cola** (121 Baker St. N.W.).

- If it's a hot day, head downtown to **Centennial Olympic Park** (265 Park Ave. West N.W.) and frolic in the Fountain of Rings. The park's lawn also happens to be a nice spot for a picnic.

- Tour the "Fabulous" **Fox Theatre** (660 Peachtree St. N.E.) an opulent throwback to the days when an old-fashioned movie premiere was a real event. The tour is a fascinating look at a building that came close to being demolished in the early '70s but staged a comeback in the '80s after an extensive, and still ongoing, renovation.

- Journey to the **Archibald Smith Plantation Home** (935 Alpharetta St. in nearby Roswell) to explore lavish antebellum mansions that were an integral part of the Deep South. Docent-led tours explore the house—complete with original furnishings—and outbuildings.

- Founded in 1850 when Atlanta outgrew its municipal graveyard and subsequently enlarged when the city needed space to lay to rest some 7,000 Civil War soldiers, **Historic Oakland Cemetery** (248 Oakland Ave. S.E.) contains rows of anonymous headstones as well as impressive marble mausoleums and monuments. "Gone With the Wind" author Margaret Mitchell is one of the notable Atlantans laid to rest here.

- Guided tours of the **Martin Luther King Jr. National Historic Site** (450 Auburn Ave. N.E.) visit King's boyhood home, his crypt and the church where he preached. Portions of the Sweet Auburn neighborhood he grew up in, which was a focal point of the city's African-American community for most of the mid- to late-20th century, have been preserved.

- Delve further into the civil rights movement—and current human rights movements—at the **Center for Civil and Human Rights** (100 Ivan Allen Jr. Blvd.). Learn how past movements have impacted society, and see how you can get involved in an issue you feel passionately about.

- Sip a specialty cocktail at the bar in **The Sun Dial** (73rd floor of **The Westin Peachtree Plaza**, 210 Peachtree St. N.W.). It's a restaurant that completes one full rotation an hour, and the panorama of downtown from this lofty perch is splendid.

- Hang out in the **Little Five Points** neighborhood, at the junction of Euclid and Moreland avenues. Bohemian is the buzzword here, from music to fashion to art, and there are some seriously funky shops selling all kinds of cool stuff.

- The Food Network has called the burger at **Holeman and Finch Public House** (2277 Peachtree Rd. N.E.) one of the country's best. It's a classic double-patty cheeseburger on a house-made bun, with hand-cut fries and homemade ketchup and mustard on the side. Make a reservation, or get there early before supplies run out.

- Get your sports fix at the **College Football Hall of Fame and Chick-fil-A Fan Experience** (250 Marietta St. N.W.). Explore the museum and have a personalized experience with exhibits highlighting your favorite team. Also participate in the fun at Skill Zone, where you get to be the player.

Georgia Aquarium

Atlanta 1-day Itinerary

AAA editors suggest these activities for a great short vacation experience. Those staying in the area for a longer visit can access a 3-day itinerary at AAA.com/TravelGuide.

Morning

- Have breakfast at the Midtown branch of the **Flying Biscuit Cafe** (1001 Piedmont Ave. N.E. at 10th Street N.E.). Atlantans love this place for good reason—the biscuits are deemed the best in town, but creamy grits, made-to-order omelets and organic oatmeal pancakes topped with warm peach compote all merit raves as well.

- Walk to Piedmont Park (1342 Worchester Dr. N.E.). It offers a big, open green space with recreational facilities, a running track, playgrounds, walking paths, bocce courts, an aquatic center and a dog park. It's a favorite destination for joggers, dog walkers, families and tourists. Take a stroll around Lake Clara Meer; the park's dogwoods bloom in spring.

- There's more greenery at ♦ **Atlanta Botanical Garden** (1345 Piedmont Ave. N.E.) adjoining Piedmont Park. Swing along the Canopy Walk, a 600-foot suspension bridge through a forest of oaks and pines giving you a bird's view of the trees from heights up to 40 feet. Another highlight is the Fuqua Orchid Center, a glass-walled conservatory filled with cascades of flowers almost too beautiful to be real.

- If you love art, make time for ♦ **High Museum of Art** (1280 Peachtree St. N.E.). The design of the dramatically white museum buildings incorporates natural light, particularly in the Meier Building's soaring atrium. Peruse works ranging from Hudson River School landscapes and African wood carvings to Southern folk art and a chandelier crafted from Murano glass.

Afternoon

- "What'll ya have?" is the first thing you'll hear when walking into the flagship branch of **The Varsity** (61 North Ave. N.E.). Known for feeding fans following Georgia Tech football games, this fast food diner built a reputation on lingo like "the heavyweight" (a hot dog with extra chili), "ring one" (onion rings) and "strings" (fries). Make sure you know the drill before you place your order. Ambience is zilch and the noise level is cacophonous, but hey-it's a landmark.

- Budget plenty of time for the sprawling and always crowded ♦ **Georgia Aquarium** (225 Baker St. N.W.). Of the many and varied exhibits, the standout is Ocean Voyager, a huge tank home to whale sharks, playful manta rays and giant groupers with lips that would put Mick Jagger's to shame. A floor-to-ceiling viewing window brings them thrillingly close. Otters, beluga whales, sea lions and penguins are some of the aquarium's other fascinating residents.

- Take a spin through adjacent Centennial Olympic Park and check out the Fountain of Rings before saluting the world's most famous

Mary Mac's Tea Room

soft drink at the ♦ **World of Coca-Cola** (121 Baker St. N.W.). It's one big tribute to the globally ubiquitous dark brown beverage that will delight kids and fans. One thing's for certain: It *is* a bit of a nostalgia rush to watch old TV commercials and hear instantly familiar catchphrases like "things go better with Coke." Don't forget to try different flavors on the tasting floor.

Evening

- Mary McKenzie opened **Mary Mac's Tea Room** (224 Ponce de Leon Ave.) in 1945, and the menu at this shrine to Southern cookery— country fried steak, cornbread stuffing, macaroni and cheese, old-fashioned peach cobbler—is not for the faint-hearted. Go ahead and indulge.

- Mary Mac's is within waddling distance of the **Fox Theatre** (660 Peachtree St. N.E.). Originally the Yaarab Temple Shrine Mosque, the "Fabulous Fox" epitomized exotic elegance in the 1930s. The building's *pièce de résistance* is the nearly 4,700-seat auditorium resembling an Arabian courtyard straight out of a Technicolor movie blockbuster like "The Ten Commandments." The entertainment lineup is eclectic; phone (855) 285-8499 for ticket and schedule information.

- Don't have tickets for a Fox show? Hang out with the hipsters in the Little Five Points neighborhood at Euclid and Moreland avenues. Everything is alternative here, from the vintage clothing, kitschy kitchen accessories and kooky novelty gifts at Junkman's Daughter to the groovy treasure trove of old vinyl records and CDs at Wax N Facts.

Top Picks for Kids

Under 13

- Say hello to Kermit the Frog, Miss Piggy and Big Bird at the **Center for Puppetry Arts** (1404 Spring St. N.W.). The museum is one of the biggest of its kind and offers a collection of puppets, shows and workshops. Live performances usually draw a crowd (advance reservations are highly recommended), so find a seat and get ready to *ooh* and *aah*. Kids can put on their own puppet shows with creations made from a hands-on workstation.

- Little Lego fans will enjoy constructing a model with a master builder, making and racing miniature cars, and playing at **LEGOLAND Discovery Center Atlanta** (3500 Peachtree Road, N.E.). They will also have fun rescuing a princess on Kingdom Quest Laser Ride and watching shorts in the 4D Cinema.

- The 21-acre **Centennial Olympic Park** (265 Park Ave. West N.W.) is close to several attractions, so no searching for another parking spot. As the staging grounds of the 1996 Summer Olympics, the area features trails and a restaurant. Bring a towel; the fountains are a perfect way to cool down in the dog days of summer. During chilly winter months, there's ice-skating to keep everyone occupied.

- Peer into the waters of the renowned ◈ **Georgia Aquarium** (225 Baker St. N.W.). The big draw is Ocean Voyager with its manta rays and whale sharks in 6.3 million gallons of water. But otters, penguins, sea lions and dolphins are crowd-pleasers, too.

Center for Puppetry Arts

Teens

- Sample beverages from around the world at the ◈ **World of Coca-Cola** (121 Baker St. N.W.). With more than 100 flavors to try, there will be lots of hits, but the inevitable misses will lead to laughs. To satisfy a thirst for retro, check out vintage Coca-Cola ads and take pictures with the iconic polar bears.

- Social media access keeps teens in the know, but get the scoop on how pros handle a 24-hour news cycle during an **Inside CNN Studio Tour** (190 Marietta St. N.W.). You'll get a "press pass" to move behind the scenes of CNN, HLN, CNN International and CNN en Español and learn about everything from teleprompters to weather maps. Time it right and you'll see newscasters and staff prepare for a show.

- Continue the educational mission at **The King Center** (449 Auburn Ave. N.E.). Established by Dr. Martin Luther King Jr.'s wife, Coretta Scott King, the center is dedicated to promoting positive change throughout the world. Though the archives are open by appointment only, stroll around Freedom Walkway's reflecting pool, the Chapel of All Faiths and Freedom Hall, where you can think about King's enduring legacy.

- Teens can further their knowledge of segregation and the fight for African-American civil rights at the ◈ **Martin Luther King Jr. National Historic Site** (450 Auburn Ave. N.E.). Exploring the visitor's center as well as the birthplace, church and grave of the assassinated civil rights leader can bring to life events they have only read about in history class.

- Learn about the human condition and the history of civil rights at the ◈ **Center for Civil and Human Rights** (100 Ivan Allen Jr. Blvd.). Teens can further explore conflicts happening today, and the center can help get them involved in a movement they're passionate about.

All Ages

- Travel back in time at the **Fernbank Museum of Natural History** (767 Clifton Rd. N.E.) where exhibits about Earth's environment take visitors from the planet's origins to the flora and fauna of Georgia. Millions of years of natural history—dinosaurs and all—are described with fossils, diagrams and sound effects.

- Have an adventure exploring ◈ **Zoo Atlanta** (800 Cherokee Ave. S.E.). You can't miss the ever-adorable pandas and otters, the large gorillas, jumping kangaroos and impressive lions as well as the many bird and reptile species.

- The **Fernbank Science Center** (156 Heaton Park Dr. N.E.) features a museum and planetarium. One highlight is the unmanned Apollo 6 space capsule, once used to prepare astronauts for manned missions. Take a guided walk through **Fernbank Forest** to learn about Atlanta's evolving ecosystem.

Arriving
By Car

Major highways provide speedy access to Atlanta from nearly all directions. Three interstate highways cross the Perimeter (I-285), which circles the city. I-75 (the Northwest Expressway) joins I-85 (the Northeast Expressway) just north of downtown to become the Downtown Connector (I-75/85), which passes to the east of downtown.

From the southeast I-75 becomes the South Expressway to the point south of downtown near the Georgia State Capitol, where it meets I-20 from the east (the East Expressway) and the west (the West Expressway).

Other roads also run from I-285 toward downtown. I-85 approaches the city from the southwest, joining the South Expressway within I-285. The Arthur Langford Parkway (SR 166) also connects the southwest portion of I-285 with the South Expressway. US 78 from the east passes Stone Mountain before crossing I-285, after which it runs into Scott Boulevard and Ponce de Leon Avenue.

Additional highways that approach the city include SR 400 from the north, which crosses I-285 and ends on I-85 just north of the I-85 and I-75 connector; US 41 from the northwest, which runs into the Northside Parkway inside I-285; and US 19, which becomes Roswell Road, Peachtree Street and finally Spring Street as it moves south. Because of the profusion of expressways, be sure to use a detailed map of the city.

Getting Around

Try to time your arrival in Atlanta after rush hours when it is easier to navigate the high-speed expressways and meandering main streets. Rush hours in general are from 6:30 to 9 a.m. and from 3:30 to 7 p.m. during which expressway traffic in both the city and the suburbs is often bumper-to-bumper. Observe posted speed limit signs.

Interstate traffic in the Metro Atlanta area is monitored and managed by NAVIGATOR, the Georgia Department of Transportation's Intelligent Transportation System (ITS). NAVIGATOR's Traffic Management Center provides 24/7 information and alerts on traffic delays, incidents and road construction.

Street System

The center of the downtown area is the Five Points Intersection, where Peachtree, Marietta, Decatur, Edgewood and Whitehall converge near the site of the original surveyor's stake. It also is where the city's four geographical divisions—N.E., N.W., S.E. and S.W.—merge.

Atlanta is not laid out in the traditional grid, so there are few rectangular blocks and square intersections. The main street is Peachtree, extending north and south through the center of the city; North and Ponce de Leon avenues are the principal east-west links. The Downtown Connector (I-75/85) skirts the business district. The East and West expressways (I-20) carry traffic from the city center.

Atlanta Streetcar

Though Peachtree Street is the main thoroughfare through the city, there are more than 65 other streets, avenues and lanes in the metro area that include the name "Peachtree." Do not be misled by West Peachtree Street, Peachtree Memorial Drive, Peachtree View, Peachtree Circle, Peachtree Heights, Peachtree Place, Peachtree Battle Avenue, Peachtree Hills Avenue or a similar name.

Parking

On-street parking in the downtown business district is virtually nonexistent. However, garages and lots are plentiful throughout the city, with rates usually $3 for the first hour or $10-$15 per day. Rates downtown, especially near the CNN Center, the Georgia World Congress Center and the Philips Arena, may be higher. Many parking lots and decks now offer "early bird specials": Drivers parking before 9 or 10 a.m. and leaving after 2 or 3 p.m. pay about $5 per day. Metered parking is available in other areas, but it is usually strictly enforced during business hours and violators' cars are often towed.

Public Transportation

Atlanta's Metropolitan Atlanta Rapid Transit Authority (MARTA) has a 47-mile Rapid Rail transit system and extensive connector bus routes. Buses are available to Six Flags Over Georgia. Minimum fare is $2.50. For information contact the route information center Mon.-Fri. 7 a.m.-7 p.m., Sat.-Sun. and most holidays 8 a.m.-5 p.m.; phone (404) 848-5000.

The Peach, or MARTA Route 110, offers bus service with frequent stops, many at some of the city's most historic and popular locations. The $2.50 fare includes transfers to other MARTA bus and rail services. The Peach is available daily 6 a.m.-1 a.m. and departs every 30 minutes.

The Buckhead Uptown Connection (BUC), a free shuttle service offering two routes and connecting directly to MARTA's rail service, transports passengers to area shopping, hotels and restaurants, including Lenox Square and Phipps Plaza. Service is available Mon.-Fri. 6:30-9:30 a.m. and 3:30-7 p.m.; phone (404) 812-7433 to confirm route, schedule and fare information.

The Atlanta Streetcar provides another convenient way to reach downtown destinations between Centennial Olympic Park and Martin Luther King Jr. National Historic Site; phone (404) 546-0311 for schedule information.

Tech Trolley bus service is provided by the Georgia Institute of Technology and offers access to Technology Square, the Midtown MARTA station and the institute's campus. The trolley runs Mon.-Fri. 5:45 a.m.-10:30 p.m., Sat. 10-6:30, Sun. 3-9:45. Phone (404) 385-7275 to confirm the schedule.

Megabus, departing from W. Peachtree Street N.W. and Pine Street N.E., offers daily departures to such cities as Birmingham, Charlotte, Chattanooga, Memphis, Nashville and Orlando; phone (877) 462-6342.

Shopping

Trying to encapsulate the shopping experience in a metro area as big and spread out as Atlanta is pretty daunting. Don't even attempt to see and do it all; instead, beam in on a couple of areas that suit your fancy.

Shop at IKEA at Atlantic Station

Buckhead, the city's No. 1 address for well-to-do residents, has loads of shopping opportunities. In addition to two major malls, you'll find numerous specialty boutiques, antique shops and galleries. Check out **Morgan Kylee** for a casual and chic designer outfit and accessorize it with a leather purse from **Mel Boteri.** The malls are conveniently located across from each other at the intersection of Peachtree and Lenox roads, and both are within walking distance of MARTA's Buckhead station. Each has a distinct personality. **Lenox Square** has everything that mallers love: big department stores (Bloomingdale's, Macy's and Neiman Marcus), major chains (everything from Ann Taylor to Williams-Sonoma) and fast-food outlets galore for pit stops.

Phipps Plaza is more sedate and more upscale. Potted palms, plush leather couches and wood-and-brass accents provide a tony backdrop for Giorgio Armani, Versace, Gucci and other top-end retailers. Belk, Nordstrom and Saks Fifth Avenue are the department stores here, and there's also that mall staple, the food court.

The **Ponce City Market,** located in a renovated 1925 Sears, Roebuck & Co. building on Ponce de Leon Ave., is an adorable and trendy space that has a variety of shops and boutiques, including **Anthropology, Boogaloos Boutique** and **Onward Reserve.** If you happen to crave a sweet retreat from your retail adventure, you can grab some candy at the **Collier Candy Company,** an ice cream from **Honeysuckle Gelato** or a Popsicle from the **King of Pops Bar & Good Grub.** Don't leave without visiting the roof. Not only will you get some great views of Atlanta, you can ride some of the old-school midway rides and play the carnival games.

If you're into antiques, definitely put Miami Circle on your shopping itinerary. Located just south off Piedmont Road, the **Shops of Miami Circle** is full of galleries, antiques, interior design shops and showrooms. The high-quality wares include imported English, French and Italian furniture, Turkish rugs, pottery and clocks. **Anne Irwin Fine Art,** which showcases emerging Southern artists, is one of Atlanta's trendiest galleries. It's fun to explore even if you don't buy anything.

The Shops Buckhead Atlanta, a six-block shopping district at jct. Peachtree and E. Paces Ferry roads, is lined with high-end retailers and eateries.

Atlantic Station (just off I-75/85 via the 17th Street Bridge) is a mixed-use retail, residential and office development. The city's first IKEA is the big draw here, but you'll also find standbys like Ann Taylor, Ann Taylor Loft, Banana Republic, Gap and Old Navy, along with a multiplex and a whole bunch of casual eateries, all in an open-air setting. If you prefer a shop a bit more unique to Atlanta, stop by **Sole Shoes and Accessories** where you will find dresses and jewelry to match the footwear. It's enough to make your shoe-loving heart pitter-patter. Those who don't want to drive can board a free shuttle at the MARTA Arts Center station (the shuttle stop is in the MARTA bus bay); it runs along 17th Street, stopping at designated bus stops along the way.

Westside Provisions District (Howell Mill Rd. at 14th St. N.W.) is a go-to place for designers. In addition to boutique shopping, the area offers award-winning dining options.

The **Mall at Peachtree Center** (Peachtree Center Avenue between Harris Street and Andrew Young International Boulevard) isn't so much a mall as it is a convenient stop-in for office workers and visitors staying at the major downtown hotels. Gift shops, business services, restaurants and a food court all can be found here.

Atlanta neighborhoods abound with quirky shopping opportunities. If you're in the market for some new ink work, stop by **Only You Tattoo** (401 Memorial Dr. across from Historic Oakland Cemetery). Don't be intimidated by the biker vibe often associated with tattoo parlors; the artists at Only You will show their body art portfolios and discuss the design beforehand, and their gentle bedside manner will ease you right through the process.

You'll find more specialty shops and eateries at **Krog St. Market** a few blocks northeast in Inman Park.

Quirkiness central, of course, is **Little Five Points**, or L5P. This neighborhood has long been a stomping ground for hippies, punks, Rastas and the artistically inclined. It's on the scruffy side, and the little plaza bounded by Moreland, Euclid and McClendon avenues attracts some shady-looking characters. But it's also got character to spare.

L5P shops and services run the alternative gamut from thrift-store duds to unusual gifts to natural foods. Serious collectors come to **Wax N Facts** (432 Moreland Ave.), one of the city's best music stores, to thumb through stacks of vintage vinyl and a great collection of used CDs. **Junkman's Daughter** (464 Moreland Ave.) is a tabernacle of kitsch—knickknacks of every stripe, '80s goth clothing, gag gifts, naughty cards, outrageous wigs, feather boas and the like. Incense wafts out the door of **Crystal Blue** (1168 Euclid Ave.), which offers pendants, glass prisms, rocks, tarot cards and other metaphysical merchandise.

If you want to find a great piece of vintage clothing like the perfect jacket or a unique, must-have bag, try searching through vintage shops. **The Lucky Exchange** (212 Ponce De Leon Ave.) has great pieces of clothing and accessories, and **The Clothing Warehouse** (420 Moreland Ave.) has two floors of merchandise that include some high-end options.

Walk due east on McClendon Avenue from Little Five Points and within minutes you'll be in **Candler Park**, a residential neighborhood with two small business districts on either side of its namesake park. Stroll around and admire the 1920s Craftsman bungalow homes, many beautifully renovated. Then stop at the original **Flying Biscuit Cafe** (1655 McLendon Ave.), a cozy-hip breakfast and lunch

Wax N Facts

spot with several Atlanta locations; their grits, biscuits and apple butter all have tasty reputations.

Virginia-Highland is another desirable residential area, located on either side of N. Highland Avenue from Ponce de Leon Avenue north to about University Drive. Virginia-Highland's symbolic center is the intersection of Highland and Virginia avenues, where there are shops specializing in gifts, home accessories, jewelry, stationery and women's fashions. Another small cluster of businesses at Highland and University includes **Alon's** (1394 N. Highland Ave.), which many Atlantans will tell you is the best bakery in town (their chocolate chunk pecan bites are legendary). A little west of this area is the Martin Luther King Jr. Historic District where the **Eastern National Bookstore,** located at 497 Auburn Ave., features some 200 titles with special emphasis on African-American history.

There are more specialty shops at the south end of the neighborhood near Ponce de Leon. **Ten Thousand Villages** (1056 St. Charles Ave.) is a fair trade retailer of handcrafted items from around the world.

You don't have to live in Atlanta to enjoy the city's farmers markets. Every day, serious cooks and dedicated foodies do their shopping at **Your Dekalb Farmers Market** (3000 E. Ponce de Leon Ave., about 2 miles west of I-285 exit 40), where you can buy just about anything under the roof of one big warehouse-like building. The produce, seafood, meat and bakery departments are extensive, but this market really shines when it comes to the amazing array of spices and international foods.

There's a similar smorgasbord at the **Buford Highway Farmers Market** (5600 Buford Hwy. N.E., just east of I-285 exit 32), where it's a treat just to wander up and down the aisles discovering stuff you've likely never encountered before. Folks in the know speak highly of the beef and cabbage piroshky freshly made and sold at the market's Eastern European bakery and deli stand. The market is open daily.

Give **Freedom Farmers' Market** (453 Freedom Pkwy. N.E.) a try. This is one of the city's newer farmers markets and is open on Saturday mornings. Most weeks there are demonstrations and a pop-up restaurant featuring a local chef. Shoppers also will find fresh pasta, pastries and local produce.

And don't forget the **Atlanta Farmers Market,** also called the Georgia State Farmers Market (on Forest Parkway just off I-75 exit 237; look for the big "State Farmers Market" sign). This is a *real* farmers market: rows and rows of stalls where growers unload truckloads of fruits and veggies every morning. In addition to produce you can find jams, jellies, baked goods, eggs, flowers, plants, trees, shrubs— even groceries. Many stalls are open by 7 a.m.

If you're spending the day at Stone Mountain Park, include a stop at **Stone Mountain Village,** at the west end of the park via Memorial Drive to Main Street. "Quaint" about describes it, so just pop into whatever shop looks interesting—crafts, collectibles and antiques are a given, and since this is Georgia there's lots of Civil War memorabilia as well. Grab a bite to eat at **The Village Corner** (6655 James B. Rivers Dr. at Main Street), a German restaurant and bakery specializing in goodies like apple and potato pancakes, sauerbraten and Bavarian-style spaetzle. It's a *gemütlich* kind of place.

Enjoy cocktails at the Hard Rock Cafe

Nightlife

Atlanta rocks, rolls, shimmies and shakes; this isn't a city where people spend the evening on the sofa watching "Everybody Loves Raymond" reruns (well, at least most people). Any pop music scholar can tell you the Atlanta area has produced such diverse artists as the Black Crowes, Collective Soul, Indigo Girls, Outkast and Sevendust. The city also has very fertile hip-hop and indie rock scenes, and a number of live music joints to boot.

Those in the musical know head for the small venues and clubs. The **Variety Playhouse** (1099 Euclid Ave.) in **Little Five Points** has been around for more than two decades. Comfortable as an old shoe, it books an impressively eclectic roster of talent—everyone from oldies but goodies like Joan Baez, Todd Rundgren and Parliament/Funkadelic to the latest up and comers. In nearby **East Atlanta Village, The Earl** (488 Flat Shoals Ave., just north of Glenwood Avenue), is the place to see buzz bands like Late of the Pier and local faves (Dead Confederate, The Black Lips) before they go on to bigger things.

There's more of the same—meaning a mix of local acts and bands passing through town—at midsize places like **The Masquerade** (695 North Ave.), which occupies a turn-of-the-20th-century former mill. **The Tabernacle** (152 Luckie St. in Centennial Olympic Park) also has a history; it opened in 1910 as part of the Georgia Baptist Medical Center and later was a church. Wood floors and a pipe organ lend a feeling of authenticity, and excellent acoustics showcase the sound, whether it's a popular hit-maker like Imagine Dragons or a more esoteric band such as The Decemberists.

Center Stage (1374 W. Peachtree St. N.E. in Midtown) is a fairly intimate (1,050 seats) theater in the round. There's not really a bad seat anywhere in the house, and the concert lineup offers a little something for everyone. Light fixtures that resemble torches give Center Stage a slightly gothic vibe. There's also a full (cash only) bar. You'll have to pay to park in the adjacent parking deck, but the building is only two blocks from MARTA's Arts Center station (North-South line).

The **Fox Theatre** (660 Peachtree St. N.E.) is perhaps the coolest place in the city for an entertainment night out. The "fabulous Fox" has it all— history, pedigree and best of all, a flamboyantly opulent interior that boasts painted plaster, bronze filigree, geometric tiles, intricately patterned carpets and other adornments. The huge auditorium, which seats nearly 4,700 people, looks like a cross between a Moorish fort and a courtyard out of "The Arabian Nights." What do the New York Metropolitan Opera, Elvis and the Stones have in common? They've all played the Fox. Besides being Atlanta's Broadway venue of choice, the performance schedule includes big-name pop, rock and country stars, movies, symphony orchestras and the **Atlanta Ballet.** Kick back and experience the "good life" at **Churchill Grounds.** Located in the north end of the

Fox, this jazz club is committed to only the very best of this musical art form from the accomplished musicians to locals. You never know, you might just see the next Miles Davis or Louis Armstrong play here before they hit it big.

If you'd rather dial it down, hit one of Atlanta's neighborhood hangouts where blues, bluegrass and other homegrown music styles are on the menu. **Blind Willie's** (828 N. Highland Ave.) is a Virginia-Highland institution and *the* place to go for blues. The club was built from the ground up by local musicians who doubled as carpenters, and the house band, the Shadows, still feature the performers who appear here. Add the fact that you can get a Chicago dog or a Memphis-style barbecue pork sandwich washed down with a bottled or draft beer, and it's no wonder Blind Willie's packs 'em in.

Food and fun also can be had at the SAVE **Hard Rock Cafe** (215 Peachtree St. N.E.); phone (404) 688-7625.

In Little Five Points, **Smith's Olde Bar** (1578 Piedmont Ave. near Ansley Mall) has five rooms. Aim for the downstairs bar first, then head upstairs to catch a show in the 350-seat **Music Room** or maybe an acoustic performance by a local musician in the **Atlanta Room** before adjourning to the **Poolroom** for a friendly game of billiards or darts. Catch live music at the **Star Community Bar** (437 Moreland Ave.) Wednesdays through Saturdays. The bands change fairly often so call ahead, but you can pretty much be sure it'll be rock, punk, rockabilly or country.

Buckhead is certainly a place to congregate, whether for dinner, drinks or just cruising around looking for action. A special occasion always seems to call for dinner with a view. Celebrate at **Nikolai's Roof Lounge,** the bar at **Nikolai's Roof** in the Hilton Atlanta (255 Courtland St. N.E.). The name is appropriate, since it offers a stunning vista of the downtown skyline from 30 floors up. Sip on a cocktail before heading to the restaurant, celebrated for its fine food and equally fine service.

Or you could take one of the scenic glass elevators a dizzying 73 stories to the top of The Westin Peachtree Plaza (210 Peachtree St.) and **The Sun Dial.** And it's quite a view indeed, whether you're sitting in the rotating cocktail lounge or gazing out from the adjacent observation deck. But sometimes you just want to chill. The **Lobby Lounge** in The Ritz-Carlton, Buckhead (3434 Peachtree Rd. N.E.) is as elegant a place as there is in the city for a cocktail or a nightcap. If it's a chilly day, sink into one of the cozy couches in front of the fireplace.

Note: *Creative Loafing,* a free newsweekly that comes out on Thursdays, has extensive arts and entertainment listings and is available all over town.

Big Events

When little white flower clusters start blooming on dogwood trees, you know spring has come to Atlanta. There's really no better way to celebrate than to attend the 🌷 **Dogwood Festival** at **Piedmont**

Dogwood Festival

Park in early April. The arts and crafts festival has taken place since 1936 at the beginning of spring, when the trees are at their prettiest. In addition to a chance to admire the delicate blooms, the event includes an artists' market, hot air balloon floats and a disc dog competition.

Auburn Avenue is the venue for 🌷 **Sweet Auburn Springfest** in early May, offering entertainment on 10 stages, the Children's Fantastic Fun Zone, a food court and a marketplace. The **Atlanta Jazz Festival,** in late May, features international artists and offers a range of activities in the metro area.

The **Peachtree Road Race 10K,** a 10-kilometer event in which 60,000 runners participate, takes place July 4 in downtown Atlanta.

The ACC and SEC square off in the 🌷 **Chick-fil-A Peach Bowl,** one of the top bowl games in college football, in December.

Sports & Rec

Atlanta's leisure activities are many. Visitors can go **fishing** in or **rafting** or **canoeing** down the Chattahoochee River, the focal point of the **Chattahoochee River National Recreation Area** *(see place listing p. 155).* Affectionately known as "the Hooch" by natives, the river is usually no more than 5 feet deep and affords excellent opportunities for year-round fishing. Trout, bass, catfish and other species of fish frequent the river. For fishing license and regulation information phone (800) 366-2661.

Trails for **jogging** border the river in the city of Roswell. Visit 🌷 **Stone Mountain Park** for an array of outdoor activities, including **hiking, bicycling** and **camping** under the stars. In summer Atlantans flock to

Lake Sidney Lanier, about 35 miles northeast of the city off US 23. Sandy beaches line the shore of this large lake, offering abundant opportunities for **fishing, boating** and **swimming.**

Six city courses offer golf opportunities. Municipal parks also provide **riding** and hiking trails, **tennis** courts and swimming pools. **Piedmont Park,** off Monroe Drive and 10th Street in midtown, is a popular spot for bicycling and jogging. **Bicycle Tours of Atlanta** offer 10-mile tours of the area's historic sites; phone (404) 273-2558.

The **Atlanta Beltline** is a series of trails that will connect many of the city's neighborhoods and parks providing green space for residents and visitors alike. While some portions are still under construction, others are open and in use. The Eastside Trail extends 2.25 miles from Piedmont Park to Inman Park. Bicycles may be rented nearby at **Atlanta Beltline Bicycle,** 151 Sampson St. N.E., (404) 588-9930, or at **Skate Escape** at 1086 Piedmont Ave. N.E., (404) 892-1292.

The West End Trail is a 2.4-mile stretch from White Street to **Westview Cemetery,** and the particularly lovely Northside Trail travels through **Tanyard Creek Park,** near the junction of Collier Road N.W. and Overbrook Drive N.W. The Beltline promises to be a vibrant, cyclist- and pedestrian-friendly part of the city with many art projects under way and with restaurants and businesses popping up nearby.

The Atlanta Beltline also includes the **Atlanta Beltline Arboretum.** This is still a work in progress, but when finished it will extend the full 22 miles of the trails. Currently the Eastside Trail has seen the planting of 43 species of grasses and wildflowers,

and at the Westside Trail, trees native to Georgia are being planted.

The National League's **Atlanta Braves** play **baseball** from early April to late September or early October. The 2017 season will be played at the new **SunTrust Park,** located near the junction of I-75 and I-285.

From early September to late December, **football** games are played in the **Georgia Dome** where the **Atlanta Falcons** of the National Football League take the field.

The National **Basketball** Association's **Atlanta Hawks** and the Women's National Basketball Association's **Atlanta Dream** host opponents downtown at the **Philips Arena,** 1 Philips Dr. (next to CNN Center).

Atlanta **racing** focuses on horsepower. Fans of the checkered flag can see it waved almost all year at Atlanta Motor Speedway *(see attraction listing in Hampton p. 189),* 20 miles south, and at **Road Atlanta,** 39 miles northeast near Braselton. The former is host to NASCAR racing; the latter offers sports car and motorcycle events on its road circuit March to early December.

Performing Arts

Atlanta's cultural offerings cover the spectrum from the grand (opera and symphony performances) to the down home (summer stock, vintage film showings). One of the oldest civic ballet companies in the country, founded in 1929, is the **Atlanta Ballet.** The company performs from October through May at the **Cobb Energy Performing Arts Centre,** 2800 Cobb Galleria Pkwy. Highlights include a holiday presentation of **The Nutcracker,** which is performed at the **Fox Theatre;** for ticket information phone the theater's information line at (404) 881-2100 Mon.-Fri. 10-6 and Sat. 10-3 or phone (855) 285-8499. Tickets for other ballet productions and fine arts events can be obtained via the **Ticketmaster Arts Line;** phone (800) 982-2787.

The renowned **Atlanta Symphony Orchestra** presents concerts October to early June, also at the Woodruff Arts Center. The series is supplemented by concerts June through August or September, when the orchestra occasionally performs in **Delta Classic Chastain Park Amphitheatre.** Seats are reserved. The Chastain concert series features headliners; for ticket information phone (404) 733-5000.

The Atlanta Opera offers four productions from October through May at the Cobb Energy Performing Arts Centre. The 2016-17 schedule includes "The Abduction from the Seraglio" in October, "Silent Night" in November and "Turandot" in April. For ticket information phone (404) 881-8801.

The **Alliance Theatre** at the Woodruff Arts Center presents performances that range from musicals to new and classic dramas.

Get thee hence to the theater! **The New American Shakespeare Tavern,** 499 Peachtree St. N.E., is home to the Atlanta Shakespeare Company.

Atlanta Symphony Orchestra

Based on the idea that the Bard's plays shouldn't be separated from the world in which they were created, the tavern creates an Elizabethan actor/audience dynamic where guests can eat, drink and watch classics come to life Thursdays through Sundays. Get tickets in advance as space is limited; phone (404) 874-5299. If a show becomes sold out, guests can add their names to a waiting list.

Dinner theater productions at **Agatha's—A Taste of Mystery**, 161 Peachtree Center Ave., feature audience participation; phone (404) 480-5244 or (877) 264-5020. Atlanta also is home to numerous professional, experimental and community theater groups. Daily and weekly newspapers have details about theater and dance productions, concerts and film showings; the free weekly *Creative Loafing* comes out on Thursdays and is a good entertainment information source.

INSIDER INFO:
CityPASS

The Atlanta CityPASS program includes the Georgia Aquarium, the Inside CNN Studio Tour and World of Coca-Cola. Also included are two option tickets for either the Fernbank Museum of Natural History or College Football Hall of Fame and Chick-fil-A Fan Experience, and either Zoo Atlanta or the Center for Civil and Human Rights.

CityPASS ticket booklets may be purchased at any participating attraction and are valid for 9 consecutive days once the first ticket is used. The Atlanta CityPASS booklets will save visitors 43 percent compared to purchasing individual tickets to the included attractions. Credit cards accepted vary with the vendor. Phone (208) 787-4300 or (888) 330-5008.

ATTRACTIONS

APEX MUSEUM, 135 Auburn Ave. N.E. at Piedmont Ave. S.E. (MARTA: Five Points station to bus #3), salutes African-Americans' contributions to history. Highlights include the exhibit "Africa: The Untold Story," which vividly documents the harrowing era of slavery, and a reproduction of the 1923 Yates & Milton Drugstore, one of Atlanta's first black-owned businesses.

Time: Allow 1 hour minimum. **Hours:** Tues.-Sat. 10-5. Last tour begins 1 hour before closing. Closed major holidays. **Cost:** $6; $5 (ages 55+ and students with ID); free (ages 0-4). **Phone:** (404) 523-2739. GT

ATLANTA BOTANICAL GARDEN is adjacent to Midtown's Piedmont Park at 1345 Piedmont Ave. N.E. (MARTA: Arts Center station). Among the garden's features are a 600-foot-long Canopy Walk through the treetops, an Edible Garden complete with outdoor kitchen, and woodland shade, parterre, Japanese rock and rose gardens.

The interactive Children's Garden has play areas designed to teach children about plants. Tropical, Mediterranean, desert and endangered plants grow in the Fuqua Conservatory. The rain forest room is populated with turtles, tropical birds and exhibits of poison dart frogs. The Fuqua Orchid Center houses rare orchids from around the world. Special events are held throughout the year.

Time: Allow 2 hours minimum. **Hours:** Tues.-Sun. 9-5 (also 5-7, Apr.-Oct.). Closed Jan. 1, Thanksgiving and Christmas. **Cost:** $18.95; $12.95 (ages 3-12). **Parking:** $2-$15. **Phone:** (404) 876-5859.

ATLANTA HISTORY CENTER is at 130 W. Paces Ferry Rd. N.W. (MARTA: Buckhead station to bus #110). Located on 33 acres in the heart of Buckhead, the history center features a museum housing exhibitions about the history of Atlanta and the Southeast, the Civil War, sports and Southern folk arts.

Six gardens and woodland trails relate the horticultural history of the area and are the setting for two historic houses: Swan House, a 1928 classically-styled mansion, and Smith Family Farm, a restored 1860 farmhouse complete with traditional outbuildings and antebellum activities. Docents are available to answer questions.

The Centennial Olympic Games Museum at the center is an exhibition capturing the spirit of the Olympic Games, especially the 1996 Atlanta Summer Games. The museum has a collection of Summer Olympic Games torches on display.

In 2017, the Atlanta Cyclorama will be on display at the museum while being restored to its original 371-feet circumference. Visitors will be totally encompassed by this massive painting depicting the Battle of Atlanta when viewing it from a circular platform.

Time: Allow 3 hours minimum. **Hours:** Mon.-Sat. 10-5:30, Sun. noon-5:30. Last admission 1 hour before closing. Closed Jan. 1, Thanksgiving, Christmas Eve and Christmas. **Cost:** (includes Margaret Mitchell House) $16.50; $13 (ages 65+ and students with ID); $11 (ages 4-12). **Parking:** Free. **Phone:** (404) 814-4000.

BUCKHEAD is concentrated along Peachtree Rd. about 4 mi. n. of downtown. Atlanta's Uptown district is a 28-square-mile area forming a "V" between I-85 and I-75, bounded by DeKalb County on the east, the Atlanta city limits on the north, Cobb County on the west, and Peachtree Creek, I-75 and I-85 on the south.

First occupied by Cherokee and Creek Native Americans, the area was used for farming and hunting and eventually became the home of a popular tavern and general store near the intersection of present-day Peachtree Street and Paces Ferry Road. The name Buckhead was adopted in 1838 after the head of a large buck was mounted on a post near the tavern.

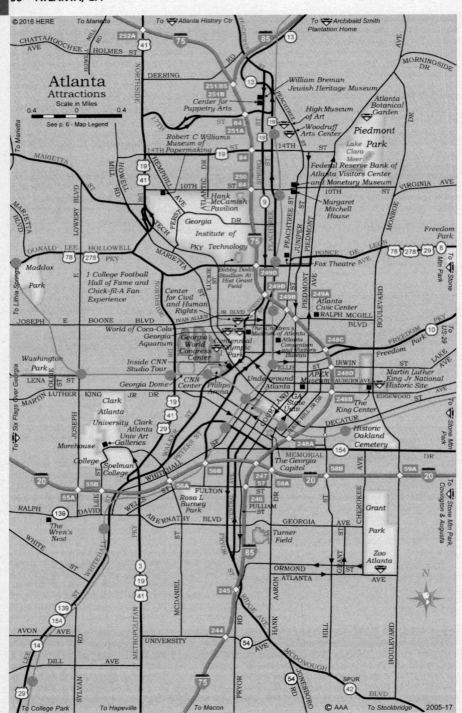

© 2016 HERE

Atlanta
Attractions
Scale in Miles
0.4   0   0.4
See p. 6 - Map Legend

A nearby vacation spot for wealthy Atlantans by the late 1800s, Buckhead was annexed to the city in 1952. One of its chief attractions for both residents and visitors is shopping; Lenox Square *(see Shopping)* is one of the Southeast's premier malls. Buckhead's mixed-use development—upscale office buildings, luxurious hotels, posh nightclubs and an eclectic variety of restaurants—has grown to the point that is boasts its own skyline.

Explore the area's past at the Atlanta History Center *(see attraction listing p. 55)*, 130 W. Paces Ferry Rd., N.W. Here you can stroll 33 acres of carefully tended gardens, walk scenic trails and view exhibits about city history, the Civil War, sports and Southern folk arts.

CDC/DAVID J. SENCER CDC MUSEUM is at CDC headquarters, 1600 Clifton Rd. N.E. at CDC Parkway (MARTA: Lindbergh Center station to bus #6). Permanent and changing exhibits focus on a variety of public health topics, as well as the history of the Centers for Disease Control and Prevention. **Note:** Visitors over age 18 must have a government-issued photo ID. **Hours:** Mon.-Fri. 9-5 (also Thurs. 5-7). Closed federal holidays. **Cost:** Free. **Phone:** (404) 639-0830.

CENTER FOR CIVIL AND HUMAN RIGHTS is at 100 Ivan Allen Jr. Blvd., near Centennial Olympic Park between the Georgia Aquarium and the World of Coca-Cola. Three floors host exhibits with interactive and hands-on technology to bring the stories of past and present to life. Colorful, eye-catching art is also on display to further inspire visitors.

Go beyond what you learned in textbooks about the Civil Rights Movement. Voice to the Voiceless: The Martin Luther King Jr. Collection reveals the life of the man through personal documents and objects. Artifacts in this collection rotate three times per year. Rolls Down Like Water: The American Civil Rights Movement not only gives the history of events from 1954-1968, but also acknowledges how those events were only one part of a larger movement in the world.

The top floor chronicles the continued struggle for civil and human rights around the world. Beginning with the events surrounding the signing of the Universal Declaration of Human Rights by the United Nations, the gallery's displays take visitors from 1948 to modern day. Spark of Conviction: The Global Human Rights Movement explores contemporary fights for human rights. Exhibits are updated regularly to remain current as events unfold around the globe.

Time: Allow 1 hour, 30 minutes minimum. **Hours:** Mon.-Sat. 10-5, Sun. noon-5. Last admission 1 hour before closing. Hours may vary seasonally. Closed Thanksgiving and Christmas. Phone ahead to confirm schedule. **Cost:** $15; $13 (ages 65+ and students with ID); $10 (ages 4-12). **Parking:** $10. **Phone:** (678) 999-8990.

CENTER FOR PUPPETRY ARTS is at 1404 Spring St. N.W. at 18th St. (MARTA: Arts Center station). Reputedly the country's largest organization dedicated to puppetry, the center's museum displays a comprehensive collection of Jim Henson puppets and artifacts and a collection of puppets from around the world. The center regularly features performances for families and adults, Create-a-Puppet workshops, Explore Puppetry adult education workshops and guided tours.

Time: Allow 30 minutes minimum. **Hours:** Tues.-Fri. 9-5, Sat. 10-5, Sun. noon-5. Ticket sales office open Mon.-Fri. 9-4:30, Sat. 9:30-5, Sun. noon-5. Closed major holidays. **Cost:** Museum $10.50. Museum and guided tour $14.50. Museum, a Family Series performance and a Create-A-Puppet workshop $20.50. Museum, a Family Series performance, a Create-A-Puppet workshop and guided tour $22.50. Free ages 0-1. Phone ahead for cost of performances. Advance reservations are highly recommended for events and activities. **Phone:** (404) 873-3391. GT

THE CHILDREN'S MUSEUM OF ATLANTA is at 275 Centennial Olympic Park Dr. N.W. (MARTA: Peachtree Center and CNN Center stations). Geared toward children 8 years of age and under, the museum offers six permanent learning zones which feature exhibits, a variety of hands-on learning activities and special programs. Participants can engage in such activities as painting on walls, creating sand sculptures, launching a rocket, operating a robot, fishing in a pond and operating pulleys and levers on a giant ball machine. Traveling exhibits also are presented. Educational programs are offered throughout the year.

Time: Allow 1 hour minimum. **Hours:** Mon.-Tues. and Thurs.-Fri. 10-4, (also select Wed., early June to mid-Aug.), Sat.-Sun. 10-5. Closed Thanksgiving and Christmas. Phone ahead to confirm schedule. **Cost:** $14.95; free (ages 0-12 months). Advance ticket purchase is recommended. **Phone:** (404) 659-5437. 🎡

CLARK ATLANTA UNIVERSITY ART GALLERIES is located on the second floor of Trevor Arnett Hall (Building #6) at 223 James P. Brawley Dr. S.W. Works in the permanent collection of 1,200 paintings, sculptures, prints, photographs and quilts constitute one of the larger and more historically significant African-American art collections. The Art of the Negro murals in the atrium, created 1950-51 by celebrated artist and teacher Hale Woodruff, illustrates African-American visual history. Changing exhibits also are featured.

Time: Allow 30 minutes minimum. **Hours:** Tues.-Fri. 11-4. Closed major holidays. **Cost:** Donations. **Phone:** (404) 880-6102 or (404) 880-6644.

COLLEGE FOOTBALL HALL OF FAME AND CHICK-FIL-A FAN EXPERIENCE is at 250 Marietta St. N.W. across from Centennial Olympic Park. Upon arrival, you will receive a fan

Federal Reserve Bank of Atlanta Visitors Center and Monetary Museum

access badge with an imbedded RFID chip that allows the exhibits to highlight your favorite team. "The Game of Your Life," a film that gives a behind-the-scenes look of game day narrated by coaches and former players, is played at the Game Day Theater.

The Skill Zone is a fun, physical adventure that allows you to test your skills in various positions, including field kicker, quarterback and wide receiver, and after the excitement of being a player, you can get a photo with the Chick-fil-A Peach Bowl trophy.

Hours: Sun.-Fri. 10-5, Sat. 9-6. Last admission 1 hour before closing. Closed Thanksgiving and Christmas. **Cost:** $19.99; $17.99 (ages 65+ and students with ID); $16.99 (ages 3-12). **Phone:** (404) 880-4800. ⑪

FEDERAL RESERVE BANK OF ATLANTA VISITORS CENTER AND MONETARY MUSEUM is at the corner of Peachtree and 10th sts. at 1000 Peachtree St. N.E. (MARTA: Midtown station). Established in 1914, the Reserve Bank is one of twelve composing the Federal Reserve System. Tours include a view of the site's automated vault and cash-processing procedures; multimedia displays focusing on the history and evolution of U.S. and global banking and currency; and Banker's Challenge, an interactive exhibit examining how banks earn profit, manage risk and provide security to customers.

Note: Due to national security concerns, tour availability is subject to change; phone ahead. **Time:** Allow 45 minutes minimum. **Hours:** Mon.-Fri. 9-4. Closed major holidays. **Cost:** Free. Parking is

available at garages near the bank for $5-$10 per day. **Phone:** (404) 498-8764 for the museum, or (404) 498-8777 for tour information. ⒼⓉ

FERNBANK MUSEUM OF NATURAL HISTORY is at 767 Clifton Rd. N.E. The museum features dioramas, interactive displays, IMAX films and traveling exhibits which explore natural history, the environment and culture.

A Walk Through Time in Georgia places visitors within re-creations of the state's diverse regions, from the coast to the mountains, to illustrate the Earth's history. Giants of the Mesozoic features the world's largest dinosaurs in a scene that highlights a 123-foot-long Argentinosaurus, the largest animal ever to walk the Earth.

The Fernbank NatureQuest children's exhibit offers hands-on opportunities to examine an interactive river, the ocean, a waterfall, a forest, a swamp, a cave, an archeology site and an activity-filled clubhouse.

Time: Allow 1 hour minimum. **Hours:** Mon.-Sat. 10-5, Sun. noon-5. Closed Thanksgiving and Christmas. **Cost:** Museum $18; $17 (ages 65+); $16 (ages 3-12); free (ages 0-2). Value Pass with one IMAX film $26; $24 (ages 65+); $22 (ages 3-12). Super Value Pass with two IMAX films $33; $30 (ages 65+); $27 (ages 3-12). **Phone:** (404) 929-6400 for tickets, or (404) 929-6300 for information. ⑪

Rankin M. Smith Sr. IMAX Theater is in the Fernbank Museum of Natural History at 767 Clifton Rd. N.E. The theater houses a five-story screen more than 70 feet wide and features a variety of nature and science films. Visitors may dine, view special screenings and experience live music during weekly Martinis & IMAX presentations.

Hours: Shows are presented on the hour Mon.-Sat. 10-5, Sun. noon-5. Closed Thanksgiving and Christmas. **Cost:** IMAX $13; $12 (ages 65+); $11 (ages 3-12); free (ages 0-2 with ticket). IMAX double feature $21; $19 (ages 65+); $17 (ages 3-12); free (ages 0-2 with ticket). **Phone:** (404) 929-6400 for tickets, or (404) 929-6300 for information. ⑪

FERNBANK SCIENCE CENTER, 156 Heaton Park Dr. N.E., offers science-related exhibits, an observatory and a planetarium. The original Apollo 6 space capsule is on display. Special events are offered throughout the year.

Time: Allow 1 hour minimum. **Hours:** Displays open Mon.-Wed. noon-5, Thurs.-Fri. noon-9, Sat. 10-5, early Jan. to mid-Dec. Phone ahead to confirm planetarium show schedule. Observatory open Thurs.-Fri. 8:30-10 p.m. (weather permitting). Center closed Martin Luther King Jr. Day, Presidents Day, school spring break, Memorial Day, July 4, Labor Day, Thanksgiving. Phone ahead to confirm schedule. **Cost:** Displays and observatory free. Planetarium $7; $5 (ages 62+ and students and military with ID); free (ages 0-2). Phone ahead to confirm rates. **Phone:** (678) 874-7102.

A Few Good Reasons to Know When Help Will Arrive

When a road trip stalls and you request AAA/CAA assistance, opt to receive text updates. Messages:

- Confirm receipt of your service request

- Alert you when a service vehicle is en route

- Provide the service vehicle's estimated arrival time

Opt in and stay informed.

AAA.com/mobile | CAA.ca/mobile

FOX THEATRE, 660 Peachtree St. N.E. (MARTA: North Avenue station), stands tall as a tribute to the heyday of the grand entertainment showplace. The "Fabulous Fox" was built in the late 1920s as the headquarters for the Shriners organization and was originally called the Yaarab Temple Shrine Mosque. It opened to great fanfare on Christmas Day 1929, changed ownership several times thereafter and came perilously close to demolition in the 1970s before a concerted grass roots effort to save the building prevailed.

Today the Fox retains all of its lavish trappings, from the imposing lobby to Egyptian-themed decorative accents to the breathtaking nearly 4,700-seat performance hall that resembles a huge Arabian courtyard, complete with a starlit ceiling and floating clouds. It's the most lavish setting in town for Broadway shows, music concerts, comedy shows, ballet performances and such special events as showings of "Gone with the Wind."

One-hour guided tours of the historic building are offered. Specialty and holiday tours also are available. Tickets for all performances are available at the Fox Theatre box office. **Hours:** Tours are given Mon., Thurs. and Sat. at 10, 11, noon and 1. **Cost:** Tour fee $18; $15 (ages 65+ and military with ID); $5 (ages 0-10). Reservations are recommended for guided tours. **Phone:** (404) 881-2100 for general information, or (855) 285-8499 for ticket information. GT

GEORGIA AQUARIUM is downtown at 225 Baker St., across from Centennial Olympic Park (MARTA: CNN Center or Peachtree Center stations). Where can you view a 24-foot-long whale shark, interact with a horseshoe crab or come face to face with creatures that bear a passing resemblance to Jar Jar Binks? The Georgia Aquarium, that's where. Its seven major exhibit galleries contain more than 10 million gallons of water and showcase a fascinating variety of marine life.

Ocean Voyager accommodates four whale sharks—the world's largest fish—along with sharks, Goliath groupers, stingrays, schools of trevally jacks and four manta rays, the only manta rays on display in a U.S. aquarium. Stand in front of the enormous viewing window or walk through a cool acrylic tunnel.

The Dolphin Tales gallery, theater and show is dedicated to creating memorable connections between humans and animals and allows guests to get an up-close look at the naturally playful behaviors of Atlantic bottlenose dolphins.

Tropical Diver boasts a living reef inhabited by thousands of colorful reef fish. Exhibits display seahorses, fairy basslets, jawfish, jellyfish, cuttlefish (not a fish but a mollusk, and the aquarium resident that fits the Jar Jar comparison) and other interesting creatures. A wave machine simulating surf conditions operates above the reef. Cold Water

Quest features harbor seals, sea otters, sea stars, anemones, a penguin habitat and white, rubbery-looking but lovable beluga whales, found in Arctic and sub-Arctic regions like Alaska, Russia and Greenland.

Electric eels, an emerald tree boa, African cichlids, albino American alligators and a tank of red piranhas are among the animals on display at River Scout, a freshwater gallery. Asian small-clawed otters energetically chase each other through the water, aided by feet that are partially webbed.

Visitors can learn about aquatic life in Aquanaut Adventure: A Discovery Zone, an interactive exhibit for all ages. Pier 225 features California sea lions, and trainer interaction sessions take place throughout the day.

There's more. The 4-D Theater combines digital projection, high-definition 3-D film and special effects in "Happy Feet," a multi-sensory experience about Mumble and the other emperor penguins in the Antarctic. For an insider's perspective of the exhibit galleries, take one of the Behind the Scenes Tours. Animal encounter programs also allow visitors to have an up-close experience with dolphins, sea otters or penguins or to swim or dive with whale sharks.

Check the schedule for fish feedings; it's quite a sight to watch all of the exhibit's inhabitants swarm when little pieces of cut-up fish are dumped into the water. The whale sharks are fed a separate meal of small crustaceans and squid, since they strain their food from the water with their gills.

Note: All tickets are non-refundable. Visitors are not permitted to bring food, beverages or gum inside. Food is available until 1 hour before closing. **Time:** Allow 5 hours minimum. **Hours:** Daily 10-8. Aquarium offers extended hours in summer and during holidays; phone ahead to verify. The 4-D Theater showings begin 30 minutes after the aquarium opens. Aquanaut Adventure schedule may vary; phone ahead. Last admission 1 hour before closing. **Cost:** $40.95; $36.95 (ages 65+); $34.95 (ages 3-12). Reservations are required for Behind the Scenes Tours and animal encounter programs and an additional fee is charged. **Parking:** $10. **Phone:** (404) 581-4000. GT ⑪

THE GEORGIA CAPITOL, 206 Washington St. between Mitchell St. and Martin Luther King Jr. Dr. (MARTA: Georgia State station), was patterned after the national Capitol. Gold leaf mined in northern Georgia covers the exterior dome. Inside, the Georgia Capitol Museum contains exhibits about the building's architecture, history and purpose; displays include rocks, minerals, Native American artifacts and colorful dioramas. The General Assembly is in session from early January to March.

An audio tour is available by cellphone. Guided tours are available by appointment (requires a minimum of 10 participants). **Note:** Visitors over age 17 must have a photo ID to enter the capitol. **Time:** Allow 1 hour, 30 minutes minimum. **Hours:** Mon.-Fri. 8-5. Closed state holidays. **Cost:** Free. **Phone:** (404) 463-4536. GT

GRANT PARK is bounded by Atlanta Ave., Sydney St., Cherokee Ave. and the Boulevard S.E. The land for this 131-acre public park was donated in 1883 by Col. Lemuel Pratt Grant, a civil engineer with the railroads, who helped bring the railroad to Atlanta and designed the defensive fortifications around Atlanta in anticipation of a Union siege during the Civil War.

The park grounds, which encompass Fort Walker and Zoo Atlanta, feature walking trails, historic structures and native plantings. A tour of the surrounding Historic District and a tour of the L.P. Grant antebellum mansion are offered by the Atlanta Preservation Center *(see Walking Tours p. 65)*. A Sunday farmers market, jct. Cherokee and Milledge aves., offers more than 30 vendors selling local products, arts and crafts activities and cooking demonstrations by local chefs.

Hours: Park open daily 6 a.m.-11 p.m. Historic District guided tours are given Mar.-Nov. (weather permitting). Farmers market Sun. 9:30-1:30, Apr.-Dec. **Cost:** Park grounds free; a fee is charged for Historic District guided tours. **Phone:** (404) 521-0938 for park information, or (404) 688-3353 for historic district tours. GT 🏕

🦎 **Zoo Atlanta,** 800 Cherokee Ave. S.E. in Grant Park, exhibits nearly 1,400 animals from around the world in naturalistic habitats. It is one of only four zoos in the country which houses giant pandas, including twins, and holds one of the nation's largest collections of Western Lowland gorillas and Bornean and Sumatran orangutans. Scaly Slimy Spectacular: The Amphibian and Reptile Experience houses more than 70 species of reptiles and amphibians in a variety of state-of-the-art habitats.

The Living Treehouse features a variety of African bird species as well as various species of smaller primates. Other animals include Asian small-clawed otters, red kangaroos and African lions. An interactive children's splash fountain is available seasonally. Wild animal encounter programs are offered.

Picnicking is permitted in the zoo and in surrounding Grant Park. **Time:** Allow 4 hours minimum. **Hours:** Ticket office open daily 9:30-4:30. Grounds remain open 1 hour after ticket office closes. Closed Thanksgiving and Christmas. **Cost:** Gate admission $25.99; $17.99 (ages 3-11); free (military with ID). Train, carousel or rock climber $3 each. **Phone:** (404) 624-9453. 🍴 🏕

HISTORIC OAKLAND CEMETERY is at 248 Oakland Ave. S.E. (MARTA: King Memorial station). Founded in 1850, this Victorian cemetery contains majestic oaks and some of the city's oldest magnolia trees. Gothic Revival and neoclassic tombs are found throughout the 48-acre cemetery as well as the graves of 27 former Atlanta mayors, six Georgia governors, "Gone With the Wind" author Margaret Mitchell, golfing great Bobby Jones and approximately 6,900 Confederate soldiers. Self-guiding walking tour brochures are available at the visitor center. Special events are held throughout the year.

Hours: Cemetery open daily dawn-dusk. Visitor center open Mon.-Fri. 9-5, Sat.-Sun. 9-8, mid-Mar. through Nov. 30; Mon.-Fri. 9-5, Sat.-Sun. 10-4, rest of year. Guided tours are given Sat.-Sun. at 10, 2 and 4, mid-Mar. to early Dec. (also at 6:30 p.m., mid-Mar. to mid-Oct.); at 2, rest of year. No tours first Sun. in Oct. and during some special events. Phone ahead to confirm schedule. **Cost:** Cemetery free. Tour fee $12; $6 (ages 6-17, ages 65+ and students with ID); $28 (family, two adults and two children). **Phone:** (404) 688-2107. GT

INSIDE CNN STUDIO TOUR is at One CNN Center/ 190 Marietta St. N.W. (MARTA: Dome/GWCC/ Philips Arena/CNN Center station). This 50-minute guided walking tour offers an up-close look behind the scenes of the CNN Worldwide networks at the company's global headquarters. Included are demonstrations of advanced weather-broadcasting technology, a teleprompter demonstration, a presentation of chroma key (green screen) effects and a look at CNN's social media presence. Viewers observe the workings of the newsrooms of CNN, HLN, CNN International and CNN en Español and get a view into CNN's HD studio with live broadcasts each weekday.

Note: The walking tour descends eight flights of stairs; comfortable attire and footwear are recommended. Elevator-assisted tours are available upon request. **Hours:** Tours, limited to 45 people, are offered approximately every 20 minutes daily 9-5. Closed Easter, Thanksgiving and Christmas. **Cost:** Tour $16; $15 (ages 13-18, ages 65+ and college students with ID); $13 (ages 4-12). Ages 0-3 are free but must have a ticket. Phone ahead to confirm rates. A limited number of same-day tickets is available on a first-come, first-served basis daily starting at 8:30 a.m. Reservations can be made at least one day in advance and are highly recommended. **Phone:** (404) 827-2300 for reservations or (877) 426-6868. GT

JIMMY CARTER PRESIDENTIAL LIBRARY & MUSEUM, at exit 248C (Freedom Pkwy.) then following signs to the Carter Center, contains interactive exhibits that chronicle Carter's life, events occurring during his 1976-81 administration and the work of the Carter Center. The beautifully landscaped grounds include two lakes and a Japanese garden.

Note: The library is open only to researchers. Food is available Mon.-Fri. 11:30-2. **Time:** Allow 1 hour, 30 minutes minimum. **Hours:** Museum open Mon.-Sat. 9-4:45, Sun. noon-4:45. Closed Jan. 1, Thanksgiving and Christmas. **Cost:** $8; $6 (ages 60+, military and students with ID); free (ages 0-16). **Phone:** (404) 865-7100. TI A

LEGOLAND DISCOVERY CENTER ATLANTA, 3500 Peachtree Rd. N.E., appeals to builders ages 3-10. Visitors get to construct and race miniature cars, test the integrity of tiny skyscrapers and attend workshops at the Master Builder Academy. On the Kingdom Quest Laser Ride they get to save the princess and compete for the high score, and at Pirate Adventure Island they can climb aboard a pirate ship and build a sandcastle with LEGO bricks. The smallest among us will enjoy Duplo Village designed for ages 1-5.

Some play areas require children to wear socks only. Adults must be with a child to visit. **Hours:** Daily 10-7 (also Sat. 7-9 p.m.). Last admission 2 hours before closing. **Cost:** $19.95; free (ages 0-2). Optional Activity Pack $4. **Phone:** (404) 848-9252. TI

MARGARET MITCHELL HOUSE is at 990 Peachtree St. N.E., at 10th St. (MARTA: Midtown station). Visitors can tour the carefully restored apartment where the Pulitzer Prize-winning novel "Gone With the Wind" was written. Two exhibits, Margaret Mitchell: A Passion for Character and The Making of a Movie Legend: Gone With the Wind, showcase Mitchell's life and the times that influenced her enduring tale of the South. Docents are available to answer questions. Parking is limited. **Hours:** Mon.-Sat. 10-5:30, Sun. noon-5:30. Closed Jan. 1, Thanksgiving, Christmas Eve and Christmas. **Cost:** $13; $10 (ages 65+ and students with ID); $8.50 (ages 4-12). **Phone:** (404) 249-7015.

MARTIN LUTHER KING JR. NATIONAL HISTORIC SITE is at 450 Auburn Ave. N.E.; the #3 Auburn Avenue bus, departing from the MARTA Five Points station, stops close to the visitor center. The 39-acre site encompasses the birthplace, church and grave of civil rights leader and Nobel Peace Prize winner Dr. Martin Luther King Jr., who paid the ultimate price as an impassioned advocate for civil rights when he was assassinated by James Earl Ray on April 4, 1968, while lending his support to a Memphis sanitation workers' strike. Coretta Scott King, who carried on her husband's work after his death, is buried beside her husband.

Dr. King's legacy endures as a source of inspiration to those who believe in social and economic equality for every American. The visitor center contains exhibits and video presentations relating to King's work and achievements and the civil rights movement. The King Center, Dr. King's final resting place, features exhibits about Coretta Scott King and Mahatma Gandhi. The surrounding district preserves sections of Sweet Auburn, the neighborhood that was the center of Atlanta's African-American community for most of the 20th century.

Hours: Site open daily 9-5. Site may offer extended hours in summer; phone ahead. Guided 30-minute tours of Dr. King's birthplace are available on a first-come, first-served basis. Reservations must be made in person the day of the tour. Closed Jan. 1, Thanksgiving and Christmas. **Cost:** Free. **Phone:** (404) 331-5190. GT

The King Center, 449 Auburn Ave. N.E., includes the Freedom Hall Complex and is part of the Martin Luther King Jr. National Historic Site. Surrounding Rev. Dr. King's crypt are the Freedom Walkway, a reflecting pool, the Chapel of All Faiths and Freedom Hall. The archives are open to the public only by appointment. Self-guiding tours are available. **Hours:** Daily 9-6, Memorial Day-Labor Day; 9-5, rest of year. Closed Jan. 1, Thanksgiving, Christmas Eve and Christmas. **Cost:** Free. **Phone:** (404) 526-8900.

MICHAEL C. CARLOS MUSEUM OF EMORY UNIVERSITY, 571 S. Kilgo Cir. on the Emory University campus, offers the art and artifacts of ancient Egypt, Nubia, the Near East, Africa, Asia, Greece, Rome and the Americas, as well as prints and drawings from the Renaissance to the present. Temporary and traveling exhibitions also are featured. Guided and MP3 audio tours are available. **Hours:** Tues.-Fri. 10-4, Sat. 10-5, Sun. noon-5. Closed university holidays. Guided tours offered Sun. at 2; phone ahead to confirm. **Cost:** $8; $6 (ages 6-17, students and senior citizens). MP3 audio tour $2. **Phone:** (404) 727-4282. GT

ROBERT C. WILLIAMS MUSEUM OF PAPER-MAKING is at 500 10th Street N.W. in the RBI Paper Tricentennial Building at the Georgia Institute of Technology. The museum houses more than 2,000 books and 10,000 items tracing the invention and evolution of paper and printing. Global artifacts dating from as early as 200 B.C. to the technology of today focus on such devices as the paper machine, as well as efforts to conserve and recycle paper. Changing exhibits feature works by contemporary and worldwide papermaking artists.

Time: Allow 1 hour minimum. **Hours:** Mon.-Fri. 9-5. Closed major holidays. **Cost:** Free. **Phone:** (404) 894-7840.

SKYVIEW ATLANTA, 168 Luckie St. N.W., is a Ferris wheel that stands about 20 stories tall and offers aerial views of downtown Atlanta. Each enclosed climate-controlled gondola features audio that helps you find such sights as the CNN Center, the Georgia Aquarium, and the Fountain of Rings in Centennial Olympic Park as well as gives facts about the sights. If you cannot hear the audio, turn up volume button located on the ceiling of the gondola, and if you did not manage to get the perfect photo on the first time around, there are more chances on the ride's four rotations.

Parking is located at 101 Cone St. Parking ticket needs to be validated for discount. **Hours:** Sun.-Thurs. 10 a.m.-midnight, Fri. 10 a.m.-1 a.m., Sat. 10 a.m.-1 a.m. **Cost:** $13.89; $12.50 (military, seniors and students with ID); $9.26 (ages 3-11). Senior and military tickets must be purchased on-site. **Parking:** $5. **Phone:** (678) 949-9023.

WILLIAM BREMAN JEWISH HERITAGE MUSEUM is in the Selig Center at 1440 Spring St. N.W. (MARTA: Arts Center station). The Blonder Heritage Gallery presents stories of the Holocaust and southern Jewish heritage. "Absence of Humanity: The Holocaust Years, 1933-1945" interprets the Holocaust through photographs, documents, memorabilia, family pictures and oral histories of survivors who rebuilt new lives in Atlanta after World War II. A special exhibition gallery and library also are available.

Guided tours are available by appointment. **Hours:** Sun.-Thurs. 10-5, Fri. 10-4. Closed major Jewish holidays and some federal holidays. **Cost:** $12; $8 (senior citizens); $6 (students and teachers with ID); $4 (ages 3-6). **Phone:** (678) 222-3700. GT

WOODRUFF ARTS CENTER is at 1280 Peachtree St. N.E. (MARTA: Arts Center station). The Woodruff combines performing and visual arts and is home to the Alliance Theatre, Arts for Learning, the Atlanta Symphony Orchestra and High Museum of Art. **Note:** The Alliance Theatre is closed due to renovations and will reopen in 2018. **Time:** Allow 2 hours minimum. **Hours:** Schedule for each facility may vary; phone ahead to confirm hours or inquire about event and performance schedule. Closed major holidays. **Cost:** Fee depends upon facilities visited. **Phone:** (404) 733-5000 for ticket information. ⊤⌐

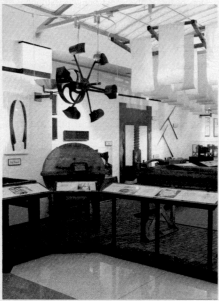

Robert C. Williams Museum of Papermaking

High Museum of Art is at 1280 Peachtree St. N.E. (MARTA: Arts Center station) in the Woodruff Arts Center. Richard Meier's stark white, porcelain-enameled building—together with three expansion buildings by renowned Italian architect Renzo Piano—is the Woodruff Arts Center's stunning focal point and a suitably dramatic showcase for more than 14,000 rotating works of art. The High complex is particularly noted for the integration of natural light into the overall design.

The Meier Building's soaring four-level atrium is probably what you'll notice first upon entering, but your attention will soon be drawn to the museum's outstanding permanent collection, noted for African, European and 19th- and 20th-century American art, civil rights photography, folk art, decorative arts, and modern and contemporary works. The contemporary galleries display paintings by such artists as Max Ernst, Robert Rauschenberg and Frank Stella, as well as highlights like Spencer Finch's "Bright Star (Sirius)," a striking hanging light sculpture made of florescent tubes.

Georgia O'Keeffe, John Singer Sargent and Childe Hassam are some of the artists spotlighted in the American art collection, which also includes Hudson River School landscape paintings. Artists from Albrecht Dürer to Claude Monet to Henri de Toulouse-Lautrec form the core of the European collection, where you'll see masterworks like Giovanni Bellini's "Madonna and Child." Another highlight is a recycled chest of drawers; Dutch artist Tejo Remy assembled that piece for a live audience in 2008.

One of the High's most popular gatherings is Friday Night Jazz on the third Friday of the month. Museum galleries are open extended hours, with live evening musical performances taking place in the atrium.

Time: Allow 2 hours minimum. **Hours:** Tues.-Sat. 10-5 (also Fri. 5-9), Sun. noon-5; also open third Fri. of the month 5-10 (except Dec.). Last admission is 1 hour before closing. Closed major holidays. Phone ahead to confirm tour schedule. **Cost:** $19.50; $16.50 (ages 65+ and students with ID); $12 (ages 6-17); half price Fri. 4-9; free (active and retired military with ID year-round and to Fulton County residents the first Sat. of the month 10-1). Fee for special programs varies; advance reservations are recommended. Admission to Friday Night Jazz includes museum access and current special exhibitions. **Phone:** (404) 733-4444, or (404) 733-5000 to purchase tickets. GT ⬛

WORLD OF COCA-COLA is at 121 Baker St. N.W. (MARTA: Dome/GWCC/Philips Arena/CNN Center or Peachtree Center stations), adjacent to the Georgia Aquarium and Center for Civil and Human Rights and across from Centennial Olympic Park. Dedicated to "the real thing," this tribute to the dark brown soft drink—which moved from its former Underground Atlanta location to the 20-acre Pemberton Place site in 2007—features more than 1,200 Coca-Cola-related artifacts that will remind you just how globally ubiquitous this product is.

The journey begins in the Coca-Cola Loft, filled with Coke logos, framed posters and all manner of memorabilia. From there visitors can trace the history of The Coca-Cola Company (chronicled in Milestones of Refreshment) and get an up-close look at the bottling process in Bottle Works.

Feel closer than ever before to Coca-Cola's most guarded trade secret and learn about the intrigue behind the secret formula in the Vault of the Secret Formula experience; visitors can see the vault where the formula is secured.

Upstairs, watching TV commercials from the past is a nostalgic trip down memory lane in the Perfect Pauses Theater (remember "I'd Like to Buy the World a Coke" sung to the tune of "I'd Like to Teach the World to Sing in Perfect Harmony"?). Coke's iconic influence is showcased in the Pop Culture Gallery. Hang on to your seat in the 4-D theater as you're taken on a breakneck quest to discover just what it is that makes Coke, well, Coke.

Don't miss Taste It!, where you can sample more than 100 different beverages from around the world. Five stations arranged geographically offer a variety of flavors unique to each region. Grab one of the small plastic cups and sip away. If you've ever wanted to know what Vegitabeta, Thums Up or Sparberry taste like, here's your chance to find out. Visitors also get to take home a commemorative bottle of you-know-what.

Food is available at the Pemberton Cafe in Pemberton Place. **Time:** Allow 1 hour, 30 minutes minimum. **Hours:** Opens Sun.-Thurs. at 10 a.m., Fri.-Sat. at 9 a.m. Usual closing time is 6:30 but varies; phone ahead for information about early closings or extended seasonal hours. Last admission is 90 minutes before closing. Closed Thanksgiving and Christmas. **Cost:** $16; $14 (ages 65+); $12 (ages 3-12). **Parking:** Parking is available at the Pemberton Place parking garage at 178 Ivan Allen Jr. Blvd.; fee $10 per vehicle. **Phone:** (404) 676-5151 or (800) 676-2653.

THE WREN'S NEST, 1050 Ralph D. Abernathy Blvd. S.W. (MARTA: West End station and bus #71), was the home of author and journalist Joel Chandler Harris from 1881 until his death in 1908. Best known as the creator of the "Uncle Remus Stories," Harris was a folklorist who preserved the Brer Rabbit stories that otherwise might have been lost. The original 1870 house was remodeled in 1884 to its current Victorian appearance and features original Harris family furnishings.

Special events are offered. **Time:** Allow 1 hour minimum. **Hours:** Tues.-Sat. 10-2:30. Storytelling sessions take place Sat. at 1 and by appointment. Closed major holidays. **Cost:** $9; $8 (ages 13-18, college students with ID and senior citizens); $6 (ages 3-12). **Phone:** (404) 753-7735. 🎫

Sightseeing
Bus and Trolley Tours

American Sightseeing Atlanta and other companies offer a variety of excursions around downtown Atlanta, to Stone Mountain and through residential areas.

THE PEACHTREE TROLLEY CO. tours depart from the Hilton Garden Inn at 275 Baker St. N.W. Sites on this narrated tour in a climate-controlled trolley include the Georgia Aquarium, World of Coca-Cola, Fox Theatre, The Georgia Capitol, Margaret Mitchell House, Martin Luther King Jr. National Historic Site, Oakland Cemetery and others.

Visitors should arrive 30 minutes early to purchase tickets. **Time:** Allow 1 hour, 30 minutes minimum. **Hours:** Tours depart Tues.-Sat. at 10:30 and 1, Sun. at 1 and 3. **Cost:** $30; $28 (ages 55+ and college students with ID); $15 (ages 7-12). Reservations are required. **Phone:** (770) 425-1006. GT

Food Tours

PEACHTREE FOOD TOURS departs from jct. Peachtree St. and 5th St. N.E. This tour is all about tasty food, interesting stories and Southern hospitality. Your guide, also the owner, will take you on a 4-hour, 2-mile walk down Peachtree Street in Midtown, stopping in five restaurants for delicious bites of food and ample sips of alcohol pairings.

All the while, he'll tell you about Atlanta, including the destruction of the city during the fire in the early 1900s and the reconstruction that followed as well as today's growth in his neighborhood. Tours are kept at 8 participants to facilitate conversation among the group and with the guide. **Hours:** Tours depart Fri.-Sat. at 11, Sun. at noon, early Jan. to mid-Dec. Tours are offered other days by request.

Phone ahead to confirm schedule. **Cost:** $100. Reservations are required. **Phone:** (770) 352-4607. GT

Segway Tours

ATL-CRUZERS ELECTRIC CAR AND SEGWAY TOURS departs from 160 Ted Turner Dr. N.W. Visitors can take a 90-minute tour of the city aboard one of the five-passenger electric cars or a 2.5-hour tour aboard two-wheeled Segway transportation devices. Tour operators give a historical overview of the city from 1837 through present-day events as they pass points of interest.

Note: Segway tours begin with a 15- to 30-minute training session. **Hours:** Electric car tours depart daily at 11, 1 and 3. Segway tours depart daily at 10 and 2. Closed Thanksgiving, Christmas Eve and Christmas. **Cost:** Electric car tour $32; $29 (ages 65+); $22 (ages 8-17); ages 0-7 are not permitted. Segway tour $59; ages 0-13 are not permitted. Reservations are recommended. **Phone:** (404) 492-7009. GT

Walking Tours

House and garden tours of Druid Hills and Ansley Park are conducted during annual events. Further information can be obtained at your hotel or from the telephone directory.

Guided walking tours of Atlanta's historic districts, downtown architecture and the Westview Cemetery are offered by the Atlanta Preservation Center March through November (weather permitting). Comfortable walking shoes should be worn; phone (404) 688-3353.

Free guided 30-minute tours of the 1967 Greek Revival-style Governor's Mansion are offered Tuesday through Thursday 10-11:30. The mansion is at 391 West Paces Ferry Rd. N.W. Phone (404) 261-1776.

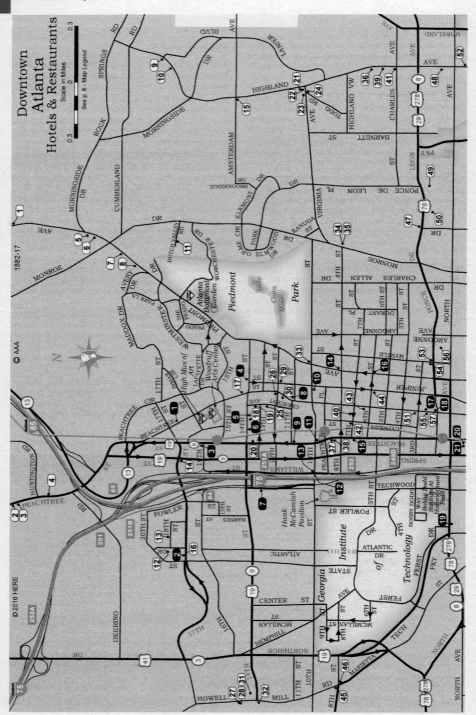

Downtown
Atlanta
Hotels & Restaurants

Scale in Miles

See p. 6 - Map Legend

© AAA

© 2016 HERE

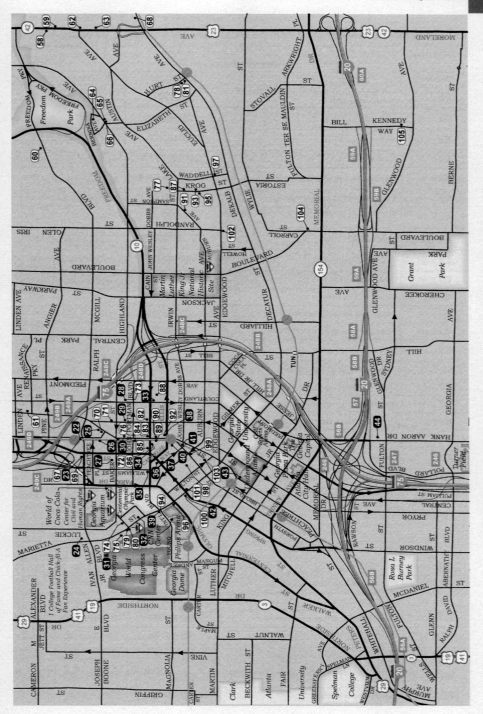

Downtown Atlanta

This index helps you "spot" where approved hotels and restaurants are located on the corresponding detailed maps. Hotel daily rate range is for comparison only. Restaurant price range is a combination of lunch and/or dinner. Turn to the listing page for more detailed rate and price information and consult display ads for special promotions.

DOWNTOWN ATLANTA

Map Page	Hotels	Diamond Rated	Rate Range	Page
1 p. 66	**Residence Inn by Marriott Atlanta Midtown Peachtree at 17th**	◇◇◇	$118-$227 SAVE	105
2 p. 66	**TWELVE Atlantic Station, Autograph Collection** *(See ad p. 106.)*	◇◇◇	$149-$409 SAVE	107
3 p. 66	Artmore Hotel	◇◇◇	Rates not provided	100
4 p. 66	**W Atlanta Midtown Hotel**	◇◇◇◇	$159-$359 SAVE	107
5 p. 66	**Four Seasons Hotel Atlanta**	◇◇◇◇◇	Rates not provided SAVE	102
6 p. 66	**Atlanta Marriott Suites Midtown**	◇◇◇	$116-$321 SAVE	101
7 p. 66	**Courtyard by Marriott Atlanta Midtown/Georgia Tech**	◇◇◇	$96-$250 SAVE	101
8 p. 66	**Loews Atlanta Hotel**	◇◇◇◇	Rates not provided SAVE	104
9 p. 66	Residence Inn by Marriott Atlanta-Midtown/Georgia Tech	◇◇◇	$125-$237	105
10 p. 66	**Hyatt Atlanta Midtown**	◇◇◇◇	$99-$449 SAVE	104
11 p. 66	Regency Suites Hotel	◇◇◇	$119-$289	105
12 p. 66	**Homewood Suites by Hilton**	◇◇◇	$149-$279 SAVE	104
13 p. 66	**Hilton Garden Inn Atlanta Midtown**	◇◇◇	$149-$269	103
14 p. 66	Stonehurst Place Bed & Breakfast	◇◇◇	Rates not provided	106
15 p. 66	**Renaissance Atlanta Midtown**	◇◇◇◇	$98-$309 SAVE	105
16 p. 66	Shellmont Inn Bed & Breakfast	◇◇◇	$185-$400	105
17 p. 66	Hotel Indigo Atlanta Midtown	◇◇◇	$99-$349	104
18 p. 66	**The Georgian Terrace Hotel** *(See ad p. 102.)*	◇◇◇	$139-$849 SAVE	103
19 p. 66	Hampton Inn Atlanta Downtown Georgia Tech	◇◇◇	$139-$300	103
20 p. 66	**Crowne Plaza Atlanta Midtown**	◇◇◇	Rates not provided SAVE	101
21 p. 66	**Staybridge Suites - Atlanta Midtown**	◇◇◇	$119-$499 SAVE	106
22 p. 66	**TWELVE Centennial Park, Autograph Collection** *(See ad p. 106.)*	◇◇◇	$170-$409 SAVE	107
23 p. 66	**W Atlanta Downtown**	◇◇◇◇	$145-$349 SAVE	107
24 p. 66	**HYATT house Atlanta Downtown**	◇◇◇	$89-$399 SAVE	104
25 p. 66	**Hyatt Place, Atlanta/Downtown**	◇◇◇	$99-$299 SAVE	104
26 p. 66	Inn at the Peachtrees	◇◇◇	$99-$299	104
27 p. 66	**Aloft Hotel Atlanta Downtown**	◇◇◇	$129-$399 SAVE	100
28 p. 66	**Hilton Atlanta**	◇◇◇	$99-$259 SAVE	103
29 p. 66	**Atlanta Marriott Marquis**	◇◇◇	$104-$321 SAVE	101
30 p. 66	**Hyatt Regency Atlanta**	◇◇◇	$109-$369 SAVE	104
31 p. 66	Hilton Garden Inn Atlanta Downtown	◇◇◇	Rates not provided	103
32 p. 66	**Embassy Suites by Hilton Centennial Olympic Park**	◇◇◇	$159-$299 SAVE	101
33 p. 66	**Sheraton Atlanta Hotel**	◇◇◇	$69-$599 SAVE	106

DOWNTOWN ATLANTA (cont'd)

Map Page	Hotels (cont'd)	Diamond Rated	Rate Range	Page
34 p. 66	**The Westin Peachtree Plaza**	◆◆◆◆	Rates not provided SAVE	107
35 p. 66	Holiday Inn Atlanta Downtown	◆◆◆	Rates not provided	103
36 p. 66	DoubleTree by Hilton Atlanta Downtown	◆◆◆	Rates not provided	101
37 p. 66	**Hampton Inn & Suites Atlanta Downtown**	◆◆◆	$229-$339 SAVE	103
38 p. 66	**The Ritz-Carlton, Atlanta**	◆◆◆◆	$169-$303 SAVE	105
39 p. 66	Omni Hotel at CNN Center	◆◆◆	Rates not provided	105
40 p. 66	**Courtyard by Marriott Atlanta Downtown**	◆◆◆	$109-$240 SAVE	101
41 p. 66	Residence Inn by Marriott Atlanta-Downtown	◆◆◆	$89-$217	105
42 p. 66	**Glenn Hotel, Autograph Collection**	◆◆◆	$121-$307 SAVE	103
43 p. 66	Fairfield Inn & Suites by Marriott Atlanta Downtown	◆◆◆	$95-$202	101
44 p. 66	Ramada Plaza Atlanta Downtown-Capitol Park	◆◆	$93-$249	105

Map Page	Restaurants	Diamond Rated	Cuisine	Price Range	Page
1 p. 66	Fat Matt's Rib Shack	◆	Barbecue	$4-$21	110
2 p. 66	Bell Street Burritos	◆	Mexican	$3-$8	108
3 p. 66	R. Thomas Deluxe Grill	◆◆	Natural/Organic	$9-$20	113
4 p. 66	Tuk Tuk Thai Food Loft	◆◆◆	Thai	$10-$21	115
5 p. 66	Atmosphere	◆◆◆	French	$11-$38	108
6 p. 66	Cowtippers	◆◆	Steak	$6-$23	109
7 p. 66	Bantam & Biddy	◆◆	Southern Comfort Food	$11-$16	108
8 p. 66	Bangkok Thai Restaurant	◆◆	Thai	$6-$25	108
9 p. 66	Doc Chey's Noodle House	◆	Asian	$8-$10	109
10 p. 66	Alon's Bakery & Market	◆	Deli	$6-$12	108
11 p. 66	ONE. midtown kitchen	◆◆◆	New American	$18-$40	112
12 p. 66	The Pig & The Pearl	◆◆◆	Barbecue Seafood	$7-$26	113
13 p. 66	Rosa Mexicano	◆◆◆	Mexican	$5-$20	113
14 p. 66	Nan Thai Fine Dining	◆◆◆◆	Thai	$17-$45	112
15 p. 66	Mali Restaurant	◆◆	Thai	$8-$17	111
16 p. 66	Lobby Bar & Bistro	◆◆	American	$8-$26	111
17 p. 66	Tamarind Seed	◆◆◆	Thai	$12-$29	114
18 p. 66	Bar Margot	◆◆◆◆	New American	$13-$36	108
19 p. 66	South City Kitchen	◆◆◆	New Southern	$12-$48	114
20 p. 66	Carolyn's Gourmet Cafe	◆	Sandwiches	$6-$18	109
21 p. 66	Fontaine's Oyster House	◆◆	Seafood	$7-$26	110
22 p. 66	Highland Tap	◆◆	American	$8-$36	110
23 p. 66	La Tavola Trattoria	◆◆◆	Italian	$8-$26	111
24 p. 66	Murphy's	◆◆◆	American	$9-$23	112
25 p. 66	Lure	◆◆◆	Seafood	$11-$34	111
26 p. 66	The Oceanaire Seafood Room	◆◆◆	Seafood	$8-$49	112

Map Page	Restaurants (cont'd)	Diamond Rated	Cuisine	Price Range	Page
(27) p. 66	Bacchanalia	◆◆◆◆	New American	$12-$85	108
(28) p. 66	JCT Kitchen & Bar	◆◆	New Southern	$7-$29	111
(29) p. 66	Einstein's	◆◆◆	American	$11-$24	110
(30) p. 66	Ribalta	◆◆◆	Italian	$10-$32	113
(31) p. 66	Cooks & Soldiers	◆◆◆	Basque	$8-$34	109
(32) p. 66	Yeah! Burger	◆	Burgers	$5-$11	115
(33) p. 66	Flying Biscuit Cafe	◆◆	American	$5-$15	110
(34) p. 66	Apres Diem	◆◆	European	$8-$25	108
(35) p. 66	F.R.O.G.S. Cantina & Tequileria	◆◆	Southwestern	$4-$20	110
(36) p. 66	Osteria 832	◆◆	Italian	$6-$15	112
(37) p. 66	dressed	◆	Sandwiches	$4-$10	109
(38) p. 66	Steel Restaurant & Sushi Lounge	◆◆◆	Asian	$5-$29	114
(39) p. 66	Surin of Thailand	◆◆	Thai	$7-$20	114
(40) p. 66	The Vortex Bar & Grill	◆◆	American	$7-$11	115
(41) p. 66	Belly General Store	◆	Sandwiches	$2-$7	109
(42) p. 66	Ecco	◆◆◆	European	$15-$50	109
(43) p. 66	Gordon Biersch Brewery Restaurant	◆◆◆	American	$10-$35	110
(44) p. 66	Mu Lan	◆◆	Chinese	$6-$20	112
(45) p. 66	The Optimist	◆◆◆	Seafood	$10-$30	112
(46) p. 66	Bocado	◆◆◆	American	$8-$22	109
(47) p. 66	Eats	◆	American	$5-$8	109
(48) p. 66	Soul Vegetarian II	◆◆	Vegan	$7-$16	114
(49) p. 66	Cameli's Gourmet Pizza Joint	◆	Pizza	$7-$23	109
(50) p. 66	Minero	◆◆	Mexican	$4-$15	112
(51) p. 66	Baraonda Caffé Italiano	◆◆	Italian	$8-$32	108
(52) p. 66	Babette's Cafe	◆◆◆	European	$16-$31	108
(53) p. 66	Mary Mac's Tea Room	◆◆	Southern	$6-$22	111
(54) p. 66	Papi's Cuban & Caribbean Grill	◆◆	Cuban	$6-$15	112
(55) p. 66	Publik Draft House	◆◆	American	$5-$15	113
(56) p. 66	Chicago's Nancy's Pizza	◆	Pizza	$8-$31	109
(57) p. 66	Livingston	◆◆◆	New American	$12-$37	111
(58) p. 66	Savage Pizza	◆◆	Pizza	$6-$22	114
(59) p. 66	Planet Bombay	◆◆	Indian	$10-$25	113
(60) p. 66	Two urban licks	◆◆◆	New American	$19-$40	115
(61) p. 66	Gladys Knight's Signature Chicken & Waffles	◆◆	Southern	$9-$17	110
(62) p. 66	Zesto	◆	Burgers	$4-$11	115
(63) p. 66	Cameli's Pizza	◆◆	Pizza	$5-$22	109
(64) p. 66	Victory Sandwich Bar	◆◆	Sandwiches	$3-$8	115
(65) p. 66	Sotto Sotto	◆◆◆	Italian	$17-$42	114
(66) p. 66	Fritti	◆◆	Regional Italian	$9-$22	110

Map Page	Restaurants (cont'd)	Diamond Rated	Cuisine	Price Range	Page
67 p. 66	Room at Twelve	▽▽▽	Steak Sushi	$10-$40	113
68 p. 66	Fox Bros Bar-B-Q	▽▽	Barbecue	$5-$17	110
69 p. 66	BLT Steak	▽▽▽▽	Steak	$14-$62	109
70 p. 66	**Max Lager's Wood-Fired Grill & Brewery**	▽▽	American	$9-$38	111
71 p. 66	Pacific Rim Bistro	▽▽▽	Pacific Rim	$9-$30	112
72 p. 66	White Oak Kitchen & Cocktails	▽▽▽	New Southern	$15-$38	115
73 p. 66	**Nikolai's Roof**	▽▽▽▽	Continental	$31-$48	112
74 p. 66	Legal Sea Foods	▽▽▽	Seafood	$10-$48	111
75 p. 66	Twin Smokers BBQ	▽▽	Barbecue	$3-$12	115
76 p. 66	Ray's in the City	▽▽▽	Seafood	$12-$65	113
77 p. 66	Kevin Rathbun Steak	▽▽▽	Steak	$19-$62	111
78 p. 66	One Eared Stag	▽▽▽	American	$9-$39	112
79 p. 66	Max's Coal Oven Pizzeria	▽▽	Pizza	$7-$18	111
80 p. 66	Stats	▽▽	American	$9-$24	114
81 p. 66	Proof Bakeshop	▽	Breads/Pastries Sandwiches	$2-$10	113
82 p. 66	CUTS Steakhouse	▽▽▽	Steak	$12-$40	109
83 p. 66	Tin Lizzy's Cantina	▽▽	Tex-Mex	$4-$10	114
84 p. 66	Hard Rock Cafe	▽▽	American	$12-$25 [SAVE]	110
85 p. 66	PittyPat's Porch	▽▽	Regional Southern	$14-$29	113
86 p. 66	The Sun Dial	▽▽▽	American	$14-$57	114
87 p. 66	Superica	▽▽▽	Mexican	$10-$32	114
88 p. 66	Fandangles Restaurant & Bar	▽▽▽	Southern American	$12-$55	110
89 p. 66	Meehan's Public House	▽▽	Irish	$10-$19	112
90 p. 66	Alma Cocina	▽▽▽	Mexican	$7-$29	108
91 p. 66	Serpas	▽▽▽	American	$16-$30	114
92 p. 66	**Atlanta Grill**	▽▽▽▽	American	$14-$69	108
93 p. 66	The Luminary	▽▽▽	French	$14-$30	111
94 p. 66	Prime Meridian	▽▽▽	Continental	$11-$36	113
95 p. 66	Rathbun's	▽▽▽	New American	$18-$43	113
96 p. 66	McCormick & Schmick's	▽▽▽	Seafood	$12-$39	111
97 p. 66	BoccaLupo	▽▽▽	Italian	$9-$19	109
98 p. 66	Slice Downtown	▽▽	Italian	$8-$20	114
99 p. 66	Landmark Diner	▽▽	Continental	$6-$25	111
100 p. 66	Glenn's Kitchen	▽▽▽	New American	$12-$40	110
101 p. 66	Thrive	▽▽▽	New American	$8-$29	114
102 p. 66	Amazza	▽▽	Italian Pizza	$5-$22	108
103 p. 66	Reuben's Deli	▽	Sandwiches Breakfast	$6-$9	113
104 p. 66	Agave	▽▽▽	Southwestern	$8-$24	107
105 p. 66	Gunshow	▽▽▽	New American	$10-$20	110

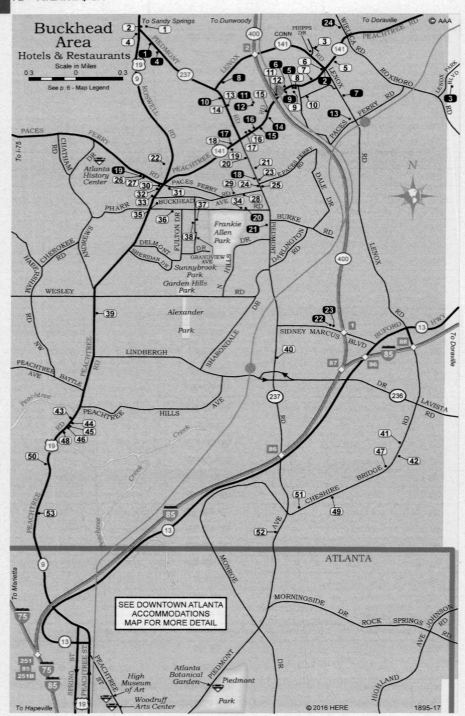

Buckhead Area
Hotels & Restaurants

Scale in Miles

0.3　0　0.3

See p. 6 - Map Legend

© AAA

Buckhead Area

This index helps you "spot" where approved hotels and restaurants are located on the corresponding detailed maps. Hotel daily rate range is for comparison only. Restaurant price range is a combination of lunch and/or dinner. Turn to the listing page for more detailed rate and price information and consult display ads for special promotions.

BUCKHEAD AREA

Map Page	Hotels	Diamond Rated	Rate Range	Page
❶ p. 72	Wingate by Wyndham Atlanta/Buckhead	◆◆◆	$139-$299	119
❷ p. 72	**The Ritz-Carlton, Buckhead**	◆◆◆◆	Rates not provided ⟨SAVE⟩	117
❸ p. 72	Residence Inn by Marriott Atlanta Buckhead/Lenox Park	◆◆◆	$89-$217	117
❹ p. 72	Homewood Suites-Atlanta Buckhead	◆◆◆	$119-$239	116
❺ p. 72	**The Westin Buckhead Atlanta**	◆◆◆◆	$139-$329 ⟨SAVE⟩	118
❻ p. 72	Mandarin Oriental, Atlanta	◆◆◆◆	Rates not provided	117
❼ p. 72	**Atlanta Marriott Buckhead Hotel & Conference Center**	◆◆◆	$111-$296 ⟨SAVE⟩	116
❽ p. 72	**SpringHill Suites by Marriott-Atlanta Buckhead**	◆◆◆	$95-$263 ⟨SAVE⟩	118
❾ p. 72	**W Atlanta Buckhead**	◆◆◆◆	Rates not provided ⟨SAVE⟩	118
❿ p. 72	Hampton Inn Atlanta Buckhead	◆◆◆	$129-$209	116
⓫ p. 72	DoubleTree by Hilton Hotel Atlanta-Buckhead	◆◆◆	Rates not provided	116
⓬ p. 72	Courtyard by Marriott-Buckhead	◆◆◆	$110-$344	116
⓭ p. 72	**JW Marriott Buckhead Atlanta**	◆◆◆◆	$140-$459 ⟨SAVE⟩	117
⓮ p. 72	**InterContinental Buckhead Atlanta**	◆◆◆◆	$159-$389 ⟨SAVE⟩	117
⓯ p. 72	**Embassy Suites Hotel by Hilton Atlanta Buckhead**	◆◆◆	$99-$259 ⟨SAVE⟩	116
⓰ p. 72	**Grand Hyatt Atlanta**	◆◆◆◆	$129-$409 ⟨SAVE⟩	116
⓱ p. 72	**Hyatt Place Atlanta/Buckhead**	◆◆◆	$109-$299 ⟨SAVE⟩	116
⓲ p. 72	Fairfield Inn & Suites by Marriott Atlanta Buckhead	◆◆	$96-$194	116
⓳ p. 72	**St. Regis Atlanta Hotel & Residences**	◆◆◆◆◆	Rates not provided ⟨SAVE⟩	117
⓴ p. 72	Staybridge Suites-Atlanta/Buckhead	◆◆◆	$109-$250	118
㉑ p. 72	**Residence Inn by Marriott Atlanta Buckhead**	◆◆	$127-$263 ⟨SAVE⟩	117
㉒ p. 72	Holiday Inn Express & Suites Atlanta Buckhead	◆◆◆	Rates not provided	116
㉓ p. 72	TownePlace Suites by Marriott Atlanta Buckhead	◆◆◆	$101-$197	118
㉔ p. 72	**AC Hotel by Marriott Atlanta Buckhead at Phipps Plaza**	◆◆◆	Rates not provided ⟨SAVE⟩	115

Map Page	Restaurants	Diamond Rated	Cuisine	Price Range	Page
① p. 72	Hal's	◆◆◆	Steak	$23-$49	121
② p. 72	FLIP burger boutique	◆◆	Burgers	$8-$14	120
③ p. 72	Davio's Northern Italian Steakhouse	◆◆◆	Northern Italian	$14-$49	120
④ p. 72	Landmark Diner	◆◆	Continental	$10-$30	121
⑤ p. 72	St. Cecilia	◆◆◆	Italian	$12-$42	122
⑥ p. 72	The Cafe	◆◆◆	American	$12-$27	120
⑦ p. 72	New York Prime	◆◆◆	Steak	$29-$60	122
⑧ p. 72	The Atlanta Palm	◆◆◆	Steak	$15-$55	119

Map Page	Restaurants (cont'd)	Diamond Rated	Cuisine	Price Range	Page
⑨ p. 72	Dantanna's Surf, Turf & Turf	◆◆	American	$10-$42	120
⑩ p. 72	True Food Kitchen	◆◆◆	Natural/Organic	$4-$24	122
⑪ p. 72	Maggiano's Little Italy	◆◆◆	Italian	$11-$46	121
⑫ p. 72	Corner Bakery Cafe	◆	Deli	$6-$12	120
⑬ p. 72	Ru San's Sushi & Sake Bar-Buckhead Tower Place	◆◆	Japanese	$7-$40	122
⑭ p. 72	Farm Burger	◆	Burgers	$7-$10	120
⑮ p. 72	Bistro Niko	◆◆◆	French	$12-$30	119
⑯ p. 72	Brick Tops	◆◆◆	Comfort Food	$14-$36	119
⑰ p. 72	Flying Biscuit Cafe - Buckhead Terminus Building	◆◆	Breakfast	$4-$12	120
⑱ p. 72	Gordon Biersch Brewery Restaurant	◆◆◆	American	$10-$35	121
⑲ p. 72	McKinnon's Louisiane Restaurant	◆◆	Creole	$18-$29	122
⑳ p. 72	Bones Restaurant	◆◆◆	Steak	$15-$55	119
㉑ p. 72	Fogo De Chao	◆◆◆	Brazilian Steak	$25-$50	120
㉒ p. 72	One Star Ranch	◆	Barbecue	$6-$29	122
㉓ p. 72	Kyma	◆◆◆	Greek	$12-$42	121
㉔ p. 72	Buckhead Bread Company & Corner Cafe	◆◆	American	$9-$18	119
㉕ p. 72	Buckhead Diner	◆◆◆	American	$13-$30	119
㉖ p. 72	Atlas	◆◆◆◆	American	$10-$59	119
㉗ p. 72	Chops Lobster Bar	◆◆◆	Steak Seafood	$15-$60	120
㉘ p. 72	Antica Posta Tuscan Restaurant & Bar	◆◆◆	Italian	$14-$34	119
㉙ p. 72	Aria	◆◆◆◆	New American	$24-$42	119
㉚ p. 72	King + Duke	◆◆◆	New Southern	$12-$54	121
㉛ p. 72	The Capital Grille	◆◆◆	Steak	$6-$47	120
㉜ p. 72	J. Christopher's	◆◆	Breakfast	$5-$11	121
㉝ p. 72	Seasons 52 Fresh Grill	◆◆◆	New American	$11-$30	122
㉞ p. 72	Pricci	◆◆◆	Italian	$13-$29	122
㉟ p. 72	Le Bilboquet	◆◆◆	French	$11-$41	121
㊱ p. 72	Atlanta Fish Market	◆◆◆	Seafood	$13-$50	119
㊲ p. 72	Basil's	◆◆◆	Mediterranean	$8-$29	119
㊳ p. 72	Anis Cafe & Bistro	◆◆	French	$11-$35	119
㊴ p. 72	**La Grotta Ristorante Italiano**	◆◆◆◆	Northern Italian	$19-$39	121
㊵ p. 72	Zesto	◆	Burgers	$4-$11	123
㊶ p. 72	Taverna Plaka	◆◆	Greek	$5-$24	122
㊷ p. 72	Taqueria del Sol	◆	Southwestern	$2-$11	122
㊸ p. 72	Georgia Grille	◆◆	Southwestern	$12-$31	121
㊹ p. 72	The Imperial Fez	◆◆	Moroccan	$12-$55	121
㊺ p. 72	Restaurant Eugene	◆◆◆◆	New American	$28-$85	122
㊻ p. 72	Holeman and Finch Public House	◆◆◆	Small Plates	$7-$31	121

Map Page	Restaurants (cont'd)	Diamond Rated	Cuisine	Price Range	Page
47 p. 72	Red Snapper	▽▽	Seafood	$8-$31	122
48 p. 72	Starfish Restaurant	▽▽▽	Japanese	$7-$30	122
49 p. 72	The Colonnade	▽▽	Southern	$12-$25	120
50 p. 72	Cafe Sunflower	▽▽	Vegetarian	$7-$17	120
51 p. 72	Nakato	▽▽▽	Japanese	$8-$50	122
52 p. 72	Grindhouse Killer Burgers	▽	Burgers	$3-$9	121
53 p. 72	Fresh 4 U	▽	Mediterranean	$5-$9	120

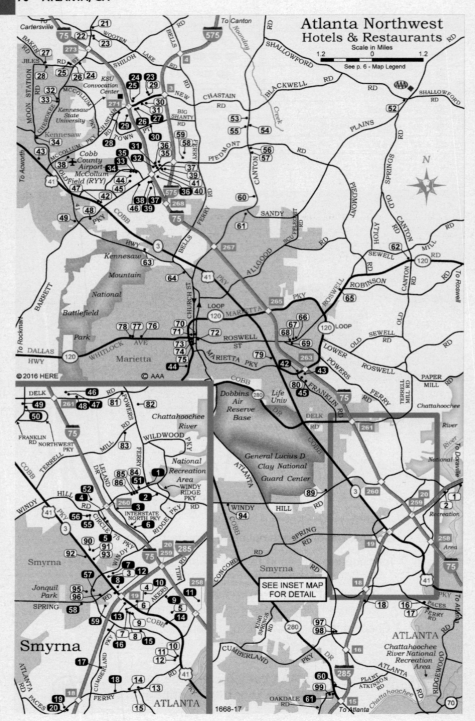

Atlanta Northwest

This index helps you "spot" where approved hotels and restaurants are located on the corresponding detailed maps. Hotel daily rate range is for comparison only. Restaurant price range is a combination of lunch and/or dinner. Turn to the listing page for more detailed rate and price information and consult display ads for special promotions.

ATLANTA NORTHWEST

Map Page	Hotels	Diamond Rated	Rate Range	Page
❶ p. 76	Hilton Garden Inn Atlanta NW/Wildwood	◆◆◆	$109-$189	124
❷ p. 76	Extended Stay America (Atlanta/Marietta/Wildwood)	◆◆	$75-$100	124
❸ p. 76	Extended Stay America (Atlanta/Marietta/Windy Hill/Int N Pkwy)	◆◆	$70-$90	124
❹ p. 76	Country Inn & Suites By Carlson, Atlanta-NW at Windy Hill Rd	◆◆◆	$89-$199	123
❺ p. 76	Days Inn-Atlanta/Marietta/Windy Hill Rd	◆◆	$57-$80	123
❻ p. 76	**Atlanta Marriott Northwest** *(See ad p. 123.)*	◆◆◆	$89-$238 SAVE	123
❼ p. 76	DoubleTree Suites by Hilton Hotel Atlanta-Galleria	◆◆◆	$99-$229	124
❽ p. 76	Hampton Inn & Suites Atlanta Galleria	◆◆◆	$159-$269	124
❾ p. 76	**Embassy Suites by Hilton Atlanta-Galleria**	◆◆◆	$119-$299 SAVE	124
❿ p. 76	**Renaissance Atlanta Waverly Hotel & Convention Center**	◆◆◆◆	$97-$314 SAVE	125
⓫ p. 76	**Hyatt House Atlanta/Cobb Galleria**	◆◆◆	$99-$309 SAVE	125
⓬ p. 76	Wingate by Wyndham Atlanta Galleria Center	◆◆◆	$109-$139	125
⓭ p. 76	**Sheraton Suites Galleria**	◆◆◆	$139-$269 SAVE	125
⓮ p. 76	Homewood Suites-Cumberland/Galleria	◆◆◆	$129-$159	124
⓯ p. 76	**Courtyard by Marriott Atlanta Cumberland/Galleria**	◆◆◆	$69-$219 SAVE	123
⓰ p. 76	Hampton Inn Cumberland	◆◆◆	$139-$189	124
⓱ p. 76	Extended Stay America Atlanta-Vinings	◆◆	$95-$115	124
⓲ p. 76	Hotel Indigo Atlanta Vinings	◆◆◆	Rates not provided	124
⓳ p. 76	La Quinta Inn & Suites Atlanta (Paces Ferry/Vinings)	◆◆◆	$86-$202	125
⓴ p. 76	Fairfield Inn & Suites by Marriott Atlanta/Vinings	◆◆◆	$80-$160	124

Map Page	Restaurants	Diamond Rated	Cuisine	Price Range	Page
① p. 76	Ray's on the River	◆◆◆	Seafood	$8-$65	126
② p. 76	Heirloom Market BBQ	◆	Barbecue	$7-$27	125
③ p. 76	Swapna Indian Cuisine	◆◆	Indian	$9-$16	126
④ p. 76	Buckhead Pizza Co.	◆◆	Pizza	$5-$22	125
⑤ p. 76	Top Spice	◆◆◆	Asian	$8-$18	126
⑥ p. 76	Stoney River	◆◆◆	Steak	$10-$34	126
⑦ p. 76	P.F. Chang's China Bistro	◆◆◆	Chinese	$8-$26	126
⑧ p. 76	The Cheesecake Factory	◆◆◆	International	$10-$30	125
⑨ p. 76	Maggiano's Little Italy	◆◆◆	Italian	$11-$46	125
⑩ p. 76	Olive Bistro	◆◆	Mediterranean	$6-$15	126
⑪ p. 76	C & S Seafood & Oyster Bar	◆◆◆	Seafood	$10-$40	125
⑫ p. 76	Thai Diner	◆◆◆	Thai	$8-$23	126
⑬ p. 76	The Old Vinings Inn	◆◆◆	Regional American	$17-$38	126
⑭ p. 76	Orient Express	◆◆	Asian	$7-$48	126

Map Page	Restaurants (cont'd)	Diamond Rated	Cuisine	Price Range	Page
⑮ p. 76	Soho	◆◆	New American	$11-$37	126
⑯ p. 76	Canoe	◆◆◆	New American	$13-$34	125
⑰ p. 76	Ray's Rio Bravo	◆◆	Tex-Mex	$4-$22	126
⑱ p. 76	Marlow's Tavern	◆◆	American	$8-$20	126

KENNESAW

Map Page	Hotels	Diamond Rated	Rate Range	Page
㉓ p. 76	Embassy Suites by Hilton Atlanta-Kennesaw Town Center	◆◆◆	$139-$299	199
㉔ p. 76	**Residence Inn by Marriott Atlanta Kennesaw/ Town Center**	◆◆◆	$102-$237 (SAVE)	200
㉕ p. 76	Fairfield Inn & Suites by Marriott Atlanta Kennesaw	◆◆◆	$85-$160	199
㉖ p. 76	**Best Western Kennesaw Inn**	◆◆	$72-$80 (SAVE)	199
㉗ p. 76	**Comfort Suites at Kennesaw State University**	◆◆◆	$99-$219 (SAVE)	199
㉘ p. 76	SpringHill Suites by Marriott	◆◆◆	$95-$171	200
㉙ p. 76	**Baymont Inn & Suites**	◆◆	$74-$125 (SAVE)	199
㉚ p. 76	Extended Stay America Atlanta Kennesaw	◆◆	$75-$100	199
㉛ p. 76	Holiday Inn Express-Town Center Mall	◆◆◆	$99-$249	200
㉜ p. 76	Comfort Inn	◆◆◆	$89-$169	199
㉝ p. 76	Hilton Garden Inn-Atlanta NW/Kennesaw Town Center	◆◆◆	$149-$199	200
㉞ p. 76	Homewood Suites-Northwest/Kennesaw	◆◆◆	Rates not provided	200
㉟ p. 76	Hampton Inn	◆◆◆	$104-$184	199
㊱ p. 76	Red Roof Inn Atlanta-Kennesaw	◆◆	$57-$100	200
㊲ p. 76	Quality Inn	◆◆	$60-$159	200
㊳ p. 76	Days Inn	◆◆	$50-$82	199
㊴ p. 76	Wingate by Wyndham	◆◆◆	$84-$139	200

Map Page	Restaurants	Diamond Rated	Cuisine	Price Range	Page
㉑ p. 76	Guston's Neighborhood Grille	◆◆	American	$9-$17	201
㉒ p. 76	Peace, Love and Pizza	◆	Pizza	$7-$21	202
㉓ p. 76	Cafe Istanbul 2	◆◆	Turkish	$5-$18	200
㉔ p. 76	Donny's Home Cooking	◆	Southern	$8	201
㉕ p. 76	Mandarin Cafe	◆◆	Asian	$5-$16	201
㉖ p. 76	Barbeque Street	◆◆	Barbecue	$8-$23	200
㉗ p. 76	Big Pie In The Sky	◆	Pizza	$4-$36	200
㉘ p. 76	La Bamba Mexican Bar & Grill	◆◆	Tex-Mex	$5-$15	201
㉙ p. 76	Ruth's Chris Steak House	◆◆◆	Steak	$11-$45	202
㉚ p. 76	Marlow's Tavern	◆◆	American	$8-$20	201
㉛ p. 76	Papi's Cuban & Caribbean Grill	◆◆	Cuban	$6-$22	202
㉜ p. 76	Bangkok Cabin	◆◆	Thai	$7-$16	200
㉝ p. 76	Big Shanty Smokehouse	◆	Barbecue	$6-$19	200
㉞ p. 76	Trackside Grill	◆◆	New Southern Comfort Food	$14-$25	202
㉟ p. 76	J. Christopher's	◆◆	Breakfast	$5-$12	201

Map Page	Restaurants (cont'd)	Diamond Rated	Cuisine	Price Range	Page
㊱ p. 76	Fuji Hana & Thai Peppers	◆◆	Asian	$7-$36	201
㊲ p. 76	Sunny's Bagels & Deli	◆	Sandwiches	$2-$8	202
㊳ p. 76	Elevation Chop House & Skybar	◆◆	American	$15-$28	201
㊴ p. 76	Ru San's-Kennesaw	◆◆	Japanese	$5-$28	202
㊵ p. 76	Penang Malaysian/Thai Cuisine	◆◆	Asian	$7-$19	202
㊶ p. 76	Ippolito's	◆◆	Italian	$8-$19	201
㊷ p. 76	Taj Mahal Grill	◆◆	Indian	$9-$15	202
㊸ p. 76	Olde Towne Grille	◆◆	American	$8-$24	201
㊹ p. 76	Kuroshio Sushi Bar & Grille	◆◆	Japanese	$9-$55	201
㊺ p. 76	Guido's Chicago Hot Dogs	◆	Hot Dogs	$2-$8	201
㊻ p. 76	Bahama Breeze	◆◆◆	Caribbean	$11-$22	200
㊼ p. 76	Whistle Stop Cafe	◆◆	Southern	$5-$9	202
㊽ p. 76	Keegan's Irish Pub	◆◆	Irish	$8-$15	201
㊾ p. 76	Caper's Restaurant & Bar	◆◆◆	American	$10-$27	201

MARIETTA

Map Page	Hotels	Diamond Rated	Rate Range	Page
㊷ p. 76	Hampton Inn Marietta	◆◆◆	$89-$139	217
㊸ p. 76	Radisson Hotel Atlanta Northwest	◆◆◆	Rates not provided	218
㊹ p. 76	Hilton Atlanta/Marietta Hotel & Conference Center	◆◆◆	$109-$159	217
㊺ p. 76	Econo Lodge Inn & Suites	◆◆	$62-$160	217
㊻ p. 76	**Ramada Marietta/Atlanta North**	◆◆	$60-$77 (SAVE)	218
㊼ p. 76	Drury Inn & Suites-Atlanta Northwest	◆◆◆	$89-$169	217
㊽ p. 76	Courtyard by Marriott-Atlanta Marietta/I-75 North	◆◆◆	$87-$206	217
㊾ p. 76	Holiday Inn Express Marietta-Atlanta NW	◆◆◆	Rates not provided	217
㊿ p. 76	**Quality Inn Atlanta/Marietta**	◆◆	$80-$140 (SAVE)	218
51 p. 76	**Hyatt Regency Suites Atlanta NW**	◆◆◆	$109-$289 (SAVE)	218
52 p. 76	Courtyard by Marriott-Windy Hill	◆◆◆	$72-$206	217

Map Page	Restaurants	Diamond Rated	Cuisine	Price Range	Page
52 p. 76	Aspens Signature Steaks	◆◆◆	American	$11-$39	218
53 p. 76	Marietta Fish Market	◆◆	Seafood	$7-$33	220
54 p. 76	Johnboy's Country Buffet	◆	Comfort Food	$8	219
55 p. 76	Frankie's Italian Restaurant	◆◆	Italian	$6-$20	219
56 p. 76	Basil Wraps	◆	Mediterranean	$5-$11	218
57 p. 76	Cherokee Cattle Company	◆◆	Steak	$9-$30	219
58 p. 76	Dogfather's	◆	Hot Dogs	$2-$6	219
59 p. 76	Pacific Buffet, Sushi & Grill	◆◆	Asian	$7-$10	220
60 p. 76	The Rib Ranch	◆◆	Barbecue	$6-$37	220
61 p. 76	Tofu Village Korean BBQ Restaurant	◆◆	Korean	$8-$35	221
62 p. 76	Los Arcos	◆◆	Tex-Mex	$2-$15	219

Map Page	Restaurants (cont'd)	Diamond Rated	Cuisine	Price Range	Page
63 p. 76	Mountain Biscuits	◆	Sandwiches	$2-$7	220
64 p. 76	Brandi's World Famous Hot Dogs	◆	Hot Dogs	$2-$3	218
65 p. 76	Lemon Grass Thai Restaurant	◆◆	Thai	$8-$15	219
66 p. 76	Rocco's Pub	◆◆	American	$6-$12	220
67 p. 76	**Cafe Life**	◆	Natural/Organic	$7-$10	218
68 p. 76	Williamson Bros Bar-B-Q	◆◆	Barbecue	$8-$23	221
69 p. 76	Chicago Delights	◆	Hot Dogs	$3-$7	219
70 p. 76	WR Social House	◆◆	Cajun	$8-$19	221
71 p. 76	Thaicoon & Sushi Bar	◆◆◆	Asian	$4-$25	220
72 p. 76	Jack's New Yorker Deli	◆	Sandwiches	$5-$12	219
73 p. 76	Marietta Pizza Co.	◆◆	Pizza	$5-$23	220
74 p. 76	La Parrilla Mexican Restaurant	◆◆	Tex-Mex	$6-$18	219
75 p. 76	Kiosco	◆◆	Colombian	$7-$27	219
76 p. 76	Dave Poe's BBQ	◆	Barbecue	$3-$21	219
77 p. 76	Chicken And The Egg	◆◆◆	American	$9-$18	219
78 p. 76	Gabriel's Restaurant & Bakery	◆	American	$4-$14	219
79 p. 76	Marietta Diner	◆◆	Continental Comfort Food	$9-$35	220
80 p. 76	Tasty China	◆◆	Chinese	$7-$18	220
81 p. 76	Sabor do Brazil	◆	Brazilian	$9-$11	220
82 p. 76	J. Christopher's	◆◆	Breakfast	$5-$12	219
83 p. 76	Vatica	◆◆	Indian	$9-$11	221
84 p. 76	George's Deli	◆	Sandwiches	$5-$7	219
85 p. 76	Barker's Red Hots	◆	Hot Dogs	$3-$9	218
86 p. 76	Red Elephant	◆◆	Thai	$7-$23	220

SMYRNA

Map Page	Hotels	Diamond Rated	Rate Range	Page
55 p. 76	Galleria/Marietta Comfort Inn & Suites	◆◆◆	$99-$214	280
56 p. 76	**Red Roof Inn-Atlanta Smyrna**	◆◆	$55-$80 SAVE	281
57 p. 76	Residence Inn by Marriott-Atlanta Cumberland	◆◆◆	$79-$206	281
58 p. 76	Extended Stay America-Atlanta-Cumberland Mall	◆◆	$75-$100	280
59 p. 76	**Hyatt Place Atlanta/Cobb Galleria**	◆◆◆	$84-$179 SAVE	281
60 p. 76	Country Inn & Suites By Carlson	◆◆◆	$90-$114	280
61 p. 76	Baymont Inn & Suites	◆◆	$69-$121	280

Map Page	Restaurants	Diamond Rated	Cuisine	Price Range	Page
89 p. 76	Siam Square	◆◆	Thai	$8-$19	281
90 p. 76	Yakitori Jinbei	◆◆	Japanese	$8-$23	282
91 p. 76	Thompson Brothers BBQ	◆	Barbecue	$6-$14	282
92 p. 76	Scalini's Italian Restaurant	◆◆	Italian	$13-$23	281
93 p. 76	House of Chan	◆◆	Chinese	$9-$30	281

Map Page	Restaurants (cont'd)	Diamond Rated	Cuisine	Price Range	Page
94 p. 76	Old South Bar-B-Q	▼	Barbecue	$6-$19	281
95 p. 76	This Is It!	▼	Soul Food	$6-$27	282
96 p. 76	Minato Japanese Restaurant	▼▼	Japanese	$5-$34	281
97 p. 76	South City Kitchen	▼▼▼	New Southern	$11-$33	282
98 p. 76	Muss & Turner's	▼▼	American	$8-$24	281
99 p. 76	Roy's Cheesesteaks	▼	Sandwiches	$3-$8	281

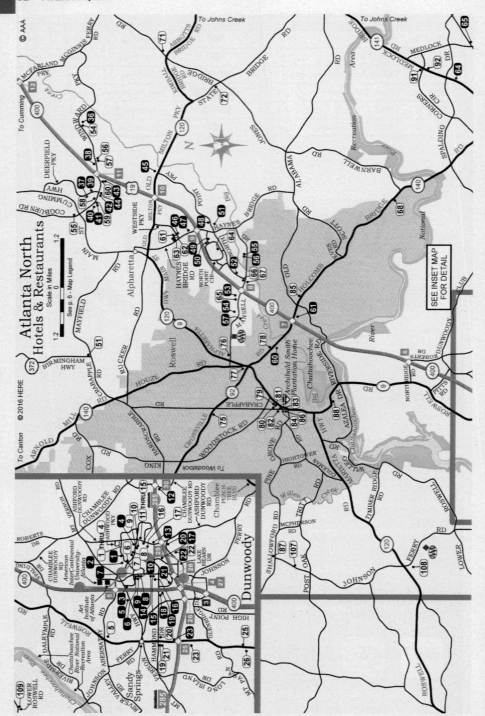

Atlanta North
Hotels & Restaurants

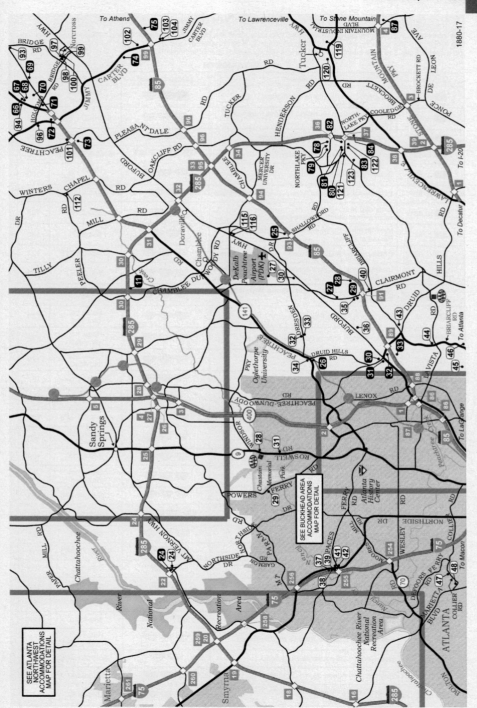

Atlanta North

This index helps you "spot" where approved hotels and restaurants are located on the corresponding detailed maps. Hotel daily rate range is for comparison only. Restaurant price range is a combination of lunch and/or dinner. Turn to the listing page for more detailed rate and price information and consult display ads for special promotions.

ATLANTA NORTH

Map Page	Hotels	Diamond Rated	Rate Range	Page
1 p. 82	Staybridge Suites Atlanta Perimeter	◆◆◆	Rates not provided	130
2 p. 82	**Embassy Suites by Hilton Atlanta Perimeter Center**	◆◆◆	$99-$299 SAVE	128
3 p. 82	**Hyatt Place Atlanta/Perimeter Center**	◆◆◆	$79-$289 SAVE	129
4 p. 82	**Le Méridien Atlanta Perimeter**	◆◆◆◆	$109-$399 SAVE	130
5 p. 82	**Sonesta ES Suites Atlanta**	◆◆◆	Rates not provided SAVE	130
6 p. 82	Extended Stay America Atlanta-Perimeter/Crestline	◆◆	$80-$105	128
7 p. 82	Extended Stay America Atlanta-Perimeter/Peachtree-Dunwoody	◆◆	$80-$105	129
8 p. 82	Microtel Inn & Suites by Wyndham Atlanta/Perimeter Center	◆◆	$59-$134	130
9 p. 82	**Courtyard by Marriott Atlanta Perimeter Center**	◆◆◆	$74-$263 SAVE	127
10 p. 82	La Quinta Inn & Suites Atlanta (Perimeter/Medical Center)	◆◆◆	$68-$202	130
11 p. 82	**Residence Inn by Marriott Atlanta Perimeter Center East**	◆◆◆	$111-$263 SAVE	130
12 p. 82	Holiday Inn Atlanta Perimeter	◆◆◆	Rates not provided	129
13 p. 82	Crowne Plaza Atlanta Perimeter at Ravinia	◆◆◆	Rates not provided	127
14 p. 82	Hilton Atlanta Perimeter Suites	◆◆◆	Rates not provided	129
15 p. 82	**Comfort Suites Hotel Perimeter Center**	◆◆◆	$84-$154 SAVE	127
16 p. 82	Extended Stay America-Atlanta-Perimeter-Hammond Drive	◆◆	$75-$110	128
17 p. 82	**Atlanta Marriott Perimeter Center**	◆◆◆	$88-$309 SAVE	127
18 p. 82	Holiday Inn Express Hotel & Suites-Perimeter	◆◆◆	Rates not provided	129
19 p. 82	Hampton Inn-Perimeter Center	◆◆◆	$89-$209	129
20 p. 82	Hilton Garden Inn-Atlanta Perimeter Center	◆◆◆	Rates not provided	129
21 p. 82	**The Westin Atlanta Perimeter North**	◆◆◆	$99-$199 SAVE	130
22 p. 82	**Hyatt Regency Atlanta Perimeter at Villa Christina**	◆◆◆◆	$109-$299 SAVE	129
23 p. 82	Comfort Inn-Buckhead North	◆◆◆	$99-$151	127
24 p. 82	**Wyndham Atlanta Galleria**	◆◆◆	$79-$175 SAVE	131
25 p. 82	Quality Inn Northeast	◆◆	$69-$84	130
26 p. 82	Extended Stay America Atlanta-Lenox	◆◆	$90-$115	128
27 p. 82	Extended Stay America Atlanta-Clairmont	◆◆	$85-$110	128
28 p. 82	Atlanta Marriott Century Center/Emory Area	◆◆◆	$69-$240	127
29 p. 82	**Holiday Inn Express Atlanta NE-Clairmont**	◆◆◆	Rates not provided SAVE	129
30 p. 82	**Red Roof PLUS+ Atlanta-Buckhead**	◆◆	$60-$150 SAVE	130
31 p. 82	Hampton Inn Atlanta-North Druid Hills	◆◆◆	$119-$249	129
32 p. 82	DoubleTree by Hilton Atlanta North Druid Hills-Emory Area	◆◆◆	$149-$189	127

ATLANTA NORTH (cont'd)

Map Page	Hotels (cont'd)	Diamond Rated	Rate Range	Page
33 p. 82	**Courtyard by Marriott Atlanta Executive Park/ Emory**	◆◆◆	$91-$206 [SAVE]	127

Map Page	Restaurants	Diamond Rated	Cuisine	Price Range	Page
1 p. 82	P.F. Chang's China Bistro	◆◆◆	Chinese	$8-$26	133
2 p. 82	Memphis Barbecue Company	◆◆	Barbecue	$4-$23	132
3 p. 82	Brio Tuscan Grille	◆◆◆	Italian	$12-$30	131
4 p. 82	McCormick & Schmick's	◆◆◆	Seafood	$12-$39	132
5 p. 82	Mirage	◆◆	Mediterranean	$8-$24	133
6 p. 82	Joey D's Oak Room	◆◆◆	American	$10-$34	132
7 p. 82	Fleming's Prime Steakhouse & Wine Bar	◆◆◆	Steak	$13-$53	132
8 p. 82	Tin Lizzy's Cantina	◆◆	Tex-Mex	$3-$10	134
9 p. 82	The Capital Grille	◆◆◆	Steak	$6-$47	131
10 p. 82	Seasons 52 Fresh Grill	◆◆◆	New American	$12-$30	133
11 p. 82	Cafe Intermezzo	◆◆	European	$8-$19	131
12 p. 82	Eclipse di Luna	◆◆	Spanish Small Plates	$3-$20	131
13 p. 82	McKendrick's Steak House	◆◆◆	Steak	$10-$53	132
14 p. 82	Alon's Bakery & Market	◆	Deli	$2-$12	131
15 p. 82	Sage Woodfire Tavern	◆◆◆	Steak	$7-$31	133
16 p. 82	The Cheesecake Factory	◆◆◆	International	$10-$30	131
17 p. 82	Maggiano's Little Italy	◆◆◆	Italian	$11-$46	132
19 p. 82	Canton Cooks	◆◆	Chinese	$7-$30	131
20 p. 82	Cafe Sunflower	◆◆	Vegetarian	$12-$22	131
21 p. 82	Mike's Hot Dogs	◆	Hot Dogs	$3-$8	132
22 p. 82	Villa Christina	◆◆◆	Italian	$14-$35	134
23 p. 82	Five Season's Brewing Company	◆◆	New American	$8-$27	131
24 p. 82	Sushi Huku	◆◆	Japanese Sushi	$8-$42	133
25 p. 82	Food 101	◆◆◆	New American	$10-$29	132
26 p. 82	Pig-N-Chik	◆	Barbecue	$6-$24	133
27 p. 82	The 57th Restuarant	◆◆	American	$4-$30	131
28 p. 82	Fellini's Pizza	◆	Pizza	$4-$24	131
29 p. 82	Horseradish Grill	◆◆◆	New Southern	$14-$28	132
30 p. 82	Pho Dai Loi	◆◆	Vietnamese	$7-$10	133
31 p. 82	10 Degrees South	◆◆◆	African	$9-$42	131
32 p. 82	Verde Taqueria	◆◆	Mexican	$4-$8	134
33 p. 82	HAVEN	◆◆◆	New American	$18-$38	132
34 p. 82	Terra Terroir Patio, Bistro & Bar	◆◆◆	American	$10-$35	133
35 p. 82	Violette	◆◆◆	French	$9-$29	134
36 p. 82	Panahar Bangladeshi Cuisine	◆◆	Indian	$10-$15	133
37 p. 82	Houston's	◆◆◆	American	$16-$44	132
38 p. 82	Pero's Pizza & Pasta	◆◆	Italian	$8-$30	133

Map Page	Restaurants (cont'd)	Diamond Rated	Cuisine	Price Range	Page
㊴ p. 82	Flying Biscuit Cafe	♦♦	American	$5-$15	132
㊵ p. 82	MesKerem Ethiopian Cuisine	♦♦	Ethiopian	$3-$32	132
㊶ p. 82	Blue Ridge Grill	♦♦♦	Regional American	$12-$40	131
㊷ p. 82	O K Cafe	♦♦	Southern	$5-$16	133
㊸ p. 82	Queen of Sheba	♦♦	Ethiopian	$6-$16	133
㊹ p. 82	Thai Chili	♦♦	Thai	$8-$27	133
㊺ p. 82	Floataway Cafe	♦♦♦	New American	$14-$26	132
㊻ p. 82	Pig-N-Chik	♦	Barbecue	$6-$26	133
㊼ p. 82	Hankook Taqueria	♦	Korean	$3-$8	132
㊽ p. 82	Nuevo Laredo Cantina	♦♦	Tex-Mex	$9-$20	133

ALPHARETTA

Map Page	Hotels	Diamond Rated	Rate Range	Page
㊱ p. 82	Hilton Garden Inn Atlanta/North Alpharetta	♦♦♦	$79-$229	32
㊲ p. 82	**SpringHill Suites by Marriott Atlanta Alpharetta**	♦♦♦	$65-$275 SAVE	34
㊳ p. 82	**Atlanta Marriott Alpharetta**	♦♦♦	$85-$309 SAVE	32
㊴ p. 82	**Courtyard by Marriott Atlanta Alpharetta**	♦♦♦	$57-$230 SAVE	32
㊵ p. 82	DoubleTree by Hilton Hotel Atlanta-Alpharetta	♦♦♦	$89-$208	32
㊶ p. 82	Holiday Inn Express & Suites	♦♦♦	Rates not provided	33
㊷ p. 82	Comfort Inn	♦♦♦	$79-$159	32
㊸ p. 82	**Hyatt Place Atlanta/Alpharetta/Windward Parkway** *(See ad p. 33.)*	♦♦♦	$59-$219 SAVE	33
㊹ p. 82	**Residence Inn by Marriott Atlanta Alpharetta/ Windward**	♦♦♦	$90-$286 SAVE	34
㊺ p. 82	Staybridge Suites	♦♦♦	Rates not provided	34
㊻ p. 82	**TownePlace Suites by Marriott Alpharetta**	♦♦	$76-$212 SAVE	34
㊼ p. 82	**Fairfield Inn & Suites by Marriott**	♦♦	$65-$202 SAVE	32
㊽ p. 82	Embassy Suites Hotel by Hilton Alpharetta	♦♦♦	$99-$269	32
㊾ p. 82	La Quinta Inn & Suites Atlanta Alpharetta	♦♦	$67-$202	34
㊿ p. 82	**Residence Inn by Marriott Atlanta Alpharetta North Point Mall**	♦♦♦	$79-$250 SAVE	34
(51) p. 82	Hilton Garden Inn-Atlanta North Point	♦♦♦	$99-$229	32
(52) p. 82	**Hyatt Place Alpharetta/North Point Mall**	♦♦♦	$79-$299 SAVE	33
(53) p. 82	Homewood Suites	♦♦♦	$119-$259	33
(54) p. 82	Hampton Inn-Alpharetta/Roswell	♦♦♦	$84-$248	32
(55) p. 82	Comfort Suites	♦♦	$89-$159	32
(56) p. 82	**Holiday Inn Express Alpharetta**	♦♦♦	Rates not provided SAVE	33
(57) p. 82	Wingate by Wyndham Alpharetta	♦♦	$74-$149	34

Map Page	Restaurants	Diamond Rated	Cuisine	Price Range	Page
(54) p. 82	J. Christopher's	♦♦	Breakfast	$5-$12	35
(55) p. 82	Ippolito's	♦♦	Italian	$8-$19	35
(56) p. 82	Sri Krishna Vilas	♦♦	Indian	$10-$18	35
(57) p. 82	Twisted Taco	♦♦	Tex-Mex	$7-$16	35

Map Page	Restaurants (cont'd)	Diamond Rated	Cuisine	Price Range	Page
58 p. 82	Nahm Fine Thai Cuisine	◆◆◆	Thai	$8-$30	35
59 p. 82	Vinny's On Windward	◆◆◆	American	$10-$30	35
60 p. 82	Cabernet	◆◆◆	Steak	$11-$44	34
61 p. 82	Village Tavern	◆◆◆	American	$9-$28	35
62 p. 82	Thai Thai	◆◆	Thai	$8-$13	35
63 p. 82	Grouchy's New York Deli & Bagels	◆	Sandwiches	$5-$9	35
64 p. 82	The Cheesecake Factory	◆◆◆	International	$10-$30	34
65 p. 82	Ray's On The Creek	◆◆◆	American	$10-$34	35
66 p. 82	P.F. Chang's China Bistro	◆◆◆	Chinese	$8-$25	35
67 p. 82	Atlantic Seafood Company	◆◆◆	Seafood	$16-$40	34
68 p. 82	di Paolo	◆◆◆	Italian	$7-$22	35

ROSWELL

Map Page	Hotels	Diamond Rated	Rate Range	Page
60 p. 82	**Best Western Plus Roswell/Alpharetta**	◆◆◆	$89-$129 [SAVE]	242
61 p. 82	Baymont Inn & Suites Roswell Atlanta North	◆◆◆	$79-$120	242

Map Page	Restaurants	Diamond Rated	Cuisine	Price Range	Page
75 p. 82	Bistro VG	◆◆◆	French	$12-$30	242
76 p. 82	The Counter	◆◆	Burgers	$6-$15	243
77 p. 82	Stoney River	◆◆◆	Steak	$15-$35	243
78 p. 82	Brookwood Grill	◆◆◆	New American	$10-$27	242
79 p. 82	Greenwood's	◆◆	Southern	$10-$25	243
80 p. 82	The Fickle Pickle	◆	Sandwiches	$5-$10	243
81 p. 82	The Swallow at the Hollow	◆◆	Barbecue	$11-$25	243
82 p. 82	Table and Main	◆◆◆	New American	$14-$28	243
83 p. 82	Little Alley Steak	◆◆◆	Steak Seafood	$16-$70	243
84 p. 82	Salt Factory	◆◆	American	$10-$28	243
85 p. 82	Aqua Blue	◆◆◆	Specialty	$14-$32	242
86 p. 82	Pastis	◆◆◆	French	$10-$28	243
87 p. 82	Chicago's Restaurant	◆◆	American	$17-$30	243
88 p. 82	Amalfi Ristorante	◆◆	Italian	$14-$21	242

NORCROSS

Map Page	Hotels	Diamond Rated	Rate Range	Page
64 p. 82	**Hyatt Place Atlanta/Norcross/Peachtree Parkway** *(See ad p. 228.)*	◆◆◆	$64-$169 [SAVE]	229
65 p. 82	Comfort Inn & Suites	◆◆	$71-$149	228
66 p. 82	Atlanta Marriott Norcross	◆◆◆	$61-$217	228
67 p. 82	Homewood Suites by Hilton	◆◆◆	$89-$189	229
68 p. 82	Hampton Inn Atlanta/Peachtree Corners/Norcross	◆◆◆	$69-$169	228
69 p. 82	Wingate by Wyndham Atlanta Norcross	◆◆◆	$70-$75	229
70 p. 82	Hilton Atlanta Northeast	◆◆◆	$79-$329	228

NORCROSS (cont'd)

Map Page	Hotels (cont'd)	Diamond Rated	Rate Range	Page
71 p. 82	Courtyard by Marriott-Atlanta Norcross/Peachtree Corners	◆◆◆	$62-$183	228
72 p. 82	Holiday Inn Express Atlanta NE-Peachtree Corners	◆◆◆	Rates not provided	229
73 p. 82	TownePlace Suites by Marriott Atlanta Norcross/Peachtree Corners	◆◆	$74-$126	229
74 p. 82	Country Inn & Suites By Carlson	◆◆◆	Rates not provided	228
75 p. 82	La Quinta Inn Norcross	◆◆◆	$71-$174	229

Map Page	Restaurants	Diamond Rated	Cuisine	Price Range	Page
91 p. 82	J. Alexander's Restaurant	◆◆◆	American	$4-$27	230
92 p. 82	Flying Biscuit Cafe	◆◆	American	$5-$15	229
93 p. 82	Thai Star	◆◆	Thai	$8-$17	230
94 p. 82	Dog Days	◆	Hot Dogs Burgers	$3-$12	229
96 p. 82	Frontera Mex-Mex Grill	◆◆	Tex-Mex	$5-$17	229
97 p. 82	Zapata Tacos and Tequila Bar	◆◆	Mexican	$8-$19	230
98 p. 82	The Crossing of Norcross	◆◆◆	American	$8-$30	229
99 p. 82	Mojitos Cuban-American Bistro	◆◆	Cuban	$5-$19	230
100 p. 82	Dominick's	◆◆	Italian	$9-$29	229
101 p. 82	JR's Log House Restaurant	◆	American	$8-$15	230
102 p. 82	Taste of Thai	◆◆	Thai	$4-$13	230
103 p. 82	Happy Valley	◆◆	Chinese	$9-$22	229
104 p. 82	Nam Phuong	◆◆	Vietnamese	$7-$13	230

TUCKER

Map Page	Hotels	Diamond Rated	Rate Range	Page
78 p. 82	Hampton Inn Atlanta-Northlake	◆◆◆	$104-$109	292
79 p. 82	TownePlace Suites by Marriott Atlanta Northlake	◆◆	$94-$144	293
80 p. 82	Holiday Inn Atlanta Northlake	◆◆◆	Rates not provided	292
81 p. 82	**Quality Inn Atlanta/Northlake**	◆◆	$75-$99 [SAVE]	292
82 p. 82	**DoubleTree by Hilton Hotel Atlanta-Northlake**	◆◆◆	Rates not provided [SAVE]	292
83 p. 82	**Courtyard by Marriott-Atlanta Northlake**	◆◆◆	$77-$160 [SAVE]	292
84 p. 82	Comfort Suites-Northlake	◆◆	$90-$140	292

Map Page	Restaurants	Diamond Rated	Cuisine	Price Range	Page
119 p. 82	Taqueria Los Hermanos	◆◆	Tex-Mex	$3-$13	293
120 p. 82	Matthews Cafeteria	◆	Comfort Food	$5-$10	293
121 p. 82	Blue Ribbon Grill	◆◆	American	$7-$20	293
122 p. 82	Fuji Ya & Lucky Key	◆◆	Asian	$7-$33	293
123 p. 82	Northlake Thai Cuisine	◆◆◆	Thai	$9-$23	293

STONE MOUNTAIN

Map Page	Hotel	Diamond Rated	Rate Range	Page
87 p. 82	Hampton Inn Stone Mountain	◆◆◆	$109-$259	286

MILTON

Map Page	Restaurant	Diamond Rated	Cuisine	Price Range	Page
(51) p. 82	Milton's Cuisine and Cocktails	▽▽▽	New Southern	$7-$32	225

JOHNS CREEK

Map Page	Restaurants	Diamond Rated	Cuisine	Price Range	Page
(71) p. 82	Bonefish Grill	▽▽▽	Seafood	$10-$28	197
(72) p. 82	Pampas Steakhouse	▽▽▽	Steak	$8-$55	198

MARIETTA

Map Page	Restaurants	Diamond Rated	Cuisine	Price Range	Page
(107) p. 82	Trattoria La Strada	▽▽▽	Italian	$12-$22	221
(108) p. 82	Seed Kitchen & Bar	▽▽▽	New American	$9-$26	220
(109) p. 82	Sam's BBQ 1	▽▽	Barbecue	$3-$20	220

DORAVILLE

Map Page	Restaurant	Diamond Rated	Cuisine	Price Range	Page
(112) p. 82	Gyro Gyro	▽	Guatemalan	$6-$13	174

CHAMBLEE

Map Page	Restaurants	Diamond Rated	Cuisine	Price Range	Page
(115) p. 82	Penang Malaysian Cuisine	▽▽	Asian	$9-$23	154
(116) p. 82	Harmony Vegetarian Chinese Restaurant	▽▽	Chinese	$5-$11	154

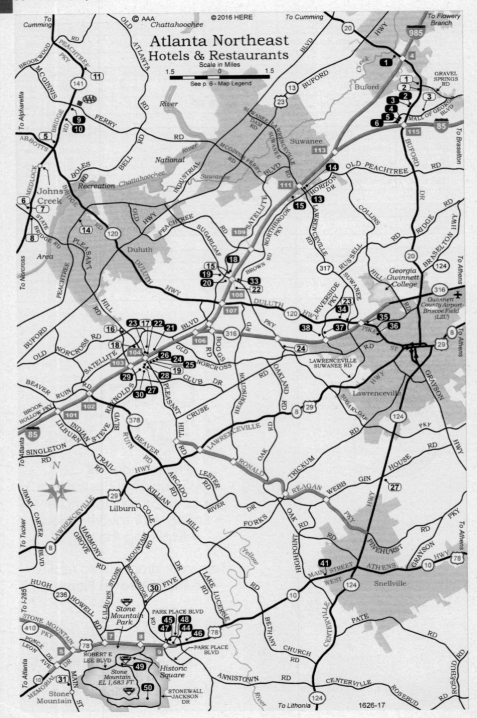

Atlanta Northeast
Hotels & Restaurants

Atlanta Northeast

This index helps you "spot" where approved hotels and restaurants are located on the corresponding detailed maps. Hotel daily rate range is for comparison only. Restaurant price range is a combination of lunch and/or dinner. Turn to the listing page for more detailed rate and price information and consult display ads for special promotions.

BUFORD

Map Page	Hotels	Diamond Rated	Rate Range	Page
1 p. 90	Holiday Inn Express Hotel & Suites Buford - Mall of GA	▼▼▼	Rates not provided	148
2 p. 90	SpringHill Suites by Marriott Atlanta/Buford-Mall of Georgia	▼▼▼	$106-$194	148
3 p. 90	Hampton Inn-Mall of Georgia	▼▼▼	$109-$189	148
4 p. 90	Courtyard by Marriott Atlanta Buford Mall of Georgia	▼▼▼	$107-$194	147
5 p. 90	Country Inn & Suites By Carlson, Buford at Mall of Georgia	▼▼▼	Rates not provided	147
6 p. 90	Fairfield Inn & Suites by Marriott	▼▼▼	$98-$151	147

Map Page	Restaurants	Diamond Rated	Cuisine	Price Range	Page
① p. 90	Bonefish Grill	▼▼▼	Seafood	$8-$29	148
② p. 90	Parma Rustic Tavern	▼▼	Italian	$7-$19	148
③ p. 90	P.F. Chang's China Bistro	▼▼▼	Chinese	$8-$26	148

JOHNS CREEK

Map Page	Hotels	Diamond Rated	Rate Range	Page
9 p. 90	Hilton Garden Inn Atlanta North-Johns Creek	▼▼▼	Rates not provided	197
10 p. 90	**Hyatt Place Atlanta/Duluth/Johns Creek**	▼▼▼	$89-$259 SAVE	197

Map Page	Restaurants	Diamond Rated	Cuisine	Price Range	Page
⑤ p. 90	Palomilla's Grillhouse	▼▼	Cuban	$3-$15	198
⑥ p. 90	Trattoria One.41	▼▼▼	Italian	$5-$39	198
⑦ p. 90	Viande Rouge	▼▼▼	French Steak	$10-$55	198
⑧ p. 90	Stoney River Legendary Steaks	▼▼▼	Steak	$15-$42	198

SUWANEE

Map Page	Hotels	Diamond Rated	Rate Range	Page
13 p. 90	**Quality Inn**	▼▼	$70-$120 SAVE	287
14 p. 90	**Comfort Inn & Suites**	▼▼▼	$100-$199 SAVE	287
15 p. 90	Courtyard by Marriott Atlanta Suwanee	▼▼▼	$98-$183	287

Map Page	Restaurant	Diamond Rated	Cuisine	Price Range	Page
⑪ p. 90	Taqueria Los Hermanos	▼▼	Tex-Mex	$4-$13	287

DULUTH

Map Page	Hotels	Diamond Rated	Rate Range	Page
18 p. 90	Residence Inn by Marriott Atlanta NE/Duluth Sugarloaf	▼▼▼	$103-$229	177
19 p. 90	Holiday Inn-Gwinnett Center	▼▼▼	Rates not provided	177
20 p. 90	Hilton Garden Inn-Atlanta NE	▼▼▼	$101-$199	177
21 p. 90	Extended Stay America-Atlanta-Gwinnett Place	▼▼	$70-$85	176
22 p. 90	**Hyatt Place Atlanta/Duluth/Gwinnett Mall**	▼▼▼	$69-$179 SAVE	177
23 p. 90	**Courtyard by Marriott Atlanta Duluth/Gwinnett Place**	▼▼▼	$79-$145 SAVE	176
24 p. 90	Holiday Inn Express & Suites Gwinnett Center	▼▼▼	Rates not provided	177
25 p. 90	Fairfield Inn & Suites by Marriott Atlanta Gwinnett Place	▼▼▼	$87-$149	176
26 p. 90	Candlewood Suites-Atlanta	▼▼	Rates not provided	176

DULUTH (cont'd)

Map Page	Hotels (cont'd)	Diamond Rated	Rate Range	Page
27 p. 90	**Best Western Gwinnett Center Hotel**	3 diamonds	$79-$129 (SAVE)	176
28 p. 90	**Sonesta Gwinnett Place Atlanta**	3 diamonds	Rates not provided (SAVE)	177
29 p. 90	Residence Inn by Marriott Atlanta Gwinnett Place	3 diamonds	$89-$183	177
30 p. 90	Hampton Inn & Suites-Gwinnett	3 diamonds	$89-$159	176

Map Page	Restaurants	Diamond Rated	Cuisine	Price Range	Page
14 p. 90	Kurt's Euro Bistro	3 diamonds	European	$12-$48	177
15 p. 90	Marlow's Tavern	2 diamonds	American	$9-$17	178
16 p. 90	Seo Ra Beol	2 diamonds	Korean	$8-$40	178
17 p. 90	Breaker's Korean Bar-B-Q	3 diamonds	Korean	$5-$35	177
18 p. 90	HARU Ichiban Japanese Restaurant	2 diamonds	Japanese	$5-$37	177
19 p. 90	Bahama Breeze	3 diamonds	Caribbean	$11-$22	177

LAWRENCEVILLE

Map Page	Hotels	Diamond Rated	Rate Range	Page
33 p. 90	Hampton Inn Lawrenceville-I-85/Sugarloaf	3 diamonds	$109-$199	206
34 p. 90	Country Inn & Suites By Carlson	3 diamonds	$129-$219	206
35 p. 90	**Days Inn**	2 diamonds	$65-$81 (SAVE)	206
36 p. 90	Holiday Inn Express Hotel & Suites	3 diamonds	$119-$154	206
37 p. 90	Hampton Inn Atlanta/Lawrenceville/Gwinnett County	2 diamonds	$94-$169	206
38 p. 90	**Comfort Suites**	3 diamonds	$94-$159 (SAVE)	206

Map Page	Restaurants	Diamond Rated	Cuisine	Price Range	Page
22 p. 90	Kingston 30 Jamaican Restaurant	1 diamond	Caribbean	$6-$9	206
23 p. 90	Papi's Cuban & Caribbean Grill	2 diamonds	Cuban	$7-$19	206
24 p. 90	Taqueria Los Hermanos	2 diamonds	Tex-Mex	$3-$13	207

SNELLVILLE

Map Page	Hotel	Diamond Rated	Rate Range	Page
41 p. 90	La Quinta Inn & Suites Snellville-Stone Mountain	3 diamonds	$101-$180	282

Map Page	Restaurant	Diamond Rated	Cuisine	Price Range	Page
27 p. 90	Bonefish Grill	3 diamonds	Seafood	$10-$28	282

STONE MOUNTAIN

Map Page	Hotels	Diamond Rated	Rate Range	Page
44 p. 90	**Quality Inn Stone Mountain**	2 diamonds	$65-$149 (SAVE)	287
45 p. 90	Holiday Inn Express	3 diamonds	Rates not provided	287
46 p. 90	Days Inn	2 diamonds	$65-$107	286
47 p. 90	Country Inn & Suites By Carlson	3 diamonds	$89-$149	286
48 p. 90	Comfort Inn & Suites at Stone Mountain	3 diamonds	$70-$210	286
49 p. 90	**Stone Mountain Inn**	2 diamonds	$86-$249 (SAVE)	287
50 p. 90	**Atlanta Evergreen Marriott Conference Center & Resort**	4 diamonds	$121-$229 (SAVE)	286

Map Page	Restaurants	Diamond Rated	Cuisine	Price Range	Page
30 p. 90	Always Fresh Neighborhood Restaurant & Market	2 diamonds	American	$6-$13	287
31 p. 90	Weeyums Philly Style	1 diamond	Sandwiches	$3-$7	287

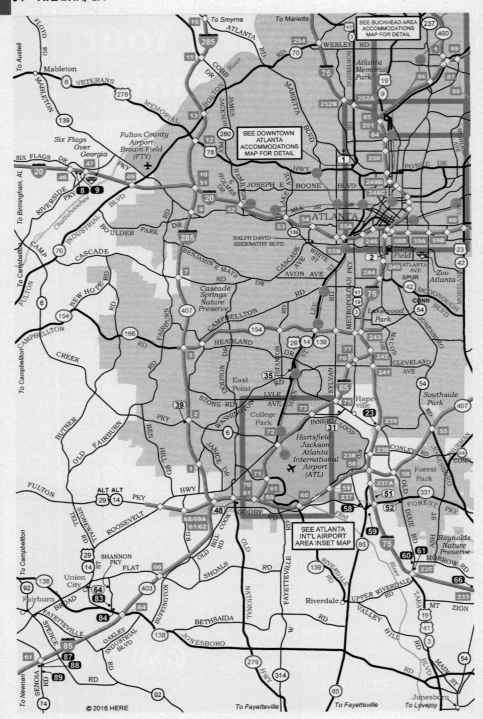

© 2016 HERE

SEE ATLANTA
NORTHEAST
ACCOMMODATIONS
MAP FOR DETAIL

Atlanta South
Hotels & Restaurants

Scale in Miles

1.5   0   1.5

See p. 6 - Map Legend

Atlanta International Airport Area

College Park

CONVENTION CENTER
CONCOURSE
CAMP CREEK

Georgia
Int'l
Convention
Center

Hartsfield-

Jackson

Atlanta

International

Airport

(ATL)

TOFFIE TER
WOOLMAN PL
DELTA BLVD

TERMINAL

MASSACHUSETTS
BLVD

© AAA

✈ Airport Hotels

Map Page	HARTSFIELD-JACKSON ATLANTA INTERNATIONAL AIRPORT (Maximum driving distance from airport: 3.4 mi)	Diamond Rated	Rate Range	Page
1 p. 94	Renaissance Concourse Atlanta Airport Hotel, 2.7 mi	◆◆◆◆	$79-$286 SAVE	134
46 p. 94	Atlanta Airport Marriott, 2.1 mi	◆◆◆	$79-$286 SAVE	157
38 p. 94	Atlanta Airport Marriott Gateway, 1.9 mi	◆◆◆	$118-$332 SAVE	157
55 p. 94	Best Western Plus Hotel & Suites Airport South, 3.4 mi	◆◆◆	$99-$149 SAVE	157
52 p. 94	Country Inn & Suites By Carlson, Atlanta Airport South, 2.8 mi	◆◆	Rates not provided	157
50 p. 94	Courtyard by Marriott Atlanta Airport South/Sullivan Road, 1.8 mi	◆◆◆	$80-$206 SAVE	157
54 p. 94	Days Inn College Park/Atlanta/Airport South, 3.4 mi	◆◆	$54-$105	157
41 p. 94	Embassy Suites Hotel by Hilton at Atlanta Airport, 1.9 mi	◆◆◆	$129-$249	157
49 p. 94	Fairfield Inn & Suites by Marriott Atlanta Airport South/Sullivan Road, 1.8 mi	◆◆◆	$86-$148 SAVE	157
47 p. 94	Hilton Garden Inn-Atlanta Airport/Millenium Center, 2.1 mi	◆◆◆	$129-$189 SAVE	158
40 p. 94	Holiday Inn-Atlanta Airport South, 1.5 mi	◆◆◆	Rates not provided	158
39 p. 94	Holiday Inn Express-Atlanta Airport, 1.9 mi	◆◆◆	Rates not provided	158
43 p. 94	Hyatt Place Atlanta Airport-South, 1.5 mi	◆◆◆	$79-$189 SAVE	158
51 p. 94	La Quinta Inn & Suites Atlanta Airport, 1.8 mi	◆◆◆	$82-$230	158
45 p. 94	Sheraton Atlanta Airport Hotel, 1.6 mi	◆◆◆	$109-$269 SAVE	158
44 p. 94	Sleep Inn/Atlanta Airport, 1.6 mi	◆◆	$81-$95	158
37 p. 94	SpringHill Suites by Marriott Atlanta Airport Gateway, 2.1 mi	◆◆◆	$110-$309 SAVE	158
48 p. 94	Super 8-Atlanta Airport, 1.7 mi	◆◆	$65-$85	158
42 p. 94	The Westin Hotel-Atlanta Airport, 1.8 mi	◆◆◆◆	$99-$289 SAVE	159
31 p. 94	Country Inn & Suites By Carlson, Atlanta-Airport North, 2.8 mi	◆◆◆	Rates not provided	178
33 p. 94	Crowne Plaza Atlanta Airport, 2.6 mi	◆◆◆	$99-$199	178
26 p. 94	DoubleTree by Hilton Hotel Atlanta Airport, 3.0 mi	◆◆◆	$109-$189	178
32 p. 94	Drury Inn & Suites-Atlanta Airport, 2.3 mi	◆◆◆	$89-$179	178
27 p. 94	Fairfield Inn & Suites by Marriott Atlanta Airport North, 2.6 mi	◆◆	$94-$156	178
29 p. 94	Hampton Inn & Suites-Atlanta Airport North, 2.5 mi	◆◆◆	$109-$179	179
30 p. 94	Hilton Garden Inn-Atlanta Airport North, 2.5 mi	◆◆◆	$162-$172	179
34 p. 94	Holiday Inn & Suites Atlanta Airport-North, 2.7 mi	◆◆◆	Rates not provided SAVE	179
28 p. 94	Hyatt Place Atlanta Airport-North, 2.5 mi	◆◆◆	$94-$189	179
20 p. 94	Courtyard by Marriott Atlanta Airport North/Virginia Avenue, 2.9 mi	◆◆◆	$76-$235 SAVE	189
22 p. 94	Hilton Atlanta Airport, 2.8 mi	◆◆◆	$99-$289 SAVE	189
21 p. 94	Residence Inn by Marriott Atlanta Airport North/Virginia Avenue, 3.0 mi	◆◆◆	$99-$240 SAVE	189

Atlanta South

This index helps you "spot" where approved hotels and restaurants are located on the corresponding detailed maps. Hotel daily rate range is for comparison only. Restaurant price range is a combination of lunch and/or dinner. Turn to the listing page for more detailed rate and price information and consult display ads for special promotions.

ATLANTA SOUTH

Map Page	Hotels	Diamond Rated	Rate Range	Page
❶ p. 94	**Renaissance Concourse Atlanta Airport Hotel**	◆◆◆◆	$79-$286 SAVE	134
❹ p. 94	Emory Conference Center Hotel	◆◆◆	Rates not provided	134
❺ p. 94	The University Inn at Emory	◆◆	Rates not provided	134

Map Page	Restaurants	Diamond Rated	Cuisine	Price Range	Page
① p. 94	Miller Union	◆◆◆	New American	$13-$34	135
② p. 94	Bullpen Rib House	◆	Barbecue	$6-$21	135
⑤ p. 94	Tin Lizzy's Cantina	◆◆	Tex-Mex	$3-$10	135
⑥ p. 94	Marlow's Tavern	◆◆	Burgers	$9-$17	135
⑦ p. 94	Flying Biscuit Cafe	◆◆	American	$8-$19	135

AUSTELL

Map Page	Hotels	Diamond Rated	Rate Range	Page
❽ p. 94	**Sleep Inn**	◆◆	$79-$119 SAVE	142
❾ p. 94	Wingate by Wyndham at Six Flags	◆◆◆	$109-$131	142

DECATUR

Map Page	Hotels	Diamond Rated	Rate Range	Page
⓬ p. 94	Holiday Inn Express, Atlanta-Emory	◆◆◆	$109-$249	173
⓭ p. 94	Super 8	◆◆	$70-$125 SAVE	173
⓮ p. 94	Courtyard by Marriott Atlanta Decatur Downtown/Emory	◆◆◆	$142-$233	173

Map Page	Restaurants	Diamond Rated	Cuisine	Price Range	Page
⑩ p. 94	Athens Pizza House	◆◆	Greek Pizza	$6-$25	173
⑪ p. 94	J. Christopher's	◆◆	Breakfast	$5-$12	174
⑫ p. 94	Café Alsace	◆◆	French	$10-$34	173
⑬ p. 94	Brick Store Pub	◆◆	American	$9-$18	173
⑭ p. 94	Farm Burger	◆	Burgers	$7-$10	173
⑮ p. 94	Cafe Lily Restaurant & Wine Bar	◆◆	Italian	$6-$29	173
⑯ p. 94	Cakes & Ale Cafe	◆	Coffee/Tea	$6-$16	173
⑰ p. 94	Cakes & Ale	◆◆◆	American	$9-$35	173
⑱ p. 94	Victory Sandwich Bar	◆◆	Sandwiches	$3-$10	174
⑲ p. 94	Revival	◆◆	Southern American	$5-$20	174
⑳ p. 94	Lawrence's Cafe	◆◆	Lebanese	$6-$21	174
㉑ p. 94	Universal Joint	◆◆	American	$7-$12	174
㉔ p. 94	The Sprig	◆◆◆	American	$9-$21	174
㉕ p. 94	Cafe Istanbul	◆◆	Turkish	$8-$19	173

LITHONIA

Map Page	Hotel	Diamond Rated	Rate Range	Page
⓱ p. 94	Holiday Inn Express & Suites Atlanta East-Lithonia	◆◆◆	$89-$109	208

Map Page	Restaurant	Diamond Rated	Cuisine	Price Range	Page
㉘ p. 94	This Is It! BBQ & Seafood	▼	Southern Soul Food	$6-$15	208

HAPEVILLE

Map Page	Hotels	Diamond Rated	Rate Range	Page
⑳ p. 94	**Courtyard by Marriott Atlanta Airport North/ Virginia Avenue**	▼▼▼	$76-$235 [SAVE]	189
㉑ p. 94	**Residence Inn by Marriott Atlanta Airport North/Virginia Avenue**	▼▼▼	$99-$240 [SAVE]	189
㉒ p. 94	**Hilton Atlanta Airport**	▼▼▼	$99-$289 [SAVE]	189
㉓ p. 94	**Best Western Plus Atlanta Airport-East**	▼▼▼	$94-$129 [SAVE]	189

Map Page	Restaurants	Diamond Rated	Cuisine	Price Range	Page
㉛ p. 94	Hambones	▼	Barbecue	$5-$20	189
㉜ p. 94	Thai Heaven	▼▼	Thai	$8-$30	190

EAST POINT

Map Page	Hotels	Diamond Rated	Rate Range	Page
㉖ p. 94	DoubleTree by Hilton Hotel Atlanta Airport	▼▼▼	$109-$189	178
㉗ p. 94	Fairfield Inn & Suites by Marriott Atlanta Airport North	▼▼	$94-$156	178
㉘ p. 94	**Hyatt Place Atlanta Airport-North**	▼▼▼	$94-$189 [SAVE]	179
㉙ p. 94	Hampton Inn & Suites-Atlanta Airport North	▼▼▼	$109-$179	179
㉚ p. 94	Hilton Garden Inn-Atlanta Airport North	▼▼▼	$162-$172	179
㉛ p. 94	Country Inn & Suites By Carlson, Atlanta-Airport North	▼▼▼	Rates not provided	178
㉜ p. 94	Drury Inn & Suites-Atlanta Airport	▼▼▼	$89-$179	178
㉝ p. 94	Crowne Plaza Atlanta Airport	▼▼▼	$99-$199	178
㉞ p. 94	**Holiday Inn & Suites Atlanta Airport-North**	▼▼▼	Rates not provided [SAVE]	179

Map Page	Restaurants	Diamond Rated	Cuisine	Price Range	Page
㉟ p. 94	Lov'n It Live	▼▼	Natural/Organic	$12-$23	179
㊱ p. 94	Benton's Grill	▼▼	American	$6-$25	179
㊲ p. 94	Malone's Steak & Seafood	▼▼	American	$9-$29	179
㊳ p. 94	Giovanna's Italian Kitchen	▼▼	Italian	$8-$24	179
㊴ p. 94	This Is It! BBQ & Seafood	▼▼	American	$7-$16	179

COLLEGE PARK

Map Page	Hotels	Diamond Rated	Rate Range	Page
㊲ p. 94	**SpringHill Suites by Marriott Atlanta Airport Gateway**	▼▼▼	$110-$309 [SAVE]	158
㊳ p. 94	**Atlanta Airport Marriott Gateway**	▼▼▼	$118-$332 [SAVE]	157
㊴ p. 94	Holiday Inn Express-Atlanta Airport	▼▼▼	Rates not provided	158
㊵ p. 94	Holiday Inn-Atlanta Airport South	▼▼▼	Rates not provided	158
㊶ p. 94	Embassy Suites Hotel by Hilton at Atlanta Airport	▼▼▼	$129-$249	157
㊷ p. 94	**The Westin Hotel-Atlanta Airport**	▼▼▼▼	$99-$289 [SAVE]	159
㊸ p. 94	**Hyatt Place Atlanta Airport-South**	▼▼▼	$79-$189 [SAVE]	158
㊹ p. 94	Sleep Inn/Atlanta Airport	▼▼	$81-$95	158
㊺ p. 94	**Sheraton Atlanta Airport Hotel**	▼▼▼	$109-$269 [SAVE]	158

COLLEGE PARK (cont'd)

Map Page	Hotels (cont'd)	Diamond Rated	Rate Range	Page
46 p. 94	**Atlanta Airport Marriott**	◆◆◆	$79-$286 SAVE	157
47 p. 94	**Hilton Garden Inn-Atlanta Airport/Millenium Center**	◆◆◆	$129-$189 SAVE	158
48 p. 94	Super 8-Atlanta Airport	◆◆	$65-$85	158
49 p. 94	**Fairfield Inn & Suites by Marriott Atlanta Airport South/Sullivan Road**	◆◆◆	$86-$148 SAVE	157
50 p. 94	**Courtyard by Marriott Atlanta Airport South/Sullivan Road**	◆◆◆	$80-$206 SAVE	157
51 p. 94	La Quinta Inn & Suites Atlanta Airport	◆◆◆	$82-$230	158
52 p. 94	Country Inn & Suites By Carlson, Atlanta Airport South	◆◆	Rates not provided	157
53 p. 94	Quality Hotel & Conference Center-Atlanta Airport	◆◆	Rates not provided	158
54 p. 94	Days Inn College Park/Atlanta/Airport South	◆◆	$54-$105	157
55 p. 94	**Best Western Plus Hotel & Suites Airport South**	◆◆◆	$99-$149 SAVE	157

Map Page	Restaurants	Diamond Rated	Cuisine	Price Range	Page
42 p. 94	Brake Pad	◆◆	American	$7-$10	159
43 p. 94	Barbeque Kitchen	◆	Southern	$5-$9	159
44 p. 94	The Pig & Pint	◆◆◆	American	$6-$28	159
45 p. 94	Simon's Steak & Seafood	◆◆◆	Steak Seafood	$11-$28	159
46 p. 94	Tony Morrow's Real Pit Barbeque	◆◆	Barbecue	$3-$15	159
47 p. 94	The Feed Store	◆◆◆	Regional American	$11-$38	159
48 p. 94	Cozumel Mexican Restaurant	◆◆	Mexican	$4-$18	159

FOREST PARK

Map Page	Hotels	Diamond Rated	Rate Range	Page
58 p. 94	Comfort Suites Atlanta Airport	◆◆◆	$74-$279	182
59 p. 94	Ramada Airport East/Forest Park	◆◆	$60-$81	182
60 p. 94	Travelodge Forest Park Atlanta South	◆◆	$60-$73	183
61 p. 94	Super 8	◆◆	$45-$100	182

Map Page	Restaurants	Diamond Rated	Cuisine	Price Range	Page
51 p. 94	Oakwood Cafe	◆◆	Southern	$6-$20	183
52 p. 94	Zesto	◆	Burgers	$4-$23	183

MORROW

Map Page	Hotels	Diamond Rated	Rate Range	Page
64 p. 94	**Best Western Southlake Inn**	◆◆	$69-$89 SAVE	225
65 p. 94	Comfort Suites Morrow	◆◆◆	$89-$149	225
66 p. 94	Red Roof Inn-Atlanta South Morrow	◆◆	$42-$69	226
67 p. 94	Drury Inn & Suites-Atlanta South	◆◆◆	$94-$134	225
68 p. 94	Quality Inn & Suites	◆◆	$70-$99	226
69 p. 94	Hampton Inn Southlake	◆◆◆	$104-$159	225
70 p. 94	Country Inn & Suites By Carlson, Atlanta I-75 South	◆◆◆	Rates not provided	225
71 p. 94	Extended Stay America-Atlanta-Morrow	◆◆	$55-$75	225

Map Page	Restaurants	Diamond Rated	Cuisine	Price Range	Page
55 p. 94	Rocky's Cafe and Pizza	◆	Italian	$5-$19	226
56 p. 94	Huynh Ky Saigon Noodle House	◆◆	Vietnamese	$3-$9	226
57 p. 94	The Sushi China Cafe	◆◆	Asian	$7-$20	226

STOCKBRIDGE

Map Page	Hotels	Diamond Rated	Rate Range	Page
74 p. 94	**Quality Inn & Suites**	◆◆	$60-$99 SAVE	284
75 p. 94	Hampton Inn-Atlanta-Stockbridge	◆◆◆	$115-$160	284
76 p. 94	**La Quinta Inn & Suites Atlanta Stockbridge**	◆◆	$86-$229 SAVE	284
77 p. 94	Sleep Inn & Suites	◆◆	$61-$119	284
78 p. 94	Comfort Suites Stockbridge	◆◆◆	$109-$169	284
79 p. 94	Holiday Inn Hotel & Suites	◆◆◆	Rates not provided	284
80 p. 94	Red Roof Inn Atlanta/Southeast	◆◆	$57-$127	284

Map Page	Restaurants	Diamond Rated	Cuisine	Price Range	Page
60 p. 94	Kazu Japanese & Chinese Restaurant	◆◆	Asian	$5-$28	284
61 p. 94	Frontera Mex-Mex Grill	◆◆	Tex-Mex	$5-$17	284

UNION CITY

Map Page	Hotels	Diamond Rated	Rate Range	Page
83 p. 94	**Days Inn & Suites**	◆◆	$70-$95 SAVE	294
84 p. 94	Magnuson Hotel Atlanta South	◆◆	$50-$125	294

Map Page	Restaurant	Diamond Rated	Cuisine	Price Range	Page
64 p. 94	The Historic Green Manor Restaurant	◆	Southern	$12-$19	294

FAIRBURN

Map Page	Hotels	Diamond Rated	Rate Range	Page
87 p. 94	Hampton Inn Atlanta/Fairburn	◆◆◆	$114-$154	180
88 p. 94	Country Inn & Suites By Carlson	◆◆◆	$89-$159	180
89 p. 94	Wingate by Wyndham Atlanta Airport Fairburn	◆◆◆	$94-$119	181

DOWNTOWN ATLANTA
• Restaurants p. 107
• Hotels & Restaurants map & index p. 66

ALOFT HOTEL ATLANTA DOWNTOWN
(678)515-0300 **27**

Hotel
$129-$399

AAA Benefit: Members save up to 15%, plus Starwood Preferred Guest® benefits!

Address: 300 Spring St NW 30308 **Location:** I-75 exit 249B (Pine St), 0.5 mi sw on Peachtree St NE, then just w. **Facility:** 254 units. 8 stories, interior corridors. **Parking:** on-site (fee) and valet. **Amenities:** safes. **Pool(s):** outdoor. **Activities:** exercise room. **Guest Services:** valet and coin laundry.

ARTMORE HOTEL 404/876-6100 **3**
◆◆◆ **Boutique Contemporary Hotel.** Rates not provided. **Address:** 1302 W Peachtree St 30309 **Location:** I-75/85 exit 250 (14th St), just e, then just n on W Peachtree St to 16th St. **Facility:** Built in 1924, this trendy retro gem sits in the midtown hotel scene. A former condominium, the property offers kitchenettes and a variety of room types, including two-bedroom suites. 102 units, some two bedrooms, efficiencies and kitchens. 3 stories, interior corridors. **Parking:** on-site (fee). **Activities:** exercise room. **Guest Services:** valet laundry.

(See map & index p. 66.)

ATLANTA MARRIOTT MARQUIS
(404)521-0000

Hotel
$104-$321

AAA Benefit:
Members save 5% or more!

Address: 265 Peachtree Center Ave 30303 **Location:** I-75/85 exit 249A, 0.3 mi s to International Blvd, just w to Peachtree Center Ave, then just n. **Facility:** 1663 units. 47 stories, interior corridors. **Parking:** valet only. **Terms:** check-in 4 pm. **Amenities:** video games, safes. **Dining:** 3 restaurants. **Pool(s):** heated outdoor, heated indoor. **Activities:** hot tub, steamroom, spa. **Guest Services:** valet laundry.

ATLANTA MARRIOTT SUITES MIDTOWN
(404)876-8888

Hotel
$116-$321

AAA Benefit:
Members save 5% or more!

Address: 35 14th St 30309 **Location:** I-75/85 exit 250 (14th St), 0.3 mi e. **Facility:** 254 units. 19 stories, interior corridors. **Parking:** on-site (fee) and valet. **Terms:** check-in 4 pm. **Pool(s):** heated indoor. **Activities:** hot tub, exercise room. **Guest Services:** valet and coin laundry.

COURTYARD BY MARRIOTT ATLANTA DOWNTOWN
(404)222-2416

Hotel
$109-$240

COURTYARD Marriott
AAA Benefit:
Members save 5% or more!

Address: 133 Carnegie Way NW 30303 **Location:** Jct Peachtree St, just w. **Facility:** 150 units. 12 stories, interior corridors. **Parking:** valet only. **Amenities:** safes. **Activities:** exercise room. **Guest Services:** valet and coin laundry.

COURTYARD BY MARRIOTT ATLANTA MIDTOWN/ GEORGIA TECH
(404)607-1112

Hotel
$96-$250

COURTYARD Marriott
AAA Benefit:
Members save 5% or more!

Address: 1132 Techwood Dr 30318 **Location:** I-75/85 exit 250 (14th St), just w. **Facility:** 168 units. 8 stories, interior corridors. **Parking:** on-site (fee). **Pool(s):** outdoor. **Activities:** hot tub, exercise room. **Guest Services:** valet and coin laundry, boarding pass kiosk, area transportation.

CROWNE PLAZA ATLANTA MIDTOWN
404/877-9000

Hotel
Rates not provided

Address: 590 W Peachtree St NW 30308 **Location:** I-75/85 exit 249D southbound; exit 249C northbound, just e. **Facility:** 358 units. 25 stories, interior corridors. **Parking:** on-site (fee) and valet. **Dining:** 2 restaurants. **Pool(s):** outdoor. **Activities:** exercise room. **Guest Services:** valet laundry.

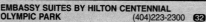

DOUBLETREE BY HILTON ATLANTA DOWNTOWN
404/688-8600 **36**

Hotel. Rates not provided. **Address:** 160 Spring St NW 30303 **Location:** I-75/85 exit 248C northbound; exit 249C (Williams St) southbound. **Facility:** 312 units. 9 stories, interior corridors. **Parking:** valet only. **Amenities:** safes. **Pool(s):** outdoor. **Activities:** exercise room. **Guest Services:** valet laundry.

AAA Benefit:
Members save 5% or more!

EMBASSY SUITES BY HILTON CENTENNIAL OLYMPIC PARK
(404)223-2300 **32**

Hotel
$159-$299

AAA Benefit:
Members save 5% or more!

Address: 267 Marietta St 30313 **Location:** Just w of International Blvd and Marietta St. **Facility:** 321 units. 8 stories, interior corridors. **Parking:** valet only. **Terms:** 1-7 night maximum stay, cancellation fee imposed. **Amenities:** safes. **Pool(s):** heated outdoor. **Activities:** hot tub, exercise room. **Guest Services:** valet and coin laundry, rental car service. **Featured Amenity:** full hot breakfast.

EMBASSY SUITES by HILTON

Recent $8 million renovation in the heart of Atlanta's Centennial Park attraction/restaurant district

---

FAIRFIELD INN & SUITES BY MARRIOTT ATLANTA DOWNTOWN
(678)702-8600 **43**

Hotel. $95-$202 **Address:** 54 Peachtree St SW 30303 **Location:** Jct Alabama St; at Underground Atlanta. **Facility:** 156 units. 17 stories, interior corridors. **Parking:** valet only. **Terms:** check-in 4:30 pm. **Activities:** exercise room. **Guest Services:** valet and coin laundry, area transportation.

AAA Benefit:
Members save 5% or more!

AAA Vacations® packages ...

exciting itineraries

and exclusive values

FOUR SEASONS HOTEL ATLANTA 404/881-9898 **5**

Hotel
Rates not provided

Address: 75 14th St NE 30309 **Location:** I-75/85 exit 250 (14th St), 0.3 mi e. Located in art and business district. **Facility:** Traditional opulence meets modern design at this luxury hotel. Rooms feature plush beds, espresso machines and views of the cityscape. The on-site spa, fine dining and service complete the package. 244 units. 19 stories, interior corridors. **Parking:** valet only. **Amenities:** video games, safes. **Dining:** Bar Margot, see separate listing. **Pool(s):** heated indoor. **Activities:** sauna, hot tub, steamroom, spa. **Guest Services:** valet laundry, boarding pass kiosk, area transportation.

▼ *See AAA listing p. 103* ▼

(See map & index p. 66.)

THE GEORGIAN TERRACE HOTEL

(404)897-1991 **18**

Classic Historic Hotel
$139-$849

Address: 659 Peachtree St NE 30308 **Location:** I-75/85 exit 249D, 0.5 mi e to Peachtree St, then just n. **Facility:** This 1911 Atlanta landmark is a favorite for weddings, special events and shows as it is located next to Fox Theatre. The entrance and lobby will make you say "wow," and rooms were recently renovated. 326 units, some two bedrooms, three bedrooms and kitchens. 19 stories, interior corridors. **Parking:** on-site (fee) and valet. **Terms:** cancellation fee imposed. **Dining:** 2 restaurants, also, Livingston, see separate listing. **Pool(s):** heated outdoor. **Activities:** exercise room. **Guest Services:** valet laundry, rental car service, area transportation. *(See ad p. 102.)*

Located in Midtown Atlanta across from the Fox Theatre & close to many Atlanta attractions.

GLENN HOTEL, AUTOGRAPH COLLECTION

(404)521-2250 **42**

Boutique Contemporary Hotel
$121-$307

AUTOGRAPH COLLECTION HOTELS
AAA Benefit: Members save 5% or more!

Address: 110 Marietta St NW 30303 **Location:** I-75/85 exit 248C northbound, 0.8 mi w, then just s; exit 249A southbound, just s to Baker St, just w, then just s. **Facility:** This contemporary boutique hotel offers the comforts of European-style bedding and pillowtop mattresses. An enclosed rooftop bar and convenient location make it a great downtown spot. 110 units. 10 stories, interior corridors. **Parking:** valet only. **Amenities:** video games, safes. **Dining:** Glenn's Kitchen, see separate listing. **Activities:** exercise room. **Guest Services:** valet laundry.

HAMPTON INN & SUITES ATLANTA DOWNTOWN

(404)589-1111 **37**

Hotel
$229-$339

Hampton by HILTON
AAA Benefit: Members save up to 10%!

Address: 161 Spring St NW 30303 **Location:** I-75/85 exit 248C northbound, 0.5 mi w, then just s; exit 249C southbound, 0.5 mi s. **Facility:** 119 units. 8 stories, interior corridors. **Parking:** on-site (fee). **Terms:** 1-7 night minimum stay, cancellation fee imposed. **Activities:** exercise room. **Guest Services:** valet and coin laundry.

HAMPTON INN ATLANTA DOWNTOWN GEORGIA TECH

(404)881-0881 **19**

Hotel. $139-$300 **Address:** 244 North Ave NW 30313 **Location:** I-75/85 exit 249D, 0.4 mi w. **Facility:** 106 units. 6 stories, interior corridors. **Parking:** no self-parking. **Terms:** 1-7 night minimum stay, cancellation fee imposed. **Activities:** game room, exercise room. **Guest Services:** valet laundry, area transportation.

AAA Benefit: Members save up to 10%!

HILTON ATLANTA

(404)659-2000 **28**

Hotel
$99-$259

Hilton HOTELS & RESORTS
AAA Benefit: Members save 5% or more!

Address: 255 Courtland St NE 30303 **Location:** I-75/85 exit 249A southbound; exit 248C northbound, just w to Piedmont Ave, just n to Baker St, then just w. **Facility:** 1242 units, some two bedrooms. 28 stories, interior corridors. **Parking:** on-site (fee) and valet. **Terms:** 1-7 night minimum stay, cancellation fee imposed. **Amenities:** safes. **Dining:** Nikolai's Roof, Trader Vic's, see separate listings. **Pool(s):** outdoor. **Activities:** tennis. **Guest Services:** valet laundry, boarding pass kiosk.

HILTON GARDEN INN ATLANTA DOWNTOWN

404/577-2001 **31**

Hotel. Rates not provided. **Address:** 275 Baker St NW 30313 **Location:** Jct Baker and Marietta sts. **Facility:** 242 units. 14 stories, interior corridors. **Parking:** on-site (fee) and valet. **Amenities:** safes. **Dining:** 2 restaurants, also, Legal Sea Foods, see separate listing. **Pool(s):** outdoor, heated indoor. **Activities:** hot tub, exercise room. **Guest Services:** valet and coin laundry.

AAA Benefit: Members save up to 10%!

HILTON GARDEN INN ATLANTA MIDTOWN

(404)524-4006 **13**

Hotel
$149-$269

Hilton Garden Inn
AAA Benefit: Members save up to 10%!

Address: 97 10th St 30309 **Location:** I-75/85 exit 250 (10th St), just e. **Facility:** 136 units. 12 stories, interior corridors. **Parking:** valet only. **Terms:** check-in 4 pm, 1-7 night minimum stay, cancellation fee imposed. **Pool(s):** outdoor. **Activities:** hot tub, exercise room. **Guest Services:** valet and coin laundry.

HOLIDAY INN ATLANTA DOWNTOWN

404/524-5555 **35**

Hotel. Rates not provided. **Address:** 101 Andrew Young International Blvd 30303 **Location:** I-75/85 exit 248C northbound, 0.6 mi w; exit 249C southbound, 0.5 mi s. **Facility:** 260 units. 11 stories, interior corridors. **Parking:** valet only. **Amenities:** video games. **Pool(s):** outdoor. **Activities:** hot tub, exercise room. **Guest Services:** valet and coin laundry.

(See map & index p. 66.)

HOMEWOOD SUITES BY HILTON   (404)524-4076   [12]

▼▼▼▼ Extended Stay Hotel
$149-$279

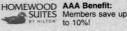
HOMEWOOD SUITES BY HILTON

AAA Benefit: Members save up to 10%!

Address: 97 10th St NW 30309 **Location:** I-75/85 exit 250 (10th St), just e. **Facility:** 92 efficiencies. 12 stories, interior corridors. **Parking:** valet only. **Terms:** 1-7 night minimum stay, cancellation fee imposed. **Pool(s):** outdoor. **Activities:** hot tub, exercise room. **Guest Services:** valet and coin laundry.

[SAVE] [⊶] [◎] CALL [&M] [⊷] [BIZ]
[◉] [⊠] [⬛] [▭] /SOME UNITS [HS]

HOTEL INDIGO ATLANTA MIDTOWN   (404)874-9200   [17]

▼▼▼▼ Boutique Hotel. $99-$349 **Address:** 683 Peachtree St NE 30308 **Location:** I-75/85 exit 249D, 0.5 mi e to Peachtree St, then just n. **Facility:** The artistic décor of the lobby and rooms reflect the trendy midtown neighborhood this small hotel is set in. Matchbox-size bathrooms reflect the historic design of the building. 140 units. 12 stories, interior corridors. *Bath:* shower only. **Parking:** on-site (fee). **Terms:** cancellation fee imposed. **Activities:** exercise room. **Guest Services:** valet laundry.

[⊶] [◎] [▭] CALL [&M] [BIZ] [HS] [◉] [⊠] [▭]
/SOME UNITS [⬛]

HYATT ATLANTA MIDTOWN   (404)443-1234   [10]

▼▼▼▼ Hotel
$99-$449

HYATT

AAA Benefit: Members save 10%!

Address: 125 10th St NE 30309 **Location:** I-85 exit 84 (10th St), 1.2 mi e. **Facility:** This impressive property has a great downtown location, luxurious décor and a full-service restaurant. Guests really enjoy the city views and comfortable, modern furnishings. 194 units. 11 stories, interior corridors. **Parking:** on-site (fee) and valet. **Amenities:** safes. **Pool(s):** heated indoor. **Activities:** exercise room. **Guest Services:** valet laundry, boarding pass kiosk.

[SAVE] [⊶] [◎] [▭] CALL [&M] [⊷] [BIZ] [HS] [◉] [⊠]
[⬛] [⬛] [▭] /SOME UNITS [⬛]

HYATT HOUSE ATLANTA DOWNTOWN   (404)332-5522   [24]

▼▼▼ Hotel
$89-$399

H HYATT house

AAA Benefit: Members save 10%!

Address: 431 Marietta St NW 30313 **Location:** I-75/85 exit 249D, take Spring St toward Centennial Olympic Park Dr NW, just s onto Ivan Allen Jr Blvd NW, just n. **Facility:** 150 units, some kitchens. 7 stories, interior corridors. **Parking:** valet only. **Pool(s):** heated outdoor. **Activities:** exercise room. **Featured Amenity:** full hot breakfast.

[SAVE] [▭] CALL [&M] [⊷] [BIZ] [◉]
[⊠] [⬛] [▭] [▭] /SOME UNITS [⬛] [HS]

HYATT PLACE, ATLANTA/DOWNTOWN   (404)577-1980   [25]

▼▼▼▼ Hotel
$99-$299

HYATT PLACE

AAA Benefit: Members save 10%!

Address: 330 Peachtree St NE 30308 **Location:** I-75/85 exit 249A to Baker St, 0.3 mi w to Peachtree St, then just n. **Facility:** 95 units. 10 stories, interior corridors. **Parking:** on-site (fee). **Terms:** cancellation fee imposed. **Amenities:** safes. **Activities:** exercise room. **Guest Services:** valet laundry, area transportation. **Featured Amenity:** full hot breakfast.

[SAVE] [⊶] [⊷] [◎] CALL [&M] [BIZ] [◉] [⊠] [⬛] [▭] [▭]
/SOME UNITS [⬛] [HS]

HYATT REGENCY ATLANTA   (404)577-1234   [30]

▼▼▼▼ Hotel
$109-$369

HYATT REGENCY

AAA Benefit: Members save 10%!

Address: 265 Peachtree St NE 30303 **Location:** I-75/85 exit 248C northbound, 0.4 mi w, then just n; exit 249A southbound, just s to Baker St, then just w; in Peachtree Center Shopping and Office Complex. **Facility:** 1260 units, some two bedrooms. 22-24 stories, interior corridors. **Parking:** valet only. **Terms:** cancellation fee imposed. **Amenities:** safes. **Dining:** 3 restaurants. **Pool(s):** outdoor. **Activities:** exercise room. **Guest Services:** valet laundry.

[SAVE] [ECO] [●] [⊶] [◎] [▭] CALL [&M] [⊷] [BIZ] [HS]
[◉] [⊠] [◎] [▭] /SOME UNITS [⬛] [▭]

INN AT THE PEACHTREES   (404)577-6970   [26]

▼▼▼ Motel. $99-$299 **Address:** 330 W Peachtree St 30308 **Location:** I-75/85 exit 248C northbound, 0.4 mi w to Peachtree St, then 0.3 mi n; exit 249C southbound, just s to Peachtree Pl, then just e. **Facility:** 109 units. 4 stories, interior/exterior corridors. **Parking:** on-site (fee). **Amenities:** safes. **Activities:** exercise room. **Guest Services:** valet laundry.

[⊶] [⊷] CALL [&M] [BIZ] [◉] [⊠] [⬛] [▭] /SOME UNITS [⬛]

LOEWS ATLANTA HOTEL   404/745-5000   [8]

▼▼▼▼ Hotel
Rates not provided

Address: 1075 Peachtree St NE 30309 **Location:** I-75/85 exit 251 (10th St), 0.5 mi e to Peachtree St NE, then just n. **Facility:** This vibrant, upscale, luxurious and uniquely Southern themed property boasts floor-to-ceiling windows in its public areas and guest rooms. The beautiful bathrooms feature a separate tub and shower. 414 units. 17 stories, interior corridors. **Parking:** on-site (fee) and valet. **Terms:** check-in 4 pm. **Amenities:** safes. **Dining:** 2 restaurants, entertainment. **Activities:** sauna, steamroom, exercise room, spa. **Guest Services:** valet laundry, area transportation.

[SAVE] [⊶] [◎] [▭] CALL [&M] [BIZ] [◉] [⊠] [▭]
/SOME UNITS [⬛] [HS] [⬛] [▭]

(See map & index p. 66.)

OMNI HOTEL AT CNN CENTER   404/659-0000 **39**
▼▼▼ ▼▼▼ **Hotel.** Rates not provided. **Address:** 190 Marrietta St 30303 **Location:** I-75/85 exit 248C northbound, 0.8 mi w; exit 249C southbound to International Blvd, 0.5 mi w. **Facility:** This luxurious hotel capitalizes on the extensive social space, marvelous Atlanta skyline and elegant rooms. An expanded fitness center and on-site spa provide physical outlets between meetings. 1059 units. 15 stories, interior corridors. **Parking:** valet only. **Amenities:** safes. **Dining:** 2 restaurants, also, Prime Meridian, see separate listing. **Pool(s):** heated outdoor. **Activities:** sauna, hot tub, spa. **Guest Services:** valet laundry.

⟨icons⟩

RAMADA PLAZA ATLANTA DOWNTOWN-CAPITOL PARK
    (404)591-2000 **44**
▼▼ ◆◆ **Hotel.** $93-$249 **Address:** 450 Capitol Ave 30312 **Location:** I-75/85 exit 246, 0.3 mi e. **Facility:** 375 units. 16 stories, interior corridors. **Terms:** check-in 4 pm. **Amenities:** video games. **Dining:** 2 restaurants. **Pool(s):** outdoor. **Activities:** exercise room. **Guest Services:** valet and coin laundry.

⟨icons⟩

REGENCY SUITES HOTEL   (404)876-5003 **11**
▼▼▼ **Boutique Hotel.** $119-$289 **Address:** 975 W Peachtree St NW 30309 **Location:** I-75/85 exit 250 (10th St), just e; corner of 10th St. Adjacent to rapid transit station. **Facility:** Converted from a European-style apartment building, this boutique hotel offers spacious rooms and a great mid-town location. Most rooms have a seating area and some have kitchenettes. 96 efficiencies. 9 stories, interior corridors. **Parking:** on-site (fee). **Terms:** cancellation fee imposed. **Amenities:** Some: safes. **Activities:** exercise room. **Guest Services:** valet and coin laundry, area transportation.

⟨icons⟩

RENAISSANCE ATLANTA MIDTOWN
    (678)412-2400 **15**

▼▼▼ ▼▼▼
Hotel
$98-$309

R
RENAISSANCE®
HOTELS

AAA Benefit:
Members save 5%
or more!

Address: 866 W Peachtree St NW 30308 **Location:** I-75/85 exit 249D, just e to W Peachtree St NW, then 0.6 mi n. **Facility:** Sleek, contemporary décor, as well as a rooftop bar, are highlights at this stylish, upscale property set in the heart of Midtown. Guests enjoy the roomy layout and upscale furniture. 304 units. 21 stories, interior corridors. **Parking:** valet only. **Amenities:** safes. **Activities:** exercise room. **Guest Services:** valet laundry, area transportation.

⟨icons⟩

RESIDENCE INN BY MARRIOTT ATLANTA-DOWNTOWN
    (404)522-0950 **41**
▼▼▼ **Extended Stay Hotel.**
$89-$217 **Address:** 134 Peachtree St NW 30303 **Location:** I-75/85 exit 248C northbound, 0.4 mi w, then just s; exit 249A southbound to International Blvd, just w, then just s. **Facility:** 160 units, some two bedrooms and efficiencies. 20 stories, interior corridors. **Parking:** valet only. **Activities:** exercise room. **Guest Services:** valet and coin laundry.

AAA Benefit:
Members save 5%
or more!

⟨icons⟩

Get up to 20 percent off Hertz rentals
PLUS exclusive everyday member benefits

RESIDENCE INN BY MARRIOTT
ATLANTA-MIDTOWN/GEORGIA TECH   (404)872-8885 **9**
▼▼▼ **Historic Extended Stay Hotel.** $125-$237 **Address:** 1041 W Peachtree St NW 30309 **Location:** I-75/85 exit 250 (10th St), just e to W Peachtree St, then just n; corner of 11th St. **Facility:** This brick, mid-rise building dates back to 1924 but has contemporary décor that appeals to modern travelers. Many rooms feature a separate sitting area and cozy bedroom layouts. 90 kitchen units. 7 stories, interior corridors. **Parking:** on-site (fee). **Activities:** exercise room. **Guest Services:** valet and coin laundry.

AAA Benefit:
Members save 5%
or more!

⟨icons⟩

RESIDENCE INN BY MARRIOTT ATLANTA MIDTOWN
PEACHTREE AT 17TH   (404)745-1000 **1**

▼▼▼ ▼▼▼
Extended Stay
Hotel
$118-$227

Residence
Inn®
Marriott

AAA Benefit:
Members save 5%
or more!

Address: 1365 Peachtree St NE 30309 **Location:** I-75/85 exit 251 northbound; exit 250 (17th St) southbound, 0.5 mi e to Peachtree St. **Facility:** 160 units, some two bedrooms, efficiencies and kitchens. 7 stories, interior corridors. **Parking:** valet only. **Terms:** check-in 4 pm. **Activities:** exercise room. **Guest Services:** valet and coin laundry. **Featured Amenity:** full hot breakfast.

⟨icons⟩

SHELLMONT INN BED & BREAKFAST   (404)872-9290 **16**
▼▼▼ **Historic Bed & Breakfast.** $185-$400 **Address:** 821 Piedmont Ave NE 30308 **Location:** I-75/85 exit 249D, just e, then 0.7 mi n. **Facility:** This home features secluded verandas, original architectural details and luxurious bathrooms. Located near downtown in the historic district, guests are within walking distance of Piedmont Park. 5 units, some two bedrooms. 2 stories (no elevator), interior corridors. **Terms:** 2 night minimum stay - weekends, 7 day cancellation notice-fee imposed. **Guest Services:** valet laundry.

⟨icons⟩

(See map & index p. 66.)

SHERATON ATLANTA HOTEL   (404)659-6500 **33**

Hotel
$69-$599

AAA Benefit:
Members save up to 15%, plus
Starwood Preferred Guest®
benefits!

Address: 165 Courtland St NE 30303 **Location:** I-75/85 exit 249A southbound; exit 248C northbound, just w. **Facility:** 763 units. 4-12 stories, interior corridors. **Parking:** on-site (fee) and valet. **Terms:** cancellation fee imposed. **Amenities:** safes. **Dining:** 2 restaurants, also, Fandangles Restaurant & Bar, see separate listing. **Pool(s):** heated indoor. **Activities:** hot tub, exercise room. **Guest Services:** valet and coin laundry, boarding pass kiosk.

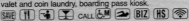

Sheraton
ATLANTA HOTEL

**763 expansive,
completely renovated
rooms and suites,
surrounded by
Atlanta's newest
attractions.**

STAYBRIDGE SUITES - ATLANTA MIDTOWN
(404)877-9495 **21**

Hotel
$119-$499

Address: 23 Linden Ave NW 30308 **Location:** I-85 exit 249D southbound; exit 249C northbound, just e. **Facility:** 102 kitchen units. 6 stories, interior corridors. **Parking:** on-site (fee) and valet. **Terms:** cancellation fee imposed. **Activities:** exercise room. **Guest Services:** valet and coin laundry. **Featured Amenity:** full hot breakfast.

STONEHURST PLACE BED & BREAKFAST
404/881-0722 **14**

Bed & Breakfast. Rates not provided. **Address:** 923 Piedmont Ave NE 30309 **Location:** I-75 exit 251 (10th St), 0.6 mi e to Juniper St, just s to 8th St, just e to Piedmont Ave, then just n. **Facility:** This historic home has been beautifully modernized to provide a unique experience for travelers tired of cookie-cutter hotels. Gather in one of the multiple social areas and relax in southern comfort. 6 units. 2 stories (no elevator), interior corridors. **Terms:** check-in 4 pm, age restrictions may apply.

TWELVE
HOTELS & RESIDENCES

TWELVE Hotel Atlantic Station
361 17th Street NW
Atlanta, GA 30363
www.marriott.com/atlas
1.887.557.0615

TWELVE Hotel Centennial Park
400 West Peachtree St.
Atlanta, GA 30308
www.marriott.com/atlpk
1.877.557.0686

Make a good trip great with insight
and ideas from AAA/CAA travel experts

(See map & index p. 66.)

TWELVE ATLANTIC STATION, AUTOGRAPH COLLECTION
(404)961-1212

Extended Stay Hotel
$149-$409

AUTOGRAPH COLLECTION® HOTELS **AAA Benefit:** Members save 5% or more!

Address: 361 17th St NW 30363 **Location:** I-75 exit 251 northbound; exit 250 southbound, just w; in Atlantic Station. **Facility:** 101 kitchen units, some two bedrooms. 6 stories, interior corridors. **Parking:** on-site (fee) and valet. **Amenities:** safes. **Dining:** Lobby Bar & Bistro, see separate listing. **Pool(s):** outdoor. **Activities:** exercise room. **Guest Services:** valet laundry. (See ad p. 106.)

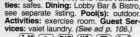

TWELVE CENTENNIAL PARK, AUTOGRAPH COLLECTION
(404)418-1212

Extended Stay Hotel
$170-$409

AUTOGRAPH COLLECTION® HOTELS **AAA Benefit:** Members save 5% or more!

Address: 400 W Peachtree St NW 30308 **Location:** I-75/85 exit 249C, 0.4 mi s; jct W Peachtree St NW. **Facility:** 102 kitchen units, some two bedrooms. 16 stories, interior corridors. **Parking:** on-site (fee) and valet. **Amenities:** safes. **Dining:** Room at Twelve, see separate listing. **Pool(s):** outdoor. **Activities:** exercise room. **Guest Services:** valet laundry. (See ad p. 106.)

W ATLANTA DOWNTOWN
(404)582-5800

Contemporary Hotel
$145-$349

W HOTELS **AAA Benefit:** Members save up to 15%, plus Starwood Preferred Guest® benefits!

Address: 45 Ivan Allen Jr Blvd 30308 **Location:** I-75/85 exit 249C, just s. **Facility:** "Sexy, sophisticated modernism" describes this ultra-contemporary urban oasis. The trendy rooms may be modestly sized, but the breathtaking cityscapes make the rooms feel spacious. 237 units. 16 stories, interior corridors. **Parking:** valet only. **Terms:** cancellation fee imposed. **Amenities:** safes. **Dining:** BLT Steak, see separate listing, entertainment. **Pool(s):** heated outdoor. **Activities:** exercise room, spa. **Guest Services:** valet laundry, area transportation.

W ATLANTA MIDTOWN HOTEL
(404)892-6000

Contemporary Hotel
$159-$359

W HOTELS **AAA Benefit:** Members save up to 15%, plus Starwood Preferred Guest® benefits!

Address: 188 14th St NE 30361 **Location:** I-75/85 exit 250 (14th St), 0.5 mi e. Adjoins a shopping mall in Art-Center District. **Facility:** With decor inspired by the trendy hotels of NYC, this property offers a hip, urban vibe unique to the property. The impressive city views make the rooms feel larger than they are in reality. 466 units. 27 stories, interior corridors. **Parking:** on-site (fee) and valet. **Terms:** cancellation fee imposed. **Amenities:** safes. **Dining:** nightclub. **Pool(s):** outdoor. **Activities:** sauna, steamroom, exercise room, spa. **Guest Services:** valet laundry, area transportation.

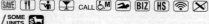

THE WESTIN PEACHTREE PLAZA
404/659-1400

Hotel
Rates not provided

AAA Benefit: Members save up to 15%, plus Starwood Preferred Guest® benefits!

Address: 210 Peachtree St NW 30303 **Location:** I-75/85 exit 248C northbound, 0.4 mi w; exit 249C southbound, 0.5 mi s. **Facility:** A visually stimulating combination of modern industrial design and organic décor accents make this a one-of-a-kind hotel. Cozy rooms feature high-end finishes and stunning views of the city skyline. 1073 units. 73 stories, interior corridors. **Parking:** on-site (fee) and valet. **Amenities:** video games, safes. **Dining:** 2 restaurants, also, The Sun Dial, see separate listing. **Pool(s):** heated indoor. **Activities:** massage. **Guest Services:** valet laundry, boarding pass kiosk.

THE WESTIN
PEACHTREE PLAZA
ATLANTA

An Atlanta icon & the ideal address in Downtown. Each room offers breathtaking views of the city.

WHERE TO EAT

AGAVE 404/588-0006
Southwestern. Fine Dining. $8-$24 **AAA Inspector Notes:** Representative of this restaurant's eclectic Southwestern cuisine is the outstanding free-range venison, which is marinated in red wine, herbs and honey and served over a spicy tomato purée. Southwestern influences also characterize the dining room, where diners can relax in front of a roaring fireplace during the winter or outdoors on the patio overlooking the city in the summer. **Features:** full bar, patio dining. **Reservations:** suggested. **Address:** 242 Boulevard SE 30312 **Location:** 0.9 mi s of jct Freedom Pkwy.

(See map & index p. 66.)

ALMA COCINA   404/968-9662   (90)

▼▼▼ Mexican. Fine Dining. $7-$29 **AAA Inspector Notes:** Fresh and contemporary Mexican cuisine is executed beautifully and deliciously at this spot with noteworthy regional and Latin influences. The ceviche is a great way to start as are inventive soups and salads. Small plates such as taquitos and huaraches are great for sharing. The chiles rellenos and the grilled pork tenderloin are creative entrées. **Features:** full bar, patio dining, happy hour. **Reservations:** suggested. **Address:** 191 Peachtree St NE 30303 **Location:** I-75/85 exit 248C northbound, 0.4 mi w, then just s; exit 249A southbound, just s to Andrew Young International Blvd, just w, then just s. **Parking:** on-site and street.

L   D   CALL &M

ALON'S BAKERY & MARKET   404/872-6000   (10)

▼ Deli. Quick Serve. $6-$12 **AAA Inspector Notes:** The bakery tempts patrons with European desserts, pastries, artisan breads, salads and sandwiches. In the market are specialty wines, cheeses and prepared to-go foods. Indoor and patio seating encourage you to relax and enjoy while you indulge! **Features:** beer & wine, patio dining. **Address:** 1394 N Highland Ave 30306 **Location:** Jct Virginia and Highland aves, 1.5 mi n. **Parking:** street only.

B   L   D   🐕

AMAZZA   404/228-1036   (102)

▼▼ Italian. Pizza. Casual Dining. $5-$22 **AAA Inspector Notes:** This trendy, artisan pizza shop offers delicious brick-oven pizza in a relaxed atmosphere. My favorite is the margherita pizza but the terra (white sauce, wild mushrooms, mozzarella, goat cheese and truffle oil) is delicious as is the spicy inferno (sopressata, mozzarella and Calabria peppers). Be sure to save room for dessert. **Features:** full bar. **Address:** 591 SE Edgewood Ave 30312 **Location:** I-75 exit 248B (Edgewood Ave), just e. **Parking:** on-site and street.

L   D   CALL &M

APRES DIEM   404/872-3333   (34)

▼▼ European. Casual Dining. $8-$25 **AAA Inspector Notes:** Enjoy the feel of a European coffee house but do not be fooled as there is much more to this unconventional eatery than that. Start the meal with some hummus, crab cakes or pâte and end it with a delicious pastry. In between there are many sandwich options including the farmer's veggie melt which I thought was off the charts. At dinner roasted lamb is a great choice. **Features:** full bar, patio dining, Sunday brunch. **Address:** 931 Monroe Dr, Suite C-103 30308 **Location:** Jct 10th St, just s; in Midtown Promenade Shopping Center.

L   D   LATE

ATLANTA GRILL   404/659-0400   (92)

▼▼▼▼ American Fine Dining $14-$69 **AAA Inspector Notes:** The charm and beauty of this restaurant is showcased in the staid décor, historic photos of downtown Atlanta and the humorous oversize caricature murals. The seasonal veranda provides diners a relaxing alfresco option or a "cheaters booth" gives a more intimate experience. The well executed menu features prime beef, chops and fresh seafood during the evening meal and a lighter fare of sandwiches, entrée salads and a few smaller entrée plates at lunch. **Features:** full bar, patio dining. **Reservations:** suggested. **Address:** 181 Peachtree St NE 30303 **Location:** I-75/85 exit 248C northbound, 0.4 mi w, then just s; exit 249A southbound, just s to International Blvd, just w, then just s; in The Ritz-Carlton, Atlanta. **Parking:** valet only.

B   L   D   CALL &M

ATMOSPHERE   678/702-1620   (5)

▼▼▼ French. Fine Dining. $11-$38 **AAA Inspector Notes:** In a charmingly restored home with a casual elegance, guests can enjoy traditional French food with a contemporary twist including excellent duck confit. Relax on the large patio area or request the back dining room for private parties. **Features:** full bar, Sunday brunch. **Address:** 1620 Piedmont Ave NE 30324 **Location:** Jct Monroe Dr, just n. **Parking:** street only.   L   D

BABETTE'S CAFE   404/523-9121   (52)

▼▼▼ European. Fine Dining. $16-$31 **AAA Inspector Notes:** This critically acclaimed bistro serves European provincial cuisine in a casual atmosphere. The mouthwatering cassoulet is popular. Tantalizing desserts include yummy homemade chocolate bread pudding with banana ice cream. **Features:** full bar, Sunday brunch. **Address:** 573 N Highland Ave NE 30307 **Location:** Jct Ponce de Leon and Highland aves, 0.5 mi s. **Parking:** valet only.

D

BACCHANALIA   404/365-0410   (27)

▼▼▼ ▼▼▼ New American. Fine Dining. $12-$85 **AAA Inspector Notes:** Gaze through a wall of windows into the chrome kitchen where the staff whips up a constantly evolving menu of creative and fresh New American cuisine with Northern California influences. Located in a transitioning warehouse district, this industrial space is softened with touches of velvet and soft lighting. On the way out, pick up items from the gourmet market up front. Note that guests enter the restaurant through the market. **Features:** full bar. **Reservations:** suggested. **Address:** 1198 Howell Mill Rd 30318 **Location:** I-75/85 exit 252, 1.4 mi w.   D

BANGKOK THAI RESTAURANT   404/874-2514   (8)

▼▼ ▼▼ Thai. Casual Dining. $6-$25 **AAA Inspector Notes:** The establishment holds the distinction of being the first Thai restaurant to open its doors in Georgia. Diners can expect friendly, dependable service and tried-and-true traditional fare. The delicious food is a good value. **Features:** beer & wine. **Address:** 1492A Piedmont Ave NE 30309 **Location:** Jct Piedmont Ave and Monroe Dr, just s; in Ansley Square.   L   D

BANTAM & BIDDY   404/907-3469   (7)

▼▼ ▼▼ Southern Comfort Food. Casual Dining. $11-$16 **AAA Inspector Notes:** Three meals a day are served at this eatery which specializes in rotisserie chicken which comes with such sauces as piri piri, wasakaka, beer mustard and sweet Blue Ridge barbecue. Duck-fat fries, deviled eggs, boiled peanuts and chipotle hummus are great ways to get started and entrées include meatloaf, sautéed Maine salmon and pork schnitzel. **Features:** full bar. **Address:** 1544 Piedmont Ave NE 30324 **Location:** Jct Monroe Dr; in Ansley Mall.

B   L   D   CALL &M

BARAONDA CAFFÉ ITALIANO   404/879-9962   (51)

▼▼ ▼▼ Italian. Casual Dining. $8-$32 **AAA Inspector Notes:** Everyone should be so lucky as to have such a warm, intimate space in their neighborhood. On the menu are more than 20 types of pizza and calzones, as well as varied pasta dishes and other Italian standards. Due to its proximity to the Fox Theatre, this restaurant is a popular stop on show nights. It is also popular for corporate events and receptions. **Features:** full bar, Sunday brunch. **Reservations:** suggested. **Address:** 710 Peachtree St NE 30308 **Location:** I-75/85 exit 249D, 0.5 mi e to Peachtree St NE, then just n. **Parking:** street only.   L   D

BAR MARGOT   404/881-5913   (18)

▼▼▼ ▼▼▼ New American. Gastropub. $13-$36 **AAA Inspector Notes:** This is a lively bar at its heart, but a sampling of the unique menu may throw you a curve ball. The food is amazing. The seasonal menu has Mediterranean and Asian influences, so you can expect complex yet robust flavors. Meat, seafood and purely vegetarian dishes are available, and to guide you, the informally dressed staff will help with their surprisingly thorough knowledge of each dish. **Features:** full bar, happy hour. **Reservations:** suggested. **Address:** 75 14th St NE 30309 **Location:** I-75/85 exit 250 (14th St), 0.3 mi e; in Four Seasons Hotel Atlanta. **Parking:** valet only.

🍷   L   D   LATE   CALL &M

BELL STREET BURRITOS   404/815-0011   (2)

▼ Mexican. Casual Dining. $3-$8 **AAA Inspector Notes:** If you want a delicious, no fuss burrito in Atlanta, this is the place to go because they utilize fresh, natural ingredients prepared when you order. Save room for the popular sopaipillas. You won't regret it. **Address:** 1816 Peachtree St NW 30309 **Location:** I-75 exit 251A (17th St), 0.5 mi n on 17th St NW, then 0.7 mi w. **Parking:** on-site and street.

L   D   CALL &M   ✂

(See map & index p. 66.)

BELLY GENERAL STORE   404/872-1003   41

Sandwiches. Quick Serve. $2-$7 **AAA Inspector Notes:** This trendy, modern take on an old fashion general store is popular for its homemade cookies, breads, artisan sandwiches and organic coffee drinks. The cupcakes have gained a rabid following as well. **Address:** 772 N Highland Ave 30306 **Location:** Ponce de Leon Ave, e to N Highland Ave, then n. **Parking:** street only. B L

BLT STEAK   404/577-7801   69

Steak. Fine Dining. $14-$62 **AAA Inspector Notes:** Integrating the traditional elements of a French bistro with an American steakhouse, this spot blends a signature rich warmth and texture with the sophistication and style of Atlanta. I recommend asking the server for guidance with the variety of Prime cuts available. **Features:** full bar. **Reservations:** suggested. **Address:** 45 Ivan Allen Jr Blvd 30308 **Location:** I-75/85 exit 249C, just s; in W Atlanta Downtown. **Parking:** valet only. B L D CALL M

BOCADO   404/815-1399   46

American. Casual Dining. $8-$22 **AAA Inspector Notes:** This trendy, boutique restaurant offers a large bar and variety of beverages to accompany the farm-to-table cuisine. They are best known for the juicy Bocado burger stack, a staple on the seasonally changing menu. For a fresh air experience ask to dine on the patio. **Features:** full bar, patio dining. **Reservations:** suggested. **Address:** 887 Howell Mill Rd NW 30318 **Location:** I-75 exit 252, 1.5 mi w, then 0.4 mi s. L D CALL M

BOCCALUPO   404/577-2332   97

Italian. Casual Dining. $9-$19 **AAA Inspector Notes:** This friendly, neighborhood restaurant is great for date night, special occasions or any time you want a creative and filling meal. The menu changes regularly so ask the server for recommendations. Guests can expect fresh homemade pasta dishes and creative seafood entrées such as tuna cruda with fried green olives. Delicious desserts include panna cotta with ink squid cookie crumbles. **Features:** full bar, patio dining. **Reservations:** suggested. **Address:** 753 Edgewood Ave NE 30307 **Location:** I-75 exit 248B (Edgewood Ave), se onto Edgewood Ave, then 0.9 mi s on Waddell St NE. **Parking:** on-site and street. D CALL M

CAMELI'S GOURMET PIZZA JOINT   404/249-9020   49

Pizza. Casual Dining. $7-$23 **AAA Inspector Notes:** This is truly a neighborhood joint, as the name implies. But do not let that fool you. Considered by many to have the best pizza in Atlanta, this spot also offers other traditional Italian dishes, panini and a good choice of appetizers. Expect to find simple, but friendly service. A nice selection of craft beers is offered. **Features:** full bar. **Address:** 699 Ponce de Leon Ave 30308 **Location:** I-75/85 exit 249D, 0.5 mi e to Piedmont Ave NE, just n to Ponce de Leon Ave, then 1.5 mi e. L D

CAMELI'S PIZZA   404/522-1624   63

Pizza. Casual Dining. $5-$22 **AAA Inspector Notes:** Menu offerings at this spacious eatery include some traditional Italian dishes and what some consider to be the best pizza in Atlanta. Service is friendly and consistent and a great selection of beers, wines and liquors is available as well. **Features:** full bar, patio dining. **Address:** 337 Moreland Ave NE 30307 **Location:** Jct Euclid Ave, just s. L D LATE CALL M

CAROLYN'S GOURMET CAFE   404/607-8100   20

Sandwiches. Quick Serve. $6-$18 **AAA Inspector Notes:** Diners can count on fast, friendly service at this small spot with deck seating and a menu of salads, sandwiches, pizzas and desserts—all made freshly each day. If visiting at lunchtime, you will be in good company. **Features:** full bar. **Address:** 1151 W Peachtree St 30309 **Location:** I-75 exit 250 (14th St), just s of jct W Peachtree and 14th sts. **Parking:** on-site and street. L D

CHICAGO'S NANCY'S PIZZA   404/254-5103   56

Pizza. Quick Serve. $8-$31 **AAA Inspector Notes:** Guests here can sample Chicago-style pizza with deep-dish, thin or super-thin crust. Most people carry out their food or request delivery, so seating is limited, yet cozy. Sandwiches, wings and desserts also are available. **Address:** 265 Ponce de Leon Ave, Suite A 30308 **Location:** I-75/85 exit 249D, 1 mi e to Penn St, then just n. L D LATE

COOKS & SOLDIERS   404/996-2623   31

Basque. Fine Dining. $8-$34 **AAA Inspector Notes:** One of the more popular restaurants in the area, this trendy eatery offers a menu focused on quality and creativity. Options change regularly, so ask your server for recommendations. A staple of the menu is the chuletón, a delicious bone-in rib-eye big enough to share. The pastry chef is constantly churning out new masterpieces such as the chocolate and corn featuring pink peppercorn gelato and corn crème Anglaise. **Features:** full bar. **Reservations:** suggested. **Address:** 691 14th St NW 30318 **Location:** I-75 exit 250 (14th St), 1.4 mi w. **Parking:** valet and street only. D CALL M

COWTIPPERS   404/874-3751   6

Steak. Casual Dining. $6-$23 **AAA Inspector Notes:** Featuring all things meat ranging from creative takes on steaks, slow-cooked beef pot roast, barbecue pulled pork, hamburgers and baby back ribs. Such seafood dishes as blackened tilapia and orange teriyaki-glazed salmon are available for landlubbers. The boisterous Texas roadhouse is as comfortable as a pair of broken-in jeans. **Features:** full bar, patio dining. **Address:** 1600 Piedmont Ave NE 30324 **Location:** Jct Monroe Dr NE, just s. L D

CUTS STEAKHOUSE   404/525-3399   82

Steak. Fine Dining. $12-$40 **AAA Inspector Notes:** The beautiful décor is the perfect complement to excellent service and delectable butcher cuts in this downtown steakhouse. The menu features classic cuts such as the juicy rib-eye or prime rib as well as some Southern-inspired dishes. The pecan salmon and Southern fried lobster tail are popular seafood options. **Features:** full bar. **Address:** 60 Andrew Young Blvd 30303 **Location:** I-75/85 exit 249A southbound; exit 248C northbound, just w. **Parking:** on-site (fee). L D CALL M

DOC CHEY'S NOODLE HOUSE   404/888-0777   9

Asian. Casual Dining. $8-$10 **AAA Inspector Notes:** This funky, crowded restaurant offers a fun mix of dishes from Asian cultures, including dim sum, soups and salads, street food, Vietnamese basil rolls, Thai curries and Szechuan vegetable stir-fry. The large patio is an ideal spot for people watching. The food is a super value. **Features:** beer & wine, patio dining. **Address:** 1424 N Highland Ave 30306 **Location:** In Virginia-Highlands at University Dr; in Highland Walk. L D

DRESSED   404/347-3636   37

Sandwiches. Quick Serve. $4-$10 **AAA Inspector Notes:** Salads with style, artisan sandwiches, panini, soups and desserts (s'mores) can be found at this eatery. Guests can customize their salad with more than 70 toppings which include veggies, meats and cheeses, top it off with one or more of some 25 dressing choices. Mango tango, minted avocado and peanut butter and jelly smoothies also are great additions to any meal. **Features:** patio dining. **Address:** 950 W Peachtree St, Suite 240 30309 **Location:** I-75/85 exit 250 (10th St), just e to Spring St, just s to 9th St, just e to W Peachtree St, then just n; in Midtown Plaza. **Parking:** street only. L D CALL M

EATS   404/888-9149   47

American. Quick Serve. $5-$8 **AAA Inspector Notes:** This is one of Midtown's best kept secrets for no fuss, quick service, home style food. Create your own pasta or get a meat-and-two (or three) plate at the chicken and veggie counter. Jerk and lemon chicken are popular as are the Southern inspired side dishes. Don't be fooled by its modest appearance, the food here will fill you up and put a smile on your face! **Features:** beer only. **Address:** 600 Ponce de Leon Ave 30308 **Location:** Jct Highland Ave, just w.

ECCO   404/347-9555   42

European. Fine Dining. $15-$50 **AAA Inspector Notes:** Upscale touches enhance this casual neighborhood-style eatery, which blends contemporary and old-style décor. Fresh seasonal cuisine includes meats and cheeses, wood-fired pizza, pasta dishes and diverse entrées. Patrons can unwind in the large lounge or enjoy the beautiful weather on the front patio. **Features:** full bar, patio dining. **Reservations:** suggested. **Address:** 40 7th St NE 30308 **Location:** Jct Peachtree and 7th sts, just w. **Parking:** street and street. D CALL M

(See map & index p. 66.)

EINSTEIN'S
404/876-7925 (29)

♥♥♥ American. Fine Dining. $11-$24 AAA Inspector Notes: The waterfall wall at the entrance of this restaurant prepares guests for the tranquil setting that awaits. The centerpiece of the restaurant is a free-standing fireplace surrounded by leather benches. Burgers, sandwiches and tacos are popular and such staples as Carolina mountain trout always satisfy. Enjoy good weather on the spacious patio or slide up to the full bar. Features: full bar, Sunday brunch. Reservations: suggested. Address: 1077 Juniper St 30309 Location: Jct 12th St. Parking: street only. (L) (D)

FANDANGLES RESTAURANT & BAR
404/659-6500 (88)

♥♥♥ Southern American. Fine Dining. $12-$55 AAA Inspector Notes: Tucked away in a hotel is this stylish restaurant serving up a modern take on Southern cuisine. The hospitable wait-staff, beautiful décor and delicious menu options attract both hotel guests and locals. The dry-aged steaks are popular as are the North Carolina mountain trout and Scottish salmon. My favorite is the roasted corn and smoked chicken chowder along with the delicious homemade desserts. Ask about the gluten-free and vegetarian menu options. Features: full bar. Reservations: suggested. Address: 165 Courtland St NE 30303 Location: I-75/85 exit 249A southbound; exit 248C northbound, just w; in Sheraton Atlanta Hotel.

(⊟) (D)

FAT MATT'S RIB SHACK
404/607-1622 (1)

♥ Barbecue. Quick Serve. $4-$21 AAA Inspector Notes: Messy ribs and down-home barbecue are a great fix at this dive, which also serves up some dynamite blues each evening. Features: beer only, patio dining. Address: 1811 Piedmont Ave NE 30324 Location: I-85 exit 86 northbound, just n to Monroe Dr, just e to Piedmont Rd NE, then just s; exit 88 southbound, just e to Cheshire Bridge Rd, 1.5 mi e to Piedmont Rd NE, then just s. (L) (D)

FLYING BISCUIT CAFE
404/874-8887 (33)

♥♥ American. Casual Dining. $5-$15 AAA Inspector Notes: Near historic Piedmont Park, the friendly neighborhood restaurant in Midtown prepares eccentric vegetarian and Southern fare. Although this place is known for its namesake biscuits, the menu also lists choices such as scrambled tofu, chipotle barbecue salmon and stoup, a combination between soup and stew. Features: beer & wine. Address: 1001 Piedmont Ave NE 30309 Location: Jct 10th St. (B) (L) (D)

FONTAINE'S OYSTER HOUSE
404/872-0869 (21)

♥♥ Seafood. Casual Dining. $7-$26 AAA Inspector Notes: Raw oysters, fried oysters, oysters Rockefeller, scampi oysters and crab and bacon oysters are some of the preparations of this mollusk that diners can find at this oyster house. The old-style bar also specializes in New Orleans-style food items, including jambalaya, po'boys and muffulettas. Combination platters are available for the table and the bar scene is quite popular. Features: full bar, patio dining. Address: 1026 1/2 N Highland Ave NE 30306 Location: Jct Virginia and Highland aves. Parking: street only.

(L) (D) (LATE) CALL (⑉M)

FOX BROS BAR-B-Q
404/577-4030 (68)

♥♥ Barbecue. Casual Dining. $5-$17 AAA Inspector Notes: This popular family joint always is filled with locals because it offers some of the best barbecue in town. The flavors are rich and the portions are generous. I recommend the beef brisket or smoked chicken. Save room for a slice of homemade pie. Address: 1238 Dekalb Ave 30307 Location: I-285 exit Moreland Ave (US 23), just w, then 6.5 mi n. Parking: on-site and street. (L) (D) CALL (⑉M)

FRITTI
404/880-9559 (66)

♥♥ Regional Italian. Casual Dining. $9-$22 AAA Inspector Notes: In a former garage, this casual Italian eatery has an operating garage door for al fresco dining when the weather is appropriate. Notable preparations include the wood-fired pizza prepared according to traditional artisanal methods, but guests also appreciate the full selection of eclectic appetizers. Features: full bar, patio dining. Address: 309 N Highland Ave NE 30307 Location: Jct US 23/SR 42 and US 29/78/278, just w to N Highland Ave NE, 0.9 mi s. Parking: valet and street only. (L) (D)

F.R.O.G.S. CANTINA & TEQUILERIA
404/607-9967 (35)

♥♥♥ Southwestern. Casual Dining. $4-$20 AAA Inspector Notes: The atmosphere is casual inside and out, but the food and more than 50 tequilas are serious. The menu comprises traditional Mexican and Southwestern favorites. Fresh is another key word here, as preservatives find no place in this food. Features: full bar, patio dining. Address: 931 Monroe Dr NE 30308 Location: Jct 10th St, just s; in Midtown Promenade Shopping Center. (L) (D)

GLADYS KNIGHT'S SIGNATURE CHICKEN & WAFFLES
404/874-9393 (61)

♥♥ Southern. Casual Dining. $9-$17 AAA Inspector Notes: Good old-fashioned Southern specialties await at this Motown-inspired spot. Enjoy such deep-fried dishes as chicken, corn, tomatoes and catfish. Baked, grilled and smothered chicken also is available. Other favorites include collard greens, barbecue turkey sandwiches and vegetable plates. Do not miss the sweet potato cheesecake. Reservations: suggested. Address: 529 Peachtree St NE 30308 Location: I-75/85 exit 249A to Barker St, 0.3 mi w to Peachtree St, then 0.5 mi n; across from Crawford-Long Hospital.

(L) (D) CALL (⑉M)

GLENN'S KITCHEN
404/469-0700 (100)

♥♥♥ New American. Fine Dining. $12-$40 AAA Inspector Notes: This casually chic kitchen of simplicity and southern comfort offers plush seating and natural light creating an open, yet intimate, ambience. Enjoy apple cider brined pork chops, Scottish salmon and Georgia trout in an atmosphere of relaxed service. The menu changes regularly. Features: full bar, Sunday brunch. Address: 110 Marietta St SW 30303 Location: I-75/85 exit 248C northbound, 0.8 mi w, then just s; exit 249A southbound, just s to Baker St, just w, then just s; in Glenn Hotel, Autograph Collection. Parking: valet and street only. (B) (L) (D)

GORDON BIERSCH BREWERY RESTAURANT
404/870-0805 (43)

♥♥♥ American. Casual Dining. $10-$35 AAA Inspector Notes: As the name implies this restaurant features fresh, brewed-on-site beer which is crafted in a German tradition. What may not be evident is the wide variety of foods like meal-sized salads, burgers and sandwiches, pizza, pastas, steaks and seafood that is also a huge draw for an upscale, casual dining experience. Features: full bar. Address: 848 Peachtree St NE 30308 Location: Jct Peachtree and 5th sts, just n. Parking: valet and street only. (L) (D) (LATE)

GUNSHOW
404/380-1886 (105)

♥♥♥ New American. Casual Dining. $10-$20 AAA Inspector Notes: Though the restaurant is the very antithesis of formal dining, diners get a unique experience in which professional chefs prepare an individual dish then present it at the table. Diners then chose if they want to accept that masterpiece or wait for another. Family style seating is an interesting social experience that adds to the casual, energetic and fast paced atmosphere. In addition to an ever changing menu, the mixologists offer a cornucopia of creative cocktails prepared tableside. Features: full bar. Reservations: suggested. Address: 924 Garrett St 30316 Location: I-285 exit Moreland Ave (US 23), 5.1 mi n on Moreland Ave SE, 0.5 mi w on Glenwood Ave SE, just n on Bill Kennedy Way SE, then just e. Parking: street only. (D) CALL (⑉M)

HARD ROCK CAFE
404/688-7625 (84)

♥♥ American. Casual Dining. $12-$25 AAA Inspector Notes: Rock 'n' roll memorabilia decorates the walls of the popular theme restaurant. Live music on the weekends contributes to the bustling atmosphere. On the menu is a wide variety of American cuisine—from burgers and sandwiches to seafood, steaks and pasta. Features: full bar. Address: 215 Peachtree St NE 30303 Location: I-75/85 exit 248C northbound, 0.4 mi w; exit 249A southbound, just s; jct International Blvd. Parking: on-site (fee).

(SAVE) (L) (D) (LATE) CALL (⑉M)

HIGHLAND TAP
404/875-3673 (22)

♥♥ American. Casual Dining. $8-$36 AAA Inspector Notes: Descend down into this subterranean pub/restaurant and enjoy the delicious steaks and martinis that are hallmarks of this local favorite. The large dining area and casual atmosphere encourage patrons to unwind and socialize. Features: full bar, Sunday brunch. Address: 1026 N Highland Ave NE 30306 Location: Jct Virginia and Highland aves. (L) (D) (LATE)

(See map & index p. 66.)

JCT KITCHEN & BAR 404/355-2252 ⟨28⟩
▼▼ New Southern. Casual Dining. $7-$29 **AAA Inspector Notes:** Contemporary style merges with comfortable warmth in the open dining room, while live music in the upstairs bar enhances the atmosphere. Fried chicken is the signature dish on a menu of New Southern food. **Features:** full bar. **Reservations:** required. **Address:** 1198 Howell Mill Rd, Suite 18 30318 **Location:** I-75 exit 252, 1.4 mi w; in Westside Urban Market. L D CALL M

KEVIN RATHBUN STEAK 404/524-5600 ⟨77⟩
▼▼▼ Steak. Fine Dining. $19-$62 **AAA Inspector Notes:** Each prime cut of beef, including dry-aged selections, comes from Allen Brothers in Chicago. Pair up the choice with such creative sides as jalapeño cream corn or smoky braised greens with Kentucky hog jowl. If diners prefer seafood, try broiled Maine lobster or blackened red fish. Among the imaginative cold appetizers is venison tataki. Contemporary appointments decorate the hugely popular restored cotton warehouse, which is known for solid service. **Features:** full bar, patio dining. **Reservations:** suggested. **Address:** 154 Krog St 30307 **Location:** Jct Edgewood Ave, 0.3 mi n. **Parking:** valet only.
D CALL M

LANDMARK DINER 404/659-1756 ⟨99⟩
▼▼ Continental. Casual Dining. $6-$25 **AAA Inspector Notes:** When you think of a traditional diner you probably think of something just like this one. From the vinyl, padded benches to the sizzle and clanking from the open kitchen, this place is just a charming relic of the past. Serving all your favorite comfort foods around the clock, portion sizes here are large and the atmosphere is laid back. **Address:** 60 Luckie St 30303 **Location:** I-75/85 exit 249A southbound; exit 248C northbound, 0.5 mi s on Courtland Ave to Auburn Ave, then 0.3 mi s. **Parking:** street only.
B L D 24 CALL M

LA TAVOLA TRATTORIA 404/873-5430 ⟨23⟩
▼▼▼ Italian. Fine Dining. $8-$26 **AAA Inspector Notes:** In the trendy Virginia-Highlands area, this sleek, contemporary restaurant has a classic interior with granite tabletops, wood accents and modern artwork. Menu favorites include seared scallops with polenta and sautéed spinach and tomato-onion compote, and ricotta and sage ravioli. To complete the experience, the chef's sampling of signature desserts cannot be missed. A truly perfect date night restaurant. **Features:** full bar, patio dining, Sunday brunch. **Address:** 992 Virginia Ave NE 30306 **Location:** Jct N Highland and Virginia aves. **Parking:** street only. D

LEGAL SEA FOODS 678/500-3700 ⟨74⟩
▼▼▼ Seafood. Casual Dining. $10-$48 **AAA Inspector Notes:** Legal prides itself on a reputation for freshness and consistency. More than 40 varieties of seafood can be grilled, broiled, fried or prepared Cajun style. Try the clam chowder that has been served at every presidential inauguration since 1981. The nautically inspired dining room is upscale and attractive with its rich cherry wood paneling and intricately detailed model ships. **Features:** full bar. **Address:** 275 Baker St NW 30313 **Location:** Jct Baker and Marietta sts; in Hilton Garden Inn Atlanta Downtown. **Parking:** on-site and street. L D CALL M

LIVINGSTON 404/897-5000 ⟨57⟩
▼▼▼ New American. Fine Dining. $12-$37 **AAA Inspector Notes:** This stunning space deftly combines contemporary styling with the historic glamour of the hotel. Exotic preparations of lobster pirogi, Georgia mountain trout, pan-seared duck and glazed beef short ribs incorporate fresh local ingredients, as do such appetizers as charred octopus and pickled shrimp. **Features:** full bar, patio dining, Sunday brunch. **Reservations:** suggested. **Address:** 659 Peachtree St NE 30308 **Location:** I-75/85 exit 249D, 0.5 mi e to Peachtree St, then just n; in The Georgian Terrace Hotel. **Parking:** on-site (fee) and valet. B L D CALL M

LOBBY BAR & BISTRO 404/961-7370 ⟨16⟩
▼▼ American. Casual Dining. $8-$26 **AAA Inspector Notes:** This casual restaurant offers a contemporary décor and is located in the lobby of the hotel. The contemporary American cuisine features popular entrées such as grilled hanger steak and lamb chops. The lemon pepper trout is an excellent seafood option. **Features:** full bar, patio dining, Sunday brunch. **Address:** 361 17th NW 30363 **Location:** I-75 exit 251 northbound; exit 250 southbound, just w; in Atlantic Station; in TWELVE Atlantic Station. **Parking:** valet and street only.
B L D CALL M

THE LUMINARY 404/600-6199 ⟨93⟩
▼▼▼ French. Fine Dining. $14-$30 **AAA Inspector Notes:** Located inside the trendy Krog Street Market, this upscale French restaurant invites guests to relax and indulge. The menu changes regularly but the fresh oyster bar and the classic steak frites are menu staples. Desserts are made in house so save room for a delicious treat. **Features:** full bar, Sunday brunch. **Reservations:** suggested. **Address:** 99 Krog St 30307 **Location:** I-75 exit 248B (Edgewood Ave), just e, then just n. **Parking:** on-site and valet.
D CALL M

LURE 404/817-3650 ⟨25⟩
▼▼▼ Seafood. Fine Dining. $11-$34 **AAA Inspector Notes:** The grilled octopus and pork lettuce wraps, served with mixed herbs and spicy Vietnamese sauce, are amazing. Only the freshest seafood is served here. Other delicious entrées include pan-roasted monkfish, seared George's Bank sea scallops and grilled Arctic char filet. The creative sandwiches found at lunch are a cannot miss as are the shrimp tacos. **Features:** full bar, Sunday brunch. **Reservations:** suggested. **Address:** 1106 Crescent Ave NE 30309 **Location:** I-75/85 exit 250 (14th St), 0.4 mi e to Crescent Ave, then just s. **Parking:** valet only. L D CALL M

MALI RESTAURANT 404/874-1411 ⟨15⟩
▼▼ Thai. Casual Dining. $8-$17 **AAA Inspector Notes:** Good takes on Thai standards can be found here, including curries, noodles, spring rolls and soups. Many creative items include shrimp and diver's scallops sautéed with asparagus, onion, carrots and mushrooms in a sweet chili sauce and fried catfish filets sautéed with roasted sweet chili sauce and red curry paste. Large soft shell crab should also be noted. Sushi is available and is very popular. The dining room is crowded with more space on the patio. Service is spotty. **Features:** full bar, patio dining. **Address:** 961 Amsterdam Ave NE 30306 **Location:** Jct N Highland Ave, just w. **Parking:** on-site and street. L D

MARY MAC'S TEA ROOM 404/876-1800 ⟨53⟩
▼▼ Southern. Casual Dining. $6-$22 **AAA Inspector Notes:** This restaurant blends traditional Southern cuisine and warm service in an atmosphere reminiscent of an old boarding house. Established in 1945, this local favorite still makes everything from scratch just like they did in the beginning. **Features:** full bar. **Reservations:** suggested. **Address:** 224 Ponce de Leon Ave 30308 **Location:** Jct Ponce de Leon Ave and Myrtle St. L D

MAX LAGER'S WOOD-FIRED GRILL & BREWERY 404/525-4400 ⟨70⟩

American Casual Dining $9-$38
AAA Inspector Notes: In the downtown area, this brewpub occupies a converted warehouse with exposed brick walls and slate floors. The restaurant specializes in wood-fired cuisine and hand-crafted beverages. **Features:** full bar, patio dining. **Reservations:** suggested. **Address:** 320 Peachtree St NW 30308 **Location:** I-75/85 exit 249A to Baker St, 0.3 mi w to Peachtree St, then just n. **Parking:** street only. L D 🍴

MAX'S COAL OVEN PIZZERIA 404/974-2941 ⟨79⟩
▼▼ Pizza. Casual Dining. $7-$18 **AAA Inspector Notes:** Pizza is the focus here and they are cooked in the only genuine coal-burning oven in Georgia. Choose from a huge selection of pizzas and toppings such as meaty, veggie and traditional or build your own pizza from the plethora of toppings. The prosciutto and arugula is excellent and the tasty wings, sandwiches and salads also are very good. **Features:** full bar, patio dining. **Address:** 300 Marietta St NW 30313 **Location:** Jct International Blvd, just w. **Parking:** street only.
L D CALL M

MCCORMICK & SCHMICK'S 404/521-1236 ⟨96⟩
▼▼▼ Seafood. Fine Dining. $12-$39 **AAA Inspector Notes:** This place is all about seafood, which is imported from all over the world. Among good choices are Washington state oysters, Maine clams, delicate Hawaiian escolar and tuna from Ecuador. The club-like decor is cozy and the staff is attentive. **Features:** full bar, happy hour. **Address:** 190 Marietta St, Suite 200 30303 **Location:** I-75/85 exit 248C northbound; exit 249C southbound to International Blvd, then 0.5 mi w. L D

(See map & index p. 66.)

MEEHAN'S PUBLIC HOUSE   404/214-9821   89
Irish. Gastropub. $10-$19 **AAA Inspector Notes:** You'll feel like you're in a true Irish pub at this bustling neighborhood spot, where you'll quaff a Guinness or other traditional draft brew in between bites of fish and chips, shepherd's pie or bangers and mash. Also offered is a great selection of burgers and other sandwiches. Try the crab and artichoke dip while you're waiting for your main course. **Features:** full bar. **Address:** 200 Peachtree St NW 30303 **Location:** I-75/85 exit 248C northbound, 0.4 mi w; exit 249C southbound, 0.5 mi s. **Parking:** street only. L D LATE

MINERO   404/900-7900   50
Mexican. Casual Dining. $4-$15 **AAA Inspector Notes:** This small Mexican eatery, located inside a converted factory known as Ponce City Market, delivers big flavors in a trendy setting. Locals rave about the tacos al pastor, tacos carnitas and the fried catfish tacos. Start out with the queso fundido and a beer or cocktail from the bar. They also offer some interesting non-alcoholic beverages. **Features:** full bar. **Address:** 675 Ponce de Leon Ave NE 30308 **Location:** I-75/85 exit 248C, just e on SR 10, 0.5 mi n on Boulevard NE, then 0.8 mi e on North Ave NE. L D CALL ⛄M

MU LAN   404/877-5797   44
Chinese. Casual Dining. $6-$20 **AAA Inspector Notes:** In a lovely converted Victorian, this place offers some upscale twists on tried-and-true Chinese and Thai cuisine, including many dishes that emphasize seafood. **Features:** full bar, patio dining. **Address:** 824 Juniper St 30308 **Location:** Jct Juniper and 5th sts; in Midtown. **Parking:** on-site and street.
L D

MURPHY'S   404/872-0904   24
American. Fine Dining. $9-$23 **AAA Inspector Notes:** A comfortable local favorite with delicious food and contemporary décor, guests can enjoy the in-house bakery and wine shop found here. Menu favorites include truffle macaroni and cheese, slow-cooked salmon steak, grilled artichokes and the uber-rich Tollhouse pie. **Features:** full bar, patio dining, Sunday brunch. **Address:** 997 Virginia Ave NE 30306 **Location:** Jct Virginia and Highland aves, just w. L D

NAN THAI FINE DINING   404/870-9933   14
Thai. Fine Dining. $17-$45 **AAA Inspector Notes:** This contemporary and stunning dining room features an upscale lounge, water wall and fresh orchids on every table. The beautifully presented food creations include braised lamb tenderloin simmered in Northern Thai red curry, peanuts, potatoes and ginger along with the fried whole red snapper with kaffir lime, basil, sweet chili and garlic. **Features:** full bar. **Reservations:** suggested. **Address:** 1350 Spring St, Suite 1 30309 **Location:** I-75/85 exit 250 (16th St), just w to 17th St, 0.5 mi e to Spring St, then just s. L D CALL ⛄M

NIKOLAI'S ROOF   404/221-6362   73
Continental Fine Dining $31-$48   **AAA Inspector Notes:** This elegant restaurant, located on the 28th floor of Hilton Atlanta, offers a breathtaking panorama of the city. The fusion of French and Russian cuisine make this a unique dining experience. Menu options change based on market availability, and you might see items such as beef tenderloin with sweet potato hash and kale, foie gras with blueberry cream or magret duck breast with farro and forest mushrooms. Ask the bartender about the house-flavored vodka, but be careful. It packs a punch. **Features:** full bar. **Reservations:** suggested. **Address:** 255 Courtland St NE 30303 **Location:** I-75/85 exit 249A southbound; exit 248C northbound, just w to Piedmont Ave, just n to Baker St, then just w; in Hilton Atlanta. **Parking:** valet only. D

Recommend places you'd like us to inspect at AAA.com/TourBookComments

THE OCEANAIRE SEAFOOD ROOM   404/475-2277   26
Seafood. Fine Dining. $8-$49 **AAA Inspector Notes:** Fresh fish and shellfish are flown in daily from around the globe. The sleek, handsomely designed dining room has a raw bar and is tastefully appointed in an Art Deco/nautical theme. The menu notes the seafood available daily and the varied preparation styles, such as broiled, grilled and blackened. **Features:** full bar, happy hour. **Reservations:** suggested. **Address:** 1100 Peachtree St NW 30309 **Location:** I-75 exit 249D, just e to Linden Ave NW, then just n. **Parking:** valet and street only. L D

ONE EARED STAG   404/525-4479   78
American. Casual Dining. $9-$39 **AAA Inspector Notes:** This trendy, neighborhood restaurant offers a cool place to relax and socialize. The bar is a popular place to gather with friends or colleagues. The menu changes regularly but guests can expect fresh, inventive menu items such as grass-fed beef short ribs with pan-fried dates with white anchovies and pistachios. **Features:** full bar, Sunday brunch. **Reservations:** suggested. **Address:** 1029 Edgewood Ave NE 30307 **Location:** I-20 exit 60B (US 23 N/Moreland Ave NE), 1.5 mi to DeKalb Ave NE, 0.5 mi to Hurt St NE, then just w. **Parking:** street only. L D CALL ⛄M

ONE. MIDTOWN KITCHEN   404/892-4111   11
New American. Fine Dining. $18-$40 **AAA Inspector Notes:** This restaurant has the perfect blend of a contemporary dining experience mixed with Southern hospitality. Tucked away in a residential area, this hidden gem offers a delicious variety of dishes such as confit rabbit leg, wood-grilled quail and chicken liver and foie gras mousse with apricot bourbon chutney and grilled farm bread. For a special treat ask to sit in the glass-enclosed patio. **Features:** full bar. **Reservations:** suggested. **Address:** 559 Dutch Valley Rd NE 30309 **Location:** Jct Monroe Dr, 0.3 mi w. D CALL ⛄M

THE OPTIMIST   404/477-6260   45
Seafood. Fine Dining. $10-$30 **AAA Inspector Notes:** This contemporary take on a fish camp offers some of the very best seafood in the city. You will definitely want to start at the oyster bar for some excellent cold water choices, and the peel-and-eat shrimp is a don't miss. Move into the dining room and enjoy both creative and simple takes on halibut, grouper, New England cod and the sublime duck fat-poached swordfish. Great sides include corn milk hushpuppies, bok choy and assorted mushrooms. Complete your meal with a sumptuous dessert. **Features:** full bar, patio dining. **Reservations:** suggested. **Address:** 914 Howell Mill Rd 30318 **Location:** Jct 10th St, just s. L D CALL ⛄M

OSTERIA 832   404/897-1414   36
Italian. Casual Dining. $6-$15 **AAA Inspector Notes:** In the historic Virginia-Highlands neighborhood, this casual Italian eatery presents a menu of pizza and pasta dishes to satisfy any appetite. Very popular with families and those looking for gluten-free options. **Features:** beer & wine, patio dining, Sunday brunch. **Address:** 832 N Highland Ave 30306 **Location:** Ponce de Leon Ave, e to N Highland Ave, then n. D

PACIFIC RIM BISTRO   404/893-0018   71
Pacific Rim. Fine Dining. $9-$30 **AAA Inspector Notes:** Chinese, Korean and Thai flavors combine in an Asian fusion that delights at this chic, downtown restaurant. The spicy seven-flavored beef is rich and flavorful and other dishes such as chin pei duck, lemon grass-crusted salmon and lamb tenderloin make for great entrées. The bento boxes are popular at lunch and the sushi is a crowd favorite. **Features:** full bar, patio dining, happy hour. **Reservations:** suggested. **Address:** 303 Peachtree Center Ave NE 30308 **Location:** I-75/85 exit 249A southbound, just s to International Blvd, just w, then 0.3 mi n; exit 248C northbound, just w, then 0.3 mi w. **Parking:** street only. L D

PAPI'S CUBAN & CARIBBEAN GRILL   404/607-1525   54
Cuban. Casual Dining. $6-$15 **AAA Inspector Notes:** The downtown location of this popular Cuban and Caribbean grill offers the same delicious cuisine as its sister restaurants in the Atlanta area. Try the classic ropa vieja or vaca frita, they are both delicious. I always save room for dessert and the flan is the perfect after-dinner treat. **Features:** full bar. **Address:** 216 Ponce De Leon Ave NE 30308 **Location:** I-75 exit 249B, stay left off exit towards Civic Center, then just e. **Parking:** street only. L D

(See map & index p. 66.)

THE PIG & THE PEARL   404/541-0930   (12)
▼▼▼ Barbecue Seafood. Casual Dining. $7-$26 **AAA Inspector Notes:** This restaurant specializes in smokehouse delights and raw oysters. You will find upscale décor and a full bar for socializing with friends. The oyster bar happy hour is a popular feature, but save room for the delicious beef brisket or St. Louis-style spare ribs. The house sauces add a real punch to the smoky goodness of the barbecue. **Features:** full bar, patio dining, Sunday brunch, happy hour. **Address:** 1380 Atlantic Dr 30363 **Location:** I-75 exit 251 northbound; exit 250 southbound, just w; in Atlantic Station. **Parking:** on-site (fee). L D CALL &M

PITTYPAT'S PORCH   404/525-8228   (85)
▼▼ ▼▼ Regional Southern. Casual Dining. $14-$29 **AAA Inspector Notes:** This quaint bistro drips Southern charm, providing a touch of country in the middle of the big city. For dinner, savor the freshness of scrumptious pork tenderloin with curried peanut sauce or house favorite, Aunt PittyPat's fried chicken. For dessert, try the Georgia peach cobbler with cinnamon ice cream. Mint Juleps are a specialty of the house. This is a popular place for locals and tourists so reservations are recommended. **Features:** full bar. **Reservations:** suggested. **Address:** 25 Andrew Young International Blvd NW 30303 **Location:** I-75/85 exit 249A southbound; exit 248C northbound, 0.5 mi w. **Parking:** on-site (fee). D

PLANET BOMBAY   404/688-0005   (59)
▼▼▼▼ Indian. Casual Dining. $10-$25 **AAA Inspector Notes:** Nibble on several varieties of naan while savoring filling lunch and dinner preparations at this spot. Traditional dishes, such as tandoori items, and some good curry entrées are offered. The samosas, both chicken and vegetable, are a good way to start the meal and homemade Indian ice cream or rice pudding are good ways to end it. **Features:** beer & wine. **Address:** 451 Moreland Ave NE 30307 **Location:** Jct Moreland and Colquitt aves, just n. **Parking:** street only. L D

PRIME MERIDIAN   404/818-4450   (94)
▼▼▼▼ Continental. Fine Dining. $11-$36 **AAA Inspector Notes:** Look out over Centennial Park and the Atlanta skyline while enjoying a meal of steak, seafood or regional fare prepared with a Southern flair. Ingredients are fresh and locally sourced. **Features:** full bar, Sunday brunch. **Reservations:** suggested. **Address:** 100 CNN Center 30303 **Location:** I-75/85 exit 248C northbound, 0.8 mi w; exit 249C southbound to International Blvd, 0.5 mi w; in Omni Hotel at CNN Center. B L D CALL &M

PROOF BAKESHOP   678/705-3905   (81)
▼ Breads/Pastries Sandwiches. Buffet Style. $2-$10 **AAA Inspector Notes:** This trendy neighborhood bakery invites patrons to gather and relax. Fresh breads, pastries and sandwiches are made with fresh, healthy ingredients. Or take your coffee to go and mosey around the historic neighborhood and enjoy the charm of Atlanta. **Address:** 100 Hurt St 30307 **Location:** US 23, w to Moreland Ave, 6.5 mi to Dekalb Ave NE, then just n to Hurt St NE.
B L CALL &M

PUBLIK DRAFT HOUSE   404/885-7505   (55)
▼▼ American. Gastropub. $5-$15 **AAA Inspector Notes:** This locally owned bar in a bustling downtown location offers a casual menu. Neighboring the historic Fox Theatre, this is a popular pre- or post-show hangout. The menu features a fresh menu with such favorites as a lamb burger, kale Caesar salad and Korean-style wings. **Features:** full bar. **Address:** 654 Peachtree St 30308 **Location:** I-75 exit 249B (Pine St), just n on Peachtree St NE. **Parking:** street only.
L D LATE

RATHBUN'S   404/524-8280   (95)
▼▼▼▼ New American. Fine Dining. $18-$43 **AAA Inspector Notes:** Highly capable servers work this trendy, warehouse-style setting, where diners review a menu of superb, highly creative American dishes. Steaks are the point of emphasis with bone-in rib-eyes, center-cut fillets and rosemary basted flat-iron steaks. The Maine lobster and roasted green chile taco is a crowd favorite as is the roasted bone marrow. **Features:** full bar, patio dining. **Reservations:** suggested. **Address:** 112 Krog St, Suite R 30307 **Location:** Jct Edgewood Ave, just n. **Parking:** valet and street only. D CALL &M

RAY'S IN THE CITY   404/524-9224   (76)
▼▼▼▼ Seafood. Fine Dining. $12-$65 **AAA Inspector Notes:** Fresh seafood arrives up to five times daily at the downtown hot spot. In addition to sushi and oyster bar offerings, the menu includes a lengthy list of fresh fish, steak and lobster. Among house specialties are shrimp and crawfish etouffee, grilled salmon Oscar and Maryland-style lump crab cakes. **Features:** full bar. **Address:** 240 Peachtree St 30303 **Location:** Jct Harris St, just n; across from Peachtree Center MARTA Station. **Parking:** street only.
L D

REUBEN'S DELI   404/589-9800   (103)
▼ Sandwiches Breakfast. Quick Serve. $6-$9 **AAA Inspector Notes:** This place has been a downtown Atlanta hot spot since 1996 for serving staples like burgers, hot dogs, wraps and breakfast. Signature sandwiches include the Godfather, American, turkey club, pastrami, corned beef and liverwurst. The Atlanta, Chicago and New York dogs are must haves and salads, soups and desserts round out the menu. Lattes, cappuccinos and hot cocoa are popular beverage choices. **Address:** 57 Broad St NW 30303 **Location:** Jct Forsyth St, just w. **Parking:** on-site and street.
B L

RIBALTA   404/249-7019   (30)
▼▼▼ Italian. Casual Dining. $10-$32 **AAA Inspector Notes:** Located in the busy downtown district, this charming, boutique restaurant is tucked away among the office buildings. Try one of the signature thin-crust pizzas or pasta dishes that will transport taste buds to the rolling hills of the Italian countryside. **Features:** full bar. **Reservations:** suggested. **Address:** 1080 Peachtree St NE, Unit 9 30309 **Location:** I-75 exit 250 (10th St/14th St), just NW on 10th St, then just n. **Parking:** street only. L D CALL &M

RISING ROLL   404/815-6787
▼ Sandwiches. Quick Serve. $7-$10 **AAA Inspector Notes:** As upscale as a self-serve delicatessen can be, this office complex location can be busy during the lunch rush. Choose a tasty sandwich made on baked-in-house bread or try soup or salad all created with distinctive and creative twists. **Address:** 1180 W Peachtree St, Suite 190 30309 **Location:** I-75/85 exit 250 (14th St), just e; in Atlantic Center Plaza Building. **Parking:** on-site and street.
B L CALL &M

ROOM AT TWELVE   404/418-1250   (67)
▼▼▼ Steak Sushi. Fine Dining. $10-$40 **AAA Inspector Notes:** A modern industrial setting provides the backdrop for this combination steakhouse and sushi restaurant. Well-prepared dishes and a semi-casual atmosphere make this an ideal place to gather with friends, co-workers or family. Try the rib-eye for melt-in-your-mouth deliciousness or the pecan-crusted Georgia trout. Cozy up to the sushi bar to watch the chefs at work on the shiro maguro roll or Mexican roll. **Features:** full bar. **Reservations:** suggested. **Address:** 400 W Peachtree St NW 30308 **Location:** I-75/85 exit 249C, 0.4 mi s; jct W Peachtree St NW; in TWELVE Centennial Park. **Parking:** on-site (fee). B L D CALL &M

ROSA MEXICANO   404/347-4090   (13)
▼▼▼ Mexican. Casual Dining. $5-$20 **AAA Inspector Notes:** This trendy restaurant offers classic Mexican cuisine with modern flair. The colorful dining room catches the eye but only until the food is served. I recommend starting with the guacamole, prepared tableside with a mortar and pestle. The mole poblano or mahi mahi tacos are excellent choices. Most dishes are served with corn tortillas but flour tortillas are available upon request. **Features:** full bar. **Address:** 245 18th St 30363 **Location:** I-75 exit 251 northbound; exit 250 southbound, just w; in Atlantic Station. **Parking:** street only. L D CALL &M

R. THOMAS DELUXE GRILL   404/872-2942   (3)
▼▼ Natural/Organic. Casual Dining. $9-$20 **AAA Inspector Notes:** In a garden atmosphere replete with exotic birds, this funky and distinctive eatery serves healthy fare and is remarkably veggie-friendly. Some tasty choices include free-range chicken, ginger salmon, ahi tuna, spicy fish tacos and a good selection of pasta dishes. Breakfast is served all day in this 24-hour spot. **Features:** beer & wine. **Address:** 1812 Peachtree Rd NW 30309 **Location:** Between Collier Rd and 26th St. B L D (24)

(See map & index p. 66.)

SAVAGE PIZZA 404/523-0500 58

WWW Pizza. Casual Dining. $6-$22 **AAA Inspector Notes:** Do not let the looks fool you. This is a busy joint but with a lot of charm and great New York-style, thin-crust pizza. Available by the slice or as a whole pie, there are many topping choices. Other menu selections include calzones and subs. Superheroes adorn the walls and ceilings throughout the dining room. **Features:** beer & wine. **Address:** 484 Moreland Ave NE 30307 **Location:** Jct Euclid and Moreland aves, just n. L D

SERPAS 404/688-0040 91

WWW American. Fine Dining. $16-$30 **AAA Inspector Notes:** Cajun and Creole influences, incorporated with Asian and Southwestern touches, can be found at this eatery. Consider highlights of slow-roasted boneless beef short ribs, flash-fried oysters and beignets with hot chocolate. The old cotton storage warehouse that houses this place has been tastefully redone while keeping the building's historical integrity intact. **Features:** full bar, patio dining, Sunday brunch. **Reservations:** suggested. **Address:** 659 Auburn Ave, Suite 501 30312 **Location:** At Pavilion in Studioplex. D CALL M

SLICE DOWNTOWN 404/917-1820 98

WWW Italian. Casual Dining. $8-$20 **AAA Inspector Notes:** Build your own whole pie or just a slice here at this appropriately named eatery. There are numerous toppings available such as potato, basil, sun-dried tomatoes, artichoke hearts, apple wood smoked bacon, goat cheese and pineapple as well as traditional favorites. There are some great sandwiches and calzones on the menu as well as spaghetti, veggie lasagna and chicken parmigiana. **Features:** full bar. **Address:** 85 Poplar St NW 30303 **Location:** Jct Fairlie St. L D LATE CALL M

SOTTO SOTTO 404/523-6678 65

WWWW Italian. Fine Dining. $17-$42 **AAA Inspector Notes:** There is something exciting about this authentic Italian eatery, from the peer-in kitchen, to the rough, sanded walls. Wood-roasted dishes, a few meats and homemade pasta in minimalist herb-enhanced sauce can be enjoyed amid bustle and a constant din. Lean on the helpful, knowledgeable staff to make the most of your meal. **Features:** full bar, patio dining. **Reservations:** suggested. **Address:** 313 N Highland Ave NE 30307 **Location:** Jct Ponce de Leon and N Highland aves, 0.8 mi s. **Parking:** valet only. D

SOUL VEGETARIAN II 404/875-0145 48

WWW Vegan. Casual Dining. $7-$16 **AAA Inspector Notes:** The vegan eatery prepares dishes with a decidedly Southern twist. Great vegetables include collards, corn and potatoes, while salads, soups, tempeh and tofu are among other choices. Everything is organic, and even the "ice cream" is free of dairy products. **Features:** Sunday brunch. **Address:** 652 N Highland Ave NE 30306 **Location:** Jct North and Highland aves, just s. L D CALL M

SOUTH CITY KITCHEN 404/873-7358 19

WWW New Southern. Fine Dining. $12-$48 **AAA Inspector Notes:** Contemporary Southern cuisine is served in a cool converted home with wide windows and high ochre-tinted walls. Food offerings are creative and complex in composition, and the servers are sharply knowledgeable of the menu and preparation styles. Ask about gluten-free menu options. **Features:** full bar, patio dining, Sunday brunch. **Reservations:** suggested. **Address:** 1144 Crescent Ave 30309 **Location:** I-75/85 exit 250 (14th St), 0.3 mi e to Crescent Ave, then just s. **Parking:** street only. L D

STATS 404/885-1472 80

WWW American. Gastropub. $9-$24 **AAA Inspector Notes:** This sprawling sports bar features five bars with numerous TV screens offering a plethora of game day options. A different take on typical bar food includes butterbean hummus, fish tacos and mountainous nachos. The atmosphere appeals to adults, yet children also are welcome. **Features:** full bar, patio dining. **Reservations:** suggested. **Address:** 300 Marietta St NW 30313 **Location:** Jct International Blvd, just w. **Parking:** street only. L D LATE

STEEL RESTAURANT & SUSHI LOUNGE 404/477-6111 38

WWW Asian. Casual Dining. $5-$29 **AAA Inspector Notes:** This modern, midtown restaurant offers an eclectic blend of Asian cuisine and an extensive sushi menu. The Mandarin chicken is a juicy blend of sweet and tangy as is the Thai coconut chicken soup. The box-pressed sushi, Mexi-Cali roll and strawberry field roll are exquisite. Also try the yellow jacket roll designed in support of nearby Georgia Tech. **Features:** full bar. **Reservations:** suggested. **Address:** 950 W Peachtree St 30309 **Location:** 1 blk s of 10th St; at Peachtree Plaza. **Parking:** on-site and street. L D CALL M

THE SUN DIAL 404/589-7506 86

WWW American. Fine Dining. $14-$57 **AAA Inspector Notes:** Romance thrives at this welcoming restaurant, where jazz infuses the dining room two nights a week. Atop the 73-story The Westin Peachtree Plaza, this restaurant rotates one full cycle per hour to treat diners to dramatic views of downtown Atlanta and beyond. Fresh ingredients enhance the flavors in contemporary American cuisine, such as the smoked trout starter and entrées of roasted lamb chops and pecan-crusted trout. The menu changes regularly to reflect market availability. **Features:** full bar, Sunday brunch. **Reservations:** suggested. **Address:** 210 Peachtree St NE 30303 **Location:** I-75/85 exit 248C northbound, 0.4 mi w; exit 249C southbound, 0.5 mi s; in The Westin Peachtree Plaza. **Parking:** valet only. L D

SUPERICA 678/791-1310 87

WWW Mexican. Casual Dining. $10-$32 **AAA Inspector Notes:** This restaurant brings the flavors of the Southwest right to the back door with a Tex-Mex-centric menu. Located inside the Krog Street Market, this is a great place to socialize, relax or bring the family. The menu features fresh, flavorful items such as hot tamales, steaming fajitas with hand-made tortillas, mesquite-grilled quail and enchiladas. They even serve breakfast food on the weekend. **Features:** full bar, Sunday brunch. **Reservations:** suggested. **Address:** 99 Krog St 30307 **Location:** I-75 exit 248B (Edgewood Ave), e on Edgewood Ave NE, then just n. **Parking:** on-site and valet. L D CALL M

SURIN OF THAILAND 404/892-7789 39

WW Thai. Casual Dining. $7-$20 **AAA Inspector Notes:** Authentic Thai cuisine is on the menu at this fashionable Virginia Highlands district restaurant. Diners can choose from various sauces, spices and marinades. The large, energetic dining room has an original tin ceiling and full bar service is available. **Features:** full bar. **Address:** 810 N Highland Ave 30306 **Location:** Jct Ponce de Leon and N Highland aves, just n. **Parking:** on-site and street. L D

TAMARIND SEED 404/873-4888 17

WWW Thai. Fine Dining. $12-$29 **AAA Inspector Notes:** A contemporary ambience, genteel service and delicious Thai dishes combine here for an exceptional experience. Favored by locals and celebrities alike, choice selections include spicy lamb with basil, roast duck panang curry and barbecue lemongrass chicken. **Features:** full bar. **Address:** 1197 Peachtree St NE, Suite 110 30361 **Location:** I-75/85 exit 250 (14th St), 0.5 mi e; in Colony Square. L D CALL M

THRIVE 404/389-1000 101

WWW New American. Fine Dining. $8-$29 **AAA Inspector Notes:** East meets West at this trendy lounge and restaurant. The menu features various sushi options and Southern favorites. While the menu changes seasonally expect options such as grilled grouper over a sushi rice cake with coconut curry and shrimp and grits. **Features:** full bar, happy hour. **Reservations:** suggested. **Address:** 101 Marietta St 30303 **Location:** I-75/85 exit 248C northbound, 0.8 mi w, then just n; exit 249A southbound, just s to Baker St, just w, then just n; in Centennial Tower. **Parking:** street only. L D CALL M

TIN LIZZY'S CANTINA 404/671-9450 83

WW Tex-Mex. Casual Dining. $4-$10 **AAA Inspector Notes:** This restaurant invites customers to relax, socialize and raise a glass to the good life. The menu features several saliva-inducing menu items such as a Korean barbecue pork taco, the "Three Little Pigs" nachos and my personal favorite, a grilled steak taco. Wash it all down with an ice-cold margarita while watching the game or swapping travel tales with your buddies. **Features:** full bar, patio dining. **Address:** 26 Andrew Young International Blvd 30303 **Location:** I-75/85 exit 249A southbound; exit 248C northbound, just w. **Parking:** street only. L D LATE CALL M

(See map & index p. 66.)

TRADER VIC'S   404/221-6339
♦♦ ♦♦ Polynesian. Casual Dining. $8-$45 **AAA Inspector Notes:** This exotic Polynesian establishment specializes in Chinese wood-fired ovens where meats are slow roasted for full flavor. The Imperial beef, miso orange glazed pork chop and macadamia crusted mahi mahi are all excellent recommendations. Try the bar's signature drink, the Peachtree Punch! **Features:** full bar. **Reservations:** suggested. **Address:** 255 Courtland St NE 30303 **Location:** I-75/85 exit 249A southbound; exit 248C northbound, just w to Piedmont Ave, just n to Baker St, then just w; in Hilton Atlanta. [D]

TUK TUK THAI FOOD LOFT   678/539-6181 [4]
♦♦♦♦♦♦ Thai. Fine Dining. $10-$21 **AAA Inspector Notes:** Named after a renowned symbol of Thailand, Tuk Tuk refers to a Thai taxi, one of which you'll see when you enter the downstairs foyer. The menu focuses on Thai street food like you might find in Bangkok. Larb kai and meing kum are favorites. The ambience offers a stylish blend of modern and traditional décor with intricate art pieces and projected images on the wall. This a popular location so be sure to call for reservations. **Features:** full bar, patio dining. **Reservations:** suggested. **Address:** 1745 Peachtree St NE, Suite Y 30309 **Location:** On Peachtree St; in Brookwood Place. [L] [D] CALL [&M]

TWIN SMOKERS BBQ   404/698-4707 [75]
♦♦ ♦♦ Barbecue. Casual Dining. $3-$12 **AAA Inspector Notes:** The great barbecue debate is settled here. It does not matter what style you prefer because you can get them all at this casual eatery—South Carolina mustard sauce, North Carolina-style vinegar sauce or the sweet/tangy taste of Kansas City and Memphis. The beef, pork and chicken always are fresh because they're smoked overnight to perfection. To finish, I recommend the trouble milk shake or the double trouble shake with a kick. **Features:** full bar. **Address:** 300 Marietta St NW 30313 **Location:** Jct International Blvd, just w. **Parking:** street only. [L] [D] CALL [&M]

TWO URBAN LICKS   404/522-4622 [60]
♦♦♦♦ New American. Casual Dining. $19-$40 **AAA Inspector Notes:** This spot is hard to find, hidden behind warehouses and industrial buildings and one might feel like a password is needed to get in. Make the effort, look for the small signs on the street and you are rewarded with bold food, friendly service and live blues in a fun, funky urban loft space. The display kitchen has a wood-fired hearth cooking up juicy, smoky steaks, roast chicken and some great fresh fish all done with a modern flair. **Features:** full bar, patio dining, Sunday brunch. **Address:** 820 Ralph McGill Blvd 30306 **Location:** Just w of Freedom Pkwy (SR 10); behind US Post office. **Parking:** valet only. [D] CALL [&M]

THE VARSITY   404/881-1706
♦♦ Hot Dogs Burgers. Quick Serve. $2-$10 **AAA Inspector Notes:** 'What'll you have?' is the question du jour at this absolute must for visitors to Atlanta. Employees shout the question from behind the long stainless steel counter, just as has been the tradition here for more than 75 years. The food is fussy, just burgers, dogs and a few other sandwiches with names like glorified burger or heavy dog, but the experience is one not to be missed. Also, the frozen orange drink is a real treat. **Address:** 61 North Ave NE 30308 **Location:** I-75/85 exit 249D, just e. [L] [D]

VICTORY SANDWICH BAR   404/709-2892 [64]
♦♦ ♦♦ Sandwiches. Casual Dining. $3-$8 **AAA Inspector Notes:** Is it a sandwich shop or is it a bar? This casual eatery serves up carbs, cocktails and conversation with a style that keeps the locals coming back daily. My favorite sandwiches are the "Mile High Club," "Porky's Revenge" and the popular "Banh Appetit for Destruction" with char-sui pork. The doors are open late for those midnight cravings or for a quick game of ping pong in the back. **Features:** full bar, patio dining. **Address:** 913 Bernina Ave NE 30307 **Location:** Jct US 23/SR 42 and US 29/78/278, just w to N Highland Ave NE, 0.9 mi s, then just ne on Copenhill Ave NE. **Parking:** on-site and street. [L] [D] [LATE] CALL [&M]

THE VORTEX BAR & GRILL   404/875-1667 [40]
♦♦ ♦♦ American. Casual Dining. $7-$11 **AAA Inspector Notes:** A huge selection of burgers and other pub fare are offered at this quirky eatery where the walls are covered in a plethora of selfie-inducing photographs, memorabilia and nostalgic items. Try the coronary bypass sirloin burger or the grilled cheesy mofo sandwich. I recommend starting with delicious turkey chili and ending with funnel cake fries. Be aware that this establishment is for guests aged 21 and over. **Features:** full bar. **Address:** 878 Peachtree St NE 30309 **Location:** Between 7th and 8th sts. **Parking:** street only. [L] [D] [LATE] [⚲]

WHITE OAK KITCHEN & COCKTAILS   404/524-7200 [72]
♦♦♦♦♦♦ New Southern. Casual Dining. $15-$38 **AAA Inspector Notes:** The ambience here is modern and casual, but guests still get warm Southern hospitality along with contemporary comfort cuisine that draws heavily on products from the local area. Creativity and culinary skill show through in dishes like rock shrimp beignets, trout with hominy, bacon and Brussels sprout leaves or fried chicken with pickled vegetables, green garlic grits and red-eye gravy. **Features:** full bar. **Reservations:** suggested. **Address:** 270 Peachtree St 30303 **Location:** Jct Baker St, just s; across from Peachtree Center. **Parking:** valet and street only. [L] [D] CALL [&M]

YEAH! BURGER   404/496-4393 [32]
♦♦ Burgers. Quick Serve. $5-$11 **AAA Inspector Notes:** You can garnish grass-fed beef, bison, turkey or veggie burger patties, as well as chicken sandwiches and hot dogs, with a wide choice of toppings and sauces. On the side, nibble fries, onion rings, fried pickles, red chili or coleslaw. All burgers are made in house with organic, natural ingredients. To drink, you can opt for a libation from the full bar. **Features:** full bar. **Address:** 1168 Howell Mill Rd, Suite E 30318 **Location:** I-75 exit 252 (Howell Mill Rd), 1.5 mi w. [L] [D] CALL [&M]

ZESTO   404/523-1973 [62]
♦♦ Burgers. Quick Serve. $4-$11 **AAA Inspector Notes:** Operating since 1949, this eatery has grown to include six locations. You can get wings, wraps, chicken, hot dogs, gyros and burgers, including the signature favorite Chubby Decker double burger. Daily specials also are tempting, as is the wonderful ice cream. Finish off the meal with an Arctic Blast made with popular candies. **Address:** 377 Moreland Ave NE 30307 **Location:** Jct Moreland and Euclid aves. [L] [D]

BUCKHEAD AREA
• **Restaurants p. 119**
• **Hotels & Restaurants map & index p. 72**

AC HOTEL BY MARRIOTT ATLANTA BUCKHEAD AT PHIPPS PLAZA   470/231-3030 [24]

♦♦♦♦♦♦
Contemporary Hotel
Rates not provided

AC HOTELS MARRIOTT

AAA Benefit: Members save 5% or more!

Address: 3600 Wieuca Rd NE 30326 **Location:** Jct Phipps Blvd NE and Peachtree Rd NE; in Phipps Plaza. **Facility:** 166 units. 6 stories, interior corridors. **Parking:** on-site and valet. **Amenities:** safes. **Pool(s):** heated indoor. **Activities:** exercise room. **Guest Services:** valet and coin laundry, area transportation. **Featured Amenity:** breakfast buffet.

[SAVE] CALL [&M] [⟷] [BIZ] [HS] [📶] [✕] [🖥] [▭]

(See map & index p. 72.)

ATLANTA MARRIOTT BUCKHEAD HOTEL & CONFERENCE CENTER   (404)261-9250

 Hotel $111-$296

AAA Benefit: Members save 5% or more!

Address: 3405 Lenox Rd NE 30326 **Location:** I-85 exit 88 southbound; exit 86 northbound, 1.8 mi n. Opposite Lenox Square. **Facility:** 349 units. 10 stories, interior corridors. **Parking:** on-site (fee) and valet. **Terms:** check-in 4 pm. **Dining:** 2 restaurants. **Pool(s):** heated outdoor. **Activities:** hot tub, exercise room. **Guest Services:** valet and coin laundry, boarding pass kiosk, area transportation.

COURTYARD BY MARRIOTT-BUCKHEAD   (404)869-0818 12

Hotel. $110-$344 **Address:** 3332 Peachtree Rd NE 30326 **Location:** SR 400 exit 2, just w to Piedmont Rd, then just e. **Facility:** 181 units. 10 stories, interior corridors. **Parking:** on-site (fee).

AAA Benefit: Members save 5% or more!

Pool(s): heated indoor. **Activities:** exercise room. **Guest Services:** valet and coin laundry, boarding pass kiosk, area transportation.

DOUBLETREE BY HILTON HOTEL ATLANTA-BUCKHEAD   404/231-1234 11

Hotel. Rates not provided. **Address:** 3342 Peachtree Rd NE 30326 **Location:** Jct Piedmont and Peachtree rds NE, just n. **Facility:** 230 units. 6 stories, interior corridors. **Parking:** on-site (fee) and valet. **Activities:** exercise room. **Guest Services:** valet laundry, area transportation.

AAA Benefit: Members save 5% or more!

EMBASSY SUITES HOTEL BY HILTON ATLANTA BUCKHEAD   (404)261-7733 15

 Hotel $99-$259

AAA Benefit: Members save 5% or more!

Address: 3285 Peachtree Rd NE 30305 **Location:** Jct Piedmont and Peachtree rds NE, 0.3 mi e. **Facility:** 316 units, some two bedrooms. 16 stories, interior corridors. **Parking:** on-site (fee) and valet. **Terms:** 1-7 night minimum stay, cancellation fee imposed. **Amenities:** video games, safes. **Pool(s):** outdoor, heated indoor. **Activities:** hot tub, exercise room. **Guest Services:** valet and coin laundry, area transportation. **Featured Amenity:** full hot breakfast.

FAIRFIELD INN & SUITES BY MARRIOTT ATLANTA BUCKHEAD   (404)846-0900 18

Hotel. $96-$194 **Address:** 3092 Piedmont Rd NE 30305 **Location:** Jct Piedmont and Peachtree rds NE, just s. **Facility:** 115 units. 5 stories, interior corridors. **Pool(s):** heated indoor. **Activities:** exercise room. **Guest Services:** valet and coin laundry, area transportation.

AAA Benefit: Members save 5% or more!

GRAND HYATT ATLANTA   (404)237-1234 16

 Hotel $129-$409

GRAND | HYATT
AAA Benefit: Members save 10%!

Address: 3300 Peachtree Rd NE 30305 **Location:** Corner of Peachtree and Piedmont rds. **Facility:** This sophisticated retreat invites you to relax in a large guest room with grand pillowtop beds and a marble accented bath. The hotel is easy walking distance to a variety of shops and restaurants. 439 units. 25 stories, interior corridors. **Parking:** on-site (fee) and valet. **Terms:** cancellation fee imposed. **Amenities:** safes. **Pool(s):** heated outdoor. **Activities:** sauna, steamroom, massage. **Guest Services:** valet laundry, boarding pass kiosk, area transportation.

HAMPTON INN ATLANTA BUCKHEAD   (404)233-5656 10

Hotel. $129-$209 **Address:** 3398 Piedmont Rd NE 30305 **Location:** SR 400 exit 2, just w to Piedmont Rd, then just e. **Facility:** 153 units. 6 stories, interior corridors. **Terms:** 1-7 night minimum stay, cancellation fee imposed. **Pool(s):** outdoor. **Activities:** exercise room. **Guest Services:** valet laundry, area transportation.

AAA Benefit: Members save up to 10%!

HOLIDAY INN EXPRESS & SUITES ATLANTA BUCKHEAD   404/949-4000 22

Hotel. Rates not provided. **Address:** 800 Sidney Marcus Blvd 30324 **Location:** I-85 exit 86 northbound, 1.9 mi n to Sidney Marcus Blvd, then just w; exit 88 southbound, just w to Sidney Marcus Blvd, then just w. **Facility:** 123 units. 6 stories, interior corridors. **Amenities:** safes. **Pool(s):** outdoor. **Activities:** exercise room. **Guest Services:** complimentary and valet laundry, area transportation.

HOMEWOOD SUITES-ATLANTA BUCKHEAD   (404)365-0001 4

Extended Stay Hotel. $119-$239 **Address:** 3566 Piedmont Rd 30305 **Location:** SR 400 exit 2, just s to Piedmont Rd, then 1 mi w. **Facility:** 92 efficiencies, some two bedrooms. 4 stories, interior corridors. **Terms:** 1-7 night minimum stay, cancellation fee imposed. **Amenities:** safes. **Pool(s):** outdoor. **Activities:** exercise room. **Guest Services:** valet and coin laundry, area transportation.

AAA Benefit: Members save up to 10%!

HYATT PLACE ATLANTA/BUCKHEAD   (404)869-6161 17

Hotel $109-$299

HYATT PLACE
AAA Benefit: Members save 10%!

Address: 3242 Peachtree Rd NE 30305 **Location:** Jct Peachtree and Piedmont rds NE, just s. **Facility:** 171 units. 8 stories, interior corridors. **Terms:** cancellation fee imposed. **Pool(s):** heated outdoor. **Activities:** exercise room. **Guest Services:** valet laundry, area transportation. **Featured Amenity:** full hot breakfast.

(See map & index p. 72.)

INTERCONTINENTAL BUCKHEAD ATLANTA
(404)946-9000 **14**

Hotel
$159-$389

Address: 3315 Peachtree Rd NE 30326 **Location:** Jct Piedmont and Peachtree rds NE, just e. **Facility:** The beautiful hotel offers a variety of luxurious amenities and a prime location in the heart of Buckhead. The incredible beds and alluring cityscape views may diminish your desire to leave the room! 422 units. 22 stories, interior corridors. **Parking:** on-site (fee) and valet. **Terms:** cancellation fee imposed. **Amenities:** safes. **Pool(s):** heated outdoor. **Activities:** hot tub, spa. **Guest Services:** valet laundry, boarding pass kiosk, area transportation.

JW MARRIOTT BUCKHEAD ATLANTA
(404)262-3344 **13**

Hotel
$140-$459

JW MARRIOTT

AAA Benefit:
Members save 5% or more!

Address: 3300 Lenox Rd NE 30326 **Location:** Jct Peachtree Rd. Adjoining Lenox Square Mall. **Facility:** A contemporary expression of elegance in stylish Buckhead, this hotel offers comfortable luxury in the guest rooms. The lobby features a restaurant and lounge perfect for socializing. 371 units, some two bedrooms. 25 stories, interior corridors. **Parking:** on-site (fee) and valet. **Terms:** check-in 4 pm. **Amenities:** video games, safes. **Dining:** 3 restaurants. **Pool(s):** heated indoor. **Activities:** sauna, hot tub, steamroom, massage. **Guest Services:** valet laundry, area transportation.

MANDARIN ORIENTAL, ATLANTA
404/995-7500 **6**

Boutique Hotel. Rates not provided. **Address:** 3376 Peachtree Rd NE 30326 **Location:** Jct Peachtree and Lenox rds, just s. **Facility:** This elegantly appointed boutique hotel offers a unique experience. One of a kind art pieces and Asian influences can be seen throughout. Relax in the English Garden, an oasis from the hectic city. 127 units. 15 stories, interior corridors. **Parking:** valet only. **Amenities:** safes. **Pool(s):** heated indoor. **Activities:** sauna, steamroom, spa. **Guest Services:** valet laundry, area transportation.

RESIDENCE INN BY MARRIOTT ATLANTA BUCKHEAD
(404)239-0677 **21**

Extended Stay Motel
$127-$263

Residence Inn Marriott

AAA Benefit:
Members save 5% or more!

Address: 2960 Piedmont Rd NE 30305 **Location:** Jct Piedmont and Pharr rds, just s. **Facility:** 136 kitchen units, some two bedrooms. 2 stories (no elevator), exterior corridors. **Pool(s):** outdoor. **Activities:** exercise room. **Guest Services:** valet and coin laundry, area transportation.

RESIDENCE INN BY MARRIOTT ATLANTA BUCKHEAD/LENOX PARK
(404)467-1660 **3**

Extended Stay Hotel.
$89-$217 **Address:** 2220 Lake Blvd 30319 **Location:** I-85 exit 89, 1.6 mi w on N Druid Hills (which becomes E Roxboro Rd), then just n on Lenox Park Blvd.

AAA Benefit:
Members save 5% or more!

Facility: 150 units, some two bedrooms, efficiencies and kitchens. 4 stories, interior corridors. **Pool(s):** heated outdoor. **Activities:** hot tub, exercise room. **Guest Services:** valet and coin laundry, area transportation.

THE RITZ-CARLTON, BUCKHEAD   404/237-2700 **2**

Hotel
Rates not provided

AAA Benefit:
Unequaled service at special member savings!

Address: 3434 Peachtree Rd NE 30326 **Location:** I-85 exit 86, 1.8 mi n on Lenox Rd. Opposite Phipps Plaza. **Facility:** This landmark has been a part of the Atlanta scene for over 30 years. The classic elegance in the lobby and the comfortable charm of the guest rooms set the hotel apart from others in the area. 510 units. 22 stories, interior corridors. **Parking:** on-site (fee) and valet. **Amenities:** safes. **Dining:** The Cafe, see separate listing, entertainment. **Pool(s):** heated indoor. **Activities:** sauna, hot tub, spa. **Guest Services:** valet laundry, boarding pass kiosk, area transportation.

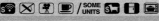

THE RITZ-CARLTON
BUCKHEAD

Our escape in the heart of Buckhead offers an indoor pool & is walking distance to shopping & dining

ST. REGIS ATLANTA HOTEL & RESIDENCES
404/563-7900 **19**

Hotel
Rates not provided

ST REGIS

AAA Benefit:
Members save up to 15%, plus Starwood Preferred Guest® benefits!

Address: 88 W Paces Ferry Rd 30305 **Location:** Jct Peachtree and W Paces Ferry rds, just w. **Facility:** Grand staircases, welcoming hearths and crystal chandeliers adorn the palatial lobby. All rooms offer spacious, luxurious marble bathrooms featuring giant soaking tubs and separate showers. 151 units. 10 stories, interior corridors. **Parking:** valet only. **Amenities:** safes. **Dining:** Atlas, see separate listing. **Pool(s):** heated outdoor. **Activities:** sauna, hot tub, steamroom, spa. **Guest Services:** valet laundry, area transportation.

Say YES to ERS text updates to stay posted when your tow truck is on the way

(See map & index p. 72.)

SPRINGHILL SUITES BY MARRIOTT-ATLANTA BUCKHEAD
(404)844-4800 **8**

Hotel
$95-$263

SPRINGHILL SUITES MARRIOTT **AAA Benefit:** Members save 5% or more!

Address: 3459 Buckhead Loop NE 30326 **Location:** SR 400 exit 2, just w on Lenox Rd. **Facility:** 220 units. 11 stories, interior corridors. **Parking:** on-site (fee). **Pool(s):** heated indoor. **Activities:** exercise room. **Guest Services:** valet and coin laundry, area transportation.

STAYBRIDGE SUITES-ATLANTA/BUCKHEAD
(404)842-0800 **20**

Extended Stay Hotel. $109-$250 **Address:** 540 Pharr Rd 30305 **Location:** Jct Pharr and Piedmont rds, just w. **Facility:** 83 efficiencies, some two bedrooms. 6 stories, interior corridors. **Amenities:** safes. **Pool(s):** heated indoor. **Activities:** hot tub, exercise room. **Guest Services:** valet laundry, area transportation.

TOWNEPLACE SUITES BY MARRIOTT ATLANTA BUCKHEAD
(404)949-4820 **23**

Extended Stay Hotel. $101-$197 **Address:** 820 Sidney Marcus Blvd 30324 **Location:** I-85 exit 86 northbound, 1.9 mi n to Sidney Marcus Blvd, then just w; exit 88 southbound, just w to Sidney Marcus Blvd, then just w. **Facility:** 75 efficiencies, some two bedrooms. 4 stories, interior corridors. **Amenities:** safes. **Activities:** exercise room. **Guest Services:** complimentary and valet laundry, area transportation.

AAA Benefit: Members save 5% or more!

W ATLANTA BUCKHEAD
678/500-3100 **9**

Contemporary Hotel
Rates not provided

W HOTELS **AAA Benefit:** Members save up to 15%, plus Starwood Preferred Guest® benefits!

Address: 3377 Peachtree Rd NE 30326 **Location:** Jct Piedmont and Peachtree rds, 0.3 mi e. **Facility:** This trendy hotel boasts luxurious and artistic touches. Guests love the pool deck's amazing metropolitan views, on-site night club and the W Insider, a fantastic personal concierge service. 291 units. 11 stories, interior corridors. **Parking:** valet only. **Amenities:** safes. **Dining:** nightclub. **Pool(s):** heated outdoor. **Activities:** exercise room. **Guest Services:** valet laundry, boarding pass kiosk, area transportation.

THE WESTIN BUCKHEAD ATLANTA
(404)365-0065 **5**

Hotel
$139-$329

WESTIN HOTELS & RESORTS **AAA Benefit:** Members save up to 15%, plus Starwood Preferred Guest® benefits!

Address: 3391 Peachtree Rd NE 30326 **Location:** Adjacent to Lenox Square Mall. **Facility:** This high-rise hotel has been recently renovated with contemporary flair and upscale finishings. The moderately sized rooms are offset with elegant comfort and style. 365 units. 22 stories, interior corridors. **Parking:** on-site (fee) and valet. **Terms:** cancellation fee imposed. **Amenities:** safes. **Dining:** The Atlanta Palm, see separate listing. **Pool(s):** heated indoor. **Activities:** sauna, steamroom, massage. **Guest Services:** valet laundry, boarding pass kiosk, area transportation.

▼ See AAA listing p. 188 ▼

(See map & index p. 72.)

WINGATE BY WYNDHAM ATLANTA/BUCKHEAD
(404)869-1100 **1**

▼▼▼▼ **Hotel.** $139-$299 **Address:** 3600 Piedmont Rd NE 30305 **Location:** SR 400 exit 2, just s to Piedmont Rd, then 1.1 mi w. **Facility:** 101 units. 5 stories, interior corridors. **Amenities:** safes. **Pool(s):** outdoor. **Activities:** hot tub, exercise room. **Guest Services:** valet laundry, area transportation.

〔▮┼〕 〔 ⟂ 〕 CALL 〔&M〕 〔⤬〕 〔BIZ〕 〔HS〕 〔📶〕 〔✕〕 〔🖥〕 〔🖼〕 〔☕〕

WHERE TO EAT

ANIS CAFE & BISTRO 404/233-9889 **38**

▼▼ ▼ French. Casual Dining. $11-$35 **AAA Inspector Notes:** Tucked away on a side street you will find this place that seems to have stepped out of the pages of a South of France travel brochure. The casual, relaxed bistro has enclosed patio seating, a full bar and intimate dining areas. Creative, well-prepared appetizers and entrées include a pate of the day, mussels, escargots, fresh seafood and a daily flatbread pizza. **Features:** full bar, patio dining, Sunday brunch. **Address:** 2974 Grandview Ave 30305 **Location:** Jct Peachtree Rd, 0.3 mi s. 〔L〕 〔D〕

ANOTHER BROKEN EGG CAFE 404/254-0219

▼ ▼ Breakfast Sandwiches. Casual Dining. $7-$16 **AAA Inspector Notes:** Enjoy a breakfast experience you will not soon forget; huge cinnamon buns, Popeye's omelet and fruit and nut pancakes or french toast are some of the menu specialties. **Features:** full bar, Sunday brunch. **Address:** 2355 Peachtree Rd NE 30305 **Location:** Jct Peachtree Battle Ave NW. 〔B〕 〔L〕

ANTICA POSTA TUSCAN RESTAURANT & BAR
404/262-7112 **28**

▼▼▼▼ Italian. Fine Dining. $14-$34 **AAA Inspector Notes:** Explore the treasures of Tuscany in fresh and authentic dishes, such as free range chicken roasted in extra virgin olive oil and Tuscan herbs, the succulent veal chop or tuna steak with black truffles. The charming converted house tucks into a quiet area just off a bustling main street. **Features:** full bar. **Reservations:** suggested. **Address:** 519 E Paces Ferry Rd NE 30305 **Location:** Jct E Paces Ferry and Piedmont rds, just w. **Parking:** valet only. 〔D〕

ARIA 404/233-7673 **29**

▼▼ ▼▼ New American. Fine Dining. $24-$42 **AAA Inspector Notes:** An unforgettable, delicious meal awaits diners at this restaurant set in a beautiful contemporary dining room with intriguing art. The executive chef is best known for his tender braised meats, and the foie gras melts in your mouth. The pastry chef's delicious warm chevre cheesecake with Oregon hazelnuts is so creamy and rich that guests will not want to miss dessert. **Features:** full bar. **Reservations:** suggested. **Address:** 490 E Paces Ferry Rd 30305 **Location:** Jct E Paces Ferry and Peachtree rds, 0.5 mi e. **Parking:** valet only. 〔D〕

ATLANTA FISH MARKET 404/262-3165 **36**

▼▼▼▼ Seafood. Fine Dining. $13-$50 **AAA Inspector Notes:** Look for a gigantic fish statue, which gives a clue that you've arrived at this popular spot in trendy Buckhead. Reminiscent of a casual Savannah-style fish market, this place whips up a wide choice of fresh fish entrées, in addition to some pasta, chicken and duck selections. Treat yourself to one of the mouthwatering desserts, such as white chocolate chunk banana crème brûlée. **Features:** full bar. **Reservations:** suggested. **Address:** 265 Pharr Rd 30305 **Location:** Jct Peachtree and Pharr rds, 2 blks e. **Parking:** valet only. 〔L〕 〔D〕

THE ATLANTA PALM 404/814-1955 **8**

▼▼▼▼ Steak. Fine Dining. $15-$55 **AAA Inspector Notes:** USDA Prime steak and seafood specialties are presented in this classic New York steakhouse setting. Steaks are cooked to order, and portions are monstrous. Particularly good is the filet, thinly sliced and served over garlic mashed potatoes, with a colossal salad. Friendly, casual and knowledgeable are characteristics of the staff here. **Features:** full bar. **Reservations:** suggested. **Address:** 3391 Peachtree Rd NE 30326 **Location:** Adjacent to Lenox Square Mall; in The Westin Buckhead Atlanta. **Parking:** on-site (fee) and valet.

〔⇇〕 〔B〕 〔L〕 〔D〕

ATLAS 404/600-6471 **26**

▼▼▼▼ ▼▼▼▼ American. Fine Dining. $10-$59 **AAA Inspector Notes:** This Buckhead hot spot offers American cuisine in trendy luxury. A constantly changing menu features fresh, seasonal ingredients, seafood and meats. As the season permits try the patio dining or seats near the exhibition kitchen for a distinctive dining experience. **Features:** full bar, patio dining. **Reservations:** suggested. **Address:** 88 W Paces Ferry Rd 30305 **Location:** Jct Peachtree and W Paces Ferry rds, just w; in St. Regis Atlanta Hotel & Residences. **Parking:** valet only. 〔⇇〕 〔D〕 CALL 〔&M〕

BASIL'S 404/233-9755 **37**

▼▼▼▼ Mediterranean. Casual Dining. $8-$29 **AAA Inspector Notes:** This cozy little restaurant serves Mediterranean dishes; many of which are not only inventive but healthy as well. The Greek shrimp with feta cheese, Kalamata olives and sun-dried tomatoes in a light white wine sauce is well-prepared and nicely presented. The Mediterranean flat bread with mushrooms, Manchego cheese and truffle oil is my recommended appetizer. In addition to the main dining room, guests may also enjoy the outdoor deck or grab a drink at the bar. **Features:** full bar, patio dining, Sunday brunch. **Reservations:** suggested. **Address:** 2985 Grandview Ave NE 30305 **Location:** Off Pharr Rd, just s on Grandview Ave; center. 〔L〕 〔D〕

BISTRO NIKO 404/261-6456 **15**

▼▼▼▼ French. Fine Dining. $12-$30 **AAA Inspector Notes:** This little slice of authentic French food offers patrons a joie de vivre in a delightful setting of mirrored walls, plush leather booths, decorative ceiling molding and twinkling lights. The menu features classic bistro cuisine and delicious pastries. Come in for a drink at the bar or a full meal in the restaurant. **Features:** full bar, Sunday brunch. **Reservations:** suggested. **Address:** 3344 Peachtree Rd NE 30326 **Location:** Jct Peachtree and Lenox rds, 0.4 mi w. **Parking:** valet only.

〔L〕 〔D〕 CALL 〔&M〕

BONES RESTAURANT 404/237-2663 **20**

▼▼▼▼ Steak. Fine Dining. $15-$55 **AAA Inspector Notes:** This restaurant has the feel of a New York club with a comfortable atmosphere and private rooms. The menu features fresh seafood and aged prime beef, including an excellent petite New York strip, cooked to perfection and served with sautéed mushrooms. Enjoy a pre-dinner drink with friends at the lounge. **Features:** full bar. **Reservations:** suggested. **Address:** 3130 Piedmont Rd NE 30305 **Location:** Jct Piedmont and Peachtree rds NE, just s. **Parking:** valet only.

〔L〕 〔D〕 CALL 〔&M〕

BRICK TOPS 404/841-2212 **16**

▼▼▼▼ Comfort Food. Casual Dining. $14-$36 **AAA Inspector Notes:** This contemporary, bright dining room is the setting for upscale, creative comfort food such as the popular deviled eggs and sugar bacon. There also is a sushi selection, a range of sandwiches and entrées including steaks, ribs and several fresh fish dishes. **Features:** full bar, Sunday brunch. **Address:** 3280 Peachtree Rd NE, Suite 100 30305 **Location:** Jct Piedmont Rd; in Terminus Building. **Parking:** on-site (fee) and valet. 〔L〕 〔D〕 CALL 〔&M〕

BUCKHEAD BREAD COMPANY & CORNER CAFE
404/240-1978 **24**

▼▼ ▼▼ American. Casual Dining. $9-$18 **AAA Inspector Notes:** Creative sandwiches and salads are featured on this appealing menu. The upbeat, bistro-style atmosphere is light and airy and features culinary murals, slate floors and wooden tables. In the heart of the city's upscale Buckhead community, this place also has a bakery that makes your mouth water at the aroma of freshly baked bread. **Features:** beer & wine, Sunday brunch. **Address:** 3070 Piedmont Rd NE 30305 **Location:** Corner of Piedmont NE and E Paces Ferry rds. 〔L〕 CALL 〔&M〕

BUCKHEAD DINER 404/262-3336 **25**

▼▼▼▼ American. Fine Dining. $13-$30 **AAA Inspector Notes:** Hop on board a reproduction of a luxury railroad dining car for a fine meal. This eclectic dining spot serves unusual, cutting-edge cuisine. The warm Maytag blue cheese chips have been an extremely popular appetizer for many years and the braised beef short rib always is a good entrée option. For a closer that cannot be beat, try the award-winning chocolate banana cream pie. **Features:** full bar, Sunday brunch. **Address:** 3073 Piedmont Rd NE 30305 **Location:** Corner of Piedmont NE and E Paces Ferry rds. **Parking:** valet and street only. 〔L〕 〔D〕 〔LATE〕

(See map & index p. 72.)

THE CAFE   404/237-2700 6

▼▼▼ American. Fine Dining. $12-$27 **AAA Inspector Notes:** This spacious restaurant is a bastion of formal service and traditional décor. A nice spot for a formal business lunch or high tea in between shopping trips at the surrounding malls. The lavish Sunday brunch is a popular draw. The menu does not stray too far from the familiar, but the quality is excellent from start to finish. **Features:** full bar, patio dining, Sunday brunch. **Reservations:** suggested. **Address:** 3434 Peachtree Rd NE 30326 **Location:** I-85 exit 86, 1.8 mi n on Lenox Rd; in The Ritz-Carlton, Buckhead. **Parking:** on-site and valet.

B   L   D   CALL ⓖM

CAFE SUNFLOWER   404/352-8859 50

▼▼ Vegetarian. Casual Dining. $7-$17 **AAA Inspector Notes:** Playful, yet sophisticated, this vegetarian restaurant's atmosphere combines sunflowers and other colorful accessories. The elaborate menu features many tasty entrées and luscious desserts such as local farm stew with Cajun vegan sausage and curry roots vegetables over organic black rice. Gluten-free options also are available. **Features:** beer & wine. **Address:** 2140 Peachtree Rd 30309 **Location:** Jct Colonial Homes Dr; in Brookwood Square Center.

L   D   CALL ⓖM

THE CAPITAL GRILLE   404/262-1162 31

▼▼▼ Steak. Fine Dining. $6-$47 **AAA Inspector Notes:** Cherry wood and red leather assist in making this clubby dining room a beautiful spot to dine on excellent cuts of dry-aged beef. The staff is highly attentive and knowledgeable. **Reservations:** suggested. **Address:** 255 E Paces Ferry Rd 30305 **Location:** Jct Peachtree and E Paces Ferry rds; in Capital Building. **Parking:** valet only.   L   D   CALL ⓖM

CHEESEBURGER BOBBY'S   678/732-9531

▼ Burgers. Quick Serve. $3-$7 **AAA Inspector Notes:** Nibble on hand-cut fries with your fresh, hand-patted burger, which you'll gussy up with onions, lettuce, tomatoes, pickles and other items on the condiment station. Other choices include hot dogs, chicken sandwiches and custard for dessert. Friendly servers tend the bright, fresh and clean dining room. **Features:** full bar. **Address:** 4365 Roswell Rd 30342 **Location:** Jct Wieuca Rd NE, just s.

L   D   CALL ⓖM

CHOPS LOBSTER BAR   404/262-2675 27

▼▼▼ Steak Seafood. Fine Dining. $15-$60 **AAA Inspector Notes:** The cosmopolitan New York-style steakhouse, with an exhibition kitchen, is a step above the everyday steakhouse. Prime beef cuts are delicious and well-prepared, as is the lobster bisque appetizer. A selection from the extensive wine list makes the meal complete. **Features:** full bar. **Reservations:** suggested. **Address:** 70 W Paces Ferry Rd NW 30305 **Location:** Just w of Peachtree Rd; in Buckhead Plaza. **Parking:** valet only.   L   D

THE COLONNADE   404/874-5642 49

▼▼ Southern. Casual Dining. $12-$25 **AAA Inspector Notes:** This family-owned favorite has been a standby for years for staples such as home-style fried chicken, seafood and Southern-style vegetables and desserts. **Features:** full bar, early bird specials. **Address:** 1879 Cheshire Bridge Rd 30324 **Location:** I-85 exit 88 southbound, 1.1 mi e; 86 northbound, 1.9 mi n to Cheshire Bridge Rd, then 1.1 mi e.   D

CORNER BAKERY CAFE   404/816-5100 12

▼ Deli. Quick Serve. $6-$12 **AAA Inspector Notes:** This restaurant specializes in sandwiches, soup, salad, freshly baked bread and desserts. All dishes are served in tasty, large portions by efficient servers. Adding in potato dill bread makes for a yummy twist on the traditional tuna sandwich. **Address:** 3368 Peachtree Rd NE 30326 **Location:** I-85 exit 88, n on Lenox Rd to Peachtree Rd NE, then 0.3 mi sw.   B   L   D   CALL ⓖM

Upgrade to Plus or Premier membership
for _more_ of the benefits you need most

DANTANNA'S SURF, TURF & TURF   404/760-8873 9

▼▼ American. Casual Dining. $10-$42 **AAA Inspector Notes:** Convenient for shoppers, this upscale sports bar offers fresh seafood and strong service. House specialties include lump crab and fresh berry salad, Zinfandel short ribs, wasabi tuna, cioppino and the "Freuben" sandwich. All steaks are USDA Choice Black Angus beef. For a sweet treat try the Krispy Kreme bread pudding with a scoop of ice cream. It's popular on game day, so arrive early to secure a spot. **Features:** full bar, Sunday brunch. **Address:** 3400 Around Lenox Dr, Suite 304 30326 **Location:** Adjacent to Lenox Square Mall.

L   D   LATE   CALL ⓖM

DAVIO'S NORTHERN ITALIAN STEAKHOUSE
                           404/844-4810 3

▼▼▼ Northern Italian. Fine Dining. $14-$49 **AAA Inspector Notes:** This beautiful upscale dining room sets the tone for the creative cuisine including handmade pastas and spring rolls which have become famous nationwide. Kobe beef meatballs are a delicious and distinctive antipasti and the fresh Maine lobster ravioli always is a big hit. Grilled USDA Prime steaks are a house specialty and the porterhouse veal chop also is a cannot miss item. **Features:** full bar, patio dining, Sunday brunch. **Reservations:** suggested. **Address:** 3500 Peachtree Rd NE 30326 **Location:** In Phipps Plaza.

L   D   CALL ⓖM

FARM BURGER   404/816-0603 14

▼ Burgers. Quick Serve. $7-$10 **AAA Inspector Notes:** The beef here is 100 percent grass fed and comes as a combo or diners can build their own with many ingredients which include jalapeños, fried farm eggs, red bean chili, local bacon and oxtail marmalade. For those not wanting beef, there is a veggie quinoa or chicken burger. Spicy garlic and pimento cheese fries are great sides. Milk shakes also are available. **Features:** beer & wine, patio dining. **Address:** 3365 Piedmont Rd 30305 **Location:** SR 400 exit 2, just w to Piedmont Rd, then just e; in Tower Place.   L   D   CALL ⓖM

FLIP BURGER BOUTIQUE   404/549-3298 2

▼▼ Burgers. Casual Dining. $8-$14 **AAA Inspector Notes:** This place boasts fine dining between two buns. Among gourmet, cooked-to-order burgers made from hanger steak are the classic, steak tartare and deluxe topped with foie gras. Other burgers have lamb, tuna, chorizo or veggies as their core ingredient. Tempting sides include french fries, fried okra, vodka-battered onion rings and fried bread and butter pickles. The contemporary atmosphere is retro hip and chic. **Features:** full bar. **Address:** 3655 Roswell Rd 30342 **Location:** SR 400 exit 2, 1 mi n to Roswell Rd, then just n.

L   D   CALL ⓖM

FLYING BISCUIT CAFE - BUCKHEAD TERMINUS BUILDING
                           404/477-0013 17

▼▼ Breakfast. Casual Dining. $4-$12 **AAA Inspector Notes:** This casual eatery serves Southern classics alongside vegetarian options proving that this cuisine doesn't have to be unhealthy, and the handmade biscuits are so good they named the restaurant after them. I recommend the "Famous Flying Biscuit Breakfast" and the "Heavenly French Toast" with raspberry sauce and honey crème anglaise. **Address:** 3280 Peachtree Rd 30305 **Location:** Corner of Peachtree and Piedmont rds.   B   L

FOGO DE CHAO   404/266-9988 21

▼▼▼ Brazilian Steak. Fine Dining. $25-$50 **AAA Inspector Notes:** This Southern Brazilian-style churrasceria features 15 select cuts of meat that gauchos serve tableside. An extremely well-stocked salad bar also is available. The service staff is most attentive. **Features:** full bar, Sunday brunch. **Reservations:** suggested. **Address:** 3101 Piedmont Rd NE 30305 **Location:** Jct Piedmont and Peachtree rds NE, just s. **Parking:** on-site and valet.   L   D

FRESH 4 U   404/603-8883 53

▼ Mediterranean. Quick Serve. $5-$9 **AAA Inspector Notes:** At this eatery, I sampled the chicken gyro, foul (chickpea) salad and baklava which were all fresh and tasty. Lamb gyros are on the menu as well as grilled chicken, beef and salmon kebabs, several types of wraps and such salads as spinach, tabouli and Greek. The pesto pasta looked good and fried wings are another choice for those who do not want Mediterranean food. **Features:** patio dining. **Address:** 1937 Peachtree St NE 30309 **Location:** Between Collier and Brighton rds.   L   D   ◤

(See map & index p. 72.)

GEORGIA GRILLE   404/352-3517   43

▼▼ Southwestern. Casual Dining. $12-$31 **AAA Inspector Notes:** This pleasant, sunny bistro features excellent, creative Southwestern cuisine. One of the most renowned dishes is the lobster enchilada, a must on a first visit, which, when followed by an exquisite chocolate mousse, makes an extraordinary meal. The highly-attentive servers are able to assist in making the proper entrée choice. **Features:** full bar. **Reservations:** suggested, weekends. **Address:** 2290 Peachtree Rd NW 30309 **Location:** Just s of Peachtree Rd and Peachtree Battle Ave; in Peachtree Square.   D

GORDON BIERSCH BREWERY RESTAURANT
404/264-0253   18

▼▼▼ American. Casual Dining. $10-$35 **AAA Inspector Notes:** As the name implies this restaurant features fresh, brewed-on-site beer which is crafted in a German tradition. What may not be evident is the wide variety of foods like meal-sized salads, burgers and sandwiches, pizza, pastas, steaks and seafood that is also a huge draw for an upscale, casual dining experience. **Features:** full bar, happy hour. **Address:** 3242 Peachtree Rd NE 30305 **Location:** Jct Peachtree and Piedmont rds NE, just s.   L   D   LATE

GRINDHOUSE KILLER BURGERS   404/254-2273   52

▼ Burgers. Quick Serve. $3-$9 **AAA Inspector Notes:** Diners can create their own burger here by choosing a grind (beef, turkey or veggie), a size and a style of burger, and then add items ranging from pico de gallo to fried green tomatoes. If deciding just what to order is difficult, then choose from such burger styles as hillbilly, Yankee or cowboy. Starters include sweet potato kettle chips and cheesy poofs. **Features:** beer & wine, patio dining. **Address:** 1842 Piedmont Ave NE 30324 **Location:** I-85 exit 86 northbound, just n to Monroe Dr, just e to Piedmont Rd NE, then just s; exit 88 southbound, just e to Lenox Rd, just e to Cheshire Bridge Rd, 1.5 mi e to Piedmont Rd, then just w.   L   D   CALL M

HAL'S   404/261-0025   1

▼▼▼ Steak. Fine Dining. $23-$49 **AAA Inspector Notes:** This is a classic steakhouse with some New Orleans accents. It's popular with locals not just for the great steaks and fresh seafood but also for the friendly, engaging staff and festive atmosphere. **Features:** full bar. **Reservations:** suggested. **Address:** 30 Old Ivy Rd 30342 **Location:** SR 400 exit 2, just s to Piedmont Rd, then 2 mi w. **Parking:** valet only.   D   CALL M

HOLEMAN AND FINCH PUBLIC HOUSE   404/948-1175   46

▼▼▼ Small Plates. Gastropub. $7-$31 **AAA Inspector Notes:** A self-described public house (an establishment that encourages diners to get to know one another) serves up a menu of American pub classics with an emphasis on seasonal ingredients and time-honored techniques. Burgers are a big deal but they are only served after 9:30 pm and they are not on the menu. A kitchen staffer bellows 'burgers' over a bullhorn and the scramble is on to get one of the two dozen limit each night. **Features:** full bar, Sunday brunch. **Reservations:** suggested. **Address:** 2277 Peachtree Rd NE, Suite B 30309 **Location:** I-75/85 exit 250 (14th St), 0.5 mi e to Peachtree St, then 2.3 mi n; in Aramore Building.   D   CALL M

THE IMPERIAL FEZ   404/351-0870   44

▼▼ Moroccan. Casual Dining. $12-$55 **AAA Inspector Notes:** Surrender your shoes and dine in an opulent nest of pillows, rugs and brilliantly patterned drapery. Five-courses of Moroccan-Mediterranean cuisine are staged in an exotic setting while belly dancers fascinate with graceful movement and colorful costumes. The servers here are warm, friendly and well-informed. A la carte items also are available. **Features:** full bar, patio dining. **Reservations:** suggested. **Address:** 2285 Peachtree Rd NE, Suite 102 30309 **Location:** Between Collier Rd and 26th St. **Parking:** on-site and valet. D

JACKS NEW YORKER DELI   404/869-7776

▼ Sandwiches. Quick Serve. $6-$12 **AAA Inspector Notes:** Part New York-style deli and part Southern-style café, this place is big on hot and cold sandwiches but also serves soups, salads, burgers, hot dogs and homemade cookies. Enjoy the best fries around with a sub, hero or panini. Breakfast is available all day. **Features:** beer & wine, patio dining. **Address:** 3333 Piedmont Rd NE, Suite 120 30305 **Location:** Jct Peachtree Rd; in Terminus Building.   B   L   D   CALL M

J. CHRISTOPHER'S   404/917-0350   32

▼▼ Breakfast. Casual Dining. $5-$11 **AAA Inspector Notes:** Blueberry crunch cakes, strawberry waffles and eggs Christopher are some of the breakfast favorites found here along with such seasonal items as pumpkin pancakes. Many traditional breakfast standards also are available. Lunch favorites include the club house burger and the classic club sandwich. Waldorf salads and signature soups are popular. **Features:** patio dining. **Address:** 3050 Peachtree Rd NW 30305 **Location:** Jct Peachtree and W Paces Ferry rds, just s.   B   L   CALL M

KING + DUKE   404/477-3500   30

▼▼▼ New Southern. Fine Dining. $12-$54 **AAA Inspector Notes:** The roaring fire of the open hearth used for cooking here sets a somewhat rustic tone, but there is a real sophistication to the knowledgeable service and bold flavors of the dishes. In keeping with current trends, the premium ingredients are all sourced from the local area and the menu changes regularly. The excellent bone-in steaks are gaining acclaim, and the menu rounds out nicely with dishes like roasted trout with bacon and almonds or Mississippi rabbit with farro salad. **Features:** full bar, patio dining. **Reservations:** suggested. **Address:** 3060 Peachtree Rd NW 30305 **Location:** Jct Peachtree and W Paces Ferry rds. **Parking:** on-site and valet.   L   D

KYMA   404/262-0702   23

▼▼▼ Greek. Fine Dining. $12-$42 **AAA Inspector Notes:** This contemporary Greek restaurant features excellent preparations of fish, which include Dover sole, skate wing, Arctic char and Maine lobster. The grilled octopus is to die for and is a favorite appetizer. Greek fish such as royal dorade and lavraki also are on the menu. The décor is chic and showcases the culture in a stylish manner. **Features:** full bar. **Reservations:** suggested. **Address:** 3085 Piedmont Rd NE 30305 **Location:** Jct Piedmont NE and E Paces Ferry rds. **Parking:** valet only.   D

LA GROTTA RISTORANTE ITALIANO
404/231-1368   39

▼▼▼ ◆▼◆
Northern
Italian
Fine Dining
$19-$39

AAA Inspector Notes: With a relaxed formal atmosphere, this local favorite always delights with Northern Italian seafood, veal, chicken and beef entrées, as well as such homemade pasta specialties as ravioli con caprino or Dover sole meuniere. Delectable homemade desserts and an excellent wine list complete a great meal. The service staff here is extremely attentive and gracious and regulars have their favorites who go out of their way to please, yet new diners will not be disappointed. **Features:** full bar. **Reservations:** suggested. **Address:** 2637 Peachtree Rd NE 30305 **Location:** Jct Peachtree and Wesley Chapel rds, just s. **Parking:** valet only.   D

LANDMARK DINER   404/816-9090   4

▼▼ Continental. Casual Dining. $10-$30 **AAA Inspector Notes:** Fresh daily specials, large portions and mountainous desserts are just a few of the reasons Atlantans have been frequenting the eatery for years. Adjoining is a lounge that has become a popular night spot. **Features:** full bar. **Address:** 3652 Roswell Rd NE 30305 **Location:** SR 400 exit 2, 1 mi n.   B   L   D   24

LE BILBOQUET   404/869-9944   35

▼▼ French. Casual Dining. $11-$41 **AAA Inspector Notes:** This French bistro-inspired restaurant serves up atmosphere, French classics and a long list of wines. Located in a trendy, high-end shopping plaza, this is Buckhead's latest hot spot. Cozy up to the bar, snuggle into the dining room or soak up fresh air on the patio. Whatever the pleasure, this place is sure to deliver. **Features:** full bar, patio dining, Sunday brunch. **Reservations:** suggested. **Address:** 3035 Peachtree Rd NE 30305 **Location:** Jct Peachtree Rd NE and Bolling Way NE, just e. **Parking:** on-site and valet.   L   D   CALL M

MAGGIANO'S LITTLE ITALY   404/816-9650   11

▼▼ Italian. Fine Dining. $11-$46 **AAA Inspector Notes:** Diners savor scrumptious, traditional favorites served in a bustling atmosphere reminiscent of Little Italy. The dining area projects an early-20th-century feel; loud conversations bouncing off high ceilings evoke a sense of the Roaring 20's. **Features:** patio dining. **Address:** 3368 Peachtree Rd NE 30328 **Location:** I-85 exit 88, n on Lenox Rd to Peachtree Rd NE, then 0.3 mi sw. **Parking:** valet only.   L   D   CALL M

(See map & index p. 72.)

MCKINNON'S LOUISIANE RESTAURANT 404/237-1313 (19)
WW WW Creole. Casual Dining. $18-$29 **AAA Inspector Notes:** Seafood items have a spicy touch, as does the homemade seasoned jambalaya. A small cocktail bar separates the elegant, candlelit dining room from the casual bistro. Service shows a touch of sophistication. **Features:** full bar, early bird specials. **Reservations:** suggested. **Address:** 3209 Maple Dr 30305 **Location:** Jct Piedmont and Peachtree rds, just s on Peachtree Rd to Maple Dr. (D)

NAKATO 404/873-6582 (51)
WW WW WW Japanese. Fine Dining. $8-$50 **AAA Inspector Notes:** A bit on the outskirts of the city, this family-owned Japanese restaurant provides a mixture of relaxed and formal experiences. Diners can choose from teppanyaki tables, a sushi bar or traditional dining room service. Teppanyaki tables provide good theatrics as the chef displays his cooking talents. Select ingredients flavor such dishes as yakitori, tempura, sushi, sashimi and varied noodles. However, my favorites are the succulent pork Kakuni and the colorful Chirashi. **Features:** full bar, patio dining. **Address:** 1776 Cheshire Bridge Rd 30324 **Location:** Between La Vista and Piedmont rds; just e of jct Cheshire Bridge and Monroe rds. **Parking:** on-site and valet. (D)

NEW YORK PRIME 404/846-0644 (7)
WW WW WW Steak. Fine Dining. $29-$60 **AAA Inspector Notes:** This classic steakhouse is a social hot spot for the professional crowd that permeates the area. The menu revolves around USDA Prime steaks which come in large, hearty portions. Seafood options also are available and highlights include live lobster, salmon and stone crab. Diners are welcome to settle into a cozy booth or light up a cigar at the bar and listen to some live music or game highlights in an upscale atmosphere. **Features:** full bar, patio dining. **Reservations:** suggested. **Address:** 3424 Peachtree Rd NE 30326 **Location:** Jct Lenox Rd, just sw; in Monarch Tower. **Parking:** valet only.
(D) CALL (&M) (\)

ONE STAR RANCH 404/233-7644 (22)
WW Barbecue. Casual Dining. $6-$29 **AAA Inspector Notes:** Simple, straightforward Texas-style barbecue makes up a menu that lists enormous ribs, brisket and such tasty sides as the popular onion rings, which go well with cold beer from the fully-stocked bar. Wings, chicken tenders and taco shell salads also are popular items here. Parking can be a challenge at busy times. **Features:** full bar, patio dining. **Address:** 25 Irby Ave 30305 **Location:** Jct Roswell Rd and Irby Ave, just w. (L) (D)

PRICCI 404/237-2941 (34)
WW WW WW Italian. Fine Dining. $13-$29 **AAA Inspector Notes:** Taste buds wake up for these Italian meals served in upscale atmosphere. Try vitello alla parmigiana or Kobe beef ravioli for dinner, and treat your sweet tooth to a luscious dessert afterward. **Features:** full bar. **Reservations:** suggested. **Address:** 500 Pharr Rd 30305 **Location:** Jct Pharr Rd and Maple Dr, just w of Piedmont Rd. **Parking:** valet only. (L) (D)

RED SNAPPER 404/634-8947 (47)
WW WW Seafood. Casual Dining. $8-$31 **AAA Inspector Notes:** Several preparations of snapper and many other succulent seafood specials are on this traditional restaurant's menu. Ginger snapper is the most popular dish while other favorites include shrimp remoulade, crabmeat en coquille, baked stuffed flounder and snapper Yvonne. A romantic ambience is part of the dining experience. **Features:** full bar. **Address:** 2100 Cheshire Bridge Rd 30324 **Location:** I-85 exit 88 southbound, 0.5 mi e; exit 86 northbound, 2.4 mi n, then 0.5 mi e. (L) (D)

RESTAURANT EUGENE 404/355-0321 (45)
WW WW WW New American. Fine Dining. $28-$85 **AAA Inspector Notes:** Located on the cusp of Midtown and Buckhead at the base of a condominium building, this restaurant features an ever-changing menu that continues to explore the boundaries of taste and creativity. Comprised of a variety of regional, global and organic products, this spot allows diners to indulge in specialty dishes such as Kumamoto oysters, caviar, Columbia River salmon, foie gras, lamb, duck, veal, Alaskan halibut, Niman Ranch rib-eye and Atlantic monkfish. **Features:** full bar. **Reservations:** suggested. **Address:** 2277 Peachtree Rd NE 30309 **Location:** I-75/85 exit 250 (14th St), 0.5 mi e to Peachtree St, then 2.3 mi n; in Aramore building. **Parking:** valet only. (D) CALL (&M)

RU SAN'S SUSHI & SAKE BAR-BUCKHEAD TOWER PLACE 404/239-9557 (13)
WW WW Japanese. Casual Dining. $7-$40 **AAA Inspector Notes:** This bustling, trendy establishment presents an extensive menu of sushi, creative appetizers, salads, fried and grilled fish and Pacific Rim seafood dinners. **Features:** beer & wine, patio dining. **Address:** 3365 Piedmont Rd 30305 **Location:** Jct Piedmont and Peachtree rds, just n. (L) (D)

ST. CECILIA 404/554-9995 (5)
WW WW WW Italian. Fine Dining. $12-$42 **AAA Inspector Notes:** From beginning to end the focus of this restaurant is on fresh, classic Italian cuisine that has stood the test of time. Guests cannot go wrong with the hand-crafted pasta or numerous seafood options which include swordfish, Maine lobster and squid ink pasta. Offerings change frequently but diners always can expect a delicious, professionally executed meal. The stylish décor and central location are popular with the after work dinner crowd, so reservations are recommended. **Features:** full bar. **Reservations:** suggested. **Address:** 3455 Peachtree Rd NE 30326 **Location:** SR 141 (Lenox Rd), just e on Peachtree Rd, 0.5 mi ne to Peachtree Rd NE. **Parking:** on-site and valet.
(L) (D) CALL (&M)

SEASONS 52 FRESH GRILL 404/846-1552 (33)
WW WW WW New American. Fine Dining. $11-$30 **AAA Inspector Notes:** Embracing a distinctive concept, this restaurant focuses entirely on calorie-conscious dishes that reflect the current season. The menu changes 52 times a year. Modern and tasty choices include several types of flatbreads, salmon, chicken and an unusual offering of novelty dessert shots. Many by-the-glass options are among selections on the wine list. **Features:** full bar, patio dining. **Address:** 3050 Peachtree Rd NW 30305 **Location:** Jct Peachtree and W Paces Ferry rds, just s. **Parking:** on-site (fee) and valet.
(L) (D) CALL (&M)

STARFISH RESTAURANT 404/350-0799 (48)
WW WW Japanese. Fine Dining. $7-$30 **AAA Inspector Notes:** The dizzying array of creative sushi and sashimi are as authentic as the bento box lunches and udon noodles. Most fish are caught in the wild and delivered daily. You'll enjoy an excellent selection of sake and Far East wines in this attractive contemporary setting. **Features:** full bar, patio dining. **Address:** 2255 Peachtree Rd NE 30309 **Location:** Between Collier Rd and 26th St. (L) (D) CALL (&M) (🐾)

TAQUERIA DEL SOL 404/321-1118 (42)
WW Southwestern. Quick Serve. $2-$11 **AAA Inspector Notes:** At lunch, lines form at the counter to order various pork, chicken, beef or fish tacos and cups of shrimp corn chowder. Guests seat themselves. The brisket enchiladas also are popular as are the sides which include jalapeño coleslaw, turnip greens and charros beans. Only dinner is served on Saturday. **Features:** full bar. **Address:** 2165 Cheshire Bridge Rd 30324 **Location:** I-85 exit 88 southbound, 0.5 mi e; exit 86 northbound, 2.4 mi n, then 0.5 mi e. (L) (D)

TAVERNA PLAKA 404/636-2284 (41)
WW WW Greek. Casual Dining. $5-$24 **AAA Inspector Notes:** For those in the mood for a casual, festive Greek dining experience, this is the place to come. I recommend starting with the wildly popular saganaki or flaming cheese—the server lights it on fire at the table and when the flame goes out everyone yells opa. Entrées include classic dishes such as gyros, moussaka (Greek lasagna), Santorini chicken and papoutsakia (stuffed eggplant). The bar serves up a wide variety of cocktails and beverages including a variety of ouzo. **Features:** full bar, patio dining. **Reservations:** suggested. **Address:** 2196 Cheshire Bridge Rd 30324 **Location:** I-85 exit 88, just e. **Parking:** valet only. (D) (LATE) CALL (&M)

TRUE FOOD KITCHEN 404/481-2980 (10)
WW WW Natural/Organic. Casual Dining. $4-$24 **AAA Inspector Notes:** Embracing a philosophy of health and healing through eating, this restaurant provides a menu of fresh, natural cuisine. Menu selections change based on market availability, so ask your server for recommendations. Selections may include the succulent bison burger, Moroccan chicken or the creamy turkey lasagna. Also try one of the specialty cocktails or fresh smoothies. **Features:** full bar. **Address:** 3393 Peachtree Rd NE 30326 **Location:** Adjacent to Lenox Square Mall. (L) (D) CALL (&M)

(See map & index p. 72.)

ZESTO   404/237-8689
Burgers. Quick Serve. $4-$11 **AAA Inspector Notes:** Serving Atlanta since 1955, this place fills you up with hot dogs, wings, roasted chicken, tacos, quesadillas, nachos and its signature ice cream. You might also try a hamburger—the Chubby Decker is a popular choice—or a daily special. **Address:** 2469 Piedmont Rd NE 30324 **Location:** Jct Sidney Marcus Blvd, just s.

ATLANTA NORTHWEST
- **Restaurants p. 125**
- **Hotels & Restaurants map & index p. 76**

ATLANTA MARRIOTT NORTHWEST
                                    (770)952-7900 **6**

Hotel
$89-$238

AAA Benefit:
Members save 5% or more!

Address: 200 Interstate North Pkwy 30339 **Location:** I-75 exit 260 (Windy Hill Rd), 0.5 mi se. Located in a corporate business park area. **Facility:** 400 units. 5-16 stories, interior corridors. **Terms:** check-in 4 pm. **Pool(s):** heated outdoor, heated indoor. **Activities:** hot tub, exercise room. **Guest Services:** valet and coin laundry, boarding pass kiosk, rental car service, area transportation. *(See ad this page.)*

COUNTRY INN & SUITES BY CARLSON, ATLANTA-NW AT WINDY HILL RD   (770)956-9919 **4**
Hotel. $89-$199 **Address:** 4500 Circle 75 Pkwy 30339 **Location:** I-75 exit 260 (Windy Hill Rd), just w to Circle 75 Pkwy, then just s. **Facility:** 149 units. 5 stories, interior corridors. **Pool(s):** heated indoor. **Activities:** hot tub, exercise room. **Guest Services:** valet and coin laundry, area transportation.

COURTYARD BY MARRIOTT ATLANTA CUMBERLAND/GALLERIA   (770)952-2555 **15**

Hotel
$69-$219

COURTYARD **Marriott**

AAA Benefit:
Members save 5% or more!

Address: 3000 Cumberland Blvd 30339 **Location:** I-285 exit 19 northbound; exit 20 southbound, 0.5 mi s to Akers Mill Rd, then just w. **Facility:** 182 units. 8 stories, interior corridors. **Pool(s):** heated indoor. **Activities:** sauna, hot tub, exercise room. **Guest Services:** valet laundry, boarding pass kiosk, area transportation.

DAYS INN-ATLANTA/MARIETTA/WINDY HILL RD   (770)541-9399 **5**
Hotel. $57-$80 **Address:** 4502 Circle 75 Pkwy 30339 **Location:** I-75 exit 260 (Windy Hill Rd), just w to Circle 75 Pkwy, then just s. **Facility:** 82 units. 3 stories, interior corridors. **Pool(s):** heated indoor. **Guest Services:** coin laundry.

(See map & index p. 76.)

DOUBLETREE SUITES BY HILTON HOTEL ATLANTA-GALLERIA (770)980-1900 **7**

WWW **Hotel.** $99-$229 **Address:** 2780 Windy Ridge Pkwy 30339 **Location:** I-285 exit 20 westbound; exit 19 eastbound, just n on US 41 (Cobb Pkwy). **Facility:** 154 units. 8 stories, interior corridors. **Terms:** 1-7 night minimum stay, cancellation fee imposed. **Pool(s):** outdoor. **Activities:** exercise room. **Guest Services:** valet laundry, area transportation.

| AAA Benefit: Members save 5% or more! |

ECO ... CALL ... BIZ ... ...

EMBASSY SUITES BY HILTON ATLANTA-GALLERIA (770)984-9300 **9**

WWW
Hotel
$119-$299

EMBASSY SUITES by HILTON

AAA Benefit: Members save 5% or more!

Address: 2815 Akers Mill Rd 30339 **Location:** I-75 exit 258, just w. **Facility:** 261 units, some two bedrooms. 9 stories, interior corridors. **Terms:** 1-7 night minimum stay, cancellation fee imposed. **Pool(s):** heated indoor. **Activities:** hot tub, exercise room. **Guest Services:** valet and coin laundry, area transportation. **Featured Amenity: breakfast buffet.**

SAVE ... CALL ... BIZ ... ... /SOME UNITS ...

EXTENDED STAY AMERICA (ATLANTA/WILDWOOD) (770)933-8010 **2**

WW **Extended Stay Hotel.** $75-$100 **Address:** 2010 Powers Ferry Rd SE 30339 **Location:** I-75 exit 260 (Windy Hill Rd), 0.5 mi e, then just s. **Facility:** 88 efficiencies. 3 stories, interior corridors. **Terms:** cancellation fee imposed. **Pool(s):** outdoor. **Activities:** limited exercise equipment. **Guest Services:** coin laundry.

... CALL ... ... /SOME UNITS ...

EXTENDED STAY AMERICA (ATLANTA/MARIETTA/WINDY HILL/INT N PKWY) (770)226-0242 **3**

WW **Extended Stay Hotel.** $70-$90 **Address:** 2225 Interstate North Pkwy 30339 **Location:** I-75 exit 260, just e to Interstate North Pkwy, then just s. **Facility:** 100 efficiencies. 3 stories, interior corridors. **Terms:** cancellation fee imposed. **Pool(s):** outdoor. **Activities:** limited exercise equipment. **Guest Services:** coin laundry.

... CALL ... ... /SOME UNITS ...

EXTENDED STAY AMERICA ATLANTA-VININGS (770)436-1511 **17**

WW WW **Extended Stay Hotel.** $95-$115 **Address:** 2474 Cumberland Pkwy SE 30339 **Location:** I-285 exit 18, just e. **Facility:** 97 kitchen units. 4 stories, interior corridors. **Terms:** cancellation fee imposed. **Pool(s):** outdoor. **Activities:** exercise room. **Guest Services:** coin laundry.

... CALL ... ... BIZ ... ... /SOME UNITS ...

FAIRFIELD INN & SUITES BY MARRIOTT ATLANTA/VININGS (770)435-4500 **20**

WWW **Hotel.** $80-$160 **Address:** 2450 Paces Ferry Rd 30339 **Location:** I-285 exit 18, just w. **Facility:** 143 units. 7 stories, interior corridors. **Pool(s):** outdoor. **Activities:** exercise room. **Guest Services:** valet and coin laundry.

| AAA Benefit: Members save 5% or more! |

... CALL ... ... BIZ ... HS ... ...

HAMPTON INN & SUITES ATLANTA GALLERIA (770)955-1110 **8**

WWW **Hotel.** $159-$269 **Address:** 2733 Circle 75 Pkwy 30339 **Location:** I-285 exit 19 eastbound; exit 20 westbound, just n. **Facility:** 106 units, some efficiencies. 8 stories, interior corridors. **Terms:** 1-7 night minimum stay, cancellation fee imposed. **Amenities:** video games. **Pool(s):** heated indoor. **Activities:** exercise room. **Guest Services:** valet and coin laundry, area transportation.

| AAA Benefit: Members save up to 10%! |

... CALL ... ... BIZ ... HS ... ...

HAMPTON INN CUMBERLAND (770)333-6006 **16**

WWW **Hotel.** $139-$189 **Address:** 2775 Cumberland Pkwy 30339 **Location:** I-285 exit 20 westbound; exit 19 eastbound, 0.5 mi s to Akers Mill Rd, just w to Cumberland Pkwy, then just s. Located behind Cumberland Mall. **Facility:** 127 units. 4 stories, interior corridors. **Terms:** 1-7 night minimum stay, cancellation fee imposed. **Pool(s):** outdoor. **Activities:** exercise room. **Guest Services:** valet and coin laundry, area transportation.

| AAA Benefit: Members save up to 10%! |

... CALL ... ... BIZ ... ...

HILTON GARDEN INN ATLANTA NW/WILDWOOD (770)953-8850 **1**

WWW **Hotel.** $109-$189 **Address:** 3045 Windy Hill Rd 30339 **Location:** I-75 exit 260 (Windy Hill Rd), 0.6 mi w; at Powers Ferry Rd. **Facility:** 123 units. 5 stories, interior corridors. **Terms:** 1-7 night minimum stay, cancellation fee imposed. **Pool(s):** heated outdoor. **Activities:** hot tub, exercise room. **Guest Services:** valet and coin laundry, area transportation.

| AAA Benefit: Members save up to 10%! |

... CALL ... ... BIZ ... HS ... ...

HOMEWOOD SUITES-CUMBERLAND/GALLERIA (770)988-9449 **14**

WWW **Extended Stay Hotel.** $129-$159 **Address:** 3200 Cobb Pkwy SE 30339 **Location:** I-285 exit 19 eastbound; exit 20 westbound, 0.7 mi s. **Facility:** 124 efficiencies, some two bedrooms. 3 stories, interior/exterior corridors. **Terms:** 1-7 night minimum stay, cancellation fee imposed. **Pool(s):** outdoor. **Activities:** exercise room. **Guest Services:** valet and coin laundry, area transportation.

| AAA Benefit: Members save up to 10%! |

... CALL ... ... BIZ ... ... /SOME UNITS ...

HOTEL INDIGO ATLANTA VININGS 770/432-5555 **18**

WWW **Hotel.** Rates not provided. **Address:** 2857 Paces Ferry Rd 30339 **Location:** I-285 exit 18, 0.6 mi e. **Facility:** 160 units. 4 stories, interior corridors. **Pool(s):** outdoor. **Activities:** hot tub, exercise room. **Guest Services:** valet laundry, area transportation.

... CALL ... ... BIZ ... ... /SOME UNITS ... ...

(See map & index p. 76.)

HYATT HOUSE ATLANTA/COBB GALLERIA
(770)541-2960 **11**

Extended Stay Hotel $99-$309

H HYATT house™
AAA Benefit: Members save 10%!

Address: 3595 Cumberland Blvd SE 30339 **Location:** I-75 exit 258, just e. **Facility:** 149 units, some two bedrooms, efficiencies and kitchens. 6 stories, interior corridors. **Terms:** cancellation fee imposed. **Pool(s):** heated indoor. **Activities:** exercise room. **Guest Services:** valet and coin laundry, area transportation. **Featured Amenity: full hot breakfast.**

SAVE ⁑ Y CALL ᴸM ⚲ BIZ HS 🛜 ✕ 🔌 🖥 🖥 / SOME UNITS 🛏

LA QUINTA INN & SUITES ATLANTA (PACES FERRY/VININGS)
(770)801-9002 **19**

Hotel. $86-$202 **Address:** 2415 Paces Ferry Rd SE 30339 **Location:** I-285 exit 18, just w. **Facility:** 140 units. 6 stories, interior corridors. **Pool(s):** outdoor. **Activities:** hot tub, exercise room. **Guest Services:** valet and coin laundry, area transportation.

⁑ CALL ᴸM ⚲ BIZ 🛜 ✕ 🔌 🖥 🖥 / SOME UNITS 🐾 HS

RENAISSANCE ATLANTA WAVERLY HOTEL & CONVENTION CENTER
(770)953-4500 **10**

Hotel $97-$314

R RENAISSANCE® HOTELS
AAA Benefit: Members save 5% or more!

Address: 2450 Galleria Pkwy 30339 **Location:** I-285 exit 20 westbound; exit 19 eastbound, just s on US 41 (Cobb Pkwy). Adjoins shopping mall and convention center. **Facility:** This beautiful mid-rise hotel is updated with many modern luxuries. The expansive meeting spaces, on-site restaurants and spa make this a great place to mix business and pampering. 522 units. 14 stories, interior corridors. **Parking:** on-site and valet. **Amenities:** safes. **Dining:** 3 restaurants. **Pool(s):** heated outdoor, heated indoor. **Activities:** steamroom, spa. **Guest Services:** valet laundry, area transportation.

SAVE ⁑ 🧖 Y CALL ᴸM ⚲ 🧍 BIZ sHS s🛜 ✕ 📷 🖥 / SOME UNITS 🔌

SHERATON SUITES GALLERIA
(770)955-3900 **13**

Hotel $139-$269

Ⓢ **Sheraton**
AAA Benefit: Members save up to 15%, plus Starwood Preferred Guest® benefits!

Address: 2844 Cobb Pkwy SE 30339 **Location:** I-285 exit 20 westbound; exit 19 eastbound, just s. Adjacent to Cumberland Mall. **Facility:** 278 units. 17 stories, interior corridors. **Parking:** on-site (fee). **Terms:** 5 day cancellation notice. **Pool(s):** heated outdoor, heated indoor. **Activities:** exercise room. **Guest Services:** valet and coin laundry, area transportation.

SAVE ⁑ 🧖 Y CALL ᴸM ⚲ s🛜 ✕ 🔌 🖥 🖥 / SOME UNITS 🛏

WINGATE BY WYNDHAM ATLANTA GALLERIA CENTER
(678)214-6000 **12**

Hotel. $109-$139 **Address:** 2762 Cobb Pkwy SE 30339 **Location:** I-285 exit 19 eastbound; 20 westbound, just n to Spring Rd, then just s. **Facility:** 103 units. 4 stories, interior corridors. **Amenities:** safes. **Pool(s):** heated indoor. **Activities:** hot tub, exercise room. **Guest Services:** valet and coin laundry, area transportation.

⁑ CALL ᴸM ⚲ BIZ HS 🛜 ✕ 🔌 🖥 🖥

WHERE TO EAT

BUCKHEAD PIZZA CO.
770/405-0722 **4**

Pizza. Casual Dining. $5-$22 **AAA Inspector Notes:** This locally owned pizza place features wood fire pizzas, pastas and calzones in a relaxed, family-friendly environment. You can nestle up the bar with friends for cocktails after work. Any of the traditional pasta dishes are sure to please or try a flatbread. The Peachtree Road and the Atlanta steak flatbreads are local favorites. **Features:** full bar. **Address:** 1 Gallery Pkwy SE 30339 **Location:** I-75 exit 258, 0.5 mi w on Cumberland Blvd, 0.4 mi e Cobb Pkwy; in Galleria Specialty Shops at the Cobb Galleria Centre. L D CALL ᴸM

C & S SEAFOOD & OYSTER BAR
770/272-0999 **11**

Seafood. Fine Dining. $10-$40 **AAA Inspector Notes:** Designed to resemble an upscale saloon—complete with large brass doors, mosaic tile floors, tin ceiling tiles and a 35-foot mahogany bar—the restaurant prepares the freshest seafood and excellent raw bar items. Market-fresh fish selections include Alaskan halibut, black grouper, organic Scottish salmon and Chilean sea bass. Meat eaters can select from several steak entrées. Oyster options change regularly so ask your server about today's offering. **Features:** full bar, patio dining. **Address:** 3240 Cobb Pkwy 30339 **Location:** I-285 exit 20 westbound; exit 19 eastbound, 1.3 mi s; in Riverview Village. L D CALL ᴸM 🐾

CANOE
770/432-2808 **16**

New American. Fine Dining. $13-$34 **AAA Inspector Notes:** This is a dining experience where the food and the ambience create a feeling of comfortable luxury. The menu reflects a cuisine inspired by the seasons and the ethnic diversity of the city. Menu items may include peppercorn encrusted kangaroo, Arctic char, Cervena venison and Georges Bank cod. Save room for dessert as the on-site pastry chef creates delicious and imaginative delights including the popular popcorn sundae. **Features:** full bar, Sunday brunch. **Reservations:** suggested. **Address:** 4199 Paces Ferry Rd NW 30339 **Location:** I-285 exit 18, 0.6 mi e, then 1 mi s. **Parking:** on-site and valet. L D

THE CHEESECAKE FACTORY
770/319-5515 **8**

International. Casual Dining. $10-$30 **AAA Inspector Notes:** What started as a small bakery in Los Angeles in the 1970s has since blossomed into one of the most recognizable restaurant chains today. Known for their large portion sizes and seemingly never-ending menu, this restaurant features over 200 selections to choose from! The "SkinnyLicious" menu options may appeal to those counting calories. **Features:** full bar, patio dining, Sunday brunch. **Address:** 1609 Cumberland Mall 30339 **Location:** I-285 exit 20, just s; at Cumberland Mall. L D

HEIRLOOM MARKET BBQ
770/612-2502 **2**

Barbecue. Quick Serve. $7-$27 **AAA Inspector Notes:** This hugely popular joint combines barbecue techniques that originate from its owner/chefs background as Texas meets Korea. Spicy Korean or North Carolina-style sandwiches are big hits as are the smoked ribs and brisket. Burgers and sausage are available as well. Various sauces include Carolina, Texas, Tennessee, Hotlanta and Korean. A local Georgia farm is the source for the sumptuous ingredients found here. The place is quite small, popular and features patio seating only. **Features:** beer only. **Address:** 2243 Akers Mill Rd 30339 **Location:** I-285 exit 22, just w. L D

MAGGIANO'S LITTLE ITALY
770/799-1580 **9**

Italian. Fine Dining. $11-$46 **AAA Inspector Notes:** Diners savor scrumptious, traditional favorites served in a bustling atmosphere reminiscent of Little Italy. The dining area projects an early-20th-century feel; loud conversations bouncing off high ceilings evoke a sense of the Roaring 20's. **Features:** full bar. **Address:** 1601 Cumberland Mall SE, Suite 200 30339 **Location:** I-285 exit 20 westbound; exit 19 eastbound, just s; in Cumberland Mall. L D CALL ᴸM

(See map & index p. 76.)

MARLOW'S TAVERN
770/432-2526 (18)
▽▽ ▽▽ American. Casual Dining. $8-$20 **AAA Inspector Notes:** This great neighborhood tavern serves tempting appetizers and tasty sides and salads as well as well-prepared entrées such as grouper. A popular dish is the succulent fish taco. The not-to-be-missed fried okra is possibly the best in the area. The dining room is casual but offers some upscale touches. **Features:** full bar, patio dining, Sunday brunch. **Address:** 2355 Cumberland Pkwy, Suite 10 30339 **Location:** I-285 exit 18, just e to Cumberland Pkwy, then 0.5 mi s.

L D CALL M

MEEHAN'S PUBLIC HOUSE
770/433-1920
▽▽ ▽▽ Irish. Casual Dining. $10-$19 **AAA Inspector Notes:** This place offers an authentic Irish pub experience featuring everything from fish and chips and Guinness to the football/soccer game on the telly. Come in for a pint and try the bangers and mash. **Features:** full bar, patio dining, happy hour. **Address:** 2810 Paces Ferry Rd, Suite 302 30339 **Location:** I-285 exit 18, 0.5 mi e; in Station at Vinings.

L D LATE CALL M ✎

THE OLD VININGS INN
770/438-2282 (13)
▽▽▽ ▽▽ Regional American. Fine Dining. $17-$38 **AAA Inspector Notes:** This cozy, established restaurant prepares some new takes on traditional Southern-style cuisine, such as the can't-miss shrimp and grits. The braised short ribs, salmon and beef stroganoff are also delicious. **Features:** full bar, Sunday brunch. **Reservations:** suggested. **Address:** 3011 Paces Mill Rd SE 30339 **Location:** I-285 exit 18, 0.8 mi e. **Parking:** valet only.

D

OLIVE BISTRO
770/272-8900 (10)
▽▽ ▽▽ Mediterranean. Casual Dining. $6-$15 **AAA Inspector Notes:** Fresh, authentic Mediterranean food is made from family recipes, such as those for lasagna with homemade tomato basil sauce. You also can opt for a gyro or other sandwich or assemble a meal of tasty small plates, including hummus, olive tapenade and tabbouleh. This casual cafe is a great place to gather, relax and converse. **Features:** beer & wine. **Address:** 3230 Cobb Pkwy 30339 **Location:** I-75 exit 258, just w to Cobb Pkwy, then just s; in Riverview Village Shopping Center.

L D CALL M

ORIENT EXPRESS
770/438-9090 (14)
▽▽ ▽▽ Asian. Casual Dining. $7-$48 **AAA Inspector Notes:** Located in a converted train car, the huge dining space here offers an area for traditional Chinese food, a sushi bar and a dining room for hibachi-style grilling. From the vast menu offerings diners can find many stir-fried dishes such as cashew chicken, hibachi filet mignon and lobster tail and sushi delights like the octopus and sea urchin. **Features:** full bar, patio dining. **Address:** 2921 Paces Ferry Rd 30339 **Location:** I-285 exit 18, 0.7 mi e.

L D CALL M

P.F. CHANG'S CHINA BISTRO
770/803-5800 (7)
▽▽▽ ▽▽ Chinese. Fine Dining. $8-$26 **AAA Inspector Notes:** Trendy, upscale decor provides a pleasant backdrop for New Age Chinese dining. Appetizers, soups and salads are a meal by themselves. Vegetarian plates and sides, noodles, chow meins, chicken and meat dishes are created from exotic, fresh ingredients. **Features:** full bar, happy hour. **Address:** 1624 Cumberland Mall, Suite LS108 30339 **Location:** I-285 exit 20, just s; in Cumberland Mall.

L D

Ask about on-the-spot

vehicle battery testing

and replacement

RAY'S ON THE RIVER
770/955-1187 (1)
▽▽ ▽▽ ▽▽ Seafood. Fine Dining. $8-$65 **AAA Inspector Notes:** On the banks of the Chattahoochee River, this upscale, bustling seafood house serves a delicious horseradish-crusted grouper and excellent sustainable fish choices such as Georges Bank scallops and Canadian salmon. Diners also can opt for a cut of Black Angus beef. Catch an early-evening sunset from the huge picture windows off of the dining room. Jazz is presented on the weekends. **Features:** full bar, patio dining, Sunday brunch, happy hour. **Address:** 6700 Powers Ferry Rd 30339 **Location:** I-285 exit 22, 0.8 mi sw; at Powers Ferry Landing.

L D

RAY'S RIO BRAVO
770/612-2829 (17)
▽▽ ▽▽ Tex-Mex. Casual Dining. $4-$22 **AAA Inspector Notes:** This local favorite is both new and old. After the original location closed the locals clamored for the return of this casual eatery until the owners once again opened the doors. Fresh ingredients, well-prepared dishes and a lively environment create the trifecta of success for this Tex-Mex eatery. The steak fajitas, street tacos and jalapeño-lime shrimp are delicious and pair well with the massive margaritas. Save room for the dessert chimichanga. **Features:** full bar, patio dining. **Address:** 6450 Paces Ferry Rd NW 30339 **Location:** I-285 exit 22, 1.2 mi sw.

L D LATE CALL M

SOHO
770/801-0069 (15)
▽▽ ▽▽ New American. Fine Dining. $11-$37 **AAA Inspector Notes:** This American bistro is a popular lunch or after work location for local residents. It is tucked away in the Vinings Jubilee shopping plaza and offers a delicious menu of modern takes on traditional comfort foods. **Features:** full bar, patio dining. **Address:** 4300 Paces Ferry Rd, Suite 107 30339 **Location:** I-285 exit 18, 0.7 mi e; in Vinings Jubilee Plaza.

L D

STONEY RIVER
678/305-9229 (6)
▽▽▽ ▽▽ Steak. Fine Dining. $10-$34 **AAA Inspector Notes:** Premium beef trimmed by hand as well as a plethora of seafood and chicken options can be found here. Guests can enjoy the extensive wine list and upscale atmosphere. **Features:** full bar, patio dining. **Reservations:** suggested. **Address:** 1640 Cumberland Mall SE 30339 **Location:** I-285 exit 20 westbound; exit 19 eastbound, just s; in Cumberland Mall.

L D CALL M

SWAPNA INDIAN CUISINE
770/956-7589 (3)
▽▽ ▽▽ Indian. Casual Dining. $9-$16 **AAA Inspector Notes:** The buffet lunch is a popular feature of this local favorite but the a la carte dinner is delicious as well. Enjoy traditional Indian cuisine in a modern yet comfortable dining room. Portions are generous and the wine list is extensive. **Features:** beer & wine. **Address:** 2655 S Cobb Pkwy 30339 **Location:** I-285 exit 19 eastbound; exit 20 westbound, just n.

L D

THAI DINER
770/859-9898 (12)
▽▽▽ ▽▽ Thai. Casual Dining. $8-$23 **AAA Inspector Notes:** Solid standards and creative specials are among the flavorful choices. A large and tastefully done dining room helps make the dining experience all the more enjoyable. I recommend the coconut soup and sesame chicken entree. **Features:** beer & wine. **Address:** 3280 Cobb Pkwy SE 30339 **Location:** I-285 exit 20 westbound; exit 19 eastbound, 1.3 mi s; in Riverview Village Shopping Center.

L D CALL M

TOP SPICE
770/988-9007 (5)
▽▽▽ ▽▽ Asian. Fine Dining. $8-$18 **AAA Inspector Notes:** Thai and Malaysian cuisine are at their finest at this restaurant and spicy is the name of the game. Creative dishes include Malaysian-style barbecue pork jerky skewers served with crispy crackers and clay-pot seafood angel hair. Also popular are curries and noodles. **Features:** full bar. **Address:** 2997 Cobb Pkwy, Suite 200 30339 **Location:** I-75 exit 258, just w to Cobb Pkwy, then just n; I-285 exit 20, 0.6 mi s; in Akers Mill Square.

L D CALL M

WILLY'S MEXICANA GRILL
770/801-8633
▽▽ Mexican. Quick Serve. $4-$9 **AAA Inspector Notes:** Massive, made-to-order burritos are the real draw, but tacos, chips and salsa also are can't-miss items on the short but sweet menu. **Features:** beer only. **Address:** 2460 Cumberland Pkwy 30339 **Location:** I-285 exit 18, just e.

L D

ATLANTA NORTH

• Restaurants p. 131
• Hotels & Restaurants map & index p. 82

ATLANTA MARRIOTT CENTURY CENTER/EMORY AREA
(404)325-0000 **28**

▽▼▽▼▽ **Hotel. $69-$240 Address:** 2000 Century Blvd NE 30345 **Location:** I-85 exit 91, 0.3 mi w to Century Blvd, then 0.5 mi n. **Facility:** 287 units. 15 stories, interior corridors. **Pool(s):** heated outdoor. **Activities:** exercise room. **Guest Services:** valet laundry, boarding pass kiosk, area transportation.

AAA Benefit: Members save 5% or more!

ATLANTA MARRIOTT PERIMETER CENTER
(770)394-6500 **17**

▽▼▽▼▽ Hotel $88-$309

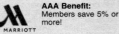

AAA Benefit: Members save 5% or more!

Address: 246 Perimeter Center Pkwy 30346 **Location:** I-285 exit 29 (Ashford-Dunwoody Rd), just n, 0.3 mi w on Hammond Dr, then just s. **Facility:** 341 units. 16 stories, interior corridors. **Terms:** check-in 4 pm. **Pool(s):** heated outdoor, heated indoor. **Activities:** hot tub, exercise room. **Guest Services:** valet and coin laundry, boarding pass kiosk, rental car service, area transportation.

COMFORT INN-BUCKHEAD NORTH
(404)252-6400 **23**

▽▼▽▼▽ **Hotel. $99-$151 Address:** 5793 Roswell Rd NE 30328 **Location:** I-285 exit 25, just n. **Facility:** 80 units. 5 stories, interior corridors. **Amenities:** safes. **Pool(s):** outdoor. **Activities:** sauna, exercise room. **Guest Services:** valet and coin laundry.

COMFORT SUITES HOTEL PERIMETER CENTER
(770)828-0330 **15**

▽▼▽▼▽ Hotel $84-$154

Address: 6110 Peachtree-Dunwoody Rd 30328 **Location:** I-285 exit 28 westbound, 1 mi n; exit 26 eastbound, 0.5 mi n to Hammond Dr, 0.7 mi e to Peachtree-Dunwoody Rd, then just n. **Facility:** 121 units. 7 stories, interior corridors. **Pool(s):** outdoor. **Activities:** sauna, exercise room. **Guest Services:** valet and coin laundry, area transportation.

COURTYARD BY MARRIOTT ATLANTA EXECUTIVE PARK/EMORY
(404)728-0708 **33**

▽▼▽▼▽ Hotel $91-$206

COURTYARD Marriott **AAA Benefit:** Members save 5% or more!

Address: 1236 Executive Park Dr 30329 **Location:** I-85 exit 89, just e to Executive Park Dr, then just s. **Facility:** 145 units. 4 stories, interior corridors. **Pool(s):** outdoor. **Activities:** exercise room. **Guest Services:** valet and coin laundry, boarding pass kiosk, area transportation.

COURTYARD BY MARRIOTT ATLANTA PERIMETER CENTER
(770)393-1000 **9**

▽▼▽▼▽ Hotel $74-$263

COURTYARD Marriott **AAA Benefit:** Members save 5% or more!

Address: 6250 Peachtree-Dunwoody Rd 30328 **Location:** I-285 exit 28 westbound, 0.8 mi n; exit 26 eastbound, 0.5 mi n, 0.7 mi e on Hammond Dr to Peachtree-Dunwoody Rd, then 0.5 mi n. **Facility:** 145 units. 4 stories, interior corridors. **Pool(s):** outdoor. **Activities:** exercise room. **Guest Services:** valet and coin laundry, boarding pass kiosk, area transportation.

CROWNE PLAZA ATLANTA PERIMETER AT RAVINIA
770/395-7700 **13**

▽▼▽▼▽ **Hotel.** Rates not provided. **Address:** 4355 Ashford-Dunwoody Rd 30346 **Location:** I-285 exit 29 (Ashford-Dunwoody Rd), just n. **Facility:** 499 units. 15 stories, interior corridors. **Parking:** on-site (fee) and valet. **Amenities:** safes. **Pool(s):** heated indoor. **Guest Services:** valet laundry, boarding pass kiosk, area transportation.

DOUBLETREE BY HILTON ATLANTA NORTH DRUID HILLS-EMORY AREA
(404)321-4174 **32**

▽▼▽▼▽ **Hotel. $149-$189 Address:** 2061 N Druid Hills Rd NE 30329 **Location:** I-85 exit 89, just w. **Facility:** 208 units. 9 stories, interior corridors. **Terms:** 1-7 night minimum stay, cancellation fee imposed. **Pool(s):** outdoor. **Activities:** exercise room. **Guest Services:** valet laundry, area transportation.

AAA Benefit: Members save 5% or more!

(See map & index p. 82.)

EMBASSY SUITES BY HILTON ATLANTA PERIMETER CENTER (770)394-5454

Hotel
$99-$299

AAA Benefit: Members save 5% or more!

Address: 1030 Crown Pointe Pkwy 30338 **Location:** I-285 exit 29 (Ashford-Dunwoody Rd), 0.5 mi n to Perimeter Center W Rd, then 0.5 mi w. Opposite Perimeter Mall. **Facility:** 241 units, some two bedrooms. 10 stories, interior corridors. **Parking:** on-site (fee). **Terms:** 1-7 night minimum stay, cancellation fee imposed. **Pool(s):** heated indoor. **Activities:** hot tub, exercise room. **Guest Services:** valet and coin laundry, area transportation. **Featured Amenity:** full hot breakfast.

Ask your AAA/CAA club

about travel money and other

financial services for travelers

EXTENDED STAY AMERICA ATLANTA-CLAIRMONT (404)679-4333 ⓐ

⬥⬥ Extended Stay Hotel. $85-$110 **Address:** 3115 Clairmont Rd 30329 **Location:** I-85 exit 91, 0.6 mi w. **Facility:** 104 efficiencies. 3 stories, interior corridors. **Terms:** cancellation fee imposed. **Guest Services:** coin laundry.

EXTENDED STAY AMERICA ATLANTA-LENOX (404)237-9100 ⓐ

⬥⬥ Extended Stay Hotel. $90-$115 **Address:** 3967 Peachtree Rd NE 30319 **Location:** I-85 exit 89, 2.8 mi w. **Facility:** 91 efficiencies. 4 stories, interior corridors. **Terms:** cancellation fee imposed. **Pool(s):** outdoor. **Activities:** limited exercise equipment. **Guest Services:** coin laundry.

EXTENDED STAY AMERICA ATLANTA-PERIMETER/CRESTLINE (770)396-5600 ⓐ

⬥⬥ Extended Stay Hotel. $80-$105 **Address:** 905 Crestline Pkwy 30328 **Location:** SR 400 exit 5A, just e to Peachtree-Dunwoody Rd, then 0.5 mi s. **Facility:** 97 efficiencies. 4 stories, interior corridors. **Terms:** cancellation fee imposed. **Guest Services:** coin laundry.

EXTENDED STAY AMERICA-ATLANTA-PERIMETER-HAMMOND DRIVE (770)522-0025 ⓐ

⬥⬥ Extended Stay Hotel. $75-$110 **Address:** 1050 Hammond Dr 30328 **Location:** I-285 exit 26 eastbound, 0.5 mi n to Hammond Dr, then 0.5 mi n; exit 28 westbound, just n to Hammond Dr, then just w. **Facility:** 129 efficiencies. 2 stories (no elevator), exterior corridors. **Terms:** cancellation fee imposed. **Guest Services:** coin laundry.

▼ See AAA listing p. 153 ▼

(See map & index p. 82.)

EXTENDED STAY AMERICA
ATLANTA-PERIMETER/PEACHTREE-DUNWOODY
(770)379-0111

▼▼▼ **Extended Stay Hotel.** $80-$105 **Address:** 6330 Peachtree-Dunwoody Rd NE 30328 **Location:** SR 400 exit 5A, just e to Peachtree-Dunwoody Rd, then 0.5 mi s. **Facility:** 100 efficiencies. 3 stories, interior corridors. **Terms:** cancellation fee imposed. **Pool(s):** outdoor. **Activities:** exercise room. **Guest Services:** coin laundry.

🛎️ CALL 🅼 🏊 BIZ 🅷🆂 📶 📶 🖨️ 📠 / SOME UNITS 🍽️

HAMPTON INN ATLANTA-NORTH DRUID HILLS
(404)320-6600

▼▼▼▼ **Hotel.** $119-$249 **Address:** 1975 N Druid Hills Rd 30329 **Location:** I-85 exit 89, just w. **Facility:** 110 units. 5 stories, interior corridors. **Terms:** 1-7 night minimum stay, cancellation fee imposed. **Pool(s):** outdoor. **Activities:** exercise room. **Guest Services:** valet laundry, area transportation.

AAA Benefit:
Members save up to 10%!

🛎️ CALL 🅼 🏊 BIZ 🅷🆂 📶 ✖️ 📶 🖨️ 📠

HAMPTON INN-PERIMETER CENTER (404)303-0014

▼▼▼▼ **Hotel.** $89-$209 **Address:** 769 Hammond Dr 30328 **Location:** I-285 exit 26 eastbound, 0.5 mi n to Hammond Dr, then 0.5 mi e; exit 28 westbound, 0.5 mi n to Hammond Dr, then 0.5 mi w. **Facility:** 131 units. 8 stories, interior corridors. **Terms:** 1-7 night minimum stay, cancellation fee imposed. **Pool(s):** outdoor. **Activities:** exercise room. **Guest Services:** valet and coin laundry, area transportation.

AAA Benefit:
Members save up to 10%!

🛎️ CALL 🅼 🏊 BIZ 📶 ✖️ 📶 🖨️ 📠

HILTON ATLANTA PERIMETER SUITES 770/668-0808

▼▼▼▼ **Hotel.** Rates not provided. **Address:** 6120 Peachtree-Dunwoody Rd 30328 **Location:** I-285 exit 28 westbound, 0.4 mi n; exit 26 eastbound, 0.5 mi n to Hammond Dr, 0.5 mi e to Peachtree-Dunwoody Rd, then just n. **Facility:** 224 units. 6 stories, interior corridors. **Amenities:** safes. **Pool(s):** heated indoor. **Activities:** hot tub, exercise room. **Guest Services:** valet laundry, area transportation.

AAA Benefit:
Members save 5% or more!

🍽️ 🛁 🍷 CALL 🅼 🏊 BIZ 🆂🅷🆂 📶 ✖️ 📶 🖨️ 📠

HILTON GARDEN INN-ATLANTA PERIMETER CENTER
404/459-0500

▼▼▼▼ **Hotel.** Rates not provided. **Address:** 1501 Lake Hearn Dr 30319 **Location:** I-285 exit 29 (Ashford-Dunwoody Rd), just s to Lake Hearn Dr, then just w. **Facility:** 193 units. 7 stories, interior corridors. **Pool(s):** heated indoor. **Activities:** hot tub, exercise room. **Guest Services:** valet and coin laundry, area transportation.

AAA Benefit:
Members save up to 10%!

🍽️ 🍷 CALL 🅼 🏊 BIZ 🅷🆂 📶 ✖️ 📶 🖨️

HOLIDAY INN ATLANTA PERIMETER 770/457-6363

▼▼▼▼ **Hotel.** Rates not provided. **Address:** 4386 Chamblee-Dunwoody Rd 30341 **Location:** I-285 exit 30 eastbound, just s; exit westbound, follow access road 1.3 mi to Chamblee-Dunwoody Rd, then just s. **Facility:** 250 units. 5 stories, interior corridors. **Pool(s):** outdoor. **Activities:** exercise room. **Guest Services:** valet and coin laundry, area transportation.

🍽️ 🛁 🍷 CALL 🅼 🏊 BIZ 🅷🆂 📶 ✖️ 📶 / SOME UNITS 🍽️ 📶 🖨️

HOLIDAY INN EXPRESS ATLANTA NE-CLAIRMONT
404/248-1550

Hotel
Rates not provided

Address: 2920 Clairmont Rd 30329 **Location:** I-85 exit 91, just w. **Facility:** 80 units. 4 stories, interior corridors. **Amenities:** safes. **Activities:** hot tub, exercise room. **Guest Services:** valet and coin laundry, area transportation. **Featured Amenity: full hot breakfast.**

SAVE 🛎️ CALL 🅼 BIZ 🅷🆂 📶 ✖️ 📶 🖨️ 📠

HOLIDAY INN EXPRESS HOTEL & SUITES-PERIMETER
404/250-4450

▼▼▼▼ **Hotel.** Rates not provided. **Address:** 765 Hammond Dr 30328 **Location:** I-285 exit 26 eastbound, 0.5 mi n, then 0.3 mi e; exit 28 westbound, 0.5 mi n to Hammond Dr, then 0.5 mi w. **Facility:** 107 units, some efficiencies. 8 stories, interior corridors. **Pool(s):** outdoor. **Activities:** exercise room. **Guest Services:** valet and coin laundry, area transportation.

🛎️ CALL 🅼 🏊 BIZ 🅷🆂 📶 ✖️ 📶 🖨️ 📠

HYATT PLACE ATLANTA/PERIMETER CENTER
(770)730-9300

Hotel
$79-$289

🏨 HYATT PLACE®
AAA Benefit: Members save 10%!

Address: 1005 Crestline Pkwy 30328 **Location:** SR 400 exit 5A (Dunwoody Rd), 0.3 mi e. **Facility:** 150 units. 3 stories, interior corridors. **Terms:** cancellation fee imposed. **Amenities:** Some: safes. **Pool(s):** outdoor. **Activities:** exercise room. **Guest Services:** valet laundry, area transportation. **Featured Amenity: full hot breakfast.**

SAVE 🛎️ 🍷 CALL 🅼 🏊 BIZ 🅷🆂 📶 ✖️ 📶 🖨️ / SOME UNITS 🍽️

HYATT REGENCY ATLANTA PERIMETER AT VILLA CHRISTINA (678)539-1234

Hotel
$109-$299

AAA Benefit:
Members save 10%!

Address: 4000 Summit Blvd 30319 **Location:** I-285 exit 29 (Ashford-Dunwoody Rd), just s to Lake Hearn Dr, follow signs to Perimeter Summit Complex, then just n. **Facility:** This beautiful hotel is a choice place for meetings, reunions and especially weddings. The elegant, contemporary design blends with lush green spaces to create a haven from the hustle of a busy city. 177 units. 1-7 stories, interior corridors. **Parking:** on-site and valet. **Amenities:** safes. **Dining:** 2 restaurants, also, Villa Christina, see separate listing. **Pool(s):** outdoor. **Activities:** exercise room, spa. **Guest Services:** valet and coin laundry, boarding pass kiosk, area transportation.

SAVE 🍽️ 🛁 🍷 CALL 🅼 🏊 📶 ✖️ 📶 🖨️ / SOME UNITS 🅷🆂 🖨️

HYATT REGENCY® ATLANTA PERIMETER

Just inside the Perimeter off Rt. 285 & GA 400. Atlanta's AAA 4-diamond "urban oasis."

(See map & index p. 82.)

LA QUINTA INN & SUITES ATLANTA (PERIMETER/MEDICAL CENTER)
(770)350-6177 **10**

 Hotel. $68-$202 **Address:** 6260 Peachtree-Dunwoody Rd 30328 **Location:** I-285 exit 28 westbound, 0.7 mi n; exit 26 eastbound, 0.5 mi n to Hammond Dr, 0.7 mi e, then 0.5 mi n. **Facility:** 142 units. 7 stories, interior corridors. **Pool(s):** outdoor. **Activities:** hot tub, exercise room. **Guest Services:** valet and coin laundry, area transportation.

LE MÉRIDIEN ATLANTA PERIMETER
(770)396-6800 **4**

Contemporary Hotel
$109-$399

Le MERIDIEN **AAA Benefit:** Members save up to 15%, plus Starwood Preferred Guest® benefits!

Address: 111 Perimeter Center W 30346 **Location:** I-285 exit 29 (Ashford-Dunwoody Rd), 0.5 mi n. **Facility:** This ultra modern, stylish hotel has an array of upscale amenities that cater to both the professional and leisure travelers. In addition to the patio lounge, guests can relax in poolside cabanas. 275 units. 12 stories, interior corridors. **Parking:** on-site (fee). **Amenities:** safes. **Pool(s):** outdoor. **Activities:** hot tub, exercise room. **Guest Services:** valet laundry, area transportation.

MICROTEL INN & SUITES BY WYNDHAM ATLANTA/PERIMETER CENTER
(678)781-4000 **8**

 Hotel. $59-$134 **Address:** 6280 Peachtree-Dunwoody Rd 30328 **Location:** SR 400 exit 5A (Dunwoody Rd), just e to Peachtree-Dunwoody Rd, then 0.5 mi s. **Facility:** 80 units. 4 stories, interior corridors. **Amenities:** safes. **Pool(s):** outdoor. **Activities:** exercise room. **Guest Services:** coin laundry, area transportation.

QUALITY INN NORTHEAST
(770)451-5231 **25**

Motel. $69-$84 **Address:** 2960 Northeast Expwy 30341 **Location:** I-85 exit 93, just w. **Facility:** 149 units. 2 stories (no elevator), exterior corridors. **Pool(s):** outdoor.

RED ROOF PLUS+ ATLANTA-BUCKHEAD
(404)321-1653 **30**

Motel
$60-$150

Address: 1960 N Druid Hills Rd 30329 **Location:** I-85 exit 89, just w. **Facility:** 115 units. 3 stories (no elevator), exterior corridors. **Amenities:** video games, safes.

Pick up colorful, top-quality
travel guides and atlases
at AAA/CAA offices

RESIDENCE INN BY MARRIOTT ATLANTA PERIMETER CENTER EAST
(770)455-4446 **11**

Extended Stay Hotel
$111-$263

Residence Inn® Marriott **AAA Benefit:** Members save 5% or more!

Address: 1901 Savoy Dr 30341 **Location:** I-285 exit 30, just e. **Facility:** 144 kitchen units, some two bedrooms. 2 stories (no elevator), exterior corridors. **Pool(s):** outdoor. **Activities:** exercise room. **Guest Services:** valet and coin laundry, area transportation. **Featured Amenity: full hot breakfast.**

SONESTA ES SUITES ATLANTA
404/250-0110 **5**

Extended Stay Hotel
Rates not provided

Address: 760 Mt Vernon Hwy NE 30328 **Location:** I-285 exit 25, 0.8 mi n on Roswell Rd, then 1 mi e. **Facility:** 122 efficiencies, some two bedrooms. 2-3 stories (no elevator), interior/exterior corridors. **Amenities:** safes. **Pool(s):** outdoor. **Activities:** exercise room. **Guest Services:** valet and coin laundry, area transportation.

STAYBRIDGE SUITES ATLANTA PERIMETER
678/320-0111 **1**

Extended Stay Hotel. Rates not provided. **Address:** 4601 Ridgeview Rd 30338 **Location:** I-285 exit 29 (Ashford-Dunwoody Rd), 0.5 mi n, 0.5 mi w on Perimeter Center W to Crowne Pointe Dr, then just n. **Facility:** 143 efficiencies, some two bedrooms. 5 stories, interior corridors. **Amenities:** video games. **Pool(s):** outdoor. **Activities:** hot tub, exercise room. **Guest Services:** valet and coin laundry, area transportation.

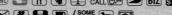

(See map & index p. 82.)

WYNDHAM ATLANTA GALLERIA (770)955-1700 24

Hotel
$79-$175

Address: 6345 Powers Ferry Rd NW 30339 **Location:** I-285 exit 22, just s. **Facility:** 296 units. 9 stories, interior corridors. **Terms:** cancellation fee imposed. **Amenities:** video games. **Pool(s):** heated outdoor, heated indoor. **Activities:** exercise room. **Guest Services:** valet and coin laundry, area transportation.

SAVE [icons] CALL [icons]
BIZ [icons]
/ SOME UNITS [icons]

WHERE TO EAT

10 DEGREES SOUTH 404/705-8870 31
African. Fine Dining. $9-$42 **AAA Inspector Notes:** The traditional South African cuisine served here is a fusion of the Portuguese, Dutch, German, Mediterranean, Malaysian, French and Indian cultures that helped to form the cultural identity of this country. This family-owned restaurant has been serving up exotic eats in a stylish setting for more than 15 years. Diners can expect bold flavors from a variety of spices, exotic ingredients such as elk and ostrich and distinctive wine selections. **Features:** full bar, patio dining. **Reservations:** suggested. **Address:** 4183 Roswell Rd NE 30342 **Location:** Between Piedmont and Wieuca rds. D LATE

THE 57TH RESTUARANT 770/234-0057 27
American. Casual Dining. $4-$30 **AAA Inspector Notes:** The smattering of Jeeps, cannons and fighter planes scattered around the lawn are the first clue that you are in for a distinctive dining experience. Walk through the sandbag-lined hallway and enter the rustic dining room decorated with pictures and memorabilia from a bygone era. The food keeps the same theme with plenty of meat and potatoes on the menu including Patton's pork (tenderloin) and Winston's chicken (breast). The best part was watching the planes take off from the adjoining airstrip. **Features:** full bar. **Reservations:** suggested. **Address:** 3829 Clairmont Rd 30341 **Location:** I-85 exit 91, 2.7 mi ne. L D CALL

ALON'S BAKERY & MARKET 678/397-1781 14
Deli. Quick Serve. $2-$12 **AAA Inspector Notes:** This bakery tempts patrons with European desserts, pastries, artisan breads, salads and sandwiches. In the market are specialty wines and cheeses as well as prepared-to-go foods. **Features:** beer & wine, patio dining, Sunday brunch. **Address:** 4505 Ashford-Dunwoody Rd NE 30346 **Location:** I-285 exit 29 (Ashford-Dunwoody Rd), 0.5 mi n; in Park Place. B L D CALL

BLUE RIDGE GRILL 404/233-5030 41
Regional American. Fine Dining. $12-$40 **AAA Inspector Notes:** This rustic Adirondack-style restaurant features creative American cuisine. Favorites of horseradish-crusted grouper and blackened mahi mahi pair well with fresh organic vegetables. Wood beams and antiques surround the dining room. **Features:** full bar, Sunday brunch. **Reservations:** suggested. **Address:** 1261 W Paces Ferry Rd 30327 **Location:** I-75 exit 255, just e. **Parking:** on-site and valet. L D

BRIO TUSCAN GRILLE 678/587-0017 3
Italian. Fine Dining. $12-$30 **AAA Inspector Notes:** While the atmosphere is casual, upscale Tuscan villa-style décor lends a sophisticated touch to the dining experience. Both lunch and dinner offer all the attentiveness a diner expects. From the garlic, spinach and artichoke dip starter to beef, chicken, veal, seafood and homemade pasta entrées, there is a selection to satisfy all tastes. Among specialties are homemade mozzarella, crisp flatbreads and wood-fired oven-baked pizza, in addition to a selection of steak. **Features:** full bar, patio dining, Sunday brunch. **Address:** 700 Ashwood Pkwy 30338 **Location:** I-285 exit 29 (Ashford-Dunwoody Rd), 0.8 mi n. L D

CAFE INTERMEZZO 770/396-1344 11
European. Casual Dining. $8-$19 **AAA Inspector Notes:** This stylish European coffee bar and restaurant serves tasty, attractively-presented dishes and delicious desserts. Crêpes, pasta, sandwiches, entrée salads and such breakfast specialties as sweet potato pancakes are the focus of the menu. Saturday and Sunday usher in a nice brunch. Friendly service rounds out an overall pleasant experience. **Features:** full bar, Sunday brunch. **Address:** 4505 Ashford-Dunwoody Rd 30346 **Location:** I-285 exit 29 (Ashford-Dunwoody Rd), 0.5 mi n; in Park Plaza Shopping Center. B L D LATE

CAFE SUNFLOWER 404/256-1675 20
Vegetarian. Casual Dining. $12-$22 **AAA Inspector Notes:** A playful yet sophisticated atmosphere blooms inside this cafe, where New Age devotees gather for elaborate and tasty vegetarian dishes and delicious desserts. Note that the restaurant is closed between lunch and dinner service. **Address:** 5975 Roswell Rd 30328 **Location:** I-285 exit 25, 0.5 mi n; in Hammonds Springs Shopping Center. L D

CANTON COOKS 404/252-0322 19
Chinese. Casual Dining. $7-$30 **AAA Inspector Notes:** The sleek, contemporary dining room is the setting for some exciting variations on basic Chinese cuisine themes. Guests rave about the salt and pepper squid, steamed sea bass, salted fried fish and the pea tips for veggie lovers. **Features:** beer & wine. **Address:** 5984 Roswell Rd 30328 **Location:** I-285 exit 25, 0.5 mi n; in The Exchange at Hammond. L D

THE CAPITAL GRILLE 770/730-8447 9
Steak. Fine Dining. $6-$47 **AAA Inspector Notes:** Cherry wood and red leather assist in making this clubby dining room a beautiful spot to dine on excellent cuts of dry-aged beef. The staff is highly attentive and knowledgeable. **Features:** full bar. **Reservations:** suggested. **Address:** 94 Perimeter Center W 30346 **Location:** I-285 exit 29 (Ashford-Dunwoody Rd), 0.5 mi n to Perimeter Center W, then 0.5 mi w. L D

THE CHEESECAKE FACTORY 678/320-0201 16
International. Casual Dining. $10-$30 **AAA Inspector Notes:** A display case of mouthwatering cheesecakes is the first thing you see as you walk through the door. The extensive menu incorporates many types of food, including Asian, Italian, Greek and Spanish dishes. **Features:** full bar, Sunday brunch. **Address:** 4400 Ashford-Dunwoody Rd 30346 **Location:** I-285 exit 29 (Ashford-Dunwoody Rd), 0.3 mi n; in Perimeter Mall. L D

ECLIPSE DI LUNA 678/205-5862 12
Spanish Small Plates. Casual Dining. $3-$20 **AAA Inspector Notes:** For those looking for a cool, trendy place to relax and let go, this is the place. Succulent flavors in tapas-size servings means guests can try a variety of items without guilt. Enjoy nightly entertainment in the dining room surrounded by Spanish-inspired art or out on the patio with a group of friends. **Features:** full bar, patio dining. Sunday brunch. **Address:** 4505 Ashford-Dunwoody Rd NE 30346 **Location:** I-285 exit 29 (Ashford-Dunwoody Rd), 0.5 mi n; in Park Place Shopping Center. L D CALL

FELLINI'S PIZZA 404/303-8248 28
Pizza. Quick Serve. $4-$24 **AAA Inspector Notes:** The menu is straightforward: just pizza, calzones and a house salad. Diners can, however, order by the slice. The dining patio allows for an al fresco meal. **Features:** beer & wine, patio dining. **Address:** 4429 Roswell Rd 30342 **Location:** Jct Roswell and Wieuca rds. L D LATE

FIVE SEASON'S BREWING COMPANY 404/255-5911 23
New American. Gastropub. $8-$27 **AAA Inspector Notes:** The brew pub serves some creative entrées, such as crispy buffalo quail, grilled pizzas and tasty handcrafted beers. Service is friendly and helpful. **Features:** full bar, patio dining. **Address:** 5600 Roswell Rd, Suite 21 30342 **Location:** I-285 exit 27, just s; in The Prado. L D

(See map & index p. 82.)

FLEMING'S PRIME STEAKHOUSE & WINE BAR
770/698-8112   7

▼▼▼ Steak. Fine Dining. $13-$53 **AAA Inspector Notes:** The warm, clubby atmosphere is the ideal setting for perfectly grilled steaks and seafood. Side dishes come in hearty portions, and salads are fresh and crisp. More than 100 wine selections are available. **Features:** full bar. **Reservations:** suggested. **Address:** 4501 Old Perimeter Pkwy 30346 **Location:** I-285 exit 29 (Ashford-Dunwoody Rd), 0.5 mi n, then 0.5 mi w on Perimeter Center W.

D   CALL M

FLOATAWAY CAFE
404/892-1414   45

▼▼▼ New American. Fine Dining. $14-$26 **AAA Inspector Notes:** In a warehouse district, the chic, contemporary digs found here are cutting-edge in style. An excellent wine list and superb cuisine make the restaurant a top choice. Desserts are exquisite. **Features:** full bar. **Reservations:** suggested. **Address:** 1123 Zonolite Rd NE 30306 **Location:** I-85 exit 89, just e on S Druid Hills Rd, 1.8 mi s on Briarcliff Rd, then 0.5 mi sw. D

FLYING BISCUIT CAFE
404/816-3152   39

▼▼ American. Casual Dining. $5-$15 **AAA Inspector Notes:** Hugely popular for breakfast and other meals serving fresh food, this place is renowned for its biscuits, which come with most courses. Bright colors and a "heavenly" ceiling with little flying biscuits make for a somewhat funky and charming atmosphere. The servers are friendly. **Features:** beer & wine, Sunday brunch. **Address:** 3515 Northside Pkwy NW, Suite 12 30327 **Location:** I-75 exit 255, just e; in Paces Ferry Plaza. B   L   CALL M

FOOD 101
404/497-9700   25

▼▼▼ New American. Fine Dining. $10-$29 **AAA Inspector Notes:** Try creative spins on old favorites, such as the interesting braised lamb shank or the buttermilk fried chicken, at this stylish, sophisticated spot in an easily accessible corner of a shopping center. Guests can expect knowledgeable, helpful service. **Features:** full bar, patio dining, Sunday brunch, happy hour. **Reservations:** suggested. **Address:** 4969 Roswell Rd, Suite 200 30342 **Location:** I-285 exit 25, 1.5 mi s; in Belle Isle Shopping Center.

L   D   CALL M 🐾

HANKOOK TAQUERIA
404/352-8881   47

▼ Korean. Quick Serve. $3-$8 **AAA Inspector Notes:** This Korean taco joint fuses Korean and Mexican influences in its fish, tofu, chicken, pork, shrimp and calamari tacos, in addition to burritos. You also can try street snacks: pork sliders with kimchee, Korean fried sweet potatoes and sesame fries. You'll have to bring your own alcohol to this simple spot, which also has a food truck that parks at various north Atlanta locations. **Address:** 1341 Collier Rd NW 30318 **Location:** I-75 exit 252, just s to Collier Rd, then 1.1 mi nw.

L   D

HAVEN
404/969-0700   33

▼▼▼ New American. Fine Dining. $18-$38 **AAA Inspector Notes:** This chic, upscale restaurant pairs creative cuisine with fine wines. Guests can enjoy the sizzle and flame emanating from the exhibition kitchen while sipping a cocktail or a glass of one of the many wine varieties. On the menu are small plates, entrées and sumptuous desserts. Among notable specialties include wild mushroom carpaccio, 30-day dry-aged steaks, wood-grilled filet mignon and praline crème brulée. **Features:** full bar, Sunday brunch. **Address:** 1441 Dresden Dr NE, Suite 160 30319 **Location:** Jct SR 141, 0.5 mi w; in Village Plaza Place. **Parking:** on-site and valet. D   CALL M

HORSERADISH GRILL
404/255-7277   29

▼▼▼ New Southern. Fine Dining. $14-$28 **AAA Inspector Notes:** The restaurant serves a taste of the New South in distinctive and imaginative regional cuisine that includes home-grown vegetables from a garden right on the premises. Beautifully decorated in wood and natural stone, the restored barn is accented with modern paintings. The staff is helpful and highly knowledgeable. **Features:** full bar, patio dining, Sunday brunch. **Reservations:** suggested. **Address:** 4320 Powers Ferry Rd 30342 **Location:** Corner of W Wieuca and Powers Ferry rds; at Chastain Park. **Parking:** valet only.

L   D

HOUSTON'S
404/262-7130   37

▼▼▼ American. Fine Dining. $16-$44 **AAA Inspector Notes:** This popular, spacious restaurant features leather booths and an open kitchen. On the menu you will find tasty burgers, steaks and salads. Portions are large, the fresh grilled fish selection changes daily, and there is a small wine list. **Features:** full bar. **Address:** 3539 Northside Pkwy NW 30327 **Location:** I-75 exit 255, just e. L   D

JOEY D'S OAK ROOM
770/512-7063   6

▼▼▼ American. Casual Dining. $10-$34 **AAA Inspector Notes:** In a bustling commercial and business park on the city's north side, this informal dining room decked out with acres of oak parquet flooring is the setting for delicious steaks and sandwiches. Try the corned beef sandwich with its massive amount of lean corned beef said to be specially flown in from the Carnegie Deli. You might also want to visit the huge, well-stocked bar for your favorite drink or try one of the bartender's creations. **Features:** full bar, patio dining. **Reservations:** suggested. **Address:** 1015 Crown Pointe Pkwy 30338 **Location:** I-285 exit 29 (Ashford-Dunwoody Rd), 0.5 mi n, then 0.5 mi w on Perimeter Center W. L   D   CALL M 🌙

MAGGIANO'S LITTLE ITALY
770/804-3313   17

▼▼▼ Italian. Fine Dining. $11-$46 **AAA Inspector Notes:** Diners savor scrumptious, traditional favorites served in a bustling atmosphere reminiscent of Little Italy. The dining area projects an early-20th-century feel; loud conversations bouncing off high ceilings evoke a sense of the Roaring 20's. **Features:** full bar. **Address:** 4400 Ashford-Dunwoody Rd 30346 **Location:** I-285 exit 29 (Ashford-Dunwoody Rd), 0.3 mi n; in Perimeter Mall. L   D

MCCORMICK & SCHMICK'S
770/399-9900   4

▼▼▼ Seafood. Fine Dining. $12-$39 **AAA Inspector Notes:** This place is all about seafood, which is imported from all over the world. Among good choices are Washington state oysters, Maine clams, delicate Hawaiian escolar and tuna from Ecuador. The clublike decor is cozy and the staff is attentive. **Features:** full bar, happy hour. **Address:** 600 Ashwood Pkwy 30338 **Location:** I-285 exit 29 (Ashford-Dunwoody Rd), 1.2 mi n. L   D

MCKENDRICK'S STEAK HOUSE
770/512-8888   13

▼▼▼ Steak. Fine Dining. $10-$53 **AAA Inspector Notes:** In an upscale shopping plaza, the posh steakhouse presents an extensive wine list to complement its Prime beef and varied seafood dishes. A good meal might include stuffed scallops, New York strip and the beefsteak tomato salad. Dressy casual is the mode of attire. Servers are highly attentive, knowledgeable and responsive. **Features:** full bar. **Reservations:** suggested. **Address:** 4505 Ashford-Dunwoody Rd NE 30346 **Location:** I-285 exit 29 (Ashford-Dunwoody Rd), 0.5 mi n. **Parking:** on-site and valet. L   D

MEMPHIS BARBECUE COMPANY
770/394-7427   2

▼▼▼ Barbecue. Casual Dining. $4-$23 **AAA Inspector Notes:** After refining the recipes and techniques on the competitive barbecue circuit, the owners of this restaurant opened their doors to the public. The delicious flavors come from a long, slow smoke over hardwoods. The baby back ribs, smoked brisket sandwich and pulled pork are the specialties of the house. Bring your appetite and leave the belt at home because you won't leave hungry. **Features:** full bar. **Address:** 4764 Ashford-Dunwoody Rd 30338 **Location:** I-285 exit 29 (Ashford-Dunwoody Rd), 1.2 mi n. L   D   CALL M

MESKEREM ETHIOPIAN CUISINE
404/417-0991   40

▼▼ Ethiopian. Casual Dining. $3-$32 **AAA Inspector Notes:** Try something exotic for dinner in this authentic Ethiopian eatery. The intimate restaurant and the friendliness of the waitstaff make this a family friendly location. **Features:** full bar, patio dining, happy hour. **Address:** 2781 Clairmont Rd NE 30329 **Location:** I-85 exit 91, just e; in Williamsburg Village Shopping Center. L   D

MIKE'S HOT DOGS
404/252-8484   21

▼ Hot Dogs. Quick Serve. $3-$8 **AAA Inspector Notes:** Slaw dogs, kraut dogs, chili dogs, stew dogs, corn dogs and veggie dogs are all to be found at this spot, but the Chicago-style dog with 100 percent Vienna beef is the crown jewel here. Polish sausage and Italian beef sandwiches are other options and sides include coleslaw, pizza puffs, fries, onion rings and some great red skin potato salad. **Features:** patio dining. **Address:** 5948 Roswell Rd NE 30328 **Location:** I-285 exit 25, 0.4 mi n; in Parkside Shopping Center.

L   D

(See map & index p. 82.)

MIRAGE   404/843-8300 (5)
▼▼ Mediterranean. Casual Dining. $8-$24 **AAA Inspector Notes:** Enjoy this Persian oasis of traditional cuisine among the hum drum culinary options of the area. Tantalizing aromas and friendly servers greet guests at this small family restaurant. The variety of traditional dishes offer plenty of options so diners are sure to find the perfect dish to satisfy. **Features:** beer & wine. **Address:** 6631 Roswell Rd, Suite B/C 30328 **Location:** I-285 exit 25, 1.6 mi n; in Abernathy Square. [L] [D]

NUEVO LAREDO CANTINA   404/352-9009 (48)
▼▼ Tex-Mex. Casual Dining. $9-$20 **AAA Inspector Notes:** In business since 1992, this award-winning restaurant centers its menu on home-style Mexican cooking. Specialties include brisket Barbacoa, chicken mole, over-stuffed poblano chiles rellenos and lobster or fish (grilled salmon) tacos. The owner refers to his cuisine as cult Mexican for die-hard fans. **Features:** full bar. **Address:** 1495 Chattahoochee Ave 30318 **Location:** I-75 exit 252, 0.4 mi s on Howell Mill Rd, nw to Chattahoochee Ave NW, then 1.5 mi nw. [L] [D]

O K CAFE   404/233-2888 (42)
▼▼ Southern. Casual Dining. $5-$16 **AAA Inspector Notes:** This well-lighted café takes guests back in time with its plaid motif and diner-style menu. Monstrous portions of fresh comfort foods such as country-fried steak and homemade desserts are dished up by fast, friendly servers. **Features:** beer & wine, Sunday brunch. **Address:** 1284 W Paces Ferry Rd 30327 **Location:** I-75 exit 255, just e. [B] [L] [D]

PANAHAR BANGLADESHI CUISINE   404/633-6655 (36)
▼▼ Indian. Casual Dining. $10-$15 **AAA Inspector Notes:** A weekday lunch buffet provides a nice alternative to the eatery's menu of exotic dinner items, including chicken and lamb karai, shrimp sagwala and many vegetarian dishes. **Address:** 3375 Buford Hwy, Suite 1060 30329 **Location:** I-85 exit 89, just w to N Druid Hills Rd, then 0.8 mi n; in North East Plaza. [L] [D]

PERO'S PIZZA & PASTA   404/261-5077 (38)
▼▼ Italian. Casual Dining. $8-$30 **AAA Inspector Notes:** This quaint eatery has been serving satisfied Atlantans tasty cuisine for more than 40 years. Chicken parmigiana is popular as is pizza. Other Italian favorites include shrimp marinara, linguine with clam sauce, baked lasagna and veal Francese. The lunch buffet is a big draw during the week. **Features:** beer & wine. **Address:** 3521 Northside Pkwy 30327 **Location:** I-75 exit 255, just e; in Regency Center. [L] [D] CALL [M] [×]

P.F. CHANG'S CHINA BISTRO   770/352-0500 (1)
▼▼▼ Chinese. Fine Dining. $8-$26 **AAA Inspector Notes:** Trendy, upscale decor provides a pleasant backdrop for New Age Chinese dining. Appetizers, soups and salads are a meal by themselves. Vegetarian plates and sides, noodles, chow meins, chicken and meat dishes are created from exotic, fresh ingredients. **Features:** full bar, happy hour. **Address:** 500 Ashwood Pkwy 30338 **Location:** I-285 exit 29 (Ashford-Dunwoody Rd), 0.8 mi n. [L] [D]

PHO DAI LOI   404/633-2111 (30)
▼▼ Vietnamese. Casual Dining. $7-$10 **AAA Inspector Notes:** Piping-hot bowls of pho and other Vietnamese favorites, including fresh basil rolls and vermicelli, satisfy patrons at this eatery. Earnest servers circulate through the dining room appointed in pleasing traditional Vietnamese décor. **Address:** 4186 Buford Hwy, Suite G 30345 **Location:** I-285 exit 32, 2.8 mi s. [B] [L] [D] CALL [M]

PIG-N-CHIK   404/255-6368 (26)
▼ Barbecue. Quick Serve. $6-$24 **AAA Inspector Notes:** Although pulled pork is the staple here, patrons averse to it can try salmon instead. Lines are a given at this popular spot. Music lends to the atmosphere on alternating Fridays. Outside seating offers no frills. **Features:** beer only, patio dining. **Address:** 4920 Roswell Rd NE 30342 **Location:** I-285 exit 25, 1.5 mi s; in Fountain Oaks Shopping Center. [L] [D] [🛒]

PIG-N-CHIK   404/474-9444 (46)
▼ Barbecue. Quick Serve. $6-$26 **AAA Inspector Notes:** Although pulled pork is the staple here, patrons averse to it can try salmon, smoked wings or a chef's salad instead. Lines are a given at this popular spot and two sister locations means there is probably one close to you if you are in the Atlanta area. **Features:** beer only, patio dining. **Address:** 1815 Briarcliff Rd NE 30329 **Location:** Jct Clifton Rd. [L] [D]

QUEEN OF SHEBA   404/321-1493 (43)
▼▼ Ethiopian. Casual Dining. $6-$16 **AAA Inspector Notes:** This restaurant provides a distinctive opportunity to get out of the dinner rut and try something exotic. The menu features authentic Ethiopian cuisine for a casual dining experience. I recommend starting with the sambasa (lentils in a deep fried phyllo dough) then moving on to the savory beef tips. The friendly staff is happy to share their culture and can help with selections. Gather up the family or have a business lunch because the large dining room can easily accommodate groups. **Features:** full bar. **Address:** 1594 Woodcliff Dr NE 30329 **Location:** I-85 exit 89, 0.5 mi e; in Briarcliff Station Shopping Center. [L] [D] [LATE]

SAGE WOODFIRE TAVERN   770/804-8808 (15)
▼▼▼ Steak. Fine Dining. $7-$31 **AAA Inspector Notes:** As the name implies, this restaurant grills most of their menu on a hickory fire which gives all the food a sweet, smoky flavor. Start the meal with the wood-fire rosemary shrimp skewers or the bruschetta. I recommend the hanger steak and the 22-ounce bone in rib-eye, but you can't go wrong with any of the steaks. The intimate setting and trendy accent pieces add to the ambience. **Features:** full bar. **Reservations:** suggested. **Address:** 4505 Ashford Dunwoody Rd NE 30346 **Location:** I-285 exit 29 (Ashford-Dunwoody Rd), just n. [L] [D] CALL [M]

SEASONS 52 FRESH GRILL   770/671-0052 (10)
▼▼▼ New American. Fine Dining. $12-$30 **AAA Inspector Notes:** Embracing a distinctive concept, this restaurant focuses entirely on calorie-conscious dishes that reflect the current season. The menu changes 52 times a year. Modern and tasty choices include several types of flatbreads, salmon, chicken and an unusual offering of novelty dessert shots. Many by-the-glass options are among selections on the wine list. **Features:** full bar, patio dining, happy hour. **Address:** 90 Perimeter Center W 30346 **Location:** I-285 exit 29 (Ashford-Dunwoody Rd), 0.5 mi n; adjacent to Perimeter Mall. [L] [D]

SUSHI HUKU   770/956-9559 (24)
▼▼ Japanese Sushi. Casual Dining. $8-$42 **AAA Inspector Notes:** Delectable sushi and tempura dishes are nicely presented and made with fresh ingredients. Well-prepared dishes include pork in ginger sauce and shrimp Sushi Huku, both delicious and highly recommended. Sake and Japanese beers pair well with the food. **Features:** beer & wine. **Address:** 6300 Powers Ferry Rd 30339 **Location:** I-285 exit 22; opposite Crowne Plaza Atlanta Perimeter Galleria; in shopping center. [L] [D]

TERRA TERROIR PATIO, BISTRO & BAR   404/841-1032 (34)
▼▼▼ American. Fine Dining. $10-$35 **AAA Inspector Notes:** Don't let the shopping center location fool you, this beautiful restaurant offers friendly service and a garden-style patio. The menu focuses on healthy, lean cuisine such as farm-raised buffalo burgers, meatloaf, chicken, trout, turkey and vegetarian dishes. Gluten-free options also are available. **Features:** full bar, patio dining. **Address:** 3974-C Peachtree Rd NE 30319 **Location:** SR 400 exit 2, just w to Peachtree Rd NE, then 1.5 mi ne; in Brookhaven Plaza. [L] [D] CALL [M]

THAI CHILI   404/315-6750 (44)
▼▼ Thai. Casual Dining. $8-$27 **AAA Inspector Notes:** Expertly prepared authentic Thai cuisine features noteworthy culinary creations daily. Start with fried tofu with a sweet peanut sauce for dipping, then indulge in an entrée of fried soft-shell crab. For the adventurous palate, try coconut milk soup. **Features:** full bar. **Address:** 2169 Briarcliff Rd NE 30329 **Location:** I-85 exit 89, 0.3 mi e to Briarcliff Rd, then 0.9 mi s; in Briar Vista Shopping Center. [L] [D]

(See map & index p. 82.)

TIN LIZZY'S CANTINA
470/514-1050 ⑧

Tex-Mex. Casual Dining. $3-$10 **AAA Inspector Notes:** This is where locals and travelers converge to feast on delicious tacos, nachos and skillet meals. Portions are generous and the flavors are bold. The steak tacos are my favorite, but the Korean BBQ and Buffalo shrimp tacos are also great. The bar churns out a variety of beverages that keep the atmosphere lively and fun. **Features:** full bar. **Address:** 121 Perimeter Center W 30346 **Location:** I-285 exit 29 (Ashford-Dunwoody Rd), just n, then 0.6 mi w.

Ⓛ Ⓓ CALL 🅼

VERDE TAQUERIA
404/254-5319 ㉜

Mexican. Casual Dining. $4-$8 **AAA Inspector Notes:** Diners can find an interesting selection of tacos including pulled pork, short rib, fried chicken and buffalo tofu. Start with some chips and salsa, or try the crispy calamari dusted in cornmeal and served with fried jalapeños, jalapeño ranch dressing and lime. A well-stocked bar includes some creative margaritas. **Features:** full bar, patio dining. **Address:** 1426 Dresden Dr 30309 **Location:** Jct Peachtree Rd, 0.5 mi e.
Ⓛ Ⓓ CALL 🅼

VILLA CHRISTINA
404/303-0133 ㉒

Italian. Fine Dining. $14-$35 **AAA Inspector Notes:** Adjacent to a luxurious hotel, this upscale Italian restaurant offers delicious cuisine in a quiet, residential area overlooking an expansive green space. Enjoy the view and the various pasta, beef, chicken and pork dishes available. The attentive waitstaff awaits your presence. **Features:** full bar, happy hour. **Reservations:** suggested. **Address:** 4000 Summit Blvd 30319 **Location:** I-285 exit 29 (Ashford-Dunwoody Rd), just s to Lake Hearn Dr, follow signs to Perimeter Summit Complex, then just n; in Hyatt Atlanta Perimeter - Villa Christina. **Parking:** on-site and valet.
Ⓛ Ⓓ

VIOLETTE
404/633-3363 ㉟

French. Casual Dining. $9-$29 **AAA Inspector Notes:** This charming French bistro has a nice selection of wines and offers a good value. Traditional favorites include coq au vin, vichyssoise, quiche Lorraine, beef bourguignon and escargot. Excellent salads are available at both lunch and dinner and the delicious desserts, such as chocolate mousse and orange-cranberry pudding, are cannot miss items. **Features:** full bar, patio dining, happy hour. **Address:** 2948 Clairmont Rd NE 30329 **Location:** I-85 exit 91, just w.

Ⓛ Ⓓ 🐾

ATLANTA SOUTH
• Hotels & Restaurants map & index p. 94

EMORY CONFERENCE CENTER HOTEL
404/712-6000 ④

Hotel. Rates not provided. **Address:** 1615 Clifton Rd 30329 **Location:** Adjacent to Emory University. Opposite Centers for Disease Control. **Facility:** 325 units. 5 stories, interior corridors. **Parking:** on-site (fee). **Terms:** check-in 4 pm. **Dining:** 2 restaurants. **Pool(s):** heated indoor. **Activities:** hot tub, exercise room. **Guest Services:** valet and coin laundry, area transportation.

ECO Ⓨ 🛏 🍽 CALL 🅼 ⊇ BIZ HS 📶 ⊠ 🖤 / SOME UNITS 🔒 🖼

RENAISSANCE CONCOURSE ATLANTA AIRPORT HOTEL
(404)209-9999 ①

Hotel
$79-$286

R RENAISSANCE° HOTELS

AAA Benefit: Members save 5% or more!

Address: One Hartsfield Centre Pkwy 30354 **Location:** I-85 exit 73A northbound; exit 73 southbound, just e to Toffie Terrace, then just se. **Facility:** Next to the airport, the hotel has some units that overlook the adjacent runways. Spacious guest units are decorated with a contemporary flair. The expansive meeting space is popular with large groups. 387 units. 11 stories, interior corridors. **Parking:** on-site (fee) and valet. **Terms:** check-in 4 pm. **Pool(s):** outdoor, heated indoor. **Activities:** sauna, hot tub. **Guest Services:** valet laundry, area transportation.

SAVE ⤝ Ⓨ 🛏 🍽 CALL 🅼 ⊇ ✚ BIZ ⒮HS 📶 ⊠ 📷 🔒 🖼

THE UNIVERSITY INN AT EMORY
404/634-7327 ⑤

Motel. Rates not provided. **Address:** 1767 N Decatur Rd NE 30307 **Location:** Adjacent to Emory University. Opposite Emory Medical Complex. **Facility:** 32 units, some efficiencies and kitchens. 2-3 stories (no elevator), interior/exterior corridors. **Pool(s):** outdoor. **Guest Services:** coin laundry.

🍽 ⊇ BIZ HS 📶 ⊠ 🔒 🖼 / SOME UNITS ⒮🖥 🖼

(See map & index p. 94.)

WHERE TO EAT

BULLPEN RIB HOUSE   404/577-5774 [2]
▼ Barbecue. Quick Serve. $6-$21 **AAA Inspector Notes:** Ribs tend to be a personal preference type of thing but these are some of the best I have found in the Atlanta area. Located across the street from Turner Field, this eatery also offers such tasty smoked barbecue items as turkey, chicken and brisket. The wings are favorites here along with burgers, all-beef hot dogs and some killer Brunswick stew. **Features:** full bar, patio dining. **Address:** 735 Pollard Blvd SW 30315 **Location:** I-75/85 exit 246, 0.3 mi e to Hank Aaron Dr, just s to Ralph D. Abernathy Blvd, just w to Pollard Blvd, then just s.
[L] [D] CALL [&M]

FLIP BURGER BOUTIQUE   404/352-3547
▼ ▼ Burgers. Casual Dining. $7-$21 **AAA Inspector Notes:** This place puts a trendy and modern spin on the common burger joint. Cooked-to-order gourmet burgers made from hanger steak include the Philly, steak tartare and Oaxaca burger. For those not in the mood for beef, try the crab, tuna, veal and veggie burgers. Tempting sides include french fries, fried okra, vodka-battered onion rings and sweet potato tots. The creative milk shakes are both distinctive and delicious. **Features:** full bar, patio dining. **Address:** 1587 Howell Mill Rd 30318 **Location:** I-75 exit 252, 0.4 mi w. [L] [D] CALL [&M]

FLYING BISCUIT CAFE   404/687-8888 [7]
▼ ▼ American. Casual Dining. $8-$19 **AAA Inspector Notes:** This cozy, hip and funky spot is known for its enormous biscuits, which practically fly out of the kitchen as soon as they are made. Examples of healthful home-style cooking include many all-day breakfast items. On weekends, expect a long wait for breakfast or brunch. **Features:** beer & wine, Sunday brunch. **Address:** 1655 McLendon Ave 30307 **Location:** In Candler Park. [B] [L] [D]

MARLOW'S TAVERN   404/343-3283 [6]
▼ ▼ Burgers. Casual Dining. $9-$17 **AAA Inspector Notes:** This great regional chain brings tavern food to a new level with tempting appetizers, yummy sides and well-prepared entrées. I like to start with asparagus fries or bruschetta before moving on to the famous fish tacos or tavern burger. Located in a trendy shopping village, parking in the garage is both incredibly close and free for diners. **Address:** 1520 Avenue Pl 30329 **Location:** Adjacent to Emory University. [L] [D] CALL [&M]

MILLER UNION   678/733-8550 [1]
▼ ▼ ▼ New American. Fine Dining. $13-$34 **AAA Inspector Notes:** The emphasis here is on the partnership between the chef and the farmer. Only the week's freshest harvest goes into dishes that bring out true flavors. Start with a farm egg baked in celery cream with rustic bread, then savor an entrée of house-made pork sausage with a side of braised local greens. For dessert, the simple scoop of the day holds its own against more creative choices. On the third Tuesday of every month, you can try the family-style harvest dinner. **Features:** full bar, patio dining. **Reservations:** suggested. **Address:** 999 Brady Ave 30318 **Location:** Jct 10th St.
[L] [D] CALL [&M]

TIN LIZZY'S CANTINA   404/537-5355 [5]
▼ ▼ Tex-Mex. Casual Dining. $3-$10 **AAA Inspector Notes:** Located in a busy shopping village, this Tex-Mex restaurant is lively, quirky and fun. The menu features several saliva-inducing menu items such as "Three Little Pigs" nachos, a Korean barbecue pork taco, the "Super Greek" taco, and my personal favorite, a grilled steak taco. Wash it all down with an ice-cold margarita. **Features:** full bar. **Address:** 1540 Avenue Pl 30329 **Location:** Adjacent to Emory University. [L] [D] [LATE] CALL [&M]

AUGUSTA (C-5) pop. 195,844, elev. 162'
• Hotels p. 137 • Restaurants p. 140

Augusta, Georgia's second oldest city, was founded in 1736, 3 years after Savannah. Long a crossroads of Native American territory, the city continued as a trading center from Colonial days until after the Revolution, becoming one of the main proponents of the New South during the post-Civil War Reconstruction era.

The city served as the colony's temporary capital before and during the Revolution, as well as the state capital from 1786-95 after the war concluded. The Declaration of Independence was signed by three Georgians, each associated with the Augusta government: Button Gwinnett, Lyman Hall and George Walton.

Augusta assumed the role of manufacturing center after a canal was built in 1845. The 9-mile Augusta Canal, now a National Heritage Area, is open for tours and features a discovery center *(see attraction listing).*

After the Civil War, many residents opened their homes to paying guests from the North who were attracted by the region's mild winters. By the 1890s Augusta had become a major winter resort area. The city has several neighborhoods on the National Register, including the Olde Towne Historic District and the Summerville neighborhood.

During this period the owner of one resort hotel built a nine-hole golf course, introducing the game to his wealthy guests. The game was so popular that the following year an 18-hole course was built at what now is the Augusta Country Club. Each April The Masters Tournament, played at the Augusta National Golf Club, attracts the country's best golfers and a number of international champions, as well as thousands of spectators.

The Augusta Futurity and Festival, occurring in January at the James Brown Arena, is one of several cutting horse competitions that takes place, and Augusta also is home to world-class water-sports events including the Augusta Southern Nationals drag boat races in July and the Head of the South Rowing Regatta in November.

Historical sites and monuments commemorate prominent figures in city history. The Monument to Georgia's Signers *(see attraction listing p. 137)* (of the Declaration of Independence, that is) stands on Greene Street between 5th and 6th streets. At the center of the Augusta Common, Broad Street between 8th and 9th streets, is a statue of Augusta founder Gen. James E. Oglethorpe. The Korean War Memorial, in the 400 block of Broad Street, honors Augusta-area Korean War soldiers.

In the 800 block of Broad Street, a life-size bronze statue of musician and singer James Brown pays tribute to the Godfather of Soul's contributions to the music industry and the Augusta community. The Lucy Craft Laney Museum of Black History, 1116 Phillips St., is housed in the former home of the influential educator. Exhibits recall her life and legacy; phone (706) 724-3576.

Springfield Village Park is adjacent to the Springfield Baptist Church. The church, at 114 12th St., is the country's oldest independently established African-American Baptist church. The adjoining park features a reflecting pool, bronze plaques and

African-American sculptor Richard Hunt's 45-foot-tall stainless steel piece "The Tower of Aspiration."

Riverwalk consists of five blocks of paved walkways, landscaped lawns and gardens on two levels along the Savannah River. The area, which is the site of a variety of festivals and events, also contains a marina, restaurants, shops, museums and the Jessye Norman Amphitheater. Performances take place at the amphitheater; phone (706) 821-1754 for events information.

The ⧉ Arts in the Heart of Augusta festival in mid-September features a parade of nations, visual and performing arts, entertainment, activities for kids, ethnic food and fireworks. Contact the Greater Augusta Arts Council for details; phone (706) 826-4702.

Augusta Visitor Center: In the lobby of the Augusta Museum of History (see attraction listing this page) at 560B Reynolds St., Augusta, GA 30901. **Phone:** (706) 724-4067 or (877) 284-8782.

Self-guiding tours: Pamphlets describing walking and driving tours of Augusta's historic districts and its special events are available at the Augusta Visitor Center within the Augusta Museum of History (see attraction listing this page).

AUGUSTA CANAL DISCOVERY CENTER is at 1450 Greene St., Suite 400. Part of the Augusta Canal National Heritage Area, the discovery center, which is housed in a renovated 19th-century cotton mill, describes the canal's 170-year history through interactive exhibits and displays of working mill machinery. "The Power of a Canal," a 10-minute film shown in a surround-sound theater, orients visitors to the 10,000-square-foot facility.

The Petersburg Boat Guided Tours depart several times daily and offer a variety of 1- to 1.5-hour narrated canal excursions (weather permitting), passing natural and historic sites along the way. Tours featuring live musical performances also are offered.

Time: Allow 1 hour minimum. **Hours:** Discovery center open Mon.-Sat. 9:30-5, Sun. 1-5, Apr.- June and Sept.-Nov.; Tues.-Sat. 9:30-5, rest of year. One-hour boat tour departs Mon.-Sat. at 10, 11:30 and 3, Sun. at 3, Apr.-June and Sept.-Nov.; Tues.-Sat. at 10 and 11:30, July-Aug.; Tues.-Sat. at 3, rest of year. One-hour Civil War-themed tours are given at 1:30. Live-music tours on select Fri. evenings in spring and fall. Closed Jan. 1, Easter, July 4, day before Thanksgiving, Thanksgiving, Christmas Eve and Christmas. Phone ahead to confirm schedule.

Cost: Discovery center $6; $4 (ages 4-18, ages 65+, military and college students with ID); free (ages 0-3 with paid adult). One-hour tour fare (includes discovery center admission) $13.75; $11.75 (ages 4-18, ages 65+, military and college students with ID); free (ages 0-3 with paid adult). Music cruise fare (includes discovery center admission) $25; $23 (ages 4-18, ages 65+, military and college students

with ID). Phone ahead to confirm rates. Reservations are recommended. **Phone:** (706) 823-0440 or (888) 659-8926. GT

AUGUSTA MUSEUM OF HISTORY, 560 Reynolds St., features Augusta's Story, an exhibit that focuses on the history of Augusta and the surrounding region. Other exhibits spotlight the history of golf and its legacy in Augusta and soul icon James Brown. The Local Legends exhibit features the accomplishments of other local residents. Life-size bronze statues of golf greats also are on display. Reminders of days gone by include a 1917 steam locomotive and a 1930s-era gas station. Historical documentaries are shown. Temporary exhibits also are available.

Time: Allow 1 hour minimum. **Hours:** Thurs.-Sat. 10-5, Sun. 1-5. Closed major holidays. **Cost:** $4; $3 (ages 65+); $2 (ages 6-18). **Phone:** (706) 722-8454.

THE BOYHOOD HOME OF PRESIDENT WOODROW WILSON is at 419 7th St.; entrance is at visitors center, 415 7th St. Built in 1859, the house was purchased by the First Presbyterian Church as the church's manse. The Rev. Dr. Joseph Ruggles Wilson lived here 1860-70 with his family, including his son Thomas Woodrow. "Tommy" was three when the family moved in, and would grow up to become the 28th president of the United States. Fourteen rooms feature Victorian furnishings, including 13 pieces that were used by the Wilson family.

Time: Allow 1 hour minimum. **Hours:** Guided 45-minute tours begin on the hour Thurs.-Sat. 10-4. Last tour departs at closing. Closed Jan. 1, July 4, Thanksgiving and Christmas. **Cost:** $5; $4 (ages 60+); $3 (grades K-12); free (ages 0-5). **Phone:** (706) 722-9828. GT

CONFEDERATE MONUMENT, Broad St. between 7th and 8th sts., is a 76-foot-high shaft of Italian marble. The monument, dominated by a statue of Confederate Sgt. Barry Greenwood Benson, includes life-size figures of Gens. Robert E. Lee, Thomas J. "Stonewall" Jackson, W.H.T. Walker and Thomas R.R. Cobb.

GERTRUDE HERBERT INSTITUTE OF ART, 506 Telfair St., is a handsome three-story Federal-style house built by Georgia legislator Nicholas Ware in 1818. Because of its huge cost of $40,000, the structure was known as "Ware's Folly." Works by local and nationally known contemporary artists are displayed. Educational programs are offered. **Hours:** Mon.-Fri. 10-5. Closed major holidays. **Cost:** Free. **Phone:** (706) 722-5495.

MEADOW GARDEN is at 1320 Independence Dr. (off 13th St. between Telfair and Walton Way), near the Augusta Canal. The 1792 home of George Walton, a signer of the Declaration of Independence, is furnished with 18th- and early 19th-century pieces. **Hours:** Guided 30-minute tours Tues.-Sat. 10-4. Last tour begins 1 hour before closing. Closed major holidays. **Cost:** $5; $4 (ages 62+ and military with ID); $1 (ages 5-18). **Phone:** (706) 724-4174. GT

MONUMENT TO GEORGIA'S SIGNERS of the Declaration of Independence, on Greene St. between 5th and 6th sts., is an 1848 marble obelisk beneath which lie the remains of George Walton and Lyman Hall. Also honored by the monument is Button Gwinnett, whose remains are believed to be buried in Savannah.

MONUMENT TO THE POETS OF GEORGIA, in the 700 block of Greene St., is a marble monument honoring 19th-century Southern poets Sidney Lanier, a native of Macon, James R. Randall and Father Abram Ryan who each lived in Augusta for a while, and Paul Hamilton Hayne who lived in Grovetown and is buried in Augusta.

MORRIS MUSEUM OF ART is on the Riverwalk at 1 Tenth St. The museum is dedicated to the art and artists of the American South. The permanent collection of nearly 5,000 paintings, drawings, prints, photographs and sculptures is displayed in themed galleries, including 19th-century portraiture, the Civil War, Southern scenes, still lifes, Impressionist paintings, landscapes, and modern and contemporary art. More than 20 special exhibitions are hosted annually. Educational programs and special events are offered.

Time: Allow 1 hour minimum. **Hours:** Tues.-Sat. 10-5, Sun. noon-5. Closed major holidays. **Cost:** $5; $3 (senior citizens and military and students with ID); free (Sun. and ages 0-12). **Phone:** (706) 724-7501.

PHINIZY SWAMP NATURE PARK, 1 mi. s. of I-520 exit 10 at 1858 Lock and Dam Rd., contains 1,150 acres of natural and constructed wetlands, swamps and streams. Several nature trails, boardwalks and four observation decks offer views of wildlife. Information kiosks throughout the park provide information about the Southeast's natural resources. **Time:** Allow 1 hour, 30 minutes minimum. **Hours:** Daily dawn-dusk. Guided tour first Sat. of the month at 9:30. Children's hike second Sat. of the month at 9:30. Stream Explorers hike fourth Sat. of the month at 9:30. Visitor center open Sat. 10-5, Sun. 1-5. **Cost:** Guided tour $2. Visitor center free. **Phone:** (706) 828-2109. (GT) (⊞)

SACRED HEART CULTURAL CENTER, 1301 Greene St., was formerly Sacred Heart Catholic Church. The 1900 Romanesque and Byzantine building features intricate brickwork, a barrel-vaulted ceiling, 92 stained-glass windows, tall turrets and graceful arches and now serves as a cultural center for the community. A Garden Festival is held on the grounds every April. Guided tours are available by appointment.

Time: Allow 30 minutes minimum. **Hours:** Mon.-Fri. 9-5. Closed holidays and during private functions. **Cost:** Free. **Phone:** (706) 826-4700. (GT)

ST. PAUL'S EPISCOPAL CHURCH, 605 Reynolds St., was founded in 1750, but the original building was destroyed during the Revolution. A second structure, built in 1819, burned down almost a century later. The present church, a classic example of Colonial-style architecture, was completed in 1919. The exterior of the building closely resembles the 1819 structure. Interred in the church's cemetery is Col. William Few Jr., Georgia's signer of the U.S. Constitution.

Hours: Mon.-Thurs. 9-3, Fri.-Sat. 9-noon (also Fri. noon-3, day after Labor Day-day before Memorial Day). Sun. services at 11 and 5:30 (also at 8 a.m., day after Labor Day-day before Memorial Day). **Cost:** Donations. **Phone:** (706) 724-2485.

SITE OF FORT AUGUSTA, at 605 Reynolds St. between St. Paul's Church and the river, is marked by a Celtic cross in the churchyard. Near the cross is a historical marker commemorating a visit by President George Washington. The fort was built in 1736. At the foot of the cross is a cannon believed to date to the 1730s. **Cost:** Free.

AUGUSTA MARRIOTT AT THE CONVENTION CENTER
(706)722-8900

Hotel
$138-$217

MARRIOTT

AAA Benefit: Members save 5% or more!

Address: 2 10th St 30901 **Location:** I-20 exit 200 (River Watch Pkwy), 5.4 mi se, then just n; downtown. **Facility:** 372 units. 11 stories, interior corridors. **Parking:** on-site (fee) and valet. **Terms:** check-in 4 pm. **Amenities:** Some: safes. **Pool(s):** heated outdoor, heated indoor. **Activities:** sauna, hot tub, exercise room. **Guest Services:** valet and coin laundry.

BAYMONT INN & SUITES AUGUSTA FORT GORDON
(706)737-2300

Motel
$80-$100

Address: 2155 Gordon Hwy 30909 **Location:** I-520 exit 3A (Gordon Hwy), just w. **Facility:** 150 units. 2 stories, exterior corridors. **Terms:** check-in 4 pm, cancellation fee imposed. **Pool(s):** outdoor. **Activities:** exercise room. **Guest Services:** valet and coin laundry, area transportation. **Featured Amenity:** breakfast buffet.

BAYMONT INN & SUITES/AUGUSTA RIVERWATCH
(706)733-5900

Hotel
$69-$135

Address: 2905 Riverwest Dr 30907 **Location:** I-20 exit 200 (River Watch Pkwy), just nw. **Facility:** 65 units. 3 stories, interior corridors. **Terms:** 3 day cancellation notice-fee imposed. **Pool(s):** outdoor. **Activities:** exercise room. **Guest Services:** valet and coin laundry. **Featured Amenity:** full hot breakfast.

CANDLEWOOD SUITES AUGUSTA   706/733-3300

▼▼▼▼ **Extended Stay Hotel.** Rates not provided. **Address:** 1080 Claussen Rd 30907 **Location:** I-20 exit 200 (River Watch Pkwy), just nw, then just sw. **Facility:** 80 units, some efficiencies. 3 stories, interior corridors. **Activities:** exercise room. **Guest Services:** complimentary laundry.

 CALL 🅜 BIZ HS 🛜 🖥 🖥 🖥 / SOME UNITS 🐾

COMFORT INN & SUITES   (706)736-6100

▼▼▼▼ **Hotel.** $95-$140 **Address:** 2121 Noland Connector 30909 **Location:** I-520 exit 3A (Gordon Hwy), just w. **Facility:** 61 units. 3 stories, interior corridors. **Pool(s):** outdoor. **Activities:** limited exercise equipment. **Guest Services:** valet and coin laundry.

CALL 🅜 🏊 BIZ HS 🛜 ✕ 🖥 🖥 🖥

COURTYARD BY MARRIOTT-AUGUSTA   (706)737-3737

 Hotel $82-$206

COURTYARD Marriott.

AAA Benefit: Members save 5% or more!

Address: 1045 Stevens Creek Rd 30907 **Location:** I-20 exit 199 (Washington Rd), just w, then just ne. **Facility:** 130 units. 2 stories (no elevator), interior corridors. **Pool(s):** outdoor. **Activities:** exercise room. **Guest Services:** valet and coin laundry, boarding pass kiosk.

SAVE 🍽 CALL 🅜 🏊 BIZ HS 🛜 ✕ 📷 🖥 🖥 🖥

DOUBLETREE BY HILTON HOTEL AUGUSTA   (706)855-8100

▼▼▼▼ **Hotel.** $109-$159 **Address:** 2651 Perimeter Pkwy 30909 **Location:** I-520 exit 1C (Wheeler Rd), just w to Perimeter Pkwy, then just n. **Facility:** 179 units. 6 stories, interior corridors. **Terms:** 1-7 night minimum stay, cancellation fee imposed. **Amenities:** safes. **Pool(s):** outdoor, heated indoor. **Activities:** hot tub, exercise room. **Guest Services:** valet and coin laundry, area transportation.

✈ 🍽 🗑 🍽 CALL 🅜 🏊 BIZ 🛜 ✕ 📷 🖥 / SOME UNITS 🐾 🖥 🖥

FAIRFIELD INN & SUITES BY MARRIOTT AUGUSTA   (706)733-2121

▼▼▼▼ Hotel $89-$164

AAA Benefit: Members save 5% or more!

Address: 2175 Gordon Hwy 30909 **Location:** I-520 exit 3A (Gordon Hwy), just w. **Facility:** 82 units. 4 stories, interior corridors. **Pool(s):** indoor. **Activities:** hot tub, exercise room. **Guest Services:** valet and coin laundry, area transportation. **Featured Amenity:** continental breakfast.

SAVE ✈ 🍽 CALL 🅜 🏊

BIZ HS 🛜 ✕ 🖥 🖥 🖥

FAIRFIELD INN & SUITES Marriott

Close to Fort Gordon, free hot breakfast buffet & WI-FI, indoor pool/whirlpool & fitness center.

Dream. Plan. Go.

TripTik® Travel Planner

AAA.com/ttp

▼ See AAA listing p. 139 ▼

HAMPTON INN
(706)737-1122

Motel
$84-$199

AAA Benefit: Members save up to 10%!

Address: 3030 Washington Rd 30907 **Location:** I-20 exit 199 (Washington Rd), just w. **Facility:** 145 units. 2 stories (no elevator), exterior corridors. **Terms:** 1-7 night minimum stay, cancellation fee imposed. **Pool(s):** outdoor. **Activities:** sauna, exercise room. **Guest Services:** valet laundry.

SAVE ▦ ⛵ BIZ 🛜 🎞 ▭ / SOME UNITS 🛡 🖨

HAMPTON INN & SUITES BY HILTON AUGUSTA-WASHINGTON RD
(706)738-4567

fyi Hotel. $129-$199 Too new to rate, opening scheduled for October 2016. **Address:** 3028 B Washington Rd 30907 **Location:** I-20 exit 199 (Washington Rd), just w. **Amenities:** 126 units. **Terms:** 1-7 night minimum stay, cancellation fee imposed. *(See ad p. 138.)*

AAA Benefit: Members save up to 10%!

HAMPTON INN GORDON HIGHWAY
(706)396-5500

Hotel. $109-$144 **Address:** 2171 Gordon Hwy 30909 **Location:** I-520 exit 3A (US 78), just w. **Facility:** 88 units. 4 stories, interior corridors. **Terms:** 1-7 night minimum stay, cancellation fee imposed. **Pool(s):** outdoor. **Activities:** hot tub, exercise room. **Guest Services:** coin laundry.

AAA Benefit: Members save up to 10%!

CALL ⛵ BIZ HS 🛜 ▭ 🛡 🖨 ▭

HILTON GARDEN INN AUGUSTA
(706)739-9990

Hotel. $109-$179 **Address:** 1065 Stevens Creek Rd 30907 **Location:** I-20 exit 199 (Washington Rd), just w, then just ne. **Facility:** 114 units. 5 stories, interior corridors. **Terms:** 1-7 night minimum stay, cancellation fee imposed. **Amenities:** safes. **Pool(s):** heated indoor. **Activities:** hot tub, exercise room. **Guest Services:** valet and coin laundry.

AAA Benefit: Members save up to 10%!

▦ 🍴 🛎 🍷 CALL ⛵ BIZ HS 🛜 ▭ 🛡 🖨 ▭

HOLIDAY INN EXPRESS AUGUSTA EAST
706/922-1414

Hotel. Rates not provided. **Address:** 444 Broad St 30901 **Location:** Between 4th and 5th sts; downtown. **Facility:** 117 units. 6 stories, interior corridors. **Pool(s):** outdoor. **Activities:** exercise room. **Guest Services:** area transportation.

➔ CALL ⛵ BIZ 🛜 ▭ 🛡 🖨 ▭

HOLIDAY INN EXPRESS AUGUSTA NORTH
(706)396-3000

Hotel. $89-$149 **Address:** 1075 Stevens Creek Rd 30907 **Location:** I-20 exit 199 (Washington Rd), just w, then just ne. **Facility:** 86 units. 3 stories, interior corridors. **Terms:** cancellation fee imposed. **Pool(s):** heated indoor. **Activities:** hot tub, exercise room. **Guest Services:** valet and coin laundry.

▦ CALL ⛵ BIZ HS 🛜 ▭ 🛡 🖨 ▭

HOME2 SUITES BY HILTON
(706)733-8787

Extended Stay Contemporary Hotel. $119-$189 **Address:** 3606 Exchange Ln 30909 **Location:** I-520 exit 1C (Wheeler Rd), just ne to Walton Rd Ext, then just nw. **Facility:** 123 units, some efficiencies. 4 stories, interior corridors. **Terms:** 1-7 night minimum stay, cancellation fee imposed. **Pool(s):** outdoor. **Activities:** exercise room. **Guest Services:** valet and coin laundry.

AAA Benefit: Members save up to 10%!

▦ CALL ⛵ BIZ 🛜 ▭ 🛡 🖨 ▭ / SOME UNITS 🛡

HOMEWOOD SUITES BY HILTON
(706)738-3131

Extended Stay Hotel. $117-$121 **Address:** 1049 Stevens Creek Rd 30907 **Location:** I-20 exit 199 (Washington Rd), just w, then n. **Facility:** 65 efficiencies, some two bedrooms. 5 stories, interior corridors. **Terms:** 1-7 night minimum stay, cancellation fee imposed. **Pool(s):** outdoor. **Activities:** exercise room. **Guest Services:** valet and coin laundry.

AAA Benefit: Members save up to 10%!

▦ CALL ⛵ BIZ HS 🛜 ▭ 🐾 🛡 🖨 ▭

JAMESON SUITES
706/733-4656

Contemporary Hotel. Rates not provided. **Address:** 1062 Clausen Rd 30907 **Location:** I-20 exit 200 (River Watch Pkwy), just nw, then just sw. **Facility:** 110 units. 6 stories, interior corridors. **Guest Services:** valet and coin laundry.

CALL ⛵ BIZ 🛜 ▭ 🛡 🖨 ▭ / SOME UNITS 🛡

THE PARTRIDGE INN, CURIO COLLECTION BY HILTON
706/737-8888

Classic Historic Hotel
Rates not provided

AAA Benefit: Members save 5% or more!

Address: 2110 Walton Way 30904 **Location:** 1.3 mi w off 15th St. **Facility:** Dating from 1890, this historic hotel overlooks the city. While the facade has Old World charm, the variety of floor plans, some with balconies, have contemporary décor. 145 units, some three bedrooms and kitchens. 6 stories, interior corridors. **Parking:** on-site and valet. **Pool(s):** outdoor. **Activities:** exercise room. **Guest Services:** valet and coin laundry, area transportation.

SAVE ▤ ➔ 🍴 🛎 🍷 ⛵ BIZ HS 🛜 ▭ ▭ / SOME UNITS 🛡 🛡 🖨

RESIDENCE INN BY MARRIOTT
(706)288-1900

Extended Stay Contemporary Hotel. $128-$195 **Address:** 1116 Marks Church Rd 30909 **Location:** I-520 exit 1C (Wheeler Rd), just e. **Facility:** 124 units, some two bedrooms, efficiencies and kitchens. 5 stories, interior corridors. **Pool(s):** heated indoor. **Activities:** hot tub, exercise room. **Guest Services:** coin laundry, boarding pass kiosk.

AAA Benefit: Members save 5% or more!

CALL ⛵ BIZ HS 🛜 ▭ 🛡 🖨 ▭ / SOME UNITS 🛡

SHERATON AUGUSTA HOTEL
(706)396-1000

Hotel. $109-$169 **Address:** 1069 Stevens Creek Rd 30907 **Location:** I-20 exit 199 (Washington Rd), just w, then just ne. **Facility:** 152 units. 5 stories, interior corridors. **Terms:** cancellation fee imposed, resort fee. **Amenities:** safes. **Pool(s):** outdoor, heated indoor. **Activities:** hot tub, exercise room. **Guest Services:** valet laundry.

AAA Benefit: Members save up to 15%, plus Starwood Preferred Guest® benefits!

▤ 🍴 🛎 CALL ⛵ BIZ HS 🛜 ▭ ▭ / SOME UNITS 🛡

Before you travel, ask your AAA/CAA club about identity theft monitoring products

SUNSET INN
706/860-8485

▼ **Motel.** Rates not provided. **Address:** 3034 Washington Rd 30907 **Location:** I-20 exit 199 (Washington Rd), just w. **Facility:** 48 units. 2 stories (no elevator), exterior corridors.

WEST BANK INN
706/733-1724

▼ ▼ **Motel.** Rates not provided. **Address:** 2904 Washington Rd 30909 **Location:** I-20 exit 199 (Washington Rd), just e. **Facility:** 46 units. 2 stories (no elevator), exterior corridors. **Activities:** exercise room. **Guest Services:** coin laundry.

WHERE TO EAT

ABLE BROWN
706/738-6491

▼▼▼ New Southern. Fine Dining. $22-$32 **AAA Inspector Notes:** The exceptional food and talented staff ensure you'll have a great night out, and if you love oysters you're in for an extra treat. Try to get a seat in the bar area, so you can be treated, as I was, to the incredible beverage knowledge of the sommelier. It's dinner and a show. On the menu you'll find a line-up of fresh seafood, beef and chops as well as a tasty selection of fresh oysters from the east coast and Canada. **Features:** full bar, happy hour. **Reservations:** suggested. **Address:** 491 Highland Ave, Suite B 30909 **Location:** Jct SR 28 (Washington Rd), 1.8 mi s on Berckmans Rd; in Surrey Center. D CALL M

THE BOLL WEEVIL-A CAFE & SWEETERY
706/722-7772

▼▼ Southern American. Casual Dining. $6-$18 **AAA Inspector Notes:** Soups, salads, sandwiches on homemade bread and a diverse variety of Southern and Creole entrées are all part of the trendy menu at this café. An on-site bakery turns out a wide selection of tantalizing desserts. Eight different homemade soups are offered daily as are jambalaya, grilled sirloin and salmon. A variety of clearly identified vegetarian selections is available in all course offerings as well. **Features:** beer & wine. **Address:** 10 9th St 30901 **Location:** Jct James Brown Blvd and Reynolds St, just n; adjacent to Riverwalk. L D

BONEFISH GRILL
706/737-2929

▼▼▼ Seafood. Fine Dining. $12-$29 **AAA Inspector Notes:** Fish is the house specialty, and the menu and nightly specials offer a variety of choices. Well-prepared food is cooked to perfection. Service is casual in nature, and the staff is skilled and attentive. **Features:** full bar, Sunday brunch, happy hour. **Address:** 2911 Washington Rd 30909 **Location:** I-20 exit 199 (Washington Rd), just e; in Washington Crossing Shopping Center. D CALL M

CALIFORNIA DREAMING
706/860-6206

▼▼ American. Casual Dining. $9-$30 **AAA Inspector Notes:** This full-service restaurant appeals to adults, particularly those with an appetite for innovative concepts in food. Revised weekly, the menu consistently incorporates sophisticated, cutting-edge California dishes with Pacific Rim influences throughout. Among house specialties are flatbread appetizers baked in a brick oven, sushi, sashimi and some vegetarian dishes. The wine list focuses primarily on California vintages. **Features:** full bar, patio dining, happy hour. **Address:** 3241 Washington Rd 30907 **Location:** I-20 exit 199 (Washington Rd), 1.2 mi nw. L D

CALVERT'S
706/738-4514

▼▼▼ Continental. Fine Dining. $23-$50 **AAA Inspector Notes:** Classic. After over 30 years of continuous service, this sophisticated, yet cozy, restaurant is truly a mainstay in the area. The food is superior and blends attractively garnished dishes that take into account texture and presentation with the freshest ingredients. Dishes such as sea bass with crab meat, cedar-plank salmon, rack of lamb and hand-cut filet of beef regularly appear on the menu along with delightful nightly specials. **Features:** full bar, early bird specials, happy hour. **Reservations:** suggested. **Address:** 475 Highland Ave 30909 **Location:** I-20 exit 199 (Washington Rd), 1.2 mi e to Berckmans Rd, then 1.8 mi s; in Surrey Center. D

CAROLINA ALE HOUSE
762/333-0019

▼▼ American. Casual Dining. $9-$18 **AAA Inspector Notes:** This popular sports bar features numerous TVs to watch your favorite game and a good line-up of craft draft and specialty cocktails to celebrate your victory. On the menu diners can find a selection of burgers, sandwiches and flatbread pizza along with full entrées like fish and chips, grilled salmon and baby back ribs. A children's menu is available. **Features:** full bar, patio dining, happy hour. **Address:** 203 Robert C. Daniel Jr. Pkwy 30909 **Location:** I-20 exit 196 (Walton Way Ext), just s. L D CALL M

CUCINA 503
762/994-0142

▼▼ Italian. Casual Dining. $17-$26 **AAA Inspector Notes:** The accomplished chef here makes all of his own breads, desserts, pastas and sauces on site so guests can expect freshness in each dish. The menu is not lengthy but is comprehensive in that it offers seafood, beef, pork and pasta dishes all prepared with the chef's interpretation of traditional food. Do not expect to find any pizza but some delicious homemade flatbreads can be ordered. **Features:** full bar, patio dining, happy hour. **Address:** 503 Fury's Ferry Rd 30907 **Location:** I-20 exit 199, SR 28 (Washington Rd), 3.3 mi nw. D CALL M

EDGAR'S GRILLE
706/854-4700

▼▼▼ Regional American. Fine Dining. $9-$32 **AAA Inspector Notes:** A delightful experience, this charming venue is situated within an upscale strip mall. Dishes are tasty and beautifully presented. Dining in a spacious, cozy booth, at a table or on the patio is enhanced by an unobtrusive and professional staff and guests can find the atmosphere to be quiet with soft music playing in the background. Start with the delicious crayfish macaroni and cheese followed by a sure-to-please entrée such as a filet with potato puree. **Features:** full bar, patio dining, Sunday brunch, happy hour. **Address:** 3165 Washington Rd 30907 **Location:** I-20 exit 199, 1 mi n; in Vaughn Square Shopping Center. L D CALL M

EMASHIYA KOREAN BBQ
706/210-7005

▼▼ Korean. Casual Dining. $9-$20 **AAA Inspector Notes:** This perennial award-winning restaurant offers a wide selection of authentic Korean cuisine in a well-appointed dining room. Service is outstanding and helpful when trying to navigate the unusual dishes. Noodles, rice, fish stir fry, soups and stews are all available along with box meal samplers. Each table receives numerous small plates of appetizers called banchan with the entrées, as is the custom. **Features:** full bar. **Address:** 4001 Columbia Rd 30907 **Location:** I-20 exit 196B (Bobby Jones Expwy), 1.4 mi n to Washington Rd, just sw to Columbia Rd, then just sw; in Columbia Place. D CALL M

EPHESUS MEDITERRANEAN
706/994-0180

▼▼ Mediterranean. Casual Dining. $14-$28 **AAA Inspector Notes:** You'll be treated to Turkish and Greek specialties at this bright little dining spot. Everything is prepared fresh on sight including the gyro meat which is comprised of freshly ground veal and lamb then packed on the traditional spit before being loaded onto the rotisserie. There are also a bunch of fresh appetizers, kabob dishes and big salads. Come hungry, courses are huge and enough for sharing. **Address:** 3102 Washington Rd 30907 **Location:** I-20 exit 199 (Washington Rd), 0.8 mi w. L D CALL M

FORMOSA'S II
706/855-8998

▼▼ Chinese. Casual Dining. $5-$13 **AAA Inspector Notes:** Family owned and operated for more than 20 years, this large restaurant features Szechuan, Hunan and Cantonese cuisine on its lengthy menu. A special and popular brunch is offered on Mother's and Father's Day. Entrée portions can only be described as enormous for dine-in customers, so be prepared. **Features:** beer & wine. **Address:** 3830 Washington Rd, Suite A-36 30907 **Location:** I-20 exit 196B (Bobby Jones Expwy), 1.4 mi n to Washington Rd, then 0.5 mi ne; in West Town Market Square. L D CALL M

FRENCH MARKET GRILLE
706/737-4865

▼▼ Cajun. Casual Dining. $7-$30 **AAA Inspector Notes:** This festive eatery nurtures a Mardi Gras theme along with an energetic attitude. Spicy cuisine, such as seafood crepes drizzled with cheese sauce, is sure to please but the menu goes on with such perfectly prepared Cajun and Creole staples as red beans and rice, jambalaya, shrimp Creole, blackened seafood dishes and seasoned steaks. The award-winning peanut butter pie is the perfect way to end a meal. **Features:** full bar, patio dining, happy hour. **Address:** 425 Highland Ave 30909 **Location:** Jct SR 28 (Washington Rd), 1.8 mi s on Berckmans Rd; in Surrey Center. L D

FRENCH MARKET GRILLE WEST   706/855-5111

▼▼ Cajun Seafood. Casual Dining. $8-$30 **AAA Inspector Notes:** Step off the sidewalk and onto Bourbon Street complete with a French Quarter motif, lively atmosphere, soothing jazz and authentic Cajun and Creole cuisine. Be prepared to be part of the Krewe and dig into some deep-fried mudbugs, Andouille sausage, jambalaya, file gumbo or a Monday night N'awlins tradition of red beans and rice. The beef and seafood menu is diverse and offers something for everyone, even for those who do not like the spicy side. **Features:** full bar, patio dining, happy hour. **Address:** 368 Fury's Ferry Rd 30907 **Location:** I-20 exit 199 (Washington Rd), 2 mi w; in Fury's Ferry Shopping Center. L D CALL M

GIUSEPPE'S PIZZA & ITALIAN SPECIALTIES   706/855-0527

▼▼ Italian Pizza. Casual Dining. $5-$16 **AAA Inspector Notes:** Serving the area continuously since 1993, this family-run restaurant features a lengthy list of pasta dishes, sandwiches and signature thin- and thick-crust pizzas. A lunchtime buffet is available during the week. **Features:** beer & wine. **Address:** 3690 Wheeler Rd 30909 **Location:** I-520 exit 1C (Wheeler Rd), 0.6 mi w. L D

MAYAKO SUSHI & STEAKHOUSE   706/755-2338

▼▼ Japanese Sushi. Casual Dining. $5-$30 **AAA Inspector Notes:** The restaurant features both a hibachi room and separate sushi bar. In the hibachi room you'll find the typically talented grill chefs wielding and banging their knives while entertaining guests with their food preparation techniques. In the sushi bar you'll be treated to an enormous menu of house specialty rolls, bento boxes and tempura dinners where you can have a regular sit down full-service meal or sit at the sushi bar and watch the imaginative creations come to life. **Features:** full bar. **Address:** 2801 Washington Rd 30909 **Location:** I-20 exit 199 (Washington Rd), just e; in Washington Walk Shopping Center. L CALL M

OLIVIANA'S PIZZERIA & GRILL   706/723-1242

▼▼▼ Northern Italian. Fine Dining. $8-$30 **AAA Inspector Notes:** Chic setting, great bar scene and well-prepared Italian menu make this restaurant a hit. The menu features a lineup of popular Italian standards with a decidedly Mediterranean influence which really makes the flavors pop. During my visit I started with the Tuscan sausage soup and stuffed pepper appetizer which was really all I needed but I persevered and had the chicken saltimbocca entrée course. Each dish was well-prepared and perfectly seasoned requiring me to do nothing but enjoy, and I did. **Features:** full bar, patio dining, Sunday brunch, happy hour. **Address:** 399 Highland Ave, Suite A 30909 **Location:** Jct SR 28 (Washington Rd), 1.8 mi s on Berckmans Rd; in Surrey Center. L D CALL M

RAES COASTAL CAFE   706/738-1313

▼▼ Caribbean. Casual Dining. $10-$32 **AAA Inspector Notes:** This café is a good place to unwind and escape to a Caribbean hideaway. Light reggae background music and a fun staff add to the comfortable atmosphere indoors and on the garden patio overlooking the tennis courts. On the menu are excellently prepared Cuban, Southeastern and Caribbean creations. Lots of seafood and jerked meats are served. **Features:** full bar, patio dining, happy hour. **Address:** 3208 W Wimbledon Dr 30909 **Location:** I-520 exit 1C (Wheeler Rd), 0.7 mi ne to Walton Way, 0.4 mi s to W Lake Forest Dr, just s to Kerry Pl, then just sw, follow signs; at Forest Hill Racquet Club. L D

RHINEHART'S OYSTER BAR   706/860-2337

▼ Seafood. Quick Serve. $7-$20 **AAA Inspector Notes:** This spot calls their style beyond casual and once diners are inside they will understand why. Picnic tables and walls covered in graffiti greet each guest and the aroma of boiled seafood is everywhere. Trays of boiled peel-and-eat shrimp, Alaskan snow crab clusters, buckets of fresh oysters and daily beer specials keep the crowds coming back for more. **Features:** full bar, patio dining, happy hour. **Address:** 3051 Washington Rd 30907 **Location:** I-20 exit 199 (Washington Rd), 0.7 mi w. L D

S & S CAFETERIA   706/736-2972

▼ Southern Comfort Food. Buffet Style. $5-$9 **AAA Inspector Notes:** A longtime favorite for comfort food, the family-owned cafeteria invites diners to load a plate with traditionally prepared chicken, beef, vegetables, salad and dessert. **Features:** senior menu. **Address:** 1616 Walton Way 30904 **Location:** Jct Bohler Ave and Walton Way. L D

THE SNUG STEAK & GRILL   706/863-1118

▼▼ Steak Seafood. Casual Dining. $10-$48 **AAA Inspector Notes:** Serving certified Angus beef and seafood, this romantic cabin-style restaurant is just northwest of the city. On the menu are such offerings as rib-eye steaks (up to 24 ounces), roasted chicken, salmon, a few pasta dishes, burgers and sandwiches. Evening specials are offered nightly. **Features:** full bar, happy hour. **Address:** 240 Davis Rd 30907 **Location:** I-20 exit 196B (Bobby Jones Expwy), just n to Scott Nixon Memorial Dr, just e to Davis Rd, then just n. L D

SOMEWHERE IN AUGUSTA BAR & GRILL   706/739-0002

▼▼ Wings Sandwiches. Casual Dining. $8-$17 **AAA Inspector Notes:** You can follow your favorite sport on TVs around the walls and at the tableside. If you don't opt for wings coated in sauce ranging from mild to suicide, you might try the signature deep-fried homewrecker hot dog, which is stuffed with cheddar, wrapped in bacon and drenched in American cheese. Still need ideas? How about a burger, sandwich, quesadilla or one of a few entrées? You won't be bored, as trivia nights, comedy nights, karaoke and other entertainment are slated nightly. **Features:** full bar, patio dining, happy hour. **Address:** 2820 Washington Rd 30909 **Location:** I-20 exit 199 (Washington Rd), 0.6 mi e. L D LATE CALL M

TAKOSUSHI   706/736-9191

▼▼ Southwestern Sushi. Casual Dining. $5-$21 **AAA Inspector Notes:** This is truly where the East meets the West, at least on the menu. Enjoy everything from fresh sushi and bento boxes to tacos and the Mexicali plate for which you get to choose your ingredients. The selection of rolls is enormous, so be prepared to spend some time reading the menu. It's a lively and upbeat environment and stays busy. I recommend getting there early for a good seat. **Features:** full bar, patio dining, happy hour. **Address:** 437 Highland Ave 30909 **Location:** Jct SR 28 (Washington Rd), 1.8 mi s on Berckmans Rd; in Surrey Center. L D LATE

TBONZ STEAKHOUSE   706/737-8325

▼▼ Steak. Casual Dining. $9-$26 **AAA Inspector Notes:** The original member of the popular family of restaurants, the atmosphere here is inviting and casual with a sports bar feel. The menu is dominated by beef dishes, yet seafood, chicken and vegetarian dishes also are offered. Wings tend to be the favorite of the bar crowd. For the hardy eater, I would recommend the signature porterhouse which is seasoned to perfection or the fall-off-the-bone baby back ribs. **Features:** full bar, happy hour. **Address:** 2856 Washington Rd 30909 **Location:** I-20 exit 199 (Washington Rd), just e. L D

TERESA'S MEXICAN RESTAURANT   706/737-8917

▼▼ Tex-Mex. Casual Dining. $5-$18 **AAA Inspector Notes:** Perennial winner of the area's best for Mexican food, this popular restaurant features an extensive menu of classic favorites and an ever-evolving list of chef's specialties. At lunchtime, guests can get an inexpensive combination plate in a hurry. Dine al fresco or sip party libations on the large, inviting gazebo patio deck. **Features:** full bar, patio dining, happy hour. **Address:** 235 Boy Scout Rd 30909 **Location:** I-20 exit 199 (Washington Rd), just e, then 0.4 mi s. L D CALL M

TIN LIZZY'S CANTINA   706/504-9767

▼▼ Tex-Mex. Casual Dining. $4-$10 **AAA Inspector Notes:** The menu features tacos, nachos, quesadillas, salads and skillets in a variety of styles that you can build on with the long list of additions. A good selection of cold craft beers and a huge variety of tequilas are also offered. The place stays lively so you can expect a good time. **Features:** full bar, patio dining, happy hour. **Address:** 2821 Washington Rd 30909 **Location:** I-20 exit 199 (Washington Rd), just w. L D LATE CALL M

VALLARTA RESTAURANTE MEXICANO   706/733-5584

▼▼ Mexican. Casual Dining. $5-$14 **AAA Inspector Notes:** The atmosphere here is so lively that even the servers get caught up in the action, which doesn't affect your meal's delivery, but you may not see the same person twice. The menu is diverse and portions are large. Along with standard fare there are lite-Mex and vegetarian offerings as well as a long list of house specials. Ingredients are top-shelf and prices can't be beat, so come and enjoy a great meal. The restaurant is known for its many types of tequila. **Features:** full bar, patio dining, happy hour. **Address:** 2808 Washington Rd 30909 **Location:** I-20 exit 199 (Washington Rd), 0.7 mi e. L D

VILLA EUROPA RESTAURANT AND LOUNGE   706/798-6211
▼▼ ⚑ European. Casual Dining. $7-$24 **AAA Inspector Notes:** Warm, pleasant servers enhance the experience at this family-owned cottage, a modest spot that families and friends have frequented since its 1974 opening. At lunch or dinner, guests can choose from an array of Bavarian, American and Italian dishes, including fried mushrooms with horseradish sauce, herring in sour cream, schnitzels, wurst, lasagna and tasty sandwiches. Of course there are plenty of steins full of beer. **Features:** full bar, patio dining, happy hour. **Address:** 3044 Deans Bridge Rd 30906 **Location:** I-520 exit 5B (US 1), 0.9 mi ne. [L] [D]

AUSTELL (H-1) pop. 6,581, elev. 927'
• Hotels & Restaurants map & index p. 76, 94
• Part of Atlanta area — see map p. 44

▼ GEM SAVE **SIX FLAGS OVER GEORGIA,** 275 Riverside Pkwy. S.W., has more than 100 acres where visitors of all ages can experience thrilling rides, games and live shows. Guests will want to be sure to bring a swimsuit and a towel to appreciate Hurricane Harbor; changing facilities are available.

Riders of The New Revolution Virtual Reality Coaster will get a wireless virtual reality headset that provides 360-degree views synchronized to the coaster's movement. The ride travels up to 50 mph while occupants battle an alien force to save Earth from destruction.

Thrill-seekers won't want to miss SkyScreamer, a swing ride that spins around a 242-foot tower at speeds up to 40 mph; Mind Bender, a triple-loop roller coaster; Dare Devil Dive, a coaster with a steeper-than-vertical plunge and three inversions; and Thunder River, a white-water rafting adventure.

Also included among the park's 11 coasters are Superman Ultimate Flight, which turns riders upside down in a pretzel-shaped loop; Batman: The Ride, which carries visitors through loops and a corkscrew spin; The Georgia Scorcher, said to be one of the region's tallest and fastest stand-up roller coasters; and Goliath, more than 200 feet tall and traveling up to 70 mph. Adults and kids alike will enjoy the surprises in Monster Mansion.

DC Super Friends and Bugs Bunny Boomtown are two areas designed for kids that have 12 rides and attractions including a bouncing drop tower, a small coaster, an interactive water ride and a Ferris wheel.

Strollers, wheelchairs and electric carts can be rented. **Hours:** Opens daily at 10:30, late May-early Aug.; Sat.-Sun. at 10:30, early Mar.-late May and early Aug.-late Sept. Closing times vary. The park also is open select days in Oct. for Fright Fest and select days Nov.-Jan. for Holiday in the Park. Phone ahead to confirm schedule. **Cost:** All-inclusive 1-day (including Hurricane Harbor) $64.99; $42.99 (children under 48 inches tall); free (ages 0-2). Prices may vary; phone ahead. AAA members save on select services and merchandise. See Guest Relations for details. **Parking:** $20. **Phone:** (770) 948-9290. ⊞ ⊞

HOLIDAY INN EXPRESS AUSTELL-POWDER SPRINGS   770/349-8000
▼▼▼ Hotel. Rates not provided. **Address:** 3741 Tramore Pointe Pkwy 30106 **Location:** Jct Powder Springs Rd, 0.5 mi s. **Facility:** 70 units, some two bedrooms. 4 stories, interior corridors. **Amenities:** video games. Some: safes. **Pool(s):** outdoor. **Activities:** exercise room. **Guest Services:** valet and coin laundry.
⊞ CALL ⓖM ⤢ BIZ HS 🛜 ✕ 🎮 🛏 🖥 🖥

SLEEP INN   (770)819-2805   **8**
▼▼ Hotel $79-$119

Address: 125 S Service Rd 30168 **Location:** I-20 exit 47 westbound; exit 46 eastbound, just s. Adjacent to Six Flags Atlanta. **Facility:** 49 units. 2 stories (no elevator), interior corridors. **Bath:** shower only. **Pool(s):** heated indoor. **Featured Amenity: full hot breakfast.**
SAVE CALL ⓖM ⤢ BIZ 🛜 🛏 🖥 🖥

WINGATE BY WYNDHAM AT SIX FLAGS   (770)948-7877   **9**
▼▼▼ Hotel. $109-$131 **Address:** 65 S Service Rd 30168 **Location:** I-20 exit 47 westbound; exit 46 eastbound, just s. **Facility:** 101 units. 4 stories, interior corridors. **Amenities:** safes. **Pool(s):** outdoor. **Activities:** game room, exercise room. **Guest Services:** valet and coin laundry.
CALL ⓖM ⤢ BIZ 🛜 ✕ 🛏 🖥 🖥 / SOME UNITS HS

WHERE TO EAT

WALLACE BARBECUE   770/739-1686
▼ Barbecue. Casual Dining. $3-$14 **AAA Inspector Notes:** Using family recipes dating back to 1947, the staff here serves traditional Georgia hickory-pit barbecue, including delicious smoked pork and beef dishes. This straightforward restaurant offers a touch of nostalgia with its fried pickles, pecan pie and a cold glass of sweet tea. Look for the original Wurlitzer jukebox in the corner. The friendly servers know how to take care of their customers. **Address:** 3035 Veterans Memorial Hwy 30168 **Location:** I-20 exit 44, 2.6 mi n on Thornton Rd, then 0.5 mi e on US 78/278. [L] [D]

BAINBRIDGE pop. 12,697

HAMPTON INN   (229)246-1341
▼▼▼ Hotel. $119-$209 **Address:** 1522 Tallahassee Hwy 39819 **Location:** On US 27. **Facility:** 71 units. 1-3 stories, interior corridors. **Terms:** 1-7 night minimum stay, cancellation fee imposed.

AAA Benefit: Members save up to 10%!

Pool(s): outdoor. **Activities:** exercise room. **Guest Services:** valet and coin laundry.
CALL ⓖM ⤢ BIZ 🛜 ✕ 🛏 🖥 / SOME UNITS 🖥

HOLIDAY INN EXPRESS HOTEL & SUITES   229/246-6771
▼▼▼ Hotel. Rates not provided. **Address:** 1413 Tallahassee Hwy 39819 **Location:** Just s of US 84 Bypass on US 27. **Facility:** 73 units. 4 stories, interior corridors. **Pool(s):** heated indoor. **Activities:** exercise room. **Guest Services:** valet and coin laundry.
⊞ CALL ⓖM ⤢ BIZ HS 🛜 ✕ 🛏 🖥 🖥

Choose real ratings you can trust from professional inspectors who've been there

QUALITY INN (229)243-7000

💎💎 **Hotel.** $67-$109 **Address:** 1403 Tallahassee Hwy 39819 **Location:** Just s of US 84 Bypass on US 27. **Facility:** 61 units. 2 stories (no elevator), exterior corridors. **Pool(s):** outdoor. **Activities:** exercise room. **Guest Services:** valet laundry.

🍴 CALL 👟M 🛥️ BIZ 📶 🔌 📺 💻 / SOME UNITS 🍽️

WHERE TO EAT

BONNIE BLUE HOUSE 229/246-9970

💎💎 American. Casual Dining. $7-$22 **AAA Inspector Notes:** The rustic décor of this café and bar is adorned with prints and memorabilia depicting the old South pre-Civil War. A good mix of meats, seafood, sandwiches and salads are offered along with a few Southern standards such as fried green tomatoes and catfish. **Features:** full bar. **Address:** 713 E Calhoun St 39817 **Location:** Jct US 27 business route and SR 309/97, just e; in The Avenues Plaza.

L D CALL 👟M

CRAVE EATERY 229/246-3195

💎💎 Southern American. Casual Dining. $6-$10 **AAA Inspector Notes:** An easy one-block walk from the town square, this is a popular luncheonette with the local residents. On a pleasant day, take advantage of dining in the yard, the fenced-in back patio. Also open on Thursday and Friday evenings from 6 to 9 pm. **Features:** beer & wine, patio dining. **Address:** 312 E Water St 39819 **Location:** Between Clark and Clay sts; in historic downtown. **Parking:** street only. L

BAXLEY pop. 4,400

CAPTAIN JOE'S SEAFOOD 912/367-7795

💎 Seafood. Casual Dining. $7-$26 **AAA Inspector Notes:** A friendly, nautical atmosphere combined with generous portions and attentive service makes for a pleasant experience. Heavenly onion rings are made from home-grown Vidalia onions and served with blue cheese dressing. **Address:** 2115 Golden Isles E 31513 **Location:** 3.5 mi se on US 341 and SR 27. L D

BLAIRSVILLE (A-3) pop. 652, elev. 1,926'

Blairsville is entirely within the Chattahoochee-Oconee National Forest *(see place listing p. 155)* and provides easy access to numerous historic buildings, scenic spots and recreational facilities. The Old Court House in the center of town contains a historical museum. Brasstown Bald, Georgia's highest mountain, provides a panorama of four states, and the Richard Russell Scenic Highway offers 14 miles of overlooks, trails and peaks.

Blairsville-Union County Chamber of Commerce: 129 Union County Recreation Rd., P.O. Box 789, Blairsville, GA 30514. **Phone:** (706) 745-5789 or (877) 745-5789.

VOGEL STATE PARK, 11 mi. s. on US 19/129, covers 233 acres adjacent to the Chattahoochee-Oconee National Forests in the Blue Ridge Mountains. There are 17 miles of hiking trails, 1 mile of which is interpreted by signs, as well as cottages and facilities for camping, fishing and swimming. Organized programs are offered during the summer. *See Recreation Areas Chart.* **Hours:** Park open daily 7 a.m.-10 p.m. Visitor center open daily 8-5, with extended hours in summer. **Cost:** $5 per private vehicle. **Phone:** (706) 745-2628, or (800) 864-7275 for reservations. 🔺 ❌ 🏕️ ⛲

BEST WESTERN MILTON INN (706)745-6995

💎💎💎 Motel $70-$130

🅱️ **Best Western.** **AAA Benefit:** Save 10% or more every day and earn 10% bonus points!

Address: 201 Hwy 515 30512 **Location:** Jct SR 19/US 129 and SR 515/US 76, just e. **Facility:** 60 units. 2 stories (no elevator), interior/exterior corridors. **Terms:** check-in 4 pm. **Pool(s):** outdoor. **Featured Amenity: full hot breakfast.**

SAVE 🍴 🛥️ BIZ 📶 🔌 📺 💻

COMFORT INN (706)745-6844

💎💎 **Hotel.** $85-$189 **Address:** 90 Fisher St 30512 **Location:** Jct SR 19/US 129 and SR 515/US 76, just e. **Facility:** 65 units. 2 stories, interior corridors. **Pool(s):** heated indoor. **Guest Services:** coin laundry.

CALL 👟M 🛥️ BIZ 📶 ❌ 🔌 💻 / SOME UNITS 🍽️

WHERE TO EAT

BLAIRSVILLE RESTAURANT 706/745-6921

💎 Southern. Casual Dining. $3-$16 **AAA Inspector Notes:** Good home-style country cooking is featured at this popular spot for breakfast and lunch. Both a buffet and full service menu are offered at lunch. The fried chicken always is a hit, as is the salad bar. If the buffet is not an option, then try a hamburger or sandwich. The atmosphere is simple and down-home with friendly servers. **Address:** 229 Earnest St 30514 **Location:** Downtown. B L

FATZ 706/781-1643

💎💎 Regional American. Casual Dining. $6-$19 **AAA Inspector Notes:** Friendly staff and appealing country decor help set the tone for a relaxed and enjoyable dining experience. It's not unusual for guests to wait to be seated at the popular spot, which earns raves for its well-prepared variations on chicken, steak, ribs and pasta, as well as salads and sandwiches. The signature Southern-style peach cobbler served with vanilla ice cream and walnuts is scrumptious. **Features:** full bar. **Address:** 206 Hwy 515 E 30512 **Location:** Jct US 76 and 19, just n on US 76. L D CALL 👟M

STEVE'S STEAKHOUSE 706/745-3600

💎 Southern. Casual Dining. $4-$17 **AAA Inspector Notes:** No Southern meal would be complete without sweet tea, so make sure you request a glass at this restaurant. Served buffet-style, fried chicken, collard greens, mashed potatoes and cornbread are plentiful. Service is friendly and the atmosphere homey and ideal for families. **Address:** 223 Wellborn St 30512 **Location:** Just off SR 515 and US 76. L D CALL 👟M

BLAKELY (E-2) pop. 5,068, elev. 270'
• Hotels p. 144

Blakely and surrounding Early County constitute one of the largest peanut-producing areas in the country. The Peanut Monument on the northeast corner of Courthouse Square was donated by citizens of the town and county.

Other sites in and near Blakely are reminders of the past. In the northwest corner of the square stands the last known Confederate flagpole, erected in 1861. Nine miles southwest, a covered bridge on Old River Road spans picturesque Coheelee Creek. Built in 1883, it is one of the few covered bridges in the South.

Blakely-Early County Chamber of Commerce: 214 Court Sq., P.O. Box 189, Blakely, GA 39823. **Phone:** (229) 723-3741.

KOLOMOKI MOUNDS STATE PARK, 6 mi. n. off US 27 at 205 Indian Mounds Rd., is an important archeological site and a popular recreation area. This 1,294-acre park contains seven mounds built by the Swift Creek and Weeden Island Native Americans. A museum at the west entrance chronicles the area's Native American cultures from 250 A.D. to 950 A.D. One exhibit shows the interior of a mound as archeologists left it. *See Recreation Areas Chart.*

Hours: Park open daily 7 a.m.-10 p.m. Museum open daily 8-5. Museum closed Christmas. **Cost:** Park $5 per private vehicle. Museum $5; $4 (ages 62+); $3.50 (ages 6-17). **Phone:** (229) 724-2150 for the park, or (800) 864-7275 for reservations.

DAYS INN OF BLAKELY   (229)723-5858
▼▼ **Hotel.** $63-$70 **Address:** 1097 Arlington Ave 39823 **Location:** On US 27. **Facility:** 30 units. 2 stories (no elevator), exterior corridors. **Pool(s):** outdoor. **Guest Services:** coin laundry.

BLUE RIDGE pop. 1,290

AMERICAS BEST VALUE INN BLUE RIDGE   706/632-2100
▼▼ **Motel.** Rates not provided. **Address:** 4970 Appalachian Hwy 30513 **Location:** On SR 515 and US 76. **Facility:** 60 units. 2 stories (no elevator), exterior corridors. **Pool(s):** outdoor.

THE BLUE RIDGE LODGE BY COMFORT INN & SUITES
         (706)946-3333
▼▼▼
Hotel
$109-$209
Address: 83 Blue Ridge Overlook 30513 **Location:** Just off SR 515 and US 76; behind Arby's. **Facility:** 68 units. 3 stories, interior corridors. **Activities:** exercise room. **Guest Services:** coin laundry. **Featured Amenity: continental breakfast.**

WHERE TO EAT

ANGELINA'S   706/632-3354
▼ Deli. Quick Serve. $4-$7 **AAA Inspector Notes:** Stop by this spot for sandwiches, soups and salads or pick up something to go along with a bottle of fine Italian wine from the great Italian market and deli. Roast beef, turkey and chicken are available as are specialty sandwiches such as the muffuletta, tuna or Italian grilled cheese. I had the veggie panini and it hit the spot as did the roasted tomato bisque. **Address:** 3640 E First St 30513 **Location:** Downtown.

BLACK SHEEP   706/946-3663
▼▼ Southern American. Fine Dining. $11-$40 **AAA Inspector Notes:** Beautifully packaged in a 100-year-old-home, this fine dining restaurant is the go-to place for special occasions and date nights. The creative menu puts a new twist on classic Southern that is sure to make you say pretty please and thank you. Ask about the house moonshine and locally-pressed olive oils. **Features:** full bar, patio dining. **Reservations:** suggested. **Address:** 480 W Main St 30513 **Location:** Historic downtown. **Parking:** on-site and street.

BLUE JEANS PIZZA AND PASTA   706/632-6503
▼▼ Italian. Casual Dining. $4-$21 **AAA Inspector Notes:** This old factory turned restaurant features décor with a hodgepodge of sports memorabilia and a large menu of Italian favorites. The portions are generous and the service is casual. Watch the game on the large flat-screens or enjoy an arcade game while awaiting brick-oven pizza or gooey chocolate cake. The restaurant has its own lot, which is helpful in an area where most only have street parking. **Features:** full bar. **Address:** Mountain St 30513 **Location:** In historic downtown. **Parking:** street only.

HARVEST ON MAIN   706/946-6164
▼▼ Regional American. Casual Dining. $8-$29 **AAA Inspector Notes:** This farm-to-table eatery features some creative and truly delicious fare. Local ingredients are used whenever possible and change seasonally. The crab ravioli is a great way to start, or share some smoked salmon and trout spread. Entrées include duck two-ways, Brasstown meatloaf and bistro steak. The homemade desserts vary from day to day and are a perfect way to complete your meal. **Features:** patio dining. **Address:** 576 E Main St 30513 **Location:** Downtown.

BRASELTON (B-3) pop. 7,511, elev. 909'

WINERIES

• **Château Élan,** SR 211 off I-85 exit 126 to 100 Rue Charlemagne. **Hours:** Tours and tastings are given Mon.-Fri. at noon and 3 (also Fri. at 6 p.m.), Sat.-Sun. at noon, 2 and 4 (also Sat. at 6 p.m.). **Phone:** (678) 425-0900 or (800) 233-9463.

BEST WESTERN BRASELTON INN   (706)654-3081

▼▼
Motel
$100-$200

(BW) **Best Western.** **AAA Benefit:** Save 10% or more every day and earn 10% bonus points!

Address: 303 Zion Church Rd 30517 **Location:** I-85 exit 129, just e, then 0.3 mi n. **Facility:** 54 units. 2 stories (no elevator), exterior corridors. **Terms:** 3 day cancellation notice-fee imposed. **Amenities:** safes. **Pool(s):** outdoor.

CHÂTEAU ÉLAN WINERY & RESORT   (678)425-0900

▼▼▼ ▼▼▼
Resort Hotel
$189-$489

Address: 100 rue Charlemagne 30517 **Location:** I-85 exit 126, just w. **Facility:** This sprawling resort, nestled among rows of grapes, transports you to the French countryside. Impressive public spaces, luxurious guest rooms and spa-like bathrooms are all designed to pamper. 301 units, some cottages. 5 stories, interior corridors. **Parking:** on-site and valet. **Terms:** 3 day cancellation notice-fee imposed. **Amenities:** safes. **Dining:** 7 restaurants, also, Paddy's Irish Pub, see separate listing. **Pool(s):** outdoor, heated indoor. **Activities:** sauna, hot tub, steamroom, regulation golf, par 3 golf, tennis, recreation programs, bicycles, playground, spa. **Guest Services:** valet laundry, area transportation. Affiliated with Preferred Hotels & Resorts.

COUNTRY INN & SUITES BY CARLSON BRASELTON
(770)868-5419

 Hotel. $109-$240 **Address:** 925 Hwy 124 30517 **Location:** I-85 exit 126, just e to SR 124, then 0.4 mi n. **Facility:** 82 units. 4 stories, interior corridors. **Terms:** cancellation fee imposed, resort fee. **Pool(s):** heated indoor. **Activities:** exercise room. **Guest Services:** valet and coin laundry.

WHERE TO EAT

HOUNDSTOOTH GRILL & TAVERN
770/967-2225

 American. Casual Dining. $8-$28 **AAA Inspector Notes:** An American version of an English restaurant and tavern, this restaurant has an English hunting theme. Surprisingly, the food does not reflect this, as menu selections include traditional American grilled foods and some Italian favorites as well as salads, sandwiches, seafood, steaks and chops. **Features:** full bar. **Address:** 6323 Grand Hickory Dr 30517 **Location:** I-85 exit 126, 1.6 mi w; in Mulberry Walk.

PADDY'S IRISH PUB
678/425-6074

Irish. Gastropub. $4-$15 **AAA Inspector Notes:** Located on the grounds of Château Élan Winery and Resort, this authentic Irish pub serves the classics. Traditional comfort food such as fish and chips, bangers and mash, and shepherd's pie along with an extensive drink menu make you feel like the pot of gold at the end of the rainbow. For an extra treat go on a night that features live music. **Features:** full bar. **Address:** 100 rue Charlemagne 30517 **Location:** I-85 exit 126, just w; in Château Élan Winery & Resort.

BREMEN pop. 6,227

HAMPTON INN
(770)537-9001

Hotel. $99-$189 **Address:** 28 Price Creek Rd 30110 **Location:** I-20 exit 11, just n. **Facility:** 56 units. 3 stories, interior corridors. **Terms:** 1-7 night minimum stay, cancellation fee imposed. **Pool(s):** outdoor. **Activities:** exercise room. **Guest Services:** valet laundry.

AAA Benefit: Members save up to 10%!

MICROTEL INN & SUITES BY WYNDHAM-BREMEN GEORGIA
(770)537-8000

Motel. $54-$90 **Address:** 104 Price Creek Rd 30110 **Location:** I-20 exit 11, just n. **Facility:** 62 units. 4 stories, interior corridors. **Pool(s):** outdoor. **Activities:** exercise room. **Guest Services:** coin laundry.

BRUNSWICK (E-5) pop. 15,383, elev. 14'
• Restaurants p. 146

Brunswick was founded in 1771 on a peninsula that juts into the Brunswick River; the city was named for Braunschweig, Germany, the ancestral home of King George II. Streets and parks named after members of England's ruling family and English places help preserve the town's past. Victorian houses remain from the late 19th century, when Brunswick was a busy shipping center for lumber and naval stores.

Shrimp- and crabmeat-processing plants are concentrated along Bay Street from Gloucester to Prince streets. In season, boats unload shrimp onto the street's docks most weekdays in the late afternoon. Charter fishing trips leave from Brunswick, St. Simons Island and Jekyll Island.

Among Brunswick's landmarks are two oak trees. Lover's Oak, at Albany and Prince streets, is thought to date from the 12th century. Local legend tells of a Native American and his love, who met beneath its branches. Lanier's Oak overlooks the marshes on US 17. It is said that under this tree the Georgia poet Sidney Lanier was inspired to write "The Marshes of Glynn." The James Oglethorpe Monument, on Newcastle Street in Queens Square, honors the founder of Georgia.

Golden Isles Convention and Visitors Bureau-Brunswick: 1505 Richmond St., Brunswick, GA 31520. **Phone:** (912) 265-0620 or (800) 933-2627.

Self-guiding tours: Brochures and maps of Brunswick, St. Simons Island, Sea Island and Jekyll Island are available at the Golden Isles Welcome Center on I-95 off the southbound lanes between exits 42 and 38 and on St. Simons Island in the village area.

HOFWYL-BROADFIELD PLANTATION STATE HISTORIC SITE, 10 mi. n. to 5556 US 17N, provides a glimpse of early 19th-century life on the Georgia rice coast as well as a chance to observe the vegetation and animal life native to this freshwater marsh country. In 1806 William Brailsford purchased a tract of land and named it Broadfield. Later generations built the present house, which they named Hofwyl, in the 1850s. The estate remained in the family until 1973.

The plantation is presently a 1,268-acre nature preserve with a museum where an orientation video introduces visitors to the site and a film presentation details the history of Hofwyl and the rice industry. Exhibits show how slaves, many of them experienced in rice cultivation in Africa, carved a thriving rice plantation from the virgin cypress swamp along the Altamaha River. The house has family furnishings from different periods. Special events are offered.

Time: Allow 1 hour, 30 minutes minimum. **Hours:** Guided 30- to 40-minute house tours depart Wed.-Sun. on the hour 9-5. First tour begins 1 hour after opening; last tour begins 1 hour before closing. Closed Jan. 1, Thanksgiving and Christmas. **Cost:** $8; $7 (ages 62+); $5 (ages 6-17). **Phone:** (912) 264-7333.

BEST WESTERN PLUS BRUNSWICK INN & SUITES
(912)265-1114

Hotel
$99-$159

Best Western PLUS

AAA Benefit: Save 10% or more every day and earn 10% bonus points!

Address: 126 Venture Dr 31525 **Location:** I-95 exit 38 (Golden Isles Pkwy), just n. **Facility:** 72 units. 3 stories, interior corridors. **Amenities:** safes. **Pool(s):** outdoor. **Activities:** exercise room. **Guest Services:** valet and coin laundry. **Featured Amenity:** full hot breakfast.

COMFORT SUITES (912)267-4440

Hotel
$85-$125

Address: 25 Ashton Dr 31523 **Location:** I-95 exit 29, just se. **Facility:** 72 units. 3 stories, interior corridors. **Amenities:** safes. **Pool(s):** heated indoor. **Activities:** hot tub, exercise room. **Guest Services:** valet and coin laundry. **Featured Amenity: full hot breakfast.**

COMFORT SUITES GOLDEN ISLES GATEWAY (912)580-4400

Contemporary Hotel. $85-$165 **Address:** 220 Gateway Center Blvd 31525 **Location:** I-95 exit 38 (Golden Isles Pkwy), just se. **Facility:** 60 units. 4 stories, interior corridors. **Amenities:** safes. **Pool(s):** heated indoor. **Activities:** exercise room. **Guest Services:** valet and coin laundry.

COURTYARD BY MARRIOTT BRUNSWICK (912)265-2644

Contemporary Hotel. $91-$171 **Address:** 580 Millennium Blvd 31525 **Location:** I-95 exit 38 (Golden Isles Pkwy), just n, then e. **Facility:** 93 units. 3 stories, interior corridors. **Amenities:** safes. **Pool(s):** heated outdoor. **Activities:** hot tub, exercise room. **Guest Services:** valet and coin laundry, boarding pass kiosk.

AAA Benefit:
Members save 5% or more!

EMBASSY SUITES HOTEL BY HILTON (912)264-6100

Hotel. $125-$195 **Address:** 500 Mall Blvd 31525 **Location:** I-95 exit 38 (Golden Isles Pkwy), 2 mi se, then just e. Adjoining Colonial Mall. **Facility:** 130 units, some two bedrooms. 5 stories, interior corridors. **Terms:** 1-7 night minimum stay, cancellation fee imposed. **Amenities:** video games. *Some:* safes. **Pool(s):** outdoor. **Activities:** exercise room. **Guest Services:** valet and coin laundry, area transportation.

AAA Benefit:
Members save 5% or more!

FAIRFIELD INN & SUITES BY MARRIOTT BRUNSWICK (912)264-2060

Hotel. $94-$147 **Address:** 107 Gateway Center Cir 31525 **Location:** I-95 exit 38 (Golden Isles Pkwy), just se. Located in a quiet area. **Facility:** 80 units. 3 stories, interior corridors. **Pool(s):** outdoor. **Activities:** hot tub, exercise room. **Guest Services:** valet and coin laundry.

AAA Benefit:
Members save 5% or more!

HAMPTON INN & SUITES BRUNSWICK. (912)261-0939

Hotel. $119-$179 **Address:** 128 Venture Dr 31525 **Location:** Waterfront. I-95 exit 38 (Golden Isles Pkwy), just n. **Facility:** 97 units. 5 stories, interior corridors. **Terms:** check-in 4 pm, 1-7 night minimum stay, cancellation fee imposed. **Amenities:** safes. **Pool(s):** heated indoor. **Activities:** hot tub, exercise room. **Guest Services:** valet and coin laundry.

AAA Benefit:
Members save up to 10%!

HOLIDAY INN HOTEL & SUITES 912/264-3300

Hotel. Rates not provided. **Address:** 138 Glynco Pkwy 31525 **Location:** I-95 exit 38 (Golden Isles Pkwy), just se. **Facility:** 103 units. 5 stories, interior corridors. **Dining:** Millhouse Steakhouse, see separate listing. **Pool(s):** indoor. **Activities:** exercise room. **Guest Services:** valet and coin laundry.

MICROTEL INN & SUITES BY WYNDHAM BRUNSWICK NORTH (912)554-1430

Hotel
$72-$130

Address: 146 Gateway Center Blvd 31525 **Location:** I-95 exit 38 (Golden Isles Pkwy), just se to Glynco Pkwy, then just ne. **Facility:** 62 units. 3 stories, interior corridors. **Activities:** exercise room. **Guest Services:** valet and coin laundry. **Featured Amenity: breakfast buffet.**

/ SOME UNITS

SUPER 8 (912)264-8800

Hotel
$50-$124

Address: 5280 New Jesup Hwy 31523 **Location:** I-95 exit 36B (New Jesup Hwy/US 25), just nw. **Facility:** 59 units. 3 stories, interior corridors. **Amenities:** *Some:* safes. **Guest Services:** coin laundry. **Featured Amenity: continental breakfast.**

/ SOME UNITS

WHERE TO EAT

BASIL THAI & SUSHI 912/342-7625

Thai Sushi. Fine Dining. $6-$30 **AAA Inspector Notes:** *Historic.* Located in the heart of downtown, this casually upscale restaurant features flavorful fresh rolled sushi, such traditional Thai dishes as national pad thai and the chef's interpretation of fresh seafood, beef, lamb and duck dishes with a decidedly Thai spin. The lunch menu is equally fleshed out with slightly smaller portions of the popular entrées. Vegetarian selections and a children's menu are available. **Features:** full bar, happy hour. **Address:** 1401 Newcastle St 31520 **Location:** Jct US 25 (Newcastle St) and SR 25 (Gloucester St); downtown. **Parking:** street only. L D

COPPER PIG 912/289-9879

Barbecue. Casual Dining. $8-$23 **AAA Inspector Notes:** This large country store, market, restaurant and bar has a lot to offer families looking for a little diversion. Enter through the store where guests can peruse all the crafts and jarred goods or proceed to the greeter's stand and get a seat in the restaurant where the lengthy menu features freshly prepared vittles. Dining options include à la carte barbecue options (platters and sandwiches) or choose from the large buffet which features a new theme daily. **Features:** full bar, patio dining, happy hour. **Address:** 704 Mall Dr 31525 **Location:** I-95 exit 38 (Golden Isles Pkwy), 2 mi se, then just e; adjoins Colonial Mall. L D CALL

JINRIGHT'S SEAFOOD HOUSE 912/267-1590

Seafood
Casual Dining
$9-$26

AAA Inspector Notes: For more than 25 years, this family-owned restaurant has served reasonably priced seafood platters in portions ample enough to satisfy any appetite. The nautical décor adds to the ambience. The menu is limited but offers a few non-seafood alternatives to broaden its appeal for the whole family. **Features:** full bar, patio dining, happy hour. **Address:** 2815 Glynn Ave 31520 **Location:** Jct US 25 Spur/Golden Isles Pkwy, 0.9 mi s on US 17; jct US 17/25, 2.6 mi n on US 17. L D

MARSHSIDE GRILL   342/342-7981
▼▼▼ Seafood. Casual Dining. $8-$30 **AAA Inspector Notes:**
Expect marsh views and great seafood at this long-time area mainstay. A few steaks, burgers and pasta dishes also are available along
with a hibachi menu and a children's menu. Live music on the back
deck is offered on Fridays and Saturdays. **Features:** full bar, patio
dining, happy hour. **Address:** 1200 Glynn Ave 31525 **Location:** Jct
SR 25 and US 17, just s on US 17. [L] [D]

MILLHOUSE STEAKHOUSE   912/264-3424
▼▼▼▼ American. Casual Dining. $10-$30 **AAA Inspector
Notes:** Wood and muted colors in a rustic theme give this restaurant
a warm country feel. The menu is focused on fresh local seafood and
Prime steaks but a world of cuisines also is listed with dishes from
Italy, Thailand, China and Japan. Specialties of the house include
Gorgonzola sirloin, seafood cioppino, pork osso buco and stir-fry. The
servers do not miss a beat and are quite friendly. Get there early be-
cause this place is popular and fills up fast. **Features:** full bar, happy
hour. **Address:** 124 Glynco Pkwy 31525 **Location:** I-95 exit 38
(Golden Isles Pkwy), just se; in Holiday Inn Hotel & Suites.
[D]

MOONDOGGY'S PIZZA & PUB   912/264-4888
▼ Italian Pizza Sandwiches. Sports Bar. $8-$13 **AAA Inspector
Notes:** The restaurant serves a long list of specialty pizzas, full hot
entrées, sandwiches and build-your-own pasta dishes in a relaxed,
friendly atmosphere. Monday is all-you-can-eat wings and beer, and
Saturday's feature is an all-day happy hour. Every Friday and most
Saturday nights, there is live entertainment. **Features:** full bar, happy
hour. **Address:** 36 Canal Rd 31525 **Location:** I-95 exit 38 (Golden
Isles Pkwy), just se, then 0.5 mi nw to jct Glynco Pkwy; in Canal Road
Plaza. [L] [D] CALL 🅢Ⓜ

SONNY'S REAL PIT BAR-B-Q   912/264-9184
▼▼ Barbecue. Casual Dining. $8-$17 **AAA Inspector Notes:**
Bearing the name after its founder, Floyd "Sonny" Tillman, this barbecue restaurant first opened its doors circa 1968 in Gainesville,
Florida and has since spawned over 150 more throughout the Southeast. The menu is steeped in finger lickin' favorites such as ribs,
pulled pork, beef brisket, burgers, catfish, shrimp and chargrilled
chicken. Let's not forget about the fried okra, which is the perfect
starter dish, and their homemade baked beans. **Features:** beer only.
Address: 5328 New Jesup Hwy 31525 **Location:** I-95 exit 36B (New
Jesup Hwy/US 25), just nw. [L] [D]

TIPSY MCSWAY'S   912/267-9991
▼▼▼ Sandwiches Burgers. Casual Dining. $7-$11 **AAA Inspector Notes:** *Historic.* This friendly downtown tavern features
sandwiches on sourdough and flatbread, salads and soups. The
menu is simple and food is well prepared. If they happen to have
Brunswick stew, go for it, it is fantastic. **Features:** full bar, patio dining,
happy hour. **Address:** 1414 Newcastle St 31520 **Location:** Between
Gloucester and Monck sts; downtown.
[L] [D] [LATE] CALL 🅢Ⓜ

TOUCANS ALE HOUSE   912/554-1937
▼▼ American. Casual Dining. $6-$20 **AAA Inspector Notes:**
A choice of more than 50 bottled beers and 25 drafts is a popular
draw at this busy, casual and lively sports bar, but the food is tasty,
too. Examples of comfort bar foods prepared with a Southern influence include fried chicken, smoked spare ribs and barbecue pulled
pork sandwiches but there also are seafood, steak and pasta entrées. **Features:** full bar, patio dining, happy hour. **Address:** 2450
Perry Lane Rd 31525 **Location:** I-95 exit 38 (Golden Isles Pkwy), just
w, then just s. [L] [D] [LATE]

ZACHRY'S SEAFOOD & STEAK   912/265-9080
▼▼ Seafood Steak. Casual Dining. $8-$27 **AAA Inspector
Notes:** Formerly located in a small shack on Jekyll Island, the family
built their own casually upscale eatery just off the island in Brunswick.
The same great food thrives here with shrimp and grits being the
house specialty. Several other local seafood dishes make an appearance including the Lowcountry boil and house crab cakes. For landlubbers grilled steaks are king and there is a 16-ounce rib-eye or a
petite six-ounce sirloin for a lighter meal. **Features:** full bar, patio
dining, happy hour. **Address:** 415 Palisade Dr 31523 **Location:** I-95
exit 29, just w. [L] [D] CALL 🅢Ⓜ

BUFORD (B-3) pop. 12,225, elev. 1,205'
- **Restaurants p. 148**
- **Hotels & Restaurants map & index p. 90**
- **Part of Atlanta area — see map p. 44**

Buford Dam is on the Chattahoochee River 5
miles northwest of town. Above the dam Lake
Sidney Lanier extends up both the Chattahoochee
and Chestatee rivers, offering some 690 miles of
shoreline.

Locals in the know rarely miss ▽ Lanier Islands
Magical Nights of Lights, mid-November through
December at Lake Lanier Islands Resort. Bearing
tailgate picnics replete with hot cocoa and holiday
treats, fans of decorative holiday excess relish this
drive-through tour of one of the country's largest animated holiday light displays. The 6.5-mile route features more than a million lights.

Shopping: Mall of Georgia, off I-85 exit 115 to 3333
Buford Dr. N.E., features more than 200 stores and
eateries, including Belk, Dillard's, JCPenney, Macy's
and Von Maur.

LAKE LANIER ISLANDS, n.w. off SR 365, were
formed when the waters of Lake Sidney Lanier failed
to cover a cluster of forested hilltops. The four
islands are connected to the mainland by cause-
ways and each offers different recreational facilities.
Facilities and amenities include a resort and rental
units, campgrounds, tennis courts, boat rentals, a
golf course and restaurants. LanierWorld offers a
beach and water park activities. Also available are
horseback riding, fishing, sailing, hiking and zipline
tours. **Cost:** $15 (per private vehicle). Fees for facili-
ties, amenities and activities vary; phone ahead.
Phone: (770) 945-8787.

COUNTRY INN & SUITES BY CARLSON, BUFORD AT MALL
OF GEORGIA   770/271-1441 [5]
▼▼▼ Hotel. Rates not provided. **Address:** 1395 Mall of
Georgia Blvd 30519 **Location:** I-85 exit 115, 1.2 mi w to Mall of
Georgia Blvd, then 0.3 mi s. **Facility:** 77 units. 4 stories, interior cor-
ridors. **Pool(s):** heated indoor. **Activities:** hot tub, exercise room.
Guest Services: valet and coin laundry.
[🍴] CALL 🅢Ⓜ [⇆] [BIZ] [HS] [📶] [✕] [🛏] [🖥] [🖥]

COURTYARD BY MARRIOTT ATLANTA BUFORD MALL OF
GEORGIA   (678)745-3380 [4]
▼▼▼ Hotel. $107-$194 **Address:**
1405 Mall of Georgia Blvd 30519 **Loca-**   **AAA Benefit:**
tion: I-85 exit 115, just w to Mall of   Members save 5%
Georgia Blvd, then 0.3 mi s. **Facility:** 110   or more!
units. 5 stories, interior corridors.
Pool(s): heated indoor. **Activities:** hot tub, exercise room. **Guest
Services:** valet and coin laundry, area transportation.
[🍴] [🍸] CALL 🅢Ⓜ [⇆] [BIZ] [HS] [📶] [✕] [🛏] [🖥]
/ SOME UNITS [🖥]

FAIRFIELD INN & SUITES BY MARRIOTT
                                  (678)714-0248 [6]
▼▼▼ Hotel. $98-$151 **Address:**
1355 Mall of Georgia Blvd 30519 **Loca-**   **AAA Benefit:**
tion: I-85 exit 115, 1.2 mi w to Mall of   Members save 5%
Georgia Blvd, then 0.3 mi s. **Facility:** 80   or more!
units. 4 stories, interior corridors. **Activ-**
ities: exercise room. **Guest Services:** valet and coin laundry.
CALL 🅢Ⓜ [BIZ] [📶] [✕] [🛏] [🖥]

(See map & index p. 90.)

HAMPTON INN-MALL OF GEORGIA (678)546-1200 [3]
▼▼▼▼ **Hotel.** $109-$189 **Address:** 3240 Buford Dr 30519 **Location:** I-85 exit 115, 0.3 mi w. **Facility:** 92 units. 5 stories, interior corridors. **Terms:** 1-7 night minimum stay, cancellation fee imposed. **Pool(s):** outdoor. **Activities:** exercise room. **Guest Services:** valet and coin laundry.

AAA Benefit: Members save up to 10%!

[icons] CALL 🔥M ➤ BIZ 🛜 ✕ ▦ /SOME UNITS ▯ ▤

HOLIDAY INN EXPRESS & SUITES BUFORD NE-LAKE LANIER AREA 678/730-5050
▼▼▼▼ **Hotel.** Rates not provided. **Address:** 4951 Bristol Industrial Way 30518 **Location:** I-985 exit 8, just w. The Facility: 60 units. 3 stories, interior corridors. **Amenities:** safes. **Pool(s):** outdoor. **Activities:** exercise room. **Guest Services:** valet and coin laundry.

[icons] CALL 🔥M ➤ BIZ HS 🛜 ✕ ▯ ▤ ▦

HOLIDAY INN EXPRESS HOTEL & SUITES BUFORD - MALL OF GA 678/318-1080 [1]
▼▼▼▼ **Hotel.** Rates not provided. **Address:** 2499 Satellite Blvd 30518 **Location:** I-985 exit 4, just w. **Facility:** 79 units. 3 stories, interior corridors. **Pool(s):** outdoor. **Activities:** exercise room. **Guest Services:** valet and coin laundry.

[icons] CALL 🔥M ➤ BIZ HS 🛜 ✕ ▯ ▤ ▦

SPRINGHILL SUITES BY MARRIOTT ATLANTA/BUFORD-MALL OF GEORGIA (678)714-2150 [2]
▼▼▼▼ **Hotel.** $106-$194 **Address:** 3250 Buford Dr 30519 **Location:** I-85 exit 115, 0.3 mi w. **Facility:** 97 units. 5 stories, interior corridors. **Pool(s):** outdoor. **Activities:** hot tub, exercise room. **Guest Services:** valet and coin laundry.

AAA Benefit: Members save 5% or more!

[icons] ECO [icons] CALL 🔥M ➤ BIZ 🛜 ✕ ▯ ▤ ▦

WHERE TO EAT

AQUA TERRA BISTRO 770/271-3000
▼▼▼▼ **New American. Fine Dining.** $10-$32 **AAA Inspector Notes:** Tucked away in the trendy historic district, in a delightful rustic setting, is this neighborhood bistro offers a flavorful menu. The chef's creative offerings include barbecue pulled pork tacos with jalapeño slaw, crunchy tilapia served over a crispy Asian salad and herb-crusted lamb chops. Menu items change periodically but guests can expect dishes that are both beautiful and delicious. **Features:** full bar. **Address:** 55 E Main St 30518 **Location:** Downtown. **Parking:** street only. [L] [D]

BONEFISH GRILL 678/546-8240 [1]
▼▼▼▼ **Seafood. Fine Dining.** $8-$29 **AAA Inspector Notes:** Fish is the house specialty, and the menu and nightly specials offer a variety of choices. Well-prepared food is cooked to perfection. Service is casual in nature, and the staff is skilled and attentive. **Features:** full bar. **Address:** 3420 Buford Dr 30519 **Location:** I-85 exit 115, 1.5 mi w; I-985 exit 4, 1.5 mi e. [D] CALL 🔥M

PARMA RUSTIC TAVERN 678/541-0908 [2]
▼▼ **Italian. Casual Dining.** $7-$19 **AAA Inspector Notes:** Come to this neighborhood dining spot ready to eat well. Try many of your Italian favorites or something unique. Two favorites include the crispy eggplant chips with chipotle sun dried tomato aïoli, and the Krispy Kreme burger, where two hot donuts provide the bun for a juicy black angus patty. Wash it down with a cool one off a diverse list of true craft beers. **Features:** beer & wine. **Address:** 3350 Buford Dr, Building B, Suite 200 30519 **Location:** I-85 exit 115, 1.3 mi w. [L] [D] CALL 🔥M

Request roadside assistance in a click — online or using the AAA or CAA apps

---

P.F. CHANG'S CHINA BISTRO 678/546-9005 [3]
▼▼▼▼ **Chinese. Fine Dining.** $8-$26 **AAA Inspector Notes:** Trendy, upscale decor provides a pleasant backdrop for New Age Chinese dining. Appetizers, soups and salads are a meal by themselves. Vegetarian plates and sides, noodles, chow meins, chicken and meat dishes are created from exotic, fresh ingredients. **Features:** full bar, happy hour. **Address:** 3333 Buford Dr 30519 **Location:** I-85 exit 115, 0.5 mi w; I-985 exit 4, 1.7 mi e; at Mall of Georgia. [L] [D] CALL 🔥M

SONNY'S REAL PIT BAR-B-Q 770/831-5002
▼▼▼▼ **Barbecue. Casual Dining.** $8-$17 **AAA Inspector Notes:** Bearing the name after its founder, Floyd "Sonny" Tillman, this barbecue restaurant first opened its doors circa 1968 in Gainesville, Florida and has since spawned over 150 more throughout the Southeast. The menu is steeped in finger lickin' favorites such as ribs, pulled pork, beef brisket, burgers, catfish, shrimp and chargrilled chicken. Let's not forget about the fried okra, which is the perfect starter dish, and their homemade baked beans. **Features:** beer only. **Address:** 1905 Buford Mill Dr 30519 **Location:** I-985 exit 4, just se. [L] [D]

BYRON pop. 4,512

BEST WESTERN INN & SUITES (478)956-3056

▼▼ Motel $75-$89

[BW] Best Western. **AAA Benefit:** Save 10% or more every day and earn 10% bonus points!

Address: 101 Dunbar Rd 31008 **Location:** I-75 exit 149 (SR 49), just e. **Facility:** 67 units. 2 stories (no elevator), exterior corridors. **Pool(s):** heated indoor. **Activities:** hot tub, exercise room. **Guest Services:** coin laundry. **Featured Amenity:** full hot breakfast.

[icons] SAVE [icons] ➤ BIZ HS 🛜 ▤ ▦ /SOME UNITS ▮

COMFORT SUITES (478)956-1222
▼▼▼ Hotel $95-$155
Address: 103 Dunbar Rd 31008 **Location:** I-75 exit 149 (SR 49), just se. **Facility:** 70 units. 4 stories, interior corridors. **Pool(s):** heated indoor. **Activities:** hot tub, exercise room. **Guest Services:** coin laundry. **Featured Amenity:** full hot breakfast.

[icons] SAVE [icons] CALL 🔥M ➤ BIZ HS 🛜 ✕ ▯ ▤ ▦

DAYS INN BYRON (478)956-5100

▼▼▼ Hotel $45-$65

Address: 246 Hwy 49 N 31008 **Location:** I-75 exit 149 (SR 49), just sw. **Facility:** 62 units. 2 stories (no elevator), exterior corridors. **Pool(s):** outdoor. **Guest Services:** coin laundry. **Featured Amenity:** continental breakfast.

[icons] SAVE [icons] CALL 🔥M ➤ 🛜 ▯ ▤ ▦ /SOME UNITS ▮

HOLIDAY INN EXPRESS HOTEL & SUITES 478/956-7829
▼▼▼▼ **Hotel.** Rates not provided. **Address:** 312 Hwy 49 N 31008 **Location:** I-75 exit 149 (SR 49), just ne. **Facility:** 61 units. 4 stories, interior corridors. **Pool(s):** outdoor. **Activities:** exercise room. **Guest Services:** coin laundry.

 [icons] CALL 🔥M ➤ BIZ HS 🛜 ✕ ▯ ▤ ▦

SUPER 8

Hotel
$54-$79

(478)956-3311

Address: 305 Hwy 49 N 31008 **Location:** I-75 exit 149 (SR 49), just e. **Facility:** 57 units. 2 stories (no elevator), exterior corridors. **Pool(s):** outdoor. **Guest Services:** coin laundry. **Featured Amenity:** continental breakfast.

WHERE TO EAT

CASA MEXICO   478/956-3044

Mexican. Casual Dining. $5-$18 **AAA Inspector Notes:** A local favorite that always is hopping, guests to this spot can try one of the traditional dishes such as a chimichangas, fajitas or enchiladas. The house specials also are delicious as are the fish tacos and carnitas. Satisfy a sweet tooth with the homemade flan or churritos. **Address:** 311 SR 49, Suite 170 31008 **Location:** I-75 exit 149 (SR 49), just ne.

MAMA MIA'S PIZZA & PASTA RESTAURANT   478/333-3700

Italian. Fine Dining. $7-$28 **AAA Inspector Notes:** This family owned and operated restaurant offers traditional homemade Italian dishes. I would start out with the lightly fried calamari or fresh baked garlic knots. Depending on how hungry you are, you can follow up with a full pasta entrée or go lighter with pizza or a sub. They offer a few healthier options such as the grilled chicken salad or wheat pasta with sauce. Save room for dessert, the chocolate cannoli is delightful. **Features:** full bar, patio dining. **Address:** 6015 Watson Blvd, Suite 440 31008 **Location:** I-75 exit 144 (Richard B Russell Pkwy), 2 mi w.

CAIRO (F-2) pop. 9,607, elev. 265'

Though the Cairo (KAY-ro) area was supposedly visited by Hernando de Soto in 1540, it was not settled until pioneers from North Carolina founded the Tired Creek Primitive Baptist Church in 1826. By 1870 the local Atlantic & Gulf Railroad station had grown large enough to support a town, and Cairo was born.

Cairo-Grady County Chamber of Commerce: 961 N. Broad St., P.O. Box 387, Cairo, GA 39828. **Phone:** (229) 377-3663.

RODDENBERY MEMORIAL LIBRARY, 320 N. Broad St., contains displays describing area history and works by local artists. **Hours:** Mon.-Thurs. 10-6 (also Tues. 6-7 p.m.), Fri. 10-3, Sat. 10-2. **Cost:** Free. **Phone:** (229) 377-3632.

BEST WESTERN EXECUTIVE INN   (229)377-8000

Hotel
$82-$102

Best Western **AAA Benefit:** Save 10% or more every day and earn 10% bonus points!

Address: 2800 Hwy 84 E 39828 **Location:** 2 mi e. **Facility:** 50 units. 2 stories (no elevator), exterior corridors. **Pool(s):** outdoor. **Activities:** sauna, limited exercise equipment. **Guest Services:** valet laundry. **Featured Amenity:** full hot breakfast.

CALHOUN (A-2) pop. 15,650, elev. 716'
• **Restaurants p. 150**

Calhoun and surrounding Gordon County were the home of the Cherokee Native Americans until 1838, when the Cherokees were forced to sell their land and move to Oklahoma. Local industry includes carpet and textile manufacturing. Resaca Confederate Cemetery, 5 miles north on I-75, was the site of the Civil War battle that opened the way to Atlanta for Gen. William Tecumseh Sherman. Nearby at Fort Wayne Civil War Historic Site, a 1-mile interpretive trail recounts the battle. The Resaca Battlefield Historic Site on Resaca Lafayette Rd. is open Fri.-Sun. dawn to dusk and has a 6-mile self-guiding trail with interpretive signs for adults and children.

Calhoun/Gordon County Convention & Visitors Bureau: 300 S. Wall St., Calhoun, GA 30701. **Phone:** (706) 625-3200 or (800) 887-3811.

NEW ECHOTA STATE HISTORIC SITE is off I-75 exit 317, 1 mi. n. on SR 225 to 1211 Chatsworth Hwy. (SR 225). Established in 1825, the capital of New Echota was the site of the *Cherokee Phoenix*, the first Native American-language newspaper office; the signing of the Treaty of New Echota; and the assembly of Native Americans for removal west on the infamous Trail of Tears.

The restored village features 12 original and reconstructed buildings, including missionary Samuel Worcester's home, Cherokee Court and Council houses, the *Cherokee Phoenix* printing office, a general store, smoke houses, barns and other outbuildings. Visitors can view exhibits and watch a 17-minute film at the on-site museum. A research library also is available. The grounds feature 1.25 miles of nature trails. **Hours:** Wed.-Sat. 9-5. Closed Jan. 1, Thanksgiving and Christmas. **Cost:** $7; $6.50 (ages 62+); $5.50 (ages 6-17). **Phone:** (706) 624-1321.

BAYMONT INN & SUITES   (706)629-8133

Motel. $59-$149 **Address:** 189 Jameson St 30701 **Location:** I-75 exit 312, just w. **Facility:** 59 units. 2 stories (no elevator), exterior corridors. **Pool(s):** outdoor. **Activities:** exercise room. **Guest Services:** valet laundry.

COUNTRY INN & SUITES BY CARLSON   (706)625-6500

Hotel. $89-$179 **Address:** 1033 Fairmount Hwy 30701 **Location:** I-75 exit 312, just w. **Facility:** 64 units. 4 stories, interior corridors. **Terms:** 3 day cancellation notice. **Pool(s):** heated indoor. **Activities:** hot tub, exercise room. **Guest Services:** coin laundry.

ECONO LODGE   (706)629-9501

Motel. $48-$60 **Address:** 915 Hwy 53 SE 30701 **Location:** I-75 exit 312, just e. **Facility:** 93 units. 2 stories (no elevator), exterior corridors. **Pool(s):** outdoor. **Guest Services:** coin laundry.

FAIRFIELD INN & SUITES BY MARRIOTT CALHOUN
(706)629-8002

Hotel
$98-$160

AAA Benefit: Members save 5% or more!

Address: 1002 GA-53 30701 **Location:** I-75 exit 312, just e. **Facility:** 73 units. 4 stories, interior corridors. **Pool(s):** heated indoor. **Activities:** exercise room. **Guest Services:** valet and coin laundry. **Featured Amenity:** full hot breakfast.

SAVE ▮▮ CALL ⬤M ⬅ BIZ HS
📶 ✕ 🖥 ⬛ ⬜

LA QUINTA INN
(706)629-2559

▼▼▼ **Hotel.** $68-$152 **Address:** 150 Cracker Barrel Dr 30701 **Location:** I-75 exit 312, just e. **Facility:** 50 units. 2 stories (no elevator), interior corridors. **Pool(s):** outdoor. **Guest Services:** coin laundry.

▮▮ CALL ⬤M ⬅ BIZ HS 📶 ✕ 🖥 ⬛ ⬜
/ SOME UNITS 🐾

QUALITY INN CALHOUN
(706)629-9207

Motel
$74-$99

Address: 1204 Red Bud Rd NE 30701 **Location:** I-75 exit 315, just w. **Facility:** 45 units. 2 stories (no elevator), exterior corridors. **Terms:** cancellation fee imposed. **Pool(s):** outdoor. **Activities:** limited exercise equipment. **Guest Services:** coin laundry. **Featured Amenity:** full hot breakfast.

SAVE ▮▮ CALL ⬤M ⬅ HS 📶
🖥 ⬛ ⬜ / SOME UNITS 🐾

SUPER 8 CALHOUN
(706)629-0999

▼▼ **Motel.** $59-$150 **Address:** 115 Hampton Dr SE 30701 **Location:** I-75 exit 312, just w. **Facility:** 58 units. 2 stories (no elevator), exterior corridors. **Pool(s):** outdoor. **Activities:** exercise room. **Guest Services:** valet laundry.

▮▮ CALL ⬤M ⬅ BIZ 📶 🖥 ⬛ ⬜ / SOME UNITS 🐾

WHERE TO EAT

B & J'S DINER
706/629-1117

▼▼ American. Casual Dining. $2-$8 **AAA Inspector Notes:** Step back in time to the 50's and enjoy burgers, hot dogs and such sandwiches as Philly cheesesteak, club, open-faced hot steak, grilled cheese and egg salad in this retro diner. French fries, chips, coleslaw and potato salad are choices of sides. The boneless fried chicken breast is available every day along with other meats and a wide selection of veggies along with a choice of cornbread or a roll. **Features:** patio dining. **Address:** 220 S Wall St 30701 **Location:** I-75 exit 312, 3 mi w following US 41; downtown. **Parking:** street only. L

CHRISTIAN & JAKE'S BISTRO
706/624-8103

▼ Sandwiches. Casual Dining. $7-$9 **AAA Inspector Notes:** This popular local eatery offers a delicious array of specialty sandwiches, soups, salads and desserts. Vegetarian and healthy options are extensive and distinctive. The small dining room fills quickly so be prepared for a little wait. Save room for the plethora of desserts—it is worth it. **Address:** 555 SR 53 SE 30701 **Location:** I-75 exit 312, 0.4 mi w. L D

DUKE'S
706/383-8270

▼▼ American. Casual Dining. $5-$24 **AAA Inspector Notes:** Come to watch a ball game while eating some great wings, seafood or other choices. All-you-can-eat catfish is available every evening starting at 4 pm. Lunch specials are available 11 am-2 pm; you can get such items as fried chicken or country fried steak with vegetables or maybe a plate of veggies will suit you. Be sure to ask about the dessert specials! **Features:** beer only. **Address:** 408 Court St 30701 **Location:** Jct River St; downtown. L D CALL ⬤M

GONDOLIER ITALIAN RESTAURANT AND PIZZA
706/625-2322

▼▼ Italian Pizza. Casual Dining. $3-$15 **AAA Inspector Notes:** In addition to daily specials, diners can select from a tempting variety of calzones and such standards as spaghetti, manicotti and ravioli. Servers are fast and friendly. **Features:** beer & wine. **Address:** 427 Hwy 53 NE 30701 **Location:** I-75 exit 312, 0.7 mi w. L D ◣

CANTON (B-2) pop. 22,958, elev. 965'

Early entrepreneurs imagined Canton as a center for the silk industry, and in fact the name Canton is derived from the famous silk manufacturing city in China, Guangzhou. However, cotton was king and the town became known for denim. Today this small town boasts a friendly downtown area and 28 acres of green space available for public use.

COUNTRY INN & SUITES BY CARLSON
(770)345-6800

▼▼▼ **Hotel.** $99-$129 **Address:** 705 Transit Ave 30114 **Location:** I-575 exit 20, just w. **Facility:** 57 units. 3 stories, interior corridors. **Terms:** cancellation fee imposed. **Pool(s):** heated indoor. **Activities:** exercise room. **Guest Services:** valet and coin laundry.

▮▮ CALL ⬤M ⬅ BIZ HS 📶 ✕ 🖥 ⬛ ⬜

DAYS INN
(770)479-0301

▼▼ **Motel.** $54-$96 **Address:** 101 Juniper St 30114 **Location:** I-575 exit 20, 1.4 mi w. **Facility:** 39 units. 2 stories (no elevator), exterior corridors. **Terms:** cancellation fee imposed. **Pool(s):** outdoor.

▮▮ CALL ⬤M ⬅ HS 📶 🖥 ⬛

HAMPTON INN
(770)345-7400

▼▼▼ **Hotel.** $99-$189 **Address:** 710 Transit Ave 30114 **Location:** I-575 exit 20, just w. **Facility:** 81 units. 5 stories, interior corridors. **Terms:** 1-7 night minimum stay, cancellation fee imposed.

AAA Benefit: Members save up to 10%!

Pool(s): outdoor. **Activities:** exercise room. **Guest Services:** valet and coin laundry.

▮▮ CALL ⬤M ⬅ BIZ HS 📶 ✕ 🎥 ⬜
/ SOME UNITS 🖥 ⬛

WHERE TO EAT

ALESSANDRO'S
770/345-4446

▼▼ Italian. Casual Dining. $7-$20 **AAA Inspector Notes:** Owned and operated by native New Yorkers, this place is the real deal. Authentic, freshly prepared Italian favorites include rave-worthy pizza and pasta dishes that are my favorite of any in the area. The staff is warm and cordial. **Address:** 10511 Bells Ferry Rd 30114 **Location:** I-575 exit 11, 2.5 mi w to Bells Ferry Rd, then 1.3 mi n; in Centre at Bridgemill. L D

CHEESEBURGER BOBBY'S
770/479-0411

▼ Burgers. Quick Serve. $3-$6 **AAA Inspector Notes:** Nibble on hand-cut fries with your fresh, hand-patted burger, which you'll gussy up with onions, lettuce, tomatoes, pickles and other items on the condiment station. Other choices include hot dogs, chicken sandwiches and custard for dessert. Friendly servers tend the bright, fresh and clean dining room. **Address:** 2060 Cumming Hwy, Suite 100 30114 **Location:** I-575 exit 19, 0.6 mi e. L D CALL ⬤M

DOWNTOWN KITCHEN
770/479-1616

▼▼▼ American. Casual Dining. $16-$40 **AAA Inspector Notes:** A downtown jewel outside the Atlanta perimeter, this restaurant serves well-prepared steaks, seafood and new takes on some traditional Southern favorites. Pair these dishes with selections from a good wine list. Funky art of music icons and exposed brick walls add to the trendy feel. **Features:** full bar. **Reservations:** suggested. **Address:** 140 E Marietta St 30114 **Location:** Downtown. D

GOIN' COASTAL
770/479-3737

▼▼ Seafood. Casual Dining. $9-$24 **AAA Inspector Notes:** Reliable servers guide you through a meal of fresh seafood, such as lobster or crab cakes, steamed seafood platters, grilled favorites and fried gator tail at this nautical, contemporary spot. **Features:** full bar. **Address:** 125 W Main St 30114 **Location:** Downtown. **Parking:** street only. L D

PROVINO'S
770/720-9676

▼▼ Italian. Casual Dining. $11-$24 **AAA Inspector Notes:** Traditional Italian favorites, such as veal parmigiana, lasagna, manicotti and fettuccine Alfredo, are served in a neighborhood-style atmosphere. Of particular interest are the bottomless house salad and garlic rolls as well as delicious cheesecake. **Features:** beer & wine, early bird specials. **Address:** 1365 Riverstone Pkwy 30144 **Location:** I-575 exit 20, 1 mi w. D CALL M

RAINBOW ASIA
770/720-0879

▼▼ Asian. Casual Dining. $7-$46 **AAA Inspector Notes:** Chinese, Thai and Japanese favorites, including sushi, are featured in this rainbow of Asian cuisine. Specials feature Peking duck, salt and pepper seafood and sizzling black pepper beef. Informed and attentive servers work the dining room, which is appointed with pleasing décor. **Features:** beer & wine, patio dining. **Address:** 3725 Sixes Rd, Suite 109 30114 **Location:** I-575 exit 11, 2.5 mi w; in Bridge Pointe Plaza. L D CALL M

R & M SANDWICH SHOP
770/479-4413

▼ Sandwiches. Quick Serve. $5-$10 **AAA Inspector Notes:** Open since the early 1970s, this bustling spot offers a great variety of traditional and creative sandwich choices as well as breakfast. The Donna special is the most popular menu item and features roast beef, Swiss, mozzarella, mushrooms, onions, jalapeños, tomato, mayonnaise and mustard. There are many types of hoagies include gyro, club and Italian. Double sandwiches feature pepperoni and roast beef and pastrami and corned beef. End with a homemade cookie. **Address:** 117 W Main St 30114 **Location:** Downtown. **Parking:** street only. B L

RIVERSTONE CORNER BISTRO
770/704-7325

▼▼ American. Casual Dining. $4-$12 **AAA Inspector Notes:** This small, family-owned establishment offers more than delicious food and a relaxing atmosphere. They have hometown charm. The lunch menu offers a variety of yummy sandwiches and salads such as the spinach salad, which is my favorite. For dinner try the North Atlantic salmon or the Southern fried chicken. Save room for desserts such as the scrumptious salted caramel bread pudding and the Key lime pie. **Features:** full bar. **Address:** 135 Reinhardt College Pkwy 30144 **Location:** I-575 exit 20, 0.5 mi w on Riverstone Pkwy, then 0.8 mi e. L D CALL M

VIVA MEXICO
770/720-3342

▼▼ Tex-Mex. Casual Dining. $6-$13 **AAA Inspector Notes:** Begin with complimentary chips and salsa, then delve into your choice of a wide array of traditional Mexican favorites such as grilled fajitas, tacos, burritos and enchiladas. You also should check out the lunch and weekend specials. Sidle up to the bar for margaritas, sangria, wine or a Mexican beer. Fast, friendly servers tend the dining room, which replicates a south-of-the-border village. **Features:** full bar. **Address:** 130 Prominence Point Pkwy 30114 **Location:** I-575 exit 14, just w; in Paradise Shops of Prominence Point. L D CALL M

WILLIAMSON BROS BAR-B-Q
770/345-9067

▼▼ Barbecue. Casual Dining. $5-$24 **AAA Inspector Notes:** This comfortable, down-home barbecue joint serves up generous portions designed to put some meat on your bones. House specialties include barbecue ribs, pork and chicken grilled over an open-pit right in the restaurant. Fried dill pickles and fried red tomatoes in a thick batter are worth a try. **Features:** full bar. **Address:** 1600 Marietta Hwy 30114 **Location:** I-575 exit 16, 0.8 mi w. L D

CARROLLTON pop. 24,388

COURTYARD BY MARRIOTT CARROLLTON
(678)664-5200

▼▼▼ Hotel. $113-$170 **Address:** 180 Barnes Ave 30117 **Location:** W on SR 61 Connector, 14 mi e. **Facility:** 109 units. 5 stories, interior corridors. **Activities:** exercise room. **Guest Services:** valet and coin laundry.

> **AAA Benefit:**
> Members save 5% or more!

CALL M BIZ HS 🛜 ✕ 📶 💻 / SOME UNITS 📷

HAMPTON INN
(770)838-7722

▼▼▼ Hotel. $99-$169 **Address:** 102 S Cottage Hill Rd 30117 **Location:** Jct US 27 and SR 166, just s. **Facility:** 77 units. 4 stories, interior corridors. **Terms:** 1-7 night minimum stay, cancellation fee imposed. **Pool(s):** outdoor. **Activities:** exercise room. **Guest Services:** valet laundry.

> **AAA Benefit:**
> Members save up to 10%!

🍴➔ CALL M 🏊 BIZ HS 🛜 ✕ 📶 📷 💻

HOLIDAY INN EXPRESS
770/838-0508

▼▼ Hotel. Rates not provided. **Address:** 104 S Cottage Hill Rd 30117 **Location:** Jct US 27 and SR 166, just s. **Facility:** 83 units. 4 stories, interior corridors. **Pool(s):** outdoor. **Activities:** exercise room. **Guest Services:** valet laundry.

🍴➔ CALL M 🏊 BIZ HS 🛜 ✕ 📶 📷 💻

QUALITY INN
(770)834-2600

▼▼ Motel. $74-$84 **Address:** 700 S Park St 30117 **Location:** On US 27, just s of downtown. **Facility:** 59 units. 2 stories (no elevator), exterior corridors. **Pool(s):** outdoor. **Activities:** exercise room. **Guest Services:** coin laundry.

🍴➔ CALL M 🏊 BIZ HS 🛜 📶 📷 💻 / SOME UNITS 🍴

WHERE TO EAT

LITTLE HAWAIIAN SEAFOOD GRILL & TIKI LOUNGE
770/838-1220

▼▼▼ Hawaiian. Casual Dining. $6-$24 **AAA Inspector Notes:** The owners of this popular local restaurant have brought the flavor and cuisine of Hawaii to Georgia. They specialize in Hawaiian fish but diners also can find a variety of other seafood, fresh meats and noodle bowls. A few vegetarian options are available as well as nightly dinner specials. **Features:** full bar, patio dining. **Address:** 206 Rome St 30117 **Location:** Jct SR 166 business/Alabama St, just nw. L D CALL M

PLATES ON THE SQUARE
770/214-5531

▼▼▼ American. Casual Dining. $7-$21 **AAA Inspector Notes:** Located on the square in a popular historic district, this trendy eatery features an eclectic menu of food and cocktails. The house specialty is the cedar plank grilled salmon. The filet mignon with fried avocado, pot roast and chicken tikka masala are also popular with the locals. **Features:** full bar. **Address:** 301 Adamson St 30117 **Location:** In historic downtown. **Parking:** on-site and street. L D LATE CALL M

**Make a good trip great with insight
and ideas from AAA/CAA travel experts**

CARTERSVILLE (B-2) pop. 19,731, elev. 787'

Only two of Cartersville's houses survived the Federal occupation of 1864, but the town's location in Bartow County's rich mineral belt led to its speedy reconstruction. Six miles east is Red Top Mountain State Park *(see Recreation Areas Chart)*.

Cartersville-Bartow County Convention and Visitors Bureau: 5450 SR 20, P.O. Box 200397, Cartersville, GA 30120. **Phone:** (770) 387-1357 or (800) 733-2280.

BOOTH WESTERN ART MUSEUM is 1 blk. n. of town square at 501 Museum Dr. The museum houses contemporary American western art along with illustrations and movie posters. Particular subjects highlighted by individual galleries within the museum include cowboys and the Civil War. One gallery features presidential photographs, letters and memorabilia; another offers interactive, hands-on exhibits for children ages 2-12. Rotating exhibits also are on display, and a sculpture garden is on the grounds.

Food is available Tues.- Sat. **Time:** Allow 1 hour minimum. **Hours:** Tues.-Sat. 10-5 (also Thurs. 5-8), Sun. 1-5; guided tours are given at 1:30. Closed Jan. 1, July 4, Thanksgiving and Christmas. **Cost:** $10; $8 (ages 65+); $7 (students with ID); free (ages 0-12, active military with ID and to all first Thurs. of the month 4-8). **Phone:** (770) 387-1300. GT ⑪

ETOWAH INDIAN MOUNDS STATE HISTORICAL SITE, 6 mi. s. of I-75 exit 288 following signs to 813 Indian Mounds Rd., preserves the remains of a Native American settlement occupied 950-1550 A.D. The 54-acre site includes six earthen mounds, a plaza, borrow pits, a fish trap in the Etowah River and a defense ditch. A museum displays artifacts excavated from the mounds and interprets religious and cultural practices of the site's former residents.

Special events are offered. **Hours:** Museum open Tues.-Sat. 9-5; grounds close 30 minutes before museum. Closed Jan. 1, Thanksgiving and Christmas. **Cost:** $6; $5 (ages 62+); $4 (ages 6-17); $2 (ages 0-5). **Phone:** (770) 387-3747. 🏛

ROSELAWN MUSEUM is at 224 W. Cherokee Ave. This restored Victorian mansion was the home of late 19th-century evangelist Samuel Porter Jones. It contains his writings and memorabilia as well as those belonging to Rebecca Latimer Felton, who in 1922 became the first woman to serve in the U.S. Senate. The 3.5-acre grounds feature a one-room schoolhouse, a brick smokehouse, a carriage house and a rose garden with nearly 250 antique roses. **Time:** Allow 45 minutes minimum. **Hours:** Guided tours Tues.-Fri. 10-noon and 1-5. The site may be closed for private events some Fri. afternoons; phone ahead. Closed major holidays. **Cost:** $5; $2 (ages 0-12). **Phone:** (770) 387-5162. GT

🔺 **TELLUS SCIENCE MUSEUM** is at 100 Tellus Dr. The museum houses four galleries. The Weinman Mineral Gallery displays gems and minerals from around the world. The Fossil Gallery takes visitors back to a time when dinosaurs, reptiles and giant mammals walked the earth. A highlight here is the 9-foot-wide jaw of a Megalodon, a shark the size of a school bus.

Science in Motion covers 100 years of transportation technology. Displays feature electric, steam and gasoline-powered cars and reflect the progress of the automotive industry as well as aviation and space exploration. The Collins Family My Big Backyard provides an interactive experience for children, letting them experiment with light, sound and electricity in a learning environment. A fossil dig and gem panning area allows young paleontologists to uncover their own buried fossils as well as sift for gems.

Special exhibits are featured in The Vault, Crossroads and Discovery Garden galleries. A 120-seat state-of-the-art digital planetarium takes visitors on a tour of the galaxy courtesy of four different shows.

Time: Allow 3 hours minimum. **Hours:** Daily 10-5. Closed Jan. 1, July 4, Thanksgiving and Christmas. **Cost:** $14; $12 (ages 65+); $10 (ages 3-17 and college students with ID). Planetarium admission $3.50. **Phone:** (770) 606-5700. ▣ ⑪ 🏛

BAYMONT INN & SUITES CARTERSVILLE　　(770)386-9259
🔷🔷 **Hotel.** $70-$95 **Address:** 11 Kent Dr 30121 **Location:** I-75 exit 296, just e. **Facility:** 54 units. 3 stories, interior corridors. **Pool(s):** outdoor. **Activities:** exercise room. **Guest Services:** coin laundry.
⑪→ CALL 🅜 ➔ BIZ 🛜 🔗 ▣ 🖨 / SOME UNITS 🔧

BEST WESTERN GARDEN INN & SUITES
　　　　　　　　　　　　　　　　(770)386-1569

🔷🔷 Motel $80-$129

🅑🅦 **Best Western.** **AAA Benefit:** Save 10% or more every day and earn 10% bonus points!

Address: 5663 Hwy 20 NE 30121 **Location:** I-75 exit 290, 0.3 mi e. **Facility:** 47 units. 3 stories, exterior corridors. **Pool(s):** outdoor. **Activities:** exercise room. **Guest Services:** valet and coin laundry.

SAVE ⑪→ CALL 🅜 ➔ BIZ HS 🛜 ✖ 🔗 🖨 ▣

CLARION INN CARTERSVILLE　　(770)386-0830
🔷🔷 **Hotel.** $119-$129 **Address:** 2336 Hwy 411 30184 **Location:** I-75 exit 293, just w. Located in a quiet rural area. **Facility:** 144 units. 2 stories (no elevator), interior corridors. **Pool(s):** outdoor. **Activities:** exercise room. **Guest Services:** valet and coin laundry.
⑪ 🍸 CALL 🅜 ➔ BIZ HS 🛜 ✖ ▣ / SOME UNITS 🔧 🔗 🖨

COUNTRY INN & SUITES BY CARLSON　　(770)386-5888
🔷🔷 **Hotel.** $99-$289 **Address:** 43 SR 20 Spur 30121 **Location:** I-75 exit 290, 0.3 mi se. **Facility:** 62 units. 3 stories, interior corridors. **Terms:** 3 day cancellation notice. **Pool(s):** heated indoor. **Activities:** hot tub, exercise room. **Guest Services:** valet and coin laundry.
⑪→ CALL 🅜 ➔ BIZ HS 🛜 ✖ 🔗 🖨 ▣ / SOME UNITS 🔧

ECONO LODGE CARTERSVILLE   (770)382-8881

▼▼▼ **Hotel.** $57-$90 **Address:** 41 SR 20 Spur SE 30121 **Location:** I-75 exit 290, 0.3 mi e. **Facility:** 58 units. 3 stories (no elevator), interior corridors. **Pool(s):** outdoor. **Guest Services:** coin laundry.

FAIRFIELD INN & SUITES BY MARRIOTT CARTERSVILLE   (770)387-0400

▼▼▼▼ **Hotel.** $94-$157 **Address:** 20 Canyon Pkwy 30120 **Location:** I-75 exit 288, just w. **Facility:** 73 units. 4 stories, interior corridors. **Pool(s):** heated indoor. **Activities:** hot tub, exercise room. **Guest Services:** coin laundry.

AAA Benefit: Members save 5% or more!

HAMPTON INN EMERSON AT LAKEPOINT   (678)792-3375

▼▼▼ **Hotel.** $109-$219 **Address:** 86 Old Allatoona Rd SE 30121 **Location:** I-75 exit 283, 0.8 mi w. **Facility:** 86 units. 4 stories, interior corridors. **Terms:** 1-7 night minimum stay, cancellation fee imposed. **Pool(s):** heated indoor. **Activities:** exercise room. **Guest Services:** coin laundry. *(See ad p. 128.)*

AAA Benefit: Members save up to 10%!

HILTON GARDEN INN CARTERSVILLE   (770)382-9787

▼▼▼ **Hotel.** $114-$214 **Address:** 24 Liberty Dr 30121 **Location:** I-75 exit 288, 1.7 mi w. **Facility:** 108 units. 4 stories, interior corridors. **Terms:** 1-7 night minimum stay, cancellation fee imposed. **Amenities:** safes. **Pool(s):** heated indoor. **Activities:** hot tub, exercise room. **Guest Services:** valet and coin laundry.

AAA Benefit: Members save up to 10%!

HOME2 SUITES BY HILTON   (678)792-3346

[fyi] Extended Stay Hotel. $119-$139 Too new to rate, opening scheduled for September 2016. **Address:** 1320 E Main St 30121 **Location:** I-75 exit 288, just w. **Amenities:** 80 units. coffeemakers, microwaves, refrigerators. **Terms:** 1-7 night minimum stay, cancellation fee imposed. *(See ad p. 128.)*

AAA Benefit: Members save up to 10%!

KNIGHTS INN   (770)386-7263

▼▼▼
Motel
$65

Address: 420 E Church St 30121 **Location:** I-75 exit 288, 1.5 mi w. **Facility:** 63 units. 1 story, exterior corridors. **Pool(s):** outdoor. **Featured Amenity: continental breakfast.**

MAINSTAY SUITES, CARTERSVILLE-EMERSON LAKEPOINT   (770)607-3005

▼▼▼▼ **Hotel.** $79-$199 **Address:** 146 Old Allatoona Rd SE 30121 **Location:** I-75 exit 283, just e. **Facility:** 80 units. 3 stories, interior corridors. **Pool(s):** heated indoor. **Activities:** exercise room. **Guest Services:** coin laundry.

MICROTEL INN & SUITES BY WYNDHAM CARTERSVILLE   (678)605-9331

▼▼▼ **Hotel.** $68-$89 **Address:** 1348 Joe Frank Harris Pkwy 30120 **Location:** I-75 exit 290, 1.8 mi w on SR 20 W, just s on Market Pl Blvd, 1.5 mi w on SR 3 N/US 41 N (Joe Frank Harris Pkwy). **Facility:** 71 units. 4 stories, interior corridors. **Guest Services:** coin laundry.

MOTEL 6 - #4046   770/386-1449

▼▼ **Motel.** Rates not provided. **Address:** 5657 Hwy 20 NE 30121 **Location:** I-75 exit 290, 0.3 mi e. **Facility:** 46 units. 2 stories (no elevator), exterior corridors. **Pool(s):** outdoor.

SLEEP INN CARTERSVILLE-EMERSON LAKEPOINT   (770)607-3005

▼▼▼ **Hotel.** $99-$189 **Address:** 146 Old Allatoona Rd SE, Bldg A 30121 **Location:** I-75 exit 283, just e. **Facility:** 40 units. 3 stories, interior corridors. **Pool(s):** heated indoor. **Activities:** exercise room. **Guest Services:** coin laundry.

WHERE TO EAT

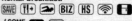

ANGELO'S NEW YORK STYLE PIZZA & BISTRO   770/387-1188

▼▼ Italian. Casual Dining. $6-$19 **AAA Inspector Notes:** Pizza is just the tip of the iceberg at this bistro and it comes with traditional toppings as well as cheeseburger, Buffalo chicken, Philly and Hawaiian. Pasta entrées include fettuccine carbonara, shrimp parmigiana, baked ziti and chicken Alfredo. Chicken wings and fried pickles are good starters and you should always leave room for dessert! **Features:** beer & wine, patio dining. **Address:** 650 Henderson Dr, Suite 101 30120 **Location:** Jct Rockmart Hwy, just s; in West End Commons.

APPALACHIAN GRILL   770/607-5357

▼▼▼ American. Casual Dining. $10-$27 **AAA Inspector Notes:** Steaks and seafood are some staples that have made this grill a favorite downtown dining spot. The pecan chicken is a favorite here. Other notable dishes include Bourbon grilled salmon, fried green tomatoes and pork stew. The rustic charm combined with upscale features provide a unique dining experience. **Features:** full bar. **Reservations:** suggested. **Address:** 14 E Church St 30120 **Location:** I-75 exit 288, 2.1 mi w to Wall St, just n; under the bridge. **Parking:** street only.

THE CITY CELLAR AND LOFT   770/334-3170

▼▼ American. Casual Dining. $9-$25 **AAA Inspector Notes:** Travel downstairs to the cellar and begin the meal at this spot with a fried green tomato tower or chicharrón. Follow up with grilled steak, pork shank or lemon-pepper salmon. The sandwiches and pasta also are popular. The candied pecan bread pudding is a must-try dessert. **Features:** full bar. **Address:** 110 S Museum Dr 30120 **Location:** I-75 exit 288, 2 mi w; downtown.

EL NOPAL MEXICAN RESTAURANT   770/382-8550

▼▼ Tex-Mex. Casual Dining. $5-$14 **AAA Inspector Notes:** This family-friendly Mexican restaurant offers all the favorites you have come to expect such as fajitas, tacos, nachos, enchiladas and burritos. For something a little different try the carnitas or a T-bone steak. For some liquid refreshment try the margaritas or ask about the Mexican beers. **Features:** full bar. **Address:** 540 Old Mill Rd 30120 **Location:** Jct Douthit Ferry Rd, just w.

JEFFERSON'S   770/334-2069

▼▼ American. Casual Dining. $4-$15 **AAA Inspector Notes:** This relaxed pub is a local favorite for burgers, sandwiches, salads, fried catfish, steaks and a variety of wings. Oysters are a house specialty. The sports-themed eatery is a great place to watch favorite teams in action. **Features:** full bar, patio dining. **Address:** 28 W Main St 30120 **Location:** I-75 exit 288, 2.1 mi w; downtown. **Parking:** street only.

MOORE'S GOURMET MARKET 770/387-0059

▼▼ ▼▼ Southern. Casual Dining. $6-$16 **AAA Inspector Notes:** The burgers alone are reason enough to dine here but there is so much more to tantalize your taste buds. Begin with roasted corn chowder or succulent Cajun shrimp dip and then dive into some fried catfish, grilled pork chops, pan-seared crab cakes, salmon patties, jambalaya with hush puppies or chopped steak. Complete your feast with almond bread pudding or cheesecake. The nostalgic market-style décor helps create a comfortable ambience. **Features:** full bar. **Address:** 227 Fite St 30120 **Location:** I-75 exit 288, 2.7 mi w to Fite St, then just s. L D

SCOTT'S WALK-UP BAR-B-Q 770/382-1600

▼▼ Barbecue. Quick Serve. $3-$22 **AAA Inspector Notes:** The pulled pork here is some of the best around. It is tender, juicy and rich in flavor and there are several sauce options. Other tempting dishes include baby back ribs, brisket, smoked sausage and barbecue chicken salad. Choose from such sides as collard greens, barbecue beans, Brunswick stew and potato salad. Be sure to save room for peach cobbler or Susan's lemon pie. **Features:** patio dining. **Address:** 206 N Tennessee St 30120 **Location:** I-75 exit 288, 2 mi w to Tennessee St, then just n. L

THE STEAK HOUSE 770/334-2623

▼▼ ▼▼ American. Casual Dining. $7-$25 **AAA Inspector Notes:** Chargrilled steaks are a big draw here and they include the T-bone, sirloin, New York strip, porterhouse, flat iron, fillet and the tasty Cajun rib-eye. Fried catfish, fresh salmon and grilled shrimp help comprise the seafood selection and specials include all-you-can-eat fried fish and shrimp on Thursday nights. Fried pickle chips and potato skins are a good way to begin the meal and molten chocolate lava cake is a great way to close it. **Features:** full bar. **Address:** 650 Henderson Dr 30120 **Location:** Jct Rockmart Hwy, just s; in West End Commons. D CALL ⑤M

SWHEAT MARKET DELI 770/607-0067

▼▼ Natural/Organic. Quick Serve. $7-$20 **AAA Inspector Notes:** Delicious and healthy food can be enjoyed at this deli, where a wide array of sandwiches includes the turkey Reuben, tuna, chicken salad and several vegetarian selections. Such daily soups as creamy broccoli are featured while chicken Caesar and chef salad are options. Rib-eyes and grilled salmon are some dinner options. Be sure to take home some fresh produce from the market. **Features:** beer & wine. **Address:** 5 E Main St 30120 **Location:** I-75 exit 288, 2.1 mi w. **Parking:** street only. L D

CEDARTOWN pop. 9,750

QUALITY INN (770)749-9951

▼▼ ▼▼ Hotel. $76-$89 **Address:** 925 N Main St 30125 **Location:** 1.5 mi n on US 27. **Facility:** 40 units. 2 stories (no elevator), interior corridors.

¶⬦ CALL ⑤M ⒣⒮ 🛜 🛗 🖼 🖵 / SOME UNITS 🕳

WHERE TO EAT

ZORBA'S 770/748-8490

▼▼ ▼▼ American. Casual Dining. $9-$24 **AAA Inspector Notes:** In addition to the tasty steaks, seafood, chicken and other American favorites, diners can enjoy a great selection of Italian cuisine here. Home-baked lasagna, veal parmigiana, manicotti and several spaghetti options all are on the menu. Numerous types of broiled steer burgers, sandwiches and daily specials are popular at lunch. Tiramisu and French chocolate silk pie are great ways to complete a satisfying meal. **Address:** 805 N Main St 30125 **Location:** 1.4 mi n on US 27. L D CALL ⑤M

CHAMBLEE pop. 9,892

- Hotels & Restaurants map & index p. 82
- Part of Atlanta area — see map p. 44

HARMONY VEGETARIAN CHINESE RESTAURANT 770/457-7288 ⑴⑴⑹

▼▼ ▼▼ Chinese. Casual Dining. $5-$11 **AAA Inspector Notes:** Succulent vegetarian dishes here include traditional Chinese soups and appetizers, as well as preparations of imitation beef, poultry, seafood and pork. Also offered are noodle platters and lunch specials. Colorful dishware enhances the presentations from the sincere staff. **Address:** 4897 Buford Hwy, Suite 109 30341 **Location:** I-285 exit 32, 1.5 mi s; in Orient Center Shopping Plaza. L D

PENANG MALAYSIAN CUISINE 770/220-0308 ⑴⑴⑸

▼▼ ▼▼ Asian. Casual Dining. $9-$23 **AAA Inspector Notes:** This eatery is nestled into a corner of a large plaza which boasts many ethnic shops and eateries. Favorites here are the whole fish with Thai sauce and pancakes with chicken curry. Enjoy the ambience which duplicates a Malaysian village, right down to the bamboo. The staff is quite capable and helpful. **Features:** beer & wine. **Address:** 4897 Buford Hwy, Suite 113 30341 **Location:** I-285 exit 32, 1.5 mi s; in Orient Center Shopping Plaza. L D

CHATSWORTH (A-2) pop. 4,299, elev. 752'

Chatsworth is noted for the Chief Vann House, the first brick home within the Cherokee Nation. Just east is Fort Mountain State Park; to the south is Carters Lake (see Recreation Areas Chart).

Chatsworth-Eton Murray County Chamber of Commerce: 126 N. 3rd Ave., Chatsworth, GA 30705. **Phone:** (706) 695-6060 or (800) 969-9490.

CHIEF VANN HOUSE STATE HISTORIC SITE, Spring Pl. 1 mi. s. at 82 SR 225N, is the restored 1804 mansion of Chief James Vann, a Cherokee who sponsored the influential Springplace Moravian Mission next to his plantation. The house is part of a memorial to the Cherokee Nation and the Trail of Tears.

Hours: Guided 45-minute tours Thurs.-Sun. 9-5. Last tour begins 1 hour before closing. Closed Jan. 1, Thanksgiving and Christmas. **Cost:** $6.50; $6 (ages 62+); $5.50 (ages 6-17). **Phone:** (706) 695-2598. ⒢⒯ 🎋

SUPER 8 CHATSWORTH (706)695-0850

▼▼ ▼▼ Hotel. $63-$80 **Address:** 613 S 3rd Ave 30705 **Location:** On US 76/441, 0.5 mi s. **Facility:** 32 units. 1 story, exterior corridors. **Pool(s):** outdoor. **Guest Services:** coin laundry.

¶⬦ CALL ⑤M 🏊 ⒣⒮ 🛜 🛗 🖼 🖵 / SOME UNITS 🕳

WHERE TO EAT

EDNA'S RESTAURANT 706/695-4960

▼▼

Southern
Casual Dining
$5-$9

AAA Inspector Notes: The long-established, straightforward eatery serves home-style Southern comfort foods such as fried chicken and ham shanks. Popular desserts are the heirloom-recipe peanut butter, coconut or chocolate pies. **Address:** 1300 Hwy 411 S 30705 **Location:** 1 mi s. L D

CHATTAHOOCHEE-OCONEE NATIONAL FOREST (A-2)

Elevations in the forests range from 500 ft. in Oconee National Forest to 4,784 ft. at Brasstown Bald in Chattahoochee National Forest. Refer to AAA maps for additional elevation information.

The 750,194 acres of the Chattahoochee National Forest are in northern Georgia, and the 115,476 acres of the Oconee National Forest are in central Georgia. Within the forests are campsites, picnic areas, wilderness areas, trails and the Chattooga National Wild and Scenic River.

The Chattahoochee National Forest includes the southern part of one of the world's most extensive and productive hardwood forests. Its Cohutta Wilderness, covering some 35,268 acres, is a popular area for fishing, hunting and hiking.

Also in the forest are the twin cascades of Anna Ruby Falls, where two creeks converge before running into Unicoi Lake and on into the Chattahoochee River. Anna Ruby Falls Recreation Area offers several hiking trails, including a quarter-mile-long paved trail and one with Braille signage, a visitor center and picnic areas. The Anna Ruby Falls Information Center has exhibits and information about the history and natural resources of the area as well as a trout-viewing pond and trails. Closed Christmas. Phone (706) 878-1448.

At 4,784 feet above sea level, Brasstown Bald is Georgia's highest mountain. The Brasstown Bald Visitor Center, off SR 180 near Blairsville, is open daily Memorial Day weekend to late November; phone (706) 896-2556 or (706) 745-6928 during the off-season. The center features a theater, a rooftop observation deck and exhibits about the relationship between people and mountains. The summit also has picnic facilities and three hiking trails, and on clear days affords views of four states.

The forest is open daily 24 hours. Forest admission free; some facilities within require a fee. Forest and area maps are sold at the Forest Supervisor's Office, 1755 Cleveland Hwy., Gainesville, GA 30501. Phone (770) 297-3000. *See Recreation Areas Chart.*

CHATTAHOOCHEE RIVER NATIONAL RECREATION AREA (G-4)

Extending along a 48-mile stretch of the Chattahoochee River from Lake Sidney Lanier to Peachtree Creek in northwest Atlanta, 7,587-acre Chattahoochee River National Recreation Area has preserved the natural riverway within an extensive metropolitan area. Its day-use trails are popular with Atlantans and tourists alike.

Designated as a National Water Trail, long scenic runs and gentle rapids offer excellent canoeing, rafting and kayaking. Small motorboats are permitted, but there is a limited number of boat ramps. The southernmost public take-out point is Paces Mill

on US 41. The park lands and waters are open for day use dawn to dusk. Island Ford visitor center open daily 9-5; closed Christmas. Recreation area admission is $3 per private vehicle, or $35 for an annual permit.

For information contact the Superintendent, Chattahoochee River National Recreation Area, 1978 Island Ford Pkwy., Sandy Springs, GA 30350; phone (678) 538-1200. *See Recreation Areas Chart.*

CHERRY LOG pop. 119

HOLLOWAY'S PINK PIG   706/632-2403

♦♦ Barbecue. Casual Dining. $5-$20 **AAA Inspector Notes:** Popular with locals and tourist since its opening in 1967, this local feed and seed turned barbecue joint has been passed down through generations. As it is tucked away in the hills, half the fun is the adventure you will take to find this local treasure. Once you arrive enjoy Brunswick stew, pulled pork or beef, fried shrimp and other Southern delicacies. The ice tea is touted as the best in the world and former President Jimmy Carter is reportedly a frequent visitor. **Address:** 824 Cherry Log St 30522 **Location:** Center. ⃞L ⃞D

◆ CHICKAMAUGA AND CHATTANOOGA NATIONAL MILITARY PARK (A-1)

Straddling the Georgia-Tennessee border, the 9,000-acre Chickamauga and Chattanooga National Military Park commemorates the September 1863 Battle of Chickamauga, the Battles for Chattanooga in November of that same year and 12,000 years of human history on Moccasin Bend. It is the oldest national military park administered by the U.S. National Park Service.

The Battle of Chickamauga occurred after Gen. William S. Rosecrans and 58,000 Union troops crossed the Tennessee River southwest of Chattanooga, forcing the Confederate troops of Gen. Braxton Bragg to abandon the city and move south to protect their Atlanta supply lines. Bragg obtained reinforcements and moved back northward hoping to retake Chattanooga. The two forces clashed at Chickamauga Creek near the Georgia-Tennessee line.

Although victorious, the Confederates suffered heavy losses. The Union forces withdrew to Chattanooga after suffering more than 16,000 casualties. The ensuing Confederate siege of the city almost subdued the Union army. However, bolstered by reinforcements and a new supply route, Union forces resumed the offensive by November.

The 3-day Battle of Chattanooga began Nov. 23, 1863, with Union forces driving the Confederates back to the base of Missionary Ridge and capturing Orchard Knob. When the Union troops assaulted the remaining Confederates in the Battle of Lookout Mountain the next day, the Confederates chose to evacuate the area rather than risk separation from their main line.

The decisive blow came a day later. Gen. Ulysses S. Grant directed the all-day Battle of Missionary Ridge, in which the Confederates were dislodged from strategic points and Union forces gained the steep slopes above the city. The Confederates withdrew after dark; their defeat opened the way to Atlanta and the heart of the Confederacy.

Much of the area in this beautiful park is kept in wartime condition. More than 1,600 markers, monuments, cannons and tablets indicate the battle lines of both sides and recount the story of the area. Self-guiding tours enable visitors to explore the battlefields of Chickamauga, Lookout Mountain and Missionary Ridge.

Among the points of interest are Orchard Knob, Grant's headquarters during the Battle of Chattanooga; Crest Road, along Missionary Ridge; Wilder Brigade Monument, commanding a good view of the Chickamauga Battlefield and its surroundings; the Brotherton House, a reconstructed prewar farmhouse marking the spot where the Union line was broken; Snodgrass Hill, the scene of the last fighting at Chickamauga; and Snodgrass House, which served as a Union field hospital during the battle.

Chickamauga Battlefield grounds and monuments are open daily 6 a.m. to dusk. Visitor center open daily 8:30-5; closed Jan. 1 and Christmas. Free. Phone (706) 866-9241.

BATTLES FOR CHATTANOOGA ELECTRIC MAP AND MUSEUM is at 1110 E. Brow Rd., next to Point Park. A miniature battlefield display with more than 5,000 soldiers and cannons depicts the Battle of Chattanooga. A narrated video presentation describes the historic conflict. **Time:** Allow 1 hour minimum. **Hours:** Daily 9-6, Memorial Day weekend-Labor Day; 10-5, rest of year. Closed Christmas. **Cost:** $8; $6 (ages 6-12). **Phone:** (423) 821-2812.

CHICKAMAUGA BATTLEFIELD VISITOR CENTER is 9 mi. s. of Chattanooga, Tenn., on US 27, near the n. end of the park on Chickamauga Battlefield. A museum has Civil War exhibits and the Fuller Gun Collection, a display of American military shoulder arms. Orientation programs are offered, including a fiber optic map and a video presentation depicting the Battle of Chickamauga. The park also offers maps and a cellphone tour of the battlefield (inquire at the information desk). **Hours:** Daily 8:30-5. Closed Jan. 1 and Christmas. **Cost:** Free. A CD narrating a self-guiding tour of the park is available for purchase at the bookstore. **Phone:** (706) 866-9241.

POINT PARK is on Lookout Mountain at 110 Point Park Rd. The park overlooks Chattanooga and the Moccasin Bend National Archeological District on the Tennessee River. The Ochs Memorial Museum and Observatory, the New York Peace Monument and Umbrella Rock are in the park. The Lookout Mountain Battlefield Visitor Center at the north end of E. Brow Road contains the restored James Walker painting "Battle of Lookout Mountain." **Hours:** Park open daily 6 a.m.-dusk. Visitor center open daily 9-5; closed Jan. 1 and Christmas. **Cost:** Admission, valid for 7 days, $5; free (ages 0-15). **Phone:** (423) 821-7786.

CLAYTON (A-3) pop. 2,047, elev. 1,925'

RECREATIONAL ACTIVITIES

White-water Rafting

- **Southeastern Expeditions,** 7 mi. e. on US 76E. **Hours:** Daily 9-5, mid-Mar. through Oct. 31. Phone for minimum age requirements and reservations. **Cost:** Excursion fees vary; advance reservations are required. **Phone:** (800) 868-7238.

AMERICAS BEST VALUE INN 706/782-4702

▼▼ **Motel.** Rates not provided. **Address:** 698 Hwy 441 S 30525 **Location:** 0.8 mi s. **Facility:** 30 units. 2 stories (no elevator), interior corridors.

DAYS INN OF CLAYTON (706)782-4258

▼ **Motel.** $65-$139 **Address:** 54 Hwy 441 N 30525 **Location:** Center. **Facility:** 59 units. 2 stories (no elevator), exterior corridors. **Pool(s):** outdoor.

QUALITY INN & SUITES (706)782-2214

▼▼ **Motel.** $75-$175 **Address:** 834 Hwy 441 S 30525 **Location:** 0.8 mi s. **Facility:** 58 units. 2 stories (no elevator), exterior corridors. **Pool(s):** outdoor.

WHERE TO EAT

FORTIFY KITCHEN & BAR 706/782-0050

▼▼▼ New American. Casual Dining. $10-$34 **AAA Inspector Notes:** Combined experience of more than 25 years in the hospitality industry and a vision of farm-to-table goodness brought the two owners together for this venture. The décor is mountain rustic with lots of wood and wrought iron, but the food is the main attraction. Regional and local farms are utilized for fresh ingredients. There also are many gluten-free offerings. Lunch is served Wednesday through Sunday in the summer and Wednesday through Saturday in the off season. **Features:** full bar, patio dining. **Reservations:** suggested, for dinner. **Address:** 69 Main St N 30525 **Location:** Center. **Parking:** street only.

COLLEGE PARK (I-2) pop. 13,942, elev. 1,047'

- **Restaurants p. 159**
- **Hotels & Restaurants map & index p. 94**
- **Part of Atlanta area — see map p. 44**

College Park is conveniently located on the west side of the Atlanta International Airport and is just south of Atlanta via I-85. Commuters can also take the MARTA train into the city. The town is a good option for travelers who are visiting Atlanta but prefer to stay outside the city.

ATLANTA AIRPORT MARRIOTT   (404)766-7900 46

Hotel
$79-$286

AAA Benefit: Members save 5% or more!

Address: 4711 Best Rd 30337 **Location:** I-85 exit 71, just w, se on access road to Best Rd, then just s. **Facility:** 638 units. 16 stories, interior corridors. **Parking:** on-site (fee) and valet. **Amenities:** video games. **Dining:** 4 restaurants. **Pool(s):** heated outdoor, heated indoor. **Activities:** tennis, exercise room. **Guest Services:** valet laundry, boarding pass kiosk.

ATLANTA AIRPORT MARRIOTT GATEWAY
(404)763-1544 38

Hotel
$118-$332

AAA Benefit: Members save 5% or more!

Address: 2020 Convention Center Concourse 30337 **Location:** I-85 exit 72 (Camp Creek Pkwy), just w. **Facility:** 403 units. 7 stories, interior corridors. **Parking:** on-site (fee) and valet. **Amenities:** safes. **Dining:** 2 restaurants. **Pool(s):** heated indoor. **Guest Services:** valet and coin laundry.

BEST WESTERN PLUS HOTEL & SUITES AIRPORT SOUTH   (770)996-5800 55

Hotel
$99-$149

Best Western PLUS

AAA Benefit: Save 10% or more every day and earn 10% bonus points!

Address: 1556 Phoenix Blvd 30349 **Location:** I-285 exit 60 (Riverdale Rd N), just s to Phoenix Blvd, then just w. **Facility:** 87 units. 5 stories, interior corridors. **Terms:** cancellation fee imposed. **Pool(s):** outdoor. **Activities:** hot tub, exercise room. **Guest Services:** valet laundry. **Featured Amenity:** full hot breakfast.

COUNTRY INN & SUITES BY CARLSON, ATLANTA AIRPORT SOUTH   770/991-1099 52

Hotel. Rates not provided. **Address:** 5100 W Fayetteville Rd 30349 **Location:** I-285 exit 60 (Riverdale Rd N), just s, then 0.5 mi w. **Facility:** 161 units. 4 stories, interior corridors. **Pool(s):** outdoor. **Activities:** exercise room. **Guest Services:** valet and coin laundry.

COURTYARD BY MARRIOTT ATLANTA AIRPORT SOUTH/SULLIVAN ROAD   (770)997-2220 50

Hotel
$80-$206

COURTYARD Marriott

AAA Benefit: Members save 5% or more!

Address: 2050 Sullivan Rd 30337 **Location:** I-85 exit 71, 0.4 mi e to Airport Rd, just s, then just w. **Facility:** 144 units. 3 stories, interior corridors. **Parking:** on-site (fee). **Pool(s):** heated indoor. **Activities:** exercise room. **Guest Services:** valet and coin laundry, boarding pass kiosk.

/ SOME UNITS

DAYS INN COLLEGE PARK/ATLANTA/AIRPORT SOUTH   (770)996-7300 54

Hotel. $54-$105 **Address:** 1540 Phoenix Blvd 30349 **Location:** I-285 exit 60 (Riverdale Rd N), just s. **Facility:** 50 units. 2 stories (no elevator), interior corridors. **Pool(s):** outdoor. **Activities:** limited exercise equipment.

EMBASSY SUITES HOTEL BY HILTON AT ATLANTA AIRPORT   (404)767-1988 41

Hotel. $129-$249 **Address:** 4700 Southport Rd 30337 **Location:** I-85 exit 71, 0.3 mi w on Riverdale Rd. **Facility:** 235 units. 5 stories, interior corridors. **Parking:** on-site (fee). **Terms:** 1-7 night minimum stay, cancellation fee imposed. **Pool(s):** outdoor, heated indoor. **Activities:** game room, exercise room. **Guest Services:** valet and coin laundry.

AAA Benefit: Members save 5% or more!

/ SOME UNITS

FAIRFIELD INN & SUITES BY MARRIOTT ATLANTA AIRPORT SOUTH/SULLIVAN ROAD   (770)994-3666 49

Hotel
$86-$148

FAIRFIELD INN & SUITES Marriott

AAA Benefit: Members save 5% or more!

Address: 2020 Sullivan Rd 30337 **Location:** I-85 exit 71, just e to Airport Rd, just s, then just w. **Facility:** 127 units. 4 stories, interior corridors. **Amenities:** safes. **Activities:** hot tub, exercise room. **Guest Services:** valet and coin laundry.

(See map & index p. 94.)

HILTON GARDEN INN-ATLANTA AIRPORT/MILLENIUM CENTER
(404)766-0303 **47**

Hotel
$129-$189

AAA Benefit: Members save up to 10%!

Address: 2301 Sullivan Rd 30337 **Location:** I-85 exit 71, just e, just s, then 0.7 mi w. **Facility:** 200 units. 6 stories, interior corridors. **Parking:** on-site (fee). **Terms:** 1-7 night minimum stay, cancellation fee imposed. **Amenities:** Some: safes. **Pool(s):** heated indoor. **Activities:** hot tub, exercise room. **Guest Services:** valet and coin laundry, area transportation.

HOLIDAY INN-ATLANTA AIRPORT SOUTH   404/763-8800 **40**

▼▼▼ **Hotel.** Rates not provided. **Address:** 4669 Airport Blvd 30337 **Location:** I-85 exit 71, just e to Airport Blvd, then just s; I-285 exit 60 (Riverdale Rd N), 1 mi n to Airport Blvd, then just s. **Facility:** 190 units. 6 stories, interior corridors. **Parking:** on-site (fee). **Pool(s):** heated indoor. **Activities:** hot tub, exercise room. **Guest Services:** valet and coin laundry.

HOLIDAY INN EXPRESS-ATLANTA AIRPORT   404/761-6500 **39**

▼▼▼ **Hotel.** Rates not provided. **Address:** 4601 Best Rd 30337 **Location:** I-85 exit 71, just w. **Facility:** 162 units. 6 stories, interior corridors. **Pool(s):** outdoor. **Activities:** exercise room. **Guest Services:** valet laundry, area transportation.

HYATT PLACE ATLANTA AIRPORT-SOUTH
(770)994-2997 **43**

Hotel
$79-$189

HYATT PLACE
AAA Benefit: Members save 10%!

Address: 1899 Sullivan Rd 30337 **Location:** I-85 exit 71, just e to Sullivan Rd, then just s; I-285 exit 60 (Riverdale Rd N), 1 mi to Sullivan Rd, then just s. **Facility:** 123 units. 6 stories, interior corridors. **Terms:** cancellation fee imposed. **Pool(s):** outdoor. **Activities:** exercise room. **Guest Services:** valet laundry. **Featured Amenity:** full hot breakfast.

Say YES to ERS text updates

to stay posted when your

tow truck is on the way

LA QUINTA INN & SUITES ATLANTA AIRPORT
(770)996-0000 **51**

▼▼▼▼ **Hotel.** $82-$230 **Address:** 4820 Massachusetts Blvd 30337 **Location:** I-85 exit 71, just e to Airport Rd, then just s. **Facility:** 70 units. 4 stories, interior corridors. **Activities:** exercise room. **Guest Services:** valet and coin laundry, area transportation.

QUALITY HOTEL & CONFERENCE CENTER-ATLANTA AIRPORT
770/996-4321 **53**

▼▼▼ **Hotel.** Rates not provided. **Address:** 1551 Phoenix Blvd 30349 **Location:** I-285 exit 60 (Riverdale Rd N), just s. **Facility:** 142 units. 6 stories, interior/exterior corridors. **Pool(s):** outdoor. **Activities:** exercise room. **Guest Services:** valet and coin laundry.

SHERATON ATLANTA AIRPORT HOTEL
(770)997-1100 **45**

Hotel
$109-$269

Sheraton
AAA Benefit: Members save up to 15%, plus Starwood Preferred Guest® benefits!

Address: 1900 Sullivan Rd 30337 **Location:** I-85 exit 71, just e to Airport Rd, then just s. **Facility:** 395 units. 12 stories, interior corridors. **Parking:** on-site (fee). **Terms:** cancellation fee imposed, resort fee. **Pool(s):** heated outdoor, heated indoor. **Activities:** exercise room. **Guest Services:** valet laundry, area transportation.

SLEEP INN/ATLANTA AIRPORT
(770)996-6100 **44**

▼▼ **Hotel.** $81-$95 **Address:** 1911 Sullivan Rd 30337 **Location:** I-85 exit 71, just e to Airport Blvd, just s to Sullivan Rd, then just w. **Facility:** 63 units. 4 stories, interior corridors. **Bath:** shower only. **Activities:** exercise room. **Guest Services:** valet and coin laundry.

SPRINGHILL SUITES BY MARRIOTT ATLANTA AIRPORT GATEWAY
(770)907-8880 **37**

Contemporary Hotel
$110-$309

SPRINGHILL SUITES MARRIOTT
AAA Benefit: Members save 5% or more!

Address: 2091 Convention Center Concourse 30337 **Location:** I-85 exit 72 (Camp Creek Pkwy), just w. **Facility:** 147 units. 6 stories, interior corridors. **Parking:** on-site (fee). **Pool(s):** heated indoor. **Activities:** exercise room. **Guest Services:** valet and coin laundry, boarding pass kiosk. **Featured Amenity:** full hot breakfast.

SUPER 8-ATLANTA AIRPORT
(770)991-8985 **48**

▼▼ **Hotel.** $65-$85 **Address:** 2010 Sullivan Rd 30337 **Location:** I-85 exit 71, just e to Airport Rd, then just sw. **Facility:** 60 units. 3 stories, interior corridors. **Guest Services:** coin laundry.

(See map & index p. 94.)

THE WESTIN HOTEL-ATLANTA AIRPORT
(404)762-7676 **42**

▼▼▼ ▼▼▼
Hotel
$99-$289

WESTIN
HOTELS & RESORTS

AAA Benefit: Members save up to 15%, plus Starwood Preferred Guest® benefits!

Address: 4736 Best Rd 30337 **Location:** I-85 exit 71, just w, se on access road to Best Rd, then just s. **Facility:** Minutes from the airport, this hotel provides luxurious amenities. The plush beds make for a delightful sleeping experience and some special rooms for allergy sufferers are offered. 500 units. 10 stories, interior corridors. **Parking:** on-site (fee) and valet. **Terms:** cancellation fee imposed. **Amenities:** video games, safes. **Pool(s):** heated outdoor, heated indoor. **Activities:** hot tub, exercise room, massage. **Guest Services:** valet laundry, boarding pass kiosk, area transportation.

[SAVE] [ECO] ⊞ ❚◍ ⬚ ⴲ CALL⬚M ⬙ [BIZ] [HS]
�꩜ ✕ ⬚ ⊟ ⬚ /SOME UNITS ⬚

WHERE TO EAT

BARBEQUE KITCHEN   404/766-9906 **43**
▼ Southern. Casual Dining. $5-$9 **AAA Inspector Notes:** This family-owned restaurant reminds me of meals at Grandmom's with all the Southern charm and delicious food I could handle. The food proves that it does not have to be fancy to be amazing. The kitchen serves up traditional, down-home favorites such as pulled pork barbecue which is a local favorite and the homemade biscuits will leave you speechless. So come on in and loosen up your belt because if you leave hungry it is your own fault. **Address:** 1437 Virginia Ave 30337 **Location:** I-85 exit 73, just w. [B] [L] [D]

BRAKE PAD   404/766-1515 **42**
▼▼ American. Casual Dining. $7-$10 **AAA Inspector Notes:** This former gas station is now a haven for burgers, wings, sandwiches, salads and healthy bar food. Tacos and quesadillas are popular items. The chicharrones or spicy egg rolls are a good way to start any meal. This is a popular local eatery and does a brisk business during peak dining times. **Features:** full bar, patio dining. **Address:** 3403 Main St 30337 **Location:** Downtown. [L] [D] [LATE]

COZUMEL MEXICAN RESTAURANT   404/559-2000 **48**
▼▼ Mexican. Casual Dining. $4-$18 **AAA Inspector Notes:** This casual eatery offers bold flavors, classic cuisine and a variety of drinks that can turn any meal into a fiesta. The extensive menu centers around burritos, tacos, quesadillas and seafood entrées. The dining room is spacious and can accommodate larger parties with ease. **Features:** full bar. **Address:** 5058 Old National Hwy 30349 **Location:** I-285 exit 62 (Old National Hwy), 1.3 mi s. [L] [D] CALL⬚M

THE FEED STORE   404/209-7979 **47**
▼▼▼ Regional American. Fine Dining. $11-$38 **AAA Inspector Notes:** This antique-feed-store-turned-chic restaurant serves up classic Southern dishes with a modern twist. The house specialty is fresh fried chicken, Coca-Cola baked beans and signature macaroni and cheese. Order the pan-seared shrimp and tilapia paired with delicious Parmesan cheese spinach risotto. **Features:** full bar. **Reservations:** suggested. **Address:** 3841 Main St 30337 **Location:** Jct Roosevelt Hwy and Main St, just n. [L] [D] CALL⬚M

THE PIG & PINT   404/549-2416 **44**
▼▼▼ American. Casual Dining. $6-$28 **AAA Inspector Notes:** Looking for a modern twist on the traditional meat and potatoes fare? This restaurant straddles the line between casual and fancy making it a perfect date night or family night out. Try the delicious smoked pork tenderloin or the chicken confit with dumplings. The extensive wine menu pairs nicely with any course. The bread and desserts are baked fresh daily. **Features:** full bar. **Address:** 1583 Virginia Ave 30337 **Location:** I-85 exit 73 (Virginia Ave), 0.7 mi w. [L] [D] CALL⬚M

SIMON'S STEAK & SEAFOOD   404/768-0143 **45**
▼▼▼ ▼▼ Steak Seafood. Casual Dining. $11-$28 **AAA Inspector Notes:** This steakhouse provides an intimate setting and generous portions. The dark wood tones, etched glass art and chrome finishing offers a distinctly masculine ambience. The menu is full of steakhouse favorites along with a generous portion of shrimp. However, the Cajun influence make this menu distinctive. House specialties include shrimp and grits, cheese garlic biscuits and the New York strip. The decadent desserts are made in house and worth every calorie. **Features:** full bar. **Address:** 3529 Main St 30337 **Location:** I-85 exit 73B northbound; exit 73 southbound, 1 mi w to Howell Slade Cir, just e to Main St, then just s. [L] [D] CALL⬚M

TONY MORROW'S REAL PIT BARBEQUE   404/996-2973 **46**
▼▼ Barbecue. Casual Dining. $3-$15 **AAA Inspector Notes:** Delicious barbecue and a dining room with a trendy vibe is what diners can expect from this restaurant. Located close to the airport in the historic district, this is a worthwhile spot to pass the time on a layover or while just visiting the area. Some of the most popular menu items are the pulled pork sandwich and the three-rib plate with oven baked macaroni and cheese or cheese fries. **Features:** full bar. **Address:** 3807 Main St 30337 **Location:** Jct Roosevelt Hwy and Main St, just n. [L] [D] ◥

COLQUITT pop. 1,992

TARRER INN   229/758-2888
▼▼▼ ▼ **Historic Country Inn.** Rates not provided. **Address:** 155 S Cuthbert St 39837 **Location:** Corner of SR 91 and 27; center of town square. **Facility:** Located on the town square, this property was built circa 1905 and is listed on the National Register of Historic Places. The main floor houses a dining facility that specializes in Southern cuisine. 17 units, some kitchens. 2 stories (no elevator), interior corridors. **Dining:** Tarrer Inn Restaurant, see separate listing. **Activities:** massage. ❚◍ ꩜ ✕ ⬚ ⬚

WHERE TO EAT

TARRER INN RESTAURANT   229/758-2888
▼ Southern Comfort Food. Quick Serve. $12-$15 **AAA Inspector Notes:** On the village square, in the heart of this small Southern town is this historic country inn. The dining room prepares a lunch of simple home-style fare, served buffet style. It always is bustling at noontime with locals enjoying a hearty feast at a reasonable price. Open on Saturday for city sponsored special events. **Features:** Sunday brunch. **Address:** 155 S Cuthbert St 39837 **Location:** Corner of SR 91 and 27; center of town square; in Tarrer Inn. **Parking:** on-site and street. [L]

COLUMBUS (D-1) pop. 189,885, elev. 261'
• Hotels p. 161 • Restaurants p. 163

Columbus, once the site of a Creek Native American village on the Chattahoochee River on the western Georgia border, later became a trading post. On April 16, 1865, in one of the final battles of the Civil War, Union troops seized the important Confederate supply depot at Columbus. Remains of the breastworks still are visible.

The restored 1871 Springer Opera House, 103 10th St., is just outside Columbus' 26-block historic district. The opera house, which once featured such prominent figures as Edwin Booth, Oscar Wilde, Lily Langtry and Irving Berlin, now offers productions on a seasonal basis. One-hour tours are offered Monday and Wednesday at 3:30; phone (706) 327-3688.

Guided Historic Columbus Heritage Tours (minimum of two people) are offered by appointment and depart from 716 Broadway. The walking tours encompass dwellings built in the 1800s. All are furnished and decorated in period. Highlights include the Walker-Peters-Langdon House, a simple Federal cottage, believed to be the oldest residence in the original city of Columbus. Phone (706) 322-0756. Also nearby, the Pemberton House, now a private residence, was occupied by Dr. J.S. Pemberton, a druggist and originator of the formula for Coca-Cola.

The Columbus Historic Riverfront Industrial District is the site of the remains of 19th-century mills and ironworks along the east bank of the Chattahoochee River, beginning at 800 Front Ave.

The Columbus, Georgia Convention & Trade Center, 801 Front Ave., operated 1853-1964 as an iron works. The breech-loading cannon, the first successful ice-making machine and the Confederate ironclad CSS *Jackson* were manufactured at the works, which is now a convention and trade center. The Chattahoochee Promenade on Front Avenue borders the river between Fifth and Ninth streets. The Chattahoochee RiverWalk is a 15-mile linear park that offers a paved walking and bicycle path.

Noteworthy events include the Thunder in the Valley Air Show, held in mid-April and featuring a variety of military and civilian aircraft and vehicles. Christmas Made in the South, a holiday arts and crafts show, occurs in late October or early November. The Steeplechase at Callaway Gardens *(see attraction listing in Pine Mountain p. 233)* attracts more than 10,000 admirers of equestrian skills the first Saturday in November.

Columbus Convention and Visitors Bureau: 900 Front Ave., P.O. Box 2768, Columbus, GA 31902. **Phone:** (706) 322-1613 or (800) 999-1613.

Self-guiding tours: Brochures detailing a walking and/or driving tour of the original city are available at the visitors bureau Mon.-Fri. 8:30-5:30, Sat., 10-2. A RiverWalk Geo Tour with stations for geocaching along the Chattahoochee River also is available.

COCA-COLA SPACE SCIENCE CENTER is at 701 Front Ave. This facility features a Challenger Learning Center and the Omnisphere Theater. Simulators and interactive displays give visitors a glimpse of the cosmos. Artifacts from the NASA space program also are on display. **Time:** Allow 1 hour minimum. **Hours:** Mon.-Fri. 10-4, Sat. 10:30-6. Theater shows Mon.-Fri. 11-3, Sat. 11-5. Closed major holidays. **Cost:** Includes Omnisphere Theater shows, $6; $5 (ages 55+ and military with ID); $4 (ages 4-12). **Phone:** (706) 649-1477.

THE COLUMBUS MUSEUM is at 1251 Wynnton Rd. Among this museum's exhibits are 18th-century through contemporary works of American art, prehistoric Native American artifacts, Civil War objects, a display of American decorative arts and regional historical items. The museum houses more than 14,000 artifacts and objects. Changing exhibits of American art and history are presented. Of interest are the children's hands-on discovery gallery and the historic Olmsted Garden. Temporary exhibits also are offered. **Time:** Allow 1 hour minimum.

Hours: Tues.-Sat. 10-5 (also Thurs. 5-8), Sun. 1-5. Closed major holidays. **Cost:** Free. **Phone:** (706) 748-2562.

FORT BENNING, s.e. of Columbus, in addition to being home of the Maneuver Center of Excellence, the only U.S. training center for infantry and armor soldiers, also trains airborne troops. Monday through Wednesday (weather permitting) visitors can go to the drop zone and watch the paratroopers land. **Phone:** (706) 545-2238.

Giant Screen Theater at Patriot Park is at 1775 Legacy Way in the National Infantry Museum next to Fort Benning. Documentaries in 3-D and 4K resolution are shown on a 40-foot-tall screen that is more than 70-feet wide. **Hours:** Shows are offered Tues.-Sun. and Mon. federal holidays. Closed Jan. 1, Easter, Thanksgiving and Christmas. Phone ahead to confirm schedule. **Cost:** $8; $7 (ages 62+ and military and students with ID); $6 (ages 4-12). **Phone:** (706) 685-5800.

National Infantry Museum & Soldier Center, adjacent to Fort Benning at 1775 Legacy Way, is dedicated to the evolution of the infantry since the French and Indian Wars. The Last 100 Yards depicts the infantry's role towards the end of any battle. Cast figures based on actual infantry soldiers bring the scenes to life. The Fort Benning Gallery presents the history of Fort Benning and the training recruits receive. Additional galleries offer interactive experiences that emphasize the sacrifices made by soldiers during times of war. The Hall of Valor shares the stories of American infantrymen who have received the Medal of Honor. Other honor galleries include Ranger Hall of Honor. Combat simulators allow visitors to experience infantry action.

The museum also pays homage to those who served in the infantry. Lined with commemorative pavers and state flags, the Heritage Walk leads guests to Inouye Field. Beyond the field is the Memorial Walk of Honor. Here guests will find monuments to infantry units and associations. The Dignity Memorial Vietnam Wall in Vietnam Memorial Plaza is inscribed with the names of more than 58,000 Vietnam War servicemen and women.

Also outside the main museum building is a World War II Company Street. Here guests can stroll through some of the restored buildings, including barracks, mess hall, supply room, orderly room and chapel, as well as headquarters used by Gen. George S. Patton before his deployment to North Africa.

Time: Allow 2 hours minimum. **Hours:** Museum Tues.-Sat. and Mon. federal holidays 9-5, Sun. 11-5. Hours vary for combat simulators; phone ahead to confirm availability. Closed Jan. 1, Easter, Thanksgiving and Christmas. **Cost:** Free. Fee for simulators. **Phone:** (706) 685-5800. 🍴

NATIONAL CIVIL WAR NAVAL MUSEUM AT PORT COLUMBUS is at 1002 Victory Dr. This 40,000-square-foot museum houses the remains of two Civil War vessels: the ironclad CSS *Jackson,* and the gunboat CSS *Chattahoochee,* a steam-powered sailing ship. The museum also contains re-created sections of the USS *Monitor,* the ironclad CSS *Albemarle,* and Adm. David Glasgow Farragut's flagship the USS *Hartford,* which visitors can enter to experience what shipboard life was like then. A multimedia show simulates a battle aboard an ironclad. Included on the Port Columbus campus is a full-scale reproduction of the USS *Water Witch,* a 160-foot Civil War side wheel steamship.

Murals depict the various craft designed for river, coastal and deep-water warfare. A chronology of the Civil War at sea is illustrated by eight wall panels. Historic items displayed include rare firearms, a uniform coat of the officer who commanded the CSS *Virginia (Merrimac)* when it fought the USS *Monitor,* and approximately 2,000 square feet of Civil War naval-related flags from ships and coastal forts throughout the South. Temporary exhibits also are offered.

An audio tour by cellphone is available. **Time:** Allow 1 hour minimum. **Hours:** Tues.-Sat. 10-4:30, Sun.-Mon. 12:30-4:30. Closed Jan. 1, Easter, Thanksgiving and Christmas. **Cost:** $7.50; $6.50 (ages 65+ and military with ID); $6 (students with ID); free (ages 0-6). **Phone:** (706) 327-9798.

COLUMBUS MARRIOTT   (706)324-1800

 Historic Hotel. $138-$223 **Address:** 800 Front Ave 31901 **Location:** Between 8th and 9th sts; north end of historic district; downtown. **Facility:** A restored 19th-century grist mill is the setting for this hotel's lobby, while guest rooms are in a 20th-century brick tower. The loft-style Governor's Suite features exposed brick and wrought iron. 177 units. 3-6 stories, interior corridors. **Parking:** on-site and valet. **Pool(s):** outdoor. **Activities:** exercise room. **Guest Services:** valet and coin laundry.

AAA Benefit: Members save 5% or more!

COMFORT INN COLUMBUS   (706)256-3093

 Hotel $64-$139

Address: 3460 Macon Rd 31907 **Location:** I-185 exit 6, just ne. **Facility:** 72 units, some kitchens. 3 stories, interior corridors. **Pool(s):** heated indoor. **Activities:** exercise room. **Guest Services:** valet and coin laundry. **Featured Amenity:** full hot breakfast.

COUNTRY INN & SUITES BY CARLSON   706/660-1880

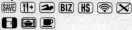 **Hotel.** Rates not provided. **Address:** 1720 Fountain Ct 31904 **Location:** I-185 exit 12, just w. Located in a quiet area across from visitor center. **Facility:** 62 units. 3 stories, interior corridors. **Pool(s):** outdoor. **Activities:** exercise room. **Guest Services:** valet and coin laundry, area transportation.

COUNTRY INN & SUITES BY CARLSON, COLUMBUS (FORT BENNING)   706/256-6390

 Hotel. Rates not provided. **Address:** 1664 Rollins Way 31904 **Location:** I-185 exit 10B (US 80 & SR 22), 1.3 mi w on US 80 to exit 3A (Bradley Park Rd), just e to Whittlesey Rd, then just n. **Facility:** 64 units. 3 stories, interior corridors. **Pool(s):** heated indoor. **Activities:** exercise room. **Guest Services:** valet and coin laundry.

COURTYARD BY MARRIOTT COLUMBUS   (706)323-2323

 Hotel $67-$171

COURTYARD Marriott

AAA Benefit: Members save 5% or more!

Address: 3501 Courtyard Way 31909 **Location:** I-185 exit 7 southbound; exit 7A northbound, 0.7 mi e. Adjacent to airport. **Facility:** 139 units. 2 stories (no elevator), interior corridors. **Pool(s):** outdoor. **Activities:** exercise room. **Guest Services:** valet and coin laundry, boarding pass kiosk.

FAIRFIELD INN & SUITES BY MARRIOTT COLUMBUS   (706)317-3600

 **Hotel.** $62-$125 **Address:** 4510 E Armour Rd 31904 **Location:** I-185 exit 7 southbound; exit 7A northbound, just w to Armour Rd, then just n. Adjacent to airport. **Facility:** 79 units. 3 stories, interior corridors. **Pool(s):** indoor. **Activities:** exercise room. **Guest Services:** valet and coin laundry.

AAA Benefit: Members save 5% or more!

HAMPTON INN AIRPORT   (706)576-5303

 Motel $79-$104

 Hampton by HILTON

AAA Benefit: Members save up to 10%!

Address: 5585 Whitesville Rd 31904 **Location:** I-185 exit 8, just w on Airport Thruway, then just n. Adjacent to Harmony Place Shops. **Facility:** 118 units. 2 stories (no elevator), exterior corridors. **Terms:** 1-7 night minimum stay, cancellation fee imposed. **Pool(s):** outdoor. **Activities:** exercise room. **Guest Services:** valet laundry. **Featured Amenity:** breakfast buffet.

HILTON GARDEN INN COLUMBUS   (706)660-1000

 Hotel. $99-$169 **Address:** 1500 Bradley Lake Blvd 31904 **Location:** Waterfront. I-185 exit 10 (US 80 and SR 22), 1.4 mi w on US 80 exit 3B, then just nw. **Facility:** 120 units. 5 stories, interior corridors. **Terms:** 1-7 night minimum stay, cancellation fee imposed. **Pool(s):** heated indoor. **Activities:** hot tub, exercise room. **Guest Services:** valet and coin laundry, area transportation.

AAA Benefit: Members save up to 10%!

HOLIDAY INN EXPRESS & SUITES   (706)507-7080

▼▼▼▼ **Hotel.** $83-$249 **Address:** 3901 Victory Dr 31903 **Location:** I-185 exit 1B, 1 mi w. **Facility:** 81 units. 5 stories, interior corridors. **Pool(s):** outdoor. **Activities:** exercise room. **Guest Services:** valet and coin laundry.

CALL 🛗Ⓜ🅱🅸🆉 🅷🆂 🛜 ❌ 🍴 🖨 🖥 / SOME UNITS 🛏

HOLIDAY INN EXPRESS HOTEL & SUITES AT NORTHLAKE
706/507-7200

▼▼▼▼ **Hotel.** Rates not provided. **Address:** 7336 Bear Ln 31909 **Location:** US 80/SR 22 exit Veterans Pkwy, 0.4 mi ne, then just se. **Facility:** 88 units. 5 stories, interior corridors. **Pool(s):** heated outdoor. **Activities:** hot tub, exercise room. **Guest Services:** valet and coin laundry.

🍴 🗐 🅱🅸🆉 🅷🆂 🛜 ❌ 🍴 🖨 🖥

HOLIDAY INN NORTH   706/324-0231

▼▼▼▼ **Hotel.** Rates not provided. **Address:** 2800 Manchester Expwy 31904 **Location:** I-185 exit 7, just w. Adjacent to airport. **Facility:** 117 units. 2 stories (no elevator), interior corridors. **Terms:** check-in 4 pm. **Pool(s):** outdoor. **Activities:** exercise room. **Guest Services:** valet and coin laundry.

🍴 📺 🍸 🗐 🅱🅸🆉 🛜 ❌ 🖥 / SOME UNITS 🛏 🍴 🖥

HOME2 SUITES BY HILTON   (706)257-6931

▼▼▼▼ **Extended Stay Hotel.** $104-$159 **Address:** 1664 Whittlesey Rd 31904 **Location:** I-185 exit 10B (US 80/SR 22), 1.3 mi w on US 80 to exit 3A (Bradley Park Rd), just e to Whittlesey Rd, then just n. **Facility:** 81 units. 4 stories, interior corridors. *Bath:* shower only. **Terms:** check-in 4 pm, 1-7 night minimum stay, cancellation fee imposed. **Pool(s):** outdoor. **Activities:** exercise room. **Guest Services:** valet and coin laundry.

> **AAA Benefit:** Members save up to 10%!

CALL 🛗Ⓜ🗐 🅱🅸🆉 🅷🆂 🛜 ❌ 🍴 🖨 🖥 / SOME UNITS 🛏

HOMEWOOD SUITES   (706)568-3545

▼▼▼▼ **Extended Stay Hotel.** $99-$169 **Address:** 6614 Whittlesey Blvd 31909 **Location:** US 80/SR 22 exit Moon Rd, just s to Whittlesey Blvd, then just w. **Facility:** 91 efficiencies, some two bedrooms. 4 stories, interior corridors. **Terms:** 1-7 night minimum stay, cancellation fee imposed. **Pool(s):** outdoor. **Activities:** exercise room. **Guest Services:** valet and coin laundry, area transportation.

> **AAA Benefit:** Members save up to 10%!

✈ 🍴 CALL 🛗Ⓜ🗐 🅱🅸🆉 🅷🆂 🛜 🍴 🖨 🖥

HYATT PLACE COLUMBUS NORTH   (706)507-5000

▼▼▼▼
Hotel
$99-$249

✧ HYATT PLACE®
AAA Benefit: Members save 10%!

Address: 2974 Northlake Pkwy 31909 **Location:** US 80/SR 22 exit Veterans Pkwy, 0.4 mi ne, then just se. **Facility:** 82 units. 5 stories, interior corridors. **Terms:** cancellation fee imposed. **Pool(s):** outdoor. **Activities:** exercise room. **Guest Services:** valet and coin laundry. **Featured Amenity:** full hot breakfast.

SAVE 🍴 🍸 CALL 🛗Ⓜ🗐 🅱🅸🆉 🅷🆂 🛜 ❌ 🍴 🖥 / SOME UNITS 🛏

LA QUINTA INN COLUMBUS FORT BENNING   (706)568-1740

▼▼ **Motel.** $67-$180 **Address:** 3201 Macon Rd, Suite 200 31906 **Location:** I-185 exit 6, just sw. **Facility:** 123 units. 2 stories (no elevator), interior/exterior corridors. **Pool(s):** outdoor. **Guest Services:** coin laundry.

🍴 🗐 🛜 🖥 / SOME UNITS 🛏 🍴 🖥

LA QUINTA INN COLUMBUS STATE UNIVERSITY
(706)323-4344

▼▼▼▼ **Hotel.** $67-$268 **Address:** 2919 Warm Springs Rd 31909 **Location:** I-185 exit 7 southbound; exit 7A northbound, just e. Adjacent to airport. **Facility:** 99 units. 3 stories, interior corridors. **Pool(s):** outdoor.

🍴 CALL 🛗Ⓜ🗐 🅱🅸🆉 🅷🆂 🛜 🖥 / SOME UNITS 🛏 🍴 🖥

MICROTEL INN & SUITES BY WYNDHAM COLUMBUS/NEAR FORT BENNING   (706)685-2305

▼▼ **Hotel.** $70-$105 **Address:** 3930 St. Mary's Rd 31907 **Location:** I-185 exit 3, just e. **Facility:** 78 units. 4 stories, interior corridors. **Amenities:** safes. **Pool(s):** outdoor. **Activities:** exercise room. **Guest Services:** valet and coin laundry.

🗐 🅱🅸🆉 🅷🆂 🛜 🖥 / SOME UNITS 🛏 🍴 🖥

MICROTEL INN & SUITES BY WYNDHAM COLUMBUS NORTH   (706)653-7004

▼▼ **Hotel.** $65-$80 **Address:** 1728 Fountain Ct 31904 **Location:** I-185 exit 12, just w. **Facility:** 56 units. 3 stories, interior corridors. **Activities:** exercise room.

CALL 🛗Ⓜ🅱🅸🆉 🅷🆂 🛜 ❌ 🖥 / SOME UNITS 🛏 🍴 🖥

QUALITY INN COLUMBUS NEAR FORT BENNING
(706)568-3300

▼▼▼
Motel
$74-$89

Address: 3443B Macon Rd 31907 **Location:** I-185 exit 6, just ne. **Facility:** 82 units. 3-4 stories, exterior corridors. **Pool(s):** outdoor. **Featured Amenity:** full hot breakfast.

SAVE 🍴 🗐 🅱🅸🆉 🛜 🍴 🖥 🖥

RESIDENCE INN BY MARRIOTT COLUMBUS
706/494-0050

▼▼▼▼
Extended Stay Hotel
$116-$198

Residence Inn Marriott
AAA Benefit: Members save 5% or more!

Address: 2670 Adams Farm Dr 31909 **Location:** US 80/SR 22 exit Veterans Pkwy, just sw, then just e. **Facility:** 78 units, some two bedrooms, efficiencies and kitchens. 3 stories, exterior corridors. **Pool(s):** outdoor. **Activities:** exercise room. **Guest Services:** valet and coin laundry.

SAVE CALL 🛗Ⓜ🗐 🅱🅸🆉 🅷🆂 🛜 ❌ 🍴 🖨 🖥 / SOME UNITS 🛏

Upgrade to Plus or Premier membership
for *more* of the benefits you need most

SLEEP INN & SUITES
(706)653-1330

Hotel. $65-$169 Address: 5100 Armour Rd 31904 Location: I-185 exit 8, just e on Airport Thruway, then 0.4 mi sw. Adjacent to airport. Facility: 61 units. 4 stories, interior corridors. Bath: shower only. Pool(s): outdoor. Guest Services: valet and coin laundry.

STAYBRIDGE SUITES
706/507-7700

Extended Stay Hotel
Rates not provided

Address: 1678 Whittlesey Rd 31904 Location: I-185 exit 10B (US 80/SR 22), 1.3 mi w on US 80 exit 3A (Bradley Park Rd), just e to Whittlesey Rd, then just 0.6 mi n. Adjacent to mall. Facility: 83 efficiencies, some two bedrooms. 4 stories, interior corridors. Pool(s): outdoor. Activities: exercise room. Guest Services: complimentary and valet laundry. Featured Amenity: breakfast buffet.

TOWNEPLACE SUITES BY MARRIOTT COLUMBUS
706/322-3001

Extended Stay Hotel
$80-$142

TOWNEPLACE SUITES MARRIOTT

AAA Benefit: Members save 5% or more!

Address: 4534 Armour Rd 31904 Location: I-185 exit 7 southbound; exit 7A northbound, just w to Armour Rd, then just n. Adjacent to airport. Facility: 86 units, some two bedrooms, efficiencies and kitchens. 3 stories, interior corridors. Activities: exercise room. Guest Services: valet and coin laundry.

WINGATE BY WYNDHAM
(706)225-1000

Hotel. $89-$160 Address: 1711 Rollins Way 31904 Location: I-185 exit 10B (US 80 and SR 22), 1.3 mi w on US 80 exit 3A (Bradley Park Rd), just e to Whittlesey Rd, then just n. Located behind Bradley Park Crossing Shopping Center. Facility: 84 units. 3 stories, interior corridors. Amenities: safes. Pool(s): outdoor. Activities: hot tub, exercise room. Guest Services: valet and coin laundry.

WHERE TO EAT

BEN'S CHOPHOUSE STEAK & SEAFOOD
706/256-0466

Steak Seafood. Casual Dining. $10-$50 AAA Inspector Notes: Upon entering this chophouse, the display of homemade desserts (red velvet, Oreo, peanut butter and banana pudding cakes) tempt guests to save room for them. The filet mignon is especially tender and comes cooked to order in a variety of sizes. Features: full bar, patio dining, happy hour. Reservations: suggested. Address: 5300 Sidney Simons Blvd 31904 Location: I-185 exit 8, just w to Sidney Simons Blvd, then just s.

THE BLACK COW
706/321-2020

American. Casual Dining. $8-$21 AAA Inspector Notes: In the heart of town, across from the post office, guests can find this cozy restaurant in a former storefront. In keeping with the establishment's name, their playful motto is amazing grazing. The menu offers steaks, poultry, seafood, sandwiches and salads—something for everyone. Features: full bar, Sunday brunch. Address: 115A 12th St, Suite A 31901 Location: Between 1st and 2nd aves; uptown. Parking: street only.

B. MERRELL'S
706/653-9464

Southern American. Casual Dining. $8-$18 AAA Inspector Notes: This locally-owned and -operated restaurant is known for its rotisserie chicken and wings. Other home-style meals include country fried steak and barbecue ribs. The strawberry shortcake, made with ice cream and an old-fashioned biscuit, is worth checking out. Features: full bar, patio dining. Address: 7600 Veterans Pkwy 31909 Location: US 80/SR 22 exit Veterans Pkwy, 0.9 mi ne.

BUCKHEAD STEAK AND WINE
706/571-9995

Steak. Casual Dining. $12-$37 AAA Inspector Notes: This restaurant is a longtime local favorite on the Columbus dining scene. It features steaks, crab cakes, pasta, chicken and other American standards. Set in a lovely wooded area, it offers a welcome respite for a weary traveler. Features: full bar, patio dining, Sunday brunch. Address: 5010 Armour Rd 31904 Location: I-185 exit 8, just w to Sidney Simons Blvd, 0.3 mi s to Armour Rd, then just w.

CAFE AMICI
706/653-6361

Italian. Casual Dining. $9-$22 AAA Inspector Notes: Established in 1996, this cozy café serves a strictly Italian menu. A nice selection of vegetarian dishes is available. Only dinner is served on Saturday. Features: full bar, patio dining. Address: 2301 Airport Thruway 31904 Location: I-185 exit 8, 0.5 mi w; in Harmony Place Shops.

CAFE LE RUE
706/507-5851

Cajun. Casual Dining. $11-$20 AAA Inspector Notes: In an upscale shopping center, a little bit of New Orleans can be experienced at this cozy bistro where traditional dishes such as gumbo, étouffee, jambalaya, shrimp boil and red beans and rice are offered. Décor also reflects the Big Easy theme with Mardi Gras accouterments throughout, including colored beads hanging off the trees shading the covered patio area. Features: beer & wine, patio dining. Address: 2523 Airport Thruway 31904 Location: I-185 exit 8, just w; in The Landings Shopping Center.

CANNON BREWPUB
706/653-2337

American. Gastropub. $10-$30 AAA Inspector Notes: Hand-crafted beers, wood-fired pizza, steak, pasta and homemade burgers are highlights at this eatery in the riverfront entertainment district. Features: full bar, patio dining, happy hour. Address: 1041 Broadway 31901 Location: In historic uptown district. Parking: street only.

COUNTRY ROAD BUFFET
706/653-5400

Southern. Casual Dining. $5-$7 AAA Inspector Notes: Simple, down-home, Southern-style cooking, can be found on the restaurant's buffet tables, such as fried chicken, fried green tomatoes, collard greens, macaroni and cheese, salad bar and desserts. As everything is ready and waiting, this is a quick and easy meal. Some items rotate daily. Address: 2509 Airport Thruway 31904 Location: I-185 exit 8, just w; in The Landings Shopping Center.

COUNTRY'S BARBECUE
706/563-7604

Barbecue. Casual Dining. $6-$19 **AAA Inspector Notes:** Since 1975, the folks here have been serving up scrumptious pulled pork, ribs and all the traditional barbecue favorites. Friendly servers and a laid back atmosphere help make diners feel at home, while the quirky country décor is sure to give guests something to talk about. **Features:** beer only. **Address:** 3137 Mercury Dr 31906 **Location:** I-185 exit 6, 0.3 mi w. L D

COUNTRY'S ON BROAD
706/596-8910

Barbecue. Casual Dining. $4-$16 **AAA Inspector Notes:** This diner-style restaurant is located in an historic bus depot. Basic country cuisine includes Brunswick stew, coleslaw and barbecue. Expect a crowd at lunchtime. **Features:** beer only, patio dining. **Address:** 1329 Broadway 31901 **Location:** Center. L D

DEORIO'S PIZZA INN
706/563-5887

Italian. Casual Dining. $2-$13 **AAA Inspector Notes:** This Columbus staple has been dishing up great pizza and pasta for more than 50 years. They are well-known for pizza, especially the taco pizza and the Krystal pizza. The lasagna and baked cheesecake also are crowd pleasers. **Features:** beer & wine. **Address:** 3201 Macon Rd, Suite 167 31906 **Location:** I-185 exit 6, 0.3 mi w; in Cross Country Plaza Shopping Center. L D

EL VAQUERO
706/569-1420

Mexican. Casual Dining. $8-$20 **AAA Inspector Notes:** Included in a great selection of Mexican favorites are tacos, burritos, enchiladas and fajitas, as well as good shrimp dishes and lunch specials. Earnest servers stay on top of things in the fast paced dining room. **Features:** full bar, happy hour. **Address:** 3135 Cross Country Plaza 31906 **Location:** I-185 exit 6, just sw; in The Hill at Cross Country Plaza, behind the main shopping center. L D

EPIC RESTAURANT
706/507-9909

New American Fine Dining

$31-$50

AAA Inspector Notes: Located on the ground level of a refurbished textile mill on the bank of Chattahoochee River, chef Jamie Keating's eclectic restaurant is for those seeking to excite their palate and discover new tastes. The atmosphere is vibrant with an upscale feel. The tall booths are perfect if you are celebrating a special occasion or for a truly distinctive experience, ask about the chef's table in the kitchen. **Features:** full bar. **Reservations:** suggested. Semiformal attire. **Address:** 1201 Front Ave 31901 **Location:** Between 12th and 13th sts; downtown. **Parking:** street only. D CALL M

EZELL'S CATFISH CABIN
706/568-1149

Southern. Casual Dining. $7-$20 **AAA Inspector Notes:** Celebrating classic country cooking and Southern hospitality, this spot offers whole or filleted catfish in fried, blackened or grilled varieties. Also on the menu are shrimp, chicken fingers and hamburger steaks. Start off with some fried dill pickles and finish up with some homemade desserts. **Features:** beer & wine. **Address:** 4001 Warm Springs Rd 31909 **Location:** I-185 exit 7 southbound; exit 7A northbound, 1.5 mi e. D CALL M

FLIP SIDE BURGERS & TACOS
706/317-0004

Burgers. Casual Dining. $5-$13 **AAA Inspector Notes:** The hip rock 'n' roll theme of this cozy café extends into its menu selections. How about trying the "Red Hot Chili Peppers burger" (warned to be extremely hot), "Sammy Hagar Cabo fish tacos" or the "Elvis burger" with peanut butter, jalapeño jelly and bacon. There are a slew of not so common "ZZ toppings" for your cooked to order burgers, a variety of tacos fillings include lobster and a good old American hot dog, plain or with chili. Eat inside, outside or to take out. **Features:** patio dining. **Address:** 1115 Broadway 31901 **Location:** Between 11th and 12th sts; uptown. **Parking:** street only. L D CALL M

IRON BANK COFFEE CO.
706/992-6609

Coffee/Tea Sandwiches. Quick Serve. $6-$10 **AAA Inspector Notes:** Start the day with one of the specialty coffees or get one as a boost to keep you going. The menu here is made up of a variety of gourmet sandwiches, including gourmet meat or vegetarian-style. If you cannot find what you are looking for, create your own. There are several salad and soup options as well as fresh baked desserts. The busy location is perfect for people watching out on the sidewalk or making new friends at the communal tables inside. **Features:** beer & wine, patio dining. **Address:** 6 11th St 31901 **Location:** Corner of Broadway; uptown. **Parking:** street only. B L D

LEMONGRASS THAI & SUSHI
706/992-6409

Asian. Casual Dining. $8-$30 **AAA Inspector Notes:** This large Asian restaurant specializes in Thai cuisine, and an expansive sushi selection, along with hibachi entrées and typical Chinese fare round out the meal selections. Be sure to specify the level of heat you desire in the preparation of the meals that have a red chili pepper next to it on the menu. **Features:** full bar, happy hour. **Address:** 2435 Wynnton Rd 31906 **Location:** Jct 13th St, just sw on SR 22; midtown. L D CALL M

THE LOFT
706/596-8141

American. Gastropub. $8-$23 **AAA Inspector Notes:** Opening in 1992, this family-operated establishment is in the heart of uptown's retail district. Whether you desire a classic burger, sandwich, salad, a steak, chicken or pasta dinner, all are options here. Sit back and enjoy live jazz music on Friday nights upstairs. **Features:** full bar, patio dining. **Address:** 1032 Broadway 31901 **Location:** Between 10th and 11th sts; in historic uptown. **Parking:** street only. L D CALL M

MARK'S CITY GRILL
706/507-3221

American. Casual Dining. $8-$21 **AAA Inspector Notes:** Known for serving up traditional Southern cuisine with a modern twist, this restaurant offers a variety of dishes such as bacon pimento cheeseburger, hamburger steak, meatloaf and shrimp and grits. This is a popular local hangout so expect a crowd during peak dining hours. **Features:** full bar, patio dining. **Address:** 7160 Moon Rd 31909 **Location:** I-185 exit 10 (US 80 and SR 22), 2.5 mi e on US 80 exit Moon Rd, then just n. L D CALL M

MERITAGE RESTAURANT & WINE BAR
706/327-0707

Small Plates. Fine Dining. $12-$36 **AAA Inspector Notes:** The modern elegance of this dining room creates a delightful setting for a glass of wine and a delicious dish. Popular menu items include duck breast, oven-roasted spaghetti squash, chicken confit and Chilean sea bass. The menu changes seasonally so ask the server for current specials. **Features:** full bar. **Address:** 1039 1st Ave 31901 **Location:** Between 11th and 12th sts; uptown. D CALL M

MINNIE'S UPTOWN RESTAURANT
706/322-2766

Southern. Casual Dining. $5-$9 **AAA Inspector Notes:** Along the edge of the historic district, the restaurant prepares traditional Southern cooking just like Mom's. Extremely friendly, helpful servers behind the lines of this cafeteria-style spot also helps in leaving patrons smiling on their way out and coming back for more. **Address:** 104 8th St 31901 **Location:** Corner of 8th St and 1st Ave. **Parking:** street only. L

THE OFFICE SPORTS BAR & GRILL
706/221-1822

American. Casual Dining. $10-$26 **AAA Inspector Notes:** This tavern has wide open space with an industrial-style décor of metal, brick and wood. The menu has something for everyone. Selections range from typical pub fare like burgers and wings to full hot entrées such as filet mignon and pork chops. With 15 TVs mounted at every angle, there is sure to be a game on to watch while munching. **Features:** full bar, patio dining. **Address:** 2979 Northlake Pkwy 31909 **Location:** I-185 exit 10B (US 80/SR 22), 1.3 mi w on US 80 exit 3A (Bradley Park Rd), just e to Whittlesey Rd, then just n. L D CALL M

RUTH ANN'S RESTAURANT
706/221-2124

Breakfast Comfort Food. Casual Dining. $4-$12 **AAA Inspector Notes:** This is where the locals come for a hearty breakfast and a home-style Southern lunch at reasonable prices. The coffee bar offers a good selection of gourmet blends and flavors. Rotating weekday lunch specials feature two entrées daily. **Address:** 941 Veterans Pkwy 31901 **Location:** Between 9th and 10th sts; in historic district. B L CALL M

STEAMY'S   706/221-7654

◆◆◆ Burgers Hot Dogs. Casual Dining. $3-$11 **AAA Inspector Notes:** They could easily film a remake of "Grease" or "Happy Days" at this '50s style retro diner. The focus of the simple menu is burgers, beef hot dogs and freshly cut fries complemented by a root beer float, old fashioned shakes and malts. On a hot, steamy day, hop on one of the shiny stainless steel stools at the counter and cool down with a banana split or sundae. Sunday the café closes earlier at 3 p.m. **Features:** patio dining. **Address:** 1204 1st Ave 31901 **Location:** Corner of 12th st; uptown. **Parking:** street only. Ⓛ Ⓓ CALL ♿Ⓜ

THAI HOUSE   706/494-5375

◆◆ Thai. Casual Dining. $9-$15 **AAA Inspector Notes:** This hugely popular strip mall restaurant offers a lengthy list of Thai specialties. Food is well prepared and simply presented. Language can be an issue so all dishes on the menu are numbered and there are many from which to choose. Try to avoid peak dining times or expect a wait. **Address:** 5592 Whitesville Rd, Suite 1 31904 **Location:** I-185 exit 8, 0.5 mi w, then just n; in The Landings Shopping Center.

Ⓛ Ⓓ

TREVIOLI ARTISAN PASTA COMPANY   706/580-8136

◆◆ Italian. Casual Dining. $10-$27 **AAA Inspector Notes:** Three adjoining suites of a storage facility might be an unorthodox location for a pasta joint, however this does not take away from the fact that the food is delicious. The owner/chef makes all the pasta and sauces from scratch using the freshest ingredients available. The portobello ravioli in a creamy mushroom sauce is yummy and satisfying. **Features:** full bar. **Address:** 3151 Tower Rd 31909 **Location:** US 80/SR 22 exit Veterans Pkwy, 1 mi ne, then just nw.

Ⓓ CALL ♿Ⓜ

WOOD STONE RESTAURANT   706/507-3993

◆◆ Mediterranean Pizza. Casual Dining. $8-$24 **AAA Inspector Notes:** This family-run restaurant offers a nice variety of Greek, Italian, Turkish and North African fare with special attention to the use of fresh herbs and spices to enhance the flavors. At lunch diners can sample a number of dishes at the daily buffet. During the dinner hour full entrées and pizza take the stage with such dishes as steak Gorgonzola, baked penne and shrimp diavolo. The chicken caprino is extremely flavorful. Vegetarian and children's selections are available. **Features:** beer & wine. **Address:** 5739 Whitesville Rd 31904 **Location:** I-185 exit 8 (Airport Thruway), just w then 0.5 mi n. Ⓛ Ⓓ

YOUR PIE   706/507-1743

◆ Pizza Sandwiches. Quick Serve. $7-$10 **AAA Inspector Notes:** No more compromising as everyone gets the pizza they want here. Each 10-inch pie is assembled at the counter right in front of you. Select the type of crust, sauce and toppings and add a salad or maybe have a panini instead. Top it all off with gelato or sorbet. **Features:** beer & wine, patio dining. **Address:** 5592 Whitesville Rd 31904 **Location:** I-185 exit 8, 0.5 mi w, then just n; in The Landings Shopping Center. Ⓛ Ⓓ

COMER (B-4) pop. 1,126, elev. 573'

WATSON MILL BRIDGE STATE OUTDOOR RECREATION AREA is 3 mi. s. on SR 22 at 650 Watson Mill Rd. A 229-foot four-span covered bridge built in 1885 crosses the South Fork Broad River. Picnicking, camping and fishing in the river are permitted. Hiking, bicycle and horse trails (no horse rental available) also are in the park. *See Recreation Areas Chart.* **Hours:** Daily 7 a.m.-10 p.m. Office daily 8-5, Mar.-Nov. Phone ahead to confirm schedule. **Cost:** $5 (per private vehicle). **Phone:** (706) 245-6270.

Take your imagination to new destinations

with the online AAA/CAA Travel Guides

COMMERCE (B-3) pop. 6,544, elev. 915'

Shopping: 🅢 Tanger Outlets, off I-85 exit 149 to 800 Steven B. Tanger Blvd., features such retailers as Chico's Outlet, The Children's Place, H&M and Polo Ralph Lauren Factory Store.

BEST WESTERN COMMERCE INN   (706)335-3640

◆◆ Hotel $75-$225

AAA Benefit: Save 10% or more every day and earn 10% bonus points!

Address: 157 Eisenhower Dr 30529 **Location:** I-85 exit 149, just ne. **Facility:** 51 units. 3 stories, interior corridors. **Terms:** check-in 4 pm. **Pool(s):** outdoor. **Activities:** exercise room. **Guest Services:** coin laundry.

🅢 🍴 CALL ♿Ⓜ 🏊 BIZ 📶 ✕ 🔧 🖼 🖵 / SOME UNITS 🐾 HS

COMFORT SUITES COMMERCE   (706)336-0000

◆◆◆ Hotel. $99-$229 **Address:** 30490 Hwy 441 S 30529 **Location:** I-85 exit 149, just w. **Facility:** 74 units. 4 stories, interior corridors. **Pool(s):** heated indoor. **Activities:** hot tub, exercise room. **Guest Services:** valet and coin laundry.

🍴 CALL ♿Ⓜ 🏊 BIZ HS 📶 ✕ 🔧 🖼 🖵 / SOME UNITS 🐾

FAIRFIELD INN & SUITES BY MARRIOTT COMMERCE
                                      (706)336-0066

◆◆◆ Hotel. $76-$126 **Address:** 137 Frontage Rd 30529 **Location:** I-85 exit 149, just w. **Facility:** 80 units. 4 stories, interior corridors. **Pool(s):** heated indoor. **Activities:** hot tub, exercise room. **Guest Services:** valet and coin laundry.

AAA Benefit: Members save 5% or more!

🍴 CALL ♿Ⓜ 🏊 HS 📶 ✕ 🔧 🖼 🖵

HAMPTON INN   (706)335-6161

◆◆◆ Hotel. $129-$149 **Address:** 153 Hampton Ct 30529 **Location:** I-85 exit 149, just e. **Facility:** 61 units. 3 stories, interior corridors. **Terms:** 1-7 night minimum stay, cancellation fee imposed. **Pool(s):** outdoor. **Activities:** exercise room. **Guest Services:** valet laundry.

AAA Benefit: Members save up to 10%!

🍴 CALL ♿Ⓜ 🏊 BIZ 📶 🔧 🖼 🖵

WHERE TO EAT

EL PARIAN MEXICAN RESTAURANT BAR & GRILL
                                      706/335-5204

◆◆ Mexican. Casual Dining. $4-$12 **AAA Inspector Notes:** This hometown Mexican cantina offers the classic cuisine you have come to love at an affordable price. Located in the historical downtown section of Commerce, this family-owned operation is a local favorite. Try the tacos al pastor on corn tortillas or any of the burritos, and of course save room for the caramel flan. **Features:** beer only. **Address:** 1662 S Broad St 30529 **Location:** Downtown. **Parking:** street only. Ⓛ Ⓓ

GRAND BUFFET   706/335-0899

◆ Chinese. Quick Serve. $6-$11 **AAA Inspector Notes:** As the restaurant's name makes clear, this place lays out an all-you-can-eat lunch and dinner buffet that includes a salad bar, a good selection of Chinese, Japanese and American entrées and a dessert bar. **Address:** 107 Pottery Factory Dr 30529 **Location:** I-85 exit 149, just se. Ⓛ Ⓓ

SONNY'S REAL PIT BAR-B-Q 706/335-4741

WW Barbecue. Casual Dining. $8-$17 **AAA Inspector Notes:** Bearing the name after its founder, Floyd "Sonny" Tillman, this barbecue restaurant first opened its doors circa 1968 in Gainesville, Florida and has since spawned over 150 more throughout the Southeast. The menu is steeped in finger lickin' favorites such as ribs, pulled pork, beef brisket, burgers, catfish, shrimp and chargrilled chicken. Let's not forget about the fried okra, which is the perfect starter dish, and their homemade baked beans. **Features:** beer only. **Address:** 30975 Hwy 441 S 30529 **Location:** I-85 exit 149, 0.5 mi se. L D

CONYERS pop. 15,195

COUNTRY INN & SUITES BY CARLSON (770)785-2400

WW **Hotel.** $87-$120 **Address:** 1312 Old Covington Hwy SE 30012 **Location:** I-20 exit 82, just n. **Facility:** 66 units. 6 stories, interior corridors. **Terms:** 3 day cancellation notice-fee imposed. **Pool(s):** heated indoor. **Activities:** hot tub, exercise room. **Guest Services:** valet and coin laundry.

Ⓣ CALL Ⓜ ⊇ BIZ HS 📶 ✕ 🛎 🖼 🖵 / SOME UNITS 🐾

HAMPTON INN (770)483-8838

WW **Hotel.** $99-$159 **Address:** 1340 Dogwood Dr SE 30013 **Location:** I-20 exit 82, just n, then just e. **Facility:** 99 units. 4 stories, interior corridors. **Terms:** 1-7 night minimum stay, cancellation fee imposed. **Pool(s):** outdoor. **Activities:** exercise room. **Guest Services:** valet and coin laundry.

AAA Benefit: Members save up to 10%!

Ⓣ CALL Ⓜ ⊇ BIZ HS 📶 ✕ 🛎 🖼 🖵 / SOME UNITS 🐾

HAWTHORN SUITES BY WYNDHAM CONYERS (770)761-9155

WWW **Hotel.** $89-$205 **Address:** 1659 Centennial Olympic Pkwy 30013 **Location:** I-20 exit 82, 3.7 mi e on SR 138, then 1.7 mi w. **Facility:** 77 units, some kitchens. 3 stories, interior corridors. **Pool(s):** outdoor. **Activities:** hot tub, regulation golf, exercise room. **Guest Services:** valet and coin laundry.

Ⓣ Ⓨ ⊇ BIZ 📶 ✕ 🛎 🖼 🖵 / SOME UNITS 🐾

LA QUINTA INN & SUITES ATLANTA CONYERS (770)918-0092

WWW **Hotel.** $86-$152 **Address:** 1184 Dogwood Dr SE 30012 **Location:** I-20 exit 82, just n to Dogwood Dr, then just w. **Facility:** 119 units. 6 stories, interior corridors. **Pool(s):** outdoor. **Activities:** hot tub, exercise room. **Guest Services:** valet and coin laundry.

Ⓣ CALL Ⓜ ⊇ BIZ 📶 ✕ 🖵 / SOME UNITS 🐾 🛎 🖼

QUALITY INN (770)760-1230

WW **Motel.** $66-$100 **Address:** 1164 Dogwood Dr SE 30012 **Location:** I-20 exit 82, just n to Dogwood Dr, then just w. **Facility:** 59 units. 2 stories (no elevator), exterior corridors. **Pool(s):** outdoor. **Activities:** exercise room. **Guest Services:** valet laundry.

Ⓣ CALL Ⓜ ⊇ BIZ 📶 🛎 🖼 🖵 / SOME UNITS 🐾

WHERE TO EAT

BAAN THAI 770/761-6161

WW Thai. Casual Dining. $8-$15 **AAA Inspector Notes:** This casual Thai restaurant is a popular choice for a quick delicious meal. The menu features traditional dishes such as pad thai, drunken Thai noodles and coconut chicken soup. There are also various vegetarian options. **Features:** beer & wine. **Address:** 1745 Hwy 138, Suite C-13 30013 **Location:** I-20 exit 82, 0.9 mi s; in Kroger Plaza.

L D

CAFE MILANO ITALIAN RESTAURANT 770/860-1144

WW Italian. Casual Dining. $4-$18 **AAA Inspector Notes:** This family, friendly restaurant is a popular local favorite for Italian cuisine. The chicken cacciatore, veal Marsala and grilled shrimp and salmon are popular. The generous portions assure that guests will not go home hungry. My favorite part is the garlic bread that comes with every order. **Address:** 875 Flat Shoals Rd 30094 **Location:** Jct SR 138 and Flat Shoals Rd. L D CALL Ⓜ

JIM 'N NICK'S BAR-B-Q 770/785-4453

WW Barbecue. Casual Dining. $6-$25 **AAA Inspector Notes:** Southern hospitality reigns at Jim 'N Nick's, where diners get neighborly treatment as they dig into huge portions of tasty lean sausage, fresh chili, juicy smoked beef and pork. A slice of sublime homemade pie ends the meal on a high note. **Features:** full bar. **Address:** 2275 GA Hwy 20 30013 **Location:** I-20 exit 82, 2 mi s. L D

SEVEN GABLES RESTAURANT 770/922-8824

WWW Continental. Casual Dining. $14-$29 **AAA Inspector Notes:** This well-known eatery has been luring folks in for more than 20 years with good food and reasonable prices. Presented in a lovely Swiss chalet setting, the European cuisine features traditional French bouillabaisse, roasted rack of lamb and grilled seafood. Try the surprisingly delicious "Pheasant Bstella" for a unique culinary experience. Menu items are based on market availability. **Features:** full bar. **Reservations:** suggested. **Address:** 1897 SR 20 SE 30013 **Location:** I-20 exit 82, 1.5 mi s. D ✎

SONNY'S REAL PIT BAR-B-Q 770/860-0099

WW Barbecue. Casual Dining. $8-$17 **AAA Inspector Notes:** Bearing the name after its founder, Floyd "Sonny" Tillman, this barbecue restaurant first opened its doors circa 1968 in Gainesville, Florida and has since spawned over 150 more throughout the Southeast. The menu is steeped in finger lickin' favorites such as ribs, pulled pork, beef brisket, burgers, catfish, shrimp and chargrilled chicken. Let's not forget about the fried okra, which is the perfect starter dish, and their homemade baked beans. **Features:** beer only. **Address:** 1870 Hwy 20 S 30013 **Location:** I-20 exit 82, 1.5 mi s. L D

THAI PALACE RESTAURANT & SUSHI BAR 770/785-7778

WW Thai. Casual Dining. $3-$15 **AAA Inspector Notes:** Away from the hustle and bustle of the city center, this family-owned restaurant serves up delicious Asian cuisine. The menu focuses on traditional Thai dishes with an expansive sushi menu as well. The coconut chicken soup is an excellent way to start the meal and the classic Thai curries are delicious. I recommend concluding the meal with the traditional dessert of sweet rice and mango. **Features:** full bar. **Address:** 968 Main St 30012 **Location:** Jct SR 138 SE and S Main St NE. L D

CORDELE (D-3) pop. 11,147, elev. 336'

GEORGIA VETERANS MEMORIAL STATE PARK is 9 mi. w. on US 280. Established in 1946, the park honors Georgia's war veterans. The 1,308-acre park includes an 18-hole golf course, a military museum with outdoor exhibits of vintage aircraft and military equipment and an indoor collection of artifacts from various wars. A marina at 8,700-acre Lake Blackshear provides boat rentals. *See Recreation Areas Chart.*

Hours: Park open daily 7 a.m.-10 p.m. Museum daily 8-5 (also Fri.-Sat. 5-7, Apr.-Sept.). **Cost:** Free. **Parking:** $5. **Phone:** (229) 276-2371.

🅰 ✕ 🐾 ⛱

BAYMONT INN & SUITES (229)273-9477

WW **Hotel.** $70-$79 **Address:** 416 S Greer St 31015 **Location:** I-75 exit 101 (US 280), just w, then just n. Adjacent to railroad tracks. **Facility:** 51 units. 2 stories (no elevator), interior corridors. **Pool(s):** heated indoor. **Activities:** exercise room.

⊇ BIZ 📶 ✕ 🛎 🖼 🖵 / SOME UNITS 🐾

BEST WESTERN COLONIAL INN   (229)273-5420

Hotel
$72-$80

AAA Benefit:
Save 10% or more every day and earn 10% bonus points!

Address: 1706 E 16th Ave (US 280) 31015 **Location:** I-75 exit 101 (US 280), just w. Across from railroad tracks. **Facility:** 93 units. 2 stories (no elevator), interior/exterior corridors. **Pool(s):** outdoor. **Activities:** playground. **Guest Services:** valet laundry. **Featured Amenity: breakfast buffet.**

ECONO LODGE   (229)273-0737

Hotel. $64-$85 **Address:** 1603 16th Ave E (US 280) 31015 **Location:** I-75 exit 101 (US 280), just w. Adjacent to railroad tracks. **Facility:** 80 units. 2 stories (no elevator), exterior corridors. **Pool(s):** outdoor. **Activities:** exercise room.

FAIRFIELD INN & SUITES BY MARRIOTT CORDELE   (229)273-0042

Hotel. $76-$140 **Address:** 2001 E 16th Ave 31015 **Location:** I-75 exit 101 (US 280), just e. **Facility:** 69 units. 3 stories, interior corridors. **Amenities:** safes. **Pool(s):** heated indoor. **Activities:** hot tub, exercise room. **Guest Services:** valet and coin laundry.

AAA Benefit:
Members save 5% or more!

HAMPTON INN & SUITES CORDELE   (229)273-7150

Hotel. $139-$179 **Address:** 1709 E 16th Ave 31015 **Location:** I-75 exit 101, just w. **Facility:** 77 units. 1-3 stories, interior corridors. **Terms:** 1-7 night minimum stay, cancellation fee imposed. **Pool(s):** outdoor. **Activities:** exercise room. **Guest Services:** coin laundry.

AAA Benefit:
Members save up to 10%!

QUALITY INN CORDELE   (229)273-2371

Hotel
$70-$750

Address: 1601 E 16th Ave (US 280) 31015 **Location:** I-75 exit 101 (US 280), just w. Adjacent to railroad tracks. **Facility:** 59 units. 2 stories (no elevator), exterior corridors. **Pool(s):** outdoor. **Featured Amenity: continental breakfast.**

WHERE TO EAT

16 EAST BAR AND GRILL   229/273-9611

Southern American. Casual Dining. $9-$27 **AAA Inspector Notes:** A delightful combination of modern décor and country charm, this local favorite has something for everyone. Try such Southern classics as shrimp and grits or modern creations like collard greens dip. Bring your big appetite and chow down on the New York strip or seafood platter. When the weather is nice ask for a seat on the covered porch or slide up to the bar for a cold beer. **Features:** full bar, patio dining. **Address:** 1309 E 16th Ave 31015 **Location:** I-75 exit 101 (US 280), 0.6 mi w.

DAPHNE LODGE RESTAURANT   229/273-2596

American. Casual Dining. $14-$38 **AAA Inspector Notes:** In a cozy red cabin nestled among pine trees, the family-owned restaurant serves award-winning regional dishes. Among favorites are baked Parmesan grouper and fried catfish. All desserts are homemade. **Features:** beer & wine. **Reservations:** suggested, weekends. **Address:** 2502 US Hwy 280 W 31015 **Location:** I-75 exit 101 (US 280), 10.2 mi w.

EL GIRASOL MEXICAN RESTAURANT   229/271-0193

Mexican. Casual Dining. $6-$10 **AAA Inspector Notes:** At this spot the bright orange stucco walls, arched doorways, terra cotta tiled floor and curved tile faux roof over the bar create a south of the border cantina atmosphere. All of the favorite dishes are available to be enjoyed in the cozy dining room or one of the more private sections. **Features:** beer only. **Address:** 102 E 14th Ave 31015 **Location:** I-75 exit 101 (US 280), 1.8 mi w, then just n; in strip mall.

LOS COMPADRES MEXICAN RESTAURANT   229/273-1350

Mexican. Casual Dining. $6-$16 **AAA Inspector Notes:** Just off the highway, the restaurant prepares traditional quick Mexican meals including quesadillas, chimichangas or carne asada. **Features:** full bar, senior menu. **Address:** 1116 E 16th Ave 31015 **Location:** I-75 exit 101 (US 280), 1.3 mi w.

SMOAKIES BAR-B-QUE   229/273-0802

Barbecue. Casual Dining. $5-$10 **AAA Inspector Notes:** A little remote but worth the short drive, this extremely casual barbecue joint features a variety of smoked meats including brisket, chicken, pork and ribs. A friendly staff will make you feel right at home so feel free to get a little messy. Try the housemade banana pudding for a sweet treat. **Address:** 602 N Greer St 31015 **Location:** I-75 exit 101 (US 280), just w.

TJ'S ITALIAN AMERICAN RESTAURANT   229/273-1160

Italian. Casual Dining. $5-$21 **AAA Inspector Notes:** For those who like their pizza thin and crispy, this family-operated restaurant is the place for you. Other traditional Italian dishes also are available along with steak and shrimp dinners. The glass-enclosed sun room is a great location to enjoy a meal. **Features:** full bar. **Address:** 1712 E 16th Ave 31015 **Location:** I-75 exit 101 (US 280), just w.

CORNELIA pop. 4,160

BAYMONT INN & SUITES   (706)778-3600

Hotel. $59-$120 **Address:** 1105 Business 441 30531 **Location:** Jct SR 365 and US 441 business route, just e. **Facility:** 60 units. 2 stories, interior corridors. **Terms:** 3 day cancellation notice. **Pool(s):** heated indoor. **Activities:** exercise room. **Guest Services:** valet laundry.

HAMPTON INN BY HILTON CORNELIA   (706)778-0040

Hotel. $129-$189 **Address:** 161 Market Corners Dr 30531 **Location:** Jct SR 365 and US 441 business route, just e. **Facility:** 81 units. 3 stories, interior corridors. **Terms:** 1-7 night minimum stay, cancellation fee imposed. **Amenities:** video games. **Pool(s):** outdoor. **Activities:** exercise room. **Guest Services:** valet laundry.

AAA Benefit:
Members save up to 10%!

SUPER 8   (706)778-9573

Hotel. $50-$111 **Address:** 2965 J Warren Rd 30531 **Location:** Jct SR 365 and US 441 business route, just w. **Facility:** 60 units, some two bedrooms and kitchens. 2 stories (no elevator), interior corridors. **Terms:** cancellation fee imposed. **Pool(s):** outdoor. **Guest Services:** valet laundry.

COVINGTON (B-3) pop. 13,118, elev. 741'

Scarcely 30 miles from the hustle and bustle of Atlanta, Covington boasts a wealth of carefully restored antebellum and Victorian-era manor homes that can be viewed on a self-guided driving or walking tour; maps are available at the visitor information center.

The 1884 Newton County Courthouse is a well-known sight to anyone who watched the TV series "In the Heat of the Night" (based on the same-named motion picture); it was filmed in Covington for eight seasons. The town also provided the setting for the first five episodes of another popular program, "The Dukes of Hazzard." The Covington Visitor Information Center offers a brochure detailing the sites of TV shows and motion pictures shot on location in Covington and Newton County. The Walk of Stars, brick pavers featuring the film industry, is found downtown.

Nearby is Hard Labor Creek State Park, a 5,804-acre complex with cottages, two lakes, a swimming beach, boat rentals, an 18-hole golf course and a bring-your-own-horse stable. *See Recreation Areas Chart.*

Covington/Newton County Visitor Information Center: 2101 Clark St., Covington, GA 30014. **Phone:** (770) 787-3868 or (800) 616-8626.

BAYMONT INN & SUITES (770)787-4900

Motel
$59-$70

Address: 10111 Alcovy Rd 30014 **Location:** I-20 exit 92, just n. **Facility:** 50 units. 2 stories (no elevator), exterior corridors. **Pool(s):** outdoor. **Activities:** exercise room. **Guest Services:** coin laundry. **Featured Amenity:** continental breakfast.

CRAWFORDVILLE (B-4) pop. 534, elev. 589'

A.H. STEPHENS STATE PARK is 2 mi. n. of I-20 via SR 22 exit at 456 Alexander St. N. Named after the vice president of the Confederacy and governor of Georgia, the park has both natural and historic features. Liberty Hall, Stephens' home, has been renovated to its 1875 appearance; tours are available of the furnished interior. A Confederate museum houses a fine collection of Civil War artifacts, including uniforms, documents and Gen. James Longstreet's battle flags. *See Recreation Areas Chart.*

Hours: Park open daily 7 a.m.-10 p.m. Historic site open Fri.-Sun. 9-5. Last tour begins 1 hour, 30 minutes before closing. Historic site closed Jan. 1, Thanksgiving and Christmas. **Cost:** $5; $4.50 (ages 62+); $3 (ages 6-17); $1 (ages 0-5). **Parking:** $5. **Phone:** (706) 456-2602.

CUMBERLAND ISLAND NATIONAL SEASHORE (F-6)
• Part of Golden Isles area — see map p. 187

The largest and southernmost of Georgia's barrier islands, Cumberland Island parallels the Georgia coast just north of the Florida border. The relatively flat island, 17.5 miles long by 3 miles wide, is separated from the mainland by several miles of salt marsh, river and sound. On its eastern side white sand beaches rise to dunes that give way to a forest of magnolias, oaks, palmettos and pines. More than 300 species of birds have been sighted on the island.

Although Cumberland Island exists in a relatively undisturbed state, Native Americans inhabited it as early as 4,000 years ago. They called the island Missoe, which meant "sassafras." These Native Americans were succeeded by the Spanish in 1566 and the English in 1736. At various times live oaks were cut for ships timbers, and land was cleared for the cultivation of fruits and sea island cotton.

The family of Revolutionary War officer Gen. Nathanael Greene built Dungeness plantation on the island in the late 18th century. Only a small building of tabby—a mixture of oyster shell, lime and sand—and a family cemetery remain, the latter the original burial site of Henry "Light-Horse Harry" Lee of Virginia, the father of Gen. Robert E. Lee and a friend of Greene.

A century later Thomas Carnegie built a lavish 30-room mansion called Dungeness as the centerpiece of an estate that covered 90 percent of Cumberland. Vegetation grows through the remains of the second Dungeness mansion, which burned in 1959. Wild horses and other wildlife roam along the beaches and throughout the ruins. Plum Orchard, another Carnegie house, survives on the banks of the Brick Hill River. A small percentage of the island is privately owned and not open to visitors.

Restricted camping is available at developed and back-country campsites; reservations are highly recommended. For further information contact Cumberland Island National Seashore, 101 Wheeler St., St. Marys, GA 31558, or phone (912) 882-4336.

A small museum houses furnishings, carriages and photographs belonging to the Carnegie family as well as exhibits about the War of 1812.

A 45-minute ferry ride provides the only access; 300 visitors are permitted per day. Private vehicles and pets are not permitted on the Island. Bicycles are permitted on the south part of the island. The ferry departs from the St. Marys Visitor Center daily at 9 a.m. and 11:45 a.m., returning from the island daily at 10:15 a.m. and 4:45 p.m. (also at 2:45, Mar.-Sept.); advance reservations are highly recommended. There is no scheduled service Christmas and Tues.-Wed., Dec.-Feb. The park and visitor center is open daily 8-4; closed Christmas. The museum is staffed by volunteers and is open Wed.-Sun. 1-4 (based on staff availability); closed Christmas.

Admission, good for 7 days, to the national seashore is $4 per person; free (ages 0-15). Round-trip ferry fare $28; $26 (ages 65+); $18 (ages 0-12). Ferry reservations are highly recommended. Phone (912) 882-4336 for information or (877) 860-6787 for ferry reservations. *See Recreation Areas Chart.*

Ranger-led walking tours that explore the Dungeness historic district depart from the Dungeness dock twice daily (based on staff availability). Reservations are not required and the tours are free. A motorized tour to the north part of the island departs from the Sea Camp ranger station. The tour takes 5 to 6 hours to complete, is an arduous journey over bumpy, unpaved roads and is not recommended for young children. Reservations are required and a fee is charged; phone (877) 860-6787.

CUMMING pop. 5,430

COMFORT SUITES (770)889-4141

 **Hotel.** $105-$190 **Address:** 905 Buford Rd 30041 **Location:** SR 400 exit 14, just e. **Facility:** 71 units. 3 stories, interior corridors. **Pool(s):** outdoor. **Activities:** exercise room. **Guest Services:** valet and coin laundry.

HAMPTON INN (770)889-0877

Hotel $119-$225

Hampton by HILTON

AAA Benefit: Members save up to 10%!

Address: 915 Ronald Reagan Blvd 30041 **Location:** SR 400 exit 14, just e. **Facility:** 71 units. 4 stories, interior corridors. **Terms:** 1-7 night minimum stay, cancellation fee imposed. **Pool(s):** outdoor. **Activities:** exercise room. **Guest Services:** valet and coin laundry. **Featured Amenity:** breakfast buffet.

HOLIDAY INN EXPRESS & SUITES CUMMING 678/845-7100

 Hotel. Rates not provided. **Address:** 870 Buford Hwy 30041 **Location:** SR 400 exit 14, just e. **Facility:** 88 units. 4 stories, interior corridors. **Pool(s):** heated indoor. **Activities:** exercise room. **Guest Services:** valet and coin laundry.

WHERE TO EAT

JIM 'N NICK'S BAR-B-Q 678/845-1565

Barbecue. Casual Dining. $6-$25 **AAA Inspector Notes:** Southern hospitality reigns at Jim 'N Nick's, where diners get neighborly treatment as they dig into huge portions of tasty lean sausage, fresh chili, juicy smoked beef and pork. A slice of sublime homemade pie ends the meal on a high note. **Features:** full bar. **Address:** 3130 Ronald Reagan Blvd 30041 **Location:** SR 400 exit 13, just e.

PROVINO'S ITALIAN RESTAURANT 770/205-5605

Italian. Casual Dining. $11-$24 **AAA Inspector Notes:** Among the hustle and bustle of the shopping plaza is this restaurant serving up traditional Italian dishes in a friendly, neighborhood atmosphere. Guests can enjoy the bottomless house salad and hot buttered garlic rolls. Popular dishes include the pasta lover's special, chicken parmigiana and veal Marsala. **Features:** beer & wine, patio dining, early bird specials. **Address:** 1610 Market Place Blvd 30041 **Location:** SR 400 exit 14, 0.3 mi e.

DAHLONEGA (A-3) pop. 5,242, elev. 1,875'
• Hotels p. 170 • Restaurants p. 170

In 1828, nearly 3 centuries after Hernando de Soto sought gold in northeastern Georgia, the area around Dahlonega (dah-LON-a-gah) boomed with the discovery of the ore. A federal mint built in 1838 coined more than $6 million before it was closed at the outbreak of the Civil War. Gold coins minted in Dahlonega are highly prized by collectors.

Gold mining continued in Dahlonega until the early 20th century when the fixing of the metal's worth at $35 an ounce made mining unprofitable. Tourism and vineyards have replaced commercial gold mining. In 1958 and again in the mid-1970s, gold donated by residents was driven to Atlanta in a mule train and used to re-cover the dome of the Capitol with gold leaf.

The price of gold is no longer fixed, and visitors can pan for the metal, take underground mine tours and see exhibits of mining equipment at Consolidated Gold Mines *(see attraction listing)*. Gold panning and mining equipment also are available at Crisson Gold Mine. An 1875 Chestatee River diving bell is on display in Hancock Park.

Every year, visitors may have another opportunity to pan for gold at the 4th of July Celebration. Other offerings include music, dancing and fireworks.

Dahlonega-Lumpkin County Chamber & Visitors Bureau: 13 S. Park St., Dahlonega, GA 30533. **Phone:** (706) 864-3711 or (800) 231-5543.

CONSOLIDATED GOLD MINES, 185 Consolidated Gold Mine Rd., offers guided 45-minute tours of a former gold mine. Demonstrations of drilling and gold-panning techniques are featured. The underground mine remains at a constant temperature of 60 F. Panning for gold and gemstones is offered.

Time: Allow 1 hour, 30 minutes minimum. **Hours:** Tours depart as needed daily 10-6, Memorial Day-Labor Day; 10-5, rest of year. Last admission 1 hour before closing. Closed Easter, Thanksgiving and Christmas. **Cost:** Tour (includes sample panning) $16; $11 (ages 4-14). Gold and gem panning $6-$11 (family buckets available). **Phone:** (706) 864-8473. **GT**

DAHLONEGA GOLD MUSEUM STATE HISTORIC SITE, 1 Public Square across from the visitors bureau, depicts America's first major gold rush through exhibits of nuggets and gold dust, Dahlonega minted gold coins, mining apparatus and photographs of early mining activities. A 17-minute film titled "America's First Gold Rush" talks about the discovery of gold in the North Georgia mountains.

Time: Allow 1 hour minimum. **Hours:** Mon.-Sat. 9-4:45, Sun. 10-4:45. Last film is shown 45 minutes before closing. Closed Jan. 1, Thanksgiving and Christmas. **Cost:** $7; $6.50 (ages 62+); $4.50 (ages 6-17). **Phone:** (706) 864-2257.

RECREATIONAL ACTIVITIES

Canoeing

- **Appalachian Outfitters** is on SR 60 S. at 2084 S. Chestatee, Dahlonega, GA 30533. **Hours:** Mon. and Thurs.-Fri. 10-3, Sat.-Sun. 9-3, Apr.-Sept. (also Tues.-Wed. 10-3, June-Aug.); Sat.-Sun. 10-3, in Mar. and Oct. **Phone:** (706) 864-7117 for reservations.

WINERIES

- **Montaluce Winery & Restaurant** is at 946 Via Montaluce. The more-than-35 acres of vineyards produce handcrafted wines. **Hours:** Daily 11-5 (also Wed.-Sun. 5-9). Tours are given Mon.-Fri. at 2, Sat.-Sun. at noon. **Phone:** (706) 867-4060. GT [I]

- **Three Sisters Vineyards** is at 439 Vineyard Way. **Hours:** Thurs.-Sat. 11-5, Sun. 1-5, Mon.-Wed. by appointment, mid-Jan. through Christmas Eve. **Phone:** (706) 865-9463. GT

- **Wolf Mountain Vineyards & Winery** is at 180 Wolf Mountain Tr. **Hours:** Tues.-Sat. 11-5, Sun. 12:30-5, Sept.-Nov.; Thurs.-Sat. 11-5, Sun. 12:30-5, Mar.-Aug.; Sat. 11-5, Sun. 12:30-5, rest of year. Last tasting begins 45 minutes before closing. Winemaker's tour Sat.-Sun. at 2. Phone ahead to confirm winter hours. **Phone:** (706) 867-9862. GT [I]

DAYS INN   (706)864-2338

▼▼ **Motel.** $60-$134 **Address:** 833 S Chestatee St 30533 **Location:** 0.5 mi s on US 19 and SR 60. **Facility:** 41 units. 2 stories (no elevator), exterior corridors. **Pool(s):** outdoor.

HOLIDAY INN EXPRESS   706/867-7777

▼▼▼ **Hotel.** Rates not provided. **Address:** 835 S Chestatee St 30533 **Location:** 0.5 mi s on US 19 and SR 60. **Facility:** 81 units. 3 stories, interior corridors. **Pool(s):** outdoor. **Activities:** exercise room. **Guest Services:** valet laundry.

LILY CREEK LODGE   (706)864-6848

▼▼▼▼▼

Bed & Breakfast
$119-$159

Address: 2608 Auraria Rd 30533 **Location:** SR 52 northbound, jct SR 400 and Burnt Stand Rd, 2.5 mi w to Auraria Rd, then 2 mi n; SR 52 southbound, jct SR 60 and 52 and 9, 1.8 mi w on SR 52 and 9 to Auraria Rd, then 2.5 mi s. **Facility:** Nestled in a quiet wooded valley, this European-style chalet features feather comforters, art, collectibles and Art Nouveau-style parlor. For a special treat, try breakfast in the treehouse or gazebo. 13 units, some efficiencies and kitchens. 3 stories (no elevator), interior corridors. **Terms:** 7 day cancellation notice-fee imposed. **Pool(s):** outdoor. **Activities:** hot tub, massage. **Featured Amenity: full hot breakfast.**

PARK PLACE HOTEL   706/864-0021

▼▼▼ **Motel.** Rates not provided. **Address:** 27 S Park St 30533 **Location:** Just off town square; downtown. **Facility:** 14 units, some two bedrooms. 2 stories (no elevator), interior/exterior corridors.

QUALITY INN DAHLONEGA   (706)864-6191

▼▼ **Motel.** $69-$160 **Address:** 619 N Grove St 30533 **Location:** 0.5 mi n on US 19 business route. **Facility:** 41 units. 2-4 stories, exterior corridors. **Pool(s):** outdoor. **Guest Services:** coin laundry.

WHERE TO EAT

CORKSCREW CAFE   706/867-8551

▼▼ American. Casual Dining. $5-$31 **AAA Inspector Notes:** This hole in the wall restaurant is a hidden treasure that the locals rave about! During good weather, try the back patio and bar. **Features:** beer & wine, patio dining, Sunday brunch. **Address:** 51 W Main St 30533 **Location:** Downtown; by the square. [L] [D] CALL [M]

YAHOOLA CREEK GRILL   706/740-4300

▼▼ Southern American. Casual Dining. $9-$24 **AAA Inspector Notes:** This small town restaurant seeks to elevate the culinary standard for the area with Southern hospitality. Featuring such classic Southern dishes as fried green tomatoes and shrimp and grits, along with New York strip and the meatloaf surprise, this restaurant has something for everyone. **Features:** wine only, patio dining, Sunday brunch. **Address:** 1810 S Chestatee St 30533 **Location:** Jct SR 400 and US 19, 3.7 mi w. [L] [D] CALL [M]

DALLAS (B-2) pop. 11,544, elev. 1,050'

PICKETT'S MILL BATTLEFIELD STATE HISTORIC SITE is 5 mi. n.e. on Dallas-Acworth Hwy. (SR 381), then 1 mi. w. on Due West Rd., then n. to 4432 Mt. Tabor Church Rd. At this site in 1864, Confederate troops defeated Union troops advancing toward Atlanta. Walking trails with explanatory markers cross the battlefield; living-history programs, a video explanation of the battle and battle artifacts also are featured.

Time: Allow 1 hour minimum. **Hours:** Thurs.-Sat. 9-5. Closed Jan. 1, Thanksgiving and Christmas. **Cost:** $5.50; $3.50 (ages 62+); $3 (ages 6-17). **Phone:** (770) 443-7850. ⟨A⟩

DALTON (A-2) pop. 33,128, elev. 767'

In the early 1900s a local farm girl sold a hand-tufted bedspread for $2.50 and unknowingly revived a century-old craft that was to become big business in Dalton. Although the bedspreads now are rare, the craft is perpetuated in the production of tufted floor coverings. Currently, Dalton supplies more than half of the world's tufted carpets.

Another craft is preserved 10 miles northeast of Dalton, off I-75 exit 341 on SR 2, at the restored Prater's Mill. Dating from the 1800s, the mill still grinds cornmeal during the annual 🐿 Prater's Mill Country Fair held at the site each October; phone (706) 694-6455.

Dalton Convention and Visitors Bureau: in the Dalton Freight Depot, 305 S. Depot St., Dalton, GA 30722. **Phone:** (706) 270-9960 or (800) 331-3258.

Ask about on-the-spot vehicle
battery testing and replacement

COMFORT INN & SUITES
(706)259-2583

Hotel. $104-$149 **Address:** 905 Westbridge Rd 30720 **Location:** I-75 exit 333, just w to Westbridge Rd, then just s. **Facility:** 76 units. 4 stories, interior corridors. **Pool(s):** heated indoor. **Activities:** hot tub, exercise room. **Guest Services:** valet and coin laundry.

COUNTRY INN & SUITES BY CARLSON-DALTON
(706)278-9700

Hotel
$99-$139

Address: 903 Westbridge Rd 30720 **Location:** I-75 exit 333, just w to Westbridge Rd, then just s. **Facility:** 68 units. 3 stories, interior corridors. **Terms:** cancellation fee imposed. **Pool(s):** heated indoor. **Activities:** exercise room. **Guest Services:** valet and coin laundry. **Featured Amenity:** full hot breakfast.

COURTYARD BY MARRIOTT DALTON
(706)275-7215

Hotel. $83-$147 **Address:** 785 College Dr 30720 **Location:** I-75 exit 333, just w, then 0.3 mi n. **Facility:** 93 units. 3 stories, interior corridors. **Pool(s):** heated indoor. **Activities:** hot tub, exercise room. **Guest Services:** valet and coin laundry.

AAA Benefit:
Members save 5% or more!

HAMPTON INN
(706)226-4333

Motel
$109-$179

AAA Benefit:
Members save up to 10%!

Address: 1000 Market St 30720 **Location:** I-75 exit 333, just e to Market St, then just s. Opposite Dalton Factory Stores Mall. **Facility:** 124 units. 3 stories, exterior corridors. **Terms:** 1-7 night minimum stay, cancellation fee imposed. **Pool(s):** outdoor. **Activities:** exercise room. **Guest Services:** valet and coin laundry. **Featured Amenity:** breakfast buffet.

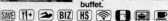

HILTON GARDEN INN DALTON
(706)529-6000

Hotel. $149-$399 **Address:** 879 College Dr 30720 **Location:** I-75 exit 333, just w. **Facility:** 110 units. 6 stories, interior corridors. **Terms:** 1-7 night minimum stay, cancellation fee imposed. **Pool(s):** heated indoor. **Activities:** hot tub, exercise room. **Guest Services:** valet and coin laundry.

AAA Benefit:
Members save up to 10%!

HOLIDAY INN EXPRESS & SUITES DALTON
(706)217-6200

Hotel. $109-$189 **Address:** 865 Holiday Inn Dr 30720 **Location:** I-75 exit 333, just w to Holiday Inn Dr, then just n. **Facility:** 67 units. 2 stories, interior corridors. **Terms:** check-in 4 pm. **Pool(s):** heated indoor. **Activities:** exercise room. **Guest Services:** valet and coin laundry.

HOWARD JOHNSON DALTON
(706)281-1880

Motel. $69-$100 **Address:** 790 College Dr 30720 **Location:** I-75 exit 333, just w, then 0.3 mi n. **Facility:** 60 units. 2 stories (no elevator), exterior corridors. **Pool(s):** outdoor. **Activities:** exercise room. **Guest Services:** coin laundry.

LA QUINTA INN & SUITES DALTON
(706)272-9099

Hotel. $102-$196 **Address:** 715 College Dr 30720 **Location:** I-75 exit 333, just w to Holiday Inn Dr, then 0.5 mi n. **Facility:** 88 units. 4 stories, interior corridors. **Amenities:** safes. **Pool(s):** outdoor. **Activities:** hot tub, exercise room. **Guest Services:** valet and coin laundry.

QUALITY INN
(706)278-0500

Motel
$69-$109

Address: 875 College Dr 30720 **Location:** I-75 exit 333, just w. **Facility:** 45 units. 2 stories (no elevator), exterior corridors. **Featured Amenity:** full hot breakfast.

SUPER 8 DALTON/CONVENTION CENTER
(706)529-7800

Hotel. $63-$70 **Address:** 869 College Dr 30720 **Location:** I-75 exit 333, just w to Holiday Inn Dr, then just n. **Facility:** 33 units. 2 stories (no elevator), exterior corridors.

WHERE TO EAT

FUJI JAPANESE STEAK HOUSE
706/281-1889

Japanese. Casual Dining. $4-$24 **AAA Inspector Notes:** For those with a craving for Japanese cuisine, this is the place. The contemporary Asian restaurant features a large selection of sushi, sizzling hibachi items and specialty drinks. Try Filet Mignon and lobster on the hibachi grill, Chilean sea bass with thick pan-fried noodles or delicious crunchy sushi rolls. For a decadent finish to the meal try the tempura cheesecake. **Features:** full bar. **Address:** 1321 W Walnut Ave 30720 **Location:** I-75 exit 333, just s to Walnut Ave, then 1 mi e.

MILLER BROTHERS RIB SHACK
706/279-3312

Barbecue. Casual Dining. $6-$18 **AAA Inspector Notes:** This hometown favorite offers good old-fashioned barbecue in a no-frills dining room. Ribs are the specialty but the catfish and barbecue pork also are crowd pleasers. Come as you are and get ready to loosen your belt. **Address:** 4109 S Dixie Hwy 30720 **Location:** I-75 exit 326, 0.4 mi e, then just s.

OAKWOOD CAFE
706/529-9663

Southern. Casual Dining. $6-$20 **AAA Inspector Notes:** Good old home-style Southern cooking comes in the form of vegetable plates or choices of meat and two (or three) vegetables, sandwiches, salads and desserts. Local favorites are meatloaf, turkey and dressing, pot roast and barbecue pork and chicken and dumplings. Locals love this place for breakfast, lunch and dinner! **Address:** 201 W Cuyler St 30720 **Location:** Downtown. **Parking:** street only.

DARIEN (E-6) pop. 1,975, elev. 30'

Established as a stronghold to protect England's rich Southern holdings from Spanish, French and Native American attacks in the 1720s, Darien was settled by Gen. James E. Oglethorpe's Scottish Highlanders. The town became a prosperous center of timber shipping and trade by the mid-1800s. The Darien River, which determined the town's location, is dotted with shrimp boats that now underpin the local economy. A 7-mile bicycle path connects the historic district with Fort King George; the path begins at the foot of the bridge at the intersection of US 17 and Fort King George Drive.

Recreational opportunities, including birdwatching, kayaking, fishing and deep-sea charter excursions, are available at downtown locations and north on US 17 at Shellman Bluff and Harris Neck National Wildlife Refuge. Harris Neck's 2,824 acres, a mix of wooded areas, grassy plains and marshes and live oaks draped with Spanish moss, offer a pleasant drive.

In summer the refuge is home to nesting egrets, herons and wood storks; in winter ducks take up residence. Open dawn-dusk; pets are not permitted. To reach the refuge take exit 67 off I-95, go south on US 17 about 1 mile and then continue east on Harris Neck Road about 7 miles. The visitor contact station is open Mon.-Sat. 9-4; closed federal holidays. Phone (843) 784-2468 to confirm staff availability.

Darien-McIntosh County Chamber and Visitor Center: 1111 Magnolia Bluff Way S.W., Suite 410, Darien, GA 31305. **Phone:** (912) 437-4837.

Self-guiding tours: A walking-tour map of the downtown historic district is available at the visitor center.

FORT KING GEORGE STATE HISTORIC SITE is 1 mi. e. of US 17 on Fort King George Dr. Serving as the Southern outpost for the British Empire 1721-27, the fort was the first English settlement in what is now the state of Georgia. It was reconstructed based on documents from the British Public Records Office. The remains of sawmills and a tabby house are on the site. A museum interprets Native American, Spanish and British occupation, as well as the history of coastal sawmills. A Highlander cottage also is on the grounds.

Time: Allow 1 hour minimum. **Hours:** Tues.-Sun. and Mon. holidays 9-5. Closed Thanksgiving, Christmas and the Tues. following some Mon. holidays. **Cost:** $7.50; $7 (ages 62+); $4.50 (ages 5-17). **Phone:** (912) 437-4770.

Ask your AAA/CAA club

about travel money and other

financial services for travelers

HOFWYL-BROADFIELD PLANTATION STATE HISTORIC SITE—see Brunswick p. 145.

COMFORT INN (912)437-4200

♥♥ ♥♥
Hotel
$81-$116

Address: 12924 GA Hwy 251 Rd 31305 **Location:** I-95 exit 49 (SR 251), just nw. Located near Darien Outlet Mall. **Facility:** 66 units. 2 stories, interior corridors. **Amenities:** safes. **Pool(s):** outdoor. **Guest Services:** coin laundry. **Featured Amenity:** continental breakfast.

[SAVE] [††] [🔧] [BIZ] [📶] [✕] [🔒]
[📷] [💻] /SOME UNITS [🔔]

WHERE TO EAT

SKIPPER'S FISH CAMP 912/437-3474

♥♥ Regional Seafood Barbecue. Casual Dining. $10-$30 **AAA Inspector Notes:** This riverfront restaurant affords views of boats and marshlands from its large wooden deck, which is great for kicking back and relaxing. Nautical appointments decorate the dining room and well-maintained landscaping showcase the inviting exterior. Comfort foods and Southern dishes, including barbecue and smoked chicken, share the menu with fresh seafood. House specialties include fresh salty oysters, smoked Boston butt and crispy local flounder. **Features:** full bar, patio dining, happy hour. **Address:** 85 Screven St 31305 **Location:** I-95 exit 49 (SR 251), 1.1 mi se to US 17, 1.2 mi s to Broad St (before bridge), then just w.
[L] [D]

DAWSONVILLE (A-3) pop. 2,536, elev. 1,376'

AMICALOLA FALLS STATE PARK is at 280 Amicalola Falls State Park Rd. The 829-acre park features a cascading waterfall—said to be the tallest east of the Mississippi River. Recreational activities include hiking, picnicking and fishing. A visitor center provides nature displays and live exhibits. Interpretive programs also are offered. See Recreation Areas Chart. **Time:** Allow 4 hours minimum. **Hours:** Park open daily 7 a.m.-10 p.m. Visitor center open daily 8:30-5. **Cost:** $5 per vehicle. **Phone:** (706) 265-4703 or (800) 573-9656. [🏕] [††] [✕] [🔔]

QUALITY INN & SUITES (706)216-1900

♥♥♥ Hotel. $91-$191 **Address:** 127 Beartooth Pkwy 30534 **Location:** Jct SR 400/53, 0.5 mi s. **Facility:** 50 units. 2 stories (no elevator), interior corridors. **Amenities:** safes. **Pool(s):** outdoor. **Activities:** exercise room. **Guest Services:** coin laundry.
[††] CALL [LM] [🔧] [BIZ] [📶] [✕] [🔒] [📷] [💻]
/SOME UNITS [🔔]

WHERE TO EAT

CHIN CHIN 706/216-2017 -

♥♥ Chinese. Casual Dining. $7-$23 **AAA Inspector Notes:** Traditional Chinese cuisine is served at this spot and includes many lunch combinations to choose from. Chef's specialties include Beijing duck and the glazed walnut mango prawns. Curries also are on the menu and there is a spa cuisine section for those seeking to dine on something a bit lighter. **Features:** beer & wine. **Address:** 837 Hwy 400 S, Suite 115 30534 **Location:** Jct SR 400/53, 0.8 mi s; in Dawson Promenade. [L] [D] CALL [LM]

EL JINETE   706/531-0012

🔻🔻🔻 Mexican. Casual Dining. $5-$16 **AAA Inspector Notes:** Enjoy Mexican favorites at this family friendly establishment such as tacos, burritos, enchiladas and fajitas as well as some vegetarian options. Yummy libations such as mango, horchata and guayaba margaritas are also popular. **Features:** full bar, patio dining. **Address:** 100 N 400 Center Ln 30534 **Location:** Jct SR 400/53, just n.

🄻 🄳 CALL 🖉M

THE VARSITY   706/265-7273

🔻 Hot Dogs Burgers. Quick Serve. $2-$10 **AAA Inspector Notes:** Be ready to order when you enter this branch of the long-time Atlanta landmark, as the service staff shouts 'What'll you have?' when you enter the line. Chili dogs, slaw dogs and naked dogs share menu space with hamburgers, chicken sandwiches and the signature frozen orange drinks. **Features:** patio dining. **Address:** 73 Bethel Dr 30534 **Location:** Jct SR 400/53, 1.5 mi s. 🄻 🄳

DECATUR pop. 19,335

- **Hotels & Restaurants map & index p. 82, 94**
- **Part of Atlanta area — see map p. 44**

COURTYARD BY MARRIOTT ATLANTA DECATUR DOWNTOWN/EMORY   (404)371-0204 [14]

🔻🔻🔻🔻 Hotel. $142-$233 **Address:** 130 Clairemont Ave 30030 **Location:** Downtown. **Facility:** 179 units. 5 stories, interior corridors. **Parking:** on-site (fee). **Terms:** check-in 4 pm. **Dining:** 2 restaurants. **Pool(s):** heated indoor. **Activities:** exercise room. **Guest Services:** valet and coin laundry, boarding pass kiosk, area transportation.

AAA Benefit: Members save 5% or more!

🍽️ 🍸 CALL 🖉M 🛥️ BIZ 📶 ✕ 🚪 🖥️ ☕ / SOME UNITS 🄷🅂 🖼️

HOLIDAY INN EXPRESS, ATLANTA-EMORY   (404)320-0888 [12]

🔻🔻🔻 Hotel. $109-$249 **Address:** 2183 N Decatur Rd 30033 **Location:** Jct N Decatur and Clairemont rds, just e. **Facility:** 62 efficiencies. 4 stories, interior corridors. **Terms:** cancellation fee imposed, resort fee. **Pool(s):** heated indoor. **Activities:** sauna, exercise room. **Guest Services:** coin laundry, area transportation.

🍽️ CALL 🖉M 🛥️ BIZ 🄷🅂 📶 ✕ 🚪 🖼️ ☕

SUPER 8   (404)378-3765 [13]

🔻🔻🔻 Motel $70-$125

Address: 917 Church St 30030 **Location:** Downtown. **Facility:** 46 units. 3 stories, exterior corridors. **Terms:** cancellation fee imposed. **Activities:** exercise room. **Guest Services:** coin laundry. **Featured Amenity:** continental breakfast.

SAVE 🍽️ CALL 🖉M BIZ 📶 🚪

🖼️ ☕

WHERE TO EAT

ATHENS PIZZA HOUSE   404/636-1100 [10]

🔻🔻🔻 Greek Pizza. Casual Dining. $6-$25 **AAA Inspector Notes:** Mediterranean pizza with gyro meat and feta, Greek salad, pita wraps and hot subs—in addition to moussaka, pastitsio and other home-style specialties prepared from family recipes that have not changed in generations—satisfy all cravings at this spot, a laid-back favorite of families and Emory students. A breezy, inviting feel envelops the spacious patio. **Features:** beer & wine, patio dining. **Address:** 1341 Clairmont Rd 30033 **Location:** Jct N Decatur Rd.

🄻 🄳

BRICK STORE PUB   404/687-0990 [13]

🔻🔻 American. Casual Dining. $9-$18 **AAA Inspector Notes:** A delightful hideaway, this local pub is atypical in that it lacks TVs or loud music. Comfort foods, and intriguing choices such as the "Tittle Pop," are made from fresh ingredients. Trout, lamb loin chops, cast-iron pot pie, pork belly or meatloaf sandwich and traditional fish and chips are just a few of the standard dishes. On hand is an excellent selection of German, English and American craft beers, and the up-stairs Belgian beer bar is specially reserved for those acclaimed Belgian beers. **Features:** full bar, patio dining. **Address:** 125 E Court Square 30030 **Location:** Just s of Ponce de Leon Ave; in historic square. **Parking:** street only. 🄻 🄳 🄻🄰🅃🄴

CAFÉ ALSACE   404/373-5622 [12]

🔻🔻 French. Casual Dining. $10-$34 **AAA Inspector Notes:** The chef here prepares food in the Alsatian style, which blends elements of French and German cuisine from the Alsace region. The dining room is appointed in a rustic French country kitchen style. A choice of quiche or escargot is a good way to begin and such entrées as the lamb loin chops or beef Wellington are quite delicious and filling. No meal here would be complete without some crème brûlée. **Features:** beer & wine, patio dining, Sunday brunch. **Address:** 121 E Ponce de Leon Ave 30030 **Location:** Just w of Church St. **Parking:** street only. 🄻 🄳

CAFE ISTANBUL   404/320-0054 [25]

🔻🔻 Turkish. Casual Dining. $8-$19 **AAA Inspector Notes:** Guests can taste succulent and satisfying Turkish cuisine here at a table or in a relaxing lounge-like setting. Traditional favorites such as hummus, falafel, lamb kebabs and vegetarian moussaka grace the menu as do Istanbul pizza, chicken calzones, salmon and red snapper. The experience is like entering a Middle Eastern habitat, and hookahs are available for smoking. Lunch is served Friday and Saturday. **Features:** beer & wine. **Address:** 1850 Lawrenceville Hwy, Suite 100 30033 **Location:** I-285 exit 39A, 2.3 mi w. 🄳 🝆

CAFE LILY RESTAURANT & WINE BAR   404/371-9119 [15]

🔻🔻 Italian. Casual Dining. $6-$29 **AAA Inspector Notes:** This neighborhood bistro and wine bar is a popular place to gather for a business lunch, a girls' night out or to celebrate with family. The menu offers a variety of classic Italian cuisine and accommodates dietary restrictions such as dairy-free, gluten-free and vegan. **Features:** full bar. **Address:** 308 W Ponce De Leon Ave 30030 **Location:** I-285 exit 48 (SR 155/Flat Shoals Rd), 5.5 mi nw on E Trinity Pl, n on Commerce Dr, then just w. **Parking:** on-site and street.

🄻 🄳 CALL 🖉M 🝆

CAKES & ALE   404/377-7994 [17]

🔻🔻🔻 American. Fine Dining. $9-$35 **AAA Inspector Notes:** Tucked away among the plethora of shops and restaurants in the pedestrian-friendly downtown, this restaurant stands out in a big way with a relaxed elegance and food that will knock your socks off. Options change regularly but some staples include wood-fire grilled rib-eye and whole roasted North Carolina trout. You also can cozy up to the bar and enjoy any one of the specialty cocktails available. Do yourself a favor and give the ecto 1 a try. **Features:** full bar. **Reservations:** suggested. **Address:** 155 Sycamore St 30030 **Location:** North on Church St. **Parking:** street only. 🄳 CALL 🖉M 🝆

CAKES & ALE CAFE   404/377-7994 [16]

🔻 Coffee/Tea. Quick Serve. $6-$16 **AAA Inspector Notes:** The neighboring sister to the popular Cake & Ale restaurant, this café offers a small menu of pastries and sandwiches as well coffee, espresso and tea. In the evenings guests also can enjoy the wine bar selections and small bar menu. The beautiful décor, friendly baristas and delicious options make this spot an excellent choice for your next coffee run. **Address:** 151 Sycamore St 30030 **Location:** Just n on Church St. **Parking:** street only. 🄱 🄻 🄳 CALL 🖉M

FARM BURGER   404/378-5077 [14]

🔻 Burgers. Quick Serve. $7-$10 **AAA Inspector Notes:** The beef here is 100 percent grass fed and comes as a combo or diners can build their own with many ingredients which include jalapeños, fried farm eggs, red bean chili, local bacon and oxtail marmalade. For those not wanting beef, there is a veggie quinoa or chicken burger. Spicy garlic and pimento cheese fries are great sides. Milk shakes also are available. **Features:** beer & wine, patio dining. **Address:** 410B W Ponce de Leon Ave 30030 **Location:** Downtown.

🄻 🄳 CALL 🖉M

(See maps & indexes p. 82, 94.)

J. CHRISTOPHER'S 404/378-2662 (11)

Breakfast. Casual Dining. $5-$12 **AAA Inspector Notes:** Blueberry crunch cakes, strawberry waffles and eggs Christopher are some of the breakfast favorites found here along with such seasonal items as pumpkin pancakes. Many traditional breakfast standards also are available. Lunch favorites include the club house burger and the classic club sandwich. Waldorf salads and signature soups are popular. **Address:** 250 E Ponce de Leon Ave 30030 **Location:** Downtown. **Parking:** street only.

B L CALL &M

LAWRENCE'S CAFE 404/320-7756 (20)

Lebanese. Casual Dining. $6-$21 **AAA Inspector Notes:** For a taste of the exotic Middle East stop into this small family restaurant. The kitchen serves up delicious dishes such as the sultan's feast with a combination of beef kebab, kafta rolls, falafel and brown rice. Vegetarians options also are available. **Features:** beer & wine. **Address:** 910 W College Ave 30030 **Location:** Between Cambridge and Feld aves. L D

REVIVAL 470/225-6770 (19)

Southern American. Casual Dining. $5-$20 **AAA Inspector Notes:** When people visit the South they often seek out an authentic Southern experience. This restaurant offers not only the classic cuisine we are known for but it provides a down-home hospitality that makes people come back for more. The menu changes regularly but they focus on locally sourced ingredients. Guests rave about Kevin's secret recipe cornbread but my mouth waters for the succulent bacon-wrapped meatloaf. Menu items are served family style so bring friends and your appetite. **Features:** full bar. **Reservations:** suggested. **Address:** 129 Church St 30030 **Location:** I-285 exit 48 (SR 155), 5.5 mi n on Chandler Rd (SR 155), just nw on Trinity Pl. **Parking:** valet and street only. D CALL &M

THE SPRIG 404/248-9700 (24)

American. Casual Dining. $9-$21 **AAA Inspector Notes:** This casual, neighborhood restaurant offers a delicious menu of fresh and innovative dishes. The friendly staff, contemporary, industrial design and spacious outdoor seating encourages guests to enjoy a culinary experience. **Features:** full bar, patio dining. **Reservations:** suggested. **Address:** 2860 La Vista Rd 30033 **Location:** Jct Lavista Rd and Oak Grove Rd; in Vista Grove Plaza.

L D CALL &M

UNIVERSAL JOINT 404/373-6260 (21)

American. Casual Dining. $7-$12 **AAA Inspector Notes:** In a converted garage, this funky joint has a large patio for outdoor dining. The atmosphere is extremely relaxed, and good, simple foods and beverages are the focus. A Mecca for burgers, wings, sandwiches, salads and healthy bar food. Tacos and quesadillas also are popular items. The chicharonnes or spicy egg rolls are a good way to start the meal. **Features:** full bar, patio dining. **Address:** 906 Oakview Rd 30030 **Location:** Corner of East Lake Dr; adjacent to Oakhurst Park. **Parking:** on-site and street. L D

VICTORY SANDWICH BAR 404/377-9300 (18)

Sandwiches. Casual Dining. $3-$10 **AAA Inspector Notes:** This fun local hangout offers a distinctive twist on pub food. It's open late to satisfy those midnight cravings for gastro delights, such as the "Beast on Yeast" pot roast sandwich or the "Banh Appetit for Destruction" (char-siu pork) sandwich. Ask about the daily flavor of popcorn or the Jack and Coke slushie for a fun treat. **Features:** full bar, patio dining. **Address:** 340 Church St 30030 **Location:** Jct Sycamore and Church sts. **Parking:** on-site and street.

L D LATE CALL &M

DILLARD pop. 339

GATEWAY HOTEL & SUITES DILLARD 706/746-3585

Hotel. Rates not provided. **Address:** 64 White Oak Ln 30537 **Location:** Just n on US 441. **Facility:** 65 units. 2 stories, interior corridors. **Terms:** check-in 4 pm. **Pool(s):** heated indoor. **Activities:** hot tub.

CALL &M

DORAVILLE pop. 8,330

- **Hotels & Restaurants map & index p. 82**
- **Part of Atlanta area — see map p. 44**

GYRO GYRO 770/352-4976 (112)

Guatemalan. Casual Dining. $6-$13 **AAA Inspector Notes:** Come in for a quick bite featuring gyros, falafel, salads and baklava. The portions are generous and there is no reason guests should leave hungry. **Address:** 5000 Winters Chapel Rd 30360 **Location:** SR 141 (Peachtree Industrial Blvd), 1.8 mi ne to Winters Chapel Rd exit, 0.8 mi n. L D CALL &M

DOUGLAS (E-4) pop. 11,589, elev. 275'

Douglas was platted in 1858 on 50 acres of land donated by J. S. Pearson and named for Stephen A. Douglas, a presidential candidate running against Abraham Lincoln. Douglas, the seat of Coffee County, has a bustling downtown and a thriving economy with a strong industrial and agricultural influence. Recreational opportunities abound in nearby General Coffee State Park *(see Recreation Areas Chart)*.

More than 500 species of plants native to Georgia may be seen at Broxton Rocks Preserve. Guided hikes of the site are provided and require a reservation; phone (404) 253-7255.

Douglas Visitor Information Center: 211 S. Gaskin Ave., Douglas, GA 31533. **Phone:** (912) 384-4555.

HAMPTON INN DOUGLAS (912)383-7550

Hotel. $119-$164 **Address:** 1604 S Peterson Ave 31533 **Location:** Jct US 221/441/SR 31 and SR 206/353, just s. **Facility:** 61 units. 3 stories, interior corridors. **Terms:** 1-7 night minimum stay, cancellation fee imposed. **Pool(s):** outdoor. **Activities:** exercise room. **Guest Services:** valet laundry.

AAA Benefit: Members save up to 10%!

CALL &M BIZ / SOME UNITS HS

HOLIDAY INN EXPRESS HOTEL & SUITES 912/384-2100

Hotel. Rates not provided. **Address:** 1636 S Peterson Ave 31535 **Location:** Jct US 221/441/SR 31 and SR 206/353, just s. **Facility:** 65 units. 4 stories, interior corridors. **Pool(s):** indoor. **Activities:** sauna, exercise room. **Guest Services:** valet and coin laundry.

CALL &M BIZ HS

WHERE TO EAT

DANNY'S PIZZA 912/384-2270

Pizza. Casual Dining. $4-$17 **AAA Inspector Notes:** The bright red wood door on this stucco, arched brick Mediterranean-style structure is a warm, welcoming invitation to enter. Inside you'll find red-and-white checker, vinyl-covered tables and walls full of memorabilia covering the span of 1973 (when the restaurant opened) to the present. This was the first pizza joint within a 50 mile radius when it first opened. Its longevity is a testament to the customer loyalty of the quality foods offered here. Expect relaxed and casual service. **Features:** beer & wine. **Address:** 218 W Ward St 31533 **Location:** Between Tanner St and Columbia Ave; downtown.

L D CALL &M

Visit the AAA and CAA senior driving websites for tips to help you drive safely longer

J&D CAFE
912/384-8948

▼▼ Southern American. Casual Dining. $6-$15 **AAA Inspector Notes:** For those who say small towns cannot have elevated eating establishments, this café proves that you can have delicious food, a stylish atmosphere and small town charm. The menu features updated Southern cuisine ranging from shrimp and grits to J&D's own interpretation of tomato pie. My personal favorite is the blue plate special and creamy grape salad. After lunch browse the shop for cookbooks, home décor and distinctive gift options. **Reservations:** suggested. **Address:** 254 S Peterson Ave 31533 **Location:** US 280 E to Peterson Ave, just s. **Parking:** on-site and street.

[L] CALL [&M]

DOUGLASVILLE pop. 30,961
• Part of Atlanta area — see map p. 44

DAYS INN
(770)949-1499

▼▼ Motel. $58-$100 **Address:** 5489 Westmoreland Plaza 30134 **Location:** I-20 exit 37, just n. **Facility:** 57 units. 2 stories (no elevator), exterior corridors. **Pool(s):** outdoor. **Guest Services:** coin laundry.

[≈] [HS] [⊚] [🛏] [▣] [▢] / SOME UNITS [⛾]

ECONO LODGE INN & SUITES
(770)489-4863

▼▼ Hotel. $60-$165 **Address:** 8304 Cherokee Blvd 30134 **Location:** I-20 exit 37, just n to Cherokee Blvd, then just e. **Facility:** 56 units. 3 stories, interior corridors. **Pool(s):** outdoor. **Activities:** exercise room. **Guest Services:** coin laundry.

CALL [&M] [≈] [BIZ] [HS] [⊚] [🛏] [▣] [▢] / SOME UNITS [⛾]

HOLIDAY INN EXPRESS-ATLANTA WEST
770/920-9228

▼▼▼ Hotel. Rates not provided. **Address:** 7101 Concourse Pkwy 30134 **Location:** I-20 exit 34, just n. **Facility:** 100 units. 5 stories, interior corridors. **Pool(s):** outdoor. **Activities:** exercise room. **Guest Services:** coin laundry.

[¶↑] CALL [&M] [≈] [BIZ] [⊚] [✕] [🛏] [▣] [▢]

LA QUINTA INN & SUITES ATLANTA DOUGLASVILLE
(770)577-3838

▼▼▼ Hotel. $75-$170 **Address:** 1000 Linnenkohl Dr 30134 **Location:** I-20 exit 34, just n. **Facility:** 90 units. 5 stories, interior corridors. **Pool(s):** outdoor. **Activities:** exercise room. **Guest Services:** coin laundry.

[¶↑] CALL [&M] [≈] [BIZ] [HS] [⊚] [✕] [🛏] [▣] [▢] / SOME UNITS [⛾]

SLEEP INN
(770)920-8887

▼▼ Hotel. $69-$89 **Address:** 7055 Concourse Pkwy 30134 **Location:** I-20 exit 34, just n to Concourse Pkwy, then just e. **Facility:** 60 units. 3 stories, interior corridors. *Bath:* shower only.

[¶↑] CALL [&M] [BIZ] [⊚] [🛏] [▣] [▢]

WHERE TO EAT

ATLANTIC BUFFET
678/838-8883

▼▼ Asian. Casual Dining. $7-$10 **AAA Inspector Notes:** Diners can find a mind-boggling assortment of sushi, shrimp, mussels and other saltwater delights. Landlubbers can choose from American, Italian, traditional Chinese and Japanese courses. Hibachi-grilled favorites can be enjoyed here as well. **Address:** 7090 Concourse Pkwy 30134 **Location:** I-20 exit 34, just n to Concourse Pkwy, then just e. [L] [D] CALL [&M]

GUMBEAUX'S, A CAJUN CAFE
770/947-8288

▼▼ Cajun. Casual Dining. $10-$30 **AAA Inspector Notes:** The spicy Cajun and New Orleans-style food is as close to authentic as diners can find without actually making the trip to Louisiana. A bayou-style atmosphere adds to the delicious food. The menu is almost exclusively traditional Cajun dishes and seafood. Make sure you save room for homemade desserts! **Features:** full bar. **Address:** 6712 E Broad St 30134 **Location:** I-20 exit 36, 2 mi n on Campbellton St, then just w. **Parking:** street only. [L] [D]

IRISH BRED PUB
678/324-1649

▼▼ Irish. Casual Dining. $9-$18 **AAA Inspector Notes:** Located along the quaint streets of historic downtown, this classic Irish pub serves up delicious favorites in a lively atmosphere. A heaping helping of fish and chips, salmon cakes and bangers and mash is sure to put guests in the Irish spirit. For those not in the mood for a meal, cozy up to the bar for a pint or gather on the patio for music and socializing. **Features:** full bar. **Address:** 6682 Broad St 31034 **Location:** I-20 exit 37, 2.1 mi n on SR 92, then just w. **Parking:** on-site and street. [L] CALL [&M]

SEA BREEZE SEAFOOD RESTAURANT
770/577-9400

▼▼ Seafood. Casual Dining. $5-$25 **AAA Inspector Notes:** This casual, family eatery serves up a variety of fresh seafood from shrimp and salmon to crab legs and lobster tails. For the land lubbers in the party there is also a generous selection of steaks, chicken and pasta dishes. **Features:** beer & wine, senior menu. **Address:** 9610 Hwy 5 30135 **Location:** I-20 exit 34, 0.4 mi s.

[L] [D] CALL [&M]

TASTE OF THAI
770/577-4142

▼▼ Thai. Casual Dining. $7-$26 **AAA Inspector Notes:** This great little find offers some delicious Thai cuisine. There are many curries, specialties and noodle dishes found here. The sea bass is pan fried and topped off with sweet, sour and ginger sauce and the lamb rack is marinated in exotic spices and served with a red curry sauce. Pan-steamed mussels are a good way to start as is the spicy seafood soup. **Features:** beer & wine. **Address:** 2911 Chapel Hill Rd, Suite 245 30135 **Location:** I-20 exit 36, 0.4 mi s; in Douglasville Promenade. [L] [D] CALL [&M]

DUBLIN pop. 16,201

HOLIDAY INN EXPRESS HOTEL & SUITES
(478)272-7862

▼▼▼ Hotel. $95-$179 **Address:** 2192 Hwy 441 S 31021 **Location:** I-16 exit 51 (US 441), just n. **Facility:** 92 units. 3 stories, interior corridors. **Terms:** cancellation fee imposed. **Pool(s):** outdoor. **Activities:** exercise room. **Guest Services:** valet and coin laundry.

[¶↑] CALL [&M] [≈] [BIZ] [HS] [⊚] [✕] [🛏] [▣] [▢]

JAMESON INN DUBLIN
478/275-1600

▼▼ Hotel. Rates not provided. **Address:** 2108 Hwy 441 S 31021 **Location:** I-16 exit 51 (US 441), 0.6 mi n. **Facility:** 71 units. 2 stories (no elevator), exterior corridors. **Pool(s):** outdoor. **Guest Services:** valet laundry.

[¶↑] CALL [&M] [≈] [BIZ] [⊚] [▢] / SOME UNITS [🛏] [▣]

LA QUINTA INN & SUITES DUBLIN
(478)272-3110

▼▼▼ Hotel. $86-$196 **Address:** 101 Travel Center Blvd 31021 **Location:** I-16 exit 51 (US 441), just s. Located behind the Cracker Barrel. **Facility:** 69 units. 3 stories, interior corridors. **Amenities:** safes. **Pool(s):** heated indoor. **Activities:** hot tub, exercise room. **Guest Services:** valet and coin laundry.

[¶↑] CALL [&M] [≈] [BIZ] [HS] [⊚] [✕] [🛏] [▣] [▢] / SOME UNITS [⛾]

WHERE TO EAT

COMPANY SUPPLY
478/353-1655

▼▼▼ Southern American. Casual Dining. $5-$22 **AAA Inspector Notes:** Proving that quality dining experiences are not limited to big cities, this small town jewel serves delicious cuisine with a heaping side of Southern hospitality. The delta chicken with roasted garlic mash potatoes is a crowd favorite as is the scrumptious sweet potato cheesecake. Menu options change depending on what is in season, so ask your server for recommendations. **Features:** full bar. **Address:** 107 W Jackson St 31021 **Location:** In historic downtown. **Parking:** street only. [L] [D] CALL [&M]

DEANO'S ITALIAN
478/275-1117

▽▽▽ Italian. Casual Dining. $7-$20 **AAA Inspector Notes:** This restaurant is worth the detour! Nestled in the quaint streets of downtown, they serve up delicious Italian favorites and brick oven pizzas. My favorite is the Margherita pizza. Fantastico! **Features:** beer & wine, patio dining. **Address:** 112 W Jackson St 31021 **Location:** US 441, just w. L D

SONNY'S REAL PIT BAR-B-Q
478/275-7180

▽▽ Barbecue. Casual Dining. $8-$17 **AAA Inspector Notes:** Bearing the name after its founder, Floyd "Sonny" Tillman, this barbecue restaurant first opened its doors circa 1968 in Gainesville, Florida and has since spawned over 150 more throughout the Southeast. The menu is steeped in finger lickin' favorites such as ribs, pulled pork, beef brisket, burgers, catfish, shrimp and chargrilled chicken. Let's not forget about the fried okra, which is the perfect starter dish, and their homemade baked beans. **Features:** beer only. **Address:** 2201 Veterans Blvd 31021 **Location:** 3 mi w on US 80/SR 26. L D

DULUTH (G-4) pop. 26,600, elev. 1,100'
• **Hotels & Restaurants map & index p. 90**
• **Part of Atlanta area — see map p. 44**

🌸 JapanFest, held in mid-September at the Gwinnett Center, celebrates Japanese cultural traditions, including clothing, cuisine, flower arrangements, martial arts, dance and music. Several workshops instruct attendees in kite construction and the paper art of origami.

Explore Gwinnett: 6500 Sugarloaf Pkwy., Suite 200, Duluth, GA 30097. **Phone:** (770) 623-3600 or (888) 494-6638.

SOUTHEASTERN RAILWAY MUSEUM is at 3595 Buford Hwy. The 35-acre site features more than 80 items of rolling stock including Pullman cars, steam locomotives and restored cabooses. Other transportation vehicles include vintage firefighting equipment, buses and streetcars. Visitors can climb aboard and explore many items. Ten- to 15-minute historic train rides and park train rides are regularly available. Closed-toe, low-heeled shoes are recommended.

Time: Allow 1 hour minimum. **Hours:** Tues.-Sat. 10-5, June-July; Wed.-Sat. 10-5, Mar.-May and Aug.-Dec.; Thurs.-Sat. 10-5, rest of year. Closed Jan. 1, Thanksgiving and Christmas. **Cost:** $10; $8 (ages 65+); $7 (ages 2-12). Historic train ride or park train ride $3. Phone ahead to confirm schedule and train ride availability. **Phone:** (770) 476-2013. GT

BEST WESTERN GWINNETT CENTER HOTEL
(770)935-7171 **27**

▽▽▽
Hotel
$79-$129

AAA Benefit: Save 10% or more every day and earn 10% bonus points!

Address: 3670 Shackleford Rd 30096 **Location:** I-85 exit 104, just e to Shackleford Rd, then just s. **Facility:** 68 units. 3 stories, interior corridors. **Terms:** cancellation fee imposed. **Pool(s):** outdoor. **Activities:** exercise room. **Guest Services:** valet laundry.

SAVE ▯↑ CALL &M 🛁 BIZ 🛜 ✕ ▯ 🍽 💻

CANDLEWOOD SUITES-ATLANTA
678/380-0414 **26**

▽▽ **Extended Stay Hotel.** Rates not provided. **Address:** 3665 Shackleford Rd 30096 **Location:** I-85 exit 104, just e, then just s. **Facility:** 122 efficiencies. 3 stories, interior corridors. **Activities:** exercise room. **Guest Services:** complimentary and valet laundry.

▯↑ CALL &M BIZ HS 🛜 ▯ 🍽 💻 / SOME UNITS 🐾

COURTYARD BY MARRIOTT ATLANTA DULUTH/ GWINNETT PLACE
(770)476-4666 **23**

▽▽▽
Hotel
$79-$145

COURTYARD Marriott
AAA Benefit: Members save 5% or more!

Address: 3550 Venture Pkwy 30096 **Location:** I-85 exit 104, just w to Venture Pkwy, then just n. **Facility:** 146 units. 3 stories, interior corridors. **Pool(s):** outdoor. **Activities:** exercise room. **Guest Services:** valet and coin laundry.

SAVE ▯↑ CALL &M 🛁 BIZ 🛜 ✕ 💻 / SOME UNITS ▯ 🍽

EXTENDED STAY AMERICA-ATLANTA-GWINNETT PLACE
(770)623-6800 **21**

▽▽ **Extended Stay Hotel.** $70-$85 **Address:** 3390 Venture Pkwy NW 30096 **Location:** I-85 exit 104, just w to Venture Pkwy, then just n. **Facility:** 114 efficiencies. 6 stories, interior corridors. **Terms:** cancellation fee imposed. **Pool(s):** outdoor. **Activities:** exercise room. **Guest Services:** coin laundry.

▯↑ CALL &M 🛁 🛜 ▯ 🍽 💻 / SOME UNITS 🐾

FAIRFIELD INN & SUITES BY MARRIOTT ATLANTA GWINNETT PLACE
(678)924-1023 **25**

▽▽▽ **Hotel.** $87-$149 **Address:** 3570 Breckinridge Blvd 30096 **Location:** I-85 exit 104, just e to Shackleford Rd, then just n. **Facility:** 112 units. 5 stories, interior corridors. **Pool(s):** heated indoor. **Activities:** exercise room. **Guest Services:** valet and coin laundry, area transportation.

AAA Benefit: Members save 5% or more!

CALL &M 🛁 BIZ HS 🛜 ✕ ▯ 🍽 💻

HAMPTON INN & SUITES-GWINNETT
(770)931-9800 **30**

▽▽▽ **Hotel.** $89-$159 **Address:** 1725 Pineland Rd 30096 **Location:** I-85 exit 104, 0.3 mi e to Crestwood, then just s. **Facility:** 136 units, some kitchens. 8 stories, interior corridors. **Terms:** 1-7 night minimum stay, cancellation fee imposed. **Pool(s):** outdoor. **Activities:** exercise room. **Guest Services:** valet and coin laundry.

AAA Benefit: Members save up to 10%!

▯↑ CALL &M 🛁 BIZ HS 🛜 ✕ 🐕 💻 / SOME UNITS ▯ 🍽

(See map & index p. 90.)

HILTON GARDEN INN-ATLANTA NE
(770)495-7600 **20**

▼▼▼ **Hotel.** $101-$199 **Address:** 2040 Sugarloaf Cir 30097 **Location:** I-85 exit 108, just w. **Facility:** 122 units. 5 stories, interior corridors. **Terms:** 1-7 night minimum stay, cancellation fee imposed. **Pool(s):** heated indoor. **Activities:** hot tub, exercise room. **Guest Services:** valet and coin laundry, area transportation.

AAA Benefit: Members save up to 10%!

HOLIDAY INN EXPRESS & SUITES GWINNETT CENTER
678/405-2900 **24**

▼▼▼ **Hotel.** Rates not provided. **Address:** 3530 Breckinridge Blvd 30096 **Location:** I-85 exit 104, just e to Shackleford Rd, then just n. **Facility:** 104 units. 5 stories, interior corridors. **Amenities:** *Some:* safes. **Pool(s):** heated indoor. **Activities:** exercise room. **Guest Services:** valet and coin laundry, area transportation.

HOLIDAY INN-GWINNETT CENTER
770/476-2022 **19**

▼▼▼ **Hotel.** Rates not provided. **Address:** 6310 Sugarloaf Pkwy 30097 **Location:** I-85 exit 108, just w. **Facility:** 143 units. 6 stories, interior corridors. **Amenities:** safes. **Pool(s):** heated indoor. **Activities:** exercise room. **Guest Services:** valet and coin laundry, area transportation.

HYATT PLACE ATLANTA/DULUTH/GWINNETT MALL
(770)623-9699 **22**

▼▼▼ Hotel $69-$179

HYATT PLACE

AAA Benefit: Members save 10%!

Address: 3530 Venture Pkwy 30096 **Location:** I-85 exit 104, just w to Venture Pkwy, then just n. **Facility:** 123 units. 6 stories, interior corridors. **Terms:** cancellation fee imposed. **Pool(s):** outdoor. **Activities:** exercise room. **Guest Services:** valet laundry, area transportation. **Featured Amenity:** full hot breakfast.

RESIDENCE INN BY MARRIOTT ATLANTA GWINNETT PLACE
(770)921-2202 **29**

▼▼▼ **Extended Stay Hotel.** $89-$183 **Address:** 1760 Pineland Rd 30096 **Location:** I-85 exit 104, just e to Shackleford Rd, just s to Pineland Rd, then just e. **Facility:** 132 units, some two bedrooms, efficiencies and kitchens. 3 stories, interior corridors. **Pool(s):** outdoor. **Activities:** playground, exercise room. **Guest Services:** valet and coin laundry, area transportation.

AAA Benefit: Members save 5% or more!

RESIDENCE INN BY MARRIOTT ATLANTA NE/DULUTH SUGARLOAF
(770)814-2929 **18**

▼▼▼ **Extended Stay Hotel.** $103-$229 **Address:** 1940 Satellite Blvd 30097 **Location:** I-85 exit 108, 0.8 mi e. **Facility:** 112 units, some two bedrooms. 6 stories, interior corridors. **Pool(s):** outdoor. **Activities:** exercise room. **Guest Services:** valet and coin laundry.

AAA Benefit: Members save 5% or more!

SONESTA GWINNETT PLACE ATLANTA
770/923-1775 **28**

▼▼▼ Hotel
Rates not provided

Address: 1775 Pleasant Hill Rd 30096 **Location:** I-85 exit 104, just e. **Facility:** 426 units. 9-17 stories, interior corridors. **Terms:** check-in 4 pm. **Dining:** 2 restaurants. **Pool(s):** heated outdoor, heated indoor. **Activities:** hot tub, exercise room. **Guest Services:** valet and coin laundry, area transportation.

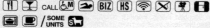
WHERE TO EAT

BAHAMA BREEZE
770/935-6509 **19**

▼▼▼ Caribbean. Casual Dining. $11-$22 **AAA Inspector Notes:** A tropical feel resonates throughout via bright colors, a Caribbean-inspired menu and music that would make Jimmy Buffett dance. The menu features something for everyone with fresh seafood, chicken dishes, pastas and steaks. The empanadas are a great way to start before moving on to the entree. Herbs and spices native to the Caribbean are used throughout the menu. **Features:** full bar, patio dining, happy hour. **Address:** 3590 Breckinridge Blvd 30096 **Location:** I-85 exit 104, just e.

BREAKER'S KOREAN BAR-B-Q
770/946-1000 **17**

▼▼▼ Korean. Fine Dining. $5-$35 **AAA Inspector Notes:** Everyone should try Korean barbecue at least once in their lives and this is the perfect place to start. The menu is full of delectable options such as lobster tails, squid, chicken and pork ribs. Classic Korean cuisine includes dwenjang jiigae (soybean paste soup), jeyuk (pork stir fry) and tofu steak for a meatless treat. Dinner turns into a dining experience when you get the opportunity to cook your desired meat on the table-top grill and then assemble each bite with a variety of toppings. **Features:** full bar. **Reservations:** suggested. **Address:** 3505 Gwinnett Place Dr 30096 **Location:** I-85 exit 104 (Pleasant Hill Rd), just n, then 0.5 mi e.

CALIFORNIA DREAMING
770/813-9240

▼▼ American. Casual Dining. $9-$30 **AAA Inspector Notes:** This full-service restaurant appeals to adults, particularly those with an appetite for innovative concepts in food. Revised weekly, the menu consistently incorporates sophisticated, cutting-edge California dishes with Pacific Rim influences throughout. Among house specialties are flatbread appetizers baked in a brick oven, sushi, sashimi and some vegetarian dishes. The wine list focuses primarily on California vintages. **Features:** full bar, patio dining. **Address:** 1630 Cross Pointe Way 30097 **Location:** I-85 exit 108, just w, then just s.

HARU ICHIBAN JAPANESE RESTAURANT
770/622-4060 **18**

▼▼ Japanese. Casual Dining. $5-$37 **AAA Inspector Notes:** This restaurant feels so authentic, like it was plucked out of Japan and plopped down here. The menu features a blend of traditional and contemporary Japanese cuisine including a wide variety of sushi, noodles and grilled favorites. Ask the server about the sake and beer selection. **Features:** beer & wine. **Address:** 3646 Satellite Blvd 30096 **Location:** I-85 exit 104, 0.3 mi w; in Mall Corners Shopping Center.

KURT'S EURO BISTRO
770/623-4128 **14**

▼▼▼ European. Fine Dining. $12-$48 **AAA Inspector Notes:** For more than 25 years this family-owned restaurant has been serving up contemporary European cuisine. Enjoy a fine dining experience with gracious servers and delicious dishes such as Wiener schnitzel, spaetzle Black Forest (with bacon and mushrooms) and a smoked pork chop with red cabbage. A flambé dessert or a Bavarian-style chocolate cake is the perfect ending to a nice meal. **Features:** full bar, patio dining, happy hour. **Reservations:** suggested. **Address:** 3305 Peachtree Industrial Blvd, Suite 100 30096 **Location:** Jct River Green Pkwy; in The Village at River Green.

(See map & index p. 90.)

LA MADELEINE COUNTRY FRENCH CAFE   770/814-0355

◈ Traditional French Breakfast. Casual Dining. $6-$13 **AAA Inspector Notes:** A fireplace creates the focal point at this cozy European style café where you can always get a quiche or savory stuffed puffed pastry on the go or stick around for a chicken crêpe or French dip sandwich. Heartier entrées like rotisserie chicken are offered and every season promises menu surprises. Whatever you decide on you probably will not get out the door without enjoying one of their tempting sweet pastries. **Features:** beer & wine. **Address:** 2255 Pleasant Hill Rd, Suite 480 30096 **Location:** I-85 exit 104, just n.

(B) (L) (D)

MARLOW'S TAVERN   770/622-2033 15

◈ ◈ American. Gastropub. $9-$17 **AAA Inspector Notes:** With the vibe of a favorite neighborhood tavern, guests quickly feel right at home at this restaurant. Stop in for lunch with the family or for a round of after-work drinks. Try the delicious asparagus fries with tarragon, citrus aioli dipping sauce or one of the classic burgers and sandwiches on the menu. This place is so popular in the evenings that there may be a wait but I think all will agree that it is worth it. **Features:** full bar. **Address:** 1950 Satellite Blvd, Suite 300 30097 **Location:** I-85 exit 108 (Sugarloaf Pkwy), 0.8 mi w, just w on W Sugarloaf Pkwy, then just n. (L) (D) CALL ⑤M

PURE TAQUERIA   770/609-2630

◈ ◈ Mexican. Casual Dining. $9-$19 **AAA Inspector Notes:** This restaurant is a blend of retro décor and classic Mexican cuisine. Set in a 1950s gas station in trendy downtown, this spot serves up food that will make your mouth water. Tacos are popular and I recommend the puerco al pastor with marinated pork, pineapple salsa and Chihuahua cheese. The fajitas, burritos and torta Cubano also are crowd favorites. **Features:** beer only. **Address:** 3108 Main St 30096 **Location:** I-85 exit 104 (Pleasant Hill Rd), 3 mi e on Buford Hwy, 1.6 mi on W Lawrence St, then just w. **Parking:** on-site and street.

(L) (D) CALL ⑤M

SEO RA BEOL   770/497-1155 16

◈ ◈ Korean. Casual Dining. $8-$40 **AAA Inspector Notes:** A mind-boggling array of menu options are available here but the authentic Korean barbecue is the big draw. I had the short ribs and they were tender and succulent. In addition to the ribs, the lunch plate comes with the standard wide array of complimentary sides as well as fried tempura items, soup, salad and sushi. The stews and bibim bap are solid choices as well. Keep in mind although this place is always open, breakfast is not served. **Features:** full bar. **Address:** 3040 Steve Reynolds Blvd 30096 **Location:** I-85 exit 104, 1 mi w.

(B) (L) (D) (24) CALL ⑤M (🍴)

EAST ELLIJAY pop. 546

BEST WESTERN MOUNTAIN VIEW INN   (706)515-1500

Hotel
$85-$150

Best Western **AAA Benefit:** Save 10% or more every day and earn 10% bonus points!

Address: 43 Coosawattee Dr 30540 **Location:** 0.8 mi s on SR 515. **Facility:** 50 units. 2 stories (no elevator), interior corridors. **Terms:** 3 day cancellation notice, resort fee. **Pool(s):** heated indoor. **Activities:** hot tub. **Guest Services:** valet laundry. **Featured Amenity:** continental breakfast.

(SAVE) CALL ⑤M (🛒) (BIZ) (HS) (📶)
(✕) (🖥) /SOME UNITS (🍴) (🔲)

EAST POINT (I-3) pop. 33,712, elev. 1,047'
- **Hotels & Restaurants map & index p. 94**
- **Part of Atlanta area — see map p. 44**

East Point is located 7 miles south of downtown and 3 miles northwest of the Atlanta International Airport and the Georgia International Convention Center. This suburb of Atlanta, with MARTA rail access, is a nice option for travelers who are looking to be close to shopping and dining options without being in the hustle and bustle of downtown Atlanta.

COUNTRY INN & SUITES BY CARLSON, ATLANTA-AIRPORT NORTH   404/767-9787 31

◈ ◈ ◈ **Hotel.** Rates not provided. **Address:** 1365 Hardin Ave 30344 **Location:** I-85 exit 73 southbound; exit 73B northbound, just w. **Facility:** 71 units. 3 stories, interior corridors. **Amenities:** safes. **Pool(s):** indoor. **Activities:** hot tub, exercise room. **Guest Services:** valet and coin laundry.

(🔀) (🍴) CALL ⑤M (🛒) (BIZ) (HS) (📶) (✕) (🔲) (🔲)
(🔲)

CROWNE PLAZA ATLANTA AIRPORT   (404)768-6660 33

◈ ◈ ◈ **Hotel.** $99-$199 **Address:** 1325 Virginia Ave 30344 **Location:** I-85 exit 73 southbound; exit 73B northbound, just w. **Facility:** 378 units. 12 stories, interior corridors. **Parking:** on-site (fee) and valet. **Terms:** cancellation fee imposed. **Dining:** Benton's Grill, see separate listing. **Pool(s):** outdoor. **Activities:** exercise room. **Guest Services:** valet and coin laundry.

(🔀) (🍴) (🏋) CALL ⑤M (🛒) (BIZ) (📶) (✕) (🖥)
/SOME UNITS (🛏) (🔲)

DOUBLETREE BY HILTON HOTEL ATLANTA AIRPORT   (404)763-1600 26

◈ ◈ ◈ **Hotel.** $109-$189 **Address:** 3400 Norman Berry Dr 30344 **Location:** I-85 exit 73B northbound; exit 73 southbound, just e to Bobby Brown Pkwy, 0.4 mi n to Norman Berry Dr, then just s. **Facility:** 220 units. 6 stories, interior corridors. **Parking:** on-site (fee). **Terms:** 1-7 night minimum stay, cancellation fee imposed. **Pool(s):** outdoor. **Activities:** hot tub, exercise room. **Guest Services:** valet laundry, area transportation.

AAA Benefit: Members save 5% or more!

(🔀) (🍴) (🏋) (🍷) CALL ⑤M (🛒) (BIZ) (HS) (📶) (✕)
(🔲) /SOME UNITS (🔲) (🔲)

DRURY INN & SUITES-ATLANTA AIRPORT   (404)761-4900 32

◈ ◈ ◈ **Hotel.** $89-$179 **Address:** 1270 Virginia Ave 30344 **Location:** I-85 exit 73 southbound; exit 73A northbound, just e. **Facility:** 151 units. 6 stories, interior corridors. **Terms:** cancellation fee imposed. **Pool(s):** heated outdoor, heated indoor. **Activities:** hot tub, exercise room. **Guest Services:** valet and coin laundry.

(🔀) (🍴) CALL ⑤M (🛒) (BIZ) (HS) (📶) (✕) (🔲) (🔲)
(🔲) /SOME UNITS (🛏)

FAIRFIELD INN & SUITES BY MARRIOTT ATLANTA AIRPORT NORTH   (404)767-5374 27

◈ ◈ **Hotel.** $94-$156 **Address:** 1255 Walker Ave 30344 **Location:** I-85 exit 73 southbound; exit 73B northbound, just e to Bobby Brown Pkwy, then just n. **Facility:** 85 units. 6 stories, interior corridors. **Pool(s):** outdoor. **Activities:** exercise room. **Guest Services:** valet and coin laundry.

AAA Benefit: Members save 5% or more!

(🔀) CALL ⑤M (🛒) (BIZ) (HS) (📶) (✕) (🔲) (🔲) (🔲)

Turn your road trip dreams into reality
with the TripTik® Travel Planner

(See map & index p. 94.)

HAMPTON INN & SUITES-ATLANTA AIRPORT NORTH
(404)767-9300 **29**

▼▼▼ **Hotel.** $109-$179 **Address:** 3450 Bobby Brown Pkwy 30344 **Location:** I-85 exit 73 southbound; exit 73B northbound, just e to Bobby Brown Pkwy, then just n. **Facility:** 105 units. 8 stories, interior corridors. **Terms:** 1-7 night minimum stay, cancellation fee imposed. **Pool(s):** outdoor. **Activities:** exercise room. **Guest Services:** valet and coin laundry, area transportation.

AAA Benefit: Members save up to 10%!

HILTON GARDEN INN-ATLANTA AIRPORT NORTH
(404)477-6600 **30**

▼▼▼ **Hotel.** $162-$172 **Address:** 3437 Bobby Brown Pkwy 30344 **Location:** I-85 exit 73 southbound; exit 73B northbound, just e to Bobby Brown Pkwy, then just n. **Facility:** 174 units. 7 stories, interior corridors. **Terms:** 1-7 night minimum stay, cancellation fee imposed. **Pool(s):** outdoor, heated indoor. **Activities:** hot tub, exercise room. **Guest Services:** valet and coin laundry.

AAA Benefit: Members save up to 10%!

HOLIDAY INN & SUITES ATLANTA AIRPORT-NORTH
404/305-9990 **34**

▼▼▼ Hotel
Rates not provided

Address: 1380 Virginia Ave 30344 **Location:** I-85 exit 73 southbound; exit 73B northbound, just w. **Facility:** 330 units. 4 stories, interior corridors. **Parking:** on-site (fee). **Pool(s):** outdoor. **Activities:** exercise room. **Guest Services:** valet and coin laundry, boarding pass kiosk.

HYATT PLACE ATLANTA AIRPORT-NORTH
(404)768-8484 **28**

▼▼▼ Hotel
$94-$189

HYATT PLACE
AAA Benefit: Members save 10%!

Address: 3415 Norman Berry Dr 30344 **Location:** I-85 exit 73B northbound; exit 73 southbound, just e to Bobby Brown Pkwy, then just n. **Facility:** 150 units. 6 stories, interior corridors. **Terms:** cancellation fee imposed. **Amenities:** safes. **Pool(s):** outdoor. **Activities:** exercise room. **Guest Services:** valet laundry. **Featured Amenity:** full hot breakfast.

WHERE TO EAT

BENTON'S GRILL
404/768-6121 **36**

▼▼ American. Casual Dining. $6-$25 **AAA Inspector Notes:** This hotel restaurant caters to guests and locals for breakfast, lunch and dinner. American favorites such as filet mignon, barbecue brisket and mahi mahi are featured. Breakfast and lunch service includes an all-you-can-eat buffet. **Address:** 1325 Virginia Ave 30344 **Location:** I-85 exit 73 southbound; exit 73B northbound, just w; in Crowne Plaza Atlanta Airport. [B] [L] [D] CALL &M

GIOVANNA'S ITALIAN KITCHEN
404/762-6755 **38**

▼▼▼ Italian. Casual Dining. $8-$24 **AAA Inspector Notes:** Menu offerings here include a great variety of classic Italian pasta dishes, steaks, seafood and other traditional American favorites. Tiramisu, Key lime pie and carrot cake are tasty dessert choices. The décor is handsome and the service competent. **Features:** full bar, patio dining. **Address:** 1375 Virginia Ave 30344 **Location:** I-85 exit 73 southbound; exit 73B northbound, just w; in Wellesley Inn (Atlanta/Hartsfield-Jackson Int'l Airport). [L] [D]

LOV'N IT LIVE
404/765-9220 **35**

▼▼ Natural/Organic. Casual Dining. $12-$23 **AAA Inspector Notes:** The eatery specializes in slow and live food that is organic, natural, whole, vegan and prepared to retain enzymes to optimize health benefits and nutrition. Popular menu items include the sage burger, pizza and mushroom steak. A great way to try a variety of dishes is the sampler platter which includes a choice of four items plus a salad. Food preparation takes additional time but your patience will be rewarded with amazing flavor. **Address:** 2796 E Point St 30344 **Location:** Just w of Main St; downtown. **Parking:** street only. [L] [D]

MALONE'S STEAK & SEAFOOD
404/762-5577 **37**

▼▼ American. Casual Dining. $9-$29 **AAA Inspector Notes:** Located near the airport, this casual restaurant features a traditional menu of certified Angus beef steak, ribs, seafood, chicken, pasta, sandwiches, burgers and salads. Shrimp and sausage jambalaya and shrimp and grits are some other regional cuisine types offered at Malone's. **Features:** full bar, patio dining. **Address:** 1258 Virginia Ave 30344 **Location:** I-85 exit 73 southbound; exit 73A northbound, just e. [L] [D] [LATE]

THIS IS IT! BBQ & SEAFOOD
404/629-1114 **39**

▼▼ American. Buffet Style. $7-$16 **AAA Inspector Notes:** Enjoy a great selection of items from the cafeteria line at this eatery, including tilapia, ribs, pork, chicken and vegetables. Any items found here also can be fried and brought to the table within five minutes. To go items such as wings and seafood baskets are popular and both chicken and pork barbecue sandwiches are good choices. The southern hospitality and common comfort foods make this a very popular stop for good food that's fast. **Address:** 3523 Camp Creek Pkwy 30344 **Location:** I-285 exit 2, just w. [L] [D] CALL &M

EATONTON (C-3) pop. 6,480, elev. 578'

Eatonton was the birthplace in 1848 of Joel Chandler Harris, creator of the popular children's characters Uncle Remus, Brer Fox, Brer Bear and Brer Rabbit. A statue of Brer Rabbit on Courthouse Square commemorates Harris' works; many originals are displayed at the Uncle Remus Museum *(see attraction listing)*. Eatonton also was home to Alice Walker, author of the 1983 Pulitzer Prize-winning novel "The Color Purple."

Fifteen miles southeast, county-owned Oconee Springs Park provides recreational facilities on Lake Sinclair *(see Recreation Areas Chart)*. Lake Oconee *(see Recreation Areas Chart)*, suitable for water skiing and other water sports, is 7 miles east.

Eatonton-Putnam Chamber of Commerce: 305 N. Madison Ave., P.O. Box 4088, Eatonton, GA 31024. **Phone:** (706) 485-7701.

Self-guiding tours: Maps outlining historic home tours and a 2.8-mile bicycle trail tour are available at the chamber of commerce.

PLAZA ARTS CENTER, 305 N. Madison Ave, housed with the Eatonton-Putnam Chamber of Commerce, is a 500-seat performing arts venue offering concerts, ballet and theater presentations. The Old School History Museum features a 1916

original classroom of the Eatonton School and houses original furnishings, a history gallery of exhibits, a vintage drugstore with a marble-topped soda fountain and various displays featuring area history.

Time: Allow 45 minutes minimum. **Hours:** Mon.-Sat. 10-4, Sun. by appointment. Guided tours are available Fri. 10-2, Sat. 10-4 and other times by advance reservations. Closed major holidays. **Cost:** Free. **Phone:** (706) 923-1655. GT

ROCK EAGLE, 7 mi. n. on US 441 to 350 Rock Eagle Rd., is a 1,428-acre state 4-H center. On the center's grounds is an effigy mound topped by a huge representation of an open-winged bird, thought to be a buzzard or a hawk, made of milky quartz stones ranging from baseball-size to boulders. Archeologists believe the Moundbuilders created the effigy A.D. 100-300. A tower affords a complete view of the structure. **Hours:** Daily dawn-dusk. **Cost:** Free. **Phone:** (706) 484-2899.

UNCLE REMUS MUSEUM is at 214 S. Oak St. in Turner Park. Housed in a log cabin built from two slave cabins, the museum recreates the setting where the little boy in Joel Chandler Harris' tales heard the stories of Uncle Remus, thought to be a composite of two slaves who excelled at storytelling. Displays include woodcarvings and paintings of Harris' characters, first editions of many of his books and Civil War memorabilia.

The fictional setting was based on Turnwold, a plantation near Eatonton where, at age 13, Harris began his apprenticeship at a weekly newspaper, *The Countryman*, in 1862. It was at the paper that Harris heard the fanciful yarns that later formed the basis of his writing. A mentor to Harris, representations of Joseph Addison Turner's library and office are on display.

Time: Allow 30 minutes minimum. **Hours:** Mon.-Sat. 10-noon and 1-5, Sun. 2-5, Mar.-Oct.; Mon.-Sat. 10-4, Sun. 1-4, rest of year. Last tour begins 30 minutes before closing. Closed Jan. 1, Easter, Thanksgiving, Christmas Eve and Christmas. Phone ahead to confirm schedule. **Cost:** $5; $4 (ages 65+ and students with ID); $3 (ages 5-12 with paid adult); $15 (family, up to five members). Phone ahead to confirm rates. **Phone:** (706) 485-6856. GT

ELBERTON (B-4) pop. 4,653, elev. 708'

ELBERTON GRANITE MUSEUM & EXHIBIT is on SR 17, .5 mi. w. of SR 77 at 1 Granite Plaza. With 45 quarries and more than 100 manufacturing plants, the Elberton area is thought to be the largest granite-producing region in the world. The museum displays interesting granite products of the past, antique working tools and a chart detailing quarrying procedures. **Time:** Allow 30 minutes minimum. **Hours:** Mon.-Sat. 2-5. Closed Jan. 1, July 4, Thanksgiving weekend and Christmas. **Cost:** Free. **Phone:** (706) 283-2551.

EVANS pop. 29,011

FATZ   706/650-2421

♦♦ ◊◊ Regional American. Casual Dining. $6-$20 **AAA Inspector Notes:** Friendly staff and appealing country decor help set the tone for a relaxed and enjoyable dining experience. It's not unusual for guests to wait to be seated at the popular spot, which earns raves for its well-prepared variations on chicken, steak, ribs and pasta, as well as salads and sandwiches. The signature Southern-style peach cobbler served with vanilla ice cream and walnuts is scrumptious. **Features:** full bar, happy hour. **Address:** 464 N Belair Rd 30809 **Location:** Center. L D CALL M

THE GARLIC CLOVE ITALIAN EATERY   706/364-7377

♦♦ ♦♦ Italian. Casual Dining. $8-$19 **AAA Inspector Notes:** Great Italian cuisine is the order of the day here. The menu offers all of the standards along with several specialties such as risotto fritters, design your own pasta dish where diners choose the sauce and additions, baked ziti Florentine Alfredo, salmon and sweet peas with beggar's pockets, lasagna sticks, an Italian mixed grill and a slew of other great dishes. I had the risotto fritters and a slightly spicy penne rustica and both were incredible. A children's menu is available. **Features:** beer & wine, happy hour. **Address:** 4534 Washington Rd 30809 **Location:** Jct N Belair Rd (SR 383) and Washington Rd (SR 104), 1.4 mi nw; in Eagle Point shopping center. L D CALL M

SHISHKEBAB RESTAURANT   706/306-8875

♦♦ ♦♦ Turkish. Casual Dining. $6-$20 **AAA Inspector Notes:** Enjoy traditional meats and spices prepared for scratch at this small, friendly restaurant. As one might expect the menu features several styles of kebabs, meat pies, falafel and salads all are prepared to order using traditional techniques. On Friday enjoy the belly dancer's entertaining act. **Address:** 648 N Belair Rd 30809 **Location:** Jct N Belair Rd (SR 383) and Washington Rd (SR 104), just nw. L D

FAIRBURN (B-2) pop. 12,950, elev. 1,033'

• Hotels & Restaurants map & index p. 94
• Part of Atlanta area — see map p. 44

The Georgia Renaissance Festival takes place on weekends from mid-April to early June. There are costumed characters, roving minstrels and jugglers as well as craft vendors and an English garden.

COUNTRY INN & SUITES BY CARLSON (678)782-4900 88

♦♦♦♦ Hotel. $89-$159 **Address:** 7815 Senoia Rd 30213 **Location:** I-85 exit 61, just e. **Facility:** 74 units. 3 stories, interior corridors. **Terms:** cancellation fee imposed. **Pool(s):** heated indoor. **Activities:** exercise room. **Guest Services:** coin laundry.

HAMPTON INN ATLANTA/FAIRBURN (678)782-4600 87

♦♦♦♦ Hotel. $114-$154 **Address:** 7790 Ella Ln 30213 **Location:** I-85 exit 61, just e. **Facility:** 99 units. 4 stories, interior corridors. **Terms:** 1-7 night minimum stay, cancellation fee imposed.

AAA Benefit: Members save up to 10%!

Amenities: video games. **Pool(s):** outdoor. **Activities:** exercise room. **Guest Services:** valet and coin laundry, area transportation.

(See map & index p. 94.)

WINGATE BY WYNDHAM ATLANTA AIRPORT FAIRBURN
(770)892-3006 **89**
▼▼▼▼ Hotel. $94-$119 Address: 7882 Senoia Rd 30213 Location: I-85 exit 61, 0.3 mi e. Facility: 66 units. 4 stories, interior corridors. Terms: cancellation fee imposed. Amenities: video games, safes. Pool(s): heated indoor. Activities: sauna, hot tub, exercise room. Guest Services: valet laundry.
▮▯ CALL 🅖M 🏊 BIZ HS 📶 ✕ 🍴 🖥 🖵
/ SOME UNITS 🐾

FAYETTEVILLE (C-2) pop. 15,945, elev. 899'

HOLLIDAY-DORSEY-FIFE HOUSE MUSEUM is at 140 Lanier Ave. W. Built in 1855, the Greek Revival antebellum house is the former residence of three famous people: John Stiles Holliday, uncle of the infamous John Henry "Doc" Holliday; Solomon Dawson Dorsey, Colonel of the state militia who helped enlist volunteers for the Confederacy; and Robert E. Lee Fife, a former member of the Fayetteville city council. Temporary exhibits also are available. A Cemetery Spirit Walk is held in late October. **Time:** Allow 1 hour, 15 minutes minimum. **Hours:** Tues.-Sat. 10-3. Closed Jan. 1, Thanksgiving and Christmas. **Cost:** $5; $4 (ages 55+, military and students with ID). **Phone:** (770) 716-5332.

HAMPTON INN FAYETTEVILLE   (770)460-6700
▼▼▼ Hotel. $99-$189 Address: 110 Meeting Place Dr 30214 Location: Jct SR 54, just s. Facility: 78 units. 3 stories, interior corridors. Terms: 1-7 night minimum stay, cancellation fee imposed. Pool(s): outdoor. Activities: exercise room. Guest Services: valet and coin laundry.

AAA Benefit:
Members save up to 10%!

▮▯ CALL 🅖M 🏊 BIZ HS 📶 ✕ 🍴 🖥 🖵

FITZGERALD (E-4) pop. 9,053, elev. 275'

Originally founded in 1896 as a colony for aging Union soldiers fleeing Midwestern droughts and frigid Northern winters, Fitzgerald features a historic downtown laid out in a perfect grid. Evidence of the city's Civil War heritage and early spirit of compromise can be seen in the street names here: seven are named for Confederate generals and seven for Union generals.

Fitzgerald Convention and Visitors Bureau: 116 N. Johnston St., Fitzgerald, GA 31750. **Phone:** (229) 426-5033 or (800) 386-4642.

BLUE AND GRAY MUSEUM is in the Municipal Building (former train Depot) at 116 N. Johnston St. The museum's centerpiece, the Hall of Honor, celebrates the Civil War veterans who founded Fitzgerald in the 1890s; veterans of other wars also are recognized. The video documentary "Marching as One" relates the city's history. The museum also features items from the estate of Confederate president Jefferson Davis as well as rare Civil War swords, guns, documents and quilts.

Time: Allow 1 hour minimum. **Hours:** Tues.-Sat. 10-4, Sun. 1-5. Closed major holidays. **Cost:** $5; $2

(students). **Phone:** (229) 426-5069 for events and special exhibits information.

JEFFERSON DAVIS MEMORIAL STATE HISTORIC SITE is at 338 Jeff Davis Park Rd. The 13-acre site contains a monument marking where Confederate President Jefferson Davis was captured by Union forces. A museum, nature trail and playground also are available. **Time:** Allow 30 minutes minimum. **Hours:** Wed.-Sun. 9-5. Closed major holidays. Phone ahead to confirm schedule. **Cost:** $4; $3.50 (ages 62+); $2.75 (ages 6-17). **Phone:** (229) 831-2335. 🏛

QUALITY INN   (229)423-5151

Hotel
$65-$97

Address: 263 Ocilla Hwy 31750 Location: US 319/107, just n. Facility: 51 units. 2 stories (no elevator), interior corridors. Pool(s): outdoor. Featured Amenity: full hot breakfast.
SAVE ▮▯ 🏊 📶 🍴 🖥 🖵
/ SOME UNITS 🐾

WESTERN MOTEL   229/424-9500
▼▼ Motel. Rates not provided. Address: 111 Bull Run Rd 31750 Location: Jct SR 107 and US 129, just nw on US 129. Located by abandoned hotels, in a commercial area. Facility: 39 units. 2 stories, exterior corridors. Pool(s): outdoor. Activities: exercise room. ▮▯ 🏊 📶 🍴 🖥 🖵 / SOME UNITS 🐾

FLOWERY BRANCH pop. 5,679

HAMPTON INN & SUITES FLOWERY BRANCH (770)965-0357
▼▼▼ Hotel. $124-$169 Address: 4660 Holland Dam Rd 30542 Location: I-985 exit 12, just e. Facility: 84 units. 5 stories, interior corridors. Terms: 1-7 night minimum stay, cancellation fee imposed. Pool(s): heated indoor. Activities: exercise room. Guest Services: valet and coin laundry.

AAA Benefit:
Members save up to 10%!

▮▯ CALL 🅖M 🏊 BIZ 📶 ✕ 🍴 🖥 🖵

WHERE TO EAT

CHEESEBURGER BOBBY'S   770/965-2250
▼ Burgers. Quick Serve. $3-$6 AAA Inspector Notes: Nibble on hand-cut fries with your fresh, hand-patted burger, which you'll gussy up with onions, lettuce, tomatoes, pickles and other items on the condiment station. Other choices include hot dogs, chicken sandwiches and custard for dessert. Friendly servers tend the bright, fresh and clean dining room. Address: 5855 Spout Springs Rd 30542 Location: I-985 exit 12, just e; in Stonebridge Village.
L D CALL 🅖M

SONNY'S REAL PIT BAR-B-Q   770/287-1622
▼▼ Barbecue. Casual Dining. $8-$17 AAA Inspector Notes: Bearing the name after its founder, Floyd "Sonny" Tillman, this barbecue restaurant first opened its doors circa 1968 in Gainesville, Florida and has since spawned over 150 more throughout the Southeast. The menu is steeped in finger lickin' favorites such as ribs, pulled pork, beef brisket, catfish, shrimp and chargrilled chicken. Let's not forget about the fried okra, which is the perfect starter dish, and their homemade baked beans. Features: beer only. Address: 3445 Mundy Mill Rd 30542 Location: I-985 exit Mundy Mill Rd, 0.4 mi sw. L D

FOLKSTON (F-5) pop. 2,502, elev. 80'

Folkston is near the eastern entrance to Okefenokee Swamp, an area of more than 600 square miles. Most of the swamp was declared a wildlife refuge in 1937.

Thanks to a track configuration that funnels railroad traffic into and out of Florida through Folkston, more than 60 trains pass through the town each day. The Folkston Funnel Train Watching Platform, near the corner of Tower and Main streets, offers a covered area from which enthusiasts can watch the trains pass by.

Okefenokee Chamber of Commerce: 3795 Main St., P.O. Box 756, Folkston, GA 31537. **Phone:** (912) 496-2536.

OKEFENOKEE ADVENTURES is 7 mi. s. on SR 121/23, then 4 mi. w. on Suwannee Canal Rd. following signs to the Okefenokee National Wildlife Refuge east entrance. Within the wildlife refuge, this company offers 90-minute guided boat tours as well as a 2- to 2.5-hour sunset tour and extended day and overnight excursions. Naturalist guides teach about the area's cultural and natural history, flora and fauna.

The refuge features walking trails, an interpretive center, an observation tower and a swamper homestead. Canoe, kayak and bicycle rentals are available.

Time: Allow 1 hour, 30 minutes minimum. **Hours:** Daily a half-hour before dawn-7:30 p.m., Mar.-Oct.; a half-hour before dawn-5:30 p.m., rest of year. Closed Thanksgiving and Christmas. **Cost:** $5 per private vehicle. Ninety-minute boat tour $19.50; $12 (ages 5-11). Sunset tour $28.50; $18 (ages 5-11). Reservations are required for sunset and extended tours. **Phone:** (912) 496-7156 or (866) 843-7926.

GT ⛽

OKEFENOKEE NATIONAL WILDLIFE REFUGE occupies 402,000 acres of the Okefenokee Swamp and surrounding uplands. The main entrance is 7 mi. s.w. on SR 121/23, then 4 mi. w. on Suwannee Canal Rd. following signs. There also is a western entrance at Stephen C. Foster State Park *(see Recreation Areas Chart)* and a northern entrance at Okefenokee Swamp Park *(see attraction listing in Waycross p. 300).*

The swamp's abundant plant and animal life can best be observed on overnight canoe trips lasting from 2 to 5 days. The trips require advance permits issued by the refuge office. Reservations are highly recommended and can be made 2 months in advance; contact the Canoe Reservation Line.

Fishing is permitted at the Suwannee Canal Recreation Area, Stephen C. Foster State Park and two unstaffed secondary entrances that provide access to the swamp's interior. All state regulations apply. Rental boats, canoes and kayaks are available at the east and west entrances; rates vary. Camping and cabins are at the western entrance.

Hours: East entrance open daily a half-hour before dawn-7:30 p.m., Mar.-Oct.; a half-hour before dawn-5:30 p.m., rest of year; closed Thanksgiving and Christmas. West entrance daily 7 a.m.-10 p.m.; closed Christmas. North entrance daily 9-5:30; hours may vary in Dec.; phone ahead. North entrance closed Jan. 1, Thanksgiving, Christmas Eve and Christmas.

Cost: A 7-day pass good for the east or west entrance to the refuge costs $5 per private vehicle. Fee at the north entrance near Waycross is $17 per person; $16 (ages 3-11, ages 62+ and active military with ID). Combination admission and boat tour (from Waycross entrance) $27; $22 (ages 3-11). **Phone:** (912) 496-7836 (east entrance), (912) 496-3331 (for overnight wilderness canoe reservations through the Refuge Manager), (912) 637-5274 (Stephen Foster entrance), or (912) 283-0583 (north entrance).

GT ⛽ ✕ ⛱

Suwannee Canal Recreation Area (east entrance), 7 mi. s.w. on SR 23/121, then 4 mi. w. on the Okefenokee National Wildlife Refuge entrance road, is the main or eastern entrance to the refuge. A visitor center offers exhibits, a 14-minute film and information about recreational activities. A wildlife drive provides access to more than 10 miles of walking trails, a restored swamp homestead and a .75-mile boardwalk leading to a 50-foot observation tower. A concessionaire offers guided boat trips as well as canoe and kayak rentals, fishing supplies and food service.

Hours: Daily a half-hour before dawn-7:30 p.m., Mar.-Oct.; a half-hour before dawn-5:30 p.m., rest of year. Visitor center daily 9-4, Mar.-May and Sept.-Nov.; Tues.-Sat. 9-4, rest of year. Closed Thanksgiving and Christmas. **Cost:** (valid for seven days) $5 per private vehicle. **Phone:** (912) 496-7836.

GT ⛽ ⛱ ✕ ⛺ ⛱

FOREST PARK pop. 18,468
- **Hotels & Restaurants map & index p. 94**
- **Part of Atlanta area — see map p. 44**

COMFORT SUITES ATLANTA AIRPORT   (404)209-7299 **58**
▼▼▼ **Hotel.** $74-$279 **Address:** 5087 Clark Howell Hwy 30297 **Location:** I-75 exit 237A southbound; exit 237 northbound, 0.5 mi w, then just n. **Facility:** 79 units. 5 stories, interior corridors. **Pool(s):** heated indoor. **Activities:** exercise room. **Guest Services:** coin laundry, area transportation.
➕ 🍴 CALL 🛗M 🛎 BIZ 🛜 ✕ 🛏 🖥 🖨

RAMADA AIRPORT EAST/FOREST PARK (404)768-7799 **59**
▼▼ **Hotel.** $60-$81 **Address:** 357 Lee St 30297 **Location:** I-75 exit 237A southbound; exit 237 northbound, 0.5 mi w. **Facility:** 77 units. 4 stories, interior corridors. **Amenities:** safes. **Pool(s):** outdoor. **Activities:** exercise room. **Guest Services:** valet and coin laundry, area transportation.
➕ 🍴 CALL 🛗M 🛎 BIZ 🛜 🛏 🖥 🖨

SUPER 8   (404)363-8811 **61**
▼▼ **Motel.** $45-$100 **Address:** 410 Old Dixie Way 30297 **Location:** I-75 exit 235, just e. **Facility:** 53 units. 2-3 stories (no elevator), exterior corridors. **Pool(s):** outdoor. **Guest Services:** coin laundry.
🍴 🛎 BIZ 🛜 🛏 🖥 🖨 /SOME UNITS 🐾

(See map & index p. 94.)

TRAVELODGE FOREST PARK ATLANTA SOUTH
(404)361-3600 **60**
 Motel. $60-$73 **Address:** 6025 Old Dixie Rd 30297 **Location:** I-75 exit 235, just n. **Facility:** 37 units. 1 story, exterior corridors. **Pool(s):** outdoor. **Guest Services:** coin laundry.
CALL ⬛ ⬛ 🛜 ⬛ ⬛ ⬛ / SOME UNITS ⬛

WHERE TO EAT

OAKWOOD CAFE
404/214-5660 **51**
 Southern. Casual Dining. $6-$20 **AAA Inspector Notes:** Good old country cooking is the staple at this hugely popular restaurant, which is set in the Farmer's Market on the south side of Atlanta. Featured are the freshest in veggies from the market next door. Favorites such as fried chicken and tasty desserts are as popular here as veggie plates. **Address:** 16 Forest Pkwy 30297 **Location:** I-75 exit 237, just e; in State Farmer's Market. ⬛B⬛ ⬛L⬛

ZESTO
404/366-0564 **52**
 Burgers. Quick Serve. $4-$23 **AAA Inspector Notes:** Serving Atlanta since 1955, this spot offers such favorites as hamburgers (the chubby decker is popular), hot dogs, wings, broasted chicken, country-fried steak, pork chops and ice cream. Daily specials include the steak burger basket and the fish filet sandwich basket. **Address:** 151 Forest Pkwy 30297 **Location:** I-75 exit 235, 2.3 mi e. **Parking:** no self-parking. ⬛B⬛ ⬛L⬛ ⬛D⬛

FORSYTH (C-3) pop. 3,788, elev. 704'
• Restaurants p. 184

Forsyth is named for Gov. John Forsyth, who served as secretary of state to Presidents Andrew Jackson and Martin Van Buren. In 1834 the town became a regional transportation center when it was linked with the railroad. It also served as a distribution point when cotton planters brought their product to Forsyth for shipment to Macon and the southern United States.

The Monroe County Courthouse, in the center of Courthouse Square, was built in 1896 and is an example of Victorian architecture. The courthouse is in the middle of an eight-block historic district that preserves late 19th- and early 20th-century buildings. The Monroe County Museum and Genealogy Room, 126 E. Johnston St., is a restored 1896 Victorian depot; phone (478) 994-5070. Its museum features railroad memorabilia and exhibits about local history.

The Rum Creek Wildlife Management Area, 7 miles east on SR 18, is 8,100 acres on Lake Juliette. High Falls State Park, 11 miles north on High Falls Road just off I-75, features a scenic waterfall *(see Recreation Areas Chart)*.

Forsyth-Monroe County Chamber of Commerce: 10 W. Chambers St., Forsyth, GA 31029. **Phone:** (478) 994-9239.

COMFORT INN FORSYTH
(478)994-3400

Hotel
$79-$89
Address: 333 Harold G Clark Pkwy 31029 **Location:** I-75 exit 185 (SR 18), just w. **Facility:** 59 units. 2 stories (no elevator), exterior corridors. **Pool(s):** outdoor. **Activities:** exercise room.

SAVE ⬛ CALL ⬛ ⬛ BIZ 🛜 ⬛ ⬛ ⬛ / SOME UNITS ⬛

COMFORT SUITES
(478)994-9494

Hotel
$79-$149
Address: 343 Harold G Clark Pkwy 31029 **Location:** I-75 exit 185 (SR 18), just w. **Facility:** 53 units. 4 stories, interior corridors. **Pool(s):** heated indoor. **Activities:** hot tub, exercise room. **Guest Services:** coin laundry. **Featured Amenity:** breakfast buffet.

SAVE ⬛ CALL ⬛ ⬛ BIZ HS 🛜 ⬛ ⬛ ⬛

DAYS INN FORSYTH
(478)994-2900

Hotel
$45-$80
Address: 343 N Lee St 31029 **Location:** I-75 exit 188, 1 mi w. **Facility:** 112 units. 2 stories (no elevator), exterior corridors. **Pool(s):** outdoor. **Guest Services:** coin laundry.

SAVE ⬛ ⬛ 🛜 ⬛ ⬛ ⬛ / SOME UNITS ⬛

HOLIDAY INN EXPRESS
(478)994-9697
 Hotel. $79-$139 **Address:** 520 Holiday Cir 31029 **Location:** I-75 exit 186 (Juliette Rd), just w, then just s on Aaron St. **Facility:** 121 units. 4 stories, interior corridors. **Terms:** cancellation fee imposed, resort fee. **Pool(s):** outdoor. **Activities:** exercise room. **Guest Services:** coin laundry.
⬛ CALL ⬛ ⬛ BIZ HS 🛜 ⬛ ⬛ / SOME UNITS ⬛ ⬛ ⬛

SUPER 8
(478)994-5101
 Motel. $57-$62 **Address:** 436 Tift College Dr 31029 **Location:** I-75 exit 186 (Juliette Rd), just w. **Facility:** 62 units. 2 stories (no elevator), interior/exterior corridors. **Pool(s):** outdoor.
⬛ ⬛ BIZ 🛜 ⬛ ⬛ ⬛ / SOME UNITS ⬛

WHERE TO EAT

GRITS CAFE   478/994-8325
▼▼▼ New Southern. Fine Dining. $10-$38 **AAA Inspector Notes:** The quality of meals surprises at the homespun-sounding cafe, where the chef takes Southern style to new heights. Hearty soups, such as cream of mushroom with roasted red peppers, warm the heart. The signature shrimp and grits combines spicy, sauced shrimp with smoked Gouda cheese-blended grit cakes. Although desserts such as homemade turtle sundae or cappuccino crème brûlée are big enough to share, diners won't want to. **Features:** full bar. **Reservations:** suggested. **Address:** 17 W Johnston St 31029 **Location:** Downtown. L D CALL &M

JONAH'S ON JOHNSTON   478/994-8844
▼▼ Pizza. Casual Dining. $3-$15 **AAA Inspector Notes:** This hometown pizzeria and bakery is a carb-lover's paradise. The brick oven churns out delicious pies such as my personal favorite, the "Margherita" and the crowd favorite, "Cheeseburger in Paradise." I recommend starting with the creamy artichoke dip and saving room for the home baked goodness of cakes, cookies and brownies. Ask about the fresh baked artisan breads to take home. **Address:** 26 E Johnston St 31029 **Location:** I-75 exit 187, 0.5 mi s on Cabaniss Rd, then just e. **Parking:** street only.
L D CALL &M

FORT FREDERICA NATIONAL MONUMENT (E-6)
• **Part of Golden Isles area — see map p. 187**

Fort Frederica National Monument is on St. Simons Island, which is reached from the mainland via the F.J. Torras Causeway.

In 1736 Gen. James E. Oglethorpe began construction of an earthwork that became one of the most important British fortifications in America. Next to the fort he laid out the town of Frederica. The settlement and fort were vital in the defense of English interests in the conflict with Spain that erupted in 1739.

On July 7, 1742, the Battle of Bloody Marsh settled the fighting. The entire Colony of Georgia remained under English rule. The Bloody Marsh Memorial Site, a separate area 6 miles south, is open daily 8:30-4.

Oglethorpe's regiment disbanded in 1749, ruining Frederica's economy. A fire in 1758 destroyed most of the town, and the last soldiers left the fort in 1763. Ruins lie atop a bluff on the island's western shore overlooking the Frederica River, and foundations of original houses have been uncovered. Field exhibits explain features of the area.

A visitor center houses pictorial panels, a diorama and artifacts pertaining to Frederica. A historical film is shown every 30 minutes. Self-guiding and audio tours are available. Allow 1 hour, 30 minutes minimum. Daily 9-5. Closed Jan. 1, Thanksgiving and Christmas. Free. Phone (912) 638-3639.

FORT GAINES (E-2) pop. 1,107, elev. 163'

At 100 Bluff St. overlooking the Chattahoochee River is Fort Gaines Frontier Village, an open-air museum with log cabins, a cane mill, a smokehouse and a Civil War cannon. A partial replica of the 1814 frontier fort and a pioneer cemetery are nearby.

Also in the area is Lake Walter F. George *(see Recreation Areas Chart)*. The 3-mile-long Walter

George Dam has a lock with what is purported to be one of the highest lifts in the world.

Clay County Chamber of Commerce: 300 Bagby Pkwy. in George T. Bagby State Park, Fort Gaines, GA 39851. **Phone:** (229) 254-0183.

FORT GORDON (C-5) elev. 469'

U.S. ARMY SIGNAL CORPS MUSEUM, in Conrad Hall (Bldg. 29807) on Chamberlain Ave., houses communications and military signal history since the corps' inception in 1860. Items displayed include signal devices from the Civil War to the present and an Oscar awarded to the movie, "Seeds of Destiny," a Signal Corps film made after World War II. Of special interest are items from Albert J. Myer, the father of the Signal Corps. **Hours:** Tues.-Fri. 8-4. Closed major holidays. **Cost:** Free. **Phone:** (706) 791-3856.

FORT OGLETHORPE pop. 9,263, elev. 728'

CHICKAMAUGA BATTLEFIELD VISITOR CENTER—see Chickamauga and Chattanooga National Military Park p. 156.

ECONO LODGE INN & SUITES   (706)866-0222
◆◆◆ **Address:** 2120 Lafayette Rd 30742 **Location:** Jct US 27 (Lafayette Rd) and SR 2, just n. **Facility:** 38 units. 1-2 stories (no elevator), exterior corridors. **Pool(s):** outdoor. **Featured Amenity:** continental breakfast.
Motel
$65-$125

WHERE TO EAT

THAI GARDEN   706/866-7025
▼▼ Asian. Casual Dining. $7-$14 **AAA Inspector Notes:** This place features a mix of Thai and Chinese cuisine with a broad cross-section of each represented. Guests will be delighted to find such typical take-out favorites as chow mein and beef and broccoli alongside well-crafted pad thai. Do not forget the soups, as the tom yum goong is awesome and comes loaded with fresh shrimp. There is a tamer Chinese wonton soup. Dishes are seasoned to your liking so kick it up a notch if you are brave. **Address:** 685 Battlefield Pkwy 30742 **Location:** Jct US 27/SR 2 and Battlefield Pkwy, 0.3 mi e; in Parkway Village Shopping Center. L D

FORT PULASKI NATIONAL MONUMENT (D-6)

Fort Pulaski National Monument, 15 miles east of Savannah via US 80, occupies Cockspur and McQueens islands at the mouth of the Savannah River. Fort Pulaski, on the eastern end of Cockspur Island, was preceded by Fort George (1761-76) and Fort Greene (1794-1804).

When a British fleet approached in 1776, American patriots dismantled Fort George. A hurricane demolished Fort Greene in 1804. Construction of Fort Pulaski began in 1829 and required 18 years and 25 million bricks to complete. The fort, in the shape of a massive irregular pentagon and surrounded by a moat crossed by drawbridges, was a link in an impressive chain of coastal forts built to protect the United States from foreign invasion. The long galleries are distinguished by fine brick arches. Today, it survives as one of the nation's best-preserved fortifications.

The Battle for Fort Pulaski, fought April 10-11, 1862, marked a turning point in military history and included the first significant use of rifled cannons. Union forces on Tybee Island bombarded the fort for 30 hours, eventually forcing the surrender of the Confederate garrison. Upon the bombardment's conclusion, the fort's southeast angle lay in ruins. The battle clearly demonstrated the improved power, range and accuracy of rifled cannons and also signaled the end of masonry fortifications.

Some 25 miles of trails crisscross Cockspur and McQueen's islands. Walking, hiking and bicycling are all popular outdoor pursuits. Vegetation on the islands—which has reverted to a more natural state since the abandonment of the fort in the late 19th century—consists of pines, grasses and other plants that grow in salt marsh and upland maritime forest habitats. This wilderness area also is home to a variety of animals, including white-tailed deer, manatees, bald eagles and loggerhead sea turtles.

The park offers daily fort tours and demonstrations of historic weapons. The visitor center has trail maps and artillery displays and shows a film about the fort's past. Picnic facilities are available. **Note:** Visitors should wear comfortable shoes and bring water and insect repellent, especially in the summer months. Allow 1 hour, 30 minutes minimum. Daily 9-5. Closed Jan. 1, Thanksgiving and Christmas. Phone ahead to confirm daily program schedule. Admission $5; free (ages 0-15). Phone (912) 786-5787.

FORT VALLEY (D-3) pop. 9,815, elev. 525'
• Hotels p. 186 • Restaurants p. 186

Legend has it that the real name of the town was Fox Valley, but when submitted to the Post Office in 1825, illegible handwriting was read as "Fort" and so it has remained.

In 1875 a new peach variety, the Elberta, was introduced. The new peach and access to railroads made Fort Valley a peach-growing center in the Peach State. The area became so successful that a new county was formed—ultimately named Peach. The Georgia Peach Festival, home to what is purported to be the world's largest peach cobbler, is held in June; for information phone the festival office at (478) 825-4002.

Peach Regional Chamber of Commerce: 201 Oakland Heights Pkwy., Fort Valley, GA 31030. **Phone:** (478) 825-3733.

MASSEE LANE GARDENS is 5.5 mi. s. on SR 49 to 100 Massee Ln. Headquarters of the American Camellia Society, the 20-acre camellia and azalea collection contains hundreds of varieties that bloom August through April. Highlights include a greenhouse, a Japanese garden, a rose garden, an environmental garden and the Children's Garden. The daylily garden blooms in summer. Two galleries house porcelains by Edward Marshall Boehm and other artists. A library has rare camellia books dating from 1863.

Guided tours are available by appointment. **Time:** Allow 30 minutes minimum. **Hours:** Tues.-Sat. 10-4:30 (also Mon. 10-4:30, in Feb.), Sun. 1-4:30. Phone ahead to confirm holiday closures. **Cost:** $5; $4 (ages 55+); free (ages 0-12). **Phone:** (478) 967-2358 or (877) 422-6355. GT

DAYS INN & SUITES (478)825-3600

▼▼ Motel. $60-$90 Address: 300 Commercial Heights 31030 Location: Jct SR 49, just se on US 341/SR 96. Facility: 40 units. 2 stories (no elevator), exterior corridors. Terms: cancellation fee imposed. Pool(s): outdoor. Guest Services: coin laundry.

WHERE TO EAT

PEACHTREE CAFÉ 478/825-3592

▼ American. Casual Dining. $5-$12 AAA Inspector Notes: Famous for peach cobbler and homemade ice cream, this café also provides tasty sandwich fare with all the fixings. A gift shop is located adjacent to the dining area, and guided and self-guided tours of the packing facilities are an interesting attraction. Features: patio dining. Address: 50 Lane Rd 31030 Location: I-75 exit 142 (SR 96), 4.9 mi w; in Lane Southern Orchard.

TAPATIO MEXICAN RESTAURANT 478/827-0250

▼▼ Mexican. Casual Dining. $6-$17 AAA Inspector Notes: Enjoy a little taste of Mexico! On the menu are such choices as fajitas, soft tacos with grilled steak or marinated pork, shrimp with rice and a variety of burritos and enchiladas. Features: beer only, patio dining, happy hour. Address: 600 Vineville St 31030 Location: Jct US 341/SR 96 (Vineville St), 0.6 mi w.

GAINESVILLE (B-3) pop. 33,804, elev. 1,227'

Gainesville, on the northeast shore of Lake Sidney Lanier, was known as Mule Camp Springs in the early 19th century. The Green Street Historical District consists of late Victorian and neoclassical revival structures along broad tree-lined Green Street. The Quinlan Visual Arts Center at 514 Green Street N.E. displays exhibits by state and local artists; phone (770) 536-2575. Road Atlanta, 10 miles south on SR 53 in Braselton, is a sanctioned road-racing course and is home to the Petit Le Mans race; phone (770) 967-6143 or (800) 849-7223.

Lake Lanier Convention and Visitors Bureau: 2875 Browns Bridge Rd., Gainesville, GA 30504. **Phone:** (770) 536-5209.

INTERACTIVE NEIGHBORHOOD FOR KIDS is at 999 S.E. Chestnut St. Several hands-on exhibits provide children with opportunities to experience adult professions and responsibilities within a fun environment. "Employees" get a taste of what it's like working on a dairy farm, in a beauty salon, or as a doctor or pilot. Special events are offered. **Time:** Allow 45 minutes minimum. **Hours:** Mon.-Sat. 10-5, Sun. 1-5. Closed major holidays. **Cost:** $8; $6 on Sundays. **Phone:** (770) 536-1900.

NORTHEAST GEORGIA HISTORY CENTER is at 322 Academy St. N.E. The center's main exhibit covers 500 years of northeast Georgia history. Highlights include a simulation of the tornado that struck in 1936; exhibits about two of the region's economic mainstays, poultry and health care; and memorabilia associated with Ed Dodd, creator of the comic strip "Mark Trail." Also on display are rotating exhibits and a collection of folk pottery created by regional artisans. The Northeast Georgia Sports Hall of Fame honors sports legends. The 1780s cabin of Cherokee Chief White Path is on the grounds. The

American Freedom Garden features a circle of 24 granite pillars engraved with the names of veterans.

Time: Allow 1 hour minimum. **Hours:** Tues.-Sat. 10-4. Closed Jan. 1, July 4, Thanksgiving, Christmas Eve and Christmas. **Cost:** $6; $5 (ages 65+ and active and retired military); $4 (ages 5-18 and college students with ID). **Phone:** (770) 297-5900.

FAIRFIELD INN & SUITES BY MARRIOTT GAINESVILLE (678)971-4670

▼▼▼ Hotel $98-$152

FAIRFIELD INN & SUITES Marriott

AAA Benefit: Members save 5% or more!

Address: 1755 Browns Bridge Rd 30501 Location: I-985 exit 20, 1.1 mi w to Pearl Nix Pkwy, 1 mi s to Browns Bridge Rd, then just s. Facility: 75 units. 4 stories, interior corridors. Pool(s): heated indoor. Activities: exercise room. Guest Services: valet and coin laundry. Featured Amenity: full hot breakfast.

THE GUEST LODGE 770/535-8100

◆ Motel Rates not provided

Address: 520 Queen City Pkwy 30501 Location: I-985 exit 20, 1.8 mi nw on SR 60/Queen City Pkwy. Facility: 96 units. 2 stories (no elevator), exterior corridors. Pool(s): outdoor. Guest Services: valet and coin laundry. Featured Amenity: continental breakfast.

HILTON GARDEN INN GAINESVILLE (770)532-3396

▼▼▼ Hotel. $109-$189 Address: 1735 Browns Bridge Rd 30501 Location: I-985 exit 20, 1.1 mi w to Pearl Nix Pkwy, 1 mi s to Browns Bridge Rd, then just s. Facility: 118 units. 6 stories, interior corridors. Terms: 1-7 night minimum stay, cancellation fee imposed. Pool(s): heated outdoor, heated indoor. Activities: exercise room. Guest Services: valet and coin laundry.

AAA Benefit: Members save up to 10%!

GARDEN CITY pop. 8,778

• Hotels & Restaurants map & index p. 260

BAYMONT INN & SUITES (912)964-8669 **54**

▼▼ Hotel $69-$250

Address: 357 Main St 31408 Location: I-95 exit 109 (SR 21), 6.5 mi se to Spur SR 21 (Brampton Rd), 0.3 mi n to Coastal Hwy/Main St, then just se. Located in a busy commercial port area. Facility: 57 units. 2 stories, interior corridors. Pool(s): outdoor. Activities: hot tub, limited exercise equipment. Guest Services: valet and coin laundry, area transportation.

GOLDEN ISLES

When Spain claimed the lovely subtropical islands along the Georgia coast as the Golden Isles of Guale in the 16th century, habitation was not new to the land. Archeological evidence traces Native American settlement to about 2500 B.C. Spain ceded the islands to Great Britain in 1763.

The term Golden Isles refers to St. Simons Island, Sea Island, Little St. Simons Island and Jekyll Island, all near the city of Brunswick. St. Simons Island is the largest of the four. St. Simons Island, Sea Island and Jekyll Island are the only islands accessible by car. Other islands in the area include Blackbeard, Cumberland, St. Catherines and Sapelo.

Just northeast of Sapelo is Blackbeard Island, where the pirate Edward Teach is said to have hidden his loot. St. Catherines Island is the former home of Button Gwinnett, one of Georgia's three signers of the Declaration of Independence. Southernmost in the chain and once the Carnegie family's private resort, Cumberland Island now is a national seashore.

This map shows cities in the Golden Isles where you will find attractions, hotels and restaurants. Cities are listed alphabetically in this book on the following pages.

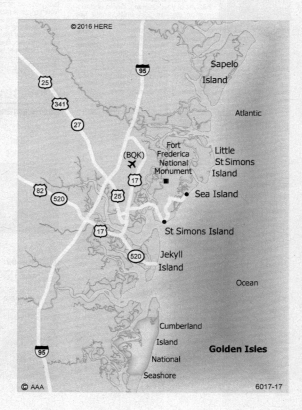

GREENSBORO pop. 3,359

THE RITZ-CARLTON REYNOLDS, LAKE OCONEE
(706)467-0600

Resort Hotel
$299-$1599

AAA Benefit:
Unequaled service at special member savings!

Address: 1 Lake Oconee Tr 30642 **Location:** I-20 exit 130, 7.2 mi sw on SR 44 (Old Eatonton Rd), 1.5 mi e on Linger Longer Rd, then 2 mi ne. **Facility:** The natural charm of Lake Oconee is reflected in the luxurious accommodations of this upscale resort that is designed to fulfill all of your sleeping, dining and recreation desires. 251 units, some two

bedrooms, three bedrooms, efficiencies, kitchens, houses and cottages. 4-5 stories, interior/exterior corridors. **Parking:** valet only. **Terms:** check-in 4 pm, 3 day cancellation notice-fee imposed, resort fee. **Amenities:** safes. **Dining:** 2 restaurants, also, Georgia's Bistro, Linger Longer Steakhouse, see separate listings. **Pool(s):** heated outdoor, heated indoor. **Activities:** sauna, hot tub, steamroom, self-propelled boats, boat dock, fishing, regulation golf, ice skating, recreation programs, kids club, bicycles, playground, trails, in-room exercise equipment, spa. **Guest Services:** valet laundry, area transportation. *(See ad p. 118.)*

(See ad p. 118.)

GEORGIA'S BISTRO
706/467-0600

Regional American. Fine Dining. $25-$38 **AAA Inspector Notes:** This casually elegant dining room specializes in Southern cuisine with a gourmet flair, incorporating such regional ingredients as pecans, peaches and Vidalia onions. Courses like Carolina rainbow trout, pork belly, Prestige Farms fried chicken and fried green tomatoes top the favorites. Homemade desserts are luscious and for those who cannot decide, the tasting trio features buttermilk pie, crème brûlée and peanut butter and jelly molten cake. **Features:** full bar, patio dining. **Address:** One Lake Oconee Tr 30642 **Location:** I-20 exit 130, 7.2 mi sw on SR 44 (Old Eatonton Rd), 1.5 mi e on Linger Longer Rd, then 2 mi ne; in The Ritz-Carlton Reynolds, Lake Oconee. **Parking:** on-site and valet.

LINGER LONGER STEAKHOUSE
706/467-7135

Steak. Fine Dining. $11-$79 **AAA Inspector Notes:** This upscale steakhouse is an excellent offering for locals and guests of the adjacent resort. Expect a relaxed formal environment with top-notch service and cuisine. The menu features some fresh, local ingredients and high-quality steak options. The wine list offers a wide range of choices of common and exotic wines. Finish the meal with the house specialty, chocolate soufflé. **Reservations:** suggested. **Address:** 1 Lake Oconee Trail 30642 **Location:** I-20 exit 130, 7.2 mi sw on SR 44 (Old Eatonton Rd), 1.5 mi e on Linger Longer Rd, then 2 mi ne; in The Ritz-Carlton Reynolds, Lake Oconee.

GRIFFIN pop. 23,643

HOLIDAY INN EXPRESS
770/228-9799

Hotel. Rates not provided. **Address:** 1900 N Expressway 30223 **Location:** 2 mi n on US 41 and 19. **Facility:** 82 units. 2 stories, interior corridors. **Amenities:** safes. **Pool(s):** heated indoor. **Activities:** hot tub, exercise room. **Guest Services:** coin laundry.

WHERE TO EAT

CORNER CAFE
678/572-4222

American. Fine Dining. $4-$12 **AAA Inspector Notes:** This small town café serves classic comfort food with generous portions at a reasonable price. The family-owned restaurant is a popular choice for locals especially for lunch and weekends. The menu features burgers, sandwiches, pasta and some salads, and they have daily specials. The desserts will taunt you from the glass case, so make sure you save room for a sweet treat. **Address:** 101 N Hill St 30223 **Location:** Downtown. **Parking:** street only.

SLICES PIZZERIA
770/227-0022

Pizza. Casual Dining. $4-$22 **AAA Inspector Notes:** This family-owned pizzeria, located in the historic district, offers delicious New York-style pizza and calzones. Order the gooey deliciousness by the slice or share a pie with friends, but be aware that the portions are massive. Save room for a slice of apple pie dessert pizza. It is so good you may never want a traditional apple pie again. This local favorite has a split-level dining room with stairs leading to the upper room. **Features:** beer only. **Address:** 136 W Solomon St 30223 **Location:** Jct Solomon and 8th sts; in historic downtown. **Parking:** street only.

GROVETOWN pop. 11,216

BEST WESTERN AUGUSTA WEST
(706)651-9100

Hotel
$89-$139

 Best Western.

AAA Benefit:
Save 10% or more every day and earn 10% bonus points!

Address: 452 Park West Dr 30813 **Location:** I-20 exit 194 (SR 383), just s. **Facility:** 58 units. 3 stories, interior corridors. **Pool(s):** outdoor. **Activities:** limited exercise equipment. **Guest Services:** coin laundry. **Featured Amenity:** full hot breakfast.

JAMESON INN
(706)855-9111

Hotel
$59-$399

Address: 461 Park West Dr 30813 **Location:** I-20 exit 194 (SR 383), just s. **Facility:** 64 units. 3 stories, interior corridors. **Pool(s):** outdoor. **Activities:** limited exercise equipment. **Guest Services:** coin laundry. **Featured Amenity:** continental breakfast.

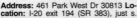

WHERE TO EAT

BIG DADDY'S BAR & GRILL
706/623-2339

Barbecue Burgers. Casual Dining. $6-$20 **AAA Inspector Notes:** This neat little restaurant is a popular watering hole where friends gather daily to unwind after work. A sit-down country menu features cooked-to-order burgers, barbecue ribs and pulled pork, po'boys, fried catfish and shrimp. The staff is friendly and the food is inexpensive. **Features:** full bar, patio dining, happy hour. **Address:** 4045 Jimmie Dyess Pkwy, Suite 101 30909 **Location:** I-20 exit 194 (SR 383), 0.5 mi s.

Visit AAA.com/searchfordiscounts to save on travel, shopping, dining and attractions

HAMPTON (C-2) pop. 6,987, elev. 890'

ATLANTA MOTOR SPEEDWAY is .2 mi. w. of jct. US 19/41 at 1500 Tara Pl. Guided van tours of the motorsport facility allow visitors to ride on the track (dependent upon availability) as well as visit the NASCAR garage, victory lane, a luxury suite and the grandstands. A small garden dedicated to Richard Petty contains a statue of the race car driver.

Hours: Guided tours every hour Mon.-Fri. 10-11 and 1-4. No tours are conducted during race weeks. Last tour departs at closing. Closed Jan. 1, Easter, Thanksgiving, Christmas and Dec. 31. Phone ahead to confirm tour availability. **Cost:** Tour $10; $5 (ages 6-12). **Phone:** (770) 707-7970. GT ⬛ ⬛

MELVIN L. NEWMAN WETLANDS CENTER is 2.2 mi. e. of SR 3/US 19/41 at 2755 Freeman Rd. The center educates visitors about such issues as the conservation of natural resources and the preservation of the environment and resident wildlife. The 32-acre site includes a half-mile nature trail with displays documenting the area's ecology and wildlife; visitors might spot beavers, deer, foxes, turtles and any of more than 150 bird species. Primitive upland trails also are available. The learning center contains exhibits about the wetlands. Educational programs are offered. Guided tours are available by appointment (requires a minimum of 15 participants).

Pets are not permitted. **Time:** Allow 1 hour minimum. **Hours:** Interpretive building open Tues.-Sat. 9-5. Phone ahead to confirm holiday closures. Nature trails open daily 7-7, Mar.-Oct.; 7-5, rest of year. **Cost:** Guided tour $1. Admission free. **Phone:** (770) 603-5603. GT ⬛

WESTERN INN   (770)707-1477
🔽🔽 Hotel. $55-$110 **Address:** 1078 Bear Creek Blvd 30228 **Location:** 1 mi w of center of town; at US 41 and 19. Opposite Atlanta Motor Speedway. **Facility:** 40 units. 2 stories (no elevator), interior corridors. **Terms:** cancellation fee imposed.

HAPEVILLE pop. 6,373
• Hotels & Restaurants map & index p. 94
• Part of Atlanta area — see map p. 44

BEST WESTERN PLUS ATLANTA AIRPORT-EAST
(404)763-8777 ㉓

Best Western PLUS **AAA Benefit:** Save 10% or more every day and earn 10% bonus points!
Address: 301 N Central Ave 30354 **Location:** I-75 exit 239, just w; I-85 exit 75, 1.5 mi e. **Facility:** 145 units. 2-10 stories, interior corridors. **Terms:** cancellation fee imposed. **Pool(s):** outdoor. **Activities:** exercise room. **Guest Services:** coin laundry. **Featured Amenity:** continental breakfast.

COURTYARD BY MARRIOTT ATLANTA AIRPORT NORTH/VIRGINIA AVENUE   (404)559-1043 ⓴

Hotel $76-$235
COURTYARD Marriott **AAA Benefit:** Members save 5% or more!
Address: 3399 International Blvd 30354 **Location:** I-85 exit 73 southbound; exit 73A northbound, 0.5 mi e to International Blvd, then just n. **Facility:** 152 units. 4 stories, interior corridors. **Pool(s):** outdoor. **Activities:** exercise room. **Guest Services:** valet and coin laundry.

HILTON ATLANTA AIRPORT   (404)767-9000 ㉒

Hotel $99-$289
Hilton HOTELS & RESORTS **AAA Benefit:** Members save 5% or more!
Address: 1031 Virginia Ave 30354 **Location:** I-85 exit 73 southbound; exit 73A northbound, just e. **Facility:** 507 units. 17 stories, interior corridors. **Parking:** on-site (fee) and valet. **Terms:** 1-7 night minimum stay, cancellation fee imposed. **Amenities:** safes. **Dining:** 3 restaurants. **Pool(s):** outdoor, heated indoor. **Activities:** hot tub, exercise room. **Guest Services:** valet laundry, area transportation.

RESIDENCE INN BY MARRIOTT ATLANTA AIRPORT NORTH/VIRGINIA AVENUE   (404)761-0511 ㉑

Extended Stay Hotel $99-$240
Residence Inn Marriott **AAA Benefit:** Members save 5% or more!
Address: 3401 International Blvd 30354 **Location:** I-85 exit 73 southbound; exit 73A northbound, 0.5 mi e to International Blvd, then just n. **Facility:** 126 units, some two bedrooms, efficiencies and kitchens. 2 stories (no elevator), interior/exterior corridors. **Pool(s):** outdoor. **Activities:** playground, exercise room. **Guest Services:** valet and coin laundry. **Featured Amenity:** full hot breakfast.

WHERE TO EAT

HAMBONES   404/767-0888 ㉛
🔽 Barbecue. Quick Serve. $5-$20 **AAA Inspector Notes:** Smoked barbecue is the specialty and diners can find pulled pork, ribs, chicken, brisket, sausage and turkey here. Also available are hamburgers, hot dogs, Brunswick stew and a good selection of such Southern sides as potato salad and baked beans. The service is fast and outdoor dining is available. **Features:** full bar. **Address:** 811 Virginia Ave 30354 **Location:** I-85 exit 73, 0.9 mi e. L

Request roadside assistance in a click — online or using the AAA or CAA apps

(See map & index p. 94.)

THAI HEAVEN   404/767-0115
♦♦ Thai. Casual Dining. $8-$30 **AAA Inspector Notes:** The chef's specialties at this spot include honey duck and hot garlic scallops. Other authentic dishes such as panang curry, basil stir fry and pad thai grace the menu. An impressive sushi bar is popular here as well. Patio dining is available. **Features:** full bar, patio dining. **Address:** 1155 Virginia Ave 30354 **Location:** I-85 exit 73 southbound; exit 73A northbound, 0.3 mi e. [L] [D] CALL &M

HARTWELL pop. 4,469

QUALITY INN   (706)376-7298
♦♦ Motel. $64-$99 **Address:** 1091 E Franklin St 30643 **Location:** Jct SR 366/US 29, 1.2 mi e on US 29 (E Franklin St). **Facility:** 40 units. 2 stories (no elevator), exterior corridors. **Pool(s):** outdoor. **Activities:** exercise room.

HAWKINSVILLE pop. 4,589

BEST WESTERN HAWKINSVILLE INN & SUITES   (478)783-1300

	AAA Benefit:
♦♦ Hotel $75-$150	Best Western. Save 10% or more every day and earn 10% bonus points!

Address: 86 Hwy 341 Bypass 31036 **Location:** 0.5 mi w on Commerce St (SR 26) to jct US 129/341, then just n. **Facility:** 26 units. 2 stories (no elevator), exterior corridors. **Pool(s):** outdoor. **Guest Services:** coin laundry. **Featured Amenity: continental breakfast.**

WHERE TO EAT

THE STEAK HOUSE RESTAURANT   478/892-3383
♦ Steak. Casual Dining. $5-$29 **AAA Inspector Notes:** Specialties at the family-run, family-friendly restaurant include char-broiled flavored steaks, a weekend seafood buffet and fresh homemade desserts. **Features:** senior menu. **Address:** 101 Buchan Rd 31036 **Location:** 0.5 mi w of downtown on Commerce St, just n on US 129/341. [L] [D] CALL &M

HAZLEHURST pop. 4,226

AMERICAS BEST VALUE INN   (912)375-3400

♦♦ Motel $60-$80	**Address:** 143 Martin Luther King Jr Blvd 31539 **Location:** Just nw of center on US 23/341. **Facility:** 42 units. 1 story, exterior corridors. **Pool(s):** outdoor. **Activities:** exercise room. **Guest Services:** coin laundry.

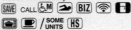

HELEN (A-3) pop. 510, elev. 1,444'

After deteriorating from an 1829 Georgia Gold Rush hot spot turned lumber mill town abandoned by 1969, the rejuvenated Helen mirrors a whimsical Alpine village. Surrounded by mountains and intersected by the Chattahoochee River, the town boasts cobblestone walkways, kaleidoscopic buildings, a market square and more than 100 specialty shops and restaurants.

Cast a line, hail a horse-drawn carriage, and pan for gold. Browse lines of shops filled with antiques, imported items and local crafts; or explore nearby Nacoochee Village, home to the 1876 Nora Mill and the 3-floor Nacoochee Antique Mall. If you're the outdoorsy type, several state parks and the surrounding Chattahoochee-Oconee National Forest (see place listing p. 155) might entice you with sightseeing, hiking, camping, canoeing and rafting.

Offering two beaches along a 53-acre lake, Unicoi State Park (see Recreation Areas Chart) is 2 miles northeast off SR 356. The park also plays host to the ♦ Fireside Art and Craft Show held in mid-February. More than 50 talented artists and skilled craftspeople participate in this juried Unicoi tradition. The Russell-Brasstown Scenic Byway (SR 348) traverses the Chattahoochee-Oconee National Forests between Helen and Brasstown Bald—at 4,784 feet, the highest point in the state—and is particularly beautiful in autumn. Hardman Farm State Historic Site, located 2 miles south at jct. SR 17 and 75, is the site of the Nacoochee Indian Mound.

And you'll be certain autumn has arrived when you hear a chorus of Prosts (the slang equivalent of Cheers) ringing through Helen during the 6-week Oktoberfest celebration, which begins in mid-September. Unwind with a beer-garden brewski or flaunt your Chicken Dance moves as you soak up the sound of genuine German tunes and the aroma of fresh wurst.

In June, bid Auf Wiedersehen to your favorite balloon at the annual Helen-to-the-Atlantic Balloon Race. Reputed to be the only long-distance hot air balloon competition in the United States, the event is conquered by the first contestant who crosses I-95.

Alpine Helen/White County Convention & Visitors Bureau: 726 Bruckenstrasse, Helen, GA 30545. **Phone:** (706) 878-2181 or (800) 858-8027.

SMITHGALL WOODS STATE PARK is 3 mi. w. on SR 75 Alt. to 61 Tsalaki Tr. Dukes Creek, one of the state's premier trout streams, runs through this north Georgia wilderness area. Hikers, bicyclists and nature photographers can take advantage of 5 miles of trails and 18 miles of roads that crisscross a region of hardwood habitats and mountain streams home to a variety of wildlife. Cottages are available.

Catch-and-release trout fishing is only allowed on certain days and reservations are required; visitors should call ahead for a current schedule and register at the visitor center. The center has a Discovery Room with exhibits. Ranger-led programs are offered. **Time:** Allow 1 hour minimum. **Hours:** Park open daily 7-7. Visitor center open 8-5; closed Christmas. **Cost:** Free. **Parking:** $5. **Phone:** (706) 878-3087.

BEST WESTERN PLUS RIVERPARK INN & CONFERENCE CENTER ALPINE HELEN   (706)878-2111

Motel
$89-$309

AAA Benefit: Save 10% or more every day and earn 10% bonus points!

Address: 8220 S Main St 30545 **Location:** 0.5 mi s on SR 17 and 75. **Facility:** 65 units. 2 stories, interior/exterior corridors. **Amenities:** safes. **Pool(s):** outdoor. **Activities:** exercise room. **Guest Services:** area transportation.

COUNTRY INN & SUITES BY CARLSON   (706)878-9000

Hotel
$59-$299

Address: 877 Edelweiss Strasse 30545 **Location:** 0.4 mi s on SR 17 and 75. **Facility:** 62 units. 3 stories, interior corridors. **Terms:** 2 night minimum stay - seasonal and/or weekends, cancellation fee imposed, resort fee. **Pool(s):** heated indoor. **Activities:** hot tub, limited exercise equipment. **Guest Services:** coin laundry. **Featured Amenity:** full hot breakfast.

HAMPTON INN   (706)878-3310

Hotel. $99-$279 Address: 147 Unicoi St 30545 **Location:** Waterfront. Jct Spring St, just e of N Main St. **Facility:** 67 units. 4 stories, interior corridors. **Terms:** check-in 4 pm, 1-7 day minimum stay, cancellation fee imposed. **Pool(s):** outdoor. **Activities:** limited exercise equipment. **Guest Services:** coin laundry.

AAA Benefit: Members save up to 10%!

THE HELENDORF RIVER INN & CONFERENCE CENTER   706/878-2271

Motel. Rates not provided. **Address:** 33 Munich Strasse 30545 **Location:** SR 17 and 75; center. **Facility:** 99 units, some kitchens. 2-3 stories, exterior corridors. **Pool(s):** heated indoor. **Activities:** fishing. **Guest Services:** coin laundry.

HOLIDAY INN EXPRESS & SUITES - HELEN CONVENTION CENTER   706/878-1084

fyi Hotel. Rates not provided. Too new to rate, opening scheduled for July 2016. **Address:** 8100 S Main St 30545 **Location:** 0.5 mi s on SR 17 and 75. **Amenities:** 86 units, coffeemakers, microwaves, refrigerators, pool, exercise facility.

QUALITY INN   (706)878-2268

Motel. $74-$259 Address: 15 Yonah St 30545 **Location:** Just w of Mack St. **Facility:** 36 units. 1-2 stories (no elevator), exterior corridors. **Pool(s):** outdoor.

WHERE TO EAT

BIGG DADDY'S   706/878-2739

American. Gastropub. $7-$24 **AAA Inspector Notes:** This popular spot promotes itself as a restaurant/tavern, while feeling like a bar with its huge dining patio. Guests can sip beers from an excellent selection while enjoying distinctive dishes that take on such classics as fried chicken, pizza, pasta, burgers, sandwiches and never frozen, jumbo wings. **Features:** full bar, patio dining, Sunday brunch. **Address:** 807 Edelweiss Strasse 30545 **Location:** 0.5 mi s.

BODENSEE RESTAURANT   706/969-8129

▼▼ German. Casual Dining. $8-$24 **AAA Inspector Notes:** The best German food I have ever had can be found here. Fresh ingredients are prepared lovingly from the owner of this eatery and everything is delicious. I had the Gypsy schnitzel which was prepared with paprika, mushrooms, onions and spicy red sauce. The German potato salad and red cabbage were excellent accompaniments and the Black Forest cake for dessert was the perfect ending to a great meal. **Features:** full bar. **Address:** 64 Munich Strasse 30545 **Location:** Just s. L D CALL &M

CAFE INTERNATIONAL   706/878-3102

▼▼ Continental. Casual Dining. $6-$18 **AAA Inspector Notes:** A nice selection of schnitzels, cheeses and side dishes, as well as sumptuous desserts, await guests of this cafe on the river. Outdoor dining is popular at this scenic spot. **Features:** beer & wine, patio dining. **Address:** 8546 Main St 30545 **Location:** Downtown. L D 🍴

HOFER'S BAKERY & CAFE   706/878-8200

▼▼ German Breads/Pastries. Casual Dining. $8-$13 **AAA Inspector Notes:** You may be lured by the bakery for yummy desserts and breads, but be sure to stay for traditional dishes from Bavaria for breakfast or lunch. There also is a butcher case full of wursts and some groceries available for those who yearn for a bit of Germany. **Features:** beer & wine, patio dining. **Address:** 8758 N Main St 30545 **Location:** Downtown. B L

LA CABANA   706/878-3456

▼▼ Tex-Mex. Casual Dining. $5-$15 **AAA Inspector Notes:** Guests can wash down chips and salsa at this eatery where traditional Tex-Mex is dished up alongside tasty margaritas. Lunch specials appeal to the midday crowd. **Features:** full bar. **Address:** 8160 S Main St 30545 **Location:** 0.6 mi s on SR 17 and 75. L D CALL &M

MULLY'S NACOOCHEE GRILL   706/878-1020

▼▼ Southern American. Casual Dining. $10-$27 **AAA Inspector Notes:** Fresh ingredients and well-prepared regional favorites are strong points at the restaurant, which features dishes such as trout and jalapeño grits. Located just south of the town limits in a historic area, the restaurant is in a converted farmhouse with multiple rooms and a large covered porch. **Features:** full bar, patio dining, Sunday brunch. **Address:** 7277 S Main St 30545 **Location:** 1.3 mi s on SR 75 and 17. L D

SPICE 55 THAI & SUSHI BAR   706/878-1010

▼▼ Thai Sushi. Casual Dining. $9-$27 **AAA Inspector Notes:** You'll find all of your favorite Thai and sushi meals including pad thai, Tom Yum soup and Fresh Basil rolls, in a town that typically features German fare. The service is friendly and the restaurant space is just off the main drag where it is a bit quieter. The restaurant is closed between the lunch and dinner hours. **Features:** full bar, patio dining. **Address:** 705 Brucken Strasse 30545 **Location:** Jct Main St, just e; across from Visitor's Center. L D

HIAWASSEE (A-3) pop. 880, elev. 1,968'

The 🎭 Georgia Mountain Fair, held from mid- to late July, attracts thousands of people with its arts and craft show, historical exhibits and live entertainment. In early December, the 🎭 Mountain Country Christmas Tour of Homes features a tour of seasonally decorated homes, a tree lighting ceremony and an art walk.

DANIELS STEAK HOUSE   706/896-8008

▼▼ American. Casual Dining. $7-$20 **AAA Inspector Notes:** The lunch buffet is quite popular here among locals and boasts such home-style cooking as fried chicken, baked fish, pork chops and meatloaf. A salad bar and a good selection of veggies also are featured. Dinner selections focus on steaks and seafood and the portions are large. Blueberry cobbler, banana pudding and various types of cake and pie help make up the tempting dessert choices. **Address:** 273 Big Sky Dr 30546 **Location:** On US 76; center. L D CALL &M

HINESVILLE (D-5) pop. 33,437, elev. 75'

Hinesville is located 40 miles southwest of Savannah. The city was devastated in Gen. Sherman's March to the Sea during the Civil War. In 1940, nearby Camp Stewart was established to provide antiaircraft training to soldiers. The town grew as people moved in and opened businesses to profit from the flood of soldiers, but the town shrank, as boomtowns do, at the end of World War II. In 1956 the camp was designated Fort Stewart, and today soldiers continue to frequent the town.

BAYMONT INN & SUITES HINESVILLE FORT STEWART AREA   (912)408-4444

◆ Hotel $62-$75

Address: 773 Frank Cochran Dr 31313 **Location:** Jct SR 119/196, 1 mi sw on SR 196, then just nw. **Facility:** 52 units. 2 stories, interior corridors. **Pool(s):** outdoor. **Guest Services:** coin laundry. **Featured Amenity:** breakfast buffet.

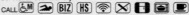

COUNTRY INN & SUITES BY CARLSON   912/877-7777

▼▼▼ Hotel. Rates not provided. **Address:** 742 General Stewart Way 31313 **Location:** Jct US 84 and SR 38C. **Facility:** 65 units, some efficiencies. 3 stories, interior corridors. **Amenities:** safes. **Pool(s):** outdoor. **Activities:** sauna, exercise room. **Guest Services:** coin laundry.

FAIRFIELD INN & SUITES BY MARRIOTT   (912)876-2003

◆◆ Hotel $84-$148

FAIRFIELD INN & SUITES Marriott

AAA Benefit: Members save 5% or more!

Address: 1494 E Oglethorpe Hwy 31313 **Location:** Waterfront. Jct US 84 and SR 38C, 0.3 mi e. **Facility:** 81 units. 3 stories, interior corridors. **Pool(s):** outdoor. **Activities:** hot tub, limited exercise equipment. **Guest Services:** valet laundry. **Featured Amenity:** full hot breakfast.

SAVE 🍴 CALL &M 🏊 BIZ HS
🛜 ✕ 🛗 🖥 🖨

HAMPTON INN   (912)877-4090

▼▼▼ Hotel. $99-$149 **Address:** 1148 E Oglethorpe Hwy 31313 **Location:** Jct US 84 and SR 38C, just ne. **Facility:** 60 units. 3 stories, interior corridors. **Terms:** 1-7 night minimum stay, cancellation fee imposed. **Pool(s):** outdoor. **Activities:** exercise room. **Guest Services:** complimentary laundry.

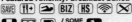

HOLIDAY INN EXPRESS HOTEL & SUITES HINESVILLE FORT STEWART 912/877-5611

▼▼▼ **Hotel.** Rates not provided. **Address:** 1388 E Oglethorpe Hwy 31313 **Location:** Jct US 84 and SR 38C, 0.3 mi ne. **Facility:** 86 units, some efficiencies. 3 stories, interior corridors. **Pool(s):** heated indoor. **Activities:** hot tub, exercise room. **Guest Services:** coin laundry.

[icons]

LA QUINTA INN & SUITES HINESVILLE/FT STEWART (912)369-3000

▼▼▼ **Contemporary Hotel.** $86-$180 **Address:** 1740 E Oglethorpe Hwy 31313 **Location:** Jct US 84 and SR 38C, 0.8 mi ne. **Facility:** 80 units. 4 stories, interior corridors. **Pool(s):** heated indoor. **Activities:** hot tub, exercise room. **Guest Services:** valet and coin laundry.

[icons]

WHERE TO EAT

KYOTO SUSHI HOUSE 2 912/369-3678

▼▼ Asian. Casual Dining. $4-$20 **AAA Inspector Notes:** No hibachi tables with knife-wielding chefs can be found here but there is a sushi bar, saki bar and a standard dining room for guests to enjoy great food. The menu is dominated by Japanese-style dishes but a few Thai plates appear as well. Lucky sushi fans will have trouble finding a wider selection of styles and sizes and, if my experience with the spicy salmon roll is any indication, they will not be disappointed. After dinner try the tempura-style cheesecake—warm, sweet deliciousness. **Features:** full bar, happy hour. **Address:** 213 W Oglethorpe Hwy 31313 **Location:** Just e of center on US 84; between SR 38 and 119. [L] [D]

RODEO MEXICAN RESTAURANT 912/877-2040

▼▼ Mexican. Casual Dining. $5-$17 **AAA Inspector Notes:** Nothing distinctive here, just a good place to get your Mexican fix. The menu has all the standard fare with no surprises. Quesadillas are the specialty of the house and specials are offered daily for lunch and dinner with a good selection of combinations. Light Mexican and vegetarian menus are available. **Features:** full bar, happy hour. **Address:** 304 W Oglethorpe Hwy 31313 **Location:** Just e of center on US 84. [L] [D] CALL [icon]

RUSTY PIG BBQ 912/368-4744

▼ Barbecue. Quick Serve. $6-$19 **AAA Inspector Notes:** The tidy restaurant features a variety of plates, wraps, sandwiches and baskets using brisket, pork and chicken. Bulk ordering is also available if you want to enjoy at home or while tailgating. **Address:** 762 Veterans Pkwy 31313 **Location:** Jct SR 119/196, 1 mi sw on SR 196, then just nw. [L] [D] CALL [icon]

THAT'S ITALIAN 912/432-7552

▼ Italian Pizza. Quick Serve. $9-$18 **AAA Inspector Notes:** This small self-service restaurant features a wide selection of pizza, sandwiches, panini and pasta dishes with surprisingly flavorful sauces. Eat in or take out. **Address:** 364 Memorial Dr 31313 **Location:** Just n of center, 0.6 mi nw. [L] [D] CALL [icon]

ZUM ROSENHOF 912/876-2191

▼▼ German. Casual Dining. $7-$22 **AAA Inspector Notes:** It's easy to fall in love with this quaint café. Guests can sit at the bar with an authentic German beer or take a seat at one of the tables to nosh on a full-course meal of bratwurst, rippchen, schnitzel or other favorites prepared by the German chef/owner. If you're pressed for time make reservations, seating is limited. **Features:** full bar, happy hour. **Reservations:** suggested. **Address:** 103 Midway St, Suite B 31313 **Location:** Downtown; adjacent to courthouse. **Parking:** street only. [L] [D]

HIRAM pop. 3,546

BEST WESTERN HIRAM INN & SUITES (770)222-9494

▼▼▼ Hotel $100-$150

AAA Benefit: Save 10% or more every day and earn 10% bonus points!

Address: 1340 Pace Rd 30141 **Location:** Jct SR 92/6 and US 278, just w. **Facility:** 62 units. 3 stories, interior corridors. **Pool(s):** outdoor. **Activities:** exercise room. **Guest Services:** valet and coin laundry. **Featured Amenity: full hot breakfast.**

[icons]

COUNTRY INN & SUITES BY CARLSON (770)222-0456

▼▼ Hotel. $95-$150 **Address:** 70 Enterprise Path 30134 **Location:** Jct SR 92/6 and US 278, 0.3 mi w. **Facility:** 51 units. 3 stories, interior corridors. **Terms:** cancellation fee imposed. **Pool(s):** heated indoor. **Activities:** hot tub. **Guest Services:** coin laundry.

[icons]

SLEEP INN & SUITES (770)222-9161

▼▼▼ Hotel. $94-$164 **Address:** 181 Metromont Rd 30141 **Location:** Jct SR 92/6 and US 278, 0.9 mi e on US 278 to Metromont Rd, then just s. **Facility:** 60 units. 3 stories, interior corridors. **Activities:** exercise room. **Guest Services:** valet and coin laundry.

[icons]

WHERE TO EAT

CHEESEBURGER BOBBY'S 678/567-2037

▼ Burgers. Quick Serve. $3-$6 **AAA Inspector Notes:** Nibble on hand-cut fries with your fresh, hand-patted burger, which you'll gussy up with onions, lettuce, tomatoes, pickles and other items on the condiment station. Other choices include hot dogs, chicken sandwiches and custard for dessert. Friendly servers tend the bright, fresh and clean dining room. **Address:** 5077 Jimmy Lee Smith Pkwy 30141 **Location:** Jct SR 92/6 and US 278, 0.6 mi e. [L] [D] CALL [icon]

HAI HAI 678/384-0096

▼▼ Japanese. Casual Dining. $2-$35 **AAA Inspector Notes:** Guests can watch as sushi and hibachi items are prepared by entertaining and friendly cooks at this contemporary Japanese restaurant. Try the Mt. Fuji, cowboy roll, crunch roll or seared tuna. Regular tables and a sushi bar are available for those not wishing to see the show. **Features:** full bar. **Address:** 5157 Jimmy Lee Smith Pkwy 30141 **Location:** Jct SR 92/6 and US 278, 0.5 mi e. [L] [D] [icon]

HUEY LUEY'S MEXICAN KITCHEN & MARGARITA BAR 678/567-0080

▼▼ Mexican. Casual Dining. $6-$14 **AAA Inspector Notes:** This festive restaurant offers classic Mexican favorites in a contemporary setting. The dishes are hearty, and the margaritas are top notch. From a heaping plate of nachos to the sizzling fajitas and creamy avocado rolls, there is something for every taste bud at this family-friendly eatery. **Features:** full bar. **Address:** 5460 Wendy Bagwell Blvd 30141 **Location:** Jct SR 92/6 and Wendy Bagwell Pkwy. [L] [D] CALL [icon]

JIM 'N NICK'S BAR-B-Q 770/439-2662

▼▼ Barbecue. Casual Dining. $6-$25 **AAA Inspector Notes:** Southern hospitality reigns at Jim 'N Nick's, where diners get neighborly treatment as they dig into huge portions of tasty lean sausage, fresh chili, juicy smoked beef and pork. A slice of sublime homemade pie ends the meal on a high note. **Features:** full bar. **Address:** 5153 Jimmy Lee Smith Pkwy 30141 **Location:** Jct SR 92/6 and US 278, 0.5 mi e. [L] [D]

HOGANSVILLE pop. 3,060

WOODSTREAM INN   706/637-9395

▼▼ ▼▼ **Motel.** Rates not provided. **Address:** 1888 E Main St 30230 **Location:** I-85 exit 28, just w. **Facility:** 35 units, some efficiencies. 2 stories (no elevator), exterior corridors. **Pool(s):** outdoor. **Guest Services:** coin laundry.

WHERE TO EAT

ROGER'S BAR-B-QUE   706/637-4100

▼▼ ▼▼ Barbecue. Casual Dining. $3-$20 **AAA Inspector Notes:** At lunch diners can sample home-style meat and veggie plates, while as with lunch or dinner, they can feast on barbecue chicken, ribs or pork. The homemade Brunswick stew is quite tasty and the catfish dinners are popular as are sandwich plates which include steak, fish, grilled cheese, hamburgers, hot dogs and BLTs. Wrap up the meal with a piece of pie or some homemade cobbler. **Address:** 1863 E Main St 30230 **Location:** I-85 exit 28, just w; in Hummingbird Station. L D

JASPER (A-2) pop. 3,684, elev. 1,467'

Named after Sergeant William Jasper who died during the Revolutionary War, the tiny town of Jasper is known as The First Mountain City as it is located at the foothills of the Appalachian Mountains. Marble mining, including rare pink marble, is a key industry with the historic jail, courthouse and Historic Tate House all faced with the stone.

Overlooking Jasper, Sharp Mountain Vineyards, at 110 Rathgeb Tr., offers tours of its facilities and tastings of the 11 varieties of wines produced; phone (770) 735-1210.

MICROTEL INN & SUITES BY WYNDHAM JASPER
    (706)299-5500

▼▼ ▼▼ **Hotel.** $60-$100 **Address:** 171 H Mullins Ct 30143 **Location:** Jct SR 515/53, 0.9 mi n. **Facility:** 70 units. 3 stories, interior corridors. **Terms:** cancellation fee imposed.

WHERE TO EAT

FATZ   706/692-0003

▼▼ ▼▼ Regional American. Casual Dining. $8-$19 **AAA Inspector Notes:** Friendly staff and appealing country decor help set the tone for a relaxed and enjoyable dining experience. It's not unusual for guests to wait to be seated at the popular spot, which earns raves for its well-prepared variations on chicken, steak, ribs and pasta, as well as salads and sandwiches. The signature Southern-style peach cobbler served with vanilla ice cream and walnuts is scrumptious. **Features:** full bar. **Address:** 800 Noah Dr 30143 **Location:** Jct SR 515/53, 0.7 mi n. L D CALL ⚡M

JEFFERSON (B-3) pop. 9,432, elev. 850'

CRAWFORD W. LONG MUSEUM, off the public square at 28 College St., honors Dr. Long who in 1842 performed the first painless surgery using sulfuric ether as an anesthesia. The three-building museum occupies the original site of Dr. Long's discovery, emphasizing his life and the history of anesthesia. The museum includes an antebellum general store. A video presentation documenting Dr. Long's achievements also is offered. Educational programs are offered throughout the year.

Time: Allow 30 minutes minimum. **Hours:** Tues.-Fri. 10-5, Sat. 10-4. Closed major holidays. **Cost:** $5; $4 (ages 65+); $3 (students and active military with ID); free (ages 0-5). **Phone:** (706) 367-5307.

QUALITY INN   (706)693-4582

▼▼ ▼▼
Hotel
$75-$119

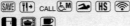

Address: 4880 US Hwy 129 N 30549 **Location:** I-85 exit 137, just e. **Facility:** 50 units. 2 stories (no elevator), interior corridors. **Pool(s):** indoor. **Activities:** hot tub, exercise room. **Guest Services:** coin laundry. **Featured Amenity:** continental breakfast.

JEKYLL ISLAND (F-6)

• Restaurants p. 197
• Part of Golden Isles area — see map p. 187

The most crowded chapter in the history of Jekyll Island began in 1886 when prominent East Coast millionaires, including Frank Henry Goodyear, Edwin and George Gould, J.P. Morgan, Joseph Pulitzer and William Rockefeller bought the island for $125,000. Naming themselves the Jekyll Island Club, they built a large clubhouse and elaborate cottages for use as a hunting preserve and family getaway.

The activities of some members while staying at this haven changed world events. In 1910 the first draft of the Federal Reserve Act, the foundation of the nation's monetary system, was drawn up. From Jekyll Island in 1915 the president of AT&T made the first transcontinental telephone call, speaking with President Woodrow Wilson in Washington, D.C., Alexander Graham Bell in New York and Bell's assistant Thomas Watson in San Francisco.

By the early 20th century Jekyll Island Club members were said to represent one-sixth of the world's wealth. By World War II, later generations had lost interest and had largely left the island, which was sold in 1947 to the state of Georgia for use as a state park.

Jekyll Island now is one of Georgia's major resort areas. The 10-mile beach offers surf fishing, swimming, bathhouses and a beach walk. The island's sand dunes form a natural buffer to protect land and buildings from tides, winds, waves and storms. Crossovers can be used for beach access. Golf, nature walks, tennis, miniature golf, sightseeing cruises and miles of bicycle trails are all available, plus picnic areas, campsites and a water park. Bicycles can be rented. Segway rentals are available seasonally (weather permitting).

Visitors traveling by private vehicle to Jekyll Island are required to pay a $6 daily parking fee at the island's entrance, at the end of the Jekyll Island Causeway.

Jekyll Island Welcome Center: 901 Downing Musgrove Causeway, Jekyll Island, GA 31527. **Phone:** (912) 635-3636 or (877) 453-5955.

GEORGIA SEA TURTLE CENTER is at 214 Stable Rd. in the Jekyll Island Historic Landmark District. The center is an educational, rehabilitation and research center for sick and injured sea turtles. An interactive exhibit gallery features engaging displays documenting the life cycle of a sea turtle. Rehabilitating turtles are displayed in several aquatic tanks. Educational talks are given throughout the day. Evening turtle walks and morning sunrise walks are offered in summer and focus on the natural history of sea turtles; a guided beach tour is included. A behind-the-scenes tour provides an up-close view of the center.

Time: Allow 1 hour minimum. **Hours:** Daily 9-5. Behind-the-scenes tour departs daily at 3. Turtle walks are scheduled daily at 8:30 and 9:30 p.m., June-July (except July 4). Sunrise walks are scheduled select days between 7 and 9 a.m. during turtle hatching season, Aug.-Sept. Closed Jan. 1, Christmas Eve and Christmas. Closes Thanksgiving at 2. Phone ahead to confirm schedule.

Cost: $7; $6 (ages 65+, teachers, active military and college students with ID); $5 (ages 4-12). Turtle walk $20. Behind-the-scenes tour $22; $17 (ages 10-12). Phone ahead to confirm rates. Reservations are required for turtle walks and behind-the-scenes tour. Turtle walks are limited to 25 persons; behind-the-scenes tour is limited to 6 persons. Children ages 0-4 are not permitted on walks. Children ages 0-9 are not permitted on behind-the-scenes tour. **Phone:** (912) 635-4444. [GT]

JEKYLL ISLAND HISTORIC LANDMARK DISTRICT TOUR, a cluster of late 19th-century cottages along Riverview Dr., is a reminder of an era when social life revolved around the Jekyll Island Club. Tours begin at the Jekyll Island Museum in the old club stables on Stable Road, where permanent exhibits explain the island's history.

A 90-minute, narrated Passport to the Century open-air tram tour of the district includes entry to two restored historic homes and a chapel. The Rockefeller Experience tour visits Indian Mound Cottage. Other programs are available seasonally. **Hours:** Museum open daily 9-5. Tours depart throughout the day; phone ahead to verify times. Closed Jan. 1, Thanksgiving, Christmas Eve and Christmas. **Cost:** Guided tour $16; $7 (ages 7-15). Rockefeller Experience tour $10; $5 (ages 7-15). **Phone:** (912) 635-4036. [GT]

SUMMER WAVES, 210 S. Riverview Dr., is an 11-acre water park. Featured attractions are six waterslides 30-50 feet high, a splash zone with a 750-gallon tipping bucket, a lazy river, a wave pool and a children's wading pool.

Hours: Mon.-Sat. 10-6 (also Sat. 6-8 p.m.), Sun. 11-7, late May-early Aug.; Sat. 10-6, Sun. 11-6, early May-late May (also Mon.-Fri. 10-5, mid- to late May) and early Aug. to mid-Sept. Phone ahead to confirm schedule. **Cost:** $19.95; $15.95 (children under 48 inches tall); $10.95 (ages 60+); free (ages 0-3 with swim diaper). Admission after 3 p.m. $11.95 (Mon.-Fri.); after 4 p.m. $13.95 (Sat.-Sun.). Two-day ticket

$26.95. A season pass is available. Phone ahead to confirm rates. **Phone:** (912) 635-2074. [ii]

JEKYLL ISLAND CLUB HOTEL   (912)635-2600

Classic Historic Hotel

$189-$519

Address: 371 Riverview Dr 31527 **Location:** 0.5 mi n of Ben Fortson Pkwy (SR 520/Beachview Dr), follow signs; in historic district. **Facility:** Offering a rare glimpse of the Gilded Age, this restored hotel and its annexes offer a variety of rooms and suites in five historic buildings, each unit is decorated in period furnishings. 157 units. 2-4 stories, interior corridors. **Parking:** on-site and valet. **Terms:** check-in 4 pm, 2 night minimum stay - weekends, 7 day cancellation notice-fee imposed, resort fee. **Amenities:** safes. **Dining:** 2 restaurants, also, Grand Dining Room, see separate listing. **Pool(s):** heated outdoor. **Activities:** fishing, recreation programs, bicycles, exercise room, massage. **Guest Services:** valet laundry, area transportation. (See ad this page.)

Jekyll Island Club Hotel

Georgia's Coastal Resort and National Historic Landmark!

VILLAS BY THE SEA   (912)635-2521

Vacation Rental Condominium

$119-$399

Address: 1175 N Beachview Dr 31527 **Location:** Oceanfront. Jct Ben Fortson Pkwy (SR 520/Beachview Dr), 4 mi n. **Facility:** The oceanside resort is set amid lush natural landscaping and towering windswept oaks. Boardwalks lead to an uncrowded wide beach. These elements combine to create a peaceful and relaxing atmosphere. 146 condominiums. 1-3 stories (no elevator), exterior corridors. **Terms:** check-in 4 pm, 2 night minimum stay - seasonal and/or weekends, 3 day cancellation notice, resort fee. **Dining:** The Driftwood Bistro, see separate listing. **Pool(s):** outdoor. **Activities:** fishing, bicycles, playground, exercise room. **Guest Services:** coin laundry.

▼ See AAA listing this page ▼

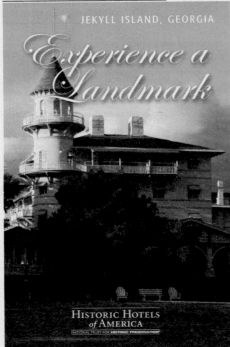

JEKYLL ISLAND, GEORGIA

Experience a Landmark

HISTORIC HOTELS of AMERICA
NATIONAL TRUST for HISTORIC PRESERVATION

Pick up colorful, top-quality travel guides and atlases at AAA/CAA offices

THE WESTIN JEKYLL ISLAND   (912)635-4545

Contemporary Hotel
$229-$349

WESTIN
HOTELS & RESORTS

AAA Benefit: Members save up to 15%, plus Starwood Preferred Guest® benefits!

Address: 110 Ocean Way 31527 **Location:** Oceanfront. Center. **Facility:** New in 2015, this beautiful property located at the convention center features upscale accommodations, beautifully appointed public spaces, upscale dining and an island location that can't be beat. 200 units. 5 stories, interior corridors. **Parking:** on-site and valet. **Terms:** check-in 4 pm, 3 day cancellation notice-fee imposed, resort fee. **Amenities:** video games, safes. **Dining:** 2 restaurants. **Pool(s):** outdoor. **Activities:** hot tub, exercise room, in-room exercise equipment. **Guest Services:** valet laundry, area transportation.

WHERE TO EAT

THE DRIFTWOOD BISTRO   912/635-3588
Comfort Food Seafood. Casual Dining. $9-$17 **AAA Inspector Notes:** Specializing in enhanced comfort food, this restaurant features casual and relaxed dining. Entrées include meatloaf, Yankee pot roast, stuffed flounder, stuffed collard greens and a fried shrimp platter. Selections are offered in petite and platter sizes which is a great option when you just want a bite. For dessert, the Georgia bourbon peach cobbler satisfies a craving for something sweet. **Features:** full bar, happy hour. **Address:** 1175 N Beachview Dr 31527 **Location:** Jct Ben Fortson Pkwy (SR 520/Beachview Dr), 4 mi n; in Villas by the Sea.

GRAND DINING ROOM   912/635-5155

Continental Fine Dining
$11-$37

AAA Inspector Notes: *Historic.* Stop by and savor a taste of creative, gourmet food, in an elegant Gilded Age dining room. Award-winning shrimp and grits, wild game, seafood, meat offerings and vegan selections are all locally sourced ensuring freshness and flavor. Service is exceptional without being stuffy and the wide menu selection offers something for everyone. Wonderful desserts are made in the house bakery. Breakfast and lunch are casual, while collared shirts and appropriate slacks are required at dinner. **Features:** full bar, early bird specials, Sunday brunch. **Reservations:** suggested. Semiformal attire. **Address:** 371 Riverview Dr 31527 **Location:** 0.5 mi n of Ben Fortson Pkwy (SR 520/Beachview Dr), follow signs; in historic district; in Jekyll Island Club Hotel. **Parking:** on-site and valet.

LATITUDE 31   912/635-3800
American. Casual Dining. $9-$36 **AAA Inspector Notes:** Dine indoors or enjoy the meal outside on the pier with summer evening entertainment at this seafood haven. Indulge in scrumptious seafood entrées and a large selection of pasta dishes with juicy chicken or marinara sauce. Closed for lunch September through May. **Features:** full bar, patio dining. **Address:** 370 Riverview Dr 31527 **Location:** 1 mi n from Jekyll Island Bridge.

MCGARVEY'S WEE PUB   912/258-5354
Sandwiches Wings. Casual Dining. $9-$18 **AAA Inspector Notes:** This welcome addition to the island is located in the new and growing central shopping district right at the island's entry point. Surrounded by shops and near the ocean, it is a great gathering spot after a day of touring the nature preserves. The menu is dominated by typical pub grub finger foods and sandwiches but a few full entrées like Irish pasta, fish and chips, steaks and shepherd's pie also are available. Large screen TVs and cold beer round out the venue. **Features:** full bar, patio dining, happy hour. **Address:** 267 Village at Glynn Pl 31527 **Location:** Jct Jekyll Island Cswy (SR 520) and Beachview Dr.

TORTUGA JACK'S BAJA MEXICAN   912/342-2600
Tex-Mex. Casual Dining. $10-$18 **AAA Inspector Notes:** Located in the dunes near the ocean, diners can relax here on the covered patio where the sound of the waves lapping the beach and the caw of the cowbirds scavenging for table crumbs can be heard. Or they can sit in the air conditioned dining room and observe through the large glass wall. The menu is limited but well prepared and features burritos, custom tacos, fajitas, tortas and a few authentic desserts. A children's menu also is available. **Features:** full bar, patio dining, happy hour. **Address:** 201 N Beachview Dr 31527 **Location:** Jct Jekyll Island Cswy (SR 520) and N Beachview Dr, just n.

JOHNS CREEK pop. 76,728
- Hotels & Restaurants map & index p. 82, 90
- Part of Atlanta area — see map p. 44

HILTON GARDEN INN ATLANTA NORTH-JOHNS CREEK
770/476-1966 9
Hotel. Rates not provided.
Address: 11695 Medlock Bridge Rd 30097 **Location:** Jct SR 141 and 120, 1 mi n. **Facility:** 122 units. 5 stories, interior corridors. **Pool(s):** outdoor. **Activities:** hot tub, exercise room. **Guest Services:** valet and coin laundry, area transportation.

AAA Benefit: Members save up to 10%!

HYATT PLACE ATLANTA/DULUTH/JOHNS CREEK
(770)622-5858 10

Hotel
$89-$259

HYATT PLACE
AAA Benefit: Members save 10%!

Address: 11505 Medlock Bridge Rd 30097 **Location:** Jct SR 141 and 120, 0.7 mi n. **Facility:** 122 units. 5 stories, interior corridors. **Terms:** cancellation fee imposed. **Pool(s):** heated outdoor. **Activities:** exercise room. **Guest Services:** valet laundry, area transportation. **Featured Amenity:** full hot breakfast.

WHERE TO EAT

BONEFISH GRILL   770/475-6668 71
Seafood. Fine Dining. $10-$28 **AAA Inspector Notes:** Fish is the house specialty, and the menu and nightly specials offer a variety of choices. Well-prepared food is cooked to perfection. Service is casual in nature, and the staff is skilled and attentive. **Features:** full bar. **Address:** 11705 C Jones Bridge Rd 30005 **Location:** SR 141 and 120, 3 mi e.

(See maps & indexes p. 82, 90.)

PALOMILLA'S GRILLHOUSE   678/710-8343   **5**
♥♥ Cuban. Casual Dining. $3-$15 **AAA Inspector Notes:** This casual grill house serves classic Cuban dishes such as vaca frita, cerdo asado (roast pork) and coconut flan. The large bar is well stocked and offers a variety of cocktails. Patio seating is popular when the weather is nice. **Features:** full bar, patio dining. **Address:** 11030 Medlock Bridge Rd 30097 **Location:** SR 141 and 120, 8.5 mi ne; in Johns Creek Commons. L D LATE CALL M

PAMPAS STEAKHOUSE   678/339-0029   **72**
♥♥♥ Steak. Fine Dining. $8-$55 **AAA Inspector Notes:** Celebrating fine dining and Argentine cuisine, this steakhouse has bold flavors and hearty portions. Sides are served family style and designed to share. Diners can enjoy the elegant dining room while watching steaks being grilled through the looking glass into the kitchen. Enhance the meal with a selection from an extensive wine list. **Features:** full bar, Sunday brunch. **Reservations:** suggested. **Address:** 10970-A State Bridge Rd 30022 **Location:** US 19 exit 10, 3.2 mi n on Old Milton Pkwy. **Parking:** on-site and valet.
D CALL M

STONEY RIVER LEGENDARY STEAKS   770/497-6676   **8**
♥♥♥ Steak. Fine Dining. $15-$42 **AAA Inspector Notes:** For more than 20 years this restaurant has been serving up legendary steaks—the seafood is pretty tempting, too. Each meal is accompanied by scrumptious poppy-seed yeast rolls with honey butter which are addictive. Try the ahi tuna roll to start off the meal and save room for one of the many decadent, homemade desserts. Favorite dishes include Scottish salmon, filet mignon and a plethora of flavorful side dishes such as sautéed spinach and onion mashed potatoes. **Features:** full bar, Sunday brunch. **Reservations:** suggested. **Address:** 5800 State Bridge Rd 30097 **Location:** Corner of State Bridge Rd and Peachtree Industrial Blvd. D

TRATTORIA ONE.41   770/497-0021   **6**
♥♥♥ Italian. Fine Dining. $5-$39 **AAA Inspector Notes:** This boutique restaurant offers classic Italian cuisine in an intimate setting. Built from quality ingredients and professional skill the menu features dishes such as homemade Italian sausage, roasted butternut squash ravioli, lobster tails and veal chop parmigiana. **Features:** full bar. **Reservations:** suggested. **Address:** 9810 Medlock Bridge Rd 30097 **Location:** I-285 exit 31B (SR 141), 4.1 mi ne. D CALL M

VIANDE ROUGE   770/623-4959   **7**
♥♥♥ French Steak. Fine Dining. $10-$55 **AAA Inspector Notes:** This French-inspired steakhouse is decadent with luscious reds, dark wood and quality art all reminiscent of a time when dining was the privilege of the elite. The menu is a blend of juicy steaks and French favorites such as escargot, crepe Florentine and bananas Foster flambé. Satisfy a taste for seafood with Maine lobster, East Coast oysters or Alaskan king crab. Portions are generous and pair well with the extensive wine and cocktail list. **Features:** full bar. **Reservations:** suggested. **Address:** 9810 Medlock Bridge Rd 30097 **Location:** I-285 exit 31B (SR 141), 4.1 mi ne. D CALL M

JONESBORO (B-2) pop. 4,724, elev. 917'
• Part of Atlanta area — see map p. 44

Clayton County Convention and Visitors Bureau: 104 N. Main St., Jonesboro, GA 30236. **Phone:** (770) 478-4800 or (800) 662-7829.

ROAD TO TARA MUSEUM is at 104 N. Main St. Housed in the 1867 Jonesboro Depot, the majority of exhibits are dedicated to the novel and movie "Gone With the Wind." Memorabilia, reproduction dresses, information about author Margaret Mitchell, collectors' items, copies of foreign translations and foreign movie posters are displayed. Also included is information about the fictional plantation Tara and the stars of the film, its premiere and awards.

Time: Allow 30 minutes minimum. **Hours:** Mon.-Fri. 8:30-5:30, Sat. 10-4. Last admission 45 minutes before closing. Closed Jan. 1, Thanksgiving, Christmas Eve and Christmas. **Cost:** $7; $6 (ages 6-12, ages 55+ and students with ID). **Phone:** (770) 478-4800 or (800) 662-7829. 🏛

SAVE **STATELY OAKS PLANTATION,** off Jodeco Rd. at 100 Carriage Ln., is an 1839 Greek Revival plantation house furnished with antiques. Also on-site are various outbuildings that include a one-room schoolhouse, original log kitchen and tenant house. Special events are held throughout the year. **Time:** Allow 1 hour minimum. **Hours:** Tours offered Mon.-Sat. 10-3. Grounds close at 4. Closed Jan. 1, Thanksgiving, day after Thanksgiving, Christmas Eve, Christmas and Dec. 31. **Cost:** Tour $12; $9 (ages 55+ and military with ID); $6 (ages 5-11). **Phone:** (770) 473-0197. GT 🏛

SONNY'S REAL PIT BAR-B-Q   770/968-0052
♥♥ Barbecue. Casual Dining. $8-$17 **AAA Inspector Notes:** Bearing the name after its founder, Floyd "Sonny" Tillman, this barbecue restaurant first opened its doors circa 1968 in Gainesville, Florida and has since spawned over 150 more throughout the Southeast. The menu is steeped in finger lickin' favorites such as ribs, pulled pork, beef brisket, burgers, catfish, shrimp and chargrilled chicken. Let's not forget about the fried okra, which is the perfect starter dish, and their homemade baked beans. **Features:** beer only. **Address:** 641 Mount Zion Rd 30236 **Location:** Jct US 19/41, just e on Morrow Industrial Blvd. L D

JULIETTE (C-3) elev. 376'

Juliette, a thriving mill town in the 1930s, fell on hard times but was revived by the local filming of the movies "A Killing Affair" in the 1980s and "Fried Green Tomatoes" in the early 1990s. Visitors can sample this Southern delicacy at the Whistle Stop Café, next to the former train depot.

JARRELL PLANTATION STATE HISTORIC SITE is 7 mi. s.e. via Round Oak-Juliette Rd. and Jarrell Plantation Rd. to 711 Jarrell Plantation Rd. An example of a self-sufficient working cotton plantation, this 236-acre historic site was settled in the 1840s and belonged to the Jarrell family until 1974. Inside the two main residences are original 19th-century furnishings. Among the 20 historic buildings on the site are a mill complex with steam engines, a cotton gin, a blacksmith and woodworking shop, a syrup evaporator and a barn. Wear a pair of comfortable shoes for exploring.

Time: Allow 1 hour minimum. **Hours:** Thurs.-Sat. 9-5. Last tour begins 1 hour before closing. Closed Jan. 1, Thanksgiving and Christmas. **Cost:** $6.50; $6 (ages 62+); $4 (ages 6-17). **Phone:** (478) 986-5172. GT 🏛

KENNESAW (G-1) pop. 29,783, elev. 1,093'
• Restaurants p. 200
• Hotels & Restaurants map & index p. 76
• Part of Atlanta area — see map p. 44

The passengers aboard a train leaving Big Shanty—modern day Kennesaw—the morning of April 12, 1862, had no idea that a dramatic episode

(See map & index p. 76.)

in the Civil War was about to begin before their breakfast coffee cooled. While the passengers and crew ate, civilian James Andrews and 21 Union soldiers, who had boarded in civilian clothes, stole the train and headed for Chattanooga, Tenn.

The conductor and crew chased the stolen train on foot, by handcar and with commandeered engines, catching Andrews just 5 miles from his goal. Andrews and seven of his "raiders" were returned to Atlanta and executed as spies. The Walt Disney movie "The Great Locomotive Chase" was based on the incident.

(SAVE) **SOUTHERN MUSEUM OF CIVIL WAR AND LOCOMOTIVE HISTORY** is at 2829 Cherokee St. This Smithsonian affiliate focuses on the history of railroads during and after the Civil War. The museum's exhibits tell the story of "The General," which was stolen during an incident known as "The Great Locomotive Chase." A 25-minute film about the chase is presented. A Civil War regimental flag is on display. Also featured is a replica of the Glover Machine Works locomotive factory complete with restored belt-driven assembly line and several trains in various stages of completion. Changing exhibits are offered as well in the Cobb Energy Gallery.

The Jolley Education Center has hands-on activities for both children and adults and showcases a restored Georgia Merci Boxcar that carried troops and aid supplies in Europe during both World Wars.

Time: Allow 1 hour, 30 minutes minimum. **Hours:** Mon.-Sat. 9:30-5, Sun. 11-6. Phone ahead to confirm tour schedule. Closed Jan. 1, Easter, Thanksgiving, Christmas Eve and Christmas. **Cost:** $7.50; $6.50 (ages 60+); $5.50 (ages 4-12). **Phone:** (770) 427-2117. (GT)

BAYMONT INN & SUITES (770)423-7105 [29]

Hotel
$74-$125

Address: 3192 Barrett Lakes Blvd 30144 **Location:** I-75 exit 271, just w to Barrett Lakes Blvd, then just s. **Facility:** 46 units. 2 stories, interior corridors. **Amenities:** safes. **Pool(s):** outdoor. **Activities:** exercise room. **Guest Services:** valet and coin laundry. **Featured Amenity:** full hot breakfast.

(SAVE) (TI→) CALL (&M) (2→) (BIZ) (HS)
(📶) (✕) (🛁) (📠) (💻)

BEST WESTERN KENNESAW INN (770)424-7666 [26]

Motel
$72-$80

(BW) Best Western. **AAA Benefit:** Save 10% or more every day and earn 10% bonus points!

Address: 3375 Busbee Dr 30144 **Location:** I-75 exit 271, just e. **Facility:** 100 units. 2 stories (no elevator), exterior corridors. **Amenities:** safes. **Pool(s):** outdoor. **Guest Services:** coin laundry. **Featured Amenity:** full hot breakfast.

(SAVE) (TI→) CALL (&M) (2→) (BIZ) (📶)
(💻) / SOME UNITS (S📞) (HS) (🛁) (📠)

COMFORT INN (770)499-9200 [32]

(♦♦♦) **Hotel.** $89-$169 **Address:** 2489 George Busbee Pkwy 30144 **Location:** I-75 exit 269, just e. Adjacent to Holiday Inn Express-Town Center Mall. **Facility:** 61 units. 5 stories, interior corridors. **Guest Services:** valet laundry.

(TI→) CALL (&M) (BIZ) (HS) (📶) (✕) (🛁) (📠) (💻)

COMFORT SUITES AT KENNESAW STATE UNIVERSITY (678)275-2090 [27]

Hotel
$99-$219

Address: 3366 Busbee Dr NW 30144 **Location:** I-75 exit 271, just e. **Facility:** 69 units. 4 stories, interior corridors. **Amenities:** *Some:* safes. **Pool(s):** heated indoor. **Activities:** exercise room. **Guest Services:** area transportation. **Featured Amenity:** breakfast buffet.

(SAVE) (TI→) CALL (&M) (2→) (BIZ) (HS)
(📶) (✕) (🛁) (📠) (💻)

DAYS INN (770)419-1576 [38]

(♦♦) **Motel.** $50-$82 **Address:** 760 Cobb Place Blvd 30144 **Location:** I-75 exit 269, just w. **Facility:** 80 units. 2 stories (no elevator), exterior corridors. **Pool(s):** outdoor. **Guest Services:** valet and coin laundry.

(TI→) CALL (&M) (2→) (BIZ) (HS) (📶) (🛁) (📠) (💻)
/ SOME UNITS (S📞)

EMBASSY SUITES BY HILTON ATLANTA-KENNESAW TOWN CENTER (770)420-2505 [23]

(♦♦♦) **Hotel.** $139-$299 **Address:** 620 Chastain Rd NW 30144 **Location:** I-75 exit 271, 0.4 mi w. **Facility:** 192 units. 7 stories, interior corridors. **Terms:** check-in 4 pm, 1-7 night minimum stay, cancellation fee imposed. **Dining:** Ruth's Chris Steak House, see separate listing. **Pool(s):** heated indoor. **Activities:** exercise room. **Guest Services:** valet and coin laundry, area transportation.

AAA Benefit: Members save 5% or more!

(TI) (🍴) (Y) CALL (&M) (2→) (BIZ) (S HS) (S📶) (🛁) (📠)
(💻)

EXTENDED STAY AMERICA ATLANTA KENNESAW (770)422-1403 [30]

(♦♦) **Extended Stay Hotel.** $75-$100 **Address:** 3000 George Busbee Pkwy 30144 **Location:** I-75 exit 269, just e to George Busbee Pkwy, then 0.8 mi n. **Facility:** 104 efficiencies. 3 stories, interior corridors. **Terms:** cancellation fee imposed. **Guest Services:** coin laundry.

(TI→) (HS) (📶) (🛁) (📠) (💻) / SOME UNITS (S📞)

FAIRFIELD INN & SUITES BY MARRIOTT ATLANTA KENNESAW (770)427-9700 [25]

(♦♦♦) **Hotel.** $85-$160 **Address:** 3425 Busbee Dr 30144 **Location:** I-75 exit 271, just e. **Facility:** 86 units. 3 stories, interior corridors. **Pool(s):** outdoor. **Activities:** hot tub, exercise room. **Guest Services:** valet and coin laundry.

AAA Benefit: Members save 5% or more!

(TI→) CALL (&M) (2→) (BIZ) (HS) (📶) (✕) (🛁) (💻)
/ SOME UNITS (📠)

HAMPTON INN (770)426-0017 [35]

(♦♦♦) **Hotel.** $104-$184 **Address:** 871 Cobb Place Blvd 30144 **Location:** I-75 exit 269, just w to Cobb Place Blvd, then just s. **Facility:** 59 units. 3 stories, interior corridors. **Terms:** 1-7 night minimum stay, cancellation fee imposed. **Pool(s):** outdoor. **Activities:** exercise room. **Guest Services:** valet laundry.

AAA Benefit: Members save up to 10%!

(TI→) CALL (&M) (2→) (BIZ) (HS) (📶) (✕) (🛁) (📠) (💻)

(See map & index p. 76.)

HILTON GARDEN INN-ATLANTA NW/KENNESAW TOWN CENTER
(678)322-1140 **33**

▼▼▼▼ **Hotel.** $149-$199 **Address:** 895 Cobb Place Blvd 30144 **Location:** I-75 exit 269, just w to Cobb Place Blvd, then just n. **Facility:** 114 units. 5 stories, interior corridors. **Terms:** 1-7 night minimum stay, cancellation fee imposed. **Pool(s):** heated indoor. **Activities:** hot tub, exercise room. **Guest Services:** valet and coin laundry, area transportation.

AAA Benefit: Members save up to 10%!

🍽 🍷 CALL ♿M 🏊 BIZ HS 🛜 ✕ 🖥 🖨 🖳

HOLIDAY INN EXPRESS-TOWN CENTER MALL
(770)427-5210 **31**

▼▼▼▼ **Hotel.** $99-$249 **Address:** 2485 George Busbee Pkwy NW 30144 **Location:** I-75 exit 269, just e. Adjacent to Town Center Mall. **Facility:** 147 units. 6 stories, interior corridors. **Terms:** cancellation fee imposed. **Pool(s):** outdoor. **Activities:** exercise room. **Guest Services:** valet and coin laundry.

🍽 CALL ♿M 🏊 BIZ HS 🛜 ✕ 🖳 /SOME UNITS 🖥 🖨

HOMEWOOD SUITES-NORTHWEST/KENNESAW
678/354-2800 **34**

▼▼▼ **Extended Stay Hotel.** Rates not provided. **Address:** 905 Cobb Place Blvd 30144 **Location:** I-75 exit 269, just w to Cobb Place Blvd, then just n. **Facility:** 100 efficiencies. 4 stories, interior corridors. **Pool(s):** outdoor. **Activities:** exercise room. **Guest Services:** valet and coin laundry, area transportation.

AAA Benefit: Members save up to 10%!

🍽 CALL ♿M 🏊 BIZ HS 🛜 🖥 🖨 🖳

QUALITY INN
(770)419-1530 **37**

▼▼▼ **Motel.** $60-$159 **Address:** 750 Cobb Place Blvd 30144 **Location:** I-75 exit 269, just w. **Facility:** 80 units. 2 stories (no elevator), exterior corridors. **Pool(s):** outdoor. **Guest Services:** valet and coin laundry.

🍽 CALL ♿M 🏊 BIZ HS 🛜 🖥 🖨 🖳 /SOME UNITS 🛏

RED ROOF INN ATLANTA-KENNESAW
(770)429-0323 **36**

▼▼ **Motel.** $57-$100 **Address:** 520 Roberts Ct NW 30144 **Location:** I-75 exit 269, just e. Opposite Town Center Mall. **Facility:** 135 units. 3 stories (no elevator), exterior corridors. **Amenities:** safes.

🍽 CALL ♿M 🛜 /SOME UNITS 🛏 🖥 🖨 🖳

RESIDENCE INN BY MARRIOTT ATLANTA KENNESAW/ TOWN CENTER
(770)218-1018 **24**

▼▼▼▼ **Extended Stay Hotel** $102-$237

Residence Inn Marriott

AAA Benefit: Members save 5% or more!

Address: 3443 NW Busbee Dr 30144 **Location:** I-75 exit 271, just e. **Facility:** 120 units, some two bedrooms, efficiencies and kitchens. 3 stories, interior corridors. **Pool(s):** outdoor. **Activities:** trails, exercise room. **Guest Services:** valet and coin laundry, area transportation. **Featured Amenity:** full hot breakfast.

SAVE 🍽 CALL ♿M 🏊 BIZ 🛜 ✕ 🖥 🖨 🖳 /SOME UNITS 🛏

SPRINGHILL SUITES BY MARRIOTT
(770)218-5550 **28**

▼▼▼▼ **Hotel.** $95-$171 **Address:** 3399 Town Point Dr 30144 **Location:** I-75 exit 271, just w. **Facility:** 90 units. 3 stories, interior corridors. **Pool(s):** outdoor. **Activities:** hot tub, exercise room. **Guest Services:** valet and coin laundry.

AAA Benefit: Members save 5% or more!

ECO 🍽 CALL ♿M 🏊 BIZ HS 🛜 ✕ 🖥 🖨 🖳

WINGATE BY WYNDHAM
(770)514-7344 **39**

▼▼▼ **Hotel.** $84-$139 **Address:** 560 Greers Chapel Dr NW 30144 **Location:** I-75 exit 269, just w. **Facility:** 84 units. 3 stories, interior corridors. **Amenities:** video games, safes. **Pool(s):** outdoor. **Activities:** exercise room. **Guest Services:** valet and coin laundry, area transportation.

🍽 CALL ♿M 🏊 BIZ HS 🛜 ✕ 🖥 🖨 🖳

WHERE TO EAT

BAHAMA BREEZE
678/354-7777 **46**

▼▼▼ Caribbean. Casual Dining. $11-$22 **AAA Inspector Notes:** A tropical feel resonates throughout via bright colors, a Caribbean-inspired menu and music that would make Jimmy Buffett dance. The menu features something for everyone with fresh seafood, chicken dishes, pastas and steaks. The empanadas are a great way to start before moving on to the entree. Herbs and spices native to the Caribbean are used throughout the menu. **Features:** full bar, patio dining, happy hour. **Address:** 755 Ernest Barrett Pkwy NW 30144 **Location:** I-75 exit 269, just w. L D

BANGKOK CABIN
770/427-5287 **32**

▼▼▼ Thai. Casual Dining. $7-$16 **AAA Inspector Notes:** Nestled in a nicely refurbished cottage with tasteful Asian décor, this restaurant prepares some of the best Thai food outside the Atlanta perimeter. Curries, noodle and rice dishes are good choices as are the ginger-roasted duck and rack of lamb. **Features:** beer & wine, patio dining. **Address:** 3413 Cherokee St 30144 **Location:** I-75 exit 273, 1.3 mi w. L D

BARBEQUE STREET
770/419-2626 **26**

▼▼ Barbecue. Casual Dining. $8-$23 **AAA Inspector Notes:** If you are craving Brunswick stew or pit-cooked barbecue—including beef, pork and chicken entrées—this family restaurant is sure to please. Rounding out the menu are sandwiches, catfish and homemade desserts. **Address:** 3815 Cherokee St 30144 **Location:** I-75 exit 273, 0.5 mi w. L D

BIG PIE IN THE SKY
770/420-8883 **27**

▼ Pizza. Quick Serve. $4-$36 **AAA Inspector Notes:** Home of the 'carnivore challenge' featured on 'Man vs. Food' TV program, Big Pie indeed is big on pies. You can get pizza ranging from a slice all the way up to the 30-inch extra-large. Specialty pizzas include the West Coast pesto, big kahuna and margherita. As for alternatives, check out the calzones, strombolis, subs and lunch specials. **Features:** beer & wine, patio dining. **Address:** 2090 Baker Rd 30144 **Location:** I-75 exit 273, 0.5 mi w to Jiles Rd, then just n. L D CALL ♿M

BIG SHANTY SMOKEHOUSE
770/499-7444 **33**

▼ Barbecue. Quick Serve. $6-$19 **AAA Inspector Notes:** In a small shanty/converted cottage, this eatery prepares hickory-smoked barbecue, including killer ribs, pork, chicken and homemade sausage. Diners also can get homemade desserts. The friendly staff is helpful. **Features:** patio dining. **Address:** 3393 Cherokee St 30144 **Location:** I-75 exit 273, 1.4 mi w. L D CALL ♿M

CAFE ISTANBUL 2
770/424-4856 **23**

▼▼ Turkish. Casual Dining. $5-$18 **AAA Inspector Notes:** Well-prepared Turkish cuisine at this café features a variety of kebabs, moussaka, falafel and stuffed grape leaves. The spicy ezme is a tasty appetizer and lamb sauté follows nicely as an entrée. Not sure what to try? I recommend the meat platter with a variety of beef, chicken and lamb. Sumptuous baklava is a great way to complete the dining experience. Singing and dancing take place nightly and the lovely dining room creates the ambience of a night under the stars in Istanbul. **Features:** full bar. **Address:** 4200 Wade Green Rd 30144 **Location:** I-75 exit 273, just e. L D LATE CALL ♿M 🍸

(See map & index p. 76.)

CAPER'S RESTAURANT & BAR   678/594-7735 ④⑨
▼▼ American. Fine Dining. $10-$27 **AAA Inspector Notes:**
This American-style grill offers patrons a variety of seafood, chicken
and meats. For those looking for lighter fare, salads and sandwiches
are available. Guest favorites include bruschetta and the Hawaiian
rib-eye. A large, stylish lounge and live music on the weekends make
this a popular place to socialize. **Features:** full bar, patio dining,
Sunday brunch. **Reservations:** suggested. **Address:** 1635 Old 41
Hwy, Suite 403 30152 **Location:** Jct Old 41 Hwy NW and Barrett
Pkwy. Ⓛ Ⓓ CALL &M

DONNY'S HOME COOKING   770/499-1111 ㉔
▼ Southern. Casual Dining. $8 **AAA Inspector Notes:** This
buffet-style eatery offers a variety of salads, entrées, veggies and
desserts. Fried chicken is available for lunch and dinner daily. Some
other choices of meat include baked chicken and fish, pork chops
and smothered steak. Veggie options feature pinto beans, mashed
potatoes, rice, green beans, corn and collard greens. **Address:** 3940
Cherokee St 30144 **Location:** I-75 exit 273, just w.

Ⓛ Ⓓ CALL &M

ELEVATION CHOP HOUSE & SKYBAR   770/485-7469 ㊳
▼▼ American. Casual Dining. $15-$28 **AAA Inspector Notes:**
At the local airport, this restaurant affords great views from its two
seating levels and bars. The progressive menu lists specialties of
wood-fired steaks and seafood along with traditional comfort foods
that reflect a new taste and presentation. Servers are informed. **Features:** full bar, Sunday brunch, happy hour. **Reservations:** suggested. **Address:** 1723 McCollum Pkwy 30144 **Location:** I-75 exit
271, 2 mi e; in McCollum Airport, entrance B. **Parking:** on-site and
valet. Ⓓ

FUJI HANA & THAI PEPPERS   770/419-9500 ㊱
▼▼ Asian. Casual Dining. $7-$36 **AAA Inspector Notes:**
Tasteful Oriental décor and casual ambiance set the stage at this restaurant for traditional Japanese favorites, excellent sushi, tried-and-
true Thai preparations and hibachi grilled items. Adjacent to the local
mall and convenient to local lodgings, the restaurant's servers please
with an attentive attitude. **Features:** beer & wine, patio dining. **Address:** 2606 George Busbee Pkwy 30144 **Location:** I-75 exit 269,
just w to George Busbee Pkwy, then just n. Ⓛ Ⓓ CALL &M

GUIDO'S CHICAGO HOT DOGS   678/581-9980 ㊺
▼ Hot Dogs. Quick Serve. $2-$8 **AAA Inspector Notes:** Yes, you
can get Vienna beef, Polish sausage, hamburgers, bratwurst and
Italian sausage at this place, but most people come for authentic,
Chicago-style hot dogs, chili dogs, slaw dogs, kraut dogs, etc. The no
frills décor gives a nod to the Windy City. **Address:** 840 Ernest Bar-
rett Pkwy, Suite 588 30144 **Location:** I-75 exit 269, 0.3 mi w; in Cobb
Place Shopping Center. Ⓛ Ⓓ

GUSTON'S NEIGHBORHOOD GRILLE   770/429-1969 ㉑
▼▼ American. Casual Dining. $9-$17 **AAA Inspector Notes:**
This friendly neighborhood eatery serves comfort food such as fried
catfish, baked meatloaf, wings, salads, burgers and luscious desserts. A lounge lets patrons kick back. **Features:** full bar, Sunday
brunch. **Address:** 4430 Wade Green Rd, Suite 90 30144 **Location:**
I-75 exit 273, 0.6 mi e; in Publix Shopping Plaza. Ⓛ Ⓓ

IPPOLITO'S   770/514-8500 ㊶
▼▼ Italian. Casual Dining. $8-$19 **AAA Inspector Notes:**
Much like the kind of intimate family restaurant that might be found in
an Italian neighborhood, this bustling café presents a good variety of
pizza, pasta, chicken and veal dishes. Chicken vodka is outstanding,
especially when accompanied by hot garlic rolls. Good desserts, such
as chocolate banana cream pie, bring the meal to a sweet end. Service is fast and friendly. **Features:** beer & wine, patio dining. **Address:** 425 Ernest Barrett Pkwy 30144 **Location:** I-75 exit 269, 0.3
mi e; in Town Center Plaza. Ⓛ Ⓓ CALL &M

J. CHRISTOPHER'S   678/213-2400 ㉟
▼▼ Breakfast. Casual Dining. $5-$12 **AAA Inspector Notes:**
Featuring classic American food but with a fresh, healthy approach,
this restaurant is a local hot spot. House specialties include eggs
Benedict, blueberry crunch cakes, quesadillas and the clubhouse
burger. Located across from the mall, this is the perfect place to fuel
up before a long day of shopping. **Features:** patio dining. **Address:**
2700 Town Center Dr 30144 **Location:** I-75 exit 269; opposite Town
Center Mall; in Esplanade. Ⓑ Ⓛ CALL &M

KEEGAN'S IRISH PUB   678/213-2460 ㊽
▼ Irish. Casual Dining. $8-$15 **AAA Inspector Notes:**
Guests can feel like they are in a true Irish pub at this bustling neighborhood spot where Guinness or other traditional draft brews, fish
and chips, shepherd's pie, bangers and mash and pot roast as well
as a great selection of other food options can be found. An Irish
breakfast is served throughout the day. **Features:** full bar. **Address:**
1625 Ridenour Blvd NW, Suite 301 30152 **Location:** I-75 exit 269,
1.6 mi w. Ⓛ Ⓓ LATE CALL &M

KUROSHIO SUSHI BAR & GRILLE   770/499-7160 ㊹
▼▼ Japanese. Casual Dining. $9-$55 **AAA Inspector Notes:**
This popular eatery features a variety of Japanese favorites such as
sushi, ramen and tempura. The extensive menu of sushi is prepared
before your eyes from quality seafood. The delicious cuisine is served
in a casual environment where guests can watch the game on TV or
enjoy the outdoor patio. **Features:** beer & wine, patio dining. **Address:** 840 Ernest Barrett Pkwy NW, Suite 500 30144 **Location:** I-75
exit 69, 0.3 mi w. Ⓛ Ⓓ CALL &M 🐾

LA BAMBA MEXICAN BAR & GRILL   770/422-1106 ㉘
▼▼ Tex-Mex. Casual Dining. $5-$15 **AAA Inspector Notes:** A
great variety of food options await at this grill. Chips and salsa are
brought to the table immediately—order some guacamole or chori dip
to complement them. Main dishes include carne asada, pork tacos or
seafood enchiladas. The sizzling fajitas always are popular and the
sopaipillas or fried ice cream is a good way to complete the meal.
Features: full bar, senior menu, happy hour. **Address:** 4100 Jiles Rd,
Suite 106 30144 **Location:** Jct Baker Rd, just e.
Ⓛ Ⓓ CALL &M

MANDARIN CAFE   770/218-1079 ㉕
▼▼ Asian. Casual Dining. $5-$16 **AAA Inspector Notes:** The
menu features both Chinese and Vietnamese cuisine at this spot with
a contemporary Asian décor. Enjoy many Chinese classics such as
sweet and sour shrimp, lo mein plus Vietnamese items such as
noodle soups, Pho and curry dishes. **Features:** patio dining. **Address:** 3895 Cherokee St NW, Suite 250 30144 **Location:** I-75 exit
273, 0.5 mi w; in Shiloh Square. Ⓛ Ⓓ CALL &M

MARLOW'S TAVERN   770/425-8777 ㉚
▼▼ American. Casual Dining. $8-$20 **AAA Inspector Notes:**
This great neighborhood tavern serves good appetizers, sides and
salads as well as well-prepared entrées such as shrimp and grits. A
popular dish is the fish taco, while the not-to-be-missed okra is possibly the best in the area. The dining room is casual but does offer
some upscale touches. **Features:** full bar, Sunday brunch, happy
hour. **Address:** 745 Chastain Rd NW, Suite 1160 30144 **Location:**
I-75 exit 271, 0.4 mi e; in Madison Place at Chastain.
Ⓛ Ⓓ CALL &M

OLDE TOWNE GRILLE   770/499-7878 ㊸
▼▼ American. Casual Dining. $8-$24 **AAA Inspector Notes:**
Besides bar food favorites like wings, burgers and sandwiches,
guests can find some very tasty entrées here. Wood-fired dishes
such as seared tuna, crab cakes, prime rib and aged steaks also
grace the extensive menu along with pizza and pasta. **Features:** full
bar. **Address:** 2500 N Cobb Pkwy 30152 **Location:** I-75 exit 271, 2.5
mi e to Cobb Pkwy (US 41), then 0.3 mi n. Ⓛ Ⓓ CALL &M

(See map & index p. 76.)

OYSTER CAFE   770/529-2196

WW WW Seafood. Casual Dining. $7-$18 AAA Inspector Notes: The modest restaurant serves a variety of menu options including boiled, grilled and fried seafood. The fried calamari and the clam chowder are good starters, and for your entrée, try the fried shrimp or the fried seafood platter. Both are popular among guests. End your meal with a selection from a variety of small desserts such as key lime and chocolate silk pies. Other menu options include wings, chicken, burgers and hot dogs. Features: full bar. Address: 3060 Cobb Pkwy NW 30152 Location: I-75 exit 271, 2.5 mi w, then 2.5 mi n on US 41. L D CALL &M

PAPI'S CUBAN & CARIBBEAN GRILL   678/797-0502 31

WW WW Cuban. Casual Dining. $6-$22 AAA Inspector Notes: Choose from either Cuban or Caribbean favorites at this Caribbean-themed grill. Highlights include Cuban sandwiches, churrasco steak, roasted pork, plantain chips and coconut flan. Guests are well tended by a thoughtful staff. This is a popular location especially during lunch. To-go orders are also available. Features: full bar. Address: 745 Chastain Rd, Suite 3001 30144 Location: I-75 exit 271, 0.4 mi w; in Madison Place at Chastain. L D CALL &M

PEACE, LOVE AND PIZZA   770/792-8989 22

W Pizza. Quick Serve. $7-$21 AAA Inspector Notes: A psyche-delic 1960s and hippie vibe weaves throughout this take-out and de-livery spot, where you can try pizzas such as the groovylicious, peaceful garden and meatasaurus Rex. You'll also find good salads, yummy cheesy bread and luscious cheesecake. Address: 4200 Wade Green Rd, Suite 10 30144 Location: I-75 exit 273, just e. L D

PENANG MALAYSIAN/THAI CUISINE   678/213-4848 40

W Asian. Casual Dining. $7-$19 AAA Inspector Notes: Take your time perusing the lengthy menu of interesting dishes while kicking back in this relaxed dining room, which resembles a banana palm and bamboo house. Curries, rice dishes, fried noodles and noodle soup all are favorites here. Features: beer & wine. Address: 2491 George Busbee Pkwy NW 30144 Location: I-75 exit 269, just e to George Busbee Pkwy, then just n. L D CALL &M

PROVINO'S   678/594-5055

W Italian. Casual Dining. $9-$23 AAA Inspector Notes: Tra-ditional Italian favorites such as veal parmigiana, lasagna, manicotti and fettuccine Alfredo are served in a neighborhood-style atmos-phere. Of particular interest are the distinctive house salad and deli-cious cheesecake. Features: beer & wine, early bird specials. Address: 440-A Ernest Barrett Pkwy NW, Suite 1 30144 Location: I-75 exit 269, just w. L D CALL &M

RAFFERTY'S RESTAURANT & BAR   770/792-8001

W American. Casual Dining. $7-$19 AAA Inspector Notes: The front door rarely stays closed for long at Rafferty's, a bustling, ca-sual spot that plies guests with hearty helpings of steak, seafood, burgers, pasta and ribs. Friendly staffers take good care of their tables. Features: full bar. Address: 2501 Cobb Place Ln NW 30144 Location: I-75 exit 269, just w to Cobb Place Ln, then just n. L D CALL &M

RU SAN'S-KENNESAW   678/766-0598 39

W Japanese. Casual Dining. $5-$28 AAA Inspector Notes: A popular regional sushi chain, this is a popular stop especially for the lunch buffet. Customer favorites include the one-dollar sushi menu, tempura and Japanese noodle dishes. The menu features a variety of fish including lobster, mackerel, sea urchin and salmon. Features: full bar. Address: 425 Ernest Barrett Pkwy, Suite H-10 30144 Loca-tion: I-75 exit 269, 0.3 mi e; in Town Center Plaza. L D

RUTH'S CHRIS STEAK HOUSE   770/420-1985 29

WW WW WW Steak. Fine Dining. $11-$45 AAA Inspector Notes: The main fare is steak, which is prepared from several cuts of Prime beef and cooked to perfection, but the menu also lists lamb, chicken and seafood dishes. Guests should come hungry because the side dishes, which are among the a la carte offerings, could make a meal in themselves. Features: full bar. Address: 620 Chastain Rd NW 30144 Location: I-75 exit 271, 0.4 mi w; in Embassy Suites by Hilton Atlanta-Kennesaw Town Center. L D CALL &M

SUNNY'S BAGELS & DELI   770/590-7590 37

W Sandwiches. Quick Serve. $2-$8 AAA Inspector Notes: Breakfast and lunch are served all day at this deli. Diners can create endless combinations of bagel sandwiches with a plethora of meats, spreads and toppings to choose from. From tuna and chicken to roast beef and turkey, enjoy the many meat options as well as any number of bagels including poppyseed, garlic, eight grain, egg, chocolate chip and spinach. Start with a salad and end with a cookie. Features: patio dining. Address: 440 Ernest Barrett Pkwy, Suite 8 30144 Loca-tion: I-75 exit 269, just w. B L

TAJ MAHAL GRILL   770/919-9990 42

WW WW Indian. Casual Dining. $9-$15 AAA Inspector Notes: De-lectables such as chicken, fish and shrimp are fresh from the tandoor and available on the popular lunch buffet at this grill. Goat, chicken and lamb curry are favorite menu items and the wide selection of naan and other bread dishes are a must. Features: beer & wine. Ad-dress: 1200 Ernest Barrett Pkwy NW, Suite 18 30144 Location: I-75 exit 269, 1.2 mi w. L D

TRACKSIDE GRILL   770/499-0874 34

WW WW New Southern Comfort Food. Casual Dining. $14-$25 AAA Inspector Notes: This Kennesaw staple is receiving good marks for its innovative interpretations of regional cuisine. The sea-food dishes, such as mango-glazed salmon, are particularly note-worthy. Comfort plates are very popular and include buttermilk fried chicken, Southern pot roast and veal meatloaf. A wide array of cre-ative sandwiches are available at lunch. Features: full bar, patio dining, Sunday brunch. Address: 2840 S Main St 30144 Location: Downtown. L D CALL &M

THE VARSITY   770/795-0802

W Hot Dogs Burgers. Quick Serve. $2-$9 AAA Inspector Notes: Guests are greeted with cries of, "What'll you have?" at this branch of a longtime Atlanta landmark. The restaurant offers such fast food favorites as hot dogs (naked, chili, slaw), hamburgers and grilled cheese sandwiches. If that is not on your radar, go with some crispy chicken tenders. Do not miss the famous frozen orange drink. Fea-tures: patio dining. Address: 2790 Town Center Dr 30144 Location: I-75 exit 269, just e; behind Town Center Mall. L D CALL &M

WHISTLE STOP CAFE   770/794-0101 47

WW WW Southern. Casual Dining. $5-$9 AAA Inspector Notes: Serious home-style Southern cooking at this café includes fried chicken, mashed potatoes, cornbread and cobblers. A railroad and Southern theme distinguishes this aptly-named spot, which always is busy. Service is fast and friendly. Address: 1200 Ernest W Bar-rett Pkwy NW, Unit 10-11 30144 Location: I-75 exit 69, 1.2 mi w; in shopping plaza. Parking: street only. B L D

WILLY'S MEXICANA GRILL   770/429-9515

W Mexican. Quick Serve. $5-$9 AAA Inspector Notes: Fast, fresh Tex-Mex includes burritos and tacos made to order in a cafeteria-style line. Beer is among the beverage choices. Varied salsas complement the chips. Features: beer only. Address: 840 Ernest Barrett Pkwy 30144 Location: I-75 exit 269, 0.3 mi w; in Cobb Place Shopping Center. L D CALL &M

KENNESAW MOUNTAIN NATIONAL BATTLEFIELD PARK (G-1)

Kennesaw Mountain National Battlefield Park oc-cupies 2,965 acres 2.5 miles northwest of Marietta off I-75 exit 269, then 4 mi. w. on Old US 41. In June 1864, Gen. Joseph E. Johnston's Confederate Army, retreating before Gen. William Tecumseh Sherman's march to Atlanta, took up a strong posi-tion on Kennesaw (KEN-uh saw) Mountain in the path of the invading forces. Sherman, however, ulti-mately forced Johnston and his troops to abandon the mountain and retreat south.

Earthworks from this battle are well preserved. A paved road to the crest of Kennesaw Mountain has fine views; around the crest is a trail with maps illustrating the conflict. The visitor center at the foot of the mountain on Old US 41 offers exhibits and a 35-minute film "Kennesaw: One Last Mountain." Living history demonstrations, educational programs and temporary exhibits also are available.

Picnicking is permitted in designated areas. The mountain road is closed weekends and major holidays; a shuttle bus provides transportation to the mountaintop during these times.

Allow 2 hours minimum. The battlefield is open daily 7:30 a.m.-8 p.m., during DST; daily 7:30-6, rest of year. Visitor Center is open daily 9-5, year-round. Visitor center is closed Jan. 1, Thanksgiving and Christmas. Free. Shuttle bus fare $3; $1.50 (ages 6-11). Phone (770) 427-4686.

KINGSLAND (F-5) pop. 15,946, elev. 47'

If you're looking for a return to nature and simpler times, Kingsland is a good place to lay your head. It lies 30 miles east of Okefenokee National Wildlife Refuge and 11 miles west of the coast where visitors can board a ferry for the 45-minute ride to Cumberland Island. The city limits are just north of the Florida-Georgia state line.

In early September, the 🐟 Labor Day Weekend Catfish Festival includes a catfish fishing tournament, arts and crafts, and Southern-fried and Cajun catfish.

BAYMONT INN & SUITES KINGSLAND (912)729-9600
🔻🔻 Hotel. $49-$75 Address: 105 May Creek Dr 31548 Location: I-95 exit 3 (SR 40), just w. Facility: 41 units. 2 stories (no elevator), exterior corridors. Pool(s): outdoor. Activities: exercise room.

BEST WESTERN PLUS KINGSLAND (912)882-8200

Hotel
$81-$129

Best Western PLUS AAA Benefit: Save 10% or more every day and earn 10% bonus points!

Address: 1375 Hospitality Ave 31548 Location: I-95 exit 3 (SR 40), just se. Facility: 54 units. 2 stories, interior corridors. Bath: shower only. Pool(s): outdoor. Activities: exercise room. Guest Services: valet and coin laundry.

COUNTRY INN & SUITES BY CARLSON 912/576-1616
🔻🔻 Hotel. Rates not provided. Address: 135 The Lakes Blvd 31548 Location: I-95 exit 3 (SR 40), just se. Facility: 64 units. 3 stories, interior corridors. Pool(s): heated indoor. Activities: hot tub, exercise room. Guest Services: coin laundry.

FAIRFIELD INN & SUITES BY MARRIOTT KINGSLAND (912)576-1010
🔻🔻🔻 Hotel. $87-$121 Address: 1319 E King Ave 31548 Location: I-95 exit 3 (SR 40), just e. Facility: 82 units. 3 stories, interior corridors. Pool(s): heated indoor. Activities: hot tub, exercise room. Guest Services: valet and coin laundry.

AAA Benefit: Members save 5% or more!

HAMPTON INN (912)729-1900
🔻🔻🔻 Hotel. $114-$144 Address: 102 Reddick Rd 31548 Location: I-95 exit 3 (SR 40), just sw. Facility: 78 units. 3 stories, interior corridors. Terms: 1-7 night minimum stay, cancellation fee imposed. Pool(s): indoor. Activities: hot tub, exercise room. Guest Services: valet and coin laundry.

AAA Benefit: Members save up to 10%!

LA QUINTA INN KINGSLAND KINGS BAY (912)882-8010
🔻🔻 Hotel. $79-$163 Address: 104 May Creek Dr 31548 Location: I-95 exit 3 (SR 40), just w. Facility: 56 units. 3 stories, interior corridors. Pool(s): outdoor. Activities: hot tub, exercise room. Guest Services: coin laundry.

MICROTEL INN & SUITES BY WYNDHAM KINGSLAND (912)729-1555

Hotel
$49-$100

Address: 1325 E King Ave 31548 Location: I-95 exit 3 (SR 40), just ne. Facility: 59 units. 3 stories, interior corridors. Amenities: safes. Pool(s): outdoor. Activities: hot tub, exercise room. Guest Services: valet and coin laundry. Featured Amenity: full hot breakfast.

QUALITY INN 912/576-9400
🔻🔻 Motel. Rates not provided. Address: 111 Robert L. Edenfield Dr 31548 Location: I-95 exit 3 (SR 40), just e. Facility: 70 units. 2 stories (no elevator), exterior corridors. Pool(s): outdoor. Activities: exercise room.

WHERE TO EAT

ANGELO'S RESTAURANT OF KINGSLAND 912/882-1212
🔻🔻 Italian Pizza. Casual Dining. $5-$18 AAA Inspector Notes: The success of this eatery is attributed to four things: freshness, quality, service and location. The diversity and length of the menu is surpassed only by the size of the portions. Diners are cautioned to come hungry or order light. Expect to find traditional pasta dishes, calzones, subs in two sizes and tasty desserts. Meals are inexpensive and the pizza is awesome. Features: beer & wine. Address: 1371A Hwy 40 E 31548 Location: I-95 exit 3 (SR 40), 0.5 mi se. L D

MILLHOUSE STEAKHOUSE 912/576-4349
🔻🔻 International. Casual Dining. $7-$29 AAA Inspector Notes: Do not be fooled by the name, steaks just scratch the surface of the menu at this popular spot. Diners can enjoy Italian and Asian fare, chicken, burgers, seafood and ribs as well as a stellar lineup of great house aged beef including a whopping signature porterhouse for two. Each steak comes with a soup or salad, a family-style side dish and fresh baked bread. There also are some wonderful house desserts for afterwards. Features: full bar, patio dining, happy hour. Address: 1215 E King Ave 31548 Location: I-95 exit 3 (SR 40), just w. D CALL

OPS PIZZA KITCHEN & CAFE   912/576-6880

▼▼ ▼▼ Italian Pizza. Casual Dining. $2-$15 **AAA Inspector Notes:** Dine in or take out at this place that is all about various styles of pizza—New York, Sicilian and gourmet concoctions. A full menu of basic Italian dishes also is featured. Daily lunch and dinner offers, by-the-slice pizza and everyday specials make for an affordable meal. **Features:** full bar, happy hour. **Address:** 1378 S Boone Ave Ext 31548 **Location:** I-95 exit 3 (SR 40), 0.4 mi se.

L D CALL M

SONNY'S REAL PIT BAR-B-Q   912/673-7262

▼▼ ▼▼ Barbecue. Casual Dining. $8-$17 **AAA Inspector Notes:** Bearing the name after its founder, Floyd "Sonny" Tillman, this barbecue restaurant first opened its doors circa 1968 in Gainesville, Florida and has since spawned over 150 more throughout the Southeast. The menu is steeped in finger lickin' favorites such as ribs, pulled pork, beef brisket, burgers, catfish, shrimp and chargrilled chicken. Let's not forget about the fried okra, which is the perfect starter dish, and their homemade baked beans. **Features:** beer only. **Address:** 1380 E Boone Ave 31548 **Location:** I-95 exit 3 (SR 40), 0.4 mi e. L D

LA FAYETTE pop. 7,121

AMERICAS BEST VALUE INN & SUITES   706/639-9362

▼▼ ▼▼ Motel. Rates not provided. **Address:** 2209 N Main St 30728 **Location:** 2.5 mi n on US 27. **Facility:** 36 units. 2 stories (no elevator), exterior corridors. **Pool(s):** outdoor.

🛬 HS 🛜 🛢 🖼 🗔 / SOME UNITS 🅂🅁

KEY WEST INN   (706)638-8200

▼▼ ▼▼ Motel. $52-$89 **Address:** 2221 N Main St 30728 **Location:** 2.5 mi n on US 27. **Facility:** 38 units. 2 stories (no elevator), exterior corridors. **Terms:** cancellation fee imposed. **Pool(s):** outdoor. **Guest Services:** coin laundry.

🍴 CALL M 🛬 🛜 🛢 🖼 / SOME UNITS 🅂🅁

WHERE TO EAT

CJ'S SOUTHERN TRADITIONS   706/639-9443

▼▼ ▼▼ Southern. Casual Dining. $4-$10 **AAA Inspector Notes:** Set in an old converted Southern mansion, this spot serves up some of the region's favorite specialties. Chicken fingers are popular and they come grilled or fried. Other mouth-watering options include fried catfish and tilapia, grilled pork chops, chicken and dressing and hamburger steaks. There are many veggie choices and peach cobbler always is a great way to top off the meal. **Address:** 640 S Main St 30728 **Location:** 0.5 mi s. L D

LAGRANGE (C-2) pop. 29,588, elev. 786'

BELLEVUE, 204 Ben Hill St., was the home of Sen. Benjamin Harvey Hill. Built in the early 1850s, the house is a fine example of Greek Revival architecture, featuring Ionic columns, porticos and elaborate millwork and ceiling medallions. **Hours:** Tues.-Sat. 10-1 and 2-5. The facility may be closed for private affairs. Closed major holidays. **Cost:** $5; $4 (ages 0-12 and students with ID). **Phone:** (706) 884-1832 to verify accessibility. GT

EXPLORATIONS IN ANTIQUITY CENTER is at 130 Gordon Commercial Dr. and provides visitors with an opportunity to view artifacts and replicas dating from about 2500 B.C.E. to 500 C.E. mostly from Israel and with a biblical focus. In the Archeological Garden view replicas of an Israeli village, including a goat hair tent, a grain silo, a grape press, a Roman theater, sheepfolds, stables and tombs.

There are 250 artifacts on loan from the Israel Antiquities Authority in the Biblical Life Artifacts Gallery. On display are items from the Roman and Byzantine periods as well as exhibits with tools used by farmers, fishermen and shepherds. A stone sarcophagus also can be seen. The Time Tunnel showcases a Byzantine church, a Canaanite temple, an Israeli shrine and a Jewish synagogue.

The center hosts special programs, including four-course biblical meals held in one of two rooms, re-creations of ones found in Pompeii and Herculaneum. Activities include bread making in the shepherd's tent and an archeological dig for kids where participants learn the rules of excavating and interpreting artifacts. **Time:** Allow 1 hour, 30 minutes minimum. **Hours:** Tues.-Sat. 10-6. **Cost:** $15; $12 (ages 6-12). Biblical meal $35; $22 (ages 6-12). Bread making $15. Archeological dig $15 (ages 4-12); $10 (adults). The cost of special programs includes entrance to museum. Reservations are recommended. **Phone:** (706) 885-0363. GT 🍴

HILLS & DALES ESTATE is off I-85 exit 18 to SR 109 (LaFayette Pkwy.), 3 mi. to SR 219 (Morgan St.) and 1 mi. on Broad St. to 1916 Hills & Dales Dr. This 1916 Italian villa with 30 rooms was the home of textile magnate Fuller E. Callaway Sr. Historic Ferrell Gardens, a highlight of the 35-acre estate grounds, includes extensive boxwood plantings, fountains, an herb garden and a greenhouse. A 14-minute film is offered. Maps for self-guiding tours of the grounds are provided, and a guided garden tour is available by advance reservation.

Time: Allow 2 hours minimum. **Hours:** Guided tours of the house (includes self-guiding garden tour) given Tues.-Sat. 10-6, Sun. 1-6, Mar.-June; Tues.-Sat. 10-5, rest of year. Last tour begins 1 hour before closing. Closed Jan. 1, Easter, July 4, Thanksgiving, Christmas Eve and Christmas. **Cost:** $15 (includes self-guiding garden tour); $7 (ages 7-18 and college students with ID). Garden only (includes audio tour) $8; $4 (ages 7-18 and college students with ID). Ages 0-6 are permitted on the grounds and in the visitor center but not on the house tour. **Phone:** (706) 882-3242. GT

LAGRANGE ART MUSEUM, 112 Lafayette Pkwy., exhibits local and nationally acclaimed artwork. Major shows include the LaGrange Southeast Regional, an art competition held even-numbered years mid-February to mid-April. Rotating exhibits also are available. **Hours:** Tues.-Fri. 9-5, third Sat. of the month 1-4. Closed major holidays. **Cost:** Donations. **Phone:** (706) 882-3267.

BAYMONT INN & SUITES   (706)885-9002

▼▼ ▼▼ Hotel. $69-$87 **Address:** 107 Hoffman Dr 30240 **Location:** I-85 exit 18 (Lafayette Pkwy), just w. **Facility:** 54 units. 2 stories (no elevator), interior corridors. **Pool(s):** heated indoor. **Activities:** hot tub, exercise room. **Guest Services:** coin laundry.

🍴 CALL M 🛬 BIZ 🛜 🛢 🖼 🗔 / SOME UNITS 🅂🅁

COMFORT INN & SUITES (706)882-7700
▼▼▼ Hotel. $84-$139 Address: 1512 Lafayette Pkwy 30241 Location: I-85 exit 18 (Lafayette Pkwy), just w. Facility: 53 units. 3 stories, interior corridors. Pool(s): outdoor. Activities: exercise room. Guest Services: valet laundry.
[▮▸] CALL [&M] [▭] [BIZ] [HS] [≋] [✕] [❙] [▤] [▭]
/ SOME UNITS [🐕]

HAMPTON INN LAGRANGE NEAR CALLAWAY GARDENS
(706)845-1115
▼▼▼ Hotel. $89-$119 Address:
100 Willis Cir 30240 Location: I-85 exit 14, just w. Facility: 81 units. 3 stories, interior corridors. Terms: 1-7 night minimum stay, cancellation fee imposed.

AAA Benefit:
Members save up to 10%!

Pool(s): outdoor. Activities: exercise room. Guest Services: valet and coin laundry.
[▮▸] [▭] [BIZ] [HS] [≋] [✕] [❙] [▤] [▭]

HOLIDAY INN EXPRESS & SUITES (706)298-4571
▼▼▼ Hotel. $99-$124 Address: 205 Cotton Rd 30241 Location: I-85 exit 18 (Lafayette Pkwy), 0.3 mi w. Facility: 73 units. 4 stories, interior corridors. Pool(s): heated indoor. Activities: exercise room. Guest Services: valet laundry.
[▮▸] CALL [&M] [▭] [BIZ] [HS] [≋] [✕] [❙] [▤] [▭]

LAFAYETTE GARDEN INN & CONFERENCE CENTER
706/884-6175
▼▼ Motel. Rates not provided. Address: 1513 Lafayette Pkwy 30241 Location: I-85 exit 18 (Lafayette Pkwy), just w. Facility: 109 units. 2 stories (no elevator), exterior corridors. Pool(s): outdoor. Activities: exercise room. Guest Services: valet and coin laundry.
[▮] [⊥] CALL [&M] [▭] [BIZ] [≋] [❙] [▤] [▭]
/ SOME UNITS [🐕] [HS]

LA QUINTA INN & SUITES (706)812-8000
▼▼▼ Hotel. $84-$169 Address: 111 Hoffman Dr 30241 Location: I-85 exit 18 (Lafayette Pkwy), just w. Facility: 74 units. 3 stories, interior corridors. Activities: exercise room. Guest Services: coin laundry.
CALL [&M] [▭] [BIZ] [≋] [❙] [▤] [▭] / SOME UNITS [🐕] [HS]

QUALITY INN (706)882-8700
▼▼ Motel. $69-$84 Address: 110 Jameson Dr 30240 Location: I-85 exit 18 (Lafayette Pkwy), 0.3 mi w. Facility: 57 units. 2 stories (no elevator), exterior corridors. Pool(s): outdoor. Activities: exercise room.
[▮▸] CALL [&M] [▭] [BIZ] [≋] [❙] [▤] [▭]
/ SOME UNITS [🐕] [HS]

RED ROOF INN LAGRANGE (706)882-9540
▼▼ Motel. $50-$100 Address: 1601 Lafayette Pkwy 30241 Location: I-85 exit 18 (Lafayette Pkwy), just e. Facility: 82 units. 2 stories, exterior corridors. Pool(s): outdoor. Activities: exercise room. Guest Services: coin laundry.
[▮▸] CALL [&M] [▭] [BIZ] [≋] [✕] [❙] [▤] [▭]
/ SOME UNITS [🐕]

WINGATE BY WYNDHAM LAGRANGE (706)298-5270
▼▼▼ Hotel. $99-$114 Address: 103 Wingate Terrace 30241 Location: I-85 exit 18 (Lafayette Pkwy), just w. Facility: 100 units. 4 stories, interior corridors. Amenities: safes. Pool(s): outdoor. Activities: exercise room. Guest Services: valet and coin laundry.
CALL [&M] [▭] [BIZ] [HS] [≋] [❙] [▤] [▭]

WHERE TO EAT

C'SONS 706/298-0892
▼▼ New American. Fine Dining. $11-$35 AAA Inspector Notes: For fine dining look no further than this establishment offering quality creations destined to delight the palate. Seared foie gras is an excellent way to begin and such items as braised lamb shank, broiled pesto mahi mahi and seared sea scallops make great entrées. There is no better way to complete the meal than with white chocolate bread pudding. An excellent wine list is available. Features: full bar, patio dining. Address: 124A Main St 30240 Location: Downtown.
[L] [D] CALL [&M]

HOG HEAVEN 706/845-7994
▼▼ Barbecue. Casual Dining. $6-$20 AAA Inspector Notes: This hometown barbecue restaurant serves up generous portions of traditional favorites like smoked pork, ribs and chicken as well as big salads, grilled steaks, burgers and specialty sandwiches. If the kitchen aroma proves too much to handle, munch on the table top bucket of full-shell peanuts while you wait. Features: beer & wine, patio dining. Address: 1302 Lafayette Pkwy, Suite A 30241 Location: I-85 exit 18 (Lafayette Pkwy), 1.5 mi w; in Lafayette Centre.
[L] [D] CALL [&M]

LOS NOPALES 706/883-8547
▼▼ Mexican. Casual Dining. $3-$13 AAA Inspector Notes: This restaurant features multiple dining areas decorated in a contemporary Mexican style and with water features. The menu includes classic Mexican cuisine, such as tacos, burritos, enchiladas and fajitas. There's a full bar and the service is friendly. Features: full bar. Address: 382 S Davis Rd 30240 Location: I-85 exit 18 (Lafayette Pkwy), 0.8 mi w to S Davis Rd, then just n.
[L] [D] CALL [&M]

LAKE PARK pop. 733

DAYS INN (229)559-0229
▼▼ Hotel. $50-$70 Address: 4913 Timber Dr 31636 Location: I-75 exit 5, just nw. Facility: 94 units. 2 stories (no elevator), exterior corridors. Pool(s): outdoor. Guest Services: coin laundry.
[▮▸] [▭] [≋] [✕] [▭] / SOME UNITS [🐕] [❙] [▤]

LAVONIA pop. 2,156
• Restaurants p. 206

HAMPTON INN & SUITES (706)460-5100
▼▼▼ Hotel. $121-$166 Address:
115 Owens Dr 30553 Location: I-85 exit 173, just w. Facility: 81 units. 4 stories, interior corridors. Terms: 1-7 night minimum stay, cancellation fee imposed.

AAA Benefit:
Members save up to 10%!

Pool(s): heated indoor. Activities: exercise room. Guest Services: valet and coin laundry.
CALL [&M] [▭] [BIZ] [≋] [❙] [▤] [▭]

HOLIDAY INN EXPRESS & SUITES 706/356-2100
▼▼▼ Hotel. Rates not provided. Address: 110 Owens Dr 30553 Location: I-85 exit 173, just w. Facility: 72 units. 4 stories, interior corridors. Pool(s): heated indoor. Activities: exercise room. Guest Services: valet and coin laundry.
[▮▸] CALL [&M] [▭] [BIZ] [HS] [≋] [✕] [❙] [▤] [▭]
/ SOME UNITS [S]

SUPER 8 (706)356-8848
▼▼ Motel. $56-$64 Address: 14227 Jones St 30553 Location: I-85 exit 173, just w. Facility: 59 units. 2 stories (no elevator), exterior corridors. Pool(s): outdoor. Activities: exercise room.
[▮▸] CALL [&M] [▭] [BIZ] [HS] [≋] [✕] [❙] [▤] [▭]
/ SOME UNITS [S]

WHERE TO EAT

J. PETERS GRILL & BAR   706/356-1179

◆◆ ◇ American. Casual Dining. $8-$25 **AAA Inspector Notes:** This neighborhood bar and grill invites you to come in, sit down and eat up. The portions are generous and options are varied. The J. Peter burger is hands down the most popular item on the menu, but the honey drizzled croissants are heavenly. **Features:** full bar, Sunday brunch. **Address:** 95 Owens Dr 30553 **Location:** I-85 exit 173, just w. L D CALL M

LAWRENCEVILLE (G-5) pop. 28,546, elev. 1,066'

• Hotels & Restaurants map & index p. 90
• Part of Atlanta area — see map p. 44

Shopping: Sugarloaf Mills, at I-85 exit 108, offers more than 180 outlet shops, eateries and movie theaters.

MEDIEVAL TIMES DINNER AND TOURNAMENT is .8 mi. n. of jct. Duluth Hwy. and Sugarloaf Pkwy. at 5900 Sugarloaf Pkwy. N.W. In a replica of a medieval-style castle, guests feast on a four-course meal and witness entertainment, grandeur and pageantry evocative of centuries ago. Knights contend in jousting tournaments, sword battles and equestrian competitions featuring Andalusian stallions. Meals for visitors with special dietary needs are available.

Time: Allow 2 hours minimum. **Hours:** Shows are presented one to three times per day. Days and times vary by season; phone ahead to confirm. **Cost:** $54.95; $36.95 (ages 4-12); free (ages 0-3 on adult's lap). Reservations are highly recommended. **Phone:** (888) 935-6878.

COMFORT SUITES   (678)377-0003 38

◆◆◆ Hotel
$94-$159

Address: 2225 Riverside Pkwy 30043 **Location:** SR 316 exit Riverside Pkwy, just n. **Facility:** 52 units. 3 stories, interior corridors. **Activities:** exercise room. **Guest Services:** valet and coin laundry. **Featured Amenity:** full hot breakfast.

SAVE Ⓣ CALL M BIZ 🛜 ✕ ▯ ▱ ▭

COUNTRY INN & SUITES BY CARLSON (770)339-1991 34

◆◆◆ Hotel. $129-$219 **Address:** 989 Duluth Hwy (SR 120) 30043 **Location:** SR 316 exit SR 120, just s. **Facility:** 49 units. 3 stories, interior corridors. **Terms:** cancellation fee imposed. **Pool(s):** outdoor. **Activities:** exercise room. **Guest Services:** valet and coin laundry.

Ⓣ CALL M 🏊 BIZ 🛜 ✕ ▯ ▱ ▭

Choose real ratings you

can trust from professional

inspectors who've been there

DAYS INN   (770)995-7782 35

◆◆ ◆◆
Motel
$65-$81

Address: 731 Duluth Hwy 30046 **Location:** SR 316 exit SR 120, just e. Across from Gwinnett Medical Center. **Facility:** 53 units. 1 story, exterior corridors. **Terms:** cancellation fee imposed. **Activities:** limited exercise equipment.

SAVE Ⓣ BIZ 🛜 ▯ ▱ ▭ / SOME UNITS 🐾

Free wi-fi. Free continental breakfast. Pet friendly. Walking distance to restaurants & mall.

HAMPTON INN ATLANTA/LAWRENCEVILLE/GWINNETT COUNTY   (770)338-9600 37

◆◆ ◆◆ Hotel. $94-$169 **Address:** 1135 Lakes Pkwy 30043 **Location:** SR 316 exit Riverside Pkwy, just n. **Facility:** 85 units. 3 stories, interior corridors. **Terms:** 1-7 night minimum stay, cancellation fee imposed. **Pool(s):** outdoor. **Activities:** exercise room. **Guest Services:** valet laundry.

AAA Benefit: Members save up to 10%!

Ⓣ CALL M 🏊 BIZ 🛜 ✕ ▯ / SOME UNITS ▱ ▭

HAMPTON INN LAWRENCEVILLE-I-85/SUGARLOAF   (678)407-0018 33

◆◆◆ Hotel. $109-$199 **Address:** 6010 Sugarloaf Pkwy 30043 **Location:** I-85 exit 108, just e. **Facility:** 127 units. 5 stories, interior corridors. **Terms:** 1-7 night minimum stay, cancellation fee imposed. **Pool(s):** outdoor. **Activities:** exercise room. **Guest Services:** valet and coin laundry, area transportation.

AAA Benefit: Members save up to 10%!

CALL M 🏊 BIZ HS 🛜 ✕ ▯ ▱ ▭

HOLIDAY INN EXPRESS HOTEL & SUITES   (770)277-8009 36

◆◆ ◆◆ Hotel. $119-$154 **Address:** 520 John B Wilson Ct 30046 **Location:** SR 316 exit SR 120, 0.6 mi s. **Facility:** 62 units. 4 stories, interior corridors. **Terms:** 1-2 night minimum stay, cancellation fee imposed, resort fee. **Pool(s):** outdoor. **Activities:** exercise room. **Guest Services:** valet laundry.

Ⓣ CALL M 🏊 BIZ 🛜 ✕ ▯ ▱ ▭

WHERE TO EAT

KINGSTON 30 JAMAICAN RESTAURANT   678/847-0465 22

◆ Caribbean. Quick Serve. $6-$9 **AAA Inspector Notes:** This super-casual eatery serves traditional Caribbean fare such as jerk chicken, oxtail, goat and curry chicken. **Features:** beer only. **Address:** 1820 Brown Rd 30044 **Location:** Just n of Sugarloaf Mills. L D

PAPI'S CUBAN & CARIBBEAN GRILL   770/237-8889 23

◆◆ ◆◆ Cuban. Casual Dining. $7-$19 **AAA Inspector Notes:** Choose from either Cuban or Caribbean favorites such as Cuban sandwiches, churrasco steak, roasted pork, plantain chips and coconut flan in this Caribbean-themed setting which is well-tended by the thoughtful staff. Daily lunch specials are quite popular and include shredded beef (ropa veija) and chicken fricassee. **Features:** full bar. **Address:** 911 Duluth Hwy, Suite A1 30043 **Location:** SR 316 exit Duluth Hwy, 0.4 mi w; in Merton Walk Shopping Plaza. L D CALL M

(See map & index p. 90.)

SONNY'S REAL PIT BAR-B-Q   770/822-3330

▼▼ ▼▼ Barbecue. Casual Dining. $8-$17 **AAA Inspector Notes:** Bearing the name after its founder, Floyd "Sonny" Tillman, this barbecue restaurant first opened its doors circa 1968 in Gainesville, Florida and has since spawned over 150 more throughout the Southeast. The menu is steeped in finger lickin' favorites such as ribs, pulled pork, beef brisket, burgers, catfish, shrimp and chargrilled chicken. Let's not forget about the fried okra, which is the perfect starter dish, and their homemade baked beans. **Features:** beer only. **Address:** 660 Duluth Hwy 30045 **Location:** I-85 exit 106 northbound, 5 mi e; exit 107 southbound, 4.5 mi e to Duluth exit, then 0.9 mi e on SR 120. ⒧ ⒟

TAQUERIA LOS HERMANOS   770/817-0363 ㉔

▼▼ ▼▼ Tex-Mex. Casual Dining. $3-$13 **AAA Inspector Notes:** Start with a cup of shrimp corn chowder at this restaurant and then try an entrée from such choices as fajitas, grilled tilapia, enchiladas rancheras or one of many taco plates available. Complimentary chips and salsa are offered. Be sure to try a tempting dessert like the coconut flan and wash it all down with a refreshing margarita. **Features:** full bar. **Address:** 4955 Sugarloaf Pkwy 30045 **Location:** SR 316 exit Sugarloaf Pkwy, 0.3 mi s; in Sugarloaf Promenade. ⒧ ⒟

LESLIE (D-3) pop. 409, elev. 344'

GEORGIA RURAL TELEPHONE MUSEUM is .2 mi. s. off US 280 on SR 195. Self-guiding tours of the museum showcase its vast collection of telephone memorabilia from the 19th and 20th centuries. Displays in a renovated 1920s cotton warehouse include early telephones, pay phones, phone booths, switchboards, a Model A Ford truck (much like those used by telephone companies in the 1920s), other vintage cars and utility vehicles and a replica of Alexander Graham Bell's workshop.

Time: Allow 1 hour minimum. **Hours:** Mon.-Fri. 9-5. Last admission 1 hour before closing. Closed major holidays. **Cost:** $7; $5 (ages 55+ and active and retired military with ID); $4 (ages 4-16). **Phone:** (229) 874-4786.

LILBURN (H-4) pop. 11,596, elev. 876'
• Part of Atlanta area — see map p. 44

YELLOW RIVER GAME RANCH is 2.5 mi. e. of Stone Mountain Park at 4525 Stone Mountain Hwy. (US 78). The ranch is a wildlife preserve that contains more than 600 animals and birds native to Georgia including bobcats, buffaloes and bears. Wild animals are enclosed, but docile, tame animals wander free. Opportunities for petting and feeding animals are available. A half-mile-long hiking trail provides a chance to see animals close up.

Time: Allow 1 hour minimum. **Hours:** Daily 10-5. Last admission 1 hour before closing. Closed Jan. 1, Easter, Thanksgiving, Christmas Eve and Christmas. **Cost:** $8; $7 (ages 2-11); free (ages 0-1 with paid adult). **Phone:** (770) 972-6643 or (877) 972-6643. ⒤⒧ 🎁

AAA Vacations® packages ...
exciting itineraries
and exclusive values

LITHIA SPRINGS (H-1) pop. 15,491, elev. 1,043'
• Part of Atlanta area — see map p. 44

SWEETWATER CREEK STATE PARK is at 1750 Mt. Vernon Rd. This 2,549-acre park offers visitors an opportunity to explore the exterior ruins of a textile mill that was burned during the Civil War. The visitor center features wildlife and historic exhibits as well as offers trail maps. Recreational activities include hiking, fishing and picnicking. Ranger-led programs also are available. See Recreation Areas Chart.

Note: The interior mill ruins are temporarily closed due to structural issues and may not be stabilized for 2-3 years. In the meantime visitors can view the exterior. **Hours:** Park open daily 7 a.m.-dusk. Visitor center open daily 9-5; closed Christmas. Trails close at dusk. **Cost:** Donations. **Parking:** $5. **Phone:** (770) 732-5871. 🗙 🎁 🎁

HILTON GARDEN INN ATLANTA WEST/LITHIA SPRINGS
          (770)949-8980

▼▼▼ ▼▼ Hotel. $109-$209 **Address:** 110 Interstate West Pkwy 30122 **Location:** I-20 exit 44, 0.5 mi s. **Facility:** 112 units. 5 stories, interior corridors. **Terms:** 1-7 night minimum stay, cancellation fee imposed. **Pool(s):** heated indoor. **Activities:** hot tub, exercise room. **Guest Services:** valet and coin laundry.

AAA Benefit: Members save up to 10%!

🍴 🍽 CALL &M ➔ BIZ HS 📶 🗙 🖥 🗔 ☕ 🖵

HOLIDAY INN EXPRESS ATLANTA I-20 WEST-THEME PARK AREA   770/941-5384

▼▼▼ ▼▼ Hotel. Rates not provided. **Address:** 850 Crestmark Dr 30122 **Location:** I-20 exit 44, just n. **Facility:** 91 units. 4 stories, interior corridors. **Pool(s):** outdoor. **Activities:** exercise room. **Guest Services:** coin laundry.

🍴 CALL &M ➔ BIZ HS 📶 🗙 🖥 🗔 🖵

SPRINGHILL SUITES BY MARRIOTT ATLANTA SIX FLAGS
          (770)819-9906

▼▼▼ ▼▼ Hotel. $83-$134 **Address:** 960 Bob Arnold Blvd 30122 **Location:** I-20 exit 44, 0.5 mi s. **Facility:** 78 units. 3 stories, interior corridors. **Pool(s):** heated indoor. **Activities:** exercise room. **Guest Services:** coin laundry.

AAA Benefit: Members save 5% or more!

CALL &M ➔ BIZ HS 📶 🗙 🖥 🗔 🖵

WHERE TO EAT

BEAVER CREEK BISCUITS & BBQ   770/739-0200

▼▼ Barbecue. Quick Serve. $4-$18 **AAA Inspector Notes:** The pulled pork here was named best in the metro area by the Atlanta Journal-Constitution. The biscuits also are quite popular as are the ribs and barbecue chicken. You can get any of these as a sandwich or by the pound. Breakfast is served beginning at 5:30 every weekday morning and at 6:30 on Saturday. **Features:** patio dining. **Address:** 1451 Six Flags Rd 30122 **Location:** I-20 exit 44, 1 mi s to Factory Shoals Rd, then just e. Ⓑ ⒧

LA FIESTA   770/732-9911

▼▼ ▼▼ Tex-Mex. Casual Dining. $4-$13 **AAA Inspector Notes:** Traditional Tex Mex with a few twists like the chorizo burrito, milanesa con papas and mole poblano can be found here. A great place to get delicious food that is quick and hot. **Features:** full bar. **Address:** 1102 Thornton Rd 30122 **Location:** I-20 exit 44, 0.5 mi s. ⒧ ⒟

LITHONIA (I-5) pop. 1,924, elev. 928'
- Hotels & Restaurants map & index p. 94
- Part of Atlanta area — see map p. 44

Lithonia is located about 18 miles east of Atlanta via SR 402 and 8 mi. south of Stone Mountain. Known as the City of Granite, locals credit the name to a teacher who combined the Greek words *lithos*, stone, and *onia*, place, to create a name fitting for this town where gneiss granite is found.

FAIRFIELD INN & SUITES BY MARRIOTT ATLANTA EAST/LITHONIA
(770)484-9993

Hotel
$88-$154

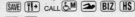
AAA Benefit: Members save 5% or more!

Address: 7850 Stonecrest Square 30038 **Location:** I-20 exit 75, just s on Turner Hill Rd, then 0.8 mi w. Located at rear of Stonecrest Mall. **Facility:** 85 units. 4 stories, interior corridors. **Amenities:** video games. **Pool(s):** heated indoor. **Activities:** exercise room. **Guest Services:** valet and coin laundry. **Featured Amenity: full hot breakfast.**

(SAVE) (¶¹→) CALL (&M) (🛄) (BIZ) (HS)
(📶) (✕) (🎦) (🛗) (🍴) (💻)

HILTON GARDEN INN-ATLANTA EAST/STONECREST
(678)526-1000

Hotel. $109-$189 **Address:** 7890 Mall Ring Rd 30038 **Location:** I-20 exit 75, just s on Turner Hill Rd, then 0.8 mi w. Located at rear of Stonecrest Mall. **Facility:** 110 units. 5 stories, interior corridors. **Terms:** 1-7 night minimum stay, cancellation fee imposed. **Pool(s):** heated indoor. **Activities:** hot tub, exercise room. **Guest Services:** valet and coin laundry.

AAA Benefit: Members save up to 10%!

(🍴) (🍸) CALL (&M) (🛟) (BIZ) (HS) (📶) (✕) (🛗)
(🍴) (💻)

HOLIDAY INN EXPRESS & SUITES ATLANTA EAST-LITHONIA
(678)325-4830 **17**

Hotel. $89-$109 **Address:** 7846 Stonecrest Square 30038 **Location:** I-20 exit 75, just s on Turner Hill Rd, then 0.8 mi w. Located at rear of Stonecrest Mall. **Facility:** 71 units. 4 stories, interior corridors. **Terms:** cancellation fee imposed. **Pool(s):** outdoor. **Activities:** exercise room. **Guest Services:** valet and coin laundry.

(¶¹→) CALL (&M) (🛟) (BIZ) (HS) (📶) (✕) (🛗) (🍴) (💻)

HYATT PLACE ATLANTA-EAST/LITHONIA
(770)484-4384

Hotel
$69-$209

HYATT PLACE®
AAA Benefit: Members save 10%!

Address: 7900 Mall Ring Rd 30038 **Location:** I-20 exit 75, just s on Turner Hill Rd, then 0.7 mi w. Located at rear of Stonecrest Mall. **Facility:** 83 units. 5 stories, interior corridors. **Terms:** cancellation fee imposed. **Pool(s):** outdoor. **Activities:** exercise room. **Guest Services:** valet laundry. **Featured Amenity: full hot breakfast.**

(SAVE) (🍸) CALL (&M) (🛟) (BIZ) (📶)

(✕) (🛗) (💻) / SOME UNITS (S↘)

WHERE TO EAT

ARIZONA'S
678/526-7775

Steak. Casual Dining. $11-$48 **AAA Inspector Notes:** Offering such classic American favorites as steaks, chops and seafood, this restaurant is a popular lunch stop. The large, casual dining room features some upscale touches. The bar area is great for meeting friends and relaxing. **Features:** full bar, Sunday brunch. **Address:** 2940 Stonecrest Cir 30038 **Location:** I-20 exit 75, just s.

(L) (D) CALL (&M)

GLADYS AND RONS CHICKEN & WAFFLES
770/482-6766

Southern. Casual Dining. $8-$17 **AAA Inspector Notes:** Good old-fashioned Southern specialties await at this spot inspired by legendary singer Gladys Knight. Enjoy such deep-fried dishes as chicken, corn, tomatoes and catfish. Baked, grilled and smothered chicken also are available. Other favorites include collard greens, barbecue turkey sandwiches and vegetable plates. And you simply do not want to miss the sweet potato cheesecake. Outdoor dining is an option. **Features:** full bar. **Address:** 7301 Stonecrest Concourse, Suite 123 30038 **Location:** I-20 exit 75, just s; adjacent to Stonecrest Mall. (L) (D) CALL (&M)

THIS IS IT! BBQ & SEAFOOD
678/526-2636

Southern Soul Food. Quick Serve. $6-$15 **AAA Inspector Notes:** Enjoy a great selection of items at this restaurant including tilapia, ribs, pork, chicken and vegetables—the Brunswick stew is not to be missed. Any items found here also can be fried and brought to your table within five minutes. To go items such as wings and seafood baskets are popular and both chicken and pork barbecue sandwiches are good choices. **Address:** 7331 Stonecrest Concourse 30038 **Location:** I-20 exit 75, 0.3 mi s; adjacent to Stonecrest Mall; in The Shops at Stonecrest. (L) (D) CALL (&M)

THIS IS IT! BBQ & SEAFOOD
770/817-5400 **28**

Southern Soul Food. Quick Serve. $6-$15 **AAA Inspector Notes:** Enjoy a great selection of items at this restaurant including tilapia, ribs, pork, chicken and vegetables—the Brunswick stew is not to be missed. Any items found here also can be fried and brought to your table within five minutes. To go items such as wings and seafood baskets are popular and both chicken and pork barbecue sandwiches are good choices. **Address:** 2853 Panola Rd 30058 **Location:** I-20 exit 71, just n. (L) (D) CALL (&M)

LITTLE ST. SIMONS ISLAND (E-6)
- Part of Golden Isles area — see map p. 187

Accessible only by boat, Little St. Simons Island is a pristine hideaway off the northern shore of St. Simons Island. What was once the exclusive retreat of a New York timber baron and his wealthy friends now is open on a limited basis to nature lovers and others who wish to enjoy the vast tracts of undeveloped tidal creeks, marshes, forests and seashell-strewn beaches. A limited number of day trips to the island are available by reservation; phone (912) 638-7472.

LOCUST GROVE (C-3) pop. 5,402, elev. 837'

Shopping: (SAVE) Tanger Outlets, off I-75 exit 212 to 1000 Tanger Dr., features nearly 70 outlet shops, including such retailers as Aéropostale, Ann Taylor, Nautica and Old Navy.

NOAH'S ARK ANIMAL SANCTUARY is at 712 L.G. Griffin Rd.; from I-75 exit 212, turn right onto Stanley K. Tanger Rd. 2 mi., then right onto L.G. Griffin Rd. 2.3 mi. This 250-acre sanctuary provides permanent housing to domestic and exotic animals including tigers, bears, wolves, cougars and monkeys. Animal habitats are open to the public. A guided Walk on the Wild Side behind-the-scenes tour (minimum of two people) also is available by reservation. **Hours:** Welcome center and grounds open Tues.-Sat. 9-4. Animal habitats can be viewed noon-3 (weather permitting). **Cost:** Donations. Fee for guided tour; phone ahead. **Phone:** (770) 957-0888.

COMFORT SUITES (678)827-7700

Hotel
$81-$179

Address: 4699 Bill Gardner Pkwy 30248 **Location:** I-75 exit 212, just w. **Facility:** 62 units. 4 stories, interior corridors. **Pool(s):** heated indoor. **Activities:** exercise room. **Guest Services:** valet and coin laundry. **Featured Amenity: full hot breakfast.**

LA QUINTA INN & SUITES LOCUST GROVE
(678)583-8088

Hotel
$82-$213

Address: 4832 Bill Gardner Pkwy 30248 **Location:** I-75 exit 212, just e. **Facility:** 65 units. 4 stories, interior corridors. **Amenities:** safes. **Pool(s):** heated indoor. **Activities:** exercise room. **Guest Services:** coin laundry.

RAMADA LIMITED (770)898-1216

Hotel. $60-$150 **Address:** 197 Stanley Tanger Blvd 30248 **Location:** I-75 exit 212, just e. **Facility:** 44 units. 2 stories (no elevator), interior corridors. **Pool(s):** heated indoor. **Activities:** exercise room. **Guest Services:** valet and coin laundry.

RED ROOF INN-LOCUST GROVE (678)583-0004

Hotel
$59-$99

Address: 4840 Bill Gardner Pkwy 30248 **Location:** I-75 exit 212, just e. **Facility:** 64 units. 3 stories, interior corridors. **Amenities:** safes. **Activities:** exercise room. **Guest Services:** coin laundry.

SUPER 8 (770)957-2936

Motel. $54-$96 **Address:** 4605 Bill Gardner Pkwy 30248 **Location:** I-75 exit 212, just w. **Facility:** 54 units. 2 stories (no elevator), exterior corridors. **Terms:** 3 day cancellation notice-fee imposed. **Guest Services:** coin laundry.

Visit AAA.com/searchfordiscounts to save on travel, shopping, dining and attractions

WHERE TO EAT

THE FRENCH MARKET AND TAVERN 770/914-9312

Southern American. Casual Dining. $8-$22 **AAA Inspector Notes:** This casual yet upscale restaurant is a delicious blend of Southern comfort food and classic New Orleans cuisine. Soak up the stylishly beautiful décor while dining on such classics as gumbo, fried green tomatoes, Andouille, crawfish and shrimp and grits. For those in the mood for a hearty meal the Jagermeister and mint barbecue lamb ribs or the Black Angus filet mignon are perfect. Before or after the meal, take time to stroll through the shop for the latest in home décor. **Features:** full bar. **Address:** 3480 Hwy 42 30248 **Location:** I-75 exit 212, just e on Bill Gardner Pkwy, then 0.5 mi se. **Parking:** on-site and street.

GABINO'S MEXICAN RESTAURANT 770/288-4300

Mexican. Casual Dining. $4-$21 **AAA Inspector Notes:** This friendly neighborhood Mexican restaurant offers all the traditional dishes that you crave. From fajitas to chunky guacamole, the food is fresh and the service makes everyone feel at home. **Features:** beer only. **Address:** 4854 Bill Gardner Pkwy 30248 **Location:** I-75 exit 212, just e.

SAN DIEGO MEXICAN RESTAURANT 678/583-4003

Mexican. Casual Dining. $3-$12 **AAA Inspector Notes:** This casual Mexican restaurant serves classic dishes such as tacos, enchiladas, nachos, quesadillas, fajitas and more. Locals rave about the margaritas and fish tacos. The portions are generous and no one walks away hungry. **Features:** full bar. **Address:** 4959 Bill Gardner Pkwy 30248 **Location:** I-75 exit 212, just e; in Walmart shopping plaza.

SLICES PIZZERIA 678/432-9498

Italian Pizza. Casual Dining. $4-$22 **AAA Inspector Notes:** This family-owned pizzeria, located in the historic district, offers delicious New York-style pizza and calzones. Order the gooey deliciousness by the slice or share a pie with friends but be aware that the portions are massive. Save room for a slice of apple pie dessert pizza. It is so good you may never want a traditional apple pie again. **Features:** full bar. **Address:** 3844 Hwy 42 30248 **Location:** I-75 exit 212, e on Bill Gardner Pkwy, then 0.5 mi s. **Parking:** on-site and street.

LOOKOUT MOUNTAIN (A-1) pop. 1,602, elev. 1,798'
• Hotels p. 210

ROCK CITY GARDENS is 5 mi. s.w. on Lookout Mountain, following signs from I-24 exit 174 or 178. The man credited with inventing miniature golf stars in the story of how a personal retreat became a symbol of American tourism. Garnet Carter purchased a large tract of land atop Lookout Mountain for residential development in the 1920s. While he built a mountaintop home, wife Frieda landscaped the grounds, weaving walkways over, under and around natural rock formations and planting native flowers and trees beside the paths. Carefully placed statuary completed the mood of a charming secret garden with whimsical fairy-tale touches.

The housing development was scrapped and a tourist attraction that has never ceased to amaze guests was born in the early 1930s. Ever the entrepreneur, Carter hatched the marketing scheme of the century when he sent one of his handymen across country to paint "See Rock City" slogans on roadside barns. Carter descendants operate the attraction today.

Rock City features more than 400 native plant species and panoramic views 1,700 feet above sea level. The Enchanted Trail leads through wonders such as Grand Corridor and Needle's Eye en route to Lover's Leap, site of the See Seven States view. Fairyland Caverns and Mother Goose Village display 3-D scenes from fairy tales and nursery rhymes. Enchanted Garden of Lights, held the Friday before Thanksgiving to early Jan., 6-9 p.m. (closed Christmas Eve), features more than 500,000 lights and some 30 holiday scenes with music.

Time: Allow 2 hours minimum. **Hours:** Open daily at 8:30. Closing times vary by season; phone ahead. **Cost:** $19.95; $11.95 (ages 3-12). Combination ticket with Ruby Falls $36.90; $21.90 (ages 3-12). Combination ticket with Lookout Mountain Incline Railway and Ruby Falls $49.90; $26.90 (ages 3-12). **Phone:** (706) 820-2531 or (800) 854-0675.

CHANTICLEER INN BED & BREAKFAST (706)820-2002
▼▼▼ **Bed & Breakfast.** $160-$265 **Address:** 1300 Mockingbird Ln 30750 **Location:** I-24 exit 178 westbound; exit 174 eastbound, follow signs to Lookout Mountain, Rock City. Adjacent to Rock City. **Facility:** These quaint cottages, circa 1930, are tucked beneath huge trees and surrounded by lush, colorful landscaping. Rooms are individually decorated, some with antique furnishings. 17 units, some cottages. 1 story, interior/exterior corridors. **Terms:** 2 night minimum stay - seasonal and/or weekends, age restrictions may apply, 7 day cancellation notice-fee imposed. **Pool(s):** outdoor.

LOUISVILLE (C-4) pop. 2,493, elev. 310'

In the heart of the cotton belt, Louisville was founded in 1786 and served as Georgia's first permanent capital from 1796 to 1807. Early settlers were reluctant to move away from the coast, so to encourage settlement of the interior an inland site was chosen as the new state capital.

A spot near Galphinton, a trading post older than some of the coastal settlements, was picked because it was in an area where Native Americans were friendly, good drinking water was available and the higher ground was away from the unhealthy swamplands. Named in honor of King Louis XVI, the new town was modeled after Philadelphia; the Capitol, governor's mansion and some houses were built before it had any residents.

Jefferson County Chamber of Commerce: 302 E. Broad St., P.O. Box 630, Louisville, GA 30434. **Phone:** (478) 625-8134 or (866) 527-2642.

THE OLD MARKET HOUSE is at Broad and Mulberry sts. Built from great oak timbers in the mid-1790s before the town was laid out, the structure once served as a market. A tower houses a bell cast in France in 1772 for a New Orleans convent. Pirates plundered the ship carrying the bell; in turn, the pirate ship was captured near Savannah. The bell was sent to the new capital, where it was rung to celebrate the independence of the 13 Colonies. **Hours:** Open daily 24 hours. **Cost:** Free. **Phone:** (478) 625-8134 or (866) 527-2642.

LUMPKIN (D-2) pop. 2,741, elev. 593'

PROVIDENCE CANYON STATE OUTDOOR RECREATION AREA, 7 mi. w. on SR 39C at 8930 Canyon Rd., is known as "Georgia's Little Grand Canyon." The park preserves a 1,003-acre area containing 16 canyons eroded to a depth of 150 feet. The still-eroding walls of the winding gullies exhibit varicolored strata. A hiking trail leads into the canyons. A visitor center offers exhibits about native wildlife, flora and fauna.

Guided hikes are available by reservation. **Hours:** Park open daily 7 a.m.-9 p.m., mid-Apr. to mid-Sept.; 7-6, rest of year. Visitor center open Sat.-Sun. 8-5 (weather permitting). Phone ahead to confirm schedule. **Cost:** Free. Guided hike $5 (per person). **Parking:** $5 per private vehicle. **Phone:** (229) 838-6870.

MACON (C-3) pop. 91,351, elev. 335'

• Hotels p. 212 • Restaurants p. 214

Macon is near Georgia's geographical center. Laid out in 1823 on the west side of the Ocmulgee River, it is one of the only cities in the Southeast that can trace its origin to a frontier fort. The remains of Fort Hawkins on Emery Highway include a replica of one of the original blockhouses.

At nearby Ocmulgee National Monument *(see place listing p. 230)*, more than 17,000 years of human habitation are celebrated and preserved. Visitors can enter a reconstructed earth lodge to see the original 1,000-year-old clay floor and seating as well as an eagle effigy.

Other city landmarks include Wesleyan College, founded in 1836 and the first college chartered specifically to grant degrees to women. Mercer University, founded in Penfield in 1833, has been in Macon since 1871. A highlight among historic buildings is the 1836 City Hall. Originally built as a fireproof bank, the Classical Revival-style building also served as the temporary state capitol during the last 2 years of the Civil War.

Older residential sections are lined with antebellum mansions spared by Gen. William Tecumseh Sherman on his March to the Sea. Outdoor recreational activities are many at nearby Lake Tobesofkee *(see Recreation Areas Chart)*.

The Allman Brothers Band Museum at the Big House, 2321 Vineville Ave., is a tribute to the local band who are considered the architects of Southern rock music. Highlights in the Grand Tudor-style mansion, once home base for the band, include posters, photographs and memorabilia as well as film footage and audio recordings; phone (478) 741-5551.

Macon celebrates the blooming of some 300,000 Yoshino cherry trees in mid-March. The International Cherry Blossom Festival features arts and children's festivals, an international food fair, concerts, evening torchlight walks, tours of historic houses and the downtown area, parades and an old-fashioned Southern ball. A designated cherry blossom trail showcases the flowering trees.

The Pan African Festival of Georgia in April celebrates a rich cultural heritage of African art, music and storytelling. Also taking place in April is Fired Works Regional Ceramics Exhibition and Sale, a show spotlighting the work of regional artists that includes a variety of ceramics demonstrations and workshops. Visitors can tour secluded gardens and view private lofts and interiors in the city's historic districts during the Spring Stroll of Macon Houses and Gardens in May.

Macon-Bibb County Convention and Visitors Bureau: 450 Martin Luther King Jr. Blvd., Macon, GA 31201. **Phone:** (478) 743-3401 or (800) 768-3401.

Self-guiding tours: Maps and brochures describing walking tours are available from the convention and visitors bureau or the welcome center north on I-75; phone (478) 743-3401.

THE CANNONBALL HOUSE is at 856 Mulberry St. This 1853 Greek Revival-style house was Macon's only home to sustain damage during the Civil War. The house contains the historic meeting parlors of the Alpha Delta Pi and Phi Mu societies, which were founded in Macon. The surrounding grounds feature a period English-style garden. The 45-minute guided tour includes the original two-story brick kitchen and servants' quarters behind the house.

Hours: Guided tours are given Mon.-Sat. 10-4. Last tour begins at 3:30. Closed major holidays. **Cost:** Tour $8; $6 (ages 65+ and military with ID); $4 (students with ID); free (ages 0-4). **Phone:** (478) 745-5982. GT

GEORGIA SPORTS HALL OF FAME is at 301 Cherry St. The museum's 14,000 square feet of exhibit space are dedicated to the history of sports in Georgia. A large interactive area includes a NASCAR simulator and basketball courts, and an 18-minute film honors hall of fame inductees. A scavenger hunt activity is available for children. **Time:** Allow 30 minutes minimum. **Hours:** Tues.-Sat. 10-5. Closed major holidays. Phone ahead to confirm holiday schedule. **Cost:** $8; $6 (ages 65+, students and military with ID); $3.50 (ages 5-16). **Phone:** (478) 752-1585. 🅰

HAY HOUSE, at 934 Georgia Ave., was built 1855-59 as a 24-room, Italian Renaissance Revival mansion that boasted many new amenities for its time, including a plumbing system with hot and cold running water in several indoor bathrooms. Mr. and Mrs. Parks Lee Hay Sr. bought and redecorated the mansion in 1926 to reflect 20th-century living. Ornate plasterwork, 19th-century faux marble *trompe l'oeil* walls, crystal chandeliers and hand-carved front doors adorn the house. The decorative arts collection includes furniture and porcelains.

Guided tours are available. A behind-the-scenes guided tour also is available seasonally by reservation. **Time:** Allow 1 hour minimum. **Hours:** Guided tours on the hour Mon.-Sat. 10-4, Sun. 1-4. Last tour begins 1 hour before closing. Closed Jan. 1, Easter,

July 4, Thanksgiving and Christmas. **Cost:** $11; $10 (ages 65+ and military with ID); $7 (ages 6-college students with ID). Top of the House tour additional $4. **Phone:** (478) 742-8155. GT

MUSEUM OF ARTS AND SCIENCES, 7.5 mi. n. on US 41 at 4182 Forsyth Rd., features four galleries with frequently changing exhibitions. The Mark Smith Planetarium and the Mini-Zoo, a live animal habitat, present daily programs. The three-story Discovery House features hands-on activities for the family. On the fourth Friday evening of the month, the planetarium features a Sky Over Macon show and an observatory opens. A nature trail also is on the grounds.

Children ages 0-2 are not permitted in the planetarium. **Hours:** Museum open Tues.-Sat. 10-5, Sun. 1-5. Planetarium shows are presented Tues.-Sat. at 11:30 and 4 (also Sat. at 2, Sun. at 2 and 4). Mini-Zoo programs are presented daily at 3 (also Sat. at 1). Additional shows may be scheduled in summer; phone ahead. Sky Over Macon show fourth Fri. of the month at 8 p.m.; observatory opens following the show (clear weather permitting). Closed major holidays. **Cost:** Museum (including all daily programs) or sky show $10; $8 (ages 62+ and military with ID); $7 (college students with ID); $5 (ages 3-17). **Phone:** (478) 477-3232. 🅰

PIEDMONT NATIONAL WILDLIFE REFUGE is approximately 25 mi. n. of Macon; from I-75 exit 186, proceed e. on Juliette Rd. 18 mi. to the refuge office and visitor center. Covering 35,000 acres, the area offers four nature trails, a scenic driving route and a visitor center with natural history exhibits. **Hours:** Refuge open daily dawn-dusk except during hunting season in spring and fall. Visitor center open Mon.-Fri. 7:30-4. Visitor center closed major holidays. Phone ahead to confirm schedule. **Cost:** Free. **Phone:** (478) 986-5441.

SIDNEY LANIER COTTAGE HOUSE MUSEUM, 935 High St. is the birthplace of Sidney Lanier—poet, musician and soldier. The house has been restored to reflect the 1840s period in which it was built. Inside, visitors will take a tour and see portraits, Lanier's silver alto flute and first editions of his published poetry while learning about his life and accomplishments. **Hours:** Thur.-Sat. 10-4. Last tour begins 30 minutes before closing. Closed major holidays. Phone ahead to confirm schedule. **Cost:** $5; $4 (senior citizens and military with ID); $3 (ages 6-18). **Phone:** (478) 743-3851. GT

TUBMAN MUSEUM, 310 Cherry St., has exhibits relating to the historic, artistic and cultural contributions of African-Americans. Among the highlights in the museum's galleries is a mural that illustrates African-American history. Special events are offered, and guided tours are available by appointment. **Time:** Allow 30 minutes minimum. **Hours:** Tues.-Sat. 9-5. Closed major holidays. **Cost:** $10; $8 (college students, senior citizens and military with ID); $6 (ages 3-17). **Phone:** (478) 743-8544. GT

1842 INN
(478)741-1842

Historic Bed & Breakfast
$189-$255

Address: 353 College St 31201 **Location:** I-75 exit 164 (US 41), 0.5 mi e, then just n. **Facility:** Built in 1842 as a private residence, this property reflects the charm and elegance of the era. Guests will enjoy spacious rooms, historic accents and the genteel hospitality of the staff. 19 units. 2 stories (no elevator), interior/exterior corridors. **Terms:** 7 day cancellation notice-fee imposed. **Guest Services:** valet laundry. **Featured Amenity: full hot breakfast.**

BEST WESTERN INN & SUITES OF MACON
(478)781-5300

Motel
$74-$90

 Best Western.

AAA Benefit: Save 10% or more every day and earn 10% bonus points!

Address: 4681 Chambers Rd 31206 **Location:** I-475 exit 3 (Eisenhower Pkwy/US 80), just ne, then just se. **Facility:** 56 units. 2 stories (no elevator), exterior corridors. **Terms:** cancellation fee imposed. **Pool(s):** heated indoor. **Activities:** hot tub, exercise room. **Guest Services:** coin laundry.

BEST WESTERN RIVERSIDE INN
(478)743-6311

Hotel
$66-$80

Best Western.

AAA Benefit: Save 10% or more every day and earn 10% bonus points!

Address: 2400 Riverside Dr 31204 **Location:** I-75 exit 167 (Riverside Dr), just w, then 0.4 mi se. **Facility:** 115 units. 2 stories (no elevator), interior corridors. **Terms:** cancellation fee imposed. **Pool(s):** outdoor. **Activities:** exercise room. **Guest Services:** coin laundry. **Featured Amenity: full hot breakfast.**

CANDLEWOOD SUITES
478/254-3530

Extended Stay Hotel. Rates not provided. **Address:** 3957 River Place Dr 31210 **Location:** I-75 exit 169 (Arkwright Rd), just e, then just s. **Facility:** 83 efficiencies. 3 stories, interior corridors. **Pool(s):** outdoor. **Activities:** hot tub, exercise room. **Guest Services:** complimentary and valet laundry.

COMFORT INN & SUITES MACON
(478)621-7977

Hotel
$100-$160

Address: 5000 Harrison Rd 31206 **Location:** I-475 exit 3 (Eisenhower Pkwy), just e on US 80, then just n. **Facility:** 79 units, some two bedrooms. 3 stories, interior corridors. **Pool(s):** heated indoor. **Activities:** hot tub, exercise room. **Guest Services:** valet and coin laundry. **Featured Amenity: full hot breakfast.**

COMFORT SUITES
(478)314-5130

Hotel
$81-$300

Address: 120 Plantation Inn Dr 31210 **Location:** I-475 exit 9 (Zebulon Rd), just e, then s. **Facility:** 75 units. 3 stories, interior corridors. **Pool(s):** heated indoor. **Activities:** hot tub, exercise room. **Guest Services:** valet and coin laundry. **Featured Amenity: full hot breakfast.**

COUNTRY INN & SUITES BY CARLSON MACON NORTH
478/803-8300

Hotel
Rates not provided

Address: 3915 Arkwright Rd 31210 **Location:** I-75 exit 169 (Arkwright Rd), just e. **Facility:** 79 units. 4 stories, interior corridors. **Pool(s):** heated indoor. **Activities:** hot tub, exercise room. **Guest Services:** valet and coin laundry. **Featured Amenity: continental breakfast.**

COURTYARD BY MARRIOTT MACON
(478)477-8899

Hotel
$76-$154

COURTYARD Marriott.

AAA Benefit: Members save 5% or more!

Address: 3990 Sheraton Dr 31210 **Location:** I-75 exit 169 (Arkwright Rd), just n, then just nw. **Facility:** 108 units. 3 stories, interior corridors. **Pool(s):** outdoor. **Activities:** exercise room. **Guest Services:** valet and coin laundry.

DAYS INN
(478)781-4343

Motel
$50-$65

Address: 4999 Eisenhower Pkwy 31206 **Location:** I-475 exit 3 (Eisenhower Pkwy/US 80), just e. **Facility:** 58 units. 2 stories (no elevator), exterior corridors. **Pool(s):** outdoor. **Guest Services:** coin laundry. **Featured Amenity: full hot breakfast.**

FAIRFIELD INN & SUITES BY MARRIOTT MACON
(478)738-9007

Hotel. $76-$111 **Address:** 4035 Sheraton Dr 31210 **Location:** I-75 exit 169 (Arkwright Rd), just n, then just nw. **Facility:** 78 units. 3 stories (no elevator), interior corridors. **Pool(s):** outdoor. **Activities:** exercise room. **Guest Services:** valet and coin laundry.

AAA Benefit: Members save 5% or more!

Request roadside assistance in a click — online or using the AAA or CAA apps

FAIRFIELD INN BY MARRIOTT MACON/WEST
(478)474-9922

Hotel
$62-$102

AAA Benefit: Members save 5% or more!

Address: 110 Plantation Inn Dr 31210 **Location:** I-475 exit 9 (Zebulon Rd), just e to Peake Rd, then just s. Located in a quiet area. **Facility:** 65 units. 3 stories, interior corridors. **Guest Services:** valet laundry.

SAVE TI→ CALL &M BIZ 🛜 ✕ ⬛ / SOME UNITS ⬛ ⬛

HAMPTON INN & SUITES MACON I-475
(478)803-4900

▽▽▽ **Hotel.** $134-$185 **Address:** 5010 Eisenhower Pkwy 31206 **Location:** I-475 exit 3, just e on US 80, then just n. **Facility:** 74 units. 3 stories, interior corridors. **Terms:** 1-7 night minimum stay, cancellation fee imposed. **Pool(s):** outdoor. **Activities:** exercise room. **Guest Services:** valet and coin laundry.

AAA Benefit: Members save up to 10%!

CALL &M 🛜 BIZ HS 🛜 ✕ ⬛ ⬛ ⬛

HILTON GARDEN INN MACON/MERCER UNIVERSITY
(478)741-5527

Hotel
$129-$185

AAA Benefit: Members save up to 10%!

Address: 1220 Stadium Dr 31204 **Location:** I-75 exit 163, just s. **Facility:** 101 units. 4 stories, interior corridors. **Terms:** 1-7 night minimum stay, cancellation fee imposed. **Pool(s):** outdoor. **Activities:** exercise room. **Guest Services:** valet and coin laundry.

SAVE TI ⬛ CALL &M 🛜 BIZ
HS 🛜 ✕ ⬛ ⬛ ⬛

HOLIDAY INN EXPRESS & SUITES MACON WEST
478/803-0033

▽▽▽ **Hotel.** Rates not provided. **Address:** 4970 Harrison Rd 31206 **Location:** I-475 exit 3 (Eisenhower Pkwy/US 80), just ne. **Facility:** 80 units. 3 stories, interior corridors. **Pool(s):** outdoor. **Activities:** exercise room. **Guest Services:** valet and coin laundry.

🛜 BIZ 🛜 ✕ ⬛ ⬛ ⬛

HOLIDAY INN MACON NORTH
478/803-8200

▽▽▽ **Hotel.** Rates not provided. **Address:** 3953 River Place Dr 31210 **Location:** I-475 exit 3 (Eisenhower Pkwy/US 80), just e, then 0.5 mi s. **Facility:** 110 units, some two bedrooms. 1-5 stories, interior corridors. **Terms:** check-in 4 pm. **Pool(s):** indoor. **Activities:** exercise room. **Guest Services:** valet and coin laundry.

TI CALL &M 🛜 BIZ 🛜 ✕ ⬛ ⬛

HOMEWOOD SUITES BY HILTON-MACON NORTH PROVIDENCE VILLAGE
478/477-9776

▽▽▽ **Extended Stay Hotel.** Rates not provided. **Address:** 1514 Bass Rd 31210 **Location:** I-75 exit 172, just w. **Facility:** 99 efficiencies, some two bedrooms. 4 stories, interior corridors. **Terms:** check-in 4 pm. **Pool(s):** outdoor. **Activities:** exercise room. **Guest Services:** valet and coin laundry.

AAA Benefit: Members save up to 10%!

TI→ CALL &M 🛜 BIZ HS 🛜 ✕ ⬛ ⬛ ⬛ ⬛

LA QUINTA INN & SUITES MACON
(478)475-0206

▽▽▽▽ **Hotel.** $82-$143 **Address:** 3944 River Place Dr 31210 **Location:** I-75 exit 169 (Arkwright Rd), just n, then e. **Facility:** 142 units. 3 stories, interior corridors. **Pool(s):** outdoor. **Activities:** exercise room. **Guest Services:** coin laundry.

TI→ CALL &M 🛜 BIZ 🛜 ⬛ / SOME UNITS 🛜 ⬛ ⬛ ⬛

LA QUINTA INN & SUITES MACON WEST
(478)788-6226

▽▽▽▽ **Hotel.** $86-$220 **Address:** 4615 Chambers Rd 31206 **Location:** I-475 exit 3 (Eisenhower Pkwy/US 80), just e, then 0.5 mi s. **Facility:** 67 units. 3 stories, interior corridors. **Pool(s):** heated indoor. **Activities:** hot tub, exercise room. **Guest Services:** coin laundry.

🛜 BIZ 🛜 ✕ ⬛ ⬛ ⬛ / SOME UNITS 🛜

MACON I-75 HAMPTON INN & SUITES
(478)803-5000

▽▽▽ **Hotel.** $119-$159 **Address:** 3954 River Place Dr 31210 **Location:** I-75 exit 169 (Arkwright Rd), just e, then just s. **Facility:** 83 units. 4 stories, interior corridors. **Terms:** 1-7 night minimum stay, cancellation fee imposed. **Pool(s):** heated indoor. **Activities:** exercise room. **Guest Services:** valet and coin laundry.

AAA Benefit: Members save up to 10%!

TI→ CALL &M 🛜 BIZ HS 🛜 ✕ ⬛ ⬛ ⬛

MAGNUSON HOTEL MACON
(478)743-1482

▽▽ **Hotel.** $79-$159 **Address:** 2720 Riverside Dr 31204 **Location:** I-75 exit 167 (Riverside Dr), just nw. **Facility:** 94 units. 6 stories, interior corridors. **Terms:** 7 day cancellation notice-fee imposed. **Activities:** exercise room. **Guest Services:** valet laundry.

TI→ CALL &M BIZ 🛜 ⬛ ⬛ ⬛

MARRIOTT MACON CITY CENTER HOTEL
(478)621-5300

Hotel
$83-$194

AAA Benefit: Members save 5% or more!

Address: 240 Coliseum Dr 31217 **Location:** I-16 exit 2, just n. **Facility:** This property offers vibrant décor with eye-catching art accents and upscale comforts. Guests will enjoy the close proximity to historic downtown and historical sights equipped with walking trails. 220 units. 8 stories, interior corridors. **Terms:** check-in 4 pm. **Amenities:** video games. **Pool(s):** heated indoor. **Activities:** hot tub, exercise room. **Guest Services:** valet and coin laundry.

SAVE TI ⬛ 🍷 CALL &M 🛜 BIZ sHS 🛜 ✕ 🎥 ⬛

MICROTEL INN & SUITES BY WYNDHAM
(478)254-3300

Motel
$60-$79

Address: 2020 Bowman Park 31210 **Location:** I-75 exit 171 (Riverside Dr), just w on Riverside Park. **Facility:** 63 units. 3 stories, interior corridors. **Activities:** exercise room. **Guest Services:** coin laundry. **Featured Amenity:** continental breakfast.

SAVE TI→ CALL &M BIZ HS 🛜 ⬛ ⬛ / SOME UNITS 🛜 ⬛

RAMADA INN   (478)788-0120

Hotel
$55-$75

Address: 4755 Chambers Rd 31206 **Location:** I-475 exit 3 (Eisenhower Pkwy/US 80), just e. **Facility:** 86 units. 2 stories (no elevator), exterior corridors. **Pool(s):** outdoor. **Activities:** exercise room. **Guest Services:** coin laundry. **Featured Amenity: continental breakfast.**

RESIDENCE INN BY MARRIOTT   (478)475-4280

Extended Stay Hotel
$116-$187

Residence Inn Marriott

AAA Benefit: Members save 5% or more!

Address: 3900 Sheraton Dr 31211 **Location:** I-75 exit 169 (Ackwright Rd), just n, then just nw. **Facility:** 78 kitchen units, some two bedrooms. 3 stories. interior corridors. **Pool(s):** heated indoor. **Activities:** exercise room. **Guest Services:** valet and coin laundry. **Featured Amenity: full hot breakfast.**

SPRINGHILL SUITES BY MARRIOTT MACON   (478)803-9100

Hotel. $90-$145 **Address:** 4630 Sheraton Dr 31210 **Location:** I-75 exit 171 (Riverside Dr), just n. **Facility:** 121 units. 4 stories, interior corridors. **Pool(s):** heated indoor. **Activities:** exercise room. **Guest Services:** valet and coin laundry.

AAA Benefit: Members save 5% or more!

SUPER 8 MACON WEST   (478)254-5290

Hotel
$49-$60

Address: 4765 Chambers Rd 31206 **Location:** I-475 exit 3, just e. **Facility:** 54 units. 2 stories (no elevator), exterior corridors. **Guest Services:** coin laundry. **Featured Amenity: continental breakfast.**

WINGATE BY WYNDHAM   (478)476-8100

Hotel. $89-$122 **Address:** 100 Northcrest Blvd 31210 **Location:** I-75 exit 169 (Arkwright Rd), just sw to Riverside Dr, then 0.4 mi nw. **Facility:** 80 units. 3 stories, interior corridors. **Amenities:** safes. **Pool(s):** heated outdoor. **Activities:** sauna, exercise room. **Guest Services:** valet laundry.

THE BACK BURNER RESTAURANT   478/746-3336

French. Casual Dining. $15-$45 **AAA Inspector Notes:** This quaint cottage's dining room has a homey feel with several small dining rooms, wood floors, artwork and comfortable furnishings. Continental dishes, which change often, reflect a heavy French influence. Delicate, perfectly prepared sauces complement such favorites as crab cakes laden with lump crab, chicken breast in Burgundy sauce, salmon in basil cream and halibut in tomato caper sauce. The waitstaff is well versed in the many wine offerings and competently make pairing suggestions. **Features:** full bar. **Reservations:** suggested. **Address:** 2242 Ingleside Ave 31204 **Location:** Jct Riverside Dr and Ingleside Ave, 0.5 mi w.

THE BEAR'S DEN   478/745-9909

American. Buffet Style. $3-$6 **AAA Inspector Notes:** This family-owned restaurant has been dishing out tasty comfort food for more than 20 years. This is a popular local place that does a brisk business all day. The food is made in house just like your grandmother used to make and no one goes away hungry. Try the fried chicken or the meatloaf and mashed potatoes. Be sure to save room for the banana pudding. **Address:** 1191 Olgethorpe St 31207 **Location:** I-75 exit 164 (SR 19/Forsyth St), 1 mi se on Forsyth St, just s on College St, take the roundabout to Oglethorpe St. **Parking:** on-site and street.

DOWNTOWN GRILL   478/742-5999

Steak. Casual Dining. $17-$28 **AAA Inspector Notes:** Located downtown in an alley, this restaurant feels like a secret only the most sophisticated patrons are privy to know. Guests enjoy the intimate dining room with muted lighting, soft jazz and gold-framed oil paintings on exposed brick walls. Whet your appetite with a cheese plate with clover honey and grill-toasted French bread. Entrées include a variety of steaks, chops and fish including filet mignon stuffed with goat cheese and cranberries or maple leaf duck breast. **Features:** full bar, happy hour. **Reservations:** suggested. **Address:** 562 Mulberry Street Ln 31201 **Location:** Center of town. **Parking:** valet and street only.

FRESH AIR BAR-B-QUE   478/477-7229

Barbecue. Casual Dining. $3-$6 **AAA Inspector Notes:** For those with a hankering for some good old fashioned barbecue, this little eatery has been serving up the goods for almost two decades. The plates are disposable and there are no fancy garnishes but the food is quick and filling. Try the Brunswick stew or chopped pork sandwich. **Address:** 3076 Riverside Dr 31210 **Location:** I-75 exit 169 (Arkwright Rd), 0.3 mi sw, then just s.

GROW   478/743-4663

Southern American. Casual Dining. $3-$8 **AAA Inspector Notes:** This home-grown restaurant offers a casual dining experience with a fresh take on Southern classics. Start off with a complimentary sample of boiled peanuts while awaiting your food. The menu features home-cooked goodness such as Mom's chicken salad, a pimento cheese sandwich or Sloppy Joe sliders. The desserts also are homemade and are a great finish to any meal. **Address:** 1019 Riverside Dr 31201 **Location:** Jct SR 23 and Riverside Dr; downtown.

INGLESIDE VILLAGE PIZZA   478/750-8488

Pizza. Casual Dining. $7-$16 **AAA Inspector Notes:** Located in a residential neighborhood, just off the beaten path, this locally popular spot always is busy. The pizza is pillowy—not too thin and not too thick—perfectly seasoned and just the right temperature. Diners can make their own or choose between several of the favorites. Those not interested in pizza are offered a few select subs and salads. An extensive selection of craft beers calls this place home. **Features:** beer only. **Address:** 2395 Ingleside Ave 31204 **Location:** Jct Corbin and Ingleside aves.

Make a good trip great with insight

and ideas from AAA/CAA travel experts

J.L.'S OPEN PIT BAR-B-Q   478/788-1989

▼ Barbecue. Casual Dining. $5-$18 **AAA Inspector Notes:** The locals love this one! Jumbo pork, beef or smoked turkey sandwiches served sliced or chopped and a large salad bar are crowd pleasers at this popular restaurant. Half and full racks of ribs, as well as Choice cut steaks and prime rib, also are available. **Features:** beer only, early bird specials. **Address:** 5001 Brookhaven Rd 31206 **Location:** I-475 exit 3 (Eisenhower Pkwy/US 80), just ne. L   D

MACON PIZZA COMPANY   478/475-0000

▼ Italian Pizza. Casual Dining. $3-$17 **AAA Inspector Notes:** This family-owned eatery is big on customer service and small on price. The cozy dining room and traditional menu favorites make this the ideal location for a family outing or casual get together with friends. I recommend the barbecue pizza and cinnamon sticks on their delicious, homemade New York-style dough. The calzone, shark bites (garlic and cheese bread bites) and people's choice pizza also are popular. **Address:** 5978 Zebulon Rd 31210 **Location:** I-475 exit 9 (Zebulon Rd), just e on Zebulon Rd; in Plantation Center.

L   D   CALL M

MARCO RISTORANTE ITALIANO   478/405-5660

▼▼▼ Northern Italian. Fine Dining. $18-$40 **AAA Inspector Notes:** The Filipponi's operate this fine dining spot, exhibiting one of their passions—fine Italian food. The modern brick storefront gives way to Old World charm and a large dark-wood bar. The interior walls of the dining room are painted to look like the outside of village buildings, creating a setting similar to dining al fresco. The menu is Northern Italian with less reliance on pasta and more on fresh vegetables, herbs, meats and seafood. Service is polished and attentive. **Features:** full bar, happy hour. **Reservations:** suggested. **Address:** 4581 Forsyth Rd 31210 **Location:** I-475 exit 9 (Zebulon Rd), 2.3 mi e, then 1.2 mi se. D

MARGARITAS MEXICAN GRILL   478/477-2410

▼ ▼ Mexican. Casual Dining. $7-$15 **AAA Inspector Notes:** Inspired by the cuisine and culture of Tequila and Guadalajara Mexico, this restaurant offers delicious dishes and friendly service. Decorative wine barrels, carved wood furniture and multi-colored brickwork transport diners to an authentic Spanish hacienda. Enjoy house specialties such as cheese dip with fresh tortilla chips, signature fajitas or Baja fish. The portions are generous and are perfectly paired with the variety of mixed drinks served from the bar. **Features:** full bar. **Address:** 6012 Zebulon Rd 31210 **Location:** I-475 exit 9 (Zebulon Rd), just e. L   D   CALL M

MOLLY'S CAFE   478/744-9898

▼ ▼ Sandwiches. Casual Dining. $6-$12 **AAA Inspector Notes:** This charming downtown café is an excellent spot for a delicious, Southern-inspired lunch. Offering a menu of gourmet salads and sandwiches, they also feature soup and a quiche of the day. Highlights include a bacon-lettuce-tomato club with pimiento cheese, chicken salad wrap, roasted turkey with apples and smoked Gouda on wheat, and roast beef with horseradish on a French baguette. The food is fresh and homemade but only available for lunch. **Features:** patio dining. **Address:** 402 Cherry St 31201 **Location:** I-16 exit 2, 0.5 mi s on Martin Luther King Jr Blvd, then just w; downtown. **Parking:** street only. L

PAPOULIS MEDITERRANEAN CAFE AND MARKET
                478/474-0204

▼ Greek. Quick Serve. $6-$20 **AAA Inspector Notes:** This is a quick way to get some favorite Greek dishes. When the weather is good, enjoy gyros outside on the picnic tables. Guests also can purchase ingredients from the market to continue the Greek experience at home. **Features:** patio dining. **Address:** 121 Tom Hill Sr Blvd 31210 **Location:** I-75 exit 169, 0.5 mi w; in shopping center.

L   D

THE ROOKERY   478/746-8658

▼ American. Casual Dining. $8-$17 **AAA Inspector Notes:** This eatery has been a fixture on the downtown scene for more than 30 years. Enjoy an array of sandwiches and burgers along with Memphis-style ribs and steaks. Homemade peach cobbler is a tasty finish to a meal. Live music is featured Saturday and Sunday. **Features:** full bar, patio dining, Sunday brunch, happy hour. **Address:** 543 Cherry St 31201 **Location:** I-16 exit 2, 0.5 mi s on Martin Luther King Jr Blvd, then just w; downtown. **Parking:** street only.

L   D

S & S CAFETERIA   478/746-9406

▼ Southern Comfort Food. Buffet Style. $6-$10 **AAA Inspector Notes:** A longtime favorite for comfort food, the family-owned cafeteria invites diners to load a plate with traditionally prepared chicken, beef, vegetables, salad and dessert. L   D

LOCATIONS:
Address: 2626 Riverside Dr 31204 **Location:** I-75 exit 167 (Riverside Dr), just w. **Phone:** 478/746-9406
Address: 3724 Bloomfield Village Dr 31206 **Location:** Jct SR 408, 2 mi e. **Phone:** 478/788-5913

MADISON (B-3) pop. 3,979, elev. 664'
• Hotels p. 216 • Restaurants p. 216

Incorporated in 1809, Madison's antebellum houses remain virtually intact, possibly due to the efforts of Sen. Joshua Hill, an anti-secessionist who resigned his seat in Congress rather than vote on the issue of secession. When Gen. William Tecumseh Sherman's Union forces approached Madison in November 1864, Hill and two other men worked to spare the town from the torch. Only the train depot, a cotton gin and a cloth factory were burned.

The Morgan County Courthouse on the downtown square is a blend of formal and country architectural styles; it is open Mon.-Fri. 9-5. Many of the historic houses are open during the Madison Tour of Homes in May and December. Tours of the antebellum homes Rose Cottage and Rogers House are offered year-round; phone (706) 342-9627.

Madison-Morgan County Welcome Center: 115 E. Jefferson St., P.O. Box 826, Madison, GA 30650. **Phone:** (706) 342-4454.

Self-guiding tours: Walking/driving tour maps and brochures are available at the welcome center.

HERITAGE HALL, 277 S. Main St., is a Greek Revival home constructed in 1811. It was originally used as a private residence, and before being converted to an inn, it was moved 200 feet to its current location. The front porch is lined with columns that are emblematic of the architectural style, and inside, the house has been restored and beautifully decorated with period-accurate furnishings including pieces from the original occupants. After the tour, visitors are invited to leisurely peruse the house.

Hours: Mon.-Sat. 11-4, Sun. 1:30-4:30. Last tour begins 45 minutes before closing. Phone ahead to confirm schedule. **Cost:** $10; $7 (students with ID); free (ages 0-11). Combination with Rose Cottage and Rogers House $15; $10 (students with ID); free (ages 0-11). **Phone:** (706) 342-9627. GT

MADISON-MORGAN CULTURAL CENTER is at 434 S. Main St. (US 441). This 1895 Romanesque Revival brick building was one of the first graded public schools in the South. Today it is a non-profit performing and visual arts center. The center contains a museum of Piedmont history with regional artifacts, displays of decorative arts and a circa 1875 Winship and Brother cotton gin; a restored early 20th-century classroom; an arts and crafts room; the original school auditorium, restored and now used for performing arts events and educational programs; and three art galleries with changing exhibits. The Boxwood Parlor is an exact replica of an 1850 Rococo Renaissance parlor, right down to the original furnishings.

Guided tours are available by appointment. **Time:** Allow 30 minutes minimum. **Hours:** Tues.-Sat. 10-5, Sun. 2-5. Closed major holidays. **Cost:** $5; $4 (ages 65+); $3 (students with ID); free (ages 0-5). **Phone:** (706) 342-4743 or (877) 233-0598. GT

HAMPTON INN AT MADISON (706)342-9003
▼▼ Hotel. $109-$319 **Address:** 2012 Eatonton Rd 30650 **Location:** I-20 exit 114, just n. **Facility:** 62 units. 3 stories, interior corridors. **Terms:** 1-7 night minimum stay, cancellation fee imposed. **Pool(s):** outdoor. **Activities:** exercise room. **Guest Services:** valet laundry.

AAA Benefit: Members save up to 10%!

HOLIDAY INN EXPRESS MADISON 706/342-9190
▼▼▼ Hotel. Rates not provided. **Address:** 1041 Ramada Way 30650 **Location:** I-20 exit 114, just e on Eatonton Rd, then just w. **Facility:** 64 units. 3 stories, interior corridors. **Terms:** check-in 3:30 pm. **Pool(s):** outdoor. **Activities:** exercise room. **Guest Services:** coin laundry.

QUALITY INN (706)342-1839
▼▼ Motel. $55-$99 **Address:** 2001 Eatonton Rd 30650 **Location:** US 129/441, 0.4 mi w. **Facility:** 69 units. 2 stories (no elevator), exterior corridors. **Pool(s):** outdoor. **Guest Services:** coin laundry.

SUPER 8 (706)438-1081
▼▼ Hotel. $54-$145 **Address:** 2091 Eatonton Rd 30650 **Location:** I-20 exit 114, 0.3 mi s. **Facility:** 58 units. 2 stories (no elevator), interior corridors. **Guest Services:** coin laundry.

WHERE TO EAT

MADISON CHOPHOUSE GRILLE 706/342-0910
▼▼ American. Casual Dining. $8-$25 **AAA Inspector Notes:** This spacious dining room bustles with an upbeat atmosphere and lively energy where guests can nosh on burgers or sandwiches or go all out with hearty portions of tasty pasta, steak, ribs or salmon dishes. End your meal here with cappuccino or espresso, or take it a step further with one of the luscious homemade desserts. **Features:** full bar, patio dining. **Address:** 202 S Main St 30650 **Location:** I-20 exit 114, 3 mi n on US 441; Historic Town Square.

MARIETTA (G-2) pop. 56,579, elev. 1,118'

• **Restaurants p. 218**
• **Hotels & Restaurants map & index p. 76, 82**
• **Part of Atlanta area — see map p. 44**

Winners of the Cherokee lands lottery settled Marietta in 1834, and the location soon attracted a seasonal population of lowland planters. The town's leisurely serenity was shattered by the Civil War. During Gen. William Tecumseh Sherman's push toward nearby Atlanta, Union and Confederate forces fought a bloody battle just beyond Marietta's boundaries at what is now Kennesaw Mountain National Battlefield Park (see place listing p. 202).

Although Marietta was spared, two of the city's cemeteries bear witness to the bitterness of the war. In 1866 Henry Cole, a local businessman, donated land for the Marietta National Cemetery as a gesture of peace so that the dead from each side could lie in the same ground. This was not to be as the Confederate Cemetery had already been established to bury soldiers killed in a nearby train wreck.

Downtown's Glover Park, complete with an ornate Victorian gazebo, recalls the late 19th century, of which few traces remain in this growing city northwest of Atlanta. Quiet walks among courtly old houses and picnics at Kennesaw Mountain National Battlefield Park are two of the area's recreational possibilities.

Held in historic Marietta, the ▼ Marietta Pilgrimage Christmas Home Tour features festively decorated private homes and historic public buildings as well as a Saturday evening candlelight tour.

Marietta Visitors Bureau: 4 Depot St., Marietta, GA 30060. **Phone:** (770) 429-1115.

Self-guiding tours: The Marietta Visitors Bureau, just off the square in the old train depot at 4 Depot St., provides brochures outlining a walking/driving tour of the historic district, which includes Sherman's former headquarters at Kennesaw House. Phone (770) 429-1115.

MARIETTA/COBB MUSEUM OF ART, 30 Atlanta St. S.E., is housed in a 1909 Greek Revival building that was the original Marietta Post Office. The museum's collection of American art spans the early 19th century to contemporary works. Temporary exhibits rotate quarterly. **Time:** Allow 30 minutes minimum. **Hours:** Tues.-Fri. 11-5, Sat. 11-4, Sun. 1-4. Closed major holidays, between exhibitions and for special events. Phone ahead to confirm exhibition schedule. **Cost:** $8; $5 (ages 6-college undergraduate students with ID and ages 65+); free (ages 0-5). **Phone:** (770) 528-1444.

MARIETTA GONE WITH THE WIND MUSEUM: SCARLETT ON THE SQUARE is at 18 Whitlock Ave. N.W. The museum houses Dr. Christopher Sullivan's collection of "Gone With The Wind" memorabilia, which includes foreign editions of the book, as well as film costumes, contracts, original scripts, personal items that belonged to cast members, and an original gown worn by Vivien Leigh as Scarlett O'Hara. Special events are offered. **Time:** Allow 30 minutes minimum. **Hours:** Mon.-Sat. 10-5. Closed Jan. 1, July 4, Thanksgiving and Christmas. Closes Christmas Eve and Dec. 31 at 4. **Cost:** $7; $6 (ages 60+ and students); free (ages 0-8). **Phone:** (770) 794-5576.

MARIETTA MUSEUM OF HISTORY is at 1 Depot St., in the 1845 Kennesaw House. The museum includes a series of galleries documenting the history of Marietta and Cobb County. Exhibits relate the development of local railroads, businesses and industries, display Civil War artifacts and showcase a variety of 19th- and 20th-century clothing, furnishings and inventions. The history of Native Americans and scouting are the subject of other permanent exhibits.

(See maps & indexes p. 76, 82.)

Time: Allow 30 minutes minimum. **Hours:** Mon.-Sat. 10-4. Closed Jan. 1, Memorial Day, July 4, Labor Day, Thanksgiving, Christmas Eve, Christmas, day after Christmas and Dec. 31. **Cost:** $7; $5 (ages 55+ and students with ID); free (ages 0-5 and active military with ID). **Phone:** (770) 794-5710.

THE ROOT HOUSE is at the intersection of Polk St. and N. Marietta Pkwy. The furnishings of this two-story house reflect the life of a middle-class merchant in the mid-19th-century. The garden contains period plants. Special events are offered. **Hours:** Wed.-Sat. 11-4. Guided tours depart at 11:30, 12:30, 1:30 and 2:30. Closed major holidays. **Cost:** $7; $6 (ages 55+ and college students with ID); $5 (ages 6-17). **Phone:** (770) 426-4982. [GT]

[SAVE] **SIX FLAGS WHITE WATER** is at 250 N. Cobb Pkwy. With more than 20 rides and 40 slides on a 50-acre site, the park is said to be the largest water park in the Southeast. On Typhoon Twister, riders in a four-person raft experience a five-story vertical drop into a huge bowl before being spun through a chute and launched into a splash pool.

Wahoo Racer is a 60-feet-tall slide in which riders can reach up to 40 feet per second while racing to the bottom on water toboggans. Standing 10-stories tall, Dive Bomber is the tallest slide at the park, and once inside a capsule, occupants are sent through a trap door to drop at nearly 90 degrees to the pool below.

Tornado is a 75-feet-tall superstructure that twists riders down into a 60-feet-tall, 130-feet-long giant funnel complete with rushing water. Other attractions include the Little Hooch lazy river and the Atlanta Ocean wave pool.

Allow a full day. **Hours:** Opens daily at 10:30, Memorial Day weekend to mid-Aug.; Sat.-Sun. and Labor Day at 10:30, mid-Aug. to mid-Sept. Closing times vary. Phone ahead to confirm schedule. **Cost:** $41.99; $36.99 (children under 48 inches tall). **Parking:** $15. **Phone:** (770) 948-9290. [🍴]

COURTYARD BY MARRIOTT-ATLANTA MARIETTA/I-75 NORTH
(770)956-1188 **48**

▼▼▼▼ Hotel. $87-$206 **Address:** 2455 Delk Rd SE 30067 **Location:** I-75 exit 261, 0.3 mi e. **Facility:** 146 units. 3 stories, interior corridors. **Pool(s):** outdoor. **Activities:** exercise room. **Guest Services:** valet and coin laundry.

| **AAA Benefit:** Members save 5% or more! |

[ECO] [🍴] CALL [&M] [🏊] [BIZ] [HS] [📶] [✕] [📶] [☕] / SOME UNITS [🖥]

COURTYARD BY MARRIOTT-WINDY HILL
(770)955-3838 **52**

▼▼▼▼ Hotel. $72-$206 **Address:** 2045 S Park Pl 30339 **Location:** I-75 exit 260, 0.3 mi w to S Park Pl, then just n. **Facility:** 127 units. 2 stories (no elevator), interior corridors. **Terms:** check-in 4 pm. **Pool(s):** outdoor. **Activities:** exercise room. **Guest Services:** valet and coin laundry.

| **AAA Benefit:** Members save 5% or more! |

[🍴] CALL [&M] [🏊] [BIZ] [📶] [✕] [📶] [☕] / SOME UNITS [🖥]

DRURY INN & SUITES-ATLANTA NORTHWEST
(770)612-0900 **47**

▼▼▼▼ Hotel. $89-$169 **Address:** 1170 Powers Ferry Pl 30067 **Location:** I-75 exit 261, just e. **Facility:** 143 units. 7 stories, interior corridors. **Terms:** cancellation fee imposed. **Pool(s):** heated outdoor, heated indoor. **Activities:** hot tub, exercise room. **Guest Services:** valet and coin laundry.

[🍴] CALL [&M] [🏊] [BIZ] [📶] [✕] [📶] [🖥] [☕] / SOME UNITS [🐕]

ECONO LODGE INN & SUITES
(678)355-5050 **45**

▼▼ Motel. $62-$160 **Address:** 639 Franklin Rd SE 30067 **Location:** I-75 exit 263, just w. **Facility:** 44 units. 3 stories, interior corridors. **Guest Services:** coin laundry.

[🍴] CALL [&M] [BIZ] [HS] [📶] [📶] [🖥] [☕]

HAMPTON INN MARIETTA
(770)425-9977 **42**

▼▼▼ Hotel. $89-$139 **Address:** 455 Franklin Rd 30067 **Location:** I-75 exit 263, just w. **Facility:** 139 units. 2-4 stories, interior/exterior corridors. **Terms:** 1-7 night minimum stay, cancellation fee imposed. **Amenities:** video games. **Pool(s):** outdoor. **Activities:** exercise room. **Guest Services:** valet laundry.

| **AAA Benefit:** Members save up to 10%! |

[🍴] CALL [&M] [🏊] [BIZ] [HS] [📶] [✕] [📹] [📶] [🖥] [☕]

HILTON ATLANTA/MARIETTA HOTEL & CONFERENCE CENTER
(770)427-2500 **44**

▼▼▼▼ Hotel. $109-$159 **Address:** 500 Powder Springs St 30064 **Location:** I-75 exit 263, 3.5 mi w to Powder Springs St, then just w. **Facility:** 198 units. 6 stories, interior corridors. **Terms:** 1-7 night minimum stay, cancellation fee imposed. **Amenities:** safes. **Dining:** 2 restaurants. **Pool(s):** outdoor. **Activities:** sauna, hot tub, regulation golf, tennis, recreation programs in season, exercise room. **Guest Services:** valet laundry.

| **AAA Benefit:** Members save 5% or more! |

[🍴] [🍴] [🍸] CALL [&M] [🏊] [BIZ] [$HS] [📶] [✕] [📶] [☕] / SOME UNITS [🐕]

HOLIDAY INN EXPRESS MARIETTA-ATLANTA NW
770/989-0071 **49**

▼▼▼▼ Hotel. Rates not provided. **Address:** 1250 Franklin Rd 30067 **Location:** I-75 exit 261, 0.3 mi w to Franklin Rd, then just s. **Facility:** 78 units. 5 stories, interior corridors. **Amenities:** safes. **Activities:** exercise room. **Guest Services:** valet and coin laundry.

[🍴] CALL [&M] [BIZ] [HS] [📶] [✕] [📶] [🖥] [☕]

Get the App

(See maps & indexes p. 76, 82.)

HYATT REGENCY SUITES ATLANTA NW
(770)956-1234

Hotel
$109-$289

 HYATT REGENCY®
AAA Benefit: Members save 10%!

Address: 2999 Windy Hill Rd 30067 **Location:** I-75 exit 260, 0.5 mi e. **Facility:** 202 units. 7 stories, interior corridors. **Parking:** no self-parking. **Terms:** 3 day cancellation notice-fee imposed. **Pool(s):** outdoor. **Activities:** exercise room. **Guest Services:** complimentary and valet laundry, area transportation.

QUALITY INN ATLANTA/MARIETTA (770)955-0004

Hotel
$80-$140

Address: 1255 Franklin Rd SE 30067 **Location:** I-75 exit 261, 0.3 mi w to Franklin Rd, then just s. **Facility:** 102 units. 3 stories, interior corridors. **Pool(s):** outdoor. **Activities:** exercise room. **Guest Services:** valet and coin laundry.

RADISSON HOTEL ATLANTA NORTHWEST
770/420-3533

Hotel. Rates not provided. **Address:** 1775 Parkway Pl SE 30067 **Location:** I-75 exit 263, just w. **Facility:** 218 units. 10 stories, interior corridors. **Pool(s):** outdoor. **Activities:** exercise room. **Guest Services:** valet laundry.

RAMADA MARIETTA/ATLANTA NORTH
(770)952-9005

Hotel
$60-$77

Address: 1175 Powers Ferry Pl 30067 **Location:** I-75 exit 261, just e. **Facility:** 88 units. 3 stories, interior corridors. *Bath:* shower only. **Pool(s):** heated indoor. **Activities:** hot tub, exercise room. **Guest Services:** valet and coin laundry. **Featured Amenity:** continental breakfast.

WHERE TO EAT

ASPENS SIGNATURE STEAKS
678/236-1400

American. Fine Dining. $11-$39 **AAA Inspector Notes:** As the name indicates, this restaurant brings to mind the rustic charm of an upscale ski lodge. Try any one of the mouthwatering steak offerings, and you won't be disappointed. The shrimp and grits, seared north Georgia trout and the braised short ribs are also very tasty. **Features:** full bar, early bird specials, Sunday brunch. **Reservations:** suggested. **Address:** 2942 Shallowford Rd 30066 **Location:** Jct Shallowford and Sandy Plains rds.

ASPENS SIGNATURE STEAKS
770/419-1744

American. Fine Dining. $14-$39 **AAA Inspector Notes:** Certified Angus steaks, palate-pleasing and imaginative appetizers and salads and mouthwatering desserts are all on this restaurant's menu. The dining room re-creates an upscale ski lodge, and the service staff is adept at pointing patrons in the right direction. **Features:** full bar, early bird specials, Sunday brunch. **Address:** 3625 Dallas Hwy 30064 **Location:** Just w of jct Due West Rd and Dallas Hwy; in Avenue of West Cobb.

BARKER'S RED HOTS
770/272-0407

Hot Dogs. Quick Serve. $3-$9 **AAA Inspector Notes:** Modeled after an old-style Coney Island stand, this quick-serve eatery has a small dining room in which patrons nosh on charcoal-broiled hot dogs, red hots, Italian sausage and even veggie dogs with all of the fixings. This place originated as a street vendor in Atlanta in 1984. **Address:** 3000 Windy Hill Rd, Suite 128 30067 **Location:** I-75 exit 260, 0.5 mi e; in Terrace at Windy Hill Plaza.

BASIL WRAPS
770/514-9990

Mediterranean. Quick Serve. $5-$11 **AAA Inspector Notes:** Everything is made from scratch at this small, family-owned and -operated Middle Eastern eatery. Guests can expect to find quick service and warm, sincere owners. Must-tries include hummus, falafel, wraps and salads. For those not as adventurous there are hamburger and hot dog options. **Address:** 2800 Canton Rd, Suite 1220 J 30066 **Location:** I-75 exit 267A, 2.6 mi ne; in Piedmont Village.

BRANDI'S WORLD FAMOUS HOT DOGS 770/422-3681

Hot Dogs. Quick Serve. $2-$3 **AAA Inspector Notes:** This popular spot has been serving hot and spicy hot dogs for many years. Chili dogs and slaw dogs are available as are hamburgers. Sides include fries, chili cheese fries, chips, onion rings and slaw. The fried apple and peach pies are tasty desserts. **Address:** 1377 Church St Ext NW 30060 **Location:** I-75 exit 267, 1.5 mi w to Church St Ext NW, then just n.

CAFE LIFE
770/977-9583

Natural/Organic
Casual Dining
$7-$10

AAA Inspector Notes: Organic, natural, whole and vegetarian options are available at this café where the food is fresh, delicious and made to order. Juices and teas also are available. **Address:** 1453 Roswell Rd 30062 **Location:** In London Square Plaza.

CHEESEBURGER BOBBY'S
770/919-9110

Burgers. Quick Serve. $3-$6 **AAA Inspector Notes:** Nibble on hand-cut fries with your fresh, hand-patted burger, which you'll gussy up with onions, lettuce, tomatoes, pickles and other items on the condiment station. Other choices include hot dogs, chicken sandwiches and custard for dessert. Friendly servers tend the bright, fresh and clean dining room. **Address:** 125 Barrett Pkwy 30066 **Location:** I-75 exit 269, 0.7 mi e.

(See maps & indexes p. 76, 82.)

CHEROKEE CATTLE COMPANY 770/427-0490 (57)
▼▼ Steak. Casual Dining. $9-$30 **AAA Inspector Notes:** Old license plates, animal heads, barbed wire and neon signs are the rustic accessories decorating the walls of this Texas-style roadhouse. Just kick back with a cold one and enjoy steak, prime rib, fish or chicken dishes all mesquite-grilled to perfection. **Features:** full bar, early bird specials. **Address:** 2710 Canton Rd 30066 **Location:** I-75 exit 267A, 2.5 mi ne. [L] [D]

CHICAGO DELIGHTS 770/420-1151 (69)
▼ Hot Dogs. Quick Serve. $3-$7 **AAA Inspector Notes:** The owner, who hails from Chicago, delivers the real deal here. Chow down on authentic Chicago-style hot dogs, bratwurst, Polish sausage and Italian beef, which is made in house. You also can get gyros, chicken tenders and pizza puffs. **Address:** 1392 Roswell Rd 30062 **Location:** Jct Cobb Pkwy and Roswell Rd; just e of Big Chicken building. [L] [D]

CHICKEN AND THE EGG 678/388-8813 (77)
▼▼▼ American. Casual Dining. $9-$18 **AAA Inspector Notes:** This farm-to-table eatery offers blue plate specials at lunch, which include a choice of a meat and two vegetables, or a good selection of soups, salads and sandwiches. Dinner options vary from such entrées such as the iron skillet fried chicken to the grilled Carolina catfish. Tempting desserts range from fried peach pie to praline bread pudding. The service staff is highly knowledgeable and attentive. **Features:** full bar, patio dining, Sunday brunch. **Address:** 800 Whitlock Ave, Suite 124 30064 **Location:** 0.8 mi w of Historic Marietta Square. [L] [D] CALL [&M] [🐾]

DAVE POE'S BBQ 770/792-2272 (76)
▼ Barbecue. Quick Serve. $3-$21 **AAA Inspector Notes:** The simple surroundings of this restaurant hides a gem with award-winning slow-smoked pork and brisket. Pulled pork, chicken, beef brisket and ribs are popular as well as delicious macaroni and cheese. For something a little different try the redneck lasagna—macaroni and cheese covered in Brunswick stew. **Address:** 660 Whitlock Ave, Suite B 30064 **Location:** 1 mi w of Historic Marietta Square. [L] [D]

DOGFATHER'S 678/354-3223 (58)
▼ Hot Dogs. Casual Dining. $2-$6 **AAA Inspector Notes:** Guests will not be able to refuse the tasty offerings found at this spot. In addition to the basic dog with chili, mustard and onions, diners can order a Black Angus dog which is a larger, beefier version of the standard option. Corn dogs and vegan dogs also are on the menu as are beer-boiled brats. The gravy or boardwalk fries make a great accompaniment to any meal and the banana split always is a good ending. **Address:** 2769 Chastain Meadows Pkwy, Suite 60 30066 **Location:** I-75 exit 269, 0.5 mi e to Chastain Meadows Pkwy, then just n. [L] [D] CALL [&M]

FRANKIE'S ITALIAN RESTAURANT 770/419-8931 (55)
▼▼ Italian. Casual Dining. $6-$20 **AAA Inspector Notes:** Diners can build their own pasta plate here from choices of several noodle and sauce combinations or opt for such favorites as shrimp scampi, chicken parmigiana, fettuccine Alfredo and veal Marsala. The New York-style pizza is a big hit as are the subs, calzones and strombolis. The service is friendly and the family atmosphere is warm and inviting. **Features:** full bar, early bird specials. **Address:** 3085 Canton Hwy 30066 **Location:** Jct Chastain Rd, just n. [L] [D] CALL [&M]

GABRIEL'S RESTAURANT & BAKERY 770/427-9007 (78)
▼ American. Quick Serve. $4-$14 **AAA Inspector Notes:** Enjoy breakfast, lunch, dinner and some of the best desserts this side of heaven at this spot. Johnnie Gabriel is Paula Deen's cousin and it must run in the family as she can flat out cook. Soups, salads and sandwiches are the primary lunch and dinner offerings. The emphasis is Southern here and they consistently win "best of" awards from their patrons. Try the fried chicken sandwich—it is divine. **Address:** 800 Whitlock Ave, Suite 135 30064 **Location:** 1.5 mi w of Historic Marietta Square. [B] [L] [D] CALL [&M]

GEORGE'S DELI 770/956-7545 (84)
▼ Sandwiches. Quick Serve. $5-$7 **AAA Inspector Notes:** This small mom-and-pop deli serves up simple, delicious soups, salads and sandwiches. It's a popular lunchtime location. **Address:** 3000 Windy Hill Rd, Suite 176 30067 **Location:** I-75 exit 260, 0.5 mi e; in Terrace at Windy Hill Plaza. [L]

JACK'S NEW YORKER DELI 770/424-1402 (72)
▼ Sandwiches. Quick Serve. $5-$12 **AAA Inspector Notes:** Part New York-style deli and part Southern-style cafe, this place is big on hot and cold sandwiches but also serves soups, salads, burgers, hot dogs and homemade cookies. Enjoy the best fries around with a sub or panini. Breakfast served all day. **Features:** patio dining. **Address:** 168 Roswell St 30060 **Location:** Just off Historic Marietta Square; downtown. **Parking:** street only. [B] [L] CALL [&M] [🐾]

J. CHRISTOPHER'S 770/953-0002 (82)
▼▼ Breakfast. Casual Dining. $5-$12 **AAA Inspector Notes:** Blueberry crunch cakes, strawberry waffles and eggs Christopher are some of the breakfast favorites found here along with such seasonal items as pumpkin pancakes. Many traditional breakfast standards are available. Lunch favorites include the club house burger and classic club sandwich. Waldorf salads and signature soups also are popular. **Address:** 1275 Powers Ferry Rd 30067 **Location:** I-75 exit 261, 1 mi e to Powers Ferry Rd, then just s. [B] [L] CALL [&M]

JOHNBOY'S COUNTRY BUFFET 770/422-6747 (54)
▼ Comfort Food. Casual Dining. $8 **AAA Inspector Notes:** This popular buffet-style eatery offers a great variety of salads, entrées, veggies and desserts. Fried chicken is available for lunch and dinner every day. Some other choices of meat include baked chicken and fish, beef tips, turkey, meatloaf and Salisbury steak. Veggie options include pinto beans, mashed potatoes, rice, rutabagas and collard greens. **Address:** 3050 Canton Rd 30066 **Location:** Between Chastain and Piedmont rds. [L] [D] CALL [&M]

KIOSCO 678/337-7999 (75)
▼▼ Colombian. Casual Dining. $7-$27 **AAA Inspector Notes:** Owned and operated by native Colombians, this restaurant focuses on such traditional fare as carnes, pescado and pollo as well as yuca and empanadas. A perfect ending consists of figs in syrup with cheese. If the salmon with fire-roasted tomato sauce is on special, be sure to order it. **Features:** wine. **Address:** 48 Powder Springs St 30064 **Location:** Just s of Historic Marietta Square; downtown. [L] [D] CALL [&M]

LA PARRILLA MEXICAN RESTAURANT 770/427-0055 (74)
▼▼ Tex-Mex. Casual Dining. $6-$18 **AAA Inspector Notes:** This Tex-Mex establishment is a cut above many in terms of food, service and décor. Patrons can sip a margarita while nibbling on chips and salsa and soak up the festive atmosphere. Guacamole is prepared tableside and the fajitas come to the table sizzling! **Features:** full bar. **Address:** 29 S Marietta Pkwy 30064 **Location:** Just w of Historic Marietta Square; downtown. [L] [D]

LEMON GRASS THAI RESTAURANT 770/973-7478 (65)
▼▼ Thai. Casual Dining. $8-$15 **AAA Inspector Notes:** This casual café offers typical Thai cuisine in a relaxed environment. The menu features favorites such as coconut chicken soup, pad thai and duck in lemon grass sauce. The entrance is a little hard to find, so keep a sharp eye out for the sign. **Features:** beer & wine. **Address:** 2145 Roswell Rd, Suite 190 30062 **Location:** I-75 exit 265, 1.6 mi se on SR 120 Loop to SR 120, then 0.6 mi e; in East Lake Shopping Center. [L] [D]

LOS ARCOS 678/560-8222 (62)
▼▼ Tex-Mex. Casual Dining. $2-$15 **AAA Inspector Notes:** This local favorite has been serving up Tex-Mex favorites such as enchiladas, fajitas, quesadillas, nachos and tacos for more than ten years. Guests enjoy a good selection of flavored margaritas and also tequilas. **Features:** full bar, patio dining. **Address:** 3101 Roswell Rd, Suite M2 30062 **Location:** Jct Old Canton Rd; in Olde Mill Shopping Center. [L] [D]

(See maps & indexes p. 76, 82.)

MARIETTA DINER   770/423-9390 **79**

🏵🏵 Continental Comfort Food. Casual Dining. $9-$35 **AAA Inspector Notes:** This beautiful chrome retro diner sits like a beacon for locals and tourists. The menu is vast and covers breakfast, lunch and dinner. Portions are huge and desserts are displayed at the entrance for all to see. **Features:** beer & wine. **Address:** 306 Cobb Pkwy 30060 **Location:** I-75 exit 263, 0.4 mi w to Cobb Pkwy, then just n. **B L D 24**

MARIETTA FISH MARKET   770/218-3474 **53**

🏵🏵 Seafood. Casual Dining. $7-$33 **AAA Inspector Notes:** A dizzying array of fresh seafood is fried, grilled, blackened or broiled. Oysters, gumbo and bisque are among choices served in enormous portions. Servers are friendly, knowledgeable and swift and the huge dining areas are done in a nautical theme. **Features:** full bar, patio dining. **Address:** 3185 Canton Rd 30066 **Location:** I-75 exit 267A, 3 mi ne. **L D CALL ♿ M**

MARIETTA PIZZA CO.   770/419-0900 **73**

🏵🏵 Pizza. Casual Dining. $5-$23 **AAA Inspector Notes:** Hummus or caprese salad is a tasty start to a meal at this bustling and fun place to eat where the bread sticks are notable, too. There are many different shapes and sizes of pizza. Diners can begin with a slice of cheese pizza and add such toppings as pepperoni, Canadian bacon, sausage and other meats and veggies, or opt for a large pizza for the family. Ice cream and ice cream bars are available as dessert choices. **Features:** beer & wine. **Address:** 3 Whitlock Ave 30064 **Location:** On Historic Marietta Square. **L D**

MOUNTAIN BISCUITS   770/419-3311 **63**

🏵 Sandwiches. Quick Serve. $2-$7 **AAA Inspector Notes:** The biscuits here are huge and delicious. There are a good variety of types that include sausage, country ham, pork and steak tenderloin, bacon, chicken and red hots. Diners can add on jalapeños, sautéed onions, cheese, chili, bacon and other toppings. Half-pound hamburgers also are on the menu as well as mountain sausage, chicken and hickory-smoked pork sandwiches. The tasty chocolate chip cookies also are enormous. **Features:** patio dining. **Address:** 1718 Old Hwy 41 30060 **Location:** Jct Bells Ferry Rd, 0.4 mi n. **B L**

PACIFIC BUFFET, SUSHI & GRILL   770/423-2238 **59**

🏵🏵 Asian. Casual Dining. $7-$10 **AAA Inspector Notes:** Upon entering this cavernous, yet tastefully done, eatery guests can find a mind-boggling assortment of sushi, snow crab legs, shrimp, mussels and other saltwater delights. For landlubbers there are American, Italian and traditional Chinese and Japanese courses. Hibachi grilled favorites also can be enjoyed. **Features:** beer & wine. **Address:** 2475 Chastain Meadows Pkwy 30066 **Location:** I-75 exit 269, 0.5 mi e to Chastain Meadows Pkwy, then just n. **L D CALL ♿ M**

PAPPADEAUX SEAFOOD KITCHEN   770/984-8899

🏵🏵 Cajun Seafood. Casual Dining. $11-$53 **AAA Inspector Notes:** A seafood lover's delight, the restaurant taps into a little bit of New Orleans with its Cajun dishes and elaborate menu selections. Patrons might start off with a creative choice of blackened oyster and shrimp fondeaux with crayfish and let the feast begin. While music plays in the background, patrons can dig into dirty rice or spicy gumbo loaded with seafood. Well-seasoned shrimp and fish are prepared in varied ways. **Features:** full bar, happy hour. **Address:** 2830 Windy Hill Rd 30067 **Location:** I-75 exit 260, just e. **L D CALL ♿ M ✑**

PAPPASITO'S CANTINA   770/541-6100

🏵🏵 Tex-Mex. Casual Dining. $11-$44 **AAA Inspector Notes:** Fine traditional offerings are served in an upscale cantina atmosphere. Often crowded during peak hours, the immensely popular stop dishes up generous portions of sizzling fajitas, enchiladas and other traditional Mexican favorites, including some shrimp specialties. The terrific margaritas are guaranteed to get attention. Tables in the large dining room are closely spaced. Ice cream with cinnamon on chocolate bread pudding shouldn't be missed. **Features:** full bar. **Address:** 2788 Windy Hill Rd 30067 **Location:** I-75 exit 260, just e. **L D**

RED ELEPHANT   770/980-1890 **86**

🏵🏵 Thai. Casual Dining. $7-$23 **AAA Inspector Notes:** Traditional Thai favorite, including curries, noodle dishes and stir-fried item, are served in a contemporary setting. Lunch specials such as pad thai and spicy basil are popular and dinner features include duck curry, grilled rack of lamb and soft shell crab. **Address:** 3000 Windy Hill Rd, Suite 152 30067 **Location:** I-75 exit 260 (Windy Hill Rd), 0.5 mi e; in Terrace at Windy Hill Plaza. **L D CALL ♿ M**

THE RIB RANCH   770/422-5755 **60**

🏵 Barbecue. Casual Dining. $6-$37 **AAA Inspector Notes:** House specialties include barbecue ribs, pork and chicken grilled over an open-pit fire and fresh homemade pie. Tex Mex favorites, quesadillas and nachos, are available as well. Rustic and comfortable, the atmosphere is perfect for family meals. **Features:** beer & wine, patio dining. **Address:** 2063 Canton Rd 30066 **Location:** I-75 exit 267A, 1 mi ne. **L D**

ROCCO'S PUB   770/971-8806 **66**

🏵🏵 American. Casual Dining. $6-$12 **AAA Inspector Notes:** This neighborhood sports bar/pub has a good selection of food offerings such as wings, burgers, wraps, sandwiches and salads as well as some classic entrées. However, the chili is the real deal. Winner of numerous awards at chili cook-offs, the restaurant has won it so consistently that they now host the International Chili Society's Georgia State Chili Cook-off. Be sure to take home a package of Rocco's gourmet blended chili mix to enjoy at home. **Features:** full bar. **Address:** 1477 Roswell Rd 30062 **Location:** I-75 exit 263 northbound, 0.5 mi w to US 41, 0.5 mi n to Roswell Rd, then 0.5 mi e; exit 265 southbound, 0.3 mi w to US 41, 0.5 mi s to Roswell Rd, then 0.5 mi e. **L D LATE**

SABOR DO BRAZIL   770/541-2625 **81**

🏵 Brazilian. Casual Dining. $9-$11 **AAA Inspector Notes:** This low key, traditional Brazilian buffet offers a variety of tantalizing flavors for a truly authentic experience. The buffet features a meat carving station with drool-inducing meat options that practically melt in your mouth. Peak dining hours can be busy as this is a popular spot. **Address:** 2858 Delk Rd SE, Suite 120 30067 **Location:** I-75 exit 261, 0.5 mi e. **B L D**

SAM'S BBQ 1   770/977-3005 **109**

🏵 Barbecue. Quick Serve. $3-$20 **AAA Inspector Notes:** This popular spot makes some of the best barbecue on the planet. Many people come here for carry-out service from the counter or have the food brought in for catering. Offerings include sandwiches, chicken, succulent pulled pork and fall-off-the-bone ribs. Be sure to ask about the redneck lasagna. **Features:** beer & wine. **Address:** 4944 Lower Roswell Rd 30068 **Location:** Jct Johnson Ferry Rd, 0.3 mi e. **L D**

SEED KITCHEN & BAR   678/214-6888 **108**

🏵🏵🏵 New American. Fine Dining. $9-$26 **AAA Inspector Notes:** This chef-driven restaurant strives to use fresh, local and organic products whenever possible. The menu changes often and there are excellent options to be found at all times. I tried the New Bedford scallops and pork belly with butternut squash, cider brown butter and fennel and apple salad. It was mouth-watering and well-prepared. The pimento crostinis come with Benton's country ham, apples and micro celery—another keeper. **Features:** full bar, patio dining, Sunday brunch. **Address:** 1311 Johnson Ferry Rd, Suite 504 30068 **Location:** Jct Roswell Rd; in Merchants Walk Shopping Center. **L D CALL ♿ M**

TASTY CHINA   770/419-9849 **80**

🏵🏵 Chinese. Casual Dining. $7-$18 **AAA Inspector Notes:** Highly acclaimed among Atlanta's restaurants, this place prepares authentic Szechuan cuisine including spicy originals as well as more Americanized dishes. Bold choices include fried dry eggplant and sharp pepper fish. **Address:** 585 Franklin Rd, Suite 215 30067 **Location:** I-75 exit 263, 0.3 mi w to Franklin Rd; in shopping plaza. **L D**

THAICOON & SUSHI BAR   678/766-0641 **71**

🏵🏵🏵 Asian. Fine Dining. $4-$25 **AAA Inspector Notes:** Visually appealing presentation and succulent cuisine are high points of this modestly upscale eatery. Various sushi options are offered as well as Japanese and Thai cuisine. Try the Thaicoon clay pot, duck curry, spicy basil leaf or Eskimo shrimp. **Features:** beer & wine. **Address:** 34 Mill St 30060 **Location:** 1 blk w of Historic Marietta Square; downtown. **Parking:** street only. **L D CALL ♿ M**

(See maps & indexes p. 76, 82.)

TOFU VILLAGE KOREAN BBQ RESTAURANT
770/426-7757 (61)

Korean. Casual Dining. $8-$35 **AAA Inspector Notes:** Barbecue short ribs, goat meat and stews can be enjoyed with the standard wide array of complimentary sides at this spot. The menu lists both vegetarian and carnivore options. The owner of this Asian/Korean restaurant is both friendly and helpful. **Features:** beer & wine. **Address:** 700 Sandy Plains Rd, Suite B-1 30066 **Location:** I-75 exit 267A, 0.7 mi ne; in Sandy Plains Connection.

L D

TRATTORIA LA STRADA
770/640-7008 (107)

Italian. Casual Dining. $12-$22 **AAA Inspector Notes:** Housed in a renovated historic home, this restaurant hugs the line between relaxed and refined and offers a cozy and intimate dining experience. The menu of classic Italian cuisine features items such as veal, gnocchi con formaggio, risotto primavera and of course a variety of delicious pasta. The locals love this place, so make reservations for peak dining times. **Features:** full bar, early bird specials. **Address:** 2930 Johnson Ferry Rd 30062 **Location:** Jct Shallowford and Johnson Ferry rds, 0.5 mi s. D

VATICA
770/955-3740 (83)

Indian. Casual Dining. $9-$11 **AAA Inspector Notes:** The Indian-vegetarian menu teems with bold, spicy and inexpensive items, such as the special vegetable curry, Indian-style pancakes and sambal. **Address:** 1475 Terrell Mill Rd, Suite 105 30067 **Location:** I-75 exit 261, 1 mi e to Powers Ferry Rd, 0.4 mi s, then just w.

L D

VINCENT'S
678/290-2031

Italian. Casual Dining. $2-$19 **AAA Inspector Notes:** The warm, bustling restaurant whips up Italian-style preparations of pasta, pizza, subs, veal, seafood and chicken. Make sure to try the delicious garlic rolls! **Features:** beer & wine, early bird specials. **Reservations:** suggested. **Address:** 3412 Earnest Barrett Pkwy 30064 **Location:** Jct Dallas Hwy, just e.

L D CALL &M

WEST COBB DINER
770/422-7717

Comfort Food. Casual Dining. $6-$16 **AAA Inspector Notes:** This popular family restaurant offers a variety of classic comfort foods. Large portions are sure to satisfy even the largest appetites. Favorites include country-fried steak, glazed meat loaf and mesquite-grilled pork chops. Save room for the homemade desserts (especially the pie). **Features:** beer & wine. **Address:** 3451 Barrett Pkwy, Suite 200 30064 **Location:** In The Pointe Shopping Center.

L D CALL &M

WILLIAMSON BROS BAR-B-Q
770/971-3201 (68)

Barbecue. Casual Dining. $8-$23 **AAA Inspector Notes:** House specialties include barbecue ribs, pork and chicken grilled over an open pit as well as fresh homemade pie. Rustic and comfortable, the atmosphere is perfect for family meals. Fried dill pickles and fried red tomatoes in a thick batter are worth a try. **Features:** beer & wine. **Address:** 1425 Roswell Rd 30062 **Location:** I-75 exit 263 northbound, 0.5 mi w to US 41, 0.5 mi n to Roswell Rd, then 0.5 mi e; exit 265 southbound, 0.3 mi e to US 41, then 0.5 mi s.

L D

WR SOCIAL HOUSE
770/792-9995 (70)

Cajun. Casual Dining. $8-$19 **AAA Inspector Notes:** This trendy eatery is situated in the pedestrian friendly downtown and recently underwent a dramatic change. The new menu features a variety of Southern favorites with an updated approach such as the boiled peanut hummus. The hand-ground hamburgers are a customer favorite as is anything off the dessert menu. **Features:** full bar, patio dining. **Address:** 25 N Park Square 30060 **Location:** On Historic Marietta Square; downtown. **Parking:** street only.

L D

MCDONOUGH (C-3) pop. 22,084, elev. 866'

• **Restaurants p. 222**

Several films and television shows have made use of McDonough's charming town square, including the 2013 comedy "A Madea Christmas" and the ABC drama "Resurrection." Historic brick buildings like the Romanesque-style Henry County Courthouse, built in 1897, and others now housing shops and eateries face the public green, the centerpiece of which is a monument to Henry County's Confederate dead. The town square also is the site of the Geranium Festival, an arts and crafts extravaganza held in mid-May.

BAYMONT INN & SUITES MCDONOUGH
(770)914-0077

Motel. $69-$180 **Address:** 855 Industrial Blvd 30253 **Location:** I-75 exit 218, just e to Industrial Blvd, then just s. **Facility:** 74 units. 2 stories, exterior corridors. **Terms:** cancellation fee imposed. **Pool(s):** outdoor. **Activities:** exercise room. **Guest Services:** valet laundry.

CALL &M BIZ HS

BEST WESTERN MCDONOUGH INN & SUITES
(770)898-1006

Hotel
$99-$129

Best Western. **AAA Benefit:** Save 10% or more every day and earn 10% bonus points!

Address: 805 Industrial Blvd 30253 **Location:** I-75 exit 218, just e to Industrial Blvd, then just s. **Facility:** 64 units, some kitchens. 3 stories, interior corridors. **Pool(s):** heated indoor. **Activities:** hot tub, exercise room. **Guest Services:** coin laundry. **Featured Amenity: breakfast buffet.**

SAVE CALL &M BIZ HS

COMFORT SUITES
(678)216-1900

Hotel. $95-$119 **Address:** 64 Hwy 81 W 30253 **Location:** I-75 exit 218, just w. **Facility:** 76 units. 4 stories, interior corridors. **Amenities:** safes. **Pool(s):** heated indoor. **Activities:** hot tub, exercise room. **Guest Services:** valet and coin laundry.

CALL &M BIZ HS

COUNTRY INN & SUITES BY CARLSON
(770)957-0082

Hotel. $75-$200 **Address:** 115 E Greenwood Rd 30253 **Location:** I-75 exit 216, just w. **Facility:** 57 units. 3 stories, interior corridors. **Pool(s):** heated indoor. **Activities:** hot tub, exercise room. **Guest Services:** valet and coin laundry.

CALL &M BIZ HS

/ SOME UNITS

COURTYARD BY MARRIOTT ATLANTA MCDONOUGH
(678)902-9000

Hotel
$105-$164

Courtyard Marriott **AAA Benefit:** Members save 5% or more!

Address: 115 Mill Rd 30253 **Location:** I-75 exit 218, 0.4 mi sw on Hampton Rd, then just nw. **Facility:** 102 units. 4 stories, interior corridors. **Pool(s):** heated indoor. **Activities:** hot tub, exercise room. **Guest Services:** valet and coin laundry.

SAVE CALL &M BIZ HS

/ SOME UNITS

ECONO LODGE (770)957-2651

Motel
$46-$55

Address: 1279 Hwy 20 W 30253 **Location:** I-75 exit 218, just w. **Facility:** 40 units. 2 stories (no elevator), exterior corridors. **Guest Services:** coin laundry. **Featured Amenity: continental breakfast.**

FAIRFIELD INN & SUITES ATLANTA MCDONOUGH
(770)305-0180

WW/WW **Hotel.** $97-$138 **Address:** 30 Mill Rd 30253 **Location:** I-75 exit 218, 0.4 mi sw on Hampton Rd, then just nw. **Facility:** 79 units. 4 stories, interior corridors. **Activities:** exercise room. **Guest Services:** valet and coin laundry.

AAA Benefit: Members save 5% or more!

    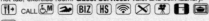

HAMPTON INN ATLANTA MCDONOUGH (770)957-5808

Hotel
$109-$169

AAA Benefit: Members save up to 10%!

Address: 250 Avalon Ct 30253 **Location:** I-75 exit 218, w on Hampton-McDonough Rd, then just se on McDonough-Lovejoy Rd. **Facility:** 80 units. 4 stories, interior corridors. **Terms:** 1-7 night minimum stay, cancellation fee imposed. **Pool(s):** heated outdoor, heated indoor. **Activities:** exercise room. **Guest Services:** valet and coin laundry.

HILTON GARDEN INN ATLANTA SOUTH (678)827-7200

WW/WW **Hotel.** $114-$209 **Address:** 95 Hwy 81 W 30253 **Location:** I-75 exit 218, 0.4 mi sw on Hampton Rd, then just nw. **Facility:** 105 units. 4 stories, interior corridors. *Bath:* shower only. **Terms:** check-in 4 pm, 1-7 night minimum stay, cancellation fee imposed. **Pool(s):** heated indoor. **Activities:** exercise room. **Guest Services:** valet and coin laundry.

AAA Benefit: Members save up to 10%!

HOLIDAY INN EXPRESS HOTEL & SUITES 678/782-1100

WW/WW **Hotel.** Rates not provided. **Address:** 1315 Hwy 20 W 30253 **Location:** I-75 exit 218, just w. **Facility:** 84 units. 4 stories, interior corridors. **Amenities:** safes. **Pool(s):** heated indoor. **Activities:** hot tub, exercise room. **Guest Services:** valet and coin laundry.

HOME2 SUITES BY HILTON ATLANTA/SOUTH MCDONOUGH (678)369-2527

WW/WW **Extended Stay Hotel.** $109-$169 **Address:** 60 Mill Rd 30253 **Location:** I-75 exit 221, 0.3 mi nw on Jonesboro Rd, then 0.4 mi s. **Facility:** 91 efficiencies. 4 stories, interior corridors. **Terms:** 1-7 night minimum stay, cancellation fee imposed. **Amenities:** safes. **Pool(s):** heated indoor. **Activities:** exercise room. **Guest Services:** valet and coin laundry.

QUALITY INN & SUITES CONFERENCE CENTER (770)957-5291

WWW **Motel.** $79-$124 **Address:** 930 Hwy 155 S 30253 **Location:** I-75 exit 216, just w. **Facility:** 90 units. 2 stories (no elevator), exterior corridors. **Pool(s):** outdoor. **Activities:** exercise room. **Guest Services:** valet and coin laundry.

SLEEP INN (770)898-0804

Hotel
$79-$94

Address: 945 Hwy 155 S 30253 **Location:** I-75 exit 216, just w. **Facility:** 50 units. 3 stories, interior corridors. *Bath:* shower only. **Pool(s):** heated indoor. **Activities:** limited exercise equipment. **Guest Services:** valet and coin laundry. **Featured Amenity: full hot breakfast.**

WHERE TO EAT

EL AGAVE 678/583-2339

WW **Tex-Mex. Casual Dining.** $6-$15 **AAA Inspector Notes:** This festive and colorful restaurant bustles with activity from patrons eager to eat Tex-Mex tacos, enchiladas and burritos. The house specialties include Cancun shrimp, Monterey steak and alambres. Guest rave about the variety of margaritas available. Vegetarian options are also available. **Features:** full bar, patio dining, happy hour. **Address:** 1381 Hwy 20 W 30253 **Location:** I-75 exit 218, 0.3 mi w; in McDonough Promenade.

GRAFFITI'S PIZZA: A GREEK TAVERNA 678/782-7533

WW **Greek Pizza. Casual Dining.** $4-$20 **AAA Inspector Notes:** This is a great neighborhood restaurant that proves that the Italians are not the only ones that can make a great pizza. The stylishly colorful décor appeals to a younger crowd while also creating an inviting atmosphere for families. The gyros are a classic choice but the Olympia, Titans and Mediterranean specials (pizza) also are crowd favorites. **Features:** beer & wine. **Address:** 1170 Hwy 155 S 30253 **Location:** 1 mi s on SR 155.

KIRBY G'S DINER & PUB 678/583-8777

WW **American. Casual Dining.** $3-$10 **AAA Inspector Notes:** The 50's are alive and well at this retro-style diner. From top to bottom the restaurant is bursting at the seams with pictures, cutouts and art of icons of the period. Even the menu is nostalgic with items such as "Rockin Robin Reuben", "Chubby Checker Chili" and the "Honeymooner" hamburger. The classic soda fountain also serves thick milk shakes and a massive sundae meant to share. If you are craving a hamburger, take a trip with the family down memory lane to Kirby G's. **Address:** 45 Macon St 30253 **Location:** Downtown. **Parking:** street only.

O.B.'S BBQ 770/954-1234

WW **Barbecue. Casual Dining.** $4-$12 **AAA Inspector Notes:** This casual, family-friendly eatery offers smokehouse delights such as brisket, Memphis-style ribs, and hickory smoked pork and chicken. Start out the meal with the crunchy and tangy fried pickles, and save room for homemade fruit cobbler. **Features:** beer only. **Address:** 1120 Hampton Rd 30253 **Location:** I-75 exit 218, just ne.

Turn your road trip dreams into reality with the TripTik® Travel Planner

PASTA MAX CAFE   770/320-9311

▼▼ Italian. Casual Dining. $8-$19 **AAA Inspector Notes:** This local favorite offers classic Northern Italian cuisine in a casual, family-friendly atmosphere. I recommend starting with savory bruschetta before moving on to either pizza or homemade pasta with herb-breaded veal. Finish the meal with the sublime strawberry sabayon (a combination of fresh strawberries, cream and chocolate sauce)—it is big enough to share but I doubt you will want to. **Features:** wine only. **Address:** 50 Griffin St 30253 **Location:** Jct Sloan St and US 23; center. **Parking:** street only. D

PJ'S CAFE   770/898-5373

▼▼ American. Casual Dining. $5-$15 **AAA Inspector Notes:** This classic small town café is a popular local favorite that does a brisk business for lunch and dinner. The beautiful painted murals depicting the town show a charming sense of community pride. The classic menu options are the epitome of comfort food and will leave your belly full and happy. The fried green tomatoes are a specialty. **Features:** patio dining. **Address:** 30 Macon St 30253 **Location:** In historic downtown. **Parking:** street only. L D CALL M

RED ORCHID THAI   770/957-9382

▼▼ Thai. Casual Dining. $8-$19 **AAA Inspector Notes:** This casual family-owned restaurant is a great choice for simply delicious food. The menu features items such as ginger catfish and mango salmon, red curry duck, lamb and spider Penang (soft-shelled crabs). Traditional offerings also include several curry and noodle dishes. The pot stickers are a good appetizer choice and desserts, such as sticky rice with mango, finish the meal off nicely. **Features:** beer & wine. **Address:** 386 SR 155 S 30253 **Location:** I-75 exit 216, 0.8 mi e; in McDonough Village South. L D CALL M

SLOWPOKE'S MEXICAN JOINT   678/782-6851

▼ Mexican. Quick Serve. $2-$8 **AAA Inspector Notes:** This casual eatery specializes in build-your-own tacos and burritos. Try the Baja burrito or fish tacos, but save room for the Oreo churros unless you are looking to cool off, then go for the King of Pops handcrafted Popsicles. **Features:** beer only. **Address:** 1160 Hwy 155 S 30253 **Location:** I-75 exit 216 (SR 155), 0.3 mi sw. L D CALL M

YUKI JAPANESE RESTAURANT   770/896-9854

▼▼ Japanese. Casual Dining. $5-$30 **AAA Inspector Notes:** This spacious Japanese steakhouse is ideal for large parties or family gatherings. The hibachi tables are a popular choice for groups and the sushi bar is great for single diners or couples. The extensive sushi menu features many traditional selections such as tiger and California rolls. The teriyaki beef or chicken on the regular menu is a personal favorite. **Features:** full bar, patio dining. **Address:** 35 Mill Rd 30253 **Location:** I-75 exit 221, just w on Jonesboro Rd, then just s. L D CALL M

MCRAE pop. 5,740

THE FAIRWAYS GRILL   229/868-7474

▼ American. Casual Dining. $9-$20 **AAA Inspector Notes:** In picturesque Little Ocmulgee State Park, this restaurant allows diners the joy of watching golfers and wildlife pass by. The menu centers around regional offerings such as Southern fried catfish and steaks. Guests can choose between the buffet or a la carte options. **Features:** beer & wine, patio dining. **Address:** US Hwy 441 31055 **Location:** On US 441, 3 mi n; in Little Ocmulgee State Park and Lodge. B L D

METTER (D-5) pop. 4,130, elev. 200'

GUIDO GARDENS is off I-16 exit 104, then 2.5 mi. n. on SR 121 to 600 N. Lewis St. This Christian-oriented garden features manicured grounds, splashing waterfalls, topiaries with Biblical themes, a small chapel and several places to sit, relax and listen to the hymns playing in the background. Guided tours are available by appointment. **Time:**

Allow 30 minutes minimum. **Hours:** Gardens open daily 24 hours. Office open Mon.-Fri. 9-5. **Cost:** Free. **Phone:** (912) 685-2222. GT

JOMAX BAR-B-QUE   912/685-3636

▼▼ Barbecue. Casual Dining. $5-$14 **AAA Inspector Notes:** Travelers on I-16 have been keeping this roadside barbecue gem a secret for more than 20 years. The log cabin motif encourages patrons to come in and make themselves at home. This family-run restaurant provides the most friendly, efficient and expedient services anywhere. Pulled pork, ribs, smoked chicken, burgers, fried chicken, homemade cream corn, cobbler and cheddar cheese sticks are samples of what this eatery is doing right. I would still be there if I had my way. **Address:** 1120 S Lewis St 30439 **Location:** I-16 exit 104, just w. L D

MIDWAY (D-6) pop. 2,121, elev. 10'

FORT MORRIS STATE HISTORIC SITE is off I-95 exit 76, 7 mi. e. via Islands Hwy. (SR 38) and Fort Morris Rd., following brown Liberty Trail signs. The Continental Congress commissioned Fort Morris in 1776, and American patriots garrisoned the post to protect the port of Sunbury against British forces in the Revolutionary War and, as Fort Defiance, in the War of 1812. A video presentation and a museum interpret the history of the site. Special events are offered throughout the year. **Time:** Allow 1 hour minimum. **Hours:** Thurs.-Sat. 9-5. Closed Jan. 1, Thanksgiving and Christmas. **Cost:** $4.50; $4 (ages 62+); $3 (ages 6-17); $1 (ages 0-5). **Phone:** (912) 884-5999. ⟨A⟩

MIDWAY CHURCH, next door to Midway Museum on US 17 and Martin Rd., was founded in 1752 by Puritans who moved to the area seeking land grants and religious freedom and became missionaries. This 1792 building is a replica of the original church, burned during the Revolution, complete with a slave gallery and high pulpit. From its congregation came Lyman Hall and Button Gwinnett, two signers of the Declaration of Independence; two Revolutionary War generals; and a U.S. senator.

Hours: The cemetery can be visited Tues.-Sat. 10-4. The keys for the church are available only at the Midway Museum Tues.-Sat. 10-4. Closed major holidays. **Cost:** Free.

MIDWAY MUSEUM, next door to Midway Church at 491 N. Coastal Hwy., was built in 1959 in the 18th-century raised-cottage style. On display are furnishings, artifacts and documents dating from the early 18th to the mid-19th centuries. **Time:** Allow 30 minutes minimum. **Hours:** Tues.-Sat. 10-4. Last tour begins 1 hour before closing. Closed major holidays. **Cost:** $10; $8 (senior citizens and military); $5 (students with ID); free (ages 0-5). **Phone:** (912) 884-5837. GT

MILLEDGEVILLE (C-4) pop. 17,715, elev. 276'
• Hotels p. 224 • Restaurants p. 225

Milledgeville looks much as it did when it was laid out as the capital of Georgia in 1803, serving in that capacity until 1868. The Old Capitol Building, built in 1807, is considered the first example of Gothic architecture utilized for a public building in the United States.

The Brown-Stetson-Sanford House, 601 W. Hancock St., is an 1825 two-story clapboard Federal house constructed by architect John Marlor. The house is open by request; phone (478) 453-1803. Also historically significant is St. Stephen's Episcopal Church on S. Wayne Street. During Gen. William Tecumseh Sherman's November 1864 occupation, his troops, who stabled their horses in the church, poured sorghum syrup down the organ pipes to prevent the organ from being used to signal Confederate sympathizers.

One notable Milledgeville resident was author Flannery O'Connor, who moved here with her family in 1938 when she was 13 and left in 1945 to attend the Iowa Writers' Workshop. She is buried in Memory Hill Cemetery (along the fence). A museum on the campus of O'Connor's *alma mater,* Georgia College, presents rotating exhibits in the Flannery O'Connor Room Monday through Saturday 10-4; phone (478) 445-4391.

Guided trolley tours that include alternating stops at Rose Hill at Lockerly Arboretum, the Old Capitol Building, St. Stephens Episcopal Church and the Brown-Stetson-Sanford House depart from the convention and visitors bureau Mon.-Fri. at 10 and Sat. at 11. Trolleys run year-round except on major holidays; the fare is $12; $10 (ages 60+); $5 (ages 6-13).

Milledgeville-Baldwin County Convention and Visitors Bureau: 200 W. Hancock St., Milledgeville, GA 31061. **Phone:** (478) 452-4687.

Self-guiding tours: A free walking-tour map of historic Milledgeville can be obtained from the convention and visitors bureau.

ANDALUSIA FARM-HOME OF FLANNERY O'CONNOR is on US 441 at 2628 N. Columbia St. Her family's dairy farm, Andalusia, was the source for many of the settings, situations and characters in O'Connor's stories; she also wrote several works here. O'Connor lived at Andalusia from 1951 until her death in 1964; the furnishings in the main house are exactly as they were when she occupied the home. The site includes a peafowl aviary, a 1-mile trail, a tenant house and other outbuildings.

Time: Allow 45 minutes minimum. **Hours:** Thurs.-Sun. 10-5 (also Thurs. 5-dusk, Apr.-Sept.). Closed federal holidays. **Cost:** Donations. **Phone:** (478) 454-4029.

GEORGIA'S OLD CAPITAL MUSEUM is at 201 E. Greene St., on the campus of the Georgia Military College. Located within a restored circa 1807 statehouse, the museum preserves the historical and cultural heritage of the area. Ten galleries interpret middle Georgia's timeline beginning with early Native American cultures through exploration and colonization of Georgia and concludes with reconstruction efforts of the late 19th century. Guided tours are available with advance reservations. **Time:** Allow 30 minutes minimum. **Hours:** Wed.-Fri. 10-3:30, Sat. noon-3:30. Closed major holidays, the week after Thanksgiving and

Christmas-early Jan. Phone ahead to confirm schedule. **Cost:** $6; $5 (ages 55+); $3 (students). **Phone:** (478) 453-1803. [GT]

GEORGIA'S OLD GOVERNORS MANSION is at 120 S. Clarke St. Guided tours share the mansion's history. Completed in 1839, the building was home to eight of Georgia's governors over the next 30 years, including George Crawford, Howell Cobb and Joseph E. Brown. In 2005 the house was restored to its 1851 appearance. The mansion features period holiday decorations in December. The behind-the-scenes Curator's Tour; the Collections Tour, which showcases the mansion's decorative arts; and the Labor Behind the Veil tour, an African-American interpretation of antebellum life, are offered by reservation.

Time: Allow 45 minutes minimum. **Hours:** Tours begin on the hour Tues.-Sat. 10-4, Sun. 2-4. Last tour begins at 4. Closed major holidays, 1 week in mid-Nov., Thanksgiving weekend and the week after Christmas. **Cost:** $10; $7 (ages 60+); $2 (students); free (ages 0-5). Curator's, Collections or Labor Behind the Veil tour $15; $8 (ages 60+); $4 (students). **Phone:** (478) 445-4545. [GT]

LOCKERLY ARBORETUM is at 1534 Irwinton Rd. An unusual variety of plants and trees grows on the 50-acre site. The centerpiece of the arboretum is Rose Hill, a Greek Revival antebellum mansion. Woodland hiking trails are on the grounds. **Time:** Allow 1 hour minimum. **Hours:** Grounds and Rose Hill Mon.-Fri. 8:30-4:30 (also Sat. 9-1, Feb.-June and Sept.-Dec.). A stop on Milledgeville's trolley tour, guided tours of Rose Hill are offered mornings, Mon.-Wed. Phone ahead to confirm holiday closures. **Cost:** Grounds free. Rose Hill $3; $1 (ages 5-college student with ID); free (veterans). **Phone:** (478) 452-2112. [GT] [⛱]

HAMPTON INN   (478)451-0050

▼▼▼▼ **Hotel.** $109-$159 **Address:** 2461 N Columbia St 31061 **Location:** US 441, 2.6 mi n of downtown. **Facility:** 75 units. 3 stories, interior corridors. **Terms:** 1-7 night minimum stay, cancellation fee imposed. **Pool(s):** outdoor. **Activities:** exercise room. **Guest Services:** valet laundry.

AAA Benefit: Members save up to 10%!

▮◆ CALL ☾M 🏊 BIZ HS 🛜 ✕ 🗎 🖼 ☕

HERITAGE INN   478/453-9491

▼▼ **Motel.** Rates not provided. **Address:** 2474 N Columbia St 31061 **Location:** US 441, 2.6 mi n of downtown. **Facility:** 49 units. 2 stories (no elevator), exterior corridors.

CALL ☾M 🛜 🗎 🖼 ☕ / SOME UNITS 🐾

WHERE TO EAT

KAI THAI RESTAURANT   478/454-1237

▼▼ Thai Sushi. Casual Dining. $4-$18 **AAA Inspector Notes:** Located in a shopping center this small restaurant may at first appear insignificant. As with most things it is what is on the inside that counts, and on the inside is great flavor, good service and generous portions. Try the chicken Chiang Mai, the Tokyo spring roll or the "Lover's Bridge" sushi plate. **Address:** 2600 N Columbia St 31061 **Location:** Jct N Columbia St and Heritage Rd NE. L D CALL ☾M

MILLEN (C-5) pop. 3,120, elev. 160'

Known as Camp Lawton during the Civil War, Magnolia Springs State Park, 5 miles north of town on US 25, offers 1,070 acres of recreational opportunities. Visitors can view the earthen breastworks which once guarded the prison stockade, see Civil War artifacts on display, take a swim in the crystal-clear springs or a hike along the boardwalk where alligators and turtles can be spotted. *See Recreation Areas Chart.*

MILTON
• **Hotels & Restaurants map & index p. 82**

MILTON'S CUISINE AND COCKTAILS   770/817-0161 51

▼▼▼ New Southern. Fine Dining. $7-$32 **AAA Inspector Notes:** Located in a quaint historic district, this restaurant focuses on providing a new twist on regionally-inspired comfort food. The menu changes seasonally and much of the produce featured on the menu comes from the restaurant's private garden. Popular dishes include sesame-crusted mountain trout, Charleston crab bisque, sweet potato shrimp fritters and espresso-rubbed apple brine pork loin. Save room for the apricot cobbler with homemade cream cheese ice cream. **Features:** full bar, patio dining, Sunday brunch. **Reservations:** suggested. **Address:** 780 Mayfield Rd 30004 **Location:** In historic downtown. D CALL ☾M

ZOLA ITALIAN BISTRO   770/360-5777

▼▼ Italian. Casual Dining. $6-$18 **AAA Inspector Notes:** Looking for a fresh American twist on traditional Italian cooking? Try this casual modern restaurant. The menu offers various entrées, pasta, salad and specialty pizzas. **Features:** full bar. **Address:** 2955 Bethany Bend 30004 **Location:** US 19 exit 11, 0.9 mi n to SR 9, 2 mi n to Bethany Bend, then just w. D CALL ☾M

MONTEZUMA pop. 3,460

YODERS DEITSCH HAUS   478/472-2024

▼ Southern Comfort Food. Buffet Style. $10-$12 **AAA Inspector Notes:** This restaurant is well-known locally for a generous buffet of homemade braised roast, fried chicken, sausages and kraut, fish and a host of savory vegetables and rolls served by young Mennonite women. Cream and fruit pies make tasty dessert choices. **Address:** 5252 SR 26 E 31063 **Location:** I-75 exit 127 (SR 26), 13.2 mi w. L D

MORROW (B-2) pop. 6,445, elev. 922'
• **Restaurants p. 226**
• **Hotels & Restaurants map & index p. 94**
• **Part of Atlanta area — see map p. 44**

Morrow, 15 miles south of Atlanta, is home to Clayton State University and is experiencing residential and commercial growth.

BEST WESTERN SOUTHLAKE INN   (770)961-6300 64

◆◆ Motel $69-$89

BW Best Western.

AAA Benefit: Save 10% or more every day and earn 10% bonus points!

Address: 6437 Jonesboro Rd 30260 **Location:** I-75 exit 233, just e. **Facility:** 113 units. 2 stories (no elevator), exterior corridors. **Pool(s):** outdoor. **Guest Services:** coin laundry.

SAVE ▮◆ 🏊 BIZ HS 🛜 🗎 🖼 ☕ / SOME UNITS 🐾

COMFORT SUITES MORROW   (678)674-1300 65

▼▼▼ **Hotel.** $89-$149 **Address:** 1444 Southlake Plaza Dr 30260 **Location:** I-75 exit 233, just e, then just n. **Facility:** 74 units. 3 stories, interior corridors. **Pool(s):** heated indoor. **Activities:** hot tub, exercise room. **Guest Services:** valet and coin laundry.

▮◆ CALL ☾M 🏊 BIZ HS 🛜 ✕ 🗎 🖼 ☕

COUNTRY INN & SUITES BY CARLSON, ATLANTA I-75 SOUTH   770/603-3232 70

▼▼▼ **Hotel.** Rates not provided. **Address:** 2192 Mt. Zion Pkwy 30260 **Location:** I-75 exit 231, just w to Mt. Zion Pkwy, then just s. **Facility:** 62 units. 3 stories, interior corridors. **Pool(s):** outdoor. **Activities:** exercise room. **Guest Services:** coin laundry.

▮◆ CALL ☾M 🏊 BIZ HS 🛜 ✕ 🗎 🖼 ☕

DRURY INN & SUITES-ATLANTA SOUTH   (770)960-0500 67

▼▼▼ **Hotel.** $94-$134 **Address:** 6520 S Lee St 30260 **Location:** I-75 exit 233, just e. **Facility:** 132 units. 7 stories, interior corridors. **Terms:** cancellation fee imposed. **Pool(s):** heated indoor. **Activities:** hot tub, exercise room. **Guest Services:** valet and coin laundry.

CALL ☾M 🏊 BIZ HS 🛜 ✕ 🗎 🖼 ☕ / SOME UNITS 🐾

EXTENDED STAY AMERICA-ATLANTA-MORROW   (770)472-0727 71

▼▼ **Extended Stay Hotel.** $55-$75 **Address:** 2265 Mt. Zion Pkwy 30260 **Location:** I-75 exit 231, just w, then just s. **Facility:** 104 efficiencies. 3 stories, interior corridors. **Terms:** cancellation fee imposed. **Guest Services:** coin laundry.

▮◆ HS 🛜 🗎 🖼 ☕ / SOME UNITS 🐾

HAMPTON INN SOUTHLAKE   (770)968-8990 69

▼▼▼ **Hotel.** $104-$159 **Address:** 1533 Southlake Pkwy 30260 **Location:** I-75 exit 233, just w, then just s. **Facility:** 126 units. 5 stories, interior corridors. **Terms:** 1-7 night minimum stay, cancellation fee imposed. **Pool(s):** outdoor. **Activities:** exercise room. **Guest Services:** valet and coin laundry.

AAA Benefit: Members save up to 10%!

▮◆ CALL ☾M 🏊 BIZ HS 🛜 🎬 🗎 🖼 ☕

Enjoy great member rates and benefits

at AAA/CAA Preferred Hotels

(See map & index p. 94.)

QUALITY INN & SUITES   (770)960-1957 68

♥♥ Motel. $70-$99 Address: 6597 Jonesboro Rd 30260 Location: I-75 exit 233, just w. Facility: 93 units. 3 stories, exterior corridors. Activities: limited exercise equipment. Guest Services: valet and coin laundry.

[icons] CALL 🅜 ⊇ BIZ HS 📶 🖥 🖩 💻 / SOME UNITS 🛢

RED ROOF INN-ATLANTA SOUTH MORROW   (770)968-1483 66

♥♥ Motel. $42-$69 Address: 1348 Southlake Plaza Dr 30260 Location: I-75 exit 233, just e to Southlake Plaza Dr, then just n. Facility: 108 units. 2 stories (no elevator), exterior corridors. Amenities: safes.

[icons] CALL 🅜 📶 📺 / SOME UNITS 🛏 🖥 🖩 💻

WHERE TO EAT

HUYNH KY SAIGON NOODLE HOUSE   678/892-1293 56

♥♥ Vietnamese. Casual Dining. $3-$9 AAA Inspector Notes: Tucked away in a small strip of shops, this family-owned restaurant serves authentic Vietnamese cuisine. Noodles are the specialty, but the yellow rice dishes and soups are also appetizing. I recommend starting off with the crispy rice cake with shredded pork and green onions. It is delicious! Address: 6284 N Lee St 30260 Location: I-75 exit 233, 0.6 mi w on Jonesboro Rd, 0.6 mi e on Lake Harbin Rd, then just w. L D

ROCKY'S CAFE AND PIZZA   404/363-4646 55

♥ Italian. Casual Dining. $5-$19 AAA Inspector Notes: The menu includes pizza, pasta and subs, including chicken parmigiana and the always popular Buffalo wings. The décor and atmosphere are not the strength here, but the owner and servers go out of their way to turn guests into repeat visitors. Features: beer & wine. Address: 2262 Lake Harbin Rd 30260 Location: I-75 exit 233, 0.4 mi e to Lake Harbin Rd, then 1.5 mi s. L D

THE SUSHI CHINA CAFE   770/968-1100 57

♥♥ Asian. Casual Dining. $7-$20 AAA Inspector Notes: Traditional Chinese cuisine—such as chow miens, egg foo young and sweet and sour dishes—and sushi is the focus of this family-owned restaurant's menu. Combinations of chicken, shrimp, pork and vegetables mingle with Chinese sauces. The décor lights up the dining room. Features: beer & wine. Address: 1500 Mt. Zion Rd, Suite 201 30260 Location: I-75 exit 233, 0.3 mi w to Mt. Zion Rd, then just s. L D

MOULTRIE (E-3) pop. 14,268, elev. 319'

ELLEN PAYNE ODOM GENEALOGY LIBRARY, 204 5th St. S.E. in the Moultrie/Colquitt County Library, houses the archives of more than 130 Scottish clans. The collection also includes genealogical research materials about families who entered the United States from the Eastern Seaboard and traces their migration routes west. Exhibits feature Cherokee and Creek Native American documents and artifacts as well as a telecommunications display.

Time: Allow 1 hour minimum. Hours: Mon.-Sat. 8:30-5:30. Closed major holidays, the first week in Aug. and the last two weeks in Dec. Phone ahead to confirm schedule. Cost: Free. Phone: (229) 985-6540.

ECONO LODGE   (229)890-8652

♥♥ Hotel. $69-$150 Address: 1300 Veterans Pkwy N 31788 Location: Northern jct US 319 and 319 business route, just e. Facility: 57 units. 2 stories (no elevator), interior corridors. Pool(s): indoor.

CALL 🅜 ⊇ 📶 ✕ 🖥 🖩 / SOME UNITS 🛢

HAMPTON INN MOULTRIE   (229)616-7777

♥♥♥ Hotel. $109-$190 Address: 441 Veterans Pkwy N 31788 Location: Jct US 319 and SR 37, just ne. Facility: 73 units, 3 stories, interior corridors. Terms: check-in 4 pm, 1-7 night minimum stay, cancellation fee imposed. Pool(s): outdoor. Activities: limited exercise equipment. Guest Services: valet and coin laundry.

> **AAA Benefit:** Members save up to 10%!

CALL 🅜 ⊇ BIZ HS 📶 ✕ 🖥 🖩 💻

HOLIDAY INN EXPRESS & SUITES MOULTRIE   229/890-9900

♥♥♥ Hotel. Rates not provided. Address: 850 Veterans Pkwy N 31788 Location: Jct US 319 and SR 37, 0.9 mi ne. Facility: 68 units, some two bedrooms. 4 stories, interior corridors. Pool(s): heated indoor. Activities: sauna, hot tub, exercise room. Guest Services: valet and coin laundry.

CALL 🅜 ⊇ BIZ HS 📶 ✕ 🖥 🖩 💻

WHERE TO EAT

THE BARBEQUE PIT   229/985-5314

♥ Barbecue. Casual Dining. $5-$16 AAA Inspector Notes: Upon approaching this barbecue shack patrons can smell the wood permeating the air from the smoker. This will get your mouth watering in anticipation of the meal that awaits. Slather on a choice of homemade sauces which come in mild, hot and sweet. Address: 311 1st Ave SE 31768 Location: 1.3 mi w of US 319. L D

MOUNTAIN CITY (A-3) pop. 1,088, elev. 2,168'

In 1966 a high school English teacher in nearby Rabun Gap helped his students publish a quarterly magazine dedicated to recording nearly forgotten Appalachian folkways. Called *Foxfire* after a lichen that glows in the dark, the publication has since grown into a popular series of books and an educational foundation.

FOXFIRE MUSEUM is off Cross St. at 98 Foxfire Ln. This museum of Southern Appalachia features a self-guiding tour around a complex of more than 20 log buildings, which are examples of authentic, replica and modern log construction. The museum includes a gristmill, a blacksmith's shop, a replica church, a wagon collection and several single- and multi-room cabins. Historic items are displayed throughout.

Time: Allow 30 minutes minimum. Hours: Mon.-Sat. 8:30-4:30. Guided tours are offered Mon.-Fri. 9-4; advance reservations are required. Phone ahead to confirm winter hours. Closed Thanksgiving and Christmas. Cost: $6; $5 (ages 62+); $3 (ages 7-10). Phone: (706) 746-5828. GT

NEWNAN (C-2) pop. 33,039, elev. 957'

Newnan's 1904 Neo-Greek Revival County Courthouse, on Courthouse Square, is one of the most well-known in the country because it has appeared in so many movies and TV shows. Four of the historic districts surrounding downtown have fine examples of antebellum and Victorian houses.

With its history rooted in the arts, Dunaway Gardens offers visitors a glimpse into the 1920s to 1940s. Created by vivacious actress Hetty Jane Dunaway, the gardens hosted ballet and theatrical troupes as well as Walt and Roy Disney and Minnie Pearl. The gardens comprise several areas: The Rockery, Arrowhead Pools, Hillside Rock Garden, Hanging Garden, Sunken Garden, Japanese Garden, Little Italy and The Rose Garden; phone (678) 423-4050.

Newnan is near the beginning of the scenic Chattahoochee-Flint Heritage Highway. This scenic route meanders through west-central Georgia from Roscoe south to West Point, Hamilton and Warm Springs.

Coweta County Convention and Visitors Bureau: 200 Court Sq., Newnan, GA 30265. **Phone:** (770) 254-2627 or (800) 826-9382.

Shopping: Ashley Park Mall, 370 Newnan Crossing Bypass/Hwy. 34, offers nearly 50 shops, eateries and theaters including Belk and Dillard's; phone (678) 423-5445.

BEST WESTERN SHENANDOAH INN   (770)304-9700

Motel
$90-$107

AAA Benefit: Save 10% or more every day and earn 10% bonus points!

Address: 620 Hwy 34 E 30265 **Location:** I-85 exit 47, just w. **Facility:** 43 units. 2 stories (no elevator), exterior corridors. **Pool(s):** outdoor. **Activities:** exercise room. **Guest Services:** coin laundry.

COUNTRY INN & SUITES BY CARLSON   770/304-8500

Hotel
Rates not provided

Address: 1125 Newnan Crossing Blvd E 30265 **Location:** I-85 exit 47, 0.3 mi e. **Facility:** 64 units. 4 stories, interior corridors. **Pool(s):** heated indoor. **Activities:** exercise room. **Guest Services:** valet and coin laundry. **Featured Amenity:** breakfast buffet.

HAMPTON INN   (770)253-9922

 Hotel. $129-$169 **Address:** 50 Hampton Way 30265 **Location:** I-85 exit 47, just e. **Facility:** 91 units. 3 stories, interior corridors. **Terms:** 1-7 night minimum stay, cancellation fee imposed. **Pool(s):** outdoor. **Activities:** exercise room. **Guest Services:** valet and coin laundry.

AAA Benefit: Members save up to 10%!

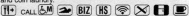

SPRINGHILL SUITES BY MARRIOTT NEWNAN   (770)254-8900

 Hotel. $106-$189 **Address:** 1119 Bullsboro Dr 30265 **Location:** I-85 exit 47, 0.3 mi e. **Facility:** 82 units. 3 stories, interior corridors. **Pool(s):** outdoor. **Activities:** hot tub, exercise room. **Guest Services:** valet and coin laundry.

AAA Benefit: Members save 5% or more!

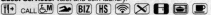

WHERE TO EAT

ASIAN CHEF   770/251-8088

Asian. Casual Dining. $5-$40 **AAA Inspector Notes:** This is a Chinese bistro, sushi bar and Japanese hibachi steakhouse all under the same roof. Contemporary Asian décor touches and an extensive variety enhance the atmosphere. **Features:** beer & wine. **Address:** 941 Bullsboro Dr, Suite B 30265 **Location:** I-85 exit 47, just e.

GOLDENS ON THE SQUARE   770/251-4300

Southern Comfort Food. Buffet Style. $5-$10 **AAA Inspector Notes:** Freshly prepared Southern favorites, such as fried chicken, mashed potatoes and greens are served cafeteria-style at this casual dining room and are sure to make you feel right at home. The rotating menu of classics means a new experience everyday which locals have enjoyed since 1972! **Address:** 9 E Court Square 30264 **Location:** Downtown. **Parking:** street only.

MAMA LUCIA'S   770/253-2501

Italian. Casual Dining. $8-$25 **AAA Inspector Notes:** The pork belly or baked Brie appetizers are just the beginning of an excellent meal here. Antipasto and Mediterranean salads are available and a huge selection of entrées include rack of lamb, shrimp scampi, veal Marsala, chicken pesto, seafood crepes, pizza and many more pasta offerings. Save room for the tiramisu or creme brûlée. **Features:** full bar, Sunday brunch. **Address:** 236 Newnan Crossing Bypass 30265 **Location:** I-85 exit 47, 0.4 mi w, then just s; in Ashley Park Mall.

MEAT 'N' GREET   770/683-4664

Burgers. Casual Dining. $5-$12 **AAA Inspector Notes:** Among the shops and restaurants of the historic downtown square sits a casual eatery specializing in craft burgers and beers. Burgers are made with a blend of Angus beef chuck, brisket and short rib making a super juicy and delicious patty. The "High West" is my favorite with its combination of fried onions, bacon, smoked tomato jam and barbecue sauce. If you are in the mood for something spicy take a chance on "El Diablo" with sambal mayo, jalapeños, ghost pepper cheese and bacon. **Features:** full bar. **Address:** 11 Jefferson St 30263 **Location:** In historic downtown. **Parking:** street only.

REDNECK GOURMET   770/251-0092

Sandwiches. Quick Serve. $6-$14 **AAA Inspector Notes:** This quirky, family-owned restaurant has been serving country classics such as fried pickles, pimento cheeseburgers and catfish po'boys since 1991. Salads, wraps, hoagies and veggie burgers round out the eclectic menu. The restaurant's location on the square gives you the opportunity to walk off those delicious calories with an after-dinner stroll through the beautiful historic downtown area. **Address:** 11 N Court Square 30263 **Location:** Downtown; on the square.

SHIRLEY'S COUNTRY KITCHEN   770/253-8914

Southern. Quick Serve. $8-$14 **AAA Inspector Notes:** For those seeking home-style cooking with no fuss then this is the place for you. Featuring homemade cakes and desserts along with several options of meat and vegetables daily. Quick and yummy. **Address:** 1485 Hwy 34 E 30264 **Location:** I-85 exit 47, 0.8 mi e.

SPRAYBERRY'S BAR-B-QUE   770/253-4421

Barbecue. Casual Dining. $8-$20 **AAA Inspector Notes:** Serving up delicious barbecue since 1926, this family-owned establishment provides three modestly furnished, clean and comfortable dining areas. For a tasty lunch, try the sliced pork sandwich with hearty onion rings and a scrumptious fried fruit pie. Steaks, catfish and Brunswick stew also are on the menu. **Features:** beer only. **Address:** 229 Jackson St 30263 **Location:** On SR 14, 1 mi n of SR 34.

SPRAYBERRY'S BAR-B-QUE/I-85   770/253-5080

Barbecue. Casual Dining. $9-$20 **AAA Inspector Notes:** This family-owned establishment provides tasty vinegar-based barbecue lunches and dinners, such as the sliced pork sandwich with hearty onion rings. Steaks, catfish and chicken are also on the menu. The fried pie is scrumptious. **Features:** beer only, senior menu. **Address:** 1060 Hwy 34 E 30263 **Location:** I-85 exit 47, just e.

NORCROSS (G-4) pop. 9,116, elev. 1,047'

- **Hotels & Restaurants map & index p. 82, 90**
- **Part of Atlanta area — see map p. 44**

Norcross, known as "Atlanta's Favorite Summer Resort" in the late-19th century, is located 20 miles north of downtown Atlanta and is populated with many Victorian and Craftsman homes. The city also has several lovely parks that contain protected, historic trees.

Norcross Welcome Center & Museum: 189 Lawrenceville St., Norcross, GA 30071. **Phone:** (678) 421-2048.

Self-guiding tours: A walking-tour map of historic homes and the historic trees is available at Norcross Welcome Center & Museum.

ATLANTA MARRIOTT NORCROSS   (770)263-8558 **66**

WWWW Hotel. $61-$217 **Address:** 475 Technology Pkwy 30092 **Location:** I-85 exit 99, 4 mi w to Peachtree Industrial Blvd, w on Holcomb Bridge Rd, then 0.8 mi n on Peachtree Pkwy (SR 141); I-285 exit 31B, 5 mi n on SR 141. **Facility:** 222 units. 6 stories, interior corridors. **Pool(s):** heated indoor. **Activities:** exercise room. **Guest Services:** valet laundry, boarding pass kiosk, area transportation.

AAA Benefit:
Members save 5% or more!

COMFORT INN & SUITES   (770)263-8883 **65**

WW Hotel. $71-$149 **Address:** 5200 Peachtree Industrial Blvd 30071 **Location:** I-85 exit 31B, 5.5 mi n; I-85 exit 99, 4 mi w to Peachtree Industrial Blvd, then 1.5 mi n. **Facility:** 62 units. 3 stories, interior corridors. **Pool(s):** outdoor. **Activities:** exercise room. **Guest Services:** coin laundry.

COUNTRY INN & SUITES BY CARLSON   770/449-5051 **74**

WWW Hotel. Rates not provided. **Address:** 5970 Jimmy Carter Blvd 30071 **Location:** I-85 exit 99, 0.8 mi w. **Facility:** 50 units. 3 stories, interior corridors. **Pool(s):** outdoor. **Activities:** exercise room. **Guest Services:** coin laundry.

COURTYARD BY MARRIOTT-ATLANTA NORCROSS/PEACHTREE CORNERS   (770)446-3777 **71**

WWW Hotel. $62-$183 **Address:** 3209 Holcomb Bridge Rd 30092 **Location:** I-85 exit 99, 4 mi w, then 0.5 mi n; I-285 exit 31B, 4 mi n to Holcomb Bridge Rd, then just w. **Facility:** 131 units. 2-3 stories, interior corridors. **Pool(s):** outdoor. **Activities:** exercise room. **Guest Services:** valet and coin laundry.

AAA Benefit:
Members save 5% or more!

HAMPTON INN ATLANTA/PEACHTREE CORNERS/NORCROSS   (770)729-0015 **68**

WWW Hotel. $69-$169 **Address:** 440 Technology Pkwy 30092 **Location:** I-85 exit 99, 4 mi w to Peachtree Industrial Blvd, then 0.8 mi n on Peachtree Pkwy (SR 141); I-285 exit 31B, 5 mi n on SR 141. **Facility:** 148 units. 5 stories, interior corridors. **Terms:** 1-7 night minimum stay, cancellation fee imposed. **Pool(s):** heated indoor. **Activities:** exercise room. **Guest Services:** valet laundry, area transportation.

AAA Benefit:
Members save up to 10%!

HILTON ATLANTA NORTHEAST   (770)447-4747 **70**

WWW Hotel. $79-$329 **Address:** 5993 Peachtree Industrial Blvd 30092 **Location:** I-285 exit 31B, 4.5 mi ne. **Facility:** 272 units. 10 stories, interior corridors. **Terms:** 1-7 night minimum stay, cancellation fee imposed. **Amenities:** safes. **Pool(s):** heated outdoor, heated indoor. **Activities:** exercise room. **Guest Services:** valet and coin laundry, area transportation.

AAA Benefit:
Members save 5% or more!

▼ *See AAA listing p. 229* ▼

(See maps & indexes p. 82, 90.)

HOLIDAY INN EXPRESS ATLANTA NE-PEACHTREE CORNERS 770/409-0004 [72]
▼▼▼▼ **Hotel.** Rates not provided. **Address:** 7035 Jimmy Carter Blvd 30092 **Location:** I-85 exit 99, 4 mi w; I-285 exit 31B, 4 mi n. **Facility:** 79 units. 3 stories, interior corridors. **Pool(s):** outdoor. **Activities:** exercise room. **Guest Services:** valet and coin laundry.

[ICONS]

HOMEWOOD SUITES BY HILTON (770)448-4663 [67]
▼▼▼▼ **Extended Stay Hotel.**
$89-$189 **Address:** 450 Technology Pkwy 30092 **Location:** I-85 exit 99, 4 mi w to Peachtree Industrial Blvd, 0.4 mi n, w on Holcomb Bridge Rd, then 2 blks n on Peachtree Pkwy; I-285 exit 31B, 5 mi n on SR 141. Located in a business park area. **Facility:** 92 efficiencies, some two bedrooms. 3 stories, interior/exterior corridors. **Terms:** 1-7 night minimum stay, cancellation fee imposed. **Pool(s):** outdoor. **Activities:** exercise room. **Guest Services:** valet and coin laundry, area transportation.

AAA Benefit:
Members save up to 10%!

[ICONS]

HYATT PLACE ATLANTA/NORCROSS/PEACHTREE PARKWAY (770)416-7655 [64]
▼▼▼ Hotel $64-$169

♦ HYATT PLACE®

AAA Benefit: Members save 10%!

Address: 5600 Peachtree Pkwy 30092 **Location:** I-285 exit 31B, 4 mi n on SR 141, then 1 mi n. **Facility:** 126 units. 6 stories, interior corridors. **Terms:** cancellation fee imposed. **Pool(s):** outdoor. **Activities:** exercise room. **Guest Services:** valet laundry, area transportation. **Featured Amenity: full hot breakfast.** *(See ad p. 228.)*

[ICONS]

LA QUINTA INN NORCROSS (770)368-9400 [75]
▼▼▼▼ **Hotel.** $71-$174 **Address:** 5945 Oakbrook Pkwy 30093 **Location:** I-85 exit 99, 0.3 mi e to Live Oak Pkwy, then 0.8 mi nw. Located in an office park area. **Facility:** 120 units. 3 stories, interior corridors. **Pool(s):** outdoor. **Activities:** exercise room. **Guest Services:** coin laundry.

[ICONS]

TOWNEPLACE SUITES BY MARRIOTT ATLANTA NORCROSS/PEACHTREE CORNERS (770)447-8446 [73]
▼▼ ▼▼ **Extended Stay Hotel.**
$74-$126 **Address:** 6640 Bay Cir 30071 **Location:** I-285 exit 31B, 3 mi n on Peachtree Industrial Blvd to Jones Mill Rd. **Facility:** 94 kitchen units, some two bedrooms. 3 stories, interior corridors. **Pool(s):** outdoor. **Activities:** exercise room. **Guest Services:** valet and coin laundry, area transportation.

AAA Benefit:
Members save 5% or more!

[ICONS]

WINGATE BY WYNDHAM ATLANTA NORCROSS (770)263-2020 [69]
▼▼▼▼ **Hotel.** $70-$75 **Address:** 5800 Peachtree Industrial Blvd 30071 **Location:** I-285 exit 31B, 5 mi n; I-85 exit 99, 4 mi w to Peachtree Industrial Blvd, then 1 mi n. **Facility:** 118 units. 4 stories, interior corridors. **Amenities:** safes. **Pool(s):** outdoor. **Activities:** hot tub, exercise room. **Guest Services:** valet and coin laundry.

[ICONS]

CHEESEBURGER BOBBY'S 770/300-0032
▼ Burgers. Quick Serve. $3-$6 **AAA Inspector Notes:** Nibble on hand-cut fries with your fresh, hand-patted burger, which you'll gussy up with onions, lettuce, tomatoes, pickles and other items on the condiment station. Other choices include hot dogs, chicken sandwiches and custard for dessert. Friendly servers tend the bright, fresh and clean dining room. **Address:** 6050 Peachtree Pkwy, Suite 140 30092 **Location:** I-85 exit 99, 4 mi w w to Peachtree Industrial Blvd, 0.4 mi n, w on Holcomb Bridge Rd, then just n; I-285 exit 31B, 5 mi n on SR 141. [L] [D] CALL [M]

THE CROSSING OF NORCROSS 678/280-9081 [98]
▼▼▼▼ American. Fine Dining. $8-$30 **AAA Inspector Notes:** This charming restaurant combines modern flavors and an historic location to create a distinctive dining experience. Situated in a remodeled train depot, the experience is made all the more real by the active train that still passes by from time to time. The kitchen serves up modern interpretations of traditional American cuisine sprinkled alongside Latin flavors from the cultural background of the owners. **Address:** 40 S Peachtree 30071 **Location:** Between Jones St NW and Holcomb Bridge Rd; in historic downtown. [L] [D] CALL [M]

DOG DAYS 770/449-7433 [94]
▼ Hot Dogs Burgers. Quick Serve. $3-$12 **AAA Inspector Notes:** Georgia dogs, Chicago dogs, pico dogs and macaroni and cheese dogs are but a few of the many types offered here. They come in small and large. Burgers come in both six- and 12-ounce sizes and include Baja, steak, chili cheese and chipotle styles. Pies, cakes and turtle candies are luscious dessert options. **Features:** patio dining. **Address:** 6025 Peachtree Pkwy 30092 **Location:** I-285 exit 31B, 5.3 mi n. [L] [D] CALL [M]

DOMINICK'S 770/449-1611 [100]
▼▼ ▼▼ Italian. Casual Dining. $9-$29 **AAA Inspector Notes:** In old town Norcross, this fun, friendly restaurant nurtures a bustling ambiance that comes straight from the heart of Little Italy. A shining example of the sumptuously prepared traditional favorites is the highly recommended veal with provolone cheese. Make sure you bring your appetite for the large portions! Lunch is served Monday through Friday. **Features:** full bar, patio dining. **Address:** 95 S Peachtree St 30071 **Location:** Corner of Peachtree St and Holcomb Bridge Rd; downtown. **Parking:** street only. [L] [D]

FLYING BISCUIT CAFE 770/407-5885 [92]
▼▼ American. Casual Dining. $5-$15 **AAA Inspector Notes:** All-day breakfast dishes and complimentary biscuits are hugely popular at this day time café. The menu focuses on fresh comfort foods that are decidedly Southern, but also offers modern trends such as gluten-free and tofu substitutes. **Features:** beer & wine, patio dining, Sunday brunch. **Address:** 5270 Peachtree Pkwy, Suite 120 30092 **Location:** I-285 exit 31B, 5.8 mi n; in The Village at Peachtree Corners. [B] [L] CALL [M]

FRONTERA MEX-MEX GRILL 770/441-3488 [96]
▼▼ ▼▼ Tex-Mex. Casual Dining. $5-$17 **AAA Inspector Notes:** A relaxed dining experience with large portions and lively Latin music playing in the background is what guests can expect at this restaurant. This regional chain has mastered the flavors and presentation we have come to expect from Tex-Mex cuisine. **Features:** full bar, patio dining, senior menu, Sunday brunch. **Address:** 7190 Jimmy Carter Blvd 30092 **Location:** I-85 exit 99, 4 mi n; I-285 exit 31B, 4 mi n, then just w. [L] [D] CALL [M]

HAPPY VALLEY 678/218-0888 [103]
▼▼ Chinese. Casual Dining. $9-$22 **AAA Inspector Notes:** The dim sum is a big draw here and a wide assortment features many types of dumplings, baked egg custard tarts, pan-fried radish cakes and barbecue pork buns. Enticing entrées include crispy whole red snapper, steamed sea bass, curry shrimp and tangerine beef. Many favorite Chinese food preparations can be found. **Features:** beer & wine. **Address:** 5495 Jimmy Carter Blvd 30093 **Location:** I-85 exit 99, 0.3 mi w to Live Oak Pkwy, then just n; in Ben Thanh Plaza. [L] [D] CALL [M]

(See maps & indexes p. 82, 90.)

J. ALEXANDER'S RESTAURANT　770/263-9755 **91**
▼▼▼ American. Casual Dining. $4-$27 **AAA Inspector Notes:** The busy and casual restaurant prepares classic fare—including steak, grilled fish and prime rib—in the open kitchen. The dessert menu is excellent. **Features:** full bar. **Reservations:** suggested. **Address:** 5245 Peachtree Pkwy 30092 **Location:** Jct Peachtree Corners Cir; in The Forum. L | D | CALL M

JR'S LOG HOUSE RESTAURANT　770/449-6426 **101**
▼ American. Casual Dining. $8-$15 **AAA Inspector Notes:** This popular local spot has been cooking and catering barbecue for more than 30 years. Three meals a day are available and daily specials are served in generous portions. The all-you-can-eat St. Louis ribs are popular, as are the daily veggies and pot roast. **Features:** beer & wine. **Address:** 6601 Peachtree Industrial Blvd 30092 **Location:** Jct Jones Mill Rd and Peachtree Industrial Blvd. B | L | D

MOJITOS CUBAN-AMERICAN BISTRO　770/441-2599 **99**
▼▼ Cuban. Casual Dining. $5-$19 **AAA Inspector Notes:** Located in the heart of the historic downtown district is this charming Cuban bistro serving up delicious cuisine that will make you want to shout delicioso. Try such classic dishes as vaca frita, ropa vieja and spicy ox-tail. Be sure to save room for the sublime mango pie. **Address:** 35 S Peachtree St 30071 **Location:** Between Jones St NW and Holcomb Bridge Rd; in historic downtown. **Parking:** street only.
L | D | CALL M

NAM PHUONG　770/409-8686 **104**
▼▼ Vietnamese. Casual Dining. $7-$13 **AAA Inspector Notes:** Piping-hot bowls of pho and other Vietnamese favorites, such as fresh basil rolls, satisfy patrons at this eatery where earnest servers circulate through a dining room appointed in pleasing traditional Vietnamese décor. The rice vermicelli dishes are not to be missed. **Features:** beer & wine. **Address:** 5495 Jimmy Carter Blvd 30093 **Location:** I-85 exit 99, 0.3 mi e to Oakbrook Pkwy; in Ben Thanh Plaza. L | D

PAPPADEAUX SEAFOOD KITCHEN　770/849-0600
▼▼ Cajun Seafood. Casual Dining. $11-$53 **AAA Inspector Notes:** A seafood lover's delight, the restaurant taps into a little bit of New Orleans with its Cajun dishes and elaborate menu selections. Patrons might start off with a creative choice of blackened oyster and shrimp fondeaux with crayfish and let the feast begin. While music plays in the background, patrons can dig into dirty rice or spicy gumbo loaded with seafood. Well-seasoned shrimp and fish are prepared in varied ways. **Features:** full bar, happy hour. **Address:** 5635 Jimmy Carter Blvd 30071 **Location:** I-85 exit 99, just w.
L | D | CALL M

TASTE OF THAI　770/662-8575 **102**
▼▼ ▼▼ Thai. Casual Dining. $4-$13 **AAA Inspector Notes:** For those who want delicious Thai cuisine in a relaxed, no-frills environment, then this family-owned restaurant is the place to try. The menu features such classic favorites as pad thai, sweet and sour pork, basil duck and spicy catfish. **Address:** 5775 Jimmy Carter Blvd 30071 **Location:** I-85 exit 99 (Jimmy Carter Blvd), just nw.
L | D | CALL M

THAI STAR　770/326-9991 **93**
▼▼ ▼▼ Thai. Casual Dining. $8-$17 **AAA Inspector Notes:** At this spot, diners can begin with some fresh basil rolls or shrimp in blankets followed by a cup of lemon grass soup and an entrée such as roasted duck curry or sea scallops in wine sauce. Lunch specials such as the pad prik and drunken noodles come with jasmine rice and either a fried spring roll or soup. **Features:** full bar. **Address:** 5370 Peachtree Industrial Blvd 30071 **Location:** I-285 exit 31B, 5.5 mi n; I-85 exit 99, 4 mi w to Peachtree Industrial Blvd, then 1.5 mi n. L | D

THE VARSITY　770/840-8519
▼ Hot Dogs Burgers. Quick Serve. $2-$10 **AAA Inspector Notes:** Be ready to order when you enter this longtime Atlanta landmark as service staff shouts 'What'll you have?' when you enter the line. Chili dogs, slaw dogs and naked dogs along with hamburgers, wings and their famous frozen orange drinks. **Address:** 6045 Dawson Blvd 30093 **Location:** I-85 exit 99, 0.3 mi e to Dawson Blvd, then just s. L | D | CALL M

ZAPATA TACOS AND TEQUILA BAR　770/248-0052 **97**
▼▼ Mexican. Casual Dining. $8-$19 **AAA Inspector Notes:** A truly distinctive Mexican menu offering authentic choices from the Guadalajara area. Their specialty, the molcajetes is delivered in a lava bowl with trimmings such as nopal, a Mexican flat cactus. The brick-lined walls and dark woods are softened by the modern amber lighting. Enjoy one of the specialty tequilas alone or in a margarita. **Features:** full bar. **Address:** 15 Jones St 30092 **Location:** I-285 exit 31B; downtown. L | D

OAKWOOD pop. 3,970

BEST WESTERN PLUS LAKE LANIER/GAINESVILLE HOTEL & SUITES　(770)535-8080

▼▼ ▼▼ ▼ Hotel $101-$116

BW Best Western PLUS.

AAA Benefit: Save 10% or more every day and earn 10% bonus points!

Address: 4535 Oakwood Rd 30566 **Location:** I-985 exit 16, just w. **Facility:** 61 units. 3 stories, interior corridors. **Pool(s):** outdoor. **Activities:** exercise room. **Guest Services:** valet and coin laundry.
SAVE | 🍴 | 🚲 | BIZ | 📶 | ✕ | 🍴
📷 | 🖥 | / SOME UNITS 🛏

JAMESON INN　770/533-9400
▼▼ ▼▼ Motel. Rates not provided. **Address:** 3530 Thurman Tanner Pkwy 30566 **Location:** I-985 exit 16, 0.4 mi w. **Facility:** 42 units. 2 stories (no elevator), exterior corridors. **Pool(s):** outdoor. **Activities:** exercise room.
🍴 | CALL M | 🚲 | BIZ | HS | 📶 | 🍴 | 🖥
/ SOME UNITS 🛏 | 🖥

 OCMULGEE NATIONAL MONUMENT (C-3)

Ocmulgee (oak-MUL-gee) National Monument is on Macon's eastern limits; take US 80 east from I-16 exit 2 and follow signs. Within the monument's 702 acres are some of the most impressive Native

American mounds and archeological remains in the Southeast. Creeks, early and late Mississippi farmers and Paleo-Indian, Archaic and Woodland hunters and gatherers are known to have inhabited the area 17,000 years.

Native American farmers migrated to central Georgia about A.D. 900 and built a large village and-ceremonial center on the Macon Plateau. Six of their temple mounds, one burial mound and one ceremonial earth lodge remain. The restored earth lodge, which dates from about 1015, was a meeting chamber. The clay floor, benches around the walls, lower portion of the walls and raised bird-shaped platform have survived.

About 1350 a new village, which archeologists named Lamar, was built 2 miles down the river. Around 1690 the Creek Native Americans built a village, and the Ocmulgee River then marked the southwestern frontier of the Carolinas and Georgia for British colonists. Charleston supported a fur-trading post in the area 1690-1715.

Foot trails connect most of the park's features, and a drive approaches the large mounds. The Opelofa Nature Trail branches off the main walking trail and explores the lowlands of Walnut Creek. The visitor center houses archeological displays and dioramas. The video "Ocmulgee: Mysteries of the Mounds" is shown upon request. An audio tour by cellphone is available.

The annual Ocmulgee Indian Celebration, held at the monument the third weekend of September, attracts one of the largest gatherings of Native Americans in the Southeast. Such activities as dancing and arts and crafts demonstrations are provided. Phone the monument office to confirm the schedule.

Events are held throughout the year. Picnic facilities are available. Daily 9-5; closed Jan. 1 and Christmas. Free. Phone (478) 752-8257.

OCONEE NATIONAL FOREST—See
Chattahoochee-Oconee National Forest p. 155

PEACHTREE CITY (C-2) pop. 34,364, elev. 899'

Made up of six villages, each with its own shopping areas, recreational facilities and elementary schools, Peachtree City was designed by real estate developers as a planned city in the 1950s. Now the film industry utilizes the picturesque city for film and TV, "Sweet Home Alabama" and "Drop Dead Diva" being two of the more notable projects to be filmed here. The Southern Hollywood Film Tour departs from the Peachtree City Convention & Visitor's Bureau Mon.-Sat. and visits the filming sets of these and the sets of other movies and TV shows such as "Fried Green Tomatoes" and "The Walking Dead." Phone (678) 216-0282 for reservations.

Peachtree City supports alternative transportation, so visitors should not be surprised by the sight of residents cruising around in golf carts.

Peachtree City Convention & Visitors Bureau: 201 McIntosh Tr., Peachtree City, GA 30269. **Phone:** (678) 216-0282 or (877) 782-4250.

CROWNE PLAZA ATLANTA SW - PEACHTREE CITY   770/487-2666
▼▼▼ **Hotel.** Rates not provided. **Address:** 201 Aberdeen Pkwy 30269 **Location:** Jct SR 74 and 54, 0.5 mi n on SR 74, then just e. **Facility:** 233 units. 2-3 stories, interior corridors. **Pool(s):** heated indoor. **Activities:** tennis, exercise room. **Guest Services:** valet and coin laundry, area transportation.

DAYS INN & SUITES PEACHTREE CITY   (770)632-9700
▼▼ **Motel.** $58-$99 **Address:** 976 Crosstown Dr 30269 **Location:** Jct SR 54 and 74, 2.1 mi s on SR 74. **Facility:** 51 units. 2 stories (no elevator), exterior corridors. **Pool(s):** outdoor. **Activities:** exercise room.

HAMPTON INN   (770)486-8800
▼▼▼ **Hotel.** $94-$209 **Address:** 300 Westpark Dr 30269 **Location:** Jct SR 74 and 54, 0.3 mi n on SR 74. **Facility:** 61 units. 2 stories, interior corridors. **Terms:** 1-7 night minimum stay, cancellation fee imposed. **Pool(s):** outdoor. **Activities:** exercise room. **Guest Services:** valet and coin laundry.

> **AAA Benefit:**
> Members save up to 10%!

SLEEP INN   (770)486-0044
▼▼ **Hotel.** $99-$109 **Address:** 109 City Cir 30269 **Location:** Jct SR 54 and 74; in The Avenue Shopping Center. **Facility:** 61 units. 2 stories, interior corridors. **Bath:** shower only. **Activities:** exercise room. **Guest Services:** valet and coin laundry.

WYNDHAM PEACHTREE HOTEL & CONFERENCE CENTER   (770)487-2000

▼▼▼▼
Resort Hotel
$99-$199

Address: 2443 Hwy 54 W 30269 **Location:** Jct SR 74 and 54, 1 mi e. **Facility:** Sprawling, well-groomed grounds with excellent recreational facilities are highlights at this hotel, which has extensive conference facilities. The modern decor is both pleasing and comfortable. 250 units. 4 stories, interior corridors. **Terms:** check-in 4 pm, cancellation fee imposed. **Pool(s):** outdoor, heated indoor. **Activities:** sauna, hot tub, steamroom, tennis, massage. **Guest Services:** valet and coin laundry, boarding pass kiosk, area transportation.

WHERE TO EAT

THE BEIRUT MEDITERREAN DINING   678/364-0707
▼▼ Lebanese. Casual Dining. $5-$21 **AAA Inspector Notes:** This casual eatery is an exotic local choice for Mediterranean and Lebanese cuisine. Menu favorites include kebabs, lamb skewers and red snapper. I recommend starting with the baba ghanoush (fire-roasted eggplant dip) and finishing the meal with the delicious taste of heaven—vanilla custard. Come for the flavors. Stay for the experience. **Features:** wine only. **Address:** 1025 N Peachtree Pkwy 30269 **Location:** SR 74 (Joel Cowan Pkwy), e on N Peachtree Pkwy; in Kendron Village shopping center.

THE ITALIAN OVEN RESTAURANT   770/486-9642

▼▼ ▼▼ Italian. Casual Dining. $4-$15 **AAA Inspector Notes:** This family restaurant serves up big portions of favorite Italian dishes in a casual and friendly atmosphere. Known for their brick-oven pizza and pasta dishes, highlights include Tuscan chicken and butternut squash ravioli. Save room for one of the decadent desserts or a delicious gelato. **Features:** full bar. **Address:** 100 Peachtree East Shopping Center 30269 **Location:** Jct SR 74 and 54, 3 mi e.

[L] [D] CALL 🛗M

J. CHRISTOPHER'S   678/216-1010

▼▼ ▼▼ Breakfast. Casual Dining. $6-$12 **AAA Inspector Notes:** Blueberry crunch cakes, strawberry waffles and eggs Christopher are some of the breakfast favorites found here along with such seasonal items as pumpkin pancakes. Many breakfast standards also are available. Lunch favorites include the club house burger and the classic club sandwich. Waldorf salads and signature soups are popular. **Address:** 264 Commerce Dr 30269 **Location:** Jct SR 54 and 74; in West Park Shopping Center. [B] [L] CALL 🛗M

PARTNERS II PIZZA   770/487-9393

▼▼ ▼▼ Italian. Casual Dining. $5-$20 **AAA Inspector Notes:** This family-owned pizzeria is the perfect place to gather with family and friends. The menu features popular pasta dishes, sandwiches and pizza. The most popular dish by far is the potato pizza with sour cream, potatoes, bacon and cheddar cheese. The "It's Greek to Me" is a popular non-meat option and there are plenty of gluten-free options as well. **Address:** 215 Northlake Dr 30269 **Location:** SR 54, just nw on Northlake Dr. [L] [D] CALL 🛗M

PASCAL'S BISTRO   770/632-0112

▼▼▼▼ New American. Fine Dining. $8-$30 **AAA Inspector Notes:** The owner/chef has been known to greet each guest at this French-influenced eatery. At lunch, the pasta buffet lines up 14 meats and vegetables, four types of pasta and four complementary sauces, Caesar salad and garlic bread. In the evening, white tablecloth service kicks in. Among flavorful dishes are braised lamb shank, steak au poivre and roasted pork tenderloin. The luscious desserts include chocolate chip bread pudding and blue ribbon carrot cake. **Features:** full bar, patio dining. **Address:** 217 Commerce Dr 30269 **Location:** Jct SR 54 and 74; in West Park Shopping Center. [L] [D]

PERRY (D-3) pop. 13,839, elev. 354'

🐎 Georgia National Junior Livestock Show and Georgia National Rodeo is held in mid-February. The livestock show is the statewide championship for Georgia's 4-H and FFA students, and men and women compete in the three-day rodeo in events such as barrel racing, bull riding and team roping. In early October, the 🐎 Georgia National Fair has midway rides, street entertainers, a circus and nightly fireworks.

BEST WESTERN BRADBURY INN & SUITES
    (478)218-5200

▼▼ ▼▼
Hotel
$70-$140

AAA Benefit: Save 10% or more every day and earn 10% bonus points!

Address: 205 Lect Dr 31069 **Location:** I-75 exit 135 (US 41), just e, then just n. **Facility:** 73 units. 3 stories, interior corridors. **Pool(s):** heated indoor. **Activities:** hot tub. **Guest Services:** coin laundry.

[SAVE] [📶↦] CALL 🛗M [🏊] [BIZ] [🛜] [✕] [🛗] [🖼] [💻]

HAMPTON INN   (478)987-7681

▼▼▼▼ Hotel. $119-$159 **Address:** 102 Hampton Ct 31069 **Location:** I-75 exit 136 (Sam Nunn Blvd), just se. **Facility:** 94 units. 2 stories, interior corridors. **Terms:** 1-7 night minimum stay, cancellation fee imposed. **Pool(s):** outdoor. **Activities:** exercise room. **Guest Services:** valet laundry.

AAA Benefit: Members save up to 10%!

[📶↦] CALL 🛗M [🏊] [BIZ] [🛜] [✕] [🛗] [🖼] [💻]

HOLIDAY INN EXPRESS PERRY   478/224-3000

▼▼ ▼▼
Hotel
Rates not provided

Address: 1502 Sam Nunn Blvd 31069 **Location:** I-75 exit 136 (Sam Nunn Blvd), just w. **Facility:** 94 units. 4 stories, interior corridors. **Pool(s):** outdoor. **Activities:** exercise room. **Featured Amenity:** full hot breakfast.

[SAVE] [📶↦] CALL 🛗M [🏊] [BIZ] [🛜] [✕] [🛗] [🖼] [💻]

MICROTEL INN & SUITES BY WYNDHAM PERRY
    (478)987-4004

▼▼ ▼▼ Hotel. $45-$144 **Address:** 110 AG Village Blvd 31069 **Location:** I-75 exit 134, just nw. **Facility:** 63 units. 3 stories, interior corridors. **Pool(s):** outdoor. **Activities:** exercise room. **Guest Services:** coin laundry.

[📶↦] CALL 🛗M [🏊] [BIZ] [HS] [🛜] [🛗] [🖼] [💻] / SOME UNITS [🐾]

RAMADA INN   (478)987-3313

▼▼ ▼▼ Motel. $66-$125 **Address:** 200 Valley Dr 31069 **Location:** I-75 exit 136 (Sam Nunn Blvd), just w, then s. **Facility:** 200 units. 2 stories, exterior corridors. **Terms:** cancellation fee imposed. **Pool(s):** outdoor. **Activities:** limited exercise equipment. **Guest Services:** valet and coin laundry.

[🍴] CALL 🛗M [🏊] [BIZ] [🛜] [💻] / SOME UNITS [🐾] [🛗] [🖼]

WHERE TO EAT

SONNY'S REAL PIT BAR-B-Q   478/218-2100

▼▼ ▼▼ Barbecue. Casual Dining. $8-$17 **AAA Inspector Notes:** Bearing the name after its founder, Floyd "Sonny" Tillman, this barbecue restaurant first opened its doors circa 1968 in Gainesville, Florida and has since spawned over 150 more throughout the Southeast. The menu is steeped in finger lickin' favorites such as ribs, pulled pork, beef brisket, burgers, catfish, shrimp and chargrilled chicken. Let's not forget about the fried okra, which is the perfect starter dish, and their homemade baked beans. **Features:** beer only. **Address:** 1001 St. Patricks Dr 31069 **Location:** I-75 exit 136 (Sam Nunn Blvd), just e, then 0.4 mi n. [L] [D]

THE SWANSON 478/987-1938

▼▼ ▼▼ Southern American. Casual Dining. $8-$15 **AAA Inspector Notes:** Housed in a historic building in the heart of downtown, the Southern-style establishment doesn't skimp on hospitality and offers delectable classic and Southern fare. Specialties include Southern-fried chicken, meatloaf and fried pork chops. At lunch, patrons with lesser appetites can opt for a salad, sandwich or the quiche of the day. Tempting homemade desserts will cap off a hearty meal. **Features:** beer & wine. **Address:** 933 Carroll St 31069 **Location:** I-75 exit 136 (Sam Nunn Blvd), 1 mi s on Sam Nunn Blvd/Ball St, then just e; downtown. ⬜L ⬜D

PINE MOUNTAIN (C-2) pop. 1,304,
elev. 1,052'
• Restaurants p. 234

◤◢ **CALLAWAY GARDENS,** 1 mi. w. at SRs 18 and 354, covers 6,500 acres in the foothills of the Appalachians. Founded in 1952 by industrialist Cason J. Callaway, the gardens feature beautiful plant and flower displays and miles of scenic woodland drives. Attractions include an early 1800s log cabin, the Ida Cason Callaway Memorial Chapel, Mr. Cason's Vegetable Garden and the Virginia Hand Callaway Discovery Center. The center offers a daily birds of prey show and serves as an information center for Callaway's recreational opportunities, which include golf, miniature golf, bicycling, walking, swimming, fishing, boating and tennis. Also available on the grounds is TreeTop Adventure, a course of aerial challenges and ziplines through the tree tops.

The gardens contain native azaleas, once plentiful in the natural woodlands of the Southeast. These rare varieties, usually purer in color than cultivated shrubs, display brilliant reds, oranges and yellows. There also are hundreds of cultivated azalea varieties found in the Callaway Brothers Azalea Bowl, purported to be the world's largest azalea garden, and the Overlook Azalea Garden, both of which bloom during Celebrate Spring. Greenhouses display native and tropical blooming plants. The 5-mile Scenic Drive winds around Mountain Creek Lake, where canoes, kayaks, paddleboats and fishing boats are available for rent. Geocache stations also are available.

The grounds are the site of many events, including a steeplechase, fairs, concerts and the Sky High Hot Air Balloon Festival, held Labor Day weekend. A large man-made sand beach borders Robin Lake, site of the Masters Water Ski & Wakeboard Tournament, a premier water ski tournament that takes place Memorial Day weekend, and shows featuring the Florida State University Flying High Circus (daily except Tues.-Wed., late May-late July). From mid-November through early January, ⬥ Callaway's Fantasy In Lights bedecks Callaway with a holiday display of more than eight million lights.

Time: Allow 4 hours minimum. **Hours:** Gardens open daily 9-6, third Sat. in Mar.-Sun. before Labor Day; 9-5, rest of year. Hours may vary early Jan. Phone ahead to confirm schedule. **Cost:** $20; $15 (ages 65+); $10 (ages 6-12); free (active and retired military with ID and spouse and half-price up to four guests in one vehicle). TreeTop Adventure admission

$35. There are separate fees for selected special events. Phone ahead to confirm rates. **Phone:** (706) 663-2281 or (855) 420-8417. ⬜↑↑ ⬜✗ ⬜⌂

Cecil B. Day Butterfly Center occupies 4.5 acres within Callaway's Meadowlark Gardens. Exotic plants provide a home for more than 1,000 tropical butterflies representing nearly 100 species in the center's octagonal, dome-shaped conservatory. The grounds surrounding the conservatory include plantings designed to attract native butterflies and birds A film documenting the lifecycle of the butterfly and interactive exhibits are available within the center.

Hours: Daily 9-6, third Sat. in Mar.-Sun. before Labor Day; 9-5, rest of year. Hours may vary early Jan. Phone ahead to confirm schedule. **Cost:** Admission is included in the Callaway Gardens entrance fee. **Phone:** (706) 663-2281 or (855) 420-8417.

WILD ANIMAL SAFARI is at 1300 Oak Grove Rd. The 500-acre park exhibits animals from six continents. The collection includes alligators, camels, deer, giraffes, bears, lions, tigers, bison and zebras. Visitors may drive through the park in a private vehicle or tour the park in a Zebra Van or on a narrated tour aboard the Zebra Bus. **Time:** Allow 2 hours minimum. **Hours:** Park open daily 10-7:30, mid-May to mid-Aug.; closing time varies rest of year. Zebra Bus availability varies seasonally; phone ahead. Last admission 1 hour before closing. Closed Christmas. Phone ahead to confirm schedule. **Cost:** $22.95; $19.95 (ages 3-12 and 65+). Additional fee for Zebra Van rental. Phone ahead to confirm rates. **Phone:** (706) 663-8744. ⬜GT ⬜↑↑

RECREATIONAL ACTIVITIES
Horseback Riding
• **Roosevelt Riding Stables** is in Franklin D. Roosevelt State Park at 1063 Group Camp Rd. **Hours:** Tues.-Sun. 10-5 (weather permitting). Last ride begins 1 hour before closing. Reservations are required. **Phone:** (706) 628-7463 for reservations. ⬜GT

CALLAWAY GARDENS - INN, COTTAGES & VILLAS
(706)663-2281

▼▼◆▼ ▼▼
Resort Hotel
$109-$996

Address: 17800 Hwy 27 31822 **Location:** Jct SR 354, 1.5 mi s on US 27/SR 1; in Callaway Gardens. **Facility:** The variety of accommodations include traditional motel-style rooms as well as larger cottages perfect for families. The appealing nostalgic charm of the 1950s design is augmented by modern décor. 241 units, some two bedrooms, three bedrooms, kitchens and cottages. 1-2 stories, interior/exterior corridors. **Terms:** check-in 4 pm, 7 day cancellation notice-fee imposed, resort fee. **Amenities:** Some: safes. **Dining:** 6 restaurants. **Pool(s):** outdoor. **Activities:** beach access, marina, fishing, regulation golf, miniature golf, tennis, recreation programs in summer, bicycles, playground, trails, exercise room. **Guest Services:** valet and coin laundry, area transportation.

⬜SAVE ⬜↑↑ ⬜ ⬜Y ⬜CALL ⬜M ⬜ ⬜BIZ ⬜HS ⬜ ⬜✗
⬜ ⬜ ⬜/SOME UNITS ⬜ ⬜ ⬜

THE LODGE AND SPA AT CALLAWAY GARDENS
(706)663-2281

Resort Hotel
$139-$289

Address: 4500 Southern Pine Dr 31822 **Location:** US 27/SR 1, 2 mi w on SR 354. **Facility:** This beautiful hotel seamlessly combines indoor luxuries with the beauty of the outdoors. Rooms are decorated in rustic charm with furnishing focused on plush comfort. Most rooms overlook the gardens. 149 units. 4 stories, interior corridors. **Parking:** on-site and valet. **Terms:** check-in 4 pm, 7 day cancellation notice-fee imposed, resort fee. **Amenities:** safes. **Pool(s):** heated outdoor. **Activities:** hot tub, regulation golf, recreation programs, spa. **Guest Services:** valet laundry, boarding pass kiosk.

[SAVE] [ECO] [▦] [☎] CALL [⌖M] [⛟] [▥] [BIZ] [HS] [◈]
[✕] [🖥] [▣] /SOME UNITS [▦]

WHITE COLUMNS MOTEL
(706)663-2312

[▼] **Motel.** $59-$79 **Address:** 524 S Main Ave 31822 **Location:** Jct SR 354, just n on US 27/SR 1. **Facility:** 14 units, some kitchens. 1-2 stories (no elevator), exterior corridors. **Terms:** 2 night minimum stay - seasonal and/or weekends, cancellation fee imposed.

[▐▌] [◈] [🖥] [▣] /SOME UNITS [S▪]

WHERE TO EAT

CRICKET'S RESTAURANT
706/663-8136

[▼▼] Cajun. Casual Dining. $5-$25 **AAA Inspector Notes:** Leave the normal hustle and bustle of the city behind and slip into nature at this New Orleans-style restaurant located in the cozy comfort of the woods. Take in a great view of nature while dining on catfish, spicy jambalaya and other Creole specialties. This family-owned restaurant is simple, home grown and filling. **Features:** beer & wine. **Address:** 14661 Hwy 18 W 31822 **Location:** Jct US 27/SR 1, 4 mi w. [L] [D]

PLAINS (D-2) pop. 776, elev. 499'

JIMMY CARTER NATIONAL HISTORIC SITE, 300 N. Bond St., consists of the restored former Plains High School, from which Jimmy and Rosalynn Carter graduated; the Plains Depot, campaign headquarters for Carter's 1976 Presidential Campaign; and the Jimmy Carter Boyhood Farm, 2 miles northwest of Plains. The high school now is a visitor center with a small museum, and a 28-minute orientation film is shown upon request. Other landmarks around Plains include brother Billy Carter's service station and the Carter Peanut Warehouse.

Note: The Carters' current residence is not open to the public. **Hours:** High school museum open daily 9-5. Plains Depot open daily 9-4:30. Farm museum open daily 10-5. Closed Jan. 1, Thanksgiving and Christmas. **Cost:** Free. **Phone:** (229) 824-4104.

Ask about on-the-spot vehicle battery testing and replacement

PLAINS HISTORIC INN
229/824-4517

[▼▼▼] **Bed & Breakfast.** Rates not provided. **Address:** 106 Main St 31780 **Location:** Center. **Facility:** This historic building was restored with the assistance of former President Jimmy Carter and his wife. The first floor houses a small museum commemorating his life along with an antique mall. 7 units. 2 stories, interior corridors. **Parking:** street only. [◈] [✕] [Z]

WHERE TO EAT

BUFFALO CAFE AT THE OLD BANK
229/824-4520

[▼] American. Casual Dining. $4-$10 **AAA Inspector Notes:** In the heart of downtown this family-owned and -operated café makes made-to-order sandwiches and salads. The walls are adorned with yearbook photographs of the town's past graduating classes. **Features:** patio dining. **Address:** 118 Main St 31780 **Location:** Center. [L] [D] [🐄]

POOLER (D-6) pop. 19,140, elev. 23'
• Hotels & Restaurants map & index p. 260

Shopping: [SAVE] Tanger Outlets, off I-95 exit 104 to 200 Tanger Outlet Blvd., features dozens of outlet shops including Coach, Michael Kors, Old Navy and Talbots.

NATIONAL MUSEUM OF THE MIGHTY EIGHTH AIR FORCE is just n.e. of I-95 exit 102 at 175 Bourne Ave. The 90,000-square-foot museum engages visitors in the story of American air power from World War II through today. Features include a World War II era B-17 Flying Fortress, Memorial Gardens, Chapel of the Fallen Eagles, which honors the 26,000 Eighth Air Force members who died in battle during World War II. Also available are Escape and Evasion, a replica of an underground escape network for downed pilots, a research center with a more than 10,000-volume library and archives containing oral histories, period photographs and wartime journals.

Additional exhibits include the Tuskegee Airmen and the Fly Girls of World War II who provided fighter support and relief to Eighth Air Force bombers.

During the "Mission Experience" multimedia presentation, visitors can relive a day in the life of a B-17 crewman; the presentation uses actual footage of a Berlin bombing run. An interactive waist gunner exhibit encourages visitors to test their skills at aerial combat. Static aircraft displayed include a B-17 Flying Fortress, an F-4C Phantom, a B-47 Stratojet Bomber, a Russian-built MiG-17 and a PT-17 Stearman Kaydet bi-plane. Many of the museum's exhibits feature video monitors showing film footage from World War II as well as personal interviews with veterans. Food is available Mon.-Fri. 11-3.

Time: Allow 2 hours minimum. **Hours:** Museum open daily 9-5. Library Tues.-Fri. 9-noon and 1-4. Closed Jan. 1, Easter, Thanksgiving and Christmas. **Cost:** $10; $9 (ages 60+ and retired military); $6 (ages 6-12 and active military); free (World War II veterans). **Phone:** (912) 748-8888. [▐▌]

(See map & index p. 260.)

BEST WESTERN PLUS SAVANNAH AIRPORT INN & SUITES
(912)330-0330

Hotel
$89-$149

Best Western PLUS.

AAA Benefit: Save 10% or more every day and earn 10% bonus points!

Address: 155 Bourne Ave 31322 **Location:** I-95 exit 102 (US 80), just e. Adjacent to Mighty 8th Air Force Museum. **Facility:** 92 units. 3 stories, interior corridors. **Terms:** cancellation fee imposed. **Pool(s):** heated indoor. **Activities:** sauna, hot tub, exercise room. **Guest Services:** coin laundry.

EMBASSY SUITES BY HILTON-SAVANNAH AIRPORT
(912)330-8222 47

Hotel. $129-$299 **Address:** 145 W Mulberry Blvd 31322 **Location:** I-95 exit 104 (Pooler Pkwy), just w, just n on Benton Blvd, then just e. **Facility:** 162 units. 7 stories, interior corridors. **Terms:** check-in 4 pm, 1-7 night minimum stay, cancellation fee imposed. **Pool(s):** heated indoor. **Activities:** hot tub, exercise room. **Guest Services:** valet and coin laundry.

AAA Benefit: Members save 5% or more!

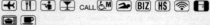

HOLIDAY INN HOTEL & SUITES-SAVANNAH/POOLER
(912)330-5100 50

Hotel
$129-$169

Address: 103 San Dr 31322 **Location:** I-95 exit 102 (US 80), just e. **Facility:** 102 units. 4 stories, interior corridors. **Terms:** check-in 4 pm, 3 day cancellation notice-fee imposed, resort fee. **Amenities:** safes. **Pool(s):** heated indoor. **Activities:** hot tub, exercise room. **Guest Services:** valet and coin laundry, area transportation.

LA QUINTA INN & SUITES SAVANNAH AIRPORT-POOLER
(912)748-3771 49

Hotel. $90-$225 **Address:** 414 Gray St 31322 **Location:** I-95 exit 102 (US 80), just w. **Facility:** 63 units. 3 stories, interior corridors. **Pool(s):** outdoor. **Activities:** hot tub, exercise room. **Guest Services:** valet and coin laundry.

MAGNOLIA INN
912/748-6883 51

Hotel. Rates not provided. **Address:** 107 San Dr 31322 **Location:** I-95 exit 102 (US 80), just w and s. **Facility:** 40 units. 2 stories, interior corridors. **Bath:** shower only. **Amenities:** safes. **Pool(s):** indoor. **Guest Services:** valet and coin laundry.

WHERE TO EAT

BAHAMA BOB'S
912/748-7777 49

Seafood. Casual Dining. $8-$20 **AAA Inspector Notes:** First a warning, there is no effort to diminish the smoke odor in the restaurant and it is active and everywhere. Now that that is out of the way, the food is good. The menu offers steamed, fried and grilled dishes featuring seafood, steaks, pork chops and chicken. Also listed are sandwiches and soups with Bob's signature seafood chowder. **Features:** full bar, happy hour. **Address:** 111 Canal St 31322 **Location:** I-95 exit 104 (Pooler Pkwy), 0.7 mi sw; in Canal Street Plaza.

B & D BURGERS BAR & GRILL
912/988-5560 48

Burgers Sandwiches. Casual Dining. $8-$17 **AAA Inspector Notes:** Naturally, it is all about the burger here. Made from Angus beef, turkey, bison or vegetarian, the burgers are available in one-third and half-pound portions. There also are a few sandwiches and signature dogs. Guests can opt for one of the many standard selections or choose to build their own from a lengthy list of topping, bun styles and sides. For those up to a challenge, try to devour a three-pound triple decker and one pound of fries in 35 minutes. **Features:** full bar, patio dining, happy hour. **Address:** 238 Pooler Pkwy, Suite G 31322 **Location:** I-95 exit 104 (Pooler Pkwy), just w; in Towne Plaza.

FATZ
912/748-2557

Regional American. Casual Dining. $6-$20 **AAA Inspector Notes:** Friendly staff and appealing country decor help set the tone for a relaxed and enjoyable dining experience. It's not unusual for guests to wait to be seated at the popular spot, which earns raves for its well-prepared variations on chicken, steak, ribs and pasta, as well as salads and sandwiches. The signature Southern-style peach cobbler served with vanilla ice cream and walnuts is scrumptious. **Features:** full bar, happy hour. **Address:** 400 Pooler Pkwy 31322 **Location:** I-95 exit 104 (Pooler Pkwy), just w.

GUERRERO MEXICAN RESTAURANT
912/748-9711 55

Mexican. Casual Dining. $4-$14 **AAA Inspector Notes:** This small, neat restaurant offers a complete lineup of well-prepared Mexican standards. An all-you-can-eat buffet is available at lunch along with a large selection of inexpensive combination dishes. The full service menu is offered during the buffet but do not expect much attentiveness. The food quality here makes the stop worthwhile. **Features:** full bar, happy hour. **Address:** 1109A E Hwy 80 31322 **Location:** I-95 exit 102 (US 80), 0.6 mi se; in Pooler Commons Shopping Center.

JALAPENO'S AUTHENTIC MEXICAN GRILL
912/988-3017 47

Mexican. Casual Dining. $8-$15 **AAA Inspector Notes:** Located across the street from the Tanger Outlets this popular cantina provides fast service and good food at reasonable prices. The menu is lengthy but contains the usual suspects with some twists like deviled shrimp, seasoned fries topped with beef and cheese with pico de gallo, spicy fish or shrimp ceviche and the Mexican egg burrito. I had the chicken soup, always a favorite on a hot day, and the huge and delicious beef fajita chimichanga. **Features:** full bar, happy hour. **Address:** 226 Pooler Pkwy 31322 **Location:** I-95 exit 104 (Pooler Pkwy), just w; in Towne Plaza.

LOS BRAVOS GRILL & CANTINA
912/748-4333 54

Tex-Mex. Casual Dining. $6-$15 **AAA Inspector Notes:** Typical fare without any menu surprises can be found at this grill. Many specialty entrées are loaded with cheese, while popular dishes like fajitas are sizable—so come hungry. What makes this place worth the trip is the staff. They are super attentive, hugely friendly and eager to please—no worries about empty beverages or having to eat something not enjoyable as they take care of everything. **Features:** full bar, happy hour. **Address:** 1108 US Hwy 80 E, Suite 600 31322 **Location:** I-95 exit 102 (US 80), 0.6 mi se.

Ask about AAA/CAA Associate membership
to share the benefits you value

(See map & index p. 260.)

LOVEZZOLA'S PIZZA RESTAURANT 912/748-6414 51
▼ Pizza Sandwiches. Casual Dining. $5-$15 **AAA Inspector Notes:** Sheltered by large old oaks, this little pizzeria, with colorful awnings and red-and-white-checkered tablecloths, serves excellent homemade pizza, an endless variety of hot and cold sandwiches and a few popular pasta dishes including lasagna, ravioli and spaghetti. A buffet is available at lunch daily and on Sunday night and a trip to the salad bar is offered with each dine-in entrée. Evening specials are offered as well. **Features:** beer & wine. **Address:** 320 E Hwy 80 31322 **Location:** I-95 exit 102 (US 80), just nw. L D

MEDITERRANEAN TAVERN 912/988-1052 43
▼▼ Mediterranean. Casual Dining. $8-$26 **AAA Inspector Notes:** Along with the standard lineup of Greek and Italian fare at this tavern, there is an adjacent hookah lounge and cigar bar that operates during the dinner hour. The menu features pasta dishes, lamb skewers, grilled steaks, seafood and sandwiches. During lunch the offerings are limited to salads, wraps and sandwiches. For those in a rush, call ahead for lunch and it will be waiting at your table when you arrive. All desserts are heavenly and made from scratch on site. **Features:** full bar, patio dining, happy hour. **Address:** 125 Foxfield Way, Suite 8 31322 **Location:** I-95 exit 104 (Pooler Pkwy), just w to Benton Blvd, then just n; in Towne Plaza. L D CALL &M

MIWA JAPANESE RESTAURANT 912/748-8228 42
▼▼ Japanese Sushi. Casual Dining. $6-$19 **AAA Inspector Notes:** Casual, cozy and relaxing describes the experience at this eatery. The menu features teriyaki, yakiniku and katsu preparations of chicken, steak and a few seafood items as well as a wide variety of made-to-order sushi. Arrive early, the restaurant tends to fill fast. **Features:** beer & wine, happy hour. **Address:** 125 Foxfield Way Towne Plaza, Suite 5 31322 **Location:** I-95 exit 104 (Pooler Pkwy), just w to Benton Blvd, then just n; in Towne Plaza. L D

MOLLY MACPHERSON'S SCOTTISH PUB & GRILL 912/348-3200 44
▼▼ Scottish. Casual Dining. $8-$18 **AAA Inspector Notes:** The pub décor and atmosphere add to the enjoyment of this casual, carefree dining experience. The restaurant boasts a large and varied selection of single malt Scotch whisky and a menu that includes an array of Scottish pub fare, such as bangers and mash and shepherd's pie, as well as more traditional American entrées. Service, while informal, is attentive. Do not forget to bring your darts for a round or two. Special events are presented nightly. Children are welcome. **Features:** full bar, patio dining, happy hour. **Address:** 110 Towne Center Dr 31322 **Location:** I-95 exit 104 (Pooler Pkwy), just w, just n on Benton Blvd; in Towne Center Entertainment Center. L D CALL &M

NAAN APPETIT 912/348-2446 50
▼▼ Indian. Casual Dining. $11-$14 **AAA Inspector Notes:** If you're a devotee of this cuisine or a beginner you won't be disappointed with the superior quality of the food that comes out of this kitchen or the friendly staff. The menu features the standard line-up of traditional tandoori dishes, stews and roasts each accompanied by a piquant sauce which is seasoned to your liking. There is also a list of fresh made breads that shouldn't be overlooked. **Features:** beer & wine. **Address:** 1024 US Hwy 80 W, Suite 118 31322 **Location:** I-95 exit 102 (US 80), 1.7 mi nw; in Pooler Park West. L D CALL &M

SAVANNAH GYRO 912/748-0675 52
▼ Sandwiches Burgers. Quick Serve. $3-$9 **AAA Inspector Notes:** This is a simple grab-and-go or dine-in sandwich shack, but don't let the gyro moniker make it seem like it's limited to Greek food only. On the menu are fresh salads, burgers, hot dogs, po'boys, subs, wraps, wings and nachos. It is a great stop for the weary traveler who's just looking for a quick bite to take back to the room. **Address:** 217 Hwy 80 E 31322 **Location:** I-95 exit 102 (US 80), just nw. L D

SMOKIN PIG THE BAR-B-Q-JOINT 912/330-0192 56
▼ Barbecue. Quick Serve. $5-$19 **AAA Inspector Notes:** For those seeking barbecue but are pressed for time, get a pulled pork sandwich or spare ribs quickly at this barbecue joint, or get a chicken and rib combo plate. Staple side dishes of macaroni and cheese, loaded baked potatoes, baked beans and banana pudding are offered. **Address:** 1215 Hwy 80 E, Suite 100 31322 **Location:** I-95 exit 102 (US 80), 1 mi se; in Coastal Crossing Shopping Center. L D

SPANKY'S PIZZA GALLEY & SALOON 912/748-8188 57
▼▼ American. Casual Dining. $9-$24 **AAA Inspector Notes:** This lively and busy restaurant offers a wide variety of American favorites infused with some international cuisine. The steaks, seafood, burgers and sandwiches are joined by pasta dishes, pizza, quesadillas and wraps on the long list of options. Whatever is chosen, do not miss the Brunswick stew, a classic and absolutely delicious. For a big appetite, try the all-in platter which comes with crab cakes, scallops, shrimp and the fresh catch. **Features:** full bar, patio dining, happy hour. **Address:** 1221 E Hwy 80 31322 **Location:** I-95 exit 102 (US 80), 0.8 mi se. L D CALL &M

SUSHI HANA 912/988-1085 45
▼▼ Japanese Sushi. Casual Dining. $4-$25 **AAA Inspector Notes:** Located across from the Tanger Outlet, this is a great spot to dine after a long day of shopping. The sushi menu runs for pages so diners certainly can find something to enjoy. If sushi is not your pick, there also is a full traditional Japanese menu featuring teriyaki, tempura, entrée soups and noodle dishes prepared with a choice of meat, seafood or vegetable. The surroundings are exotic, the food is wonderful and if you like sake there is a wide variety to select from, warm or cold. **Features:** full bar, happy hour. **Address:** 238 Pooler Pkwy, Suite B 31322 **Location:** I-95 exit 104 (Pooler Pkwy), just w. L D CALL &M

TERRA MIA 912/748-1702 53
▼▼ Italian Pizza. Casual Dining. $9-$24 **AAA Inspector Notes:** Don't let the fast food facade fool you, the quality of the food you'll get here is outstanding. The owner has other long successful restaurants in Charleston and Savannah, and he brings the same quality and service to Pooler guests. The menu features well prepared Italian standards like fettuccine Alfredo, spaghetti and meatballs, veal Parmesan, pizza and salads. The sauces are rich and authentic, and during the lunch period you can also order panini if you need a quick bite. **Features:** beer & wine, patio dining. **Address:** 1009 US 80 E 31322 **Location:** I-95 exit 102 (US 80), just e. L D

WORLD OF BEER 912/348-3079 46
▼▼ Small Plates Sandwiches. Gastropub. $8-$15 **AAA Inspector Notes:** It goes without saying that guests will not have any trouble finding a favorite beer here—there are more than 500 available with 40 on tap. The menu comes complete with pairing suggestions to enjoy distinctive tavern grub with the perfect suds. Some options include a sausage board, spicy macaroni and cheese, fish tacos, burgers and sandwiches and wings. Consider the huge German pretzel with beer cheddar dip—you will not want to share. **Features:** full bar, patio dining, Sunday brunch, happy hour. **Address:** 238 Pooler Pkwy, Suite A 31322 **Location:** I-95 exit 104 (Pooler Pkwy), just w. L D LATE CALL &M

PORT WENTWORTH (D-6) pop. 5,359, elev. 23'
• Hotels & Restaurants map & index p. 260

Ten miles upstream from Savannah, Port Wentworth accesses the 29,175-acre Savannah National Wildlife Refuge (see attraction listing p. 253), an area composed largely of marshes, tidal rivers and creeks in both Georgia and South Carolina. The refuge is home to such threatened and endangered species as wood storks and manatees, as well as more common residents like ducks, wading and shorebirds, turkeys, deer and the American alligator. Bird-watching opportunities, plentiful all year, are especially rewarding in April, when birds that have wintered at the refuge are about to migrate and birds already on a migratory journey use the refuge as a stopover.

A great way to experience the refuge is via Laurel Hill Wildlife Drive, 1 mile east of Port Wentworth off North Coastal Highway/US 17. This scenic drive follows 4 miles of earthen dikes through freshwater pools; fishing from the dike banks is permissible

(See map & index p. 260.)

year-round. Fishing elsewhere is permitted on a seasonal basis, as is hunting waterfowl, turkeys, deer and feral hogs. Defined time periods are set aside for archery and gun hunts. For 2 days in November, several areas are specifically designated for use by wheelchair-dependent hunters.

For more information contact the Savannah Coastal Refuges, 694 Beech Hill Ln., Hardeeville, SC 29927; phone (843) 784-2468 Mon.-Sat. 9-4.

Port Wentworth Chamber of Commerce/Welcome Center: 7532 SR 21, Port Wentworth, GA 31407. **Phone:** (912) 965-1999.

BEST WESTERN PLUS NORTH SAVANNAH
(912)964-0840 **44**

Hotel
$90-$100

Best Western PLUS AAA Benefit: Save 10% or more every day and earn 10% bonus points!

Address: 115 O' Leary Rd 31407 **Location:** I-95 exit 109 (SR 21), just s, then just n. **Facility:** 83 units. 4 stories, interior corridors. **Amenities:** safes. **Pool(s):** outdoor. **Activities:** exercise room. **Guest Services:** valet and coin laundry. **Featured Amenity: full hot breakfast.**

COMFORT SUITES SAVANNAH NORTH (912)965-1445 **41**
Hotel. $89-$179 **Address:** 115 Travelers Way 31407 **Location:** I-95 exit 109 (SR 21), just n. **Facility:** 83 units. 3 stories, interior corridors. **Pool(s):** heated indoor. **Activities:** hot tub, exercise room. **Guest Services:** valet and coin laundry.

COUNTRY INN & SUITES BY CARLSON SAVANNAH NORTH
912/964-2300 **42**
Hotel. Rates not provided. **Address:** 200 Raley Rd 31407 **Location:** I-95 exit 109 (SR 21), just s. **Facility:** 61 units. 3 stories, interior corridors. **Pool(s):** heated indoor. **Activities:** hot tub, exercise room. **Guest Services:** valet and coin laundry.

HAMPTON INN SAVANNAH NORTH (912)966-2000 **43**
Hotel. $115-$219 **Address:** 7050 Hwy 21 31407 **Location:** I-95 exit 109 (SR 21), just s. **Facility:** 106 units. 3 stories, interior corridors. **Terms:** 1-7 night minimum stay, cancellation fee imposed. **Pool(s):** outdoor. **Activities:** exercise room. **Guest Services:** valet laundry.

AAA Benefit: Members save up to 10%!

HOLIDAY INN EXPRESS SAVANNAH NORTH
(912)964-8900 **39**
Hotel. $119-$189 **Address:** 7210 Hwy 21 31407 **Location:** I-95 exit 109 (SR 21), just n. **Facility:** 82 units. 2 stories, interior corridors. **Terms:** cancellation fee imposed, resort fee. **Pool(s):** outdoor. **Activities:** exercise room. **Guest Services:** valet and coin laundry.

SLEEP INN I-95 NORTH SAVANNAH (912)966-9800 **40**
Hotel. $59-$129 **Address:** 7206 Hwy 21 N 31407 **Location:** I-95 exit 109 (SR 21), just n. **Facility:** 84 units. 2 stories (no elevator), interior corridors. **Amenities:** safes. **Pool(s):** outdoor. **Guest Services:** coin laundry.

WHERE TO EAT

DELI MART NORTH 912/777-6298
Sandwiches Pizza. Quick Serve. $5-$13 **AAA Inspector Notes:** This deli serves surprisingly flavorful pizza and sandwiches as well as burgers, wings and salads. At lunchtime enjoy an inexpensive pizza buffet and salad bar. The pizza goes fast, so it's always freshly made. **Features:** beer only. **Address:** 7306 Hwy 21, Suite 204 31407 **Location:** I-95 exit 109 (SR 21), 0.5 mi n to SR 30, then just e; in shopping center. **L D**

EL RANCHITO 912/965-0270
Mexican. Casual Dining. $6-$15 **AAA Inspector Notes:** This storefront restaurant features a menu with the typical fare expected but with a few surprises such as a wide selection of vegetarian dishes and build-your-own plates from a mix-and-match menu selection. Food is well prepared and the staff is fun and friendly. **Features:** full bar, patio dining, happy hour. **Address:** 7306 Hwy 21, Suite 201 31407 **Location:** I-95 exit 109 (SR 21), 0.5 mi n to SR 30, then just e; in shopping center. **L D** CALL **M**

PORT SIDE SEAFOOD 912/964-2722 **38**
Seafood Sandwiches. Casual Dining. $10-$22 **AAA Inspector Notes:** Just off the interstate, this full-service restaurant offers a variety of local seafood dishes, including clams, crab, fish, scallops and shrimp. Also available are a few pasta dishes, burgers, po'boys and salads. Consider trying the fried catfish, a house specialty. Tuesday is taco night, Thursday night is all you can eat crab legs, and various other specials are offered throughout the week. Live entertainment can be found on most weekends. **Features:** full bar, patio dining, happy hour. **Address:** 7202 Hwy 21 31407 **Location:** I-95 exit 109 (SR 21), just n. **L D LATE**

SWEET TEA GRILLE 912/200-4480 **39**
Southern. Casual Dining. $9-$20 **AAA Inspector Notes:** The diverse menu here has something for everyone, and the friendly staff will have diners coming back for more. The food is freshly prepared and it all is awesome. I started with the grilled pimiento-stuffed jalapeños wrapped in bacon—not too spicy but very flavorful. I then moved on to chicken and sausage gumbo and polished off the meal with voodoo pasta. Everything was absolutely great and my server was anxious to know how I enjoyed my meal. Free Wi-Fi is available. **Features:** full bar, patio dining, happy hour. **Address:** 109 Travelers Way 31407 **Location:** I-95 exit 109 (SR 21), just n. **L D** CALL **M**

RICHMOND HILL (D-6) pop. 9,281, elev. 17'
• Hotels p. 238 • Restaurants p. 238

Once known as Ways Station, a winter home for industrialist Henry Ford, Richmond Hill was incorporated in 1962. A few miles north of Richmond Hill, US 17 crosses the Ogeechee River near the site of the Battle of Kings Ferry, an audacious 18th-century defeat of the British by a Colonial colonel, two other officers and three enlisted men. Using widely spaced watch fires and misleading shouts to imaginary sentinels, the Americans convinced the British commander that they vastly outnumbered the five ships and 130 men intended to capture Savannah.

Riding alone into the British camp the next morning, the American leader informed the British commander that the bloodthirsty Colonial soldiers would accept nothing but unconditional surrender. The erstwhile invader handed over his entire force, which was marched away by the lone American while the other five followed behind to restrain their nonexistent restless troops.

Richmond Hill Convention & Visitors Bureau: 2591 Hwy. 17, Suite 100, Richmond Hill, GA 31324. **Phone:** (912) 756-2676.

FORT MCALLISTER STATE PARK is 4.5 mi. s.e. on SR 144, then 4 mi. e. on SR 144 Spur to 3894 Fort McAllister Rd. On a bank of the Great Ogeechee River, the fort is an example of Confederate earthwork fortifications; it withstood bombardments by the Union navy on Mar. 3, 1863. The fort finally fell before Gen. William Tecumseh Sherman's army on Dec. 13, 1864. A museum contains exhibits and artifacts. *See Recreation Areas Chart.*

Hours: Park open daily 7 a.m.-10 p.m. Museum and fort open daily 8-5. Guided tours are given daily at 2. Historical presentations are given most Fri.-Sun. at 10; phone ahead to confirm schedule. Museum and fort closed Thanksgiving and Christmas. **Cost:** $9; $8 (ages 62+); $5 (ages 6-17); $2 (ages 2-5). **Parking:** $5. **Phone:** (912) 727-2339.

BEST WESTERN PLUS RICHMOND HILL INN
(912)756-7070

Hotel
$69-$159

AAA Benefit: Save 10% or more every day and earn 10% bonus points!

Address: 4564 Hwy 17 31324 **Location:** I-95 exit 87 (Ocean Hwy/US 17), just w. **Facility:** 59 units. 3 stories, interior corridors. **Pool(s):** heated indoor. **Activities:** hot tub, game room, exercise room. **Guest Services:** coin laundry. **Featured Amenity:** full hot breakfast. *(See ad p. 265.)*

BW Best Western PLUS. 40 Item Breakfast Buffet. Nightly "Nacho's Social Hour" & Fresh Baked Cookies. Dining options nearby

ECONO LODGE-RICHMOND HILL
(912)756-3312

Motel
$56-$130

Address: 4701 US 17 31324 **Location:** I-95 exit 87 (Ocean Hwy/US 17), 0.4 mi sw. **Facility:** 47 units. 2 stories (no elevator), exterior corridors. **Guest Services:** coin laundry. **Featured Amenity:** continental breakfast.

Choose real ratings you can trust from professional inspectors who've been there

HAMPTON INN
(912)756-2272

Hotel
$99-$194

AAA Benefit: Members save up to 10%!

Address: 4679 US Hwy 17 31324 **Location:** I-95 exit 87 (Ocean Hwy/US 17), 0.4 mi sw. **Facility:** 64 units. 3 stories, interior corridors. **Terms:** 1-7 night minimum stay, cancellation fee imposed. **Pool(s):** outdoor. **Activities:** exercise room. **Guest Services:** coin laundry.

HOLIDAY INN EXPRESS
(912)756-6668

Hotel
$99-$199

Address: 4601 US Hwy 17 31324 **Location:** I-95 exit 87 (Ocean Hwy/US 17), 0.4 mi sw. **Facility:** 65 units. 3 stories, interior corridors. **Terms:** cancellation fee imposed. **Pool(s):** outdoor. **Activities:** sauna, hot tub, exercise room. **Guest Services:** coin laundry. **Featured Amenity:** full hot breakfast.

WHERE TO EAT

MELODY'S COASTAL CAFE   912/459-6357

Burgers Sandwiches. Casual Dining. $9-$19 **AAA Inspector Notes:** Stop in for some Southern hospitality and a tasty bite. The menu features sandwiches, po'boys, burgers, tacos, wings, baskets and blue plate specials like the cowboy cut bone-in rib-eye and the lamb shank over grits. I had the banh mi sandwich, which was rich and flavorful with a nice hint of spice. Give it a try. You'll fall in love with the friendly staff and the food. **Features:** full bar, happy hour. **Address:** 2518 US Hwy 17 31324 **Location:** Jct SR 144 and US 17/SR 25, just sw.   L D

MOLLY MACPHERSON'S SCOTTISH PUB & GRILL
912/459-9600

Scottish. Gastropub. $9-$18 **AAA Inspector Notes:** The pub décor and atmosphere add to the enjoyment of this casual, care-free dining experience. The restaurant boasts a large and varied selection of single malt scotches and a menu that includes an array of Scottish pub fare, including bangers and mash and shepherd's pie, as well as more traditional American entrées. Service, while informal, is attentive. Do not forget to bring your darts for a round or two. Special events nightly. Children welcome. **Features:** full bar, patio dining, happy hour. **Address:** 3742 Hwy 17 S 31324 **Location:** I-95 exit 87 (Ocean Hwy/US 17), 0.5 mi ne; in Park South Plaza.   L D CALL

SMOKIN PIG THE BAR-B-Q-JOINT   912/756-7850

Barbecue. Quick Serve. $5-$19 **AAA Inspector Notes:** For those seeking barbecue but are pressed for time, get a pulled pork sandwich or spare ribs quickly at this barbecue joint. Staple side dishes of macaroni and cheese, baked beans and banana pudding are offered along with a tasty Brunswick stew. Bulk orders available if you want to carry some home or get ready to tailgate. **Features:** patio dining. **Address:** 3986 Hwy 17 31324 **Location:** I-95 exit 87 (Ocean Hwy/US 17), just e.   L D

SOUTHERN IMAGE RESTAURANT   912/756-3535

Comfort Food. Casual Dining. $4-$20 **AAA Inspector Notes:** The accent here is on Southern preparations of chicken, fried seafood, steaks and sandwiches. Daily multi-course buffet lunch and dinner specials are popular and reasonably priced. A full a la carte menu is available as well as steaks and chops. With a casual, relaxed and friendly atmosphere, guests always are welcome. **Features:** senior menu. **Address:** 3881 Coastal Hwy 31324 **Location:** I-95 exit 87 (Ocean Hwy/US 17), just e.   B L D CALL

THE UPPER CRUST 912/756-6990

◆ Italian. Casual Dining. $5-$21 **AAA Inspector Notes:** This comfortable, family spot is all about the pizza though a few Italian pasta dishes also are available. Cold drinks are served in mason jars fitting the country theme of the décor. **Features:** beer & wine. **Address:** 1702 US 17 31324 **Location:** I-95 exit 87 (Ocean Hwy/US 17), 2.5 mi ne. [L] [D]

RINGGOLD pop. 3,580

HAMPTON INN (706)935-4800

Hotel
$109-$169

AAA Benefit: Members save up to 10%!

Address: 6875 Battlefield Pkwy 30736 **Location:** I-75 exit 350, just e to Smitherman Rd, then just n. **Facility:** 78 units. 4 stories, interior corridors. **Terms:** 1-7 night minimum stay, cancellation fee imposed. **Pool(s):** heated indoor. **Activities:** hot tub, exercise room. **Guest Services:** coin laundry. **Featured Amenity:** full hot breakfast.

[SAVE] CALL [&M] [⌨] [BIZ] [HS] [📶]

HOMETOWN INN 706/937-7070

◆◆ **Hotel**
Rates not provided

Address: 22 Gateway Business Park Dr 30736 **Location:** I-75 exit 350, just e to Smitherman Rd, then just n. **Facility:** 40 units, some efficiencies. 2 stories, interior corridors. **Pool(s):** outdoor. **Guest Services:** coin laundry.

[SAVE] CALL [&M] [⌨] [BIZ] [HS] [📶]

/ SOME UNITS

SUPER 8 RINGGOLD (706)965-7080

◆ **Hotel.** $60-$70 **Address:** 5400 Alabama Hwy 30736 **Location:** I-75 exit 348, just e. **Facility:** 40 units. 2 stories (no elevator), exterior corridors.

[†+] CALL [&M] [📶] [🖥] [⌨] / SOME UNITS [🔒] [HS]

WHERE TO EAT

BAILEY'S BBQ 706/935-2969

◆◆ Barbecue. Casual Dining. $7-$15 **AAA Inspector Notes:** Travelers from all around stop here to sample some of the best barbecue in north Georgia. The pulled pork is delicious and comes in a sandwich or as a plate. The ribs and beef come highly recommended as well. Sides include baked beans, tater tots, onion rings and french fries. Meat and three lunch specials are available throughout the week and the pies (chocolate, coconut and pecan) are a must. **Address:** 5540 US 41 30736 **Location:** I-75 exit 350, 2 mi e to US 41, then 0.7 mi n. [B] [L] [D]

ROCKMART pop. 4,199

LINDA'S PLACE 770/684-3467

◆◆ Southern. Casual Dining. $4-$8 **AAA Inspector Notes:** Come get some down-home Southern fare. You can choose from the standard soups, salads, sandwiches, burgers and hot dogs, but it's always worth considering daily lunch-plate specials such as fried chicken and meatloaf. Pair them with vegetables such as collards, lima beans, mashed potatoes or corn. Give in to the temptation of pecan pie. The staff carries out competent service. **Address:** 480 Nathan Dean Pkwy 30153 **Location:** Jct US 278 and SR 101, 1 mi w. [B] [L]

ROME (B-1) pop. 36,303, elev. 603'
• Hotels p. 240 • Restaurants p. 240

Rome's name is apt, for like its Italian counterpart it is built upon seven hills. The city was founded in 1834 when three men stopped to provide water for their horses where the Etowah and Oostanaula rivers become the Coosa River. The men laid out a townsite and drew a name for it from a hat.

Rome's importance to the Confederacy as a rail and manufacturing center led to the 1863 ride of John Wisdom. Wearing out five horses and a mule in 11 hours, Wisdom rode 67 miles from Alabama to Rome to warn of an impending Union attack. A giant cannon lathe atop Civic Center Hill survived even Gen. William Tecumseh Sherman. Marks made by the sledgehammers of Union soldiers who tried to destroy it can be seen on the lathe's sides.

There are other reminders of the past, including Boswell Cabin, a mid-19th-century log house; a cotton gin next to the lathe; and Myrtle Hill Cemetery that contains 368 Confederate and Union graves and those of two of Rome's founders. Ellen Louise Axson Wilson, wife of President Woodrow Wilson, also is buried in this cemetery. A map of the 40 types of trees in the cemetery is available from the Rome-Floyd Visitor Center (402 Civic Center Dr.) and the Downtown Welcome Center (300 W. 1st St.). Atop the water tower on another of the city's seven hills is the Old Town Clock, dating from 1871.

Early 20th-century houses and commercial buildings can be seen in downtown Rome along Broad Street. In front of City Hall is the Capitoline Wolf, a bronze replica of the Roman statue depicting a she-wolf nursing Romulus and Remus, the legendary founders of Rome, Italy. It was given to the city by the Italian government in 1929.

Rome-Floyd Visitor Center: 402 Civic Center Dr., Rome, GA 30161. **Phone:** (706) 295-5576 or (800) 444-1834.

CHIEFTAINS MUSEUM/MAJOR RIDGE HOME, 501 Riverside Pkwy., is the early 19th-century home of Cherokee leader Major Ridge, who struggled to maintain his Native American heritage while adapting to the white man's culture. Ridge is best known for his leadership of the Treaty Party in the years preceding the Cherokee removal from their homeland. Ridge was killed in 1839 by Cherokee who felt betrayed by the Treaty Party. The original early 19th-century log cabin remains at the center of this gracious mansion. On display is A Witness to History, an exhibit that documents the history of the house.

Hours: Wed.-Sat. 10-5. Closed major holidays. **Cost:** $5; $3 (ages 62+); $2 (students with ID). **Phone:** (706) 291-9494.

GEM ◆ **OAK HILL AND THE MARTHA BERRY MUSEUM** are 3 mi. n. on US 27/SR 1 (Martha Berry Blvd.) to 24 Veterans Memorial Hwy. N.E. on the campus of Berry College. Oak Hill was the home of Martha Berry, a cotton broker's daughter who began teaching local children in a one-room log cabin in the late 19th century. Her school eventually developed into Berry College, and her former home is furnished and maintained as it was during her lifetime.

The Martha Berry Museum contains memorabilia of the school and its founder, including paintings, portraits of philanthropists and furniture made by students. Three exhibit rooms chronicle Miss Berry's life. Visitors can take a guided tour of Oak Hill and a tour of five gardens, including a sunken garden with Japanese cherry trees. The college's 28,000-acre campus, near Oak Hill on US 27, also features nature trails, buildings constructed by students and a gristmill with a 42-foot wheel, said to be one of the largest in the world.

Time: Allow 2 hours minimum. **Hours:** Open Mon.-Sat. 10-5. Last tour begins at 3:30. Closed major holidays, Sat. preceding Mon. holidays, during the university Christmas break and during special events; phone ahead to confirm tour availability. **Cost:** $8; $7 (ages 55+); $5 (students); free (ages 0-5). **Phone:** (706) 368-6789. GT

ROME AREA HISTORY MUSEUM is at 305 Broad St. in the city's historic section. Organized in chronological order, the museum's exhibits form a historical timeline beginning with the Native Americans, the region's original inhabitants, and proceeding to the founding of Floyd County and Rome. Through original blueprints, maps and photographs, visitors can trace how Rome grew during the 1800s.

Hours: Wed.-Fri. 10-4; Sat. 11-2. Guided tours are available with advance reservations. Phone to confirm holiday schedule. **Cost:** Free. **Phone:** (706) 235-8051. GT

BEST WESTERN EXECUTIVE INN   (706)234-3161

Motel
$59-$79

AAA Benefit: Save 10% or more every day and earn 10% bonus points!

Address: 217 Hwy 411 E 30161 **Location:** 2.3 mi e. **Facility:** 45 units. 2 stories (no elevator), exterior corridors. **Pool(s):** outdoor. **Guest Services:** valet laundry.

COMFORT SUITES   (706)232-6055
Hotel. $79-$189 **Address:** 23 Chateau Dr 30161 **Location:** 2 mi e on US 411. **Facility:** 64 units, some two bedrooms. 3 stories, interior corridors. **Pool(s):** heated indoor. **Activities:** hot tub, exercise room. **Guest Services:** valet and coin laundry.

COUNTRY INN & SUITES BY CARLSON   (706)232-3380
Hotel. $94-$139 **Address:** 15 Hobson Way SE 30161 **Location:** 2.3 mi e. **Facility:** 60 units. 3 stories, interior corridors. **Terms:** cancellation fee imposed. **Pool(s):** outdoor. **Activities:** exercise room. **Guest Services:** valet and coin laundry.

DAYS INN ROME   (706)295-0400
Hotel. $66-$99 **Address:** 840 Turner McCall Blvd 30161 **Location:** On SR 20 and US 27; downtown. **Facility:** 105 units. 5 stories, interior corridors. **Amenities:** safes. **Pool(s):** outdoor. **Activities:** exercise room. **Guest Services:** coin laundry.

HAMPTON INN   706/232-9551
Hotel. Rates not provided. **Address:** 21 Chateau Dr 30161 **Location:** 2 mi e on US 411. **Facility:** 64 units. 2 stories, interior corridors. **Pool(s):** outdoor. **Activities:** exercise room. **Guest Services:** valet and coin laundry.

AAA Benefit: Members save up to 10%!

HAMPTON INN & SUITES DOWNTOWN ROME   (706)622-5631
Hotel. $109-$189 **Address:** 875 W 1st St 30161 **Location:** US 27, 2.1 mi w. **Facility:** 90 units. 5 stories, interior corridors. **Terms:** 1-7 night minimum stay, cancellation fee imposed. **Pool(s):** heated indoor. **Activities:** exercise room.

AAA Benefit: Members save up to 10%!

HAWTHORN SUITES BY WYNDHAM ROME   (706)378-4837
Hotel. $126-$225 **Address:** 100-110 W 2nd Ave 30161 **Location:** Downtown. **Facility:** 65 units, some efficiencies and kitchens. Interior corridors. **Amenities:** safes. **Dining:** 2 restaurants. **Activities:** exercise room. **Guest Services:** valet and coin laundry.

HOLIDAY INN EXPRESS & SUITES   (706)232-0021
Hotel. $119-$149 **Address:** 35 Hobson Way 30161 **Location:** 2.3 mi e. **Facility:** 81 units. 4 stories, interior corridors. **Terms:** cancellation fee imposed. **Activities:** exercise room. **Guest Services:** valet and coin laundry.

LA QUINTA INN & SUITES   (706)291-1034
Hotel. $67-$174 **Address:** 15 Chateau Dr 30161 **Location:** 2 mi e on US 411. **Facility:** 48 units. 3 stories, interior corridors. **Pool(s):** outdoor. **Activities:** exercise room. **Guest Services:** valet and coin laundry.

QUALITY INN   (706)291-7797
Hotel. $69-$163 **Address:** 40 Grace Dr 30161 **Location:** 2.2 mi e on US 411. **Facility:** 67 units. 3 stories, interior corridors. **Pool(s):** heated indoor. **Activities:** exercise room.

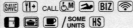

HARVEST MOON   706/292-0099
Southern. Casual Dining. $6-$23 **AAA Inspector Notes:** You will find delicious, fresh homemade food with a flair here. Favorites include fried catfish, hot pimento cheese with tortilla chips for dipping, roasted barbecue pork and meat and veggie plates as well as many other veggie dishes. You can also build your own sandwich by choosing a protein, a bread, a topping and add a cheese. Burgers, meatloaf, Carolina crab cakes and fish or shrimp tacos are other options. Outdoor dining is available, too. **Features:** full bar, Sunday brunch. **Address:** 234 Broad St 30161 **Location:** Downtown. **Parking:** street only. L D

LA SCALA MEDITERRANEAN RESTAURANT   706/238-9000
Italian. Casual Dining. $8-$32 **AAA Inspector Notes:** Located among the charm of historic downtown, this is a popular date night restaurant with a focus on classic Italian dishes such as risotto, linguine and clams, ravioli, and lasagna. The lounge is a popular place to socialize and occasionally features live music. **Features:** full bar. **Address:** 413 Broad St 30161 **Location:** Jct SR 27 and Broad St. D

THE SHRIMP BOAT 706/291-7500

▼ Seafood. Quick Serve. $5-$10 **AAA Inspector Notes:** This modest restaurant is a fisherman's delight with a plethora of fish-inspired knickknacks. Enjoy delicious home-style cooking featuring a range of fried menu items such as wild caught Alaskan pollock and U.S. farm-raised catfish. Not in the mood for seafood? The menu also features sandwiches, hamburgers, hot dogs and salads. **Address:** 402 E 2nd Ave 30161 **Location:** Jct 4th St. ⬜ L ⬜ D

SONNY'S REAL PIT BAR-B-Q 706/234-1441

▼▼ Barbecue. Casual Dining. $8-$17 **AAA Inspector Notes:** Bearing the name after its founder, Floyd "Sonny" Tillman, this barbecue restaurant first opened its doors circa 1968 in Gainesville, Florida and has since spawned over 150 more throughout the Southeast. The menu is steeped in finger lickin' favorites such as ribs, pulled pork, beef brisket, burgers, catfish, shrimp and chargrilled chicken. Let's not forget about the fried okra, which is the perfect starter dish, and their homemade baked beans. **Features:** beer only. **Address:** 2103 Shorter Ave 30165 **Location:** 3.3 mi w on SR 20.

⬜ L ⬜ D

ROSWELL (G-3) pop. 88,346, elev. 1,059'

- **Hotels p. 242 • Restaurants p. 242**
- **Hotels & Restaurants map & index p. 82**
- **Part of Atlanta area — see map p. 44**

In Roswell you can practically hear the past whispering in your ear. Cherokee Native Americans called the verdant banks of the Chattahoochee River the "Enchanted Land." The first Native Americans to create and use a written language and alphabet, the Cherokee were a very progressive tribe. And as the white man began infiltrating their Georgia homeland, members of the Cherokee Nation began adopting the white man's ways, becoming shopkeepers, farmers and mill operators in an attempt to survive the encroachment.

There was no turning back, however, once gold was discovered in northern Georgia in 1828. Settlers began flooding in, among them one Roswell King, who recognized the untapped potential of the region's rich natural resources and built a water-powered cotton mill. By 1850, the mills of the Roswell Manufacturing Co. were churning out cloth, flannel, yarn and rope, and a mill town was on the map.

At first glance Roswell, about 20 miles north of downtown Atlanta, seems swallowed up by the metro area's inexorable outward push. Neighboring Alpharetta Highway and Holcomb Bridge Road are a sea of businesses, office buildings and tightly packed strip centers. Even Canton and Atlanta streets, which pass right through the middle of Roswell's historic district, are busy thoroughfares. To do this town right you need to explore at least some of it on foot.

Make your first stop Town Square (Atlanta and Sloan streets), which has a layout that's a bit reminiscent of a New England village. Before you set off exploring, pick up maps and information at the Historic Roswell Visitors Center across the street. Within walking distance of Town Square are a trio of gracious old antebellum mansions, the Archibald Smith Plantation Home, Barrington Hall and Bulloch Hall *(see attraction listings).*

Some 16 miles of scenic hiking trails meander throughout town. Just off Mill Street is Old Mill Park, where you can follow an interpretive trail to the ruins of Ivy Mill. A covered bridge links the park to the Chattahoochee River National Recreation Area. During the Civil War, Confederate soldiers burned a bridge at the river crossing to try and slow down the Union army's progress toward Atlanta.

Come face to face with Roswell's spooky past on the Roswell Ghost Tour, which departs from the bandstand in Roswell Square (across from the Roswell Visitors Center). A highlight of this tour through the city's historic district is a visit to Founders Cemetery. The tour is not recommended for young children. Phone (770) 649-9922 for schedule information.

Enjoy guided historic home tours and witness the lighting of the town square during Christmas in Roswell in November and December. The best part? Actors re-enact the 1853 wedding of Mittie Bulloch and Theodore Roosevelt.

Historic Roswell Convention and Visitors Bureau: 617 Atlanta St., Roswell, GA 30075. **Phone:** (770) 640-3253 or (800) 776-7935.

Self-guiding tours: If it's about Roswell the visitors center (617 Atlanta St.) has it: brochures outlining the historic district and Roswell Mill Village, audio tours, promotional videos, event information and the Southern Trilogy Pass that offers discounted admission to three historic houses.

Shopping: Have fun shopping on Canton Street, lined with specialty stores like The Chandlery (950 Canton St.) and the Shoppes of Plumtree Village (1035-1065 Canton St.).

When you feel like taking a break, head to the Land of a Thousand Hills Coffee House (352 S. Atlanta St.). Their motto is "drink coffee, do good," and the reason is that money from coffee bean purchases is funneled back to growers and home-based small business owners in Rwanda; Land of a Thousand Hills uses only premium Rwandan beans for their lattes, espressos and other brews. This comfy place (it occupies a restored house) has couches, a patio out back and free Wi-Fi, plus live music on Friday and Saturday nights.

◆ **ARCHIBALD SMITH PLANTATION HOME,** 935 Alpharetta St., is the preserved former home of one of Roswell's founding families. The 1845 house features original furnishings, clothing and family possessions kept intact by descendants of the Smiths. An 1840s piano, a Civil War soldier's trunk and a walnut plantation desk are among the antiques and artifacts displayed.

The property also features several original buildings, including a barn, carriage house, greenhouse, corn crib, kitchen, slave cabin and spring house. Docents convey generations of history regarding the house and its inhabitants.

An audio tour of the grounds is available by cellphone. **Time:** Allow 1 hour minimum. **Hours:** Guided tours Mon.-Sat. on the hour 10-3, Sun. 1-3.

(See map & index p. 82.)

Last tour begins at closing. Closed major holidays. **Cost:** $8; $7 (senior citizens and military with ID); $6 (ages 6-18 and college students with ID). Combination ticket with Barrington Hall and Bulloch Hall $18; $15 (ages 6-18). Cash only. **Phone:** (770) 641-3978. GT

BARRINGTON HALL is at jct. SRs 120 and 9 (Atlanta St.) at 535 Barrington Dr. Constructed by Barrington King in 1842, the restored Greek Revival hall was the home of the King family—whose wealth came from textile mills—for more than 160 years. During the Civil War, Union troops occupied the home and burned the mills. The home opened to the public in 2005 and now displays original family furniture and possessions. Visitors can stroll the grounds and see a restored 1842 boxwood formal garden.

An audio tour of the grounds is available by cellphone. **Time:** Allow 1 hour minimum. **Hours:** Guided tours are given on the hour Mon.-Sat. 10-3, Sun. 1-3. Last tour begins at closing. Closed major holidays. **Cost:** $8; $7 (ages 65+); $6 (ages 6-18 and college students with ID); free (active and retired military with ID and family). Combination ticket with Archibald Smith Plantation Home and Bulloch Hall $18; $15 (ages 6-18). **Phone:** (770) 640-3855. GT

BULLOCH HALL, 1 blk. w. of the Old Square at 180 Bulloch Ave., was the girlhood home of President Theodore Roosevelt's mother, Martha (Mittie) Bulloch. This 1839 Greek Revival house features restored rooms with period furnishings. Special events are held. An audio tour of the grounds is available by cellphone. **Time:** Allow 1 hour minimum. **Hours:** Tours on the hour Mon.-Sat. 10-3, Sun. 1-3. Last tour begins at closing. Closed major holidays. Phone ahead to confirm schedule. **Cost:** $8; $7 (ages 65+); $6 (ages 6-18). Combination ticket with Archibald Smith Plantation Home and Barrington Hall $18; $15 (ages 6-18). **Phone:** (770) 992-1731. GT

CHATTAHOOCHEE NATURE CENTER, off SR 120 at 9135 Willeo Rd., encompasses 127 acres and has gardens, a river boardwalk and several nature trails that wind through wetlands, wildlife areas and woodlands; markers identify native plants. The Interpretive Center has a terrace with a green roof, a resource gallery and interactive exhibits. Carnivorous plants can be seen in the wetland demonstration area. Live reptiles and birds are exhibited. Guided walks, canoe trips, entertainment and special events are offered on weekends.

Bicycles, pets and smoking are not permitted. **Time:** Allow 1 hour minimum. **Hours:** Mon.-Sat. 10-5, Sun. noon-5. Closed Jan. 1, Thanksgiving, Christmas Eve and Christmas. **Cost:** $10; $7 (ages 13-18 and 65+); $6 (ages 3-12). **Phone:** (770) 992-2055, ext. 238.

BAYMONT INN & SUITES ROSWELL ATLANTA NORTH
(770)992-7200 **61**

WWWW **Hotel.** $79-$120 **Address:** 1500 Market Blvd 30076 **Location:** SR 400 exit 7A northbound; exit 7 southbound, just e. Located in a commercial/business area. **Facility:** 154 units. 2-4 stories, interior corridors. **Pool(s):** outdoor. **Activities:** exercise room. **Guest Services:** valet laundry.

[icons] CALL / SOME UNITS HS

BEST WESTERN PLUS ROSWELL/ALPHARETTA
(770)552-5599 **60**

WWWW
Hotel
$89-$129

BW Best Western PLUS

AAA Benefit: Save 10% or more every day and earn 10% bonus points!

Address: 907 Holcomb Bridge Rd 30076 **Location:** SR 400 exit 7B, 0.7 mi w. **Facility:** 93 units. 3 stories, interior corridors. **Pool(s):** outdoor. **Activities:** exercise room. **Guest Services:** valet and coin laundry, area transportation. **Featured Amenity:** breakfast buffet.

SAVE [icons] CALL BIZ HS [icons] / SOME UNITS

WHERE TO EAT

AMALFI RISTORANTE 770/645-9983 **88**

WW **Italian. Casual Dining. $14-$21 AAA Inspector Notes:** If you are looking for traditional Italian cuisine with an intimate dining room then this is the place. Start with complimentary olives and then dive right into some antipasto or calamari. Rigatoni with meatballs is representative of the nightly specials and the Southern Italian cooking offered. Desserts are delectable. **Features:** full bar. **Address:** 292 S Atlanta St 30075 **Location:** 1 mi s of town square. D

AQUA BLUE 770/643-8886 **85**

WW **Specialty. Fine Dining. $14-$32 AAA Inspector Notes:** This upscale spot is known for its killer sushi and romantic ambience. The heavily Asian-influenced menu also features Maine lobster ravioli, pan-seared Chilean sea bass, six-spice hanger steak and fries and braised lamb shank. Its widely varied and eclectic offerings are sure to please everyone. There also are nightly specials such as half-price bottles of wine. **Features:** full bar. **Address:** 1564 Holcomb Bridge Rd 30076 **Location:** SR 400 exit 7 southbound; exit 7A northbound, just e. D CALL

BISTRO VG 770/993-1156 **75**

WWW **French. Casual Dining. $12-$30 AAA Inspector Notes:** A northern-suburb favorite for many years, this eatery never seems to disappoint with its consistently great food and top-notch service. Do not miss dishes include domestic lamb chops and the excellent grilled Mediterranean octopus. Charcuterie items are popular as well. Artwork enhances the intimate atmosphere. **Features:** full bar, patio dining. **Reservations:** suggested. **Address:** 70 W Crossville Rd 30075 **Location:** SR 400 exit 7B, 2.7 mi w, follow via Holcomb Bridge Rd (SR 92); jct Crabapple Rd. **Parking:** valet only.

L D CALL

BROOKWOOD GRILL 770/587-0102 **78**

WWW **New American. Fine Dining. $10-$27 AAA Inspector Notes:** This classy neighborhood grill is a local favorite for family dinners and business lunches. Diners cannot go wrong with any of the creative options but I highly recommend starting with the chicken skewers. The hickory-grilled chicken and steak are crowd pleasers. The portions are large and the desserts are decadent so make sure to bring your appetite. **Features:** full bar, patio dining, Sunday brunch, happy hour. **Reservations:** suggested. **Address:** 880A Holcomb Bridge Rd 30076 **Location:** SR 400 exit 7B, 0.8 mi w.

L D [icon]

(See map & index p. 82.)

CHICAGO'S RESTAURANT   770/993-7464   87

▼▼ American. Casual Dining. $17-$30 **AAA Inspector Notes:** Seafood mixed grill, sautéed shrimp and scallops, stockyard steak and a variety of quality menu items are popular at this casual, neighborhood-style restaurant. The filet is tasty and cooked to order. Fresh ground espresso or cappuccino also is available. Join them in the lounge on Friday and Saturday evenings for live entertainment. **Features:** full bar, early bird specials, Sunday brunch. **Reservations:** suggested. **Address:** 4401 Shallowford Rd, Suite 106 30075 **Location:** Jct Shallowford and Johnson's Ferry rds; in Shallowford Corners Shopping Center. D CALL ♿M

THE COUNTER   678/461-9661   76

▼▼ Burgers. Casual Dining. $6-$15 **AAA Inspector Notes:** Get just the burger you want with this eatery's build a burger concept. The server gives diners an easy-to-use worksheet to choose everything from the bun to the meat to the condiments. Or choose a pre-set offering while relaxing in the industrialist décor with a touch of California. My perfect burger consisted of a Hawaiian bun, turkey burger with Gouda and applewood-smoked bacon. Top it off with a side of sweet potato fries and a peanut butter and Nutella shake. **Features:** wine only. **Address:** 850 Mansell Rd 30076 **Location:** SR 400 exit 8, 1.7 mi w; in Mansell Oaks Shopping Center. L D CALL ♿M

DREAMLAND BAR-B-QUE   678/352-7999

▼ Barbecue. Casual Dining. $8-$20 **AAA Inspector Notes:** "Ain't nothing like 'em nowhere" is the motto at this barbecue cafe. The menu is small, but that is okay because everybody comes for one thing: the ribs. Barbecue dishes come with white bread and a kicking sauce. Friendly Southern hospitality and a casual backdrop help make this place a favorite. **Features:** beer only, patio dining. **Address:** 10730 Alpharetta Hwy 30076 **Location:** SR 400 exit 7B, 1.5 mi w to Alpharetta Hwy, then just n. L D

THE FICKLE PICKLE   770/650-9838   80

▼ Sandwiches. Quick Serve. $5-$10 **AAA Inspector Notes:** In a restored old house in the historic district, this self-service bakery/sandwich shop is a delightful find. The menu is limited to soups, salads and sandwiches, as well as a wonderful array of homemade desserts and goodies, including pies, cookies and scrumptious brownies. All orders are made to order. **Features:** beer & wine, patio dining. **Address:** 1085 Canton St 30075 **Location:** Downtown. L D CALL ♿M

GREENWOOD'S   770/992-5383   79

▼▼ Southern. Casual Dining. $10-$25 **AAA Inspector Notes:** When you find yourself dreaming about the crispy fried chicken served here, you know it must be good. Maybe the huge slice of delicious homemade coconut cream pie is just as dream-worthy. They believe in sourcing local products and making food when you order it so sit back, relax and enjoy the experience. This historic restaurant makes its home in a 150-year-old clapboard house and displays many distinctive and quirky art pieces. **Features:** beer & wine, patio dining. **Address:** 1087 Green St 30075 **Location:** SR 400 exit 7B, 1.5 mi w to Alpharetta Hwy, 1 mi s to Green St, then just w. L D

LITTLE ALLEY STEAK   770/998-0440   83

▼▼▼ Steak Seafood. Fine Dining. $16-$70 **AAA Inspector Notes:** USDA Prime beef steaks are both wet aged and dry aged here. Whether it is a rib-eye, New York strip or fillet, guests cannot go wrong. Kobe beef burgers also are available. There are many other great options like shellfish pappardelle, tuna tartare, Berkshire pork chops, Springer Mountain chicken, duck confit, roasted bone marrow and for vegetarians, tandoori spiced tofu steaks. **Features:** full bar, Sunday brunch. **Address:** 955 Canton St 30075 **Location:** Downtown. **Parking:** street only. D CALL ♿M

PASTIS   770/640-3870   86

▼▼▼ French. Fine Dining. $10-$28 **AAA Inspector Notes:** This appealing French bistro offers a Mediterranean feel and delicious, authentic cuisine. Diners can choose to sit upstairs on the balcony or in the downstairs lounge. Casual and friendly servers dish up fresh salads, cheese plates and such dishes as salmon en croute, tuna nicoise and filet mignon. **Features:** full bar, patio dining, Sunday brunch. **Address:** 928 Canton St 30075 **Location:** Downtown. **Parking:** street only. L D 🛒

SALT FACTORY   770/998-4850   84

▼▼ American. Gastropub. $10-$28 **AAA Inspector Notes:** This contemporary gastropub is a local favorite and can fill up quickly. The starters, specialties, pizza, burgers and aged meats are all highly popular. The cured and aged meats include sweet cappicola, liverwurst and serrano ham. Try the Thai-style braised beef short ribs, dubbed the area's best or the double-chicken pot pie which also has received rave reviews. **Features:** full bar. **Address:** 952 Canton St 30075 **Location:** Downtown. **Parking:** street only. L D CALL ♿M

STONEY RIVER   678/461-7900   77

▼▼▼ Steak. Fine Dining. $15-$35 **AAA Inspector Notes:** Flagstone, leather and polished wood contribute to the appeal of this upscale lodge. In addition to well-prepared cuts of steak, patrons can choose from tempting side dishes such as sautéed spinach and onion mashed potatoes. Other entrées include pecan-encrusted swordfish and baby back ribs. **Features:** full bar. **Address:** 10524 Alpharetta Hwy 30076 **Location:** SR 400 exit 7B, 1.5 mi w. D CALL ♿M

THE SWALLOW AT THE HOLLOW   678/352-1975   81

▼▼ Barbecue. Casual Dining. $11-$25 **AAA Inspector Notes:** This eatery serves savory barbecue, such as baby back ribs and pork, in addition to grilled portobello mushroom sandwiches and mouth-watering banana chocolate chip pudding. Nashville songwriters perform on Friday and Saturday evenings in the rustic setting, and fast, friendly servers make the down-home dining experience even more enjoyable. Family friendly. **Features:** beer & wine. **Address:** 1072 Green St 30075 **Location:** SR 400 exit 4, 1.5 mi w to Alpharetta St, 1.2 mi s to Green St, then 0.3 mi w. L D

TABLE AND MAIN   678/869-5178   82

▼▼▼ New American. Fine Dining. $14-$28 **AAA Inspector Notes:** This spot offers American farm-to-table cuisine with heavy Southern influences. Grilled Carolina grouper, country-fried biscuit-breaded veal tenderloin and Charleston she-crab soup are menu items that exemplify the style here. The menu changes seasonally and the bourbon bar is quite popular. **Features:** full bar, patio dining. **Reservations:** required. **Address:** 1028 Canton St 30075 **Location:** Downtown. **Parking:** street only. D CALL ♿M

JILLY'S CUPCAKERY   770/645-1500

fyi Not evaluated. A plethora of cupcake styles and types awaits at this sweet spot. Choose from the most popular red velvet, cookies and cream, chocolate peanut butter, salted caramel and ultimate chocolate. Daily special flavors range from carrot to lemon to Boston cream pie. Get them to go by the dozen. Limited seating. **Address:** 10800 Alpharetta Hwy, Suite 300 30076 **Location:** Jct Mansell Rd; in Roswell Market Place.

ROYSTON (B-4) pop. 2,582, elev. 898'

TY COBB MUSEUM is at 461 Cook St. The museum promotes education and understanding of baseball and professional baseball hitter Ty Cobb. Exhibits include rare photographs, memorabilia, books and archives. A video presentation and temporary exhibits also are featured. A vintage-style baseball game takes place in September or October, every other year. **Time:** Allow 30 minutes minimum. **Hours:** Mon.-Fri. 9-4, Sat. 10-4. Closed major holidays. **Cost:** $5; $4 (ages 62+); $3 (students); free (ages 0-5 and active military with ID). **Phone:** (706) 245-1825.

ST. MARYS (F-5) pop. 17,121, elev. 11'
• Hotels p. 244 • Restaurants p. 244

From treasure-smuggling pirates to commercial fishermen, St. Marys' past blends into its present. Many shrimp and fishing boats line the docks along the St. Marys River. It's the gateway to Cumberland Island National Seashore and also is home to the

Kings Bay Naval Submarine Base, the Atlantic Coast home base of Trident nuclear submarines.

McIntosh Sugar Mill Tabby Ruins, on Spur 40, is the largest structure in the region constructed from tabby, a building material made by combining oyster shells, sand and water. Built by John Houston McIntosh in the 18th century, the mill was used for cane grinding and the boiling and processing of sugar products. Ten miles north on SR 40, Crooked River State Park offers year-round recreational opportunities *(see Recreation Areas Chart)*.

The Cumberland Island National Seashore Museum, a block from the waterfront at 129 Osborne St., has an exhibit about one of the last battles of the War of 1812, which was fought not in New Orleans but 5 days later at Point Peter, where British troops vanquished a fort that had defended coastal Georgia. Artifacts retrieved from the site tell the story of the "forgotten invasion"; phone (912) 882-4336 or (877) 860-6787. The 1812 Binational Heritage Peace Garden commemorates the war, and the adjacent St. Marys History Walk features 24 interpretive panels that describe community milestones.

Howard Gilman Memorial Park on the waterfront hosts a variety of seasonal festivities, including fireworks on the Fourth of July. Near downtown, the St. Marys Aquatic Center, a water park featuring slides, pools and seasonal activities, opens in May; phone (912) 673-8118.

St. Marys Convention and Visitors Bureau: 400 Osborne St., St. Marys, GA 31558. **Phone:** (912) 882-4000 or (866) 868-2152.

Self-guiding tours: Maps and brochures for a walking tour of the National Historic District featuring houses dating from 1801 are available at the welcome center.

ORANGE HALL HOUSE MUSEUM is just n. of the waterfront at 311 Osborne St. The stately house, with its white Doric columns and wide steps leading to a main entrance on the second floor, is considered a fine example of Greek Revival architecture. The house, believed to have undergone its last enlargement and remodeling in 1856, is furnished with 19th-century items. **Time:** Allow 30 minutes minimum. **Hours:** Mon.-Fri. 10-3, Sat. 10-4, Sun. 1-4. Closed Jan. 1, Easter, Thanksgiving, Christmas Eve, Christmas and Dec. 31. **Cost:** $4 (ages 62+ and active and retired military with ID); $3 (ages 6-18). Cash only. **Phone:** (912) 576-3644.

ST. MARYS SUBMARINE MUSEUM, 102 St. Marys St. W., displays items from both United States and foreign military submarines including a hands-on periscope, a control room and other major submarine shipboard components. Also on the premises are a reading library, photos, models and plaques. **Hours:** Tues.-Sat. 10-5, Sun. noon-5, mid-Jan. to late Dec. Closed Easter, July 4 and Thanksgiving. Phone ahead to confirm schedule. **Cost:** $5; $4 (ages 13-18, ages 62+, college students with ID,

and active and retired military with ID); $3 (ages 6-12). **Phone:** (912) 882-2782.

SPENCER HOUSE INN BED & BREAKFAST   (912)882-1872
▼▼▼▼ **Historic Bed & Breakfast.** $155-$295 **Address:** 200 Osborne St 31558 **Location:** I-95 exit 3 (SR 40), 9 mi se. Located in heart of St. Marys historic district. **Facility:** This beautiful Victorian home built in 1872 is within walking distance to the Cumberland Island Ferry. The Inn features individually decorated rooms, a wonderful breakfast and an elevator. 14 units. 3 stories, interior corridors. **Terms:** 7 day cancellation notice-fee imposed.

GREYFIELD INN   904/261-6408
[fyi] Not evaluated. **Address:** Cumberland Island 31558 **Location:** Park at Amelia Island Deck D, board ferry to Cumberland Island. Facilities, services, and décor characterize an upscale property. This elegant former Carnegie family mansion built in 1901 is located in a national wilderness forest and seashore, accessible only by ferry. The price includes upscale accommodations and all meals.

WHERE TO EAT

BORRELL CREEK LANDING RESTAURANT   912/673-6300
▼▼▼ American. Casual Dining. $8-$27 **AAA Inspector Notes:** This waterfront restaurant sustains a cozy feel that lends to its popularity as an exceptional dining spot. Good preparations of beef, poultry and seafood are complemented by a broad wine list of potential pairings by the bottle or glass. Shrimp Grand Marnier, chicken Borrell and broiled salmon Monte Carlo are signature dishes. **Features:** full bar, patio dining, happy hour. **Reservations:** suggested, weekends. **Address:** 2715 Osborne Rd E 31558 **Location:** I-95 exit 3 (SR 40), 6 mi se, then just sw to Borrell Creek Landing. [D]

OPS PIZZA KITCHEN & CAFE   912/882-8558
▼ Italian Pizza. Casual Dining. $7-$14 **AAA Inspector Notes:** This place is all about the pizza in all its variations—New York, Sicilian and gourmet concoctions. A full menu of basic Italian dishes also are featured. Daily lunch and dinner offers, by-the-slice pizza and everyday specials make for an affordable meal. Dine in or take out. **Features:** full bar, patio dining. **Address:** 231 Charlie Smith Sr Hwy 31558 **Location:** Jct Osborne Rd (SR 40) and Charlie Smith Sr Hwy (SR 40 Spur), just n. [L] [D]

PAPA LUIGI'S PIZZA   912/673-1557
▼▼ Italian Pizza. Casual Dining. $7-$19 **AAA Inspector Notes:** Specialties of the house include sautéed baby clams in white wine sauce, sautéed mussels and chicken cacciatore. Chicken and veal entrées also are available as well as subs, pizza and calzones, and the red sauce here is very tasty. This small dine in/take out pizzeria is located in the back of a large shopping center. **Features:** beer & wine. **Address:** 143 City Smitty Dr 31558 **Location:** Jct Osborne Rd (SR 40) and Charlie Smith Sr Hwy (SR 40 Spur), just se on Osborne Rd; in Kings Bay Village. [L] [D]

RIVERSIDE CAFE & RESTAURANT   912/882-3466
▼▼ American. Casual Dining. $7-$20 **AAA Inspector Notes:** This downtown waterfront restaurant features a wide selection of Greek-influenced American favorites, all prepared to order. Gyros, burgers, seafood, big salads and breakfast all day, plus a long list of daily specials, appeal to all. **Features:** beer & wine, patio dining. **Address:** 106 St Marys St 31558 **Location:** I-95 exit 3 (SR 40), 9 mi se. **Parking:** street only. [L] [D]

ST. MARY'S SEAFOOD & MORE   912/467-4217
▼▼ Regional Seafood. Casual Dining. $7-$30 **AAA Inspector Notes:** This popular restaurant serves up a wide variety of shellfish and finfish specialties in lunch, dinner and light portions. Full entrées and sandwiches are both available as are a few steak, chicken and gator dishes. The soups are made with real cream and are sinfully delicious. **Features:** full bar, patio dining, happy hour. **Address:** 1837 Osborne Rd 31558 **Location:** Jct Osborne Rd (SR 40) and Charlie Smith Sr Hwy (SR 40 Spur), 1.1 mi se. [L] [D]

ST. SIMONS ISLAND (E-6) elev. 7'
* Restaurants p. 246
* Part of Golden Isles area — see map p. 187

St. Simons Island had an active Colonial period. The area around Gascoigne Bluff served as the headquarters for English ships after 1736. Land disputes between Spain and England exploded in 1742 with the Battle of Bloody Marsh *(see Fort Frederica National Monument p. 184)*. Timber cut on the island was used in the first ships of the U.S. Navy, including the USS *Constitution.*

Aaron Burr sought refuge along the shores of St. Simons Island after his duel with Alexander Hamilton. British actress Fanny Kemble Butler penned many of her anti-slavery letters at the Hampton Plantation. Near the remains of the moat that surrounded the town of Frederica stand ancient live oaks under which John and Charles Wesley, the Anglican ministers who founded Methodism, once preached.

The village, at the island's southern tip, includes an 1872 working lighthouse, coastal history museum and fishing pier. St. Simons Island provides an appropriate setting for such activities as golf, tennis, fishing and boating. Bicycle trails parallel many of the roads on the island.

St. Simons Island Visitors Center: 529 Beachview Dr., St. Simons Island, GA 31522. **Phone:** (912) 638-9014.

ARTHUR J. MOORE METHODIST MUSEUM, is
from entrance to St. Simons Island via F.J. Torras Cswy., .2 mi. e. to Sea Island Rd., .4 mi. n.e. to Epworth Rd./Methodist Center Booth Gate and .2 mi. n. to 100 Arthur J. Moore Dr. The museum is part of the Epworth-by-the-Sea Methodist Center and displays an assortment of Methodist artifacts, a nativity collection and a history of St. Simons Island. It also houses a 10,000-volume library pertaining to Methodist and general church history. Video presentations relate to the role of the Wesleys in Georgia.

Time: Allow 1 hour minimum. **Hours:** Mon.-Sat. 10-4. Closed Thanksgiving weekend and Christmas-Jan. 4. **Cost:** Grounds free. Museum by donation. Fee for guided tours (reservations required). **Phone:** (912) 638-4050. GT

CHRIST CHURCH, FREDERICA, just s. of Fort
Frederica National Monument at 6329 Frederica Rd., was established in 1736. Charles Wesley, chaplain to Gen. James E. Oglethorpe's settlers at Fort Frederica, was the first priest. After building the present edifice in 1884 as a memorial to his wife, Anson Green Phelps Dodge Jr. took Holy Orders and served as rector until 1898. His life was the subject of the 1977 novel "Beloved Invader" by local writer Eugenia Price; Ms. Price is buried in the church cemetery. **Hours:** Tues.-Sun. 2-5. Closed Thanksgiving, Christmas Eve, Christmas and Dec. 31. **Cost:** Donations. **Phone:** (912) 638-8683.

MARITIME MUSEUM AT THE HISTORIC COAST GUARD STATION is at 4201 1st St. Seven galleries
depict the station's history and the natural history of Georgia's barrier islands through interactive exhibits and activities. A 12-minute video presentation introduces visitors to the museum. **Time:** Allow 1 hour minimum. **Hours:** Mon.-Sat. 10-noon and 1-5, Sun. 1:30-5. Closed Jan. 1, Easter, Thanksgiving, Christmas Eve and Christmas. **Cost:** (includes admission to the St. Simons Island Lighthouse Museum) $12; $5 (ages 6-12). **Phone:** (912) 638-4666.

ST. SIMONS ISLAND LIGHTHOUSE MUSEUM AND A.W. JONES HERITAGE CENTER, 101 12th
St., is in a restored 1872 lighthouse keeper's house. Exhibits depict local history and the life of a lighthouse keeper and his family. Visitors should begin their visit at the heritage center, 610 Beachview Dr., that contains additional exhibits. A research library is open to the public by appointment. The adjacent lighthouse offers a fine view of the island. A lighthouse built here in 1810 was destroyed during the Civil War.

Hours: Museum and lighthouse open Mon.-Sat. 10-5, Sun. 1:30-5. Last admission 30 minutes before closing. Closed Jan. 1, Easter, Thanksgiving, Christmas Eve and Christmas. **Cost:** (includes admission to the Maritime Museum at the Historic Coast Guard Station) $12; $5 (ages 6-12). **Phone:** (912) 638-4666.

ST. SIMONS TROLLEY TOURS departs from the
pier in the village at 117 Mallery St. This charming and humorous narrated tour aboard an air-conditioned trolley includes the St. Simons Lighthouse, the Battle of Bloody Marsh site, Fort Frederica, Christ Church and the ruins at Retreat Plantation. Visitors should arrive 15 minutes prior to departure. **Time:** Allow 1 hour, 30 minutes minimum. **Hours:** Daily at 11 (also at 1, Apr.-Aug.). **Cost:** $20; $10 (ages 4-12). **Phone:** (912) 638-8954. GT

Visit the AAA and CAA senior
driving websites for tips
to help you drive safely longer

THE LODGE AT SEA ISLAND   (912)634-3992

Hotel
$325-$850

Address: 100 Retreat Ave 31522 **Location:** Waterfront. FJ Torras Cswy, 1.6 mi se on Kings Way, just s; on Sea Island Club golf course. **Facility:** This sanctuary is the epitome of living in the lap of luxury with personalized service by experienced butlers. The stately English country estate offers large, tastefully embellished rooms. 40 units. 3 stories, interior corridors. **Parking:** valet only. **Terms:** check-in 4 pm, 3-5 night minimum stay - seasonal and/or weekends, 7 day cancellation notice-fee imposed, resort fee. **Amenities:** safes. **Dining:** 2 restaurants, entertainment. **Activities:** steamroom, regulation golf, recreation programs, bicycles, exercise room, spa. **Guest Services:** valet laundry, area transportation.

[SAVE] [↔] [¶] [⚓] [Y] [🍴] [BIZ] [HS] [📶] [✕] [🛎]
[🛏]/SOME UNITS [S🔦]

VILLAGE INN & PUB   (912)634-6056

▼▼▼ Bed & Breakfast. $160-$285 **Address:** 500 Mallory St 31522 **Location:** Jct Frederica Rd and Kings Way, 0.7 mi s on Kings Way, then just n. **Facility:** Nestled among live oaks, this property was designed to complement the natural environment. It's within walking distance of the Pier Village entertainment district. 28 units. 2 stories (no elevator), exterior corridors. **Terms:** 7 day cancellation notice-fee imposed. **Pool(s):** outdoor. **Guest Services:** valet laundry.

[¶+] [Y] [🏊] [📶] [✕]

WHERE TO EAT

BARBARA JEAN'S RESTAURANTS   912/634-6500

▼▼ Regional Comfort Food. Casual Dining. $9-$25 **AAA Inspector Notes:** This small, downtown eatery boasts friendly service and down-home, Southern country cooking. Some favorite menu items are salmon, crab cakes, fried catfish, meatloaf and fruit cobbler. Many galleries and shops are within walking distance. **Features:** full bar, patio dining, happy hour. **Address:** 214 Mallery St 31522 **Location:** Between Beachview Dr and Lord Ave; on south side of island. **Parking:** street only. [L] [D] [🐾]

BENNIE'S RED BARN DINNER CLUB   912/638-2844

▼▼ American. Casual Dining. $13-$32 **AAA Inspector Notes:** *Historic.* A Golden Isles tradition since 1954, the restaurant builds its menu around fresh local seafood and steaks cooked over a wood fire. Servers deliver a pleasant recitation of the menu and don't make a request to repeat it. **Features:** full bar, happy hour. **Address:** 5514 Frederica Rd 31522 **Location:** Jct Demere and Frederica rds, 3.5 mi n. [D]

BLACKWATER GRILL   912/634-6333

▼▼ Cajun. Casual Dining. $14-$30 **AAA Inspector Notes:** The menu here centers on fresh Creole and Cajun specialties like boudin, gumbo, jambalaya and a few Lowcountry specialties like shrimp and grits. All of it is flavorful and can be spiced up or toned down to your liking since each dish is made to order. The décor has a casual nautical theme which is perfect for this island location. Each meal is enhanced by friendly servers who kick off the meal with a small treat. **Features:** full bar, patio dining, early bird specials, happy hour. **Address:** 260 Redfern Village 31522 **Location:** Jct Demere and Frederica rds, just n. [D]

BONEFISH GRILL   912/634-0246

▼▼ Seafood. Fine Dining. $12-$29 **AAA Inspector Notes:** Fish is the house specialty, and the menu and nightly specials offer a variety of choices. Well-prepared food is cooked to perfection. Service is casual in nature, and the staff is skilled and attentive. **Features:** full bar, Sunday brunch, happy hour. **Address:** 202 Retreat Village, Unit 3 31522 **Location:** Jct Demere and Frederica rds, just s. [D] CALL [🍷M]

BUBBA GARCIA'S   912/634-0073

▼ Mexican. Casual Dining. $9-$14 **AAA Inspector Notes:** This small cantina is a party bar that happens to serve some awfully good tacos, fajitas, burritos and quesadillas. The menu is a little more limited than the average Tex-Mex or traditional Mexican places but still offers some great choices. A good place to get together with friends and relax on the large covered patio (children are welcome). Try the fried jalapeños with Manchego cheese, a little bit of fire and a whole lot of flavor. **Features:** full bar, happy hour. **Address:** 200 Redfern Village 31522 **Location:** Jct Demere and Frederica rds, just n.
[L] [D]

CRABDADDY'S SEAFOOD GRILL   912/634-1120

▼▼ Regional Seafood. Casual Dining. $16-$27 **AAA Inspector Notes:** Come enjoy dining in this popular nautical-themed island mainstay, pleasing locals and visitors since 1988. The seafood offerings are available grilled, blackened, steamed or sautéed. There also are a variety of pasta-inspired seafood dishes. A few beef and chicken dishes make an appearance, but are limited. The specialty of the house is soft shell crab, availability is limited so call ahead if that is what you are after. A wide selection of off-menu specials are available nightly. **Features:** full bar, happy hour. **Reservations:** suggested, in season. **Address:** 1217 Ocean Blvd 31522 **Location:** Jct Arnold Rd. [D]

DELANEY'S BISTRO AND BAR   912/638-1330

▼▼ Continental. Casual Dining. $10-$37 **AAA Inspector Notes:** This pleasant, contemporary bistro is located in a small business center. The French-influenced dinner menu has a selection of seafood, duck, chicken, veal, beef and lamb all accompanied by well-crafted sauces. Entrées are carefully prepared to ensure a flavorful, palate-pleasing experience. Service is casual and informal. **Features:** full bar, happy hour. **Reservations:** suggested. **Address:** 3415 Frederica Rd, Suite C 31522 **Location:** Jct Ocean Rd, just n; in Plantation Center in Plantation Place. [L] [D]

DEL SUR ARTISAN EATS   912/638-1223

▼▼ Argentine. Casual Dining. $10-$30 **AAA Inspector Notes:** This small corner bistro is a favorite for a lunch date whether dining on the sidewalk patio or in the busy dining room. The menu focuses on traditional Argentinian and Italian specialties which have been enhanced by the chef and prepared fresh to order. The menu features fresh pasta dishes, grilled dishes, poultry and risotto. During lunch diners also can find gourmet sandwiches. I tried the spinach empanadas and shredded short rib sandwich which were unbelievably delicious. **Features:** beer & wine, patio dining. **Reservations:** suggested, in season. **Address:** 321 Mallery St 31522 **Location:** Corner of Kings Way; on southern tip of island. **Parking:** on-site and street.
[L] [D]

THE FREDERICA HOUSE   912/638-6789

▼▼ Seafood Steak. Casual Dining. $11-$30 **AAA Inspector Notes:** Guests find a bustling atmosphere at the cozy, family dining establishment. Taking pride in its fresh seafood selections, the restaurant has crab soup with a thick, white cream broth. The rustic setting attracts locals and tourists alike. **Features:** full bar, early bird specials, happy hour. **Reservations:** suggested, in season. **Address:** 3611 Frederica Rd 31522 **Location:** Jct Demere and Frederica rds, 2.3 mi n. [L] [D]

IGUANAS SEAFOOD RESTAURANT   912/638-9650

▼▼ Seafood. Casual Dining. $9-$37 **AAA Inspector Notes:** With a great location and continuous party atmosphere, the entire family can enjoy a visit to this spot. The menu is centered around fresh Georgia shrimp and offers them in a wide variety of styles from boiled, peel and eat, bacon wrapped, fried and traditional shrimp and grits. A few fish entrées also are available as well as sandwiches and burgers. Grab a seat on the covered patio to enjoy the fresh sea air and people watching on the busy street. **Features:** full bar, patio dining, happy hour. **Address:** 303 Mallery St 31522 **Location:** Jct Kings Way, just sw; on southern tip of island; in Pier Village. **Parking:** street only. [L] [D] CALL [🍷M] [🐾]

LOCO'S GRILL & PUB   912/634-2002

▼▼ American. Casual Dining. $6-$16 **AAA Inspector Notes:** The big draw here is the bar and drink specials but for those in the mood for some light fare, they offer a good-sized menu of finger foods and sandwiches along with a few full entrées. **Features:** full bar, patio dining, happy hour. **Address:** 2463 Demere Rd 31522 **Location:** Jct Demere and Frederica rds, just w. [L] [D] CALL [🍷M]

NAZZARO'S RISTORANTE ITALIANO   912/634-6161

♥♥ Italian. Casual Dining. $15-$30 **AAA Inspector Notes:** This full-service Italian restaurant has been serving the area since 2000 and is one of only a handful serving the area. The menu features a wide range of such standard fare as veal, chicken, steaks and pasta with the veal osso buco Milanese being the specialty of the house. For those in the mood for a lighter meal there is a bar menu with equally well-prepared finger foods that can be enjoyed with a favorite libation. **Features:** full bar, patio dining, happy hour. **Reservations:** suggested, in season. **Address:** 196 Retreat Village 31522 **Location:** Jct Demere and Frederica Rd Circle, just sw on Demere Rd; across from airport. [D] CALL [&M]

SAPELO ISLAND (E-6) elev. 7'
• Part of Golden Isles area — see map p. 187

SAPELO ISLAND NATIONAL ESTUARINE RESEARCH RESERVE is reached by a 30-minute ferry ride. To reach the dock take I-95 exit 58, then SR 99 s. 9.1 mi. to Landing Rd. in Meridian, then left to the Sapelo Island Visitors Center. The visitor center at the dock features exhibits and information about the area. Bus tours may include the Palladian-style R.J. Reynolds mansion, the Sapelo Lighthouse, the University of Georgia Marine Institute and Hog Hammock, a small community of Sapelo Plantation slave descendants.

Time: Allow 4 hours minimum. **Hours:** Mansion tour departs Wed. at 8:30 and returns at 12:30. Lighthouse tour departs Sat. at 9 and returns at 1 (also Fri. 8:30-12:30, June 1-Labor Day). Extended tour departs at 8:30 and returns at 3 the last Tues. of the month, Mar.-Oct. Visitor center open Tues.-Fri. 7:30-5:30, Sat. 8-5:30. Closed federal and state holidays. **Cost:** Visitor center free. Ferry $15; $10 (ages 6-12). Credit cards are not accepted for tours. Reservations are required. **Phone:** (912) 437-3224. [GT]

SAVANNAH (D-6) pop. 136,286, elev. 43'
• Hotels p. 264 • Restaurants p. 270
• Attractions map p. 251
• Hotels & Restaurants map & index p. 257, 260

Gen. James E. Oglethorpe and his settlers founded Savannah, England's 13th and last colony, in February 1733. Forgoing the usual village grid system, Oglethorpe and Col. William Bull laid out their new settlement in a series of wards in which commercial and residential buildings centered on a public square. This visionary plan has survived as the city's blueprint because of Oglethorpe's choice of location.

GET REAL
REAL INSPECTORS, REAL RATINGS

AAA's in-person inspections ensure the places you select provide what you expect.

AAA.com/Diamonds

On a bluff overlooking the Savannah River, the new settlement soon prospered as a crossroads of trade with England and the new communities of the interior. Port traffic, begun in 1744, experienced a steady increase along with the plantation economy of tobacco and cotton.

Residents eagerly embraced the revolt against England, and Savannah was garrisoned by some 900 Colonial troops under Gen. Robert Howe. British forces captured the city by surprise in December 1778 and made it a base for their operations against the Colonies until their departure in 1782.

Nineteenth-century Savannah grew and flourished with King Cotton, becoming a vital port. In 1862 Union forces closed the port to all but blockade runners when they captured Fort Pulaski *(see Fort Pulaski National Monument, p. 184)*. Two years later Gen. William Tecumseh Sherman blazed a trail of destruction across Georgia to the city. Confederate forces fought stubbornly, but with the fall of Fort McAllister, Gen. William J. Hardee realized further resistance was futile and withdrew his troops to prevent the city's destruction. Sherman entered Savannah on Christmas Day 1864 and offered it to President Abraham Lincoln as a present.

Cotton again came to the rescue after the war as the city grew into a major trading center. The collapse of the cotton market at the beginning of the 20th century left Savannah languishing until just before World War II, when other industries began to develop. Almost lost to the wrecking ball, however, was what Sherman had spared some 100 years earlier: its squares, its houses and its heritage.

In a drive to reshape the city's skyline, developers began to tear down historic structures. The proposed demolition of the Davenport House, now a museum *(see attraction listing p. 252)*, sparked the founding of the Historic Savannah Foundation. This dedicated group of women organized one of the country's first and most successful urban restoration programs, buying hundreds of properties and selling them to private parties along with a covenant to restore and repair them.

Today 22 of Oglethorpe's original 24 squares survive, lined with handsome town houses, bedecked with fountains and statues and beautified by live oaks and azaleas. The success of the Historic Savannah Foundation's early efforts spawned other civic renewal projects.

The cleanup of the river and the restoration of the warehouses and cotton brokerage offices along Bay Street, Factor's Walk and River Street revived the city's historic waterfront. Instead of the commerce associated with cotton trade buying and selling, these renovated 19th-century buildings now house specialty shops, restaurants and nightspots.

Notable landmarks include Solomon's Lodge No. 1, Free & Accepted Masons, in the 1886 Cotton and Naval Stores Exchange at 100 E. Bay St. The Masonic lodge, organized in 1734, is the country's oldest in continuous operation, and the old exchange is said

(See maps & indexes p. 257, 260.)
to be the first building to straddle a public street according to the legal principle of air rights.

River Street's Waving Girl statue is evocative of Savannah's romantic character. In the early years of the 20th century the city light tender's sister, Florence Martus, became known to sailors all over the world for waving at every ship. One legend maintains that she promised her sweetheart to greet every ship until his return.

Another historic building is Christ Church, on Johnson Square at Bull and East St. Julian streets. The congregation—the first in the Georgia colony—organized in 1733, and in 1736 established what is believed to have been the first Protestant Sunday school for children in the New World. The present structure was built in 1838; the interior was renovated following a fire in 1895. The church is open to the public by appointment; phone (912) 236-2500.

Colonial Park, East Oglethorpe Avenue and Abercorn Street, is the site of the old Christ Episcopal Church cemetery, for many years the only public burying ground in the colony. Closed to interment in 1853, the cemetery suffered much damage when Gen. William Tecumseh Sherman's troops used it as a stabling ground.

Founded in 1755 by members of the Church of Scotland, Independent Presbyterian Church is at the corner of Bull Street and West Oglethorpe Avenue. The building and steeple were re-created after the original structure, built in 1829, was destroyed by an 1889 fire; the original was modeled after St. Martin-in-the-Fields Church in London's Trafalgar Square; phone (912) 236-3346.

First African Baptist Church, at 23 Montgomery St., was established in 1775. The church is housed in a brick sanctuary built in 1859 by congregation members. It is reputedly North America's oldest African-American church and has a museum containing archives and memorabilia dating from the 18th century. Guided tours are available; phone (912) 233-6597.

Since 1839, the Georgia Historical Society Research Center library and archives has preserved state history. The collection includes more than 4 million manuscripts, 100,000 photographs, 30,000 architectural drawings, 15,000 rare books, and thousands of maps, portraits, and artifacts. Across from Forsyth Park at 501 Whitaker St., it is housed in an 1876 structure designed by American Institute of Architects founder Detlef Lienau. The library is open Wed.-Fri. noon-5, first and third Sat. 10-5; phone (912) 651-2128.

Writer Mary Flannery O'Connor was born in Savannah in 1925 and lived at 207 East Charlton St. on Lafayette Square until 1938 *(see attraction listing)*. A more recent local celebrity is chef, restaurateur and cookbook author Paula Deen. Born in Albany but a longtime Savannah resident, the ebullient Deen owns a popular downtown restaurant.

As you might imagine, Savannah has a packed events calendar. In mid-February the ⚑ Savannah Irish Festival is celebrated with traditional folk dances, music and food. The city dons green during a festive ⚑ St. Patrick's Day Celebration on the River held in mid-March. The 4-day ⚑ Savannah Tour of Homes and Gardens, during which numerous private houses are open to the public, begins the fourth Thursday in March; for more information phone (912) 234-8054.

The holidays are celebrated in festive style in November and December. Individual events include the Savannah Harbor Foundation Annual Boat Parade of Lights, Christmas on the River and the Holiday Tour of Homes; for more information contact the visitor information center.

Savannah Visitor Information Center: 301 Martin Luther King Jr. Blvd., Savannah, GA 31402. **Phone:** (912) 944-0455.

Self-guiding Tours

Information about Savannah's scenic tour route is available at the visitor information centers at 301 Martin Luther King Jr. Blvd. and 1 W. River St. Audio tours from Savannah Story Tours can be purchased on CD at 301 Martin Luther King Jr. Blvd. for $18.95.

Shopping

Unless your heart is set on a classic mall, outlet mall or shopping center experience, you'll be more than content exercising your purchasing power within the boundaries of Savannah's walkable downtown historic district. While great places to swipe your credit card are found on nearly every street, there are a few areas you should definitely zero in on.

Sure, River Street is a tourist trap, but for good reason: This bustling waterfront promenade is easily navigable and has a little something for everyone. Formerly cotton warehouses, the multilevel 19th-century buildings lining the famed cobblestone street have been transformed into restaurants, bars, galleries, specialty stores and, as you'd expect, souvenir emporiums cluttered with T-shirts and pirate tchotchkes. Art aficionados should stop by Gallery 209 for a look at two floors' worth of local photography, sculpture, woodcrafts and other pieces as well as the chance to meet one of the artists. Suckers for sweets, take note: the aroma of fresh pralines and saltwater taffy wafting from the doors of confectioneries River Street Sweets and Savannah's Candy Kitchen makes it nearly impossible to pop in just for the free samples.

River Street Market Place, at the east end of the street, is an open-air bazaar of booths hawking everything from wind spinners to handcrafted jewelry. Situated on the level between River and Bay streets is Factor's Walk, with its alleyways and network of cobblestone, iron and concrete walkways leading to antiques dealers, specialty shops and other businesses.

You'll notice the shopping scene gets less touristy the farther south from the Savannah River you go—

(See maps & indexes p. 257, 260.)

that is, until you set foot in City Market. This four-block conglomeration of refurbished warehouses and storefronts between Ellis and Franklin squares has been a gathering place ever since the mid-18th century. Walking through the courtyard amid info kiosks and wooden planters, you'll see galleries, gift shops, sweets shops and eateries on each side. In the two-story City Market Art Center Studios, you can view and buy the works of more than 50 local artists, many of whom are on-site to chat with visitors.

At the Paula Deen Store, just south of City Market at 108 W. Congress St., fans of the local celebrity chef scope out her line of cookbooks, kitchen essentials and signature "Hey Y'all" mugs. Another block south at 38 Barnard Street is the quirky Kitchens on the Square, where even the most clueless of cooks enjoy perusing displays of cute cookie cutters, innovative gadgets, silly refrigerator magnets and vintage-style decor.

Those seeking to spruce up their homes and wardrobes with one-of-a-kind finds head to Whitaker Street, which runs parallel to Barnard. Known as the Downtown Design District, the segment between Charlton and Gaston streets is home to 20 or so indie retailers specializing in everything from antiques, folk art and vintage clothing to painted furniture, trendy lighting fixtures and fine linens. The exclusive boutiques, showrooms and galleries are definitely worth a peek inside, even if you've vowed to keep the credit card holstered.

Going back north on Bull Street toward Liberty Street, you'll come across two noteworthy stops for discerning antique hounds: Alex Raskin Antiques, housed in a 12,000-square-foot 1860s Italianate mansion, and George Davis Antiques & Interiors. Another Bull Street highlight is the 1892 brick Savannah Volunteer Guards Armory building, which shopSCAD—a funky, colorful co-op gallery selling all sorts of items made by talented Savannah College of Art and Design (SCAD) students, faculty, staff and alumni—calls home. Nearby, bibliophiles can easily spend hours in two thoughtfully stocked independent bookstores: E. Shaver, Bookseller, 326 Bull St., and The Book Lady Bookstore, 6 E. Liberty St. Occupying the ground floor of a Greek Revival mansion on Madison Square, the former is beloved for its cheery atmosphere and excellent selection of local, regional, Civil War and children's reads. The latter, a cozy nook packed with 50,000-plus new, used and out-of-print texts, encourages customers to linger in its Wi-Fi cafe and reading garden.

Just a hop, skip and jump away from The Book Lady Bookstore is Fabrika Fine Fabrics, a true DIY fashion/interior designer's delight. This bright, fun little gem of a space offers sewing tools and equipment in addition to unique, high-quality textiles running the gamut from bridal silks to wools to cutesy-print cottons. Budget-minded fashionistas desiring the finished product procure super-chic looks for less at Red Clover, 244 Bull St., while the ladies' sportswear and formal wear across the street at

Gaucho appeal to those with fatter wallets. If you're searching for the perfect gift, Magnolia's of Savannah, 137 Bull St., carries holiday merch, old-school toys, candles, stationery and the like.

For more than a century, Levy Jewelers has dazzled Savannahians with its diamonds, watches, sterling silver and other precious pieces. In 2012 the family-owned retailer opened a new flagship location in a 20,000-square-foot midcentury modern building at the corner of Bull and E. Broughton streets. Also on E. Broughton is the exclusive Globe Shoe Company, which has helped hipsters complete their outfits since 1892. If you have a few bucks left after exploring the retail offerings on this side of Broughton, go ahead and indulge in an old-fashioned soda fountain fave at Leopold's Ice Cream, next to SCAD's Trustees Theater.

More shopportunities—from gourmet food stores to independent boutiques and interior design galleries to clothiers like GAP, Banana Republic, Urban Outfitters, Palm Avenue, Kate Spade and Free People—await you on W. Broughton Street. French flair and Southern charm come together at The Paris Market, a two-story emporium/coffee bar filled with tons of old and new treasures—bedding, estate jewelry, antique Egyptian chandeliers, English candles, baby items, you name it—inspired by the owner's travels. At Savannah Bee Company's flagship store, you can peruse the selection of honey, body care products and bee-themed gifts; watch videos about bees; and let the kids play inside a giant faux hive. Lowcountry Gourmet Foods has an array of specialty balsamic vinegars, olive oils and seasonings. Stop in for a tasting to find the perfect product to delight your taste buds.

Malls outside Savannah's downtown historic district offer the usual mix of nationally recognized department, clothing and specialty stores. Oglethorpe Mall, 7804 Abercorn Ext., is anchored by Belk, Macy's, JCPenney and Sears; Savannah Mall, 14045 Abercorn St., includes Dillard's, Bass Pro Shops Outdoor World and Burlington Coat Factory. One of the city's newer shopping complexes, Abercorn Walk (5525 Abercorn St.) counts upscale Jos. A. Bank and Williams-Sonoma among its retailers. Bargain hunters bag discounted name-brand items at The Shoppes of Savannah, 11 Gateway Blvd.

Nightlife

Running the gamut from restaurant bars to cozy little neighborhood pubs to martini and dessert lounges to hot dance clubs, Savannah's nighttime entertainment options are primarily concentrated in the downtown historic district. The district's walkability makes barhopping easy, and for many, the lax open-container regulations make it more fun. Two pieces of safety-related advice for those who plan to hoof it after dusk: wear comfortable shoes (cobblestones, bricks and 4-inch stilettos just don't mesh well) and stay within the district's boundaries.

Inside **The Distillery**, (912) 236-1772, a sign above the front door explains in four simple words what this casual W. Liberty Street restaurant/bar is all about: "No Crap Just Craft." While you can't order a Bud at

(See maps & indexes p. 257, 260.)
the long mahogany bar (which is usually jam-packed on weekends), you *can* take your pick of 100-plus craft beers, about two dozen of which are on tap. Almost as diverse as the suds selection is the clientele—artsy types, preppies, T-shirted twenty-somethings and everyone in between come here to bond over Fat Tires and Golden Monkeys.

Also hailed for its custom-crafted brews is **Moon River Brewing Company,** (912) 447-0943. Occupying a W. Bay Street space that originally served as a hotel, Savannah's only brewery attracts a multifarious crowd—and not just of the townie and tourist variety. Rumor has it that there's paranormal activity (and lots of it) here. Don't let that scare you away, though—the drinks and grub are definitely worth a try, and the 5,400-square-foot attached beer garden is a fun place to unwind if the weather's nice. A Moon River tradition since the 1990s, a weekend-welcoming toast takes place every Friday at 6 p.m.

Named for the first Irish Republican Army volunteer executed by the British during the War of Independence, **Kevin Barry's Pub** is a happening W. River Street hangout serving up not only Guinness, bangers and mash and other traditional Irish faves, but also nightly live Celtic tunes. Upstairs, a nicely done display of military memorabilia pays homage to members of the armed forces; phone (912) 233-9626.

Other good spots to grab a stout are **Molly MacPherson's Scottish Pub & Grill,** 311 W. Congress St., where you'll find kilted waiters and an outstanding selection of single malt whiskeys; and **Six Pence Pub,** a small, laid-back British tavern on Bull Street (you can't miss the old-school red telephone booth outside). Phone (912) 239-9600 for Molly MacPherson's and (912) 233-3151 for Six Pence.

For a bar experience that's sweet in every sense of the word, check out **Lulu's Chocolate Bar,** 42 Martin Luther King Jr. Blvd. The comfy, retro-chic joint entices all sorts of night owls looking for a slice or sip of heaven in the form of a dangerously delectable martini or homemade dessert. The prices can be on the steep side, but there are some great daily specials; phone (912) 480-4564.

You can also satiate your sweet tooth at **Jen's and Friends,** (912) 238-5367, which has more than 300 specialty martinis to choose from. This reasonably priced, eclectic Bull Street bar is a popular girls'-night-out destination, but take one glance at the extensive craft beer list and it's plenty obvious that the guys, too, are welcome here. Jen's and Friends' "Enter as Strangers, Leave as Friends" motto rings true, thanks not only to the glasses of strong, sugary goodness, but also to the friendly bartenders and the maximum seating capacity of 37.

Wet Willie's, (912) 233-5650, is *the* place to hang on sultry summer nights when ice cream just won't do the trick. The main draw of the brick-walled E. River Street location (there's a second location in City Market) is the rainbow of machines dispensing curiously named frozen drinks—from Attitude Improvement to Call a Cab. Be forewarned: these "adult Slurpees" are potent!

Gorgeous views of the Savannah River can be enjoyed at **Rocks on the Roof,** The Bohemian Hotel Savannah Riverfront, Autograph Collection's sexy rooftop lounge located at 102 W. Bay St. and accessible from River Street. You can sit inside at the bar or a table or sink into a cushioned wicker couch or chair on the deck amid potted trees ablaze with Christmas lights. When it's warm outside, the lively lounge's transparent roll-up doors stay open; on nippy nights, a fire pit takes the chill out of the air. Along with beer, wine and some killer cocktails, appetizers are served; phone (912) 721-3800.

Super-sexy nightlife options can also be found *below* street level, as **Jazz'd Tapas Bar,** 52 Barnard St., proves. After descending an outdoor staircase, you'll find yourself in a modern, colorfully lit and painted bar and dining area. Live blues, jazz and swing melodies fill the place 5 days a week, and dancing is always encouraged. You can order a variety of wines, martinis and other specialty drinks in addition to, of course, tapas; phone (912) 236-7777.

If doing JELL-O shots and bumping and grinding to Latin, Top 40 and house music under strobe lights sounds like a good time to you, then get dolled up, make sure you have some cash (there's a cover charge most nights) and head to **Club 51 Degrees** on W. Congress Street. Open Thursday through Saturday, this loud, raucous and usually packed dance club caters to an under-30 (but over-21) crowd and is split into three levels, each with its own DJ; phone (912) 234-7265.

ANDREW LOW HOUSE, 329 Abercorn St. at Lafayette Sq., was built by Andrew Low, a wealthy cotton merchant said to be the richest man in Savannah at the time this three-story Italianate residence was built in 1849. At the time of Low's death his son William inherited the house and shortly thereafter married Juliette Gordon. It was from this stuccoed brick house, noted for its well-proportioned rooms with plaster cornices, carved woodwork and crystal chandeliers, that widowed Juliette later organized the Girl Scouts of the USA in 1912. Guests have included Gen. Robert E. Lee and novelist William Makepeace Thackeray. A historic garden is on the grounds.

Time: Allow 30 minutes minimum. **Hours:** Guided 25-minute tours are given every half-hour Mon.-Sat. 10-4, Sun. noon-4. Last tour departs at closing. Closed major holidays and the first two weeks in Jan. **Cost:** $10; $9 (senior citizens); $8 (students with ID); $7 (ages 6-18); free (active military with ID). A combination ticket with Davenport House and Ships of the Sea Maritime Museum is available. **Phone:** (912) 233-6854. GT

BIRTHPLACE OF JULIETTE GORDON LOW is at 10 E. Oglethorpe Ave. Founder of the Girl Scouts of the USA, Juliette Gordon Low was born in this elegant 1821 English Regency house in 1860. The home has been restored to its appearance in 1886, the year of

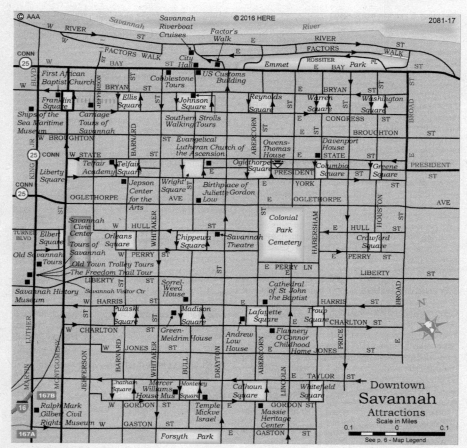

© AAA   Savannah   Savannah Riverboat Cruises   © 2016 HERE   River   2081-17

Downtown
Savannah
Attractions
Scale in Miles
0.1   0   0.1
See p. 6 - Map Legend

(See maps & indexes p. 257, 260.)

Juliette Low's marriage. Exhibits include period arrangements of original Gordon family furnishings, artwork by Juliette Low, a Victorian garden, a stable and a carriage house. Guided 30- to 40-minute tours offer insight into the lives of Low, the Gordon family and early history of the Girl Scouts.

Hours: Walk-in tours are offered Mon.-Sat. 10:15-4:15, mid-Jan. through Dec. 30. Tours with advance reservations are given Mon.-Sat. 12:15-4:15, mid-Jan. through Dec. 30; tickets can be purchased up to 6 months in advance. The site may have visiting Girl Scout troops some mornings; phone ahead. Closed Mar. 17, July 4, Thanksgiving, Christmas Eve and Christmas. Phone ahead to confirm schedule. **Cost:** $15; $12 (ages 5-21, active military with ID and senior citizens); $10 (Girl Scouts). **Phone:** (912) 233-4501. GT

BONAVENTURE CEMETERY is at 330 Bonaventure Rd. This former plantation has been a cemetery since the mid-19th century. The site, which encompasses 100 acres, overlooks the Wilmington River

and has an abundance of live oak trees, some of which are 250 years old. Many of the graves incorporate beautiful statues and ornate carvings. Among the famous persons interred here are author Conrad Aiken and composer Johnny Mercer. One-hour guided walking tours are offered.

Note: Visitors should be aware of the potential for theft and are not advised to travel alone. Valuables should not be left in automobiles. **Time:** Allow 1 hour minimum. **Hours:** Daily 8-5. Volunteers from the Bonaventure Historical Society are available in the office Sat.-Sun. 10-4 to provide maps and a brief overview of the cemetery and former plantation. During second Sun. weekends, walking tours are given Sat. at 2 and Sun. at 2, 2:30 and 3. **Cost:** Donations. **Phone:** (912) 651-6843. GT 🎋

CATHEDRAL OF ST. JOHN THE BAPTIST, 222 E. Harris St. at Abercorn St., is a Gothic-style cathedral completed in 1896, then rebuilt in 1899 after a severe fire. One of the largest cathedrals in the South, it features marble railings, floors and altar. In addition there are murals, stained-glass windows, large

(See maps & indexes p. 257, 260.)

carved-wood stations of the cross, and a solid white-oak 2,081-pipe Noack tracker organ. **Time:** Allow 30 minutes minimum. **Hours:** Open Mon.-Sat. 9-5, Sun. 8-5; no tours available during church services. Phone ahead to confirm holiday closures. **Cost:** Donations. **Phone:** (912) 233-4709. GT

CITY HALL, jct. Bull and Bay sts., was built in the Renaissance Revival style and completed in 1906 on the site of the 1799 City Exchange. Bronze tablets attached to the building's front commemorate the 1834 launching of the SS *John Randolph*, the first iron ship seen in American waters, and the 1819 SS *Savannah*, the first steam-propelled ship to cross the Atlantic. On the first floor visitors can view original architectural details, including a four-story rotunda crowned by a stained-glass dome, mechanical clockworks, tile mosaics, a bronze fountain, and rotating art and history exhibits. **Hours:** Mon.-Fri. 8:30-5. Guided tours are offered the first Tues. of each month at noon; reservations are required. Closed major holidays. **Cost:** Free. **Phone:** (912) 651-6565, or (912) 651-6412 for tour information. GT

DAVENPORT HOUSE is on Columbia Square at 324 E. State St. Master builder Isaiah Davenport finished his Federal-style home in 1820. The finely proportioned house is noted for its historically accurate interiors, delicate ironwork, elliptical stairway and handsome plasterwork. Guides point out the vast differences between how certain rooms looked while the Davenports lived here and after it became a tenement house in the early 1900s. The building was saved from demolition in 1955 by seven women who went on to form the Historic Savannah Foundation—one of the earliest preservation movements in the United States.

Hours: Guided 30-minute tours depart every half-hour Mon.-Sat. 10-4, Sun. 1-4 (10-1 on day before Thanksgiving, Christmas Eve and Dec. 31). Last tour begins at closing. Closed Jan. 1 and 11-15, Mar. 17, Thanksgiving and Christmas. **Cost:** $9; $8.10 (ages 65+ and active military with ID); $7 (students ages 18-21 with ID); $5 (ages 6-17). A combination ticket with Andrew Low House and Ships of the Sea Maritime Museum is available. **Phone:** (912) 236-8097. GT

EVANGELICAL LUTHERAN CHURCH OF THE ASCENSION, on Wright Sq. at Bull and E. State sts., combines Norman and Gothic architectural features. The 1844 structure is noted for its stained-glass windows and exhibits about church history. The congregation was founded in 1741. **Hours:** Mon.-Fri. 9-1. Closed major holidays. **Cost:** Donations. **Phone:** (912) 232-4151.

FACTOR'S WALK, a row of narrow buildings along the river bluff on the north side of Bay St., acquired its name in the 19th century when it was the meeting place for factors—sales agents and commission brokers such as cotton merchants—and was the center of commercial activities. Today it contains shops, restaurants and bars. A network of iron and concrete bridgeways connects the buildings to the bluff. The cobblestone streets were made from the ballast of ships from Europe.

FLANNERY O'CONNOR CHILDHOOD HOME, 207 E. Charlton St. on Lafayette Square, is a four-story house where author Mary Flannery O'Connor's family lived from her birth in 1925 until 1938. The two floors open to the public have been restored to reflect the appearance during the O'Connor occupancy. The bedrooms are furnished with family pieces, and in other parts of the residence are the future author's perambulator; two childhood books; and Kiddie-Koop, a screen-enclosed crib.

Flannery O'Connor's "The Complete Stories" won the National Book Award's fiction category in 1972. **Hours:** Fri.-Tues. 1-4 and by appointment. Closed major holidays. Phone ahead to confirm schedule. **Cost:** $6; $5 (students and active military with ID); free (ages 0-15). **Phone:** (912) 233-6014.

FORSYTH PARK, on Gaston St. between Whitaker and Drayton sts., is particularly lovely in early spring during the azalea season and includes a fragrance garden and a playground for children. A circa 1858 fountain featuring a fanciful grouping of mermen, swans and a lone water nymph is the centerpiece of the original tract, laid out in 1851. The Confederate Monument is in the park extension. **Hours:** Daily 24 hours. **Cost:** Free.

FORT MCALLISTER STATE PARK—see attraction listing in Richmond Hill p. 238.

GREEN-MELDRIM HOUSE, on Madison Sq. at 14 W. Macon St., was Gen. William Tecumseh Sherman's headquarters during his 1864 occupation of Savannah. The 1850 house is a fine example of neo-Gothic Revival architecture. Today the house is used by the parish of St. John's Episcopal Church for church functions.

Hours: Guided tours every half-hour Tues. and Thurs.-Fri. 10-4, Sat. 10-1 (unless a church function is scheduled), early Jan. to mid-Dec. Last tour begins 30 minutes before closing. Closed major holidays, the week before Easter, the second week in Nov. and Thanksgiving week. **Cost:** $10; $5 (students with ID); free (ages 0-5). Cash only. **Phone:** (912) 232-1251 to confirm availability. GT

SAVE **JEPSON CENTER FOR THE ARTS** is on Telfair Square at 207 W. York St. (at Barnard St.). The 64,000-square-foot building is one of three venues that together comprise the Telfair Museums. In addition to showcasing terraces and gardens, the center has galleries that display permanent and temporary exhibitions. On the second level is a children's area, ArtZeum, with interactive exhibits. Visitors can also create art projects in the Drop-In Studio.

Time: Allow 1 hour minimum. **Hours:** Tues.-Sat. 10-5, Sun.-Mon. noon-5. Guided architectural tours are given daily at 11 and 3. Special exhibition tours are given Mon.-Fri. at 2. Drop-In Studio daily 1-4.

(See maps & indexes p. 257, 260.)

Closed major holidays. **Cost:** (includes 1-week access to the Jepson Center, Owens-Thomas House and Telfair Academy) $20; $18 (ages 65+ and military with ID); $15 (ages 13-college students with ID); free (ages 0-12). $40 (family, two adults and two children). **Phone:** (912) 790-8800. GT ¶

MASSIE HERITAGE CENTER is at 207 E. Gordon St. (street parking only). The center, a unit of the Savannah-Chatham County Public Schools, is housed in three 19th-century Greek Revival buildings situated on Calhoun Square in the Historic Landmark District. Massie School served as a public elementary school, Savannah's first from its opening in 1856, until it was closed in 1974. Building highlights include a 19th-century classroom, a 3-D interactive laser show of Savannah's city plan, the Native American Room, artifacts from the Victorian era, examples of city architectural styles and hands-on activities for children. In the Massie Maritime Gallery, nineteen handmade model ships are on display.

Time: Allow 45 minutes minimum. **Hours:** Mon.-Sat. 10-4, Sun. noon-4. Docent-led tours are offered Mon.-Tues. and Thurs.-Fri. 10-2. Closed major holidays. **Cost:** $8; $7 (ages 63+); $5 (ages 4-12 and students with ID); $2 (ages 1-3). **Phone:** (912) 395-5070. GT

MERCER WILLIAMS HOUSE MUSEUM is at 429 Bull St. Antiques dealer, preservation expert and social gadfly Jim Williams restored this 1860 mansion built for Gen. Hugh W. Mercer, great-grandfather of singer and songwriter Johnny Mercer. Events central to the book "Midnight in the Garden of Good and Evil" took place in the house. Guides provide tours of the garden and first floor while offering insight about the architecture, interior furnishings and Williams' life. Highlights include a spiral stairway below a stained-glass dome and the original English ceramic tile in the 60-foot entryway. Tours depart from the carriage house gift shop.

Time: Allow 30 minutes minimum. **Hours:** Mon.-Sat. 10:30-4:10, Sun. noon-4. Closed major holidays. Phone ahead to confirm schedule. **Cost:** $12.50; $8 (active military and students with ID). **Phone:** (912) 236-6352 or (877) 430-6352. GT

NATIONAL MUSEUM OF THE MIGHTY EIGHTH AIR FORCE—see Pooler p. 234.

OLD FORT JACKSON, 3 mi. e. via President St., was built between 1808 and 1812. On the banks of the Savannah River and surrounded by a moat, the fort is the oldest remaining brickwork fort in Georgia. Exhibits depict the history of the fort's construction and its garrison during the War of 1812 and the Civil War.

Interpretive presentations and cannon firings take place throughout the year. **Time:** Allow 30 minutes minimum. **Hours:** Daily 9-5. Closed Jan. 1, Thanksgiving, Christmas Eve and Christmas; phone ahead to confirm holiday hours. **Cost:** $7; $4 (ages 2-12).

A combination ticket is available that offers admission to three of the following five sites: Georgia State Railroad Museum, Savannah Children's Museum, Savannah History Museum, Old Fort Jackson and Pin Point Heritage Museum. **Phone:** (912) 232-3945. GT

⚜ SAVE **OWENS-THOMAS HOUSE,** 124 Abercorn St. on Oglethorpe Sq., was designed by English architect William Jay. Influenced by classical antiquity, he built the elegant residence over a 4-year period beginning in 1816 using both domestic and imported materials, and designed an innovative plumbing system. In 1825 the Marquis de Lafayette was a guest here.

The English Regency house is furnished with rare antiques and contains decorative arts owned by 19th-century city residents. The carriage house, also the departure point for tours, contains an orientation gallery and the original slave quarters. An English-inspired parterre garden connects the main buildings.

Hours: Guided tours every 15 minutes Tues.-Sat. 10-5, Sun.-Mon. noon-5; last tour begins at 4:30. Tours often sell out during the peak summer season; arrive early. Closed major holidays. **Cost:** (includes 1-week access to Jepson Center, Owens-Thomas House and Telfair Academy) $20; $18 (ages 65+ and military with ID); $15 (ages 13-college students with ID); free (ages 0-12). $40 (family, two adults and two children). **Phone:** (912) 790-8800. GT

PIN POINT HERITAGE MUSEUM, 9924 Pin Point Ave., chronicles the life and culture of the Gullah Geechee community settled by freedmen in 1890. The museum is located in what was once the A.S. Varn & Son Oyster and Crab Factory, the main source of income of the fishing community until 1985 when the factory shut its doors.

Hours: Thurs.-Sat. 9-5. Closed Jan. 1, Thanksgiving and Christmas. **Cost:** $8; $4 (ages 2-12). A combination ticket is available that offers admission to three of the following five sites: Georgia State Railroad Museum, Savannah Children's Museum, Savannah History Museum, Old Fort Jackson and Pin Point Heritage Museum. **Phone:** (912) 355-0064.

RALPH MARK GILBERT CIVIL RIGHTS MUSEUM is at 460 Martin Luther King Jr. Blvd. The museum, named in honor of the late Dr. Ralph Mark Gilbert, NAACP leader and father of Georgia's civil rights movement, recounts the civil rights struggle of Georgia's oldest African-American community. Guided, narrated tours take visitors through three floors of interactive exhibits, videos and memorabilia.

Time: Allow 30 minutes minimum. **Hours:** Tues.-Sat. 10-5. Closed Jan. 1, July 4, Labor Day, Thanksgiving and Christmas. **Cost:** $10; $8 (ages 65+); $6 (students with ID). **Phone:** (912) 777-6099. GT

SAVANNAH NATIONAL WILDLIFE REFUGE is one part of the Savannah Coastal Refuge Complex,

(See maps & indexes p. 257, 260.)

which extends from Pinckney Island National Wildlife Refuge near Hilton Head Island, S.C., to Wolf Island National Wildlife Refuge near Darien, Ga.; a visitor center is at 694 Beech Hill Ln. in Hardeeville, S.C. Freshwater marshes, tidal rivers and forests provide sanctuary for waterfowl, deer, turkey and feral hogs. Many of the freshwater impoundments were originally created as plantation rice fields. The surrounding dikes and earthen berms create good trails for hiking and wildlife viewing.

Bird-watching is best October through April. On the South Carolina side is the Laurel Hill Wildlife Drive, a scenic 4-mile route off SR 170. The refuge visitor center, on US 17 6 miles north of downtown Savannah and 7 miles south of Hardeeville, has a museum-quality exhibit hall where an 11-minute video about the refuge is shown. Various interpretive programs and special events are conducted throughout the year. Pets (including horses) are not permitted on refuge grounds. **Time:** Allow 30 minutes minimum. **Hours:** Grounds daily dawn-dusk. Center Mon.-Sat. 9-4. **Cost:** Free. **Phone:** (843) 784-2468.

SAVANNAH RIVERBOAT CRUISES departs from the dock at 9 E. River St. behind City Hall. Excursions aboard the 600-passenger vessels *Savannah River Queen* and *Georgia Queen* include a 90-minute narrated sightseeing harbor cruise, a 2-hour gospel entertainment and Southern buffet dinner cruise, 90-minute Monday-Saturday lunch and Sunday brunch cruises, a 2-hour dinner/entertainment cruise, a 2-hour sunset cruise, a 90-minute moonlight cruise and several other specialty cruises.

Hours: Sightseeing cruises depart daily at 1 and 3:30, Mar.-Nov.; Wed.-Sun. at 1 (also Sat. at 3:30), in Feb.; Sat.-Sun. at 1, rest of year (also Mon.-Fri. at 1, Christmas week). Phone for dinner and specialty cruise schedules.

Cost: Sightseeing cruise $22.95; $13.95 (ages 5-12). Sunset cruise $32.95; $23.95 (ages 5-12). Moonlight cruise $22.95; $13.95 (ages 5-12). Luncheon cruise $41.95; $24.15 (ages 5-12). Gospel dinner cruise $49.95; $30.35 (ages 5-12). Sunday brunch cruise $49.95; $33.45 (ages 5-12). Dinner entertainment cruise Sun.-Fri. $59.95; $35.95 (ages 5-12). Dinner entertainment cruise Sat. $65.95; $39.25 (ages 5-12). Reservations are required for meal cruises. **Phone:** (912) 232-6404 or (800) 786-6404. GT

SAVANNAH THEATRE is at 222 Bull St. in the historic district that centers on Chippewa Square. Rotating 2-hour musical productions staged in this restored 1818 theater are performed year-round. **Hours:** Performances Wed.-Sat. and select Tues. at 8 p.m., Sun. and select Sat. at 3. Matinee performances are presented on select Sat. **Cost:** $37; $18 (ages 0-17). **Phone:** (912) 233-7764.

SHIPS OF THE SEA MARITIME MUSEUM, 41 Martin Luther King Jr. Blvd., is in Scarbrough House, built in 1819 for William Scarbrough, a principal owner

of the *Savannah,* the first steamship to cross the Atlantic. Exhibitions include ship models, maritime artifacts and paintings from the 18th and 19th centuries. Four different videos are shown, and rotating exhibits are on display. Also of interest is the 1.2-acre garden, the largest private garden in the historic district.

Special events are offered. **Time:** Allow 30 minutes minimum. **Hours:** Garden open daily 10-5. Museum Tues.-Sun. 10-5. Last admission is 45 minutes before closing. Closed major holidays; phone ahead. **Cost:** Garden free. Museum $9; $7 (ages 65+ and students and military with ID); free (ages 0-5); $21 (family, two adults and up to three children ages 0-17). A combination ticket with Andrew Low House and Davenport House is available. **Phone:** (912) 232-1511.

SORREL-WEED HOUSE is at 6 W. Harris St. A 6-minute video presentation introduces visitors to the house. A guided tour follows and shares the history, architecture and antiques of the former residence of Francis Sorrel and his family. One-hour ghost tours of the Sorrel-Weed House and carriage house also are offered. A 2-hour ghost walking tour includes the surrounding neighborhood. **Time:** Allow 45 minutes minimum. **Hours:** Daily 10-4:30. Ghost tours depart nightly and generally begin after 6 p.m. Reservations are required for ghost tours. Closed Thanksgiving and Christmas; phone ahead to confirm holiday hours. **Cost:** House tour $12; $5 (ages 7-11). Ghost tours $20-$28; $10-$12 (ages 7-11). **Phone:** (912) 257-2223. GT

SAVE **TELFAIR ACADEMY** is at 121 Barnard St. on Telfair Sq. Designed by William Jay in 1819, this Regency-style mansion includes two rooms furnished in period, including the impressive Octagon Room. The permanent collection features works by American Impressionists and European artists such as George Bellows, Chuck Close, Childe Hassam, Robert Henri and Roy Lichtenstein. On long-term loan is the Bird Girl statue popularized by the book "Midnight in the Garden of Good and Evil." Traveling exhibitions also are presented.

Hours: Tues.-Sat. 10-5, Sun.-Mon. noon-5. Guided Mansion to Museum tours are given daily at 10, noon, 2 and 4. Special exhibition tours are given Mon.-Fri. at 1. Closed major holidays. **Cost:** (includes 1-week access to Telfair Academy, Jepson Center and Owens-Thomas House) $20; $18 (ages 65+ and military with ID); $15 (ages 13-college students with ID); free (ages 0-12). $40 (family, two adults and two children). **Phone:** (912) 790-8800. GT

TEMPLE MICKVE ISRAEL is in the historic district on Monterey Sq. on Bull St. (at Gordon and Wayne sts.). This 1876 neo-Gothic-style synagogue contains an archival museum displaying the Torah that the founders of the congregation brought to Savannah from England in 1733. Other items of interest are letters from George Washington, Thomas Jefferson, James Madison and several other presidents. A tour of the temple includes an audio tour followed by a docent-led tour.

(See maps & indexes p. 257, 260.)

Hours: Guided 45-minute tours are given Mon.-Fri. 10-12:30 and 2-3:30. Closed Jewish holidays and federal holidays. **Cost:** $7. **Phone:** (912) 233-1547. GT

TOURS OF SAVANNAH, departing from various locations, are conducted by several different companies and offer sightseeing tours of Savannah's historic district. Some feature nature tours, island tours, coastal low-country tours or specialty tours. Many include admission to one or two historic buildings. GT

Carriage Tours of Savannah departs from the City Market at Jefferson St. and W. Saint Julian St. Narrated 50-minute tours in horse-drawn carriages cover major points of interest in the historic district. **Hours:** Tours depart daily every 30 to 60 minutes 9-3 and 6-9 p.m. Ghost tours are given 6-9 p.m. Closed Mar. 17, Easter, Thanksgiving and Christmas. **Cost:** $22; $12 (ages 5-11). Reservations are recommended. **Parking:** Garage or metered parking is available. **Phone:** (912) 236-6756. GT

Cobblestone Tours departs from various city locations. The 90-minute Savannah Haunted History walking tour is given by guides in period costume. The tour begins at Colonial Park Cemetery and includes city history, local folklore and ghost stories. A 2-hour walking tour of local pubs, which is accompanied by local ghost stories, is available for those 21 and over.

Time: Allow 2 hours minimum. **Hours:** Haunted history tour departs daily at 7 and 9 p.m. Pub tour departs Mon.-Sat. at 8 and 9 p.m., Sun. at 8 only. Tour departures may vary seasonally; phone ahead. **Cost:** Haunted history tour $25; $20 (ages 65+ and active military with ID); $15 (ages 5-12). Pub tour $25; $20 (ages 65+ and active military with ID). Reservations are required. **Phone:** (912) 604-3007. GT

The Freedom Trail Tour departs the Savannah Visitor Information Center at 301 Martin Luther King Jr. Blvd. This 2-hour, narrated van or bus tour passes and stops at historic sites important in the experiences and contributions of African Americans to the city and the region, from the founding of Savannah the present. **Time:** Allow 2 hours minimum. **Hours:** Tours depart daily at 10, 1 and 3, Apr.-Sept.; daily at 1 and 3, rest of year. **Cost:** $25; $22 (ages 65+); $20 (college students with ID); $15 (ages 14-17); $13 (ages 7-13). **Phone:** (912) 398-2785. GT

Gray Line/Oglethorpe Tours departure points are from 526 Turner Blvd., 215 W. Boundary St. and the Savannah Visitor Information Center, as well as all historic district hotels. A 90-minute narrated tour of the city's historic downtown includes such highlights as River Street, Colonial Cemetery, Forsyth Park,

City Market and the Waving Girl statue. The tour fee includes free on/off boarding privileges until 5:30 at selected downtown trolley stops.

Time: Allow 1 hour, 30 minutes minimum. **Hours:** Narrated tours depart daily every 25 minutes 9-4. Evening Haunted Trolley Tours daily at 7 p.m. (also Fri.-Sat. at 9 p.m.). Closed Mar. 17 and Christmas; phone ahead to confirm holiday closures. **Cost:** $19; $11 (ages 5-11). Haunted Trolley Tour $20; $12 (ages 5-11). **Phone:** (912) 233-8380 or (866) 374-8687. GT

Old Savannah Tours departs the Savannah Visitor Information Center, 301 Martin Luther King Jr. Blvd.; the ticket office is across the street, 250 Martin Luther King Jr. Blvd. Tours include a 90-minute narrated historic tour aboard open-air trolley cars and a tour with on/off privileges at 16 stops in the historic district. Specialty excursions include a ghost tour, a land and sea tour and a 3-hour Savannah Experience tour aboard a climate-controlled minibus.

Hours: Trolley tours depart every 15-20 minutes daily 9-4:30. Phone for specialty tour schedules. Closed Mar. 17, Thanksgiving and Christmas. **Cost:** On/off tour $29; $12 (ages 5-11). Narrated tour $23; $10 (ages 5-11). Specialty tours $30-$47; $14-$32 (ages 5-11). Reservations are required for specialty tours. **Phone:** (912) 234-8128 or (800) 517-9007. GT

Old Town Trolley Tours departs from various downtown locations. The 90-minute narrated tours with all-day on/off privileges feature more than 100 points of interest and pass through Savannah's city squares and Colonial, Historic, Victorian and waterfront districts. The Paula Deen Tour, which includes dinner at The Lady & Sons, and an evening Ghosts & Gravestones tour, which includes a visit to the Andrew Low House, are available by reservation.

Hours: On/off tours depart at least every 20 minutes daily 9-6, Apr.-July; 9-5, rest of year. Other tours are by reservation. Closed St. Patrick's Day. Phone ahead to confirm schedule. **Cost:** Trolley on/off fare $29.91; $11.68 (ages 4-12). Ghosts & Gravestones fare $28.04; $11.68 (ages 4-12). Paula Deen fare $50; $26 (ages 4-12). **Phone:** (912) 233-0083. GT

Southern Strolls Walking Tours departs from the east side of Johnson Sq. near the fountain and the marble bench dedicated to songwriter Johnny Mercer. Savannah has been called one of the country's most haunted cities, and this ghost tour shows why. Knowledgeable guides lead visitors on a 90-minute tour of various city haunts, recounting historical anecdotes, ghost stories and local legends along the way.

Hours: Tours depart Mon.-Sat. at 8 p.m. Closed major holidays. Phone ahead to confirm schedule. **Cost:** $16; $8 (ages 6-13). Reservations are required. **Phone:** (912) 480-4477. GT

TRICENTENNIAL PARK is a family-friendly attraction where visitors can learn about the history of Savannah, including the American Revolution and Civil War, as well as the rich culture of Georgia's coast.

(See maps & indexes p. 257, 260.)

The park consists of Savannah History Museum, 303 Martin Luther King Jr. Blvd., and Georgia State Railroad Museum and Savannah Children's Museum, both at 655 Louisville Rd.

Hours: Georgia State Railroad Museum daily 9-5. Savannah Children's Museum (weather permitting) Mon.-Sat. 9-2, June-Aug; Wed.-Sat. 10-4, Sun. 11-4, rest of year. Savannah History Museum daily 9-5:30. Closed Jan. 1, Thanksgiving and Christmas; phone ahead to confirm holiday hours. **Cost:** Georgia State Railroad Museum $10; $6 (ages 2-12). Savannah Children's Museum $7.50; free (under 18 months). Savannah History Museum $7; $4 (ages 2-12). A combination ticket is available that offers admission to three of the following five sites: Georgia State Railroad Museum, Savannah Children's Museum, Savannah History Museum, Old Fort Jackson and Pin Point Heritage Museum. **Phone:** (912) 651-6823.

Georgia State Railroad Museum, in Tricentennial Park at 655 Louisville Rd., is one of the nation's oldest and most complete railroad complexes; more than a dozen buildings survive. Restored locomotives, rail cars, machinery, and a working handcar and model train are displayed. A site tour aboard a train is available.

Time: Allow 30 minutes minimum. **Hours:** Daily 9-5. Closed Jan. 1, Thanksgiving and Christmas; phone ahead to confirm holiday hours and train schedule. **Cost:** $10; $6 (ages 2-12). A combination ticket is available that offers admission to three of the following five sites: Georgia State Railroad Museum, Savannah Children's Museum, Savannah History Museum, Old Fort Jackson and Pin Point Heritage Museum. **Phone:** (912) 651-6823. GT

Savannah Children's Museum is in Tricentennial Park at 655 Louisville Rd. The outdoor museum is home to more than one dozen interactive exhibits just for kids. Children can run, explore and touch various educational displays and participate in daily programs. Highlights include a walk-through maze, a sensory garden, playable musical instruments from around the world, building with blocks and LEGOS, learning through play in Exploration Station, dress-up and story time.

Time: Allow 1 hour minimum. **Hours:** (weather permitting) Mon.-Sat. 9-2, June-Aug; Wed.-Sat. 10-4, Sun. 11-4, rest of year. **Cost:** $7.50; free (under 18 months). A combination ticket is available that offers admission to three of the following five sites: Georgia State Railroad Museum, Savannah Children's Museum, Savannah History Museum, Old Fort Jackson and Pin Point Heritage Museum. **Phone:** (912) 651-4292.

Savannah History Museum is housed in a restored mid-19th century passenger train station at 303 Martin Luther King Jr. Blvd. within Tricentennial Park. Artifacts, exhibits and an 18-minute film presentation tell Savannah's story from Native American settlement to the city's founding in 1733 to the present day. Exhibits include the cotton legacy, waterfront commerce, the railroad and railroad travel, the Revolutionary War, a couple of motor car displays and a haberdashery where children can try on period hats.

Battlefield Memorial Park, across the street, is dedicated to the 800 men who were killed and wounded in the Battle of Savannah during the American Revolution.

Time: Allow 1 hour minimum. **Hours:** Daily 9-5:30. Closed Jan. 1, Thanksgiving and Christmas; phone ahead to confirm holiday hours. **Cost:** $7; $4 (ages 2-12). A combination ticket is available that offers admission to three of the following five sites: Georgia State Railroad Museum, Savannah Children's Museum, Savannah History Museum, Old Fort Jackson and Pin Point Heritage Museum. **Parking:** $1 per hour after first hour. **Phone:** (912) 651-6825.

THE UNIVERSITY OF GEORGIA MARINE EDUCATION CENTER & AQUARIUM, on Skidaway Island at 30 Ocean Science Cir., features saltwater aquariums displaying local marine life with additional exhibits focusing on the ecology, marine science, archeology and fossils of the coastal region. A touch tank lets visitors interact with marine invertebrates. A self-guiding nature trail and boardwalk winds through maritime forest and salt marsh ecosystems. The 680-acre property, formerly portions of two plantations, is shared with the Skidaway Institute of Oceanography.

Hours: Mon.-Fri. 9-4, Sat. 10-5. Closed major holidays and most Sat. preceding Mon. holidays; phone ahead. **Cost:** $6; $3 (ages 3-12, ages 55+ and military with ID). Cash or check only. **Phone:** (912) 598-2496, or (912) 598-3474 for recorded information. 🎫

WORMSLOE STATE HISTORIC SITE, 10 mi. s.e. at 7601 Skidaway Rd. on the Isle of Hope, was established in 1736 by Noble Jones, one of 114 colonists who came to Georgia with Gen. James E. Oglethorpe. The vestiges of his fortified tabby house, constructed 1739-45, are all that remain architecturally in Savannah of Georgia's first decade. A 1.5-mile oak-lined avenue leads to the plantation's ruins.

A museum presents excavated artifacts and an audiovisual show about early settlement in Georgia. This scenic site also has nature trails, a re-created homesite, a blacksmith area and a living-history area. Interpreters dressed in period costumes demonstrate colonial crafts some mornings and afternoons.

Guided tours are available (staffing and weather permitting). **Time:** Allow 1 hour minimum. **Hours:** Tues.-Sun. and Mon. holidays 9-5. Closed Jan. 1, Thanksgiving and Christmas. **Cost:** $10; $9 (ages 62+); $4.50 (ages 6-17); $2 (ages 0-5). **Phone:** (912) 353-3023. GT 🎫

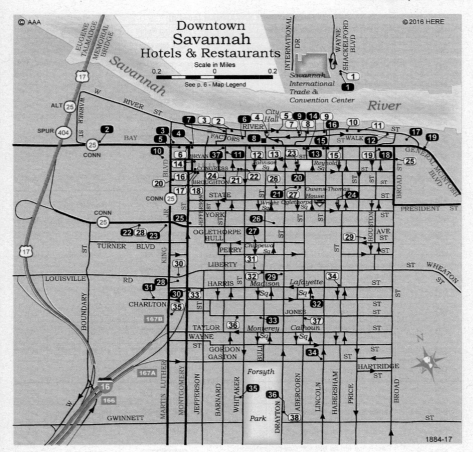

Downtown Savannah

This index helps you "spot" where approved hotels and restaurants are located on the corresponding detailed maps. Hotel daily rate range is for comparison only. Restaurant price range is a combination of lunch and/or dinner. Turn to the listing page for more detailed rate and price information and consult display ads for special promotions.

DOWNTOWN SAVANNAH

Map Page	Hotels	Diamond Rated	Rate Range	Page
1 this page	The Westin Savannah Harbor Golf Resort and Spa	▽▽▽▽	$179-$479 SAVE	270
2 this page	Comfort Suites Historic District	▽▽▽	$79-$399 SAVE	266
3 this page	Best Western Plus Savannah Historic District	▽▽▽	$79-$309 SAVE	264
4 this page	Quality Inn Savannah Historic District *(See ad p. 269.)*	▽▽	$99-$289 SAVE	269
5 this page	DoubleTree by Hilton Savannah Historic District	▽▽▽	Rates not provided SAVE	266
6 this page	The Bohemian Hotel Savannah Riverfront, Autograph Collection	▽▽▽	$171-$458 SAVE	264
7 this page	Hilton Garden Inn Savannah Historic District	▽▽▽	Rates not provided SAVE	267
8 this page	Hyatt Regency Savannah	▽▽▽	$109-$369 SAVE	268
9 this page	River Street Inn	▽▽▽	Rates not provided	269

DOWNTOWN SAVANNAH (cont'd)

Map Page	Hotels (cont'd)	Diamond Rated	Rate Range	Page
10 p. 257	**Holiday Inn Savannah Historic District**	◆◆◆	Rates not provided [SAVE]	268
11 p. 257	**Andaz Savannah**	◆◆◆◆	$179-$429 [SAVE]	264
12 p. 257	Olde Harbour Inn	◆◆◆	$180-$450	269
13 p. 257	Holiday Inn Express Historic District	◆◆◆	Rates not provided	268
14 p. 257	Hampton Inn-Savannah Historic District	◆◆◆	$129-$429	267
15 p. 257	East Bay Inn	◆◆◆	$169-$400	266
16 p. 257	Staybridge Suites Savannah Historic District	◆◆◆	Rates not provided	270
17 p. 257	**Homewood Suites Savannah Historic District/ River Street**	◆◆◆	Rates not provided [SAVE]	268
18 p. 257	**The Brice**	◆◆◆◆	Rates not provided [SAVE]	266
19 p. 257	**Savannah Marriott Riverfront**	◆◆◆	$163-$261 [SAVE]	270
20 p. 257	Planters Inn at Reynolds Square	◆◆◆	$109-$399	269
21 p. 257	Marshall House	◆◆◆	$169-$400	269
22 p. 257	**Embassy Suites by Hilton Savannah Historic District**	◆◆◆	$139-$279 [SAVE]	267
23 p. 257	**Hampton Inn & Suites Downtown Savannah Historic District**	◆◆◆	$109-$219 [SAVE]	267
24 p. 257	**Kehoe House**	◆◆◆◆	$209-$459 [SAVE]	268
25 p. 257	SpringHill Suites by Marriott Savannah Downtown/ Historic District	◆◆◆	$99-$241	270
26 p. 257	**Ballastone Inn**	◆◆◆◆	$249-$415 [SAVE]	264
27 p. 257	**Foley House Inn**	◆◆◆	Rates not provided [SAVE]	267
28 p. 257	Courtyard by Marriott Savannah Downtown/ Historic District	◆◆◆	$90-$235	266
29 p. 257	**Hilton Savannah DeSoto**	◆◆◆	$139-$299 [SAVE]	268
30 p. 257	B Historic Savannah (See ad p. 265.)	◆◆◆	Rates not provided	264
31 p. 257	Residence Inn by Marriott Downtown/Historic District	◆◆◆	$137-$248	269
32 p. 257	**Hamilton-Turner Inn**	◆◆◆	Rates not provided [SAVE]	267
33 p. 257	Eliza Thompson House Inn	◆◆◆	$149-$399	266
34 p. 257	**The Gastonian**	◆◆◆◆	$179-$525 [SAVE]	267
35 p. 257	The Forsyth Park Inn	◆◆◆	$210-$345	267
36 p. 257	**Mansion on Forsyth Park, Autograph Collection**	◆◆◆◆	$125-$352 [SAVE]	268
37 p. 257	**Hotel Indigo Savannah Historic District**	◆◆◆	$129-$799 [SAVE]	268

Map Page	Restaurants	Diamond Rated	Cuisine	Price Range	Page
1 p. 257	Aqua Star Restaurant	◆◆◆	American	$13-$44	270
2 p. 257	River House Seafood & Bakery	◆◆◆	Seafood	$10-$30	272
3 p. 257	Chart House	◆◆◆	Seafood	$11-$42	271
4 p. 257	Olympia Cafe	◆◆	Greek	$5-$26	272
5 p. 257	Vic's on the River Restaurant & Bar	◆◆◆	New Southern	$8-$38	273
6 p. 257	John Ryan's Bistro & Pub	◆◆	Regional American	$9-$27	271
7 p. 257	Huey's New Orleans Cafe	◆◆	Creole	$10-$32	271

Map Page	Restaurants (cont'd)	Diamond Rated	Cuisine	Price Range	Page
⑧ p. 257	The Cotton Exchange	◈◈	American	$9-$30	271
⑨ p. 257	Boar's Head Grill & Tavern	◈◈	New American Seafood	$9-$34	271
⑩ p. 257	Shrimp Factory	◈◈◈	Regional Seafood	$10-$36	273
⑪ p. 257	One-Eyed Lizzy's Grille & Bar	◈◈	American	$8-$24	272
⑫ p. 257	Moon River Brewing Company	◈◈	American	$7-$24	272
⑬ p. 257	Tondee's Tavern	◈◈	American	$8-$35	273
⑭ p. 257	Vinnie Van Go Go	◈	Pizza	$3-$16	273
⑮ p. 257	B. Matthew's Eatery	◈◈	New American	$8-$30	271
⑯ p. 257	Belford's Savannah	◈◈◈	American	$11-$42	270
⑰ p. 257	Garibaldi's Cafe	◈◈◈	Italian Seafood	$8-$90	271
⑱ p. 257	Molly MacPherson's Scottish Pub & Grill	◈◈	Scottish	$8-$19	272
⑲ p. 257	Pacci Italian Kitchen + Bar	◈◈◈	Italian	$11-$32	272
⑳ p. 257	Corleone's Trattoria	◈◈	Mediterranean	$6-$28	271
㉑ p. 257	Sapphire Grill	◈◈◈	New American	$23-$45	273
㉒ p. 257	The Lady & Sons	◈◈	Southern	$10-$30	271
㉓ p. 257	The Olde Pink House	◈◈◈	Regional Seafood	$15-$35	272
㉔ p. 257	Goose Feathers	◈	Breakfast Sandwiches	$4-$10	271
㉕ p. 257	The Pirates' House	◈◈◈	Regional Seafood	$10-$27	272
㉖ p. 257	B&D Burgers	◈◈	Burgers	$9-$19	270
㉗ p. 257	45 Bistro	◈◈◈	American Pizza	$12-$45	270
㉘ p. 257	39 Rue de Jean	◈◈◈	French Sushi	$8-$32	270
㉙ p. 257	Ta Ca Sushi & Japanese Fusion	◈◈	Japanese Sushi Fusion	$8-$28	273
㉚ p. 257	The Distillery	◈◈	Burgers Sandwiches	$8-$18	271
㉛ p. 257	Soho South Cafe	◈◈	Sandwiches	$9-$14	273
㉜ p. 257	The Public Kitchen & Bar	◈◈	New American	$10-$24	272
㉝ p. 257	Noble Fare	◈◈◈	Regional American	$29-$39	272
㉞ p. 257	Firefly Cafe	◈◈	American	$11-$32	271
㉟ p. 257	Rancho Alegre Cuban Restaurant	◈◈	Cuban	$8-$25	272
㊱ p. 257	Mrs. Wilkes' Dining Room	◈◈	Southern Comfort Food	$22	272
㊲ p. 257	Clary's Cafe	◈	Breakfast Sandwiches	$6-$13	271
㊳ p. 257	700 Drayton	◈◈◈	Southern American	$13-$43	270

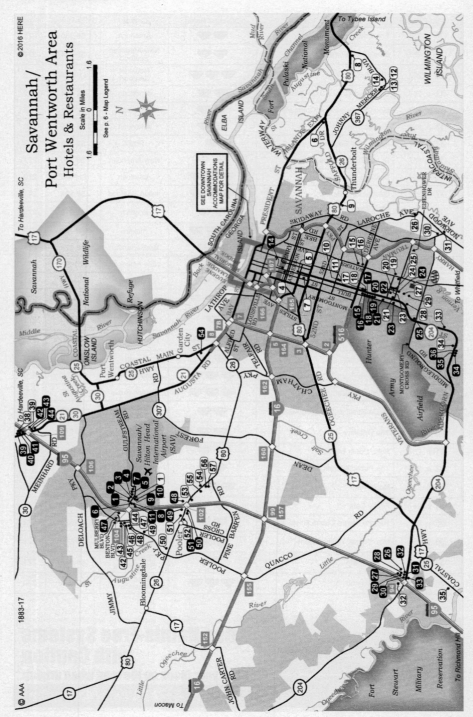

Savannah/
Port Wentworth Area
Hotels & Restaurants

©2016 HERE

See p. 6 - Map Legend

Scale in Miles

SEE DOWNTOWN
SAVANNAH
ACCOMMODATIONS
MAP FOR DETAIL.

1883-17

✈ Airport Hotels

Map Page	SAVANNAH/HILTON HEAD INTERNATIONAL AIRPORT (Maximum driving distance from airport: 3.2 mi)	Diamond Rated	Rate Range	Page
47 p. 260	Embassy Suites by Hilton-Savannah Airport, 3.2 mi	◈◈◈	$129-$299	235
2 p. 260	**Comfort Inn & Suites Savannah Airport, 1.9 mi**	◈◈◈	$79-$199 SAVE	274
5 p. 260	Country Inn & Suites By Carlson, Savannah Airport, 1.9 mi	◈◈◈	Rates not provided	274
7 p. 260	**DoubleTree by Hilton Hotel Savannah Airport, 1.9 mi**	◈◈◈	$109-$219 SAVE	275
6 p. 260	**Fairfield Inn & Suites by Marriott Savannah Airport, 2.0 mi**	◈◈◈	$89-$167 SAVE	275
11 p. 260	Hampton Inn & Suites Savannah Airport, 2.4 mi	◈◈◈	$114-$299	275
8 p. 260	Hilton Garden Inn Savannah Airport, 2.1 mi	◈◈◈	$119-$139	275
4 p. 260	Holiday Inn Express Savannah Airport, 1.9 mi	◈◈◈	$109-$209	276
9 p. 260	**Hyatt Place Savannah Airport, 1.9 mi**	◈◈◈	$79-$299 SAVE	276
1 p. 260	SpringHill Suites by Marriott Savannah Airport, 2.0 mi	◈◈◈	$104-$171	277
3 p. 260	TownePlace Suites by Marriott Savannah Airport, 1.9 mi	◈◈◈	$106-$171	277
10 p. 260	Wingate by Wyndham Savannah Airport, 2.0 mi	◈◈◈	$69-$279	277

Savannah/Port Wentworth Area

This index helps you "spot" where approved hotels and restaurants are located on the corresponding detailed maps. Hotel daily rate range is for comparison only. Restaurant price range is a combination of lunch and/or dinner. Turn to the listing page for more detailed rate and price information and consult display ads for special promotions.

SAVANNAH

Map Page	Hotels	Diamond Rated	Rate Range	Page
1 p. 260	SpringHill Suites by Marriott Savannah Airport	◈◈◈	$104-$171	277
2 p. 260	**Comfort Inn & Suites Savannah Airport**	◈◈◈	$79-$199 SAVE	274
3 p. 260	TownePlace Suites by Marriott Savannah Airport	◈◈◈	$106-$171	277
4 p. 260	Holiday Inn Express Savannah Airport	◈◈◈	$109-$209	276
5 p. 260	Country Inn & Suites By Carlson, Savannah Airport	◈◈◈	Rates not provided	274
6 p. 260	**Fairfield Inn & Suites by Marriott Savannah Airport**	◈◈◈	$89-$167 SAVE	275
7 p. 260	**DoubleTree by Hilton Hotel Savannah Airport**	◈◈◈	$109-$219 SAVE	275
8 p. 260	Hilton Garden Inn Savannah Airport	◈◈◈	$119-$139	275
9 p. 260	**Hyatt Place Savannah Airport**	◈◈◈	$79-$299 SAVE	276
10 p. 260	Wingate by Wyndham Savannah Airport	◈◈◈	$69-$279	277
11 p. 260	Hampton Inn & Suites Savannah Airport	◈◈◈	$114-$299	275
14 p. 260	Catherine Ward House Inn	◈◈◈	Rates not provided	273
15 p. 260	Extended Stay America Savannah-Midtown	◈◈	$80-$115	275
16 p. 260	**Hampton Inn & Suites Savannah Midtown**	◈◈◈	$119-$279 SAVE	275
17 p. 260	**Hilton Garden Inn Savannah Midtown**	◈◈◈	Rates not provided SAVE	275
18 p. 260	Residence Inn by Marriott Savannah Midtown	◈◈◈	$119-$234	277
19 p. 260	**Homewood Suites by Hilton** *(See ad p. 276.)*	◈◈◈	$99-$239 SAVE	276
20 p. 260	Baymont Inn & Suites Savannah Midtown	◈◈	$76-$140	273

SAVANNAH (cont'd)

Map Page	Hotels (cont'd)	Diamond Rated	Rate Range	Page
21 p. 260	**Courtyard by Marriott Savannah Midtown**	◆◆◆	$90-$191 (SAVE)	274
22 p. 260	Days Inn & Suites Midtown	◆◆	$50-$250	274
23 p. 260	**Best Western Central Inn**	◆◆	$74-$149 (SAVE)	273
24 p. 260	Comfort Inn	◆◆	Rates not provided	274
25 p. 260	La Quinta Inn & Suites	◆◆	$67-$284	276
26 p. 260	Hampton Inn & Suites I-95 Gateway	◆◆◆	$109-$199	275
27 p. 260	Clarion Suites & Conference Center	◆◆	$74-$209	274
28 p. 260	**Country Inn & Suites By Carlson-Savannah Gateway**	◆◆◆	Rates not provided (SAVE)	274
29 p. 260	Holiday Inn Savannah S I-95	◆◆◆	Rates not provided	276
30 p. 260	**Best Western Savannah Gateway**	◆◆	$75-$122 (SAVE)	273
31 p. 260	SpringHill Suites by Marriott Savannah I-95 South	◆◆◆	$98-$157	277
32 p. 260	Fairfield Inn & Suites by Marriott Savannah I-95 South	◆◆	$69-$138	275
33 p. 260	Baymont Inn & Suites	◆◆	$69-$275	273
34 p. 260	**Holiday Inn Express Inn & Suites Savannah Midtown**	◆◆◆	Rates not provided (SAVE)	276
35 p. 260	SpringHill Suites by Marriott Savannah/Midtown	◆◆	$82-$171	277
36 p. 260	TownePlace Suites by Marriott Savannah Midtown	◆◆	$80-$182	277

Map Page	Restaurants	Diamond Rated	Cuisine	Price Range	Page
1 p. 260	Sam Snead's Oak Grill & Tavern	◆◆◆	American	$10-$29	279
4 p. 260	Local 11 Ten	◆◆◆	New American	$16-$45	279
5 p. 260	Elizabeth on 37th	◆◆◆	Regional Southern	$25-$40	278
6 p. 260	Wiley's Championship BBQ	◆◆	Barbecue	$4-$30	280
7 p. 260	Back in the Day Bakery	◆	Sandwiches Breads/Pastries	$7-$9	277
8 p. 260	Ele Fine Fusion	◆◆◆	Thai Fusion	$15-$90	278
9 p. 260	Chiriya's Thai Cuisine	◆◆	Asian	$12-$30	278
10 p. 260	Bella's Italian Cafe	◆◆	Italian	$9-$24	277
11 p. 260	The 5 Spot	◆◆	American	$9-$17	277
12 p. 260	Kanpai	◆◆	Japanese Sushi	$7-$28	278
13 p. 260	Little Italy	◆◆	Italian Pizza	$10-$29	279
14 p. 260	Lili's Restaurant & Bar	◆◆	Fusion	$9-$30	278
15 p. 260	Barnes Restaurant	◆◆	Regional Barbecue	$6-$25	277
16 p. 260	Saigon Bistro	◆◆	Vietnamese	$8-$15	279
17 p. 260	Bonefish Grill	◆◆◆	Seafood	$12-$29	277
18 p. 260	Cancun Mexican Restaurant	◆◆	Mexican	$4-$12	278
19 p. 260	The Exchange on Waters Restaurant & Bar	◆◆	American	$7-$22	278
20 p. 260	The Noodle Bowl	◆◆	Asian	$6-$25	279
21 p. 260	Toni Steakhouse	◆◆◆	Steak Seafood	$9-$55	280
23 p. 260	Caribbean Cuisine Restaurant	◆◆	Caribbean	$8-$15	278

Map Page	Restaurants (cont'd)	Diamond Rated	Cuisine	Price Range	Page
㉔ p. 260	The King and I	◆◆	Thai	$9-$23	278
㉕ p. 260	**Sweet Potatoes Kitchen**	◆◆	Regional Comfort Food	$8-$12	279
㉖ p. 260	Pearl's Saltwater Grille Seafood & Steaks	◆◆	Seafood	$9-$26	279
㉗ p. 260	Fiddler's Seafood Southside	◆◆	Seafood	$8-$30	278
㉘ p. 260	La Parrilla Mexican Restaurant	◆◆	Mexican	$6-$18	278
㉙ p. 260	Taste of India	◆◆	Indian	$8-$25	279
㉚ p. 260	Fiore Italian Bar & Grill	◆◆◆	Italian	$9-$26	278
㉛ p. 260	Driftaway Cafe	◆◆	Seafood	$11-$24	278
㉜ p. 260	The Shell House Restaurant	◆◆	Seafood	$13-$40	279
㉝ p. 260	Troy Mediterranean Cuisine	◆◆	Mediterranean	$8-$24	280
㉞ p. 260	B&D Burgers	◆◆	Burgers	$9-$19	277
㉟ p. 260	Love's Seafood Restaurant	◆◆	Seafood	$11-$30	279

PORT WENTWORTH

Map Page	Hotels	Diamond Rated	Rate Range	Page
㊴ p. 260	Holiday Inn Express Savannah North	◆◆◆	$119-$189	237
㊵ p. 260	Sleep Inn I-95 North Savannah	◆◆	$59-$129	237
㊶ p. 260	Comfort Suites Savannah North	◆◆◆	$89-$179	237
㊷ p. 260	Country Inn & Suites By Carlson Savannah North	◆◆◆	Rates not provided	237
㊸ p. 260	Hampton Inn Savannah North	◆◆◆	$115-$219	237
㊹ p. 260	**Best Western Plus North Savannah**	◆◆◆	$90-$100 SAVE	237

Map Page	Restaurants	Diamond Rated	Cuisine	Price Range	Page
㊳ p. 260	Port Side Seafood	◆◆	Seafood Sandwiches	$10-$22	237
㊴ p. 260	Sweet Tea Grille	◆◆	Southern	$9-$20	237

POOLER

Map Page	Hotels	Diamond Rated	Rate Range	Page
㊼ p. 260	Embassy Suites by Hilton-Savannah Airport	◆◆◆	$129-$299	235
㊽ p. 260	**Best Western Plus Savannah Airport Inn & Suites**	◆◆◆	$89-$149 SAVE	235
㊾ p. 260	La Quinta Inn & Suites Savannah Airport-Pooler	◆◆◆	$90-$225	235
㊿ p. 260	**Holiday Inn Hotel & Suites-Savannah/Pooler**	◆◆◆	$129-$169 SAVE	235
(51) p. 260	Magnolia Inn	◆◆	Rates not provided	235

Map Page	Restaurants	Diamond Rated	Cuisine	Price Range	Page
㊷ p. 260	MIWA Japanese Restaurant	◆◆	Japanese Sushi	$6-$19	236
㊸ p. 260	Mediterranean Tavern	◆◆	Mediterranean	$8-$26	236
㊹ p. 260	Molly MacPherson's Scottish Pub & Grill	◆◆	Scottish	$8-$18	236
㊺ p. 260	Sushi Hana	◆◆◆	Japanese Sushi	$4-$25	236
㊻ p. 260	World of Beer	◆◆	Small Plates Sandwiches	$8-$15	236
㊼ p. 260	Jalapeno's Authentic Mexican Grill	◆◆	Mexican	$8-$15	235
㊽ p. 260	B & D Burgers Bar & Grill	◆◆	Burgers Sandwiches	$8-$17	235
㊾ p. 260	Bahama Bob's	◆◆	Seafood	$8-$20	235
㊿ p. 260	Naan Appetit	◆◆	Indian	$11-$14	236

Map Page	Restaurants (cont'd)	Diamond Rated	Cuisine	Price Range	Page
51 p. 260	Lovezzola's Pizza Restaurant	▽	Pizza Sandwiches	$5-$15	236
52 p. 260	Savannah Gyro	▽	Sandwiches Burgers	$3-$9	236
53 p. 260	Terra Mia	▽▽	Italian Pizza	$9-$24	236
54 p. 260	Los Bravos Grill & Cantina	▽▽	Tex-Mex	$6-$15	235
55 p. 260	Guerrero Mexican Restaurant	▽▽	Mexican	$4-$14	235
56 p. 260	Smokin Pig The Bar-B-Q-Joint	▽	Barbecue	$5-$19	236
57 p. 260	Spanky's Pizza Galley & Saloon	▽▽	American	$9-$24	236

GARDEN CITY					
Map Page	Hotel		Diamond Rated	Rate Range	Page
54 p. 260	Baymont Inn & Suites		▽▽	$69-$250 SAVE	186

DOWNTOWN SAVANNAH
- Restaurants p. 270
- Hotels & Restaurants map & index p. 257

ANDAZ SAVANNAH
(912)233-2116 **11**

Hotel
$179-$429

ANDAZ.

AAA Benefit: Members save 10%!

Address: 14 Barnard St 31401 **Location:** Jct Barnard and W Bryan sts. **Facility:** This modern hotel offers a prime downtown location, upscale accommodations and added amenities. Standard rooms and large two-room suites are offered. Some have private balconies providing city views. 151 units, some efficiencies. 6 stories, interior corridors. **Parking:** valet only. **Terms:** check-in 4 pm, cancellation fee imposed. **Amenities:** safes. **Pool(s):** heated outdoor. **Activities:** exercise room. **Guest Services:** valet laundry.

SAVE ▯ ▯ ▯ CALL ▯M ▯ BIZ HS ▯ ▯
▯ / SOME UNITS ▯ ▯ ▯

BALLASTONE INN
(912)236-1484 **26**

Historic Bed
& Breakfast
$249-$415

Address: 14 E Oglethorpe Ave 31401 **Location:** Between Bull and Drayton sts. **Facility:** This restored antebellum inn, built in 1838, was Savannah's first B&B. Its large rooms are tastefully furnished with Victorian antiques and reproductions. 16 units. 4 stories, interior corridors. **Parking:** on-site and street. **Terms:** 2 night minimum stay - seasonal and/or weekends, cancellation fee imposed. **Activities:** massage. **Guest Services:** valet laundry. **Featured Amenity:** full hot breakfast.

SAVE ▯ ▯ ▯

BEST WESTERN PLUS SAVANNAH HISTORIC DISTRICT
(912)233-1011 **3**

▽▽▽
Motel
$79-$309

Best Western PLUS

AAA Benefit: Save 10% or more every day and earn 10% bonus points!

Address: 412 W Bay St 31401 **Location:** Jct Montgomery St. **Facility:** 89 units. 3 stories, exterior corridors. **Parking:** on-site (fee). **Terms:** check-in 4 pm. **Pool(s):** heated outdoor. **Activities:** exercise room. **Guest Services:** valet laundry.

SAVE ▯ ▯ BIZ ▯ ▯ ▯
▯ / SOME UNITS ▯

B HISTORIC SAVANNAH
912/921-5300 **30**

Contemporary Hotel. Rates not provided. **Address:** 320 Montgomery St 31401 **Location:** Just s of W Liberty St. **Facility:** 101 units. 5 stories, interior corridors. **Parking:** on-site (fee). **Terms:** check-in 4 pm. **Pool(s):** heated indoor. **Activities:** exercise room. **Guest Services:** valet and coin laundry. (See ad p. 265.)

▯ CALL ▯M ▯ BIZ HS ▯
▯ ▯ ▯

THE BOHEMIAN HOTEL SAVANNAH RIVERFRONT, AUTOGRAPH COLLECTION
(912)721-3800 **6**

▽▽▽
Boutique
Contemporary
Hotel
$171-$458

AUTOGRAPH COLLECTION HOTELS

AAA Benefit: Members save 5% or more!

Address: 102 E Bay St 31401 **Location:** Waterfront. Between Bull and Whitaker sts. **Facility:** This beautiful and unusual hotel features original artwork in its public areas and rooms, a web-based entertainment system in each room, a rooftop lounge, and a street-level lounge and restaurant. 75 units. 9 stories, interior corridors. **Parking:** valet only. **Terms:** check-in 4 pm, 3 day cancellation notice. **Amenities:** safes. **Dining:** 2 restaurants. **Activities:** exercise room. **Guest Services:** valet laundry.

SAVE ▯ ▯ ▯ CALL ▯M BIZ HS ▯ ▯ ▯

▯ / SOME UNITS ▯

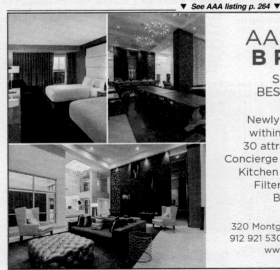
Before you travel, ask your AAA/CAA club
about identity theft monitoring products

(See map & index p. 257.)

THE BRICE
912/238-1200 **18**

Boutique
Contemporary
Retro Hotel
Rates not provided

Address: 601 E Bay St 31401 **Location:** Between Houston and E Broad sts. **Facility:** You will enjoy the comfortable, uniquely decorated standard rooms and larger suites with pull-out sofas. The public areas are beautiful and include a large outdoor courtyard as the centerpiece. 145 units. 3 stories, interior corridors. **Parking:** valet only. **Terms:** check-in 4 pm. **Amenities:** safes. **Dining:** Pacci Italian Kitchen + Bar, see separate listing. **Pool(s):** outdoor. **Guest Services:** valet laundry.

COMFORT SUITES HISTORIC DISTRICT
(912)629-2001 **2**

Hotel
$79-$399

Address: 630 W Bay St 31401 **Location:** Between Fahm and W Boundary sts; on west side of historic district. **Facility:** 76 units. 3 stories, interior corridors. **Parking:** on-site (fee). **Pool(s):** heated indoor. **Activities:** hot tub, bicycles, exercise room. **Guest Services:** valet and coin laundry, area transportation. **Featured Amenity:** full hot breakfast.

COURTYARD BY MARRIOTT SAVANNAH DOWNTOWN/ HISTORIC DISTRICT
(912)790-8287 **28**

Hotel. $90-$235 **Address:** 415 W Liberty St 31401 **Location:** Between Martin Luther King Jr Blvd and Montgomery St. **Facility:** 156 units. 5 stories, interior corridors. **Parking:** valet only. **Terms:** check-in 4 pm. **Pool(s):** heated outdoor. **Activities:** hot tub, exercise room. **Guest Services:** valet and coin laundry, boarding pass kiosk.

AAA Benefit:
Members save 5%
or more!

DOUBLETREE BY HILTON SAVANNAH HISTORIC DISTRICT
912/790-7000 **5**

Contemporary
Hotel
Rates not provided

AAA Benefit:
Members save 5% or more!

Address: 411 W Bay St 31401 **Location:** Jct Montgomery St. **Facility:** 150 units. 6 stories, interior corridors. **Parking:** valet only. **Terms:** check-in 4 pm. **Amenities:** video games. **Dining:** John Ryan's Bistro & Pub, see separate listing. **Pool(s):** heated outdoor. **Activities:** hot tub, exercise room. **Guest Services:** valet and coin laundry.

Location. Location. Location. Full service by River Street and City Market! Great rates!!

EAST BAY INN
(912)238-1225 **15**

Historic Country Inn. $169-$400 **Address:** 225 E Bay St 31401 **Location:** Between Abercorn and Lincoln sts. **Facility:** Four-poster rice beds and 18-foot ceilings are among the elegant features found in this restored 1853 cotton warehouse's individually decorated rooms. It's walking distance to popular attractions. 28 units. 3 stories, interior corridors. **Parking:** on-site (fee). **Terms:** 2-3 night minimum stay - seasonal and/or weekends, 7 day cancellation notice-fee imposed. **Amenities:** safes. **Guest Services:** valet laundry.

ELIZA THOMPSON HOUSE INN
(912)236-3620 **33**

Historic Bed & Breakfast. $149-$399 **Address:** 5 W Jones St 31401 **Location:** Between Whitaker and Bull sts. **Facility:** Located in the center of the residential historic district, this restored 1847 home features an attractive courtyard area with a fountain where breakfast is served daily. 25 units. 3 stories (no elevator), interior/exterior corridors. **Parking:** on-site (fee) and street. **Terms:** 2 night minimum stay - seasonal and/or weekends, 7 day cancellation notice-fee imposed. **Amenities:** safes.

▼ See AAA listing p. 275 ▼

(See map & index p. 257.)

EMBASSY SUITES BY HILTON SAVANNAH HISTORIC DISTRICT (912)721-6900 🔢22

Hotel
$139-$279

AAA Benefit:
Members save 5% or more!

Address: 605 W Oglethorpe Ave 31401 **Location:** Jct Martin Luther King Jr Blvd, just w. **Facility:** 150 units, some two bedrooms. 6 stories, interior corridors. **Parking:** on-site (fee) and valet. **Terms:** check-in 4 pm, 1-7 night minimum stay, cancellation fee imposed. **Amenities:** safes. **Dining:** 39 Rue de Jean, see separate listing. **Pool(s):** outdoor. **Activities:** exercise room. **Guest Services:** valet and coin laundry. **Featured Amenity:** breakfast buffet.

E EMBASSY SUITES by HILTON

Located in Downtown Historic Savannah, walking distance to City Market, Riverfront & attractions.

FOLEY HOUSE INN 912/232-6622 🔢27

Historic Bed & Breakfast

Rates not provided

Address: 14 W Hull St 31401 **Location:** Between Bull and Whitaker sts; on Chippewa Square. **Facility:** Located in the center of the historic district, this inn offers upscale accommodations furnished with period antiques and luxurious amenities. Two private garden courtyards also are on the premises. 19 units. 2-4 stories (no elevator), interior/exterior corridors. **Parking:** on-site (fee) and street. **Amenities:** safes. **Guest Services:** valet laundry. **Featured Amenity:** full hot breakfast.

THE FORSYTH PARK INN (912)233-6800 🔢35

Historic Bed & Breakfast. $210-$345 **Address:** 102 W Hall St 31401 **Location:** Between Whitaker and Howard sts; across from Forsyth Park. **Facility:** An original oak staircase, 12-foot-tall solid oak doors and a garden patio distinguish this restored Victorian mansion overlooking Savannah's largest park in the historic residential district. 12 units, some cottages. 3 stories (no elevator), interior corridors. **Parking:** street only. **Terms:** 2 night minimum stay - seasonal and/or weekends, 14 day cancellation notice-fee imposed. **Guest Services:** valet laundry.

THE GASTONIAN (912)232-2869 🔢34

Classic Historic Bed & Breakfast

$179-$525

Address: 220 E Gaston St 31401 **Location:** Between Abercorn and Lincoln sts. **Facility:** All accommodations in this inn's conjoined 1868 houses are furnished with English antiques and include a functional fireplace. The main public rooms are decorated in a subdued elegance. 17 units. 4 stories (no elevator), interior/exterior corridors. **Parking:** on-site and street. **Terms:** 2 night minimum stay - seasonal and/or weekends, 7 day cancellation notice-fee imposed. **Amenities:** safes. **Guest Services:** valet laundry. **Featured Amenity:** full hot breakfast.

HAMILTON-TURNER INN 912/233-1833 🔢32

Historic Bed & Breakfast

Rates not provided

Address: 330 Abercorn St 31401 **Location:** Between E Charlton and E Harris sts; overlooking Lafayette Square. **Facility:** A Southern ambiance is evident in this converted Second French Empire-style mansion circa 1873 that's furnished with period antiques from area estates and features a hand illustrated parlor. 17 units. 4 stories (no elevator), interior/exterior corridors. **Parking:** street only. **Terms:** age restrictions may apply. **Guest Services:** valet laundry.

HAMPTON INN & SUITES DOWNTOWN SAVANNAH HISTORIC DISTRICT (912)721-1600 🔢23

Hotel
$109-$219

AAA Benefit:
Members save up to 10%!

Address: 603 W Oglethorpe Ave 31401 **Location:** Jct Martin Luther King Jr Blvd. **Facility:** 154 units. 6 stories, interior corridors. **Parking:** on-site (fee) and valet. **Terms:** check-in 4 pm, 1-7 night minimum stay, cancellation fee imposed. **Amenities:** video games. **Pool(s):** outdoor. **Activities:** exercise room. **Guest Services:** valet and coin laundry.

Hampton by HILTON

Located in Downtown Savannah's Historic District, just blocks from shopping and dining.

HAMPTON INN-SAVANNAH HISTORIC DISTRICT (912)231-9700 🔢14

Hotel. $129-$429 **Address:** 201 E Bay St 31401 **Location:** Corner of Abercorn St. **Facility:** 144 units. 7 stories, interior corridors. **Parking:** valet only. **Terms:** check-in 4 pm, 1-7 night minimum stay, cancellation fee imposed. **Pool(s):** outdoor. **Activities:** exercise room. **Guest Services:** valet laundry.

AAA Benefit:
Members save up to 10%!

HILTON GARDEN INN SAVANNAH HISTORIC DISTRICT 912/721-5000 🔢7

Hotel
Rates not provided

Hilton Garden Inn

AAA Benefit:
Members save up to 10%!

Address: 321 W Bay St 31401 **Location:** Jct Montgomery St. **Facility:** 133 units. 6 stories, interior corridors. **Parking:** valet only. **Terms:** check-in 4 pm. **Pool(s):** heated outdoor. **Activities:** hot tub, exercise room. **Guest Services:** valet and coin laundry.

Ask your AAA/CAA club about travel money and other financial services for travelers

(See map & index p. 257.)

HILTON SAVANNAH DESOTO　(912)232-9000　29

Hotel
$139-$299

AAA Benefit:
Members save 5% or more!

Address: 15 E Liberty St 31401 **Location:** Between Bull and Drayton sts. **Facility:** 246 units. 15 stories, interior corridors. **Parking:** valet only. **Terms:** check-in 4 pm, 1-7 night minimum stay, cancellation fee imposed. **Amenities:** safes. **Pool(s):** outdoor. **Activities:** exercise room. **Guest Services:** valet laundry.

Downtown Historic Savannah. Convenient to City Market & River St. Outdoor pool & patio. Free Wi-Fi.

HOLIDAY INN EXPRESS HISTORIC DISTRICT
912/231-9000　13

Hotel. Rates not provided. **Address:** 199 E Bay St 31401 **Location:** Jct Abercorn St. **Facility:** 143 units. 8 stories, interior corridors. **Parking:** valet only. **Terms:** check-in 4 pm. **Pool(s):** heated outdoor. **Activities:** hot tub, exercise room. **Guest Services:** valet laundry.

HOLIDAY INN SAVANNAH HISTORIC DISTRICT
912/790-1000　10

Contemporary Hotel
Rates not provided

Address: 520 W Bryan St 31401 **Location:** Between Olive and Bryan sts. **Facility:** 127 units. 5 stories, interior corridors. **Parking:** on-site (fee) and valet. **Pool(s):** outdoor. **Activities:** exercise room. **Guest Services:** valet and coin laundry.

HOMEWOOD SUITES SAVANNAH HISTORIC DISTRICT/RIVER STREET　912/355-0025　17

Extended Stay Hotel
Rates not provided

AAA Benefit:
Members save up to 10%!

Address: 611 E River St 31401 **Location:** Waterfront. Terminus of River St; at E Bay St. **Facility:** 162 efficiencies. 7 stories, interior corridors. **Parking:** valet only. **Pool(s):** outdoor. **Activities:** exercise room. **Guest Services:** valet and coin laundry. **Featured Amenity:** breakfast buffet.

HOMEWOOD SUITES BY HILTON
Brand NEW. Located on River Street. Rooftop pool. Free breakfast.

HOTEL INDIGO SAVANNAH HISTORIC DISTRICT
(912)236-4440　37

Historic Hotel
$129-$799

Address: 201 W Bay St 31401 **Location:** Between Barnard and Jefferson sts; enter at Barnard St and W Bay Ln. **Facility:** This hotel, newly built in 2016, has a facade that matches the historic area but with a contemporary décor inside. Standard rooms and suites are offered. The double queen rooms have limited seating. 252 units. 3-7 stories, interior corridors. *Bath:* shower only. **Parking:** valet only. **Terms:** check-in 4 pm, cancellation fee imposed. **Activities:** exercise room. **Guest Services:** valet laundry.

HYATT REGENCY SAVANNAH　(912)238-1234　8

Hotel
$109-$369

HYATT REGENCY

AAA Benefit: Members save 10%!

Address: 2 W Bay St 31401 **Location:** Waterfront. Jct Whitaker St. Next to City Hall. **Facility:** 351 units. 7 stories, interior corridors. **Parking:** valet only. **Terms:** 3 day cancellation notice-fee imposed. **Amenities:** safes. **Dining:** 2 restaurants. **Pool(s):** heated indoor. **Activities:** boat dock. **Guest Services:** valet laundry.

KEHOE HOUSE　(912)232-1020　24

Historic Bed & Breakfast
$209-$459

Address: 123 Habersham St 31401 **Location:** Between E President and E State sts; on Columbia Square. **Facility:** An elegantly furnished European-style inn is contained within this meticulously restored 1892 Victorian mansion featuring a red brick exterior with ornate architectural accents. 13 units. 4 stories, interior corridors. **Parking:** on-site (fee). **Terms:** 2 night minimum stay - seasonal and/or weekends, 7 day cancellation notice-fee imposed. **Amenities:** safes. **Guest Services:** valet laundry. **Featured Amenity:** full hot breakfast.

MANSION ON FORSYTH PARK, AUTOGRAPH COLLECTION　(912)238-5158　36

Classic Historic Hotel
$125-$352

AUTOGRAPH COLLECTION HOTELS

AAA Benefit: Members save 5% or more!

Address: 700 Drayton St 31401 **Location:** Between E Hall and E Gwinnett sts; on Forsyth Park. **Facility:** This lushly appointed Victorian mansion exudes an aura of refinement and class in its high-end appointments and amenities. All rooms offer original works of art, plush bedding and oversize tubs. 125 units. 4 stories, interior corridors. **Parking:** valet only. **Terms:** check-in 4 pm. **Amenities:** safes. **Dining:** 700 Drayton, see separate listing. **Pool(s):** heated outdoor. **Activities:** exercise room, spa. **Guest Services:** valet laundry, area transportation.

(See map & index p. 257.)

MARSHALL HOUSE (912)644-7896
 Classic Historic Country Inn. $169-$400 **Address:** 123 E Broughton St 31401 **Location:** Between Drayton and Abercorn sts. **Facility:** The restored 1851 property offers the charm and friendly warmth of a country inn with all the amenities expected of a modern hotel. A variety of room styles are offered from petite to two-room suites. 68 units. 4 stories, interior corridors. **Parking:** valet only. **Terms:** 2 night minimum stay - seasonal and/or weekends, 7 day cancellation notice-fee imposed. **Amenities:** safes. **Dining:** 45 Bistro, see separate listing. **Guest Services:** valet laundry.

OLDE HARBOUR INN (912)234-4100 12
 Historic Bed & Breakfast. $180-$450 **Address:** 508 E Factors Walk 31401 **Location:** Waterfront. Lincoln St ramp off E Bay St. **Facility:** The inn offers one- and two-bedroom accommodations with living rooms. A few of the studios have a kitchen, and some afford river views. The two-bedroom suites have a standard bedroom and an open loft. 24 units, some two bedrooms and kitchens. 3 stories (no elevator), exterior corridors. **Parking:** on-site (fee). **Terms:** 2 night minimum stay - seasonal and/or weekends, 7 day cancellation notice-fee imposed. **Amenities:** safes. **Guest Services:** valet laundry.

PLANTERS INN AT REYNOLDS SQUARE (912)232-5678 20
 Historic Boutique Hotel. $109-$399 **Address:** 29 Abercorn St 31401 **Location:** Corner of E Congress; on Reynolds Square. **Facility:** Individually decorated rooms with 18-foot ceilings add charm to this historic inn. Guests will appreciate its location, across from Reynolds Park and just blocks from the riverfront. 60 units. 7 stories, interior corridors. **Parking:** on-site (fee) and valet. **Terms:** check-in 4 pm, 3 day cancellation notice. **Amenities:** safes. **Guest Services:** valet laundry.

Say YES to ERS text updates
to stay posted when your
tow truck is on the way

QUALITY INN SAVANNAH HISTORIC DISTRICT
(912)236-6321 4
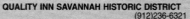
Motel
$99-$289

Address: 300 W Bay St 31401 **Location:** Between N Montgomery and N Jefferson sts. **Facility:** 52 units. 2 stories (no elevator), exterior corridors. **Parking:** on-site (fee). **Terms:** check-in 4 pm. *(See ad this page.)*

Steps from River Street & City Market. Free Breakfast. Trolley pick up at hotel.

RESIDENCE INN BY MARRIOTT DOWNTOWN/HISTORIC DISTRICT (912)233-9996 31
Extended Stay Hotel. $137-$248 **Address:** 500 W Charlton St 31401 **Location:** Jct Martin Luther King Jr Blvd. **Facility:** 109 efficiencies, some two bedrooms and cottages. 3 stories, interior corridors. **Parking:** on-site (fee) and valet. **Pool(s):** outdoor. **Activities:** exercise room. **Guest Services:** valet and coin laundry.

AAA Benefit:
Members save 5% or more!

RIVER STREET INN 912/234-6400 9
Historic Country Inn. Rates not provided. **Address:** 124 E Bay St 31401 **Location:** Waterfront. Between Abercorn and Drayton sts. **Facility:** Southern grace and simple charm can be found at this historic former warehouse with rooms that feature period furnishings and four-poster beds. Some riverfront and riverview rooms have a balcony. 86 units. 5 stories, interior corridors. **Parking:** on-site (fee) and street. **Terms:** check-in 4 pm. **Amenities:** safes. **Dining:** Huey's New Orleans Cafe, see separate listing. **Activities:** exercise room. **Guest Services:** valet laundry.

▼ See AAA listing this page ▼

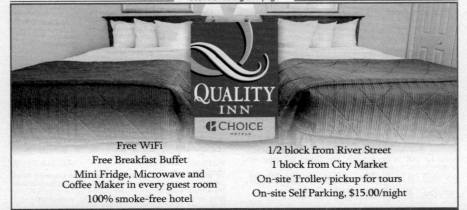

(See map & index p. 257.)

SAVANNAH MARRIOTT RIVERFRONT
(912)233-7722

Hotel
$163-$261

AAA Benefit: Members save 5% or more!

Address: 100 General McIntosh Blvd 31401 **Location:** Waterfront. East end of E Bay St. **Facility:** 387 units. 8 stories, interior corridors. **Parking:** on-site (fee) and valet. **Terms:** check-in 4 pm. **Pool(s):** outdoor. **Activities:** exercise room, spa. **Guest Services:** valet and coin laundry.

/ SOME UNITS

SPRINGHILL SUITES BY MARRIOTT SAVANNAH
DOWNTOWN/HISTORIC DISTRICT
(912)629-5300

Contemporary Hotel. $99-$241 **Address:** 150 Montgomery St 31401 **Location:** I-16 exit 167B, just ne; jct E Oglethorpe Ave. **Facility:** 160 units. 6 stories, interior corridors. **Parking:** on-site and valet. **Terms:** check-in 4 pm. **Pool(s):** heated outdoor. **Activities:** hot tub, exercise room. **Guest Services:** valet and coin laundry.

AAA Benefit: Members save 5% or more!

STAYBRIDGE SUITES SAVANNAH HISTORIC DISTRICT
912/721-9000

Extended Stay Hotel. Rates not provided. **Address:** 301 E Bay St 31401 **Location:** Corner of Lincoln St. **Facility:** 104 efficiencies. 2-5 stories, interior corridors. **Parking:** on-site (fee). **Activities:** exercise room. **Guest Services:** complimentary and valet laundry.

/ SOME UNITS

THE WESTIN SAVANNAH HARBOR GOLF RESORT AND SPA
(912)201-2000

Resort Hotel
$179-$479

WESTIN HOTELS & RESORTS **AAA Benefit:** Members save up to 15%, plus Starwood Preferred Guest® benefits!

Address: 1 Resort Dr 31421 **Location:** Waterfront. On Hutchinson Island; 1 mi se of first exit after Eugene Talmadge Memorial Bridge and US 17. **Facility:** The resort offers oversize rooms and upgraded suites that overlook river and harbor activities. A water-taxi service to historic River Street is available at the resort's dock. 403 units. 16 stories, interior corridors. **Parking:** on-site (fee) and valet. **Terms:** 3 day cancellation notice-fee imposed, resort fee. **Amenities:** safes. **Dining:** Aqua Star Restaurant, see separate listing. **Pool(s):** heated outdoor. **Activities:** sauna, hot tub, steamroom, boat dock, regulation golf, tennis, bicycles, spa. **Guest Services:** valet laundry, boarding pass kiosk.

/ SOME UNITS

39 RUE DE JEAN
912/721-0595

French Sushi. Fine Dining. $8-$32 **AAA Inspector Notes:** French brasserie cuisine, a sophisticated but unpretentious atmosphere, and an extensive wine list are featured in this distinctively decorated and decidedly European restaurant. On the menu are classically prepared entrées and hors d'oeuvres, such as pork Brittany, escargot, boudin blanc, braised rabbit and salmon béarnaise along center cut steaks. There also are several sushi and nigiri offerings for diversity. Meals are enhanced by complex yet delicate sauces which really add a wow factor. **Features:** full bar, happy hour. **Address:** 605 W Oglethorpe Ave 31401 **Location:** Jct Martin Luther King Jr Blvd, just w; in Embassy Suites by Hilton Savannah Historic District. **Parking:** valet and street only.

45 BISTRO
912/234-3111

American Pizza. Fine Dining. $12-$45 **AAA Inspector Notes:** Classic Historic. This dining spot is a popular downtown venue. The atrium garden setting, professional waitstaff and gourmet a la carte menu combine to create a relaxing dining experience and a great meal. Highlights include Cervena venison chop, king crab omelet, duck two ways and grilled black Angus fillet. All dishes are well prepared and presented with an imaginative array of accompaniments. **Features:** full bar, happy hour. **Reservations:** suggested. **Address:** 123 E Broughton St 31401 **Location:** Between Drayton and Abercorn sts; in Marshall House. **Parking:** valet and street only.

700 DRAYTON
912/721-5002

Southern American. Fine Dining. $13-$43 **AAA Inspector Notes:** Historic. This restaurant offers an upscale and sophisticated atmosphere with beautiful art work, high ceilings, polished wood floors and walls, custom chairs and sofas in the lounge area and distinctive lighting accents. The food is prepared to perfection with tempting appetizers like Kessler calamari with sweet olives and tomato concasse or choose hand-harvested Carolina scallops with Madagascar vanilla-corn emulsion, wild mushrooms and asparagus. The wine list is extensive. **Features:** full bar, patio dining, Sunday brunch, happy hour. **Reservations:** suggested. **Address:** 700 Drayton St 31401 **Location:** Between E Hall and E Gwinnett sts; on Forsyth Park; in Mansion on Forsyth Park, Autograph Collection. **Parking:** valet and street only.

AQUA STAR RESTAURANT
912/201-2000

American. Fine Dining. $13-$44 **AAA Inspector Notes:** Enjoy fine dining at this casually elegant signature restaurant. Diners can choose from a selection of fresh local seafood, beef and chicken served with organic and heirloom vegetables while watching the ships sail by against the backdrop of Savannah's historic skyline. The second-story location and large picture windows overlooking the river give the effect of dining on the water. **Features:** full bar, Sunday brunch, happy hour. **Reservations:** suggested. **Address:** 1 Resort Dr 31421 **Location:** On Hutchinson Island; 1 mi se of first exit after Eugene Talmadge Memorial Bridge and US 17; in The Westin Savannah Harbor Golf Resort and Spa. **Parking:** on-site (fee) and valet.

B&D BURGERS
912/231-0986

Burgers. Casual Dining. $9-$19 **AAA Inspector Notes:** More than 33 burger combinations can be found on the menu at this spot and there is an option to create your own from the toppings listed. Some toppers include olives, mushrooms, pineapple, egg, salsa, ham and sun-dried tomatoes. **Features:** beer & wine, happy hour. **Address:** 13 E Broughton St 31401 **Location:** Jct Broughton and Drayton sts. **Parking:** on-site and street.

BELFORD'S SAVANNAH
912/233-2626

American. Fine Dining. $11-$42 **AAA Inspector Notes:** Historic. Boasting brick walls, large arched windows and wood floors, this restaurant resides in a historic building built around 1902. Features include a well-rounded menu of steaks, seafood and pastas. During lunch diners can find lighter fare with sandwiches and salads dominating but a few full entrée menu favorites remain available. Specialties include crab cakes, shrimp and grits and smoked salmon which is the size of a main course. **Features:** full bar, patio dining, Sunday brunch, happy hour. **Reservations:** suggested. **Address:** 315 W Saint Julian St 31401 **Location:** Between Montgomery and Jefferson sts; at City Market. **Parking:** street only.

(See map & index p. 257.)

B. MATTHEW'S EATERY   912/233-1319   ⑮
🍷🍷 New American. Casual Dining. $8-$30 **AAA Inspector Notes:** *Historic.* The shop is in a historic building with exposed brick walls and dark wood appointments, somewhat reminiscent of a roadside inn of bygone days. The quality of the products, as well as the skill of the chef, combine to create flavorful, upscale cuisine for evening diners and standard fare for the lunch crowd. On the lunch menu you'll find the infamous tur-duck-en burger and the black-eyed pea cake sandwich but come evening the upscale elements set in with dishes like rosemary confit lamb shank. **Features:** full bar, patio dining, Sunday brunch. **Address:** 325 E Bay St 31401 **Location:** Between Habersham and Price sts; on east side of historic district. **Parking:** street only. Ⓑ Ⓛ Ⓓ

BOAR'S HEAD GRILL & TAVERN   912/651-9660   ⑨
🍷🍷 New American Seafood. Casual Dining. $9-$34 **AAA Inspector Notes:** *Historic.* The restored cotton warehouse affords nice views of the river. A Southern chef infuses the award-winning chef-owner's New American cuisine, which is beautifully presented. The menu is diverse, service is good, and the distinctive dessert creations merit the indulgence. **Features:** full bar, patio dining, happy hour. **Address:** 1 N Lincoln St 31401 **Location:** Jct River St. **Parking:** street only. Ⓛ Ⓓ

CHART HOUSE   912/234-6686   ③
🍷🍷 Seafood. Fine Dining. $11-$42 **AAA Inspector Notes:** *Historic.* Examples of the fabulous food include prime rib, filet mignon, tomato-basil chicken and varied fresh fish and seafood dishes. **Features:** full bar, patio dining, early bird specials, happy hour. **Reservations:** suggested. **Address:** 202 W Bay St 31401 **Location:** Between Montgomery and Whitaker sts. **Parking:** street only. Ⓛ Ⓓ

CLARY'S CAFE   912/233-0402   ㊲
🍷 Breakfast Sandwiches. Casual Dining. $6-$13 **AAA Inspector Notes:** Serving the area since 1903, and at this location since the 1940s, this one-time drug store soda fountain was featured in the book "Midnight in the Garden of Good and Evil." Cuisine is simple and service is inconsistent at times, but guests still enjoy all day breakfast offerings and house desserts like the super-sized éclairs. The soda fountain still is in operation for those in the mood for a float or banana split. **Features:** patio dining. **Address:** 404 Abercorn St 31401 **Location:** Jct Jones St. **Parking:** on-site and street. Ⓑ Ⓛ 🐾

CORLEONE'S TRATTORIA   912/232-2720   ⑳
🍷🍷 Mediterranean. Casual Dining. $6-$28 **AAA Inspector Notes:** This downtown corner eatery offers a lengthy menu of traditional pasta dishes, panini and a few Greek entrées. Ciabatta pizzas also are available during lunch service only. Each dish is prepared to order with homemade sauces and served with delicious warm bread. The friendly, efficient floor staff adds to the experience and is eager to ensure your visit is thoroughly enjoyable. Portions tend to be huge so order with care or ask to downsize. There is no lunch service on Sunday. **Features:** full bar, patio dining, happy hour. **Address:** 44 Martin Luther King Jr Blvd 31401 **Location:** Jct W Congress Ln. **Parking:** street only. Ⓛ Ⓓ 🐾

THE COTTON EXCHANGE   912/232-7088   ⑧
🍷🍷 American. Casual Dining. $9-$30 **AAA Inspector Notes:** *Historic.* Operating since 1971, this waterfront dining room is located in a restored 1790s cotton warehouse. The dining room has a rustic appeal with exposed old brick and stone walls. Specializing in fresh seafood, entrées are prepared in a variety of ways such as fried, baked and steamed. Other options include oysters on the half shell and steamed oysters by the bucket. For the landlubber, there is a selection of chicken, steaks, salads, sandwiches and burgers. The Tybee crab chowder is a crowd-pleaser. **Features:** full bar. **Address:** 201 E River St 31401 **Location:** On historic riverfront. **Parking:** street only. Ⓛ Ⓓ

Check DrivingLaws.AAA.com

for local motor vehicle laws

when traveling

THE DISTILLERY   912/236-1772   ㉚
🍷🍷 Burgers Sandwiches. Casual Dining. $8-$18 **AAA Inspector Notes:** *Historic.* You won't want for beverage options, as your choices include 21 draft microbrews, more than 50 craft bottled beers and a short wine list. The menu is your standard lineup of bar foods, with sandwiches and burgers playing the dominant role but a few entrées also listed. Regardless of what you order, portions tend to be large. **Features:** full bar, patio dining, happy hour. **Address:** 416 W Liberty St 31401 **Location:** Jct W Broad St. **Parking:** street only. Ⓛ Ⓓ CALL &Ⓜ 🐾

FIREFLY CAFE   912/234-1971   ㉞
🍷🍷 American. Casual Dining. $11-$32 **AAA Inspector Notes:** *Historic.* This eatery is located in a building originally constructed in 1869. This casual neighborhood café serves comfort foods, seafood and other favorites prepared with creative touches. Vegan-friendly options are available. There are a few tables on the sidewalk for al fresco dining. **Features:** wine only, patio dining, Sunday brunch. **Address:** 321 Habersham St 31401 **Location:** S of E Liberty St; at Harris St; on Troup Square. **Parking:** street only. Ⓛ Ⓓ

GARIBALDI'S CAFE   912/232-7118   ⑰
🍷🍷🍷 Italian Seafood. Fine Dining. $8-$90 **AAA Inspector Notes:** *Historic.* In a restored 1871 German firehouse, guests will find a bustling bar and dining area downstairs. Upstairs is more traditional and formal in what was once the firemen's ballroom. The menu is a mix of local seafood and steak dishes alongside traditional pastas like five-layer lasagna, veal parmigiana and linguine with clam sauce. On the seafood side there is the restaurant's premiere dish, diamond-scored flounder. **Features:** full bar. **Reservations:** required. **Address:** 315 W Congress St 31401 **Location:** Between Montgomery and Jefferson sts; on southeast side of Franklin Square; at city market. **Parking:** street only. Ⓓ

GOOSE FEATHERS   912/233-4683   ㉔
🍷 Breakfast Sandwiches. Casual Dining. $4-$10 **AAA Inspector Notes:** This coffee house café has been serving the downtown area homemade pastries, desserts and sandwiches for more than 26 years. This is a great place to gather and charge your batteries before your big day on the town. **Features:** patio dining. **Address:** 39 Barnard St 31405 **Location:** Between Barnard and Congress sts. **Parking:** street only. Ⓑ Ⓛ

HUEY'S NEW ORLEANS CAFE   912/234-7385   ⑦
🍷🍷 Creole. Casual Dining. $10-$32 **AAA Inspector Notes:** *Historic.* This popular restaurant serves authentic New Orleans-style fare such as gumbo, red beans and rice and shrimp Creole. Steaks, chicken and pasta dishes round out the offerings. French doors provide light and beautiful views of the riverfront and in cool weather they are open to the waterfront activity. Sidewalk seating is the perfect setting to enjoy incredible bloody Marys. Brunch is served daily until 3 pm and offers omelets and beignets. **Features:** full bar, patio dining, Sunday brunch, happy hour. **Address:** 115 E River St 31401 **Location:** On historic riverfront; under River Street Inn. **Parking:** street only. Ⓑ Ⓛ Ⓓ 🐾

JOHN RYAN'S BISTRO & PUB   912/790-7000   ⑥
🍷🍷 Regional American. Casual Dining. $9-$27 **AAA Inspector Notes:** This hotel restaurant prepares a nice selection of local favorites for dinner with a wide variety of specialty sandwiches. Expect to find crab cakes, fried chicken and catfish as the dinner mainstays. **Features:** full bar, happy hour. **Address:** 411 W Bay St 31401 **Location:** Jct Montgomery St; in DoubleTree by Hilton Savannah Historic District. **Parking:** valet and street only. Ⓑ Ⓓ CALL &Ⓜ

THE LADY & SONS   912/233-2600   ㉒
🍷🍷 Southern. Casual Dining. $10-$30 **AAA Inspector Notes:** *Historic.* The upbeat atmosphere and bustling activity here make for a contagiously enjoyable dining experience where the waitstaff may surprise you by simply bursting into song. Appetizers include crispy fried green tomatoes and crab-stuffed portobello mushrooms. Barbecue shrimp over grits and chicken pot pie are two house specialties that give guests a sample of Southern cooking at its best. Cheese biscuits melt in your mouth, and the pear cobbler and sock-it-to-me cake are fitting finales. **Features:** full bar. **Reservations:** suggested. **Address:** 102 W Congress St 31401 **Location:** Jct Whitaker St. **Parking:** street only. Ⓛ Ⓓ

(See map & index p. 257.)

MOLLY MACPHERSON'S SCOTTISH PUB & GRILL
912/239-9600 (18)

▼▼▼ Scottish. Casual Dining. $8-$19 **AAA Inspector Notes:** *Historic.* The pub décor and atmosphere add to the enjoyment of a casual, carefree dining experience. A large and varied selection of single malt scotches, in addition to many international beers, complements the Scottish pub fare, such as bangers and mash and shepherd's pie, as well as more traditional American entrées. Service is very casual so don't be afraid to flag someone down if you need something. Don't forget to bring your darts if you dare to compete. **Features:** full bar, happy hour. **Address:** 311 W Congress St 31401 **Location:** Just e of Montgomery St; across from city market. **Parking:** street only. [L] [D]

MOON RIVER BREWING COMPANY   912/447-0943 (12)

▼▼ American. Gastropub. $7-$24 **AAA Inspector Notes:** *Historic.* The great variety of food here pleases meat eaters, seafood lovers and vegans alike. An impressive selection of beers complements dishes that cover the spectrum from comfort food to eclectic gourmet fare, sandwiches and burgers. Atmosphere is part of the draw here, too: Several passed visitors, including the lady in white, are rumored to haunt this place. **Features:** full bar, patio dining, happy hour. **Reservations:** suggested. **Address:** 21 W Bay St 31401 **Location:** Between Bull and Whitaker sts. **Parking:** street only. [L] [D] [🐾]

MRS. WILKES' DINING ROOM   912/232-5997 (36)

▼▼ Southern Comfort Food. Casual Dining. $22 **AAA Inspector Notes:** A line forms down the sidewalk for a seat at this Savannah institution that has been serving delicious Southern fare for more than 60 years. If the aromas wafting out of the kitchen have not sold you, the exiting guests will by telling you the food is worth the wait. A bounty of dishes like fried chicken, black-eyed peas, sweet potatoes, collards and cornbread are preset on the tables of ten, and diners pass the bowls just like at grandma's house on Thanksgiving at this family-style eatery. **Address:** 107 W Jones St 31401 **Location:** Jct Whitaker St, just w. **Parking:** street only. [L]

NOBLE FARE   912/443-3210 (33)

▼▼▼ Regional American. Fine Dining. $29-$39 **AAA Inspector Notes:** *Historic.* Low light lends to the intimate feel in the dining room, a prime destination for that special occasion. A thoughtfully crafted menu lines up well-prepared duck, beef, chicken and catch-of-the-day dishes, each served with an original accompaniment. You can test the chef's diverse skills via the seven-course tasting menu, an experience that won't leave you disappointed. The tasting menu may be paired with wine if you choose. **Features:** full bar. **Reservations:** suggested. **Address:** 321 Jefferson St 31401 **Location:** Jct W Harris St. **Parking:** street only. [D]

THE OLDE PINK HOUSE   912/232-4286 (23)

▼▼▼ Regional Seafood. Fine Dining. $15-$35 **AAA Inspector Notes:** *Historic.* Hearty, new interpretations of classic Southern cuisine, tip-top service and historic décor are the cornerstones of this restaurant's draw. Housed in a converted 18th-century mansion, the restaurant consists of nine separate dining rooms, a casual lounge and sidewalk dining areas. Menu favorites are pan-seared salmon, crispy scored flounder, braised pork shank and Kobe beef burgers. Live piano music from the lounge wafts through the restaurant every evening. **Features:** full bar, patio dining. **Reservations:** suggested. **Address:** 23 Abercorn St 31401 **Location:** Between E Bryan and E Saint Julian sts; facing Reynolds Square. **Parking:** street only. [L] [D] [🐾]

OLYMPIA CAFE   912/233-3131 (4)

▼▼ Greek. Casual Dining. $5-$26 **AAA Inspector Notes:** Located on the historic waterfront, this casual eatery serves up a wide variety of traditional authentic Greek dishes and desserts—there are 32 flavors of ice cream. Guests can either dine in the casual sit-down venue or opt for a quick meal at the express annex next door. Along with the gyro, kebab and pastitsio standards are house specialties including the popular scored flounder and whole red snapper, each prepared with a Grecian spin. **Features:** full bar, patio dining. **Address:** 5 E River St 31401 **Location:** Jct Bull St; on historic riverfront. **Parking:** street only. [L] [D]

ONE-EYED LIZZY'S GRILLE & BAR   912/341-8897 (11)

▼▼ American. Casual Dining. $8-$24 **AAA Inspector Notes:** This restaurant has dining on two levels, as well as balcony seating. The atmosphere and ambience are casual and relaxing—a perfect setting for sipping one the flavored margaritas. The menu specializes in Tex-Mex dishes, as well as local seafood, steaks, sandwiches and salads. A popular entrée is the outrageous burrito, big enough for two to share. The distinctive quesadillas and famous fajitas keep the crowds coming back for more. **Features:** full bar, patio dining, happy hour. **Address:** 417 E River St 31401 **Location:** East end of River St. **Parking:** street only. [L] [D]

PACCI ITALIAN KITCHEN + BAR   912/233-6002 (19)

▼▼▼ Italian. Casual Dining. $11-$32 **AAA Inspector Notes:** Not a typical hotel restaurant, the bright playful atmosphere of this casual, chic facility is well complemented by the skilled chef's talents. Though the dishes are indulgent, the focus remains on healthy eating which means diners can count on only fresh, local ingredients and made-from-scratch dishes. If you are in the mood for spaghetti and meatballs, you will have to go elsewhere. **Features:** full bar, patio dining, Sunday brunch, happy hour. **Address:** 601 E Bay St 31401 **Location:** Between Houston and E Broad sts; in The Brice. **Parking:** valet and street only.

[⊟] [B] [L] [D] CALL [🔊M]

THE PIRATES' HOUSE   912/233-5757 (25)

▼▼▼ Regional Seafood. Casual Dining. $10-$27 **AAA Inspector Notes:** *Classic Historic.* Dating back to the early 1700s, this spot began as a tavern and now that same yesteryear charm greets diners in historic Savannah. The menu is dominated by seafood dishes but steak, chicken and sandwiches are served alongside Southern-style side dishes also are available. There are 15 dining rooms decorated with period pieces and memorabilia and the floor staff is well versed in the building's colorful history and eager to pass it along with all the sordid details. **Features:** full bar. **Reservations:** suggested. **Address:** 20 E Broad St 31401 **Location:** Between E Bay and E Broughton sts; on east side of historic district at Trustees' Garden. [L] [D]

THE PUBLIC KITCHEN & BAR   912/200-4045 (32)

▼▼▼ New American. Casual Dining. $10-$24 **AAA Inspector Notes:** The small, chic corner restaurant features simple fare made with high-quality ingredients and prepared by highly skilled chefs. During the lunch cycle you'll be treated to a selection of sandwiches, a few entrées and daily specials. After 5 pm, sandwich selections are replaced by a good variety of full entrées like paella, lasagna, stuffed chicken breast and a seasonal risotto. The signature free-range grass-fed beef burgers are always available. **Features:** full bar, patio dining, Sunday brunch, happy hour. **Address:** 1 W Liberty St 31401 **Location:** Jct Bull St. **Parking:** street only. [L] [D]

RANCHO ALEGRE CUBAN RESTAURANT   912/292-1656 (35)

▼▼ Cuban. Casual Dining. $8-$25 **AAA Inspector Notes:** Serving the area since 1999 and from this location since 2012, this small corner restaurant features friendly service and traditionally prepared food. Though guests can find the popular pressed Cuban sandwich, the menu is much broader with wonderfully flavorful dishes featuring chicken, beef, pork and lots of fresh fish all topped with fruits and rich sauces. It is a Caribbean adventure. The signature dish is paella, a melange of seafood and rice. **Features:** full bar, happy hour. **Address:** 402 Martin Luther King Jr Blvd 31402 **Location:** Jct W Jones St. **Parking:** street only. [L] [D]

RIVER HOUSE SEAFOOD & BAKERY   912/234-1900 (2)

▼▼▼ Seafood. Casual Dining. $10-$30 **AAA Inspector Notes:** This riverfront eatery offers fresh and flavorful entrées in a nautical atmosphere complete with views of the river activity. The seafood could not be fresher unless you brought it with you. Dishes like iron skillet blackened mahi mahi, scored whole flounder (sweet and delicious), grouper Florentine and herb-baked tilapia share menu space with a few steaks and chops for the landlubbers. A children's menu is available for the fussy tots. **Features:** full bar, patio dining, happy hour. **Address:** 125 W River St 31401 **Location:** On historic riverfront. **Parking:** street only.

[B] [L] [D] [🐾]

(See map & index p. 257.)

SAPPHIRE GRILL 912/443-9962 21
▼▼▼▼ New American. Fine Dining. $23-$45 **AAA Inspector Notes:** *Historic.* This historic building's dining rooms combine the charm of original exposed brick walls and wood plank floors with a distinctive, upscale décor featuring accent lighting and original art pieces. The talented and busy chef uses only fresh ingredients to create his innovative contemporary cuisine. Artistic presentations are a feast for the eyes, as well as a treat for the palate as diners sample something off the seasonal menu. **Features:** full bar. **Reservations:** suggested. **Address:** 110 W Congress St 31401 **Location:** Jct Whitaker St; 2 blks s of Bay St. **Parking:** street only.
D LATE

SHRIMP FACTORY 912/236-4229 10
▼▼▼▼ Regional Seafood. Casual Dining. $10-$36 **AAA Inspector Notes:** *Historic.* This dining spot with a classic nautical décor is located in a former 1820s cotton warehouse and provides river views of passing commercial vessels. As one might expect the menu is rife with original shrimp concoctions such as the shrimp trio, Creole peppered shrimp and shrimp and crab au gratin. The signature dish is the historic pine bark stew made from a recipe dating back hundreds of years; it can be plated up as an appetizer for four. Raw bar selections are also available. **Features:** full bar, happy hour. **Reservations:** suggested. **Address:** 313 E River St 31401 **Location:** On historic riverfront. **Parking:** street only. L D

SOHO SOUTH CAFE 912/233-1633 31
▼▼ Sandwiches. Casual Dining. $9-$14 **AAA Inspector Notes:** This popular bistro and collectibles gallery serves up a creative selection of gourmet sandwiches, soups, salads, quiche and homemade desserts. This is a great stop for a quick business lunch or a casual respite with friends to catch up in person or text while you taste without the hustle and noise of the street. A children's menu is available. **Features:** beer & wine, patio dining, Sunday brunch. **Address:** 12 W Liberty St 31401 **Location:** Between Bull and Whitaker sts. **Parking:** street only. L

TA CA SUSHI & JAPANESE FUSION 912/232-8222 29
▼▼ Japanese Sushi Fusion. Casual Dining. $8-$28 **AAA Inspector Notes:** This restaurant features a lengthy sushi menu and wide selection of Japanese beers and sake (purportedly the largest in the city). The fusion portion of the menu is due to the Vietnamese pho offerings which are a big draw for those seeking a simple, healthy meal. Typical hibachi dishes and combinations also are available and make for a quick lunch for those in a rush. **Features:** full bar, happy hour. **Address:** 513 E Oglethorpe Ave, Suite A 31401 **Location:** Between Price and Houston sts.
L D CALL M

TONDEE'S TAVERN 912/341-7427 13
▼▼ American. Casual Dining. $8-$35 **AAA Inspector Notes:** *Historic.* Located in the center of the city in an historic bank building, circa 1850, this tavern features a good selection of above average bar fare. Grilled steaks, seafood specialty dishes, sandwiches, burgers and salads are available all day. Lunch specials are offered during the work week. The building is said to be haunted so guests may want to try some of the artillery punch to calm the nerves. **Features:** full bar, happy hour. **Address:** 7 E Bay St 31401 **Location:** Jct Bull St. **Parking:** street only.
L D LATE

VIC'S ON THE RIVER RESTAURANT & BAR
912/721-1000 5
▼▼▼ New Southern. Fine Dining. $8-$38 **AAA Inspector Notes:** *Historic.* Entry to this restaurant is via Bay Street or from an elevator on River Street. The historic building once served as a warehouse and a gathering place for Union officers during the Civil War. During a renovation, a portion of a wall-drawn map chronicling General Sherman's march through the South was uncovered; patrons are invited to take a peek. Waits are not unusual at the popular spot, which earns praise for its professional service and diverse, regionally-influenced menu. **Features:** full bar, patio dining, happy hour. **Reservations:** suggested. **Address:** 26 E Bay St 31401 **Location:** On historic riverfront; alternate entrance at 15 E River St. **Parking:** valet and street only. L D CALL M

VINNIE VAN GO GO 912/233-6394 14
▼▼ Pizza. Quick Serve. $3-$16 **AAA Inspector Notes:** Pizza, pizza, pizza is what they do at this busy spot. Bring an appetite (even the single slices are huge) and some patience as seating is limited on the interior (patrons getting to-go orders are not permitted to wait in the dining room or bar area due to the size restrictions). The pizza is really good and features old-style toppings—the most adventurous of which is pineapple. Lunch is only available on weekends. Also bring cash as they do not accept credit cards. **Features:** beer & wine, patio dining. **Address:** 317 W Bryan St 31401 **Location:** Between Montgomery and Jefferson sts; at City Market. **Parking:** street only.
D LATE 🐾

SAVANNAH
- **Restaurants p. 277**
- **Hotels & Restaurants map & index p. 260**

BAYMONT INN & SUITES (912)925-9494 33
▼▼ Hotel. $69-$275 **Address:** 393 Canebrake Rd 31419 **Location:** I-95 exit 94 (SR 204/Abercom St), just se. **Facility:** 70 units. 3 stories, interior corridors. **Pool(s):** outdoor. **Activities:** exercise room.
🍽➜ 🏊 BIZ HS 🛜 ✕ 🖥 🖨 🖥 / SOME UNITS 🐾

BAYMONT INN & SUITES SAVANNAH MIDTOWN
(912)353-7100 20
▼▼ Hotel. $76-$140 **Address:** 2 Lee Blvd 31405 **Location:** Jct SR 21 and 204 (Abercom St), 0.6 mi s on Abercom St, just e. **Facility:** 131 units. 3 stories, interior/exterior corridors. **Terms:** check-in 4 pm. **Pool(s):** outdoor. **Activities:** exercise room. **Guest Services:** valet and coin laundry.
🏊 BIZ 🛜 ✕ 🖥 / SOME UNITS 🖨 🖥

BEST WESTERN CENTRAL INN (912)355-1000 23
▼▼ Motel $74-$149
BW Best Western.
AAA Benefit: Save 10% or more every day and earn 10% bonus points!

Address: 45 Eisenhower Dr 31406 **Location:** 1.3 mi s of jct SR 21 and 204 (Abercom), just w. Adjacent to Hunter Army Air Field. **Facility:** 129 units. 2 stories (no elevator), exterior corridors. **Pool(s):** outdoor. **Guest Services:** valet laundry. **Featured Amenity: continental breakfast.**
SAVE 🍽➜ 🏊 BIZ 🛜 🖥 / SOME UNITS 🖨 🖥

BEST WESTERN SAVANNAH GATEWAY
(912)925-2420 30
▼▼ Motel $75-$122
BW Best Western.
AAA Benefit: Save 10% or more every day and earn 10% bonus points!
Address: 1 Gateway Blvd E 31419 **Location:** I-95 exit 94 (SR 204/Abercom St), just e. **Facility:** 120 units. 2 stories (no elevator), exterior corridors. **Pool(s):** outdoor. **Featured Amenity: full hot breakfast.**
SAVE 🍽 🏊 BIZ HS 🛜 🖨 🖥 / SOME UNITS 🖥 🖥

CATHERINE WARD HOUSE INN 912/234-8564 14
▼▼▼ Historic Bed & Breakfast. Rates not provided. **Address:** 118 E Waldburg St 31401 **Location:** Between Drayton and Abercom sts. **Facility:** Originally built in 1886, this house is an example of Italianate architecture. Gingerbread embellishments, a parlor filled with fine antiques and beautifully decorated rooms make this a great choice. 9 units. 3 stories (no elevator), interior/exterior corridors. **Parking:** street only. **Terms:** age restrictions may apply.
🛜 ✕ ✏ 🖥 / SOME UNITS 🖨 🖥

(See map & index p. 260.)

CLARION SUITES & CONFERENCE CENTER
(912)925-2700 **27**

◆◆◆ **Hotel.** $74-$209 **Address:** 17 Gateway Blvd E 31419 **Location:** I-95 exit 94 (SR 204/Abercorn St), just e, then ne. **Facility:** 96 units. 3 stories, interior corridors. **Amenities:** safes. **Pool(s):** outdoor. **Guest Services:** coin laundry.

[icons]

COMFORT INN
912/354-8560 **24**

◆◆◆ **Hotel.** Rates not provided. **Address:** 7110 Hodgson Memorial Dr 31406 **Location:** Jct SR 21 and 204 (Abercorn Dr), 1.3 mi s, just e on Eisenhower Dr, then just s. **Facility:** 52 units. 3 stories (no elevator), interior corridors. **Pool(s):** outdoor. **Activities:** exercise room. **Guest Services:** coin laundry.

[icons] / SOME UNITS

COMFORT INN & SUITES SAVANNAH AIRPORT
(912)629-1500 **2**

Hotel
$79-$199

Address: 15 Jay R Turner Dr 31408 **Location:** I-95 exit 104, 0.4 mi e. **Facility:** 79 units. 3 stories, interior corridors. **Terms:** check-in 4 pm. **Pool(s):** outdoor. **Activities:** exercise room. **Guest Services:** valet laundry, area transportation. **Featured Amenity:** full hot breakfast.

[icons] / SOME UNITS

COUNTRY INN & SUITES BY CARLSON, SAVANNAH AIRPORT
912/966-1717 **5**

◆◆◆ **Hotel.** Rates not provided. **Address:** 21 Yvette Johnson Hagins Dr 31408 **Location:** I-95 exit 104, just se to Crossroads Pkwy, then just ne. Adjacent to Savannah/Hilton Head International Airport. **Facility:** 82 units. 3 stories, interior corridors. **Pool(s):** heated indoor. **Activities:** hot tub, exercise room. **Guest Services:** valet and coin laundry.

[icons]

COUNTRY INN & SUITES BY CARLSON-SAVANNAH GATEWAY
912/920-3200 **28**

Hotel
Rates not provided

Address: 16 Gateway Blvd E 31419 **Location:** I-95 exit 94 (SR 204/Abercorn St), just e, then ne. **Facility:** 72 units. 3 stories, interior corridors. **Pool(s):** heated indoor. **Activities:** hot tub, exercise room. **Guest Services:** coin laundry. **Featured Amenity:** full hot breakfast.

[icons]

COURTYARD BY MARRIOTT SAVANNAH MIDTOWN
(912)354-7878 **21**

Hotel
$90-$191

COURTYARD Marriott

AAA Benefit: Members save 5% or more!

Address: 6703 Abercorn St 31405 **Location:** Jct SR 21 and 204 (Abercorn St), 0.8 mi s. **Facility:** 144 units. 3 stories, interior corridors. **Activities:** exercise room. **Guest Services:** valet and coin laundry, boarding pass kiosk.

[icons] / SOME UNITS

DAYS INN & SUITES MIDTOWN
(912)352-9884 **22**

◆◆ **Motel.** $50-$250 **Address:** 211 Stephenson Ave 31405 **Location:** Jct Abercorn St, just e. **Facility:** 60 units. 2 stories (no elevator), exterior corridors. **Amenities:** safes. **Pool(s):** outdoor.

[icons]

For identification in more than 150 countries, purchase an International Driving Permit

(See map & index p. 260.)

DOUBLETREE BY HILTON HOTEL SAVANNAH AIRPORT
(912)965-9595

Contemporary Hotel
$109-$219

 AAA Benefit: Members save 5% or more!

Address: 50 Yvette Johnson Hagins Dr 31408 **Location:** I-95 exit 104, just se to Crossroads Pkwy, then just ne. Adjacent to Savannah/Hilton Head International Airport. **Facility:** 97 units, some two bedrooms. 4 stories, interior corridors. **Terms:** 1-7 night minimum stay, cancellation fee imposed. **Pool(s):** heated indoor. **Activities:** hot tub, exercise room. **Guest Services:** valet and coin laundry, area transportation.

EXTENDED STAY AMERICA SAVANNAH-MIDTOWN
(912)692-0076   **15**

Extended Stay Hotel. $80-$115 **Address:** 5511 Abercorn St 31405 **Location:** Jct SR 21 and 204 (Abercorn St), just s. **Facility:** 104 efficiencies. 3 stories, interior corridors. **Terms:** cancellation fee imposed. **Guest Services:** coin laundry.

FAIRFIELD INN & SUITES BY MARRIOTT SAVANNAH AIRPORT
(912)965-9777   **6**

Hotel
$89-$167

FAIRFIELD INN & SUITES Marriott **AAA Benefit:** Members save 5% or more!

 Address: 10 Stephen S Green Dr 31408 **Location:** I-95 exit 104, just se to Crossroads Pkwy, just sw to Stephen S Green Dr, just nw. Adjacent to Savannah/Hilton Head International Airport. **Facility:** 80 units. 3 stories, interior corridors. **Pool(s):** heated indoor. **Activities:** hot tub, exercise room. **Guest Services:** valet and coin laundry. **Featured Amenity:** full hot breakfast.

FAIRFIELD INN & SUITES BY MARRIOTT SAVANNAH I-95 SOUTH
(912)925-5050   **32**

Hotel. $69-$138 **Address:** 17027 Abercorn St 31419 **Location:** I-95 exit 94 (SR 204/Abercorn St), just e. **Facility:** 80 units. 3 stories, interior corridors. **Pool(s):** heated indoor. **Activities:** hot tub, exercise room. **Guest Services:** valet and coin laundry.

AAA Benefit: Members save 5% or more!

FAIRFIELD INN & SUITES BY MARRIOTT SAVANNAH MIDTOWN
(912)298-0800

fyi **Hotel.** $70-$251 Too new to rate, opening scheduled for October 2016. **Address:** 5801 Abercorn St 31405 **Location:** Jct SR 21 and 204 (Abercorn St), just s. **Amenities:** coffeemakers, microwaves, refrigerators, exercise facility. **Terms:** check-in 4 pm. *(See ad p. 266.)*

AAA Benefit: Members save 5% or more!

Crossing borders or traveling abroad?
Arrive ready with foreign currency

HAMPTON INN & SUITES I-95 GATEWAY   (912)921-1515   **26**

Hotel. $109-$199 **Address:** 591 Al Henderson Blvd 31419 **Location:** I-95 exit 94 (SR 204/Abercorn St), just ne. **Facility:** 92 units. 6 stories, interior corridors. **Terms:** 1-7 night minimum stay, cancellation fee imposed. **Amenities:** safes. **Pool(s):** heated indoor. **Activities:** hot tub, exercise room. **Guest Services:** coin laundry.

AAA Benefit: Members save up to 10%!

HAMPTON INN & SUITES SAVANNAH AIRPORT
(912)966-1240   **11**

Hotel. $114-$299 **Address:** 70 Stephen S Green Dr 31408 **Location:** Waterfront. I-95 exit 104, just se to Crossroads Pkwy, sw to Stephen S Green Dr, follow road nw, then s. Adjacent to Savannah/Hilton Head International Airport. **Facility:** 102 units. 4 stories, interior corridors. **Terms:** check-in 4 pm, 1-7 night minimum stay, cancellation fee imposed. **Pool(s):** outdoor. **Activities:** exercise room. **Guest Services:** valet laundry.

AAA Benefit: Members save up to 10%!

HAMPTON INN & SUITES SAVANNAH MIDTOWN
(912)721-3700   **16**

Hotel
$119-$279

Hampton **AAA Benefit:** Members save up to 10%!

Address: 20 Johnston St 31405 **Location:** Jct SR 21, 0.5 mi s on SR 204 (Abercorn St), then just w. **Facility:** 120 units. 6 stories, interior corridors. **Terms:** 1-7 night minimum stay, cancellation fee imposed. **Pool(s):** heated indoor. **Activities:** hot tub, exercise room. **Guest Services:** valet and coin laundry. **Featured Amenity:** full hot breakfast.

HILTON GARDEN INN SAVANNAH AIRPORT
(912)964-5550   **8**

 Hotel. $119-$139 **Address:** 80 Clyde E Martin Dr 31408 **Location:** I-95 exit 104, just se to Crossroads Pkwy, sw to Stephen S Green Dr, then just nw. Adjacent to Savannah/Hilton Head International Airport. **Facility:** 105 units. 3 stories, interior corridors. **Terms:** check-in 4 pm, 1-7 night minimum stay, cancellation fee imposed. **Pool(s):** outdoor. **Activities:** hot tub, exercise room. **Guest Services:** valet and coin laundry, area transportation.

AAA Benefit: Members save up to 10%!

HILTON GARDEN INN SAVANNAH MIDTOWN
912/652-9300   **17**

Hotel
Rates not provided

Hilton Garden Inn **AAA Benefit:** Members save up to 10%!

 Address: 5711 Abercorn St 31405 **Location:** Jct SR 21 and 204 (Abercorn St), just s. **Facility:** 132 units. 6 stories, interior corridors. **Terms:** check-in 4 pm. **Amenities:** video games. **Pool(s):** heated outdoor. **Activities:** hot tub, exercise room. **Guest Services:** valet and coin laundry.

(See map & index p. 260.)

HOLIDAY INN EXPRESS INN & SUITES SAVANNAH MIDTOWN
912/629-0900 **34**

Hotel
Rates not provided

Address: 11325 Abercorn St 31419 **Location:** Jct SR 21 and 204 (Abercorn St), 4.6 mi s. **Facility:** 88 units. 4 stories, interior corridors. **Pool(s):** heated outdoor. **Activities:** exercise room. **Guest Services:** valet laundry. **Featured Amenity: breakfast buffet.**

HOLIDAY INN EXPRESS SAVANNAH AIRPORT
(912)721-9100 **4**

Hotel. $109-$209 **Address:** 1 Yvette Johnson Hagins Dr 31408 **Location:** I-95 exit 104, 0.4 mi e. Adjacent to Savannah/Hilton Head International Airport. **Facility:** 80 units. 3 stories, interior corridors. **Activities:** hot tub, exercise room. **Guest Services:** valet and coin laundry.

HOLIDAY INN SAVANNAH S I-95
912/925-2525 **29**

Hotel. Rates not provided. **Address:** 11 Gateway Blvd E 31419 **Location:** I-95 exit 94 (SR 204/Abercorn St), just e, then ne. **Facility:** 101 units. 4 stories, interior corridors. **Terms:** check-in 4 pm. **Amenities:** safes. **Pool(s):** outdoor. **Activities:** exercise room. **Guest Services:** valet laundry.

Use travel time to share

driving tips and rules

of the road with your teens

HOMEWOOD SUITES BY HILTON
(912)353-8500 **19**

Extended Stay Hotel
$99-$239

HOMEWOOD SUITES BY HILTON
AAA Benefit: Members save up to 10%!

Address: 5820 White Bluff Rd 31405 **Location:** Jct SR 21 and 204 (Abercorn St), 0.5 mi s. **Facility:** 106 efficiencies, some two bedrooms. 2-3 stories, interior/exterior corridors. **Terms:** 1-7 night minimum stay, cancellation fee imposed. **Amenities:** video games. **Pool(s):** heated outdoor. **Activities:** hot tub, exercise room. **Guest Services:** valet and coin laundry. *(See ad this page.)*

HYATT PLACE SAVANNAH AIRPORT
(912)966-0020 **9**

Hotel
$79-$299

HYATT PLACE
AAA Benefit: Members save 10%!

Address: 4 Stephen S Green Dr 31408 **Location:** I-95 exit 104, just se to Crossroads Pkwy, then just sw. Adjacent to Savannah/Hilton Head International Airport. **Facility:** 81 units. 3 stories, interior corridors. **Pool(s):** outdoor. **Activities:** exercise room. **Guest Services:** valet and coin laundry, area transportation. **Featured Amenity: full hot breakfast.**

LA QUINTA INN & SUITES
(912)927-7660 **25**

Hotel. $67-$284 **Address:** 8484 Abercorn St 31406 **Location:** 2.4 mi s of jct SR 21 and 204 (Abercorn St). **Facility:** 100 units. 3 stories, interior corridors. **Pool(s):** outdoor. **Activities:** exercise room. **Guest Services:** coin laundry.

(See map & index p. 260.)

RESIDENCE INN BY MARRIOTT SAVANNAH MIDTOWN
(912)356-3266 **18**

WWW **Extended Stay Hotel.** $119-$234 **Address:** 5710 White Bluff Rd 31405 **Location:** Jct SR 21, 0.5 mi s. **Facility:** 66 units, some two bedrooms, efficiencies and kitchens. 3 stories, interior corridors. **Terms:** check-in 4 pm. **Pool(s):** heated indoor. **Activities:** hot tub, exercise room. **Guest Services:** valet and coin laundry.

AAA Benefit: Members save 5% or more!

CALL 🛗M 🛏 BIZ HS 🛜 ✕ 🖪 🖼 🖳
/ SOME UNITS 🛏

SPRINGHILL SUITES BY MARRIOTT SAVANNAH AIRPORT
(912)330-5555 **1**

WWW **Hotel.** $104-$171 **Address:** One Jay R Turner Dr 31408 **Location:** I-95 exit 104, just e. **Facility:** 92 units. 3 stories, interior corridors. **Pool(s):** heated indoor. **Activities:** hot tub, exercise room. **Guest Services:** valet and coin laundry.

AAA Benefit: Members save 5% or more!

🛫 🍴 CALL 🛗M 🛏 BIZ HS 🛜 ✕ 🖪 🖼
🖳

SPRINGHILL SUITES BY MARRIOTT SAVANNAH I-95 SOUTH
(912)629-7777 **31**

WWW **Hotel.** $98-$157 **Address:** 4 Gateway Blvd E 31419 **Location:** I-95 exit 94 (SR 204/Abercorn St), just ne. Next to Cracker Barrel and Houlihan's restaurants. **Facility:** 86 units. 3 stories, interior corridors. **Pool(s):** heated indoor. **Activities:** hot tub, exercise room. **Guest Services:** valet and coin laundry.

AAA Benefit: Members save 5% or more!

🍴 CALL 🛗M 🛏 BIZ HS 🛜 ✕ 🖪 🖼 🖳

SPRINGHILL SUITES BY MARRIOTT SAVANNAH/MIDTOWN
(912)920-3787 **35**

WWW **Hotel.** $82-$171 **Address:** 11317 Abercorn St 31419 **Location:** Jct SR 21 and 204 (Abercorn St), 4.6 mi s. **Facility:** 79 units. 3 stories, interior corridors. **Pool(s):** indoor. **Activities:** hot tub, exercise room. **Guest Services:** valet and coin laundry.

AAA Benefit: Members save 5% or more!

🍴 🛏 BIZ 🛜 ✕ 🖪 🖼 🖳

TOWNEPLACE SUITES BY MARRIOTT SAVANNAH AIRPORT
(912)629-7775 **3**

WWW **Extended Stay Hotel.** $106-$171 **Address:** 4 Jay R Turner Dr 31408 **Location:** I-95 exit 104, just e. Adjacent to Savannah/Hilton Head International Airport. **Facility:** 63 efficiencies. 4 stories, interior corridors. **Activities:** hot tub, exercise room. **Guest Services:** valet and coin laundry.

AAA Benefit: Members save 5% or more!

🛫 🍴 CALL 🛗M BIZ HS 🛜 ✕ 🖪 🖼 🖳
/ SOME UNITS 🛏

TOWNEPLACE SUITES BY MARRIOTT SAVANNAH MIDTOWN
(912)920-9080 **36**

WW **Extended Stay Hotel.** $80-$182 **Address:** 11309 Abercorn St 31419 **Location:** Jct SR 21 and 204 (Abercorn St), 4.6 mi s. **Facility:** 95 kitchen units, some two bedrooms. 3 stories, interior corridors. **Terms:** check-in 4 pm. **Pool(s):** outdoor. **Activities:** limited exercise equipment. **Guest Services:** valet and coin laundry.

AAA Benefit: Members save 5% or more!

🍴 CALL 🛗M 🛏 BIZ HS 🛜 ✕ 🖪 🖼 🖳
/ SOME UNITS 🛏

WINGATE BY WYNDHAM SAVANNAH AIRPORT
(912)544-1180 **10**

WWW **Hotel.** $69-$279 **Address:** 50 Sylvester C Formey Dr 31408 **Location:** Waterfront. I-95 exit 104, just se to Crossroads Pkwy, sw to Stephen S Green Dr, then just se. Adjacent to Savannah/Hilton Head International Airport. **Facility:** 81 units. 4 stories, interior corridors. **Amenities:** safes. **Pool(s):** outdoor. **Activities:** hot tub, exercise room. **Guest Services:** valet and coin laundry, area transportation.

🛫 🍴 🛏 BIZ HS 🛜 ✕ 🕱 🖪 🖼 🖳
/ SOME UNITS 🛏

WHERE TO EAT

THE 5 SPOT   912/777-3021 **11**

WW American. Casual Dining. $9-$17 **AAA Inspector Notes:** This neighborhood kitchen and bar is the place to get a hearty breakfast on the way to work or unwind with a cold beverage afterward. The all-day menu features breakfast until 11 am, sandwiches, burgers and such full entrée selections as shrimp and grits, meatloaf and the signature Low County catfish or smothered boneless pork chops. A children's menu is available. Live entertainment is offered on Thursday and Friday evenings. **Features:** full bar, patio dining, happy hour. **Address:** 4430 Habersham St 31405 **Location:** Between 60th and 61st sts; midtown; in Habersham Village. **Parking:** street only.

B L D

BACK IN THE DAY BAKERY   912/495-9292 **7**

W Sandwiches Breads/Pastries. Quick Serve. $7-$9 **AAA Inspector Notes:** Stop by this knickknack-filled shop and let the aromas guide you through the flavorful light lunch fare. Freshly prepared sandwiches served on homemade breads are available daily after 11 am. Peruse the deli cases filled with tempting desserts to complete your meal or save for an after work treat. **Address:** 2403 Bull St 31401 **Location:** Corner W 40th St. **Parking:** street only. B L

BARNES RESTAURANT   912/354-8745 **15**

WW Regional Barbecue. Casual Dining. $6-$25 **AAA Inspector Notes:** *Classic.* Serving the area for more than 40 years, this popular restaurant provides consistently reliable food, friendly seasoned service and great family value. Though they promote themselves as a barbecue restaurant the menu is actually much broader and caters to any taste. Not holding to the barbecue moniker are distinctive salads such as the tropical salad with grilled pineapple, Southern fried chicken, seafood platters and grilled steaks. **Address:** 5320 Waters Ave 31401 **Location:** Jct De Renne Ave, just n; between E 67th and E 68th sts; midtown. L D

B&D BURGERS   912/927-8700 **34**

WW Burgers. Casual Dining. $9-$19 **AAA Inspector Notes:** More than 33 burger combinations are on the menu here and there is an option to create your own from the toppings listed. Some toppers include olives, mushrooms, pineapple, eggs, salsa, ham and sun-dried tomatoes. Seating is limited and at times filled with starving college students as there is a mini meals and starving student menu. Burgers are offered in one-third, one-half and one-pound versions with a choice of beef, turkey or vegetarian patties. **Features:** full bar, patio dining, happy hour. **Address:** 11108 Abercorn St 31416 **Location:** Jct SR 21 and 204 (Abercorn St), 4.6 mi s. L D LATE

BELLA'S ITALIAN CAFE   912/354-4005 **10**

WW Italian. Casual Dining. $9-$24 **AAA Inspector Notes:** Well worth the short drive from downtown, this popular restaurant serves up robustly flavored pasta dishes, pizza and sandwiches. Signature dishes include Florentine chicken, three-cheese manicotti, the antipasto sandwich and New York-style cheese pizza. The popularity of the place cannot be underestimated, so get there early. A diverse wine list is offered to complement the meal and can be ordered by the bottle or glass. **Features:** beer & wine. **Address:** 4420 Habersham St 31405 **Location:** Between 60th and 61st sts; Midtown; in Habersham Village. **Parking:** street only. L D

BONEFISH GRILL   912/691-2575 **17**

WWW Seafood. Fine Dining. $12-$29 **AAA Inspector Notes:** Fish is the house specialty, and the menu and nightly specials offer a variety of choices. Well-prepared food is cooked to perfection. Service is casual in nature, and the staff is skilled and attentive. **Features:** full bar, Sunday brunch, happy hour. **Address:** 5500 Abercorn St, Suite 44 31405 **Location:** Jct SR 21 and 204 (Abercorn St), 0.4 mi s. L D

(See map & index p. 260.)

CANCUN MEXICAN RESTAURANT 912/356-1333 (18)

▼▼ Mexican. Casual Dining. $4-$12 AAA Inspector Notes: This restaurant offers a variety of Mexican standards in a somewhat stark dining room. Food is well prepared and service is swift. Great place for a quick bite especially at lunch where an inexpensive combination menu is offered. Children's selections are available. Features: full bar, patio dining, happy hour. Address: 5500 Abercorn St 31405 Location: Jct SR 21 and 204 (Abercorn St), just s; in Twelve Oaks Shopping Center. [L] [D] CALL [M]

CARIBBEAN CUISINE RESTAURANT 912/335-7629 (23)

▼▼ Caribbean. Casual Dining. $8-$15 AAA Inspector Notes: The exterior of this restaurant is not the most inviting—a storefront in a small strip mall with dark tinted windows and full-length curtains. However, once inside, guests can find an immaculately clean, vibrantly colored dining room complete with a beautiful smiling Jamaican hostess welcoming all. The menu features traditional stuffed beef pies, curried meat balls, Creole shrimp and chicken dishes, marinated turkey wings, ox tail stew, fried pork and daily specials. Address: 7094 Hodgson Memorial Dr 31406 Location: Jct SR 21 and 204 (Abercorn St), 1.3 mi s to Eisenhower Dr, just e; in Eisenhower Shopping Plaza. [L] [D]

CHIRIYA'S THAI CUISINE 912/691-2080 (9)

▼▼ Asian. Casual Dining. $12-$30 AAA Inspector Notes: The menu here features comprehensive Thai listings as well as a few Vietnamese, Hawaiian and Korean. Although I had the Thai, many of the guests there during my visit were returning customers for such Hawaiian dishes as huli huli chicken, kalua pig and cabbage (slow roasted in banana leaves) and Hawaiian fried rice. The Thai was excellent so I fully expected guests will enjoy the Hawaiian options as well. Features: beer & wine, patio dining. Address: 3017 E Victory Dr 31404 Location: Jct Truman Hwy and US 80 (Victory Dr), 1 mi e. [L] [D]

DRIFTAWAY CAFE 912/303-0999 (31)

▼▼ Seafood. Casual Dining. $11-$24 AAA Inspector Notes: This popular gathering spot offers a lengthy selection of appetizers, salads and sandwiches while having a modest line-up of full entrées dominated by specialty seafood dishes. A few chicken, tenderloin and short rib plates also are available nightly. Some interesting house sangrias, craft beers and an international selection of wine vintages are presented. Features: full bar, patio dining, Sunday brunch, happy hour. Address: 7400 Skidaway Rd 31406 Location: Harry S Truman Pkwy exit E Montgomery Crossroad, 0.4 mi e to Skidaway Rd, then just se; in the Sandfly area. [L] [D]

ELE FINE FUSION 912/898-2221 (8)

▼▼▼ Thai Fusion. Fine Dining. $15-$90 AAA Inspector Notes: The menu here features locally raised organic vegetables and meats along with high-end imports. The herbs used in the preparations are grown in the backyard garden and the chefs are skilled professionals. For starters try the sushi—some rolls may seem expensive but they are enormous and can be shared. The aromatic entrée selections show Thai and Vietnamese influences. There also is a separate steak and seafood section which is where the kitchen really shows off the fabled Kobe beef. Features: full bar. Address: 7815 US 80 E 31410 Location: Jct Harry Truman Pkwy and US 80, 6.6 mi w; on Wilmington Island just before crossing over to Tybee Island. [D] CALL [M]

ELIZABETH ON 37TH 912/236-5547 (5)

▼▼▼ Regional Southern. Fine Dining. $25-$40 AAA Inspector Notes: Historic. This restaurant blends Southern charm, accomplished service and a sophisticated menu with imaginative creations featuring local seafood, poultry, beef, lamb and pork. Each meal comes with a fresh salad picked from the chef's private garden and it is a great kick-off for the meal to come. Dusted Parmesan red snapper, pepper-crusted tenderloin and roasted chicken with exotic mushrooms are just a few of the selections on the seasonal menu, each served with appropriate accompaniments. Features: full bar. Reservations: suggested. Address: 105 E 37th St 31401 Location: Corner of Drayton and 37th sts. Parking: street only. [D]

THE EXCHANGE ON WATERS RESTAURANT & BAR 912/525-1148 (19)

▼▼ American. Casual Dining. $7-$22 AAA Inspector Notes: A sister property to The Cotton Exchange on River Street, this is a locally popular restaurant and waiting to be seated can be expected. Most appetites can be satisfied with varied and extensive menu selections offering fresh seafood dinners and baskets, stir-fry, pasta, chicken, steaks, salads, burgers and sandwiches. A popular item is the Tybee crab chowder made fresh with local crab. Features: full bar, happy hour. Address: 6710 Waters Ave 31406 Location: Just s of Stephenson Ave; in Midtown at Eisenhower Square. [L] [D] CALL [M]

FIDDLER'S SEAFOOD SOUTHSIDE 912/351-2274 (27)

▼▼ Seafood. Casual Dining. $8-$30 AAA Inspector Notes: This restaurant's exterior resembles an old fish camp. An additional distinctive feature is a waterfall that descends from the roof and flows into a small pond in front of the porch. The fish camp ambience continues inside, with rustic wood plank walls and ceilings and a nautical themed maritime décor with historic sepia photographs. The menu emphasizes fresh seafood with lobster, oysters, shrimp and the incredible seafood tower being house specialties. Features: full bar, patio dining, happy hour. Address: 7201 Hodgson Memorial Dr 31406 Location: Jct SR 21 and 204 (Abercorn St), 1.4 mi s, just e on Mall Blvd. [L] [D] CALL [M]

FIORE ITALIAN BAR & GRILL 912/349-2609 (30)

▼▼▼ Italian. Casual Dining. $9-$26 AAA Inspector Notes: This is great old-style Italian in a contemporary restaurant that is a wonderful setting for a night out with friends. The all-day menu features pasta, sandwiches, hoagies and panini. The dinner menu broadens the offerings with more complex entrées like cioppino, shrimp fra diavolo and lemon rosemary-roasted chicken. Sauces are rich and the pasta is al dente. Features: full bar, patio dining, happy hour. Address: 7360 Skidaway Rd, Suite E-4 31406 Location: Harry S Truman Pkwy exit E Montgomery Crossroad, 0.4 mi e to Skidaway Rd, then just se; in Norwood Shopping Plaza in the Sandfly. [L] [D] CALL [M]

KANPAI 912/898-7778 (12)

▼▼ Japanese Sushi. Casual Dining. $7-$28 AAA Inspector Notes: Of the many sushi offerings, I had the spicy tuna, and it was quite possibly the best I've ever had. The menu also includes all of the items typically found at a Japanese steakhouse like hibachi offerings, noodle dishes, tempura, bento boxes and rice dishes. A children's menu is available. Features: beer & wine, happy hour. Address: 140 Johnny Mercer Blvd, Suite 1 31410 Location: Jct US 80 and SR 367 (Johnny Mercer Blvd), 2.7 mi se; on Whitemarsh Island. [L] [D]

THE KING AND I 912/355-2100 (24)

▼▼ Thai. Casual Dining. $9-$23 AAA Inspector Notes: Traditional cuisine is made to order and spiced to preference at this place, which resides in a small shopping center. Address: 7098 Hodgson Memorial Dr 31406 Location: Jct SR 21 and 204 (Abercorn St), 1.3 mi s to Eisenhower Dr, then just e; in Eisenhower Shopping Plaza. [L] [D]

LA PARRILLA MEXICAN RESTAURANT 912/354-3757 (28)

▼▼ Mexican. Casual Dining. $6-$18 AAA Inspector Notes: This above-average cantina offers a large menu of extraordinarily prepared Mexican standards and Americanized interpretations. The dining room is bright and welcoming as is the casually uniformed staff. I tried the potato soup and marinated skirt steak on the chilly evening of my visit and was really impressed by the depth of flavor of both dishes, and the tenderness of the steak. The well-developed menu includes something for everyone along with a special selection for youngsters. Features: full bar, patio dining, happy hour. Address: 7804 Abercorn St 31406 Location: 1.7 mi s of jct SR 21 and 204 (Abercorn St); at Oglethorpe Mall. [L] [D] CALL [M]

LILI'S RESTAURANT & BAR 912/235-2664 (14)

▼▼ Fusion. Casual Dining. $9-$30 AAA Inspector Notes: With his talented fusion of French, Indian, Pakistani, Middle Eastern, Caribbean and Southern cooking techniques and spices, the chef/owner produces flavors like I have never experienced before. I stopped for a quick bite and chose the slider trio. Each was a separate delight. The daily lunch menu is comprised of sandwiches, flatbreads and curries. For dinner the finger foods disappear and heavenly entrées featuring seafood, lamb, beef and risotto take their place for a more robust experience. Features: full bar, patio dining. Address: 326 Johnny Mercer Blvd 31410 Location: Jct US 80 and SR 367 (Johnny Mercer Blvd), 2.7 mi se; on Whitemarsh Island. [L] [D]

(See map & index p. 260.)

LITTLE ITALY 912/201-3805 [13]
▼▼ ▼▼ Italian Pizza. Casual Dining. $10-$29 **AAA Inspector Notes:** The surroundings are comfortable, the marsh views are enjoyable and the red sauce is flavorful. All the standards are here along with nightly specials and several pizza selections. Start with a shareable antipasto, choose a pasta, veal, chicken or seafood dish then cap off the evening with a rich dessert like limoncello cake. **Features:** full bar, patio dining, happy hour. **Address:** 138 Johnny Mercer Blvd, Suite 16 31410 **Location:** Jct US 80 and SR 367 (Johnny Mercer Blvd), 2.7 mi SE; on Whitemarsh Island. [D]

LOCAL 11 TEN 912/790-9000 [4]
▼▼▼ New American. Fine Dining. $16-$45 **AAA Inspector Notes:** This restaurant is located in a restored and converted bank building, although there is little evidence of the building's former use. The upscale, yet comfortable, décor blends mixed mediums to create a modern visual. The cuisine draws on the chef's creative talents and combines French and Italian influences with upscale Southern flavors, using local and regional products as much as possible. The menu changes seasonally and offers daily specials driven by market availability. **Features:** full bar, patio dining, happy hour. **Address:** 1110 Bull St 31401 **Location:** Jct W Duffy Ln, 1 blk s of Forsyth Park. **Parking:** on-site and street. [D]

LOVE'S SEAFOOD RESTAURANT 912/925-3616 [35]
▼▼ ▼▼ Seafood. Casual Dining. $11-$30 **AAA Inspector Notes:** This lovely location overlooks scenic Ogeechee River. Family operated since 1949, this restaurant specializes in golden-fried river catfish, huge seafood platters, alligator, shrimp and just about anything else that comes out of the water. You'll also find some hand-cut steaks and pasta dishes for diversity. Four indoor dining rooms and a cozy patio offer a rustic atmosphere and great views of the activity on the water, including gators and the occasional manatee. **Features:** full bar, patio dining, happy hour. **Address:** 6817 Chief O.F. Love Rd 31419 **Location:** I-95 exit 94 (SR 204/Abercorn St), 1.9 mi e to US 17 S, 2.8 mi sw to Basin Rd; just ne of Ogeechee River at Kings Ferry Bridge. [D] CALL [&M] [🐾]

THE NOODLE BOWL 912/692-1394 [20]
▼▼ ▼▼ Asian. Casual Dining. $6-$25 **AAA Inspector Notes:** The popularity of this former self-serve, predominantly take-out restaurant required it to expand to a full service sit-down eatery where guests are treated to a diverse menu from all parts of Asia. Relax and enjoy a Singaporean laksa soup, Vietnamese pho, pad thai see ew, Japanese udon, Korean bulgogi or any of the many other dishes and nations represented. Service is provided by the owners and other than ensuring the food is prepared well they also make sure it is enjoyable. **Features:** beer & wine. **Address:** 7052 Hodgson Memorial Dr 31406 **Location:** Just e of jct SR 204 (Abercorn St) and Eisenhower Dr; in Eisenhower Shopping Plaza. [L] [D]

PEARL'S SALTWATER GRILLE SEAFOOD & STEAKS 912/352-8221 [26]
▼▼ ▼▼ Seafood. Casual Dining. $9-$26 **AAA Inspector Notes:** This bustling eatery on the river is known for its seafood, but the menu has diverse enough offerings to satisfy any palate. Subtle nautical appointments and freshly caught seafood nicely complement each other. A good variety of homemade desserts is available to top off a great meal. Large wrap-around windows offer relaxing scenery of the river, but after sunset there is not much activity so get there early for the views. **Features:** full bar. **Reservations:** suggested. **Address:** 7000 LaRoche Ave 31406 **Location:** 5.8 mi sw via SR 204 (Abercorn St) to Eisenhower Dr (which becomes Nottingham Rd), 2.5 mi e to LaRoche Ave, then just s. [D] CALL [&M]

SAIGON BISTRO 912/335-2025 [16]
▼▼ ▼▼ Vietnamese. Casual Dining. $8-$15 **AAA Inspector Notes:** Freshly prepared dishes made with equally fresh ingredients are the hallmarks of success at this little corner restaurant. Expect hand-rolled spring rolls, a wide variety of pho specialty soups and rice and noodle dishes. It not only is delicious and inexpensive but it is healthy. **Address:** 5700 Waters Ave 31404 **Location:** Jct De Renne Ave, just n at E 71st St; midtown. **Parking:** on-site and street. [L] [D]

SAM SNEAD'S OAK GRILL & TAVERN 912/963-0797 [1]
▼▼▼ American. Fine Dining. $10-$29 **AAA Inspector Notes:** I'm not sure which I enjoyed more, the wonderful food or the museum-quality interior with its walls lined with golf memorabilia as homage to the great Slammin' Sammy. The menu is diverse and will certainly please most palates with its selection of steak, seafood, ribs, pastas and signature flatbreads. I had the Asian shrimp and onion soup with Emmentaler cheeses topping; both were simply divine. Checking out the many wall displays is encouraged. **Features:** full bar, patio dining, happy hour. **Address:** 7 Sylvester C. Formey Dr 31408 **Location:** I-95 exit 104, just se to Crossroads Pkwy, then just sw. [L] [D] CALL [&M] [🐾]

THE SHELL HOUSE RESTAURANT 912/927-3280 [32]
▼▼ ▼▼ Seafood. Casual Dining. $13-$40 **AAA Inspector Notes:** The seafood offerings at this family-oriented restaurant encourage you to eat with your fingers and push the trash through the hole in the center of your table. Snow crab legs, peel-and-eat shrimp, fresh oysters and crab cakes are menu favorites at this waterfront eatery. Serving the area for more than 25 years, it must be doing something right. This place is not fancy, just filling. **Features:** full bar, happy hour. **Address:** 8 Gateway Blvd 31419 **Location:** I-95 exit 94 (SR 204/Abercorn St), just w, then just n. [D]

STICKY FINGERS RIB HOUSE 912/925-7427
▼▼ ▼▼ Barbecue. Casual Dining. $9-$21 **AAA Inspector Notes:** Diners can put down their silverware and get their fingers ready for classic Carolina sweet ribs, as well as ribs cooked in the Texas and Tennessee styles. Hearty sides of baked beans and coleslaw complement the entrees. **Features:** full bar, happy hour. **Address:** 7921 Abercorn St 31406 **Location:** Jct SR 204 (Abercorn St) and White Bluff Rd, just sw. [L] [D] CALL [&M]

SWEET POTATOES KITCHEN 912/352-3434 [25]
◆◆◆
Regional Comfort Food Casual Dining $8-$12
AAA Inspector Notes: The menu in this laid-back, easy-going kitchen boasts comfort foods and seafood marked by home-style and Southern influences. The namesake sweet potato is highlighted in such items as the sweet potato of the day and sweet potato cake. The primary décor feature is the field of flowers painted along the walls. The banana pudding is regarded as the best on earth by 'Man v. Food' on the Travel Channel. **Features:** beer & wine. **Address:** 6825 Waters Ave 31405 **Location:** SR 21 and 204 (Abercorn St), 1.2 mi s, 0.9 mi e on Eisenhower Dr. [L] [D] CALL [&M]

TASTE OF INDIA 912/356-1020 [29]
▼▼ ▼▼ Indian. Casual Dining. $8-$25 **AAA Inspector Notes:** Guests peruse an extensive menu of well-prepared dishes here, including lamb, chicken, goat, seafood and vegetarian specialties—all spiced to the requested level. Attentive servers are knowledgeable about menu preparations. Casual and relaxed dining combines with prepared-to-order cuisine for a pleasurable experience. A lunch buffet is offered daily as is a Dosa street food menu featuring light crepes and eaten-by-hand favorites. **Features:** full bar, patio dining. **Address:** 401 Mall Blvd, Suite 102C 31406 **Location:** Just e of SR 204 (Abercorn St); jct Hodgson Memorial Dr; in Southpoint. [L] [D] CALL [&M]

(See map & index p. 260.)

TONI STEAKHOUSE   912/691-8748 21
▼▼▼ Steak Seafood. Casual Dining. $9-$55 AAA Inspector Notes: Known for its chic interior, attentive service and great steaks, this small restaurant urges diners to come in and meet the family, who are eager to prepare you a great meal. Opt for anything from a petite filet to a 34-ounce cowboy rib-eye with traditional accompaniments. A nice selection of equally well-prepared fresh catches, a few pasta and chicken dishes and some strictly vegetarian appetizers and salads also are offered. Features: full bar, happy hour. Address: 110 Eisenhower Dr 31406 Location: Jct SR 21, 1.2 mi s on SR 204 (Abercorn St), just e. [L] [D] CALL [&M]

TROY MEDITERRANEAN CUISINE   912/921-5117 33
▼▼ Mediterranean. Casual Dining. $8-$24 AAA Inspector Notes: This storefront restaurant features a takeout area in the entryway and a large comfortable dining room to the side. The menu is huge and specializes in Italian-style pasta dishes, Greek and Turkish kebabs, salads, wraps, burgers and sandwiches. Try the mix meze appetizer for a variety of specialty treats to kick off the meal. Features: beer & wine. Address: 10510 Abercorn St 31419 Location: Between W Magnolia Ave and Wilshire Blvd on the south-side; in D & B Plaza. [L] [D]

WILEY'S CHAMPIONSHIP BBQ   912/201-3259 6
▼▼ Barbecue. Casual Dining. $4-$30 AAA Inspector Notes: The name says championship while the awards on the wall attest to that fact. This spot is barbecue worthy of blue ribbons on a national level. Rev up the taste buds with some Brunswick stew or redneck nachos, then dig into one of the many hearty portions of beef, pork or chicken, all cooked to tender perfection and served with Texas toast. For those who are really hungry, ask for the big Wiley which adds an additional half-pound of meat to any selection. Features: beer & wine. Address: 4700 Hwy 80 E, Suite N 31410 Location: On Whitemarsh Island; jct Islands Expwy and US 80, just w on US 80; in Whitemarsh Shopping Center. [L] [D]

SEA ISLAND (E-6) elev. 7'
• Part of Golden Isles area — see map p. 187

Seaward of St. Simons Island and accessible from there by causeway, Sea Island is an all-year resort in a lush garden setting of flowering shrubs, ancient oaks, palms and pines. The private island lies between the Atlantic Ocean and the marshes of Glynn, the subject of Sidney Lanier's poem.

Sea Island has long been a favorite with heads of state. Presidents Calvin Coolidge, Herbert Hoover, Dwight Eisenhower, Richard Nixon, Gerald Ford, Jimmy Carter and George H.W. Bush all vacationed on the island. In addition to a smooth 5-mile beach and a spa, there are excellent facilities for golf, skeet shooting, horseback riding, tennis and fishing.

THE CLOISTER   912/638-3611
▼▼▼▼▼ Resort Hotel
Rates not provided

Address: 100 Cloister Dr 31561 Location: Waterfront. Just over Sea Island Bridge Cswy. Facility: Rooms are as large and luxurious as you would expect but you will only need them to relax after your full day of activities and upscale dining. Expect the best; you will not be disappointed. 102 units, some two bedrooms. 3 stories, interior/exterior corridors. Parking: valet only. Terms: check-in 4 pm. Amenities: safes. Dining: 5 restaurants, also, The Georgian Room, Tavola, see separate listings. Pool(s): outdoor. Activities: hot tub, boat dock, fishing, regulation golf, tennis, recreation programs, bicycles, trails, spa. Guest Services: valet laundry, luggage security pick-up, area transportation.

[SAVE] [✕] [✈] [↑↓] [♿] [☰] CALL [&M] [≈] [♨] [BIZ]
[HS] [≈] [✕] [♨] [▭] /SOME UNITS [🐾]

WHERE TO EAT

THE GEORGIAN ROOM   912/638-3611
▼▼▼▼ New Southern. Fine Dining. $45-$51 AAA Inspector Notes: Diners should prepare for an experience like none other when stepping through the doors of The Georgian Room. Gorgeous antique gold and crystal chandeliers, grand molded stone columns, majestic arches and a stately fireplace create an impressive backdrop for the equally magnificent menu. A highly trained staff provides unparalleled tableside service and impressive knowledge of New Southern cuisine and world-class wine. Features: full bar. Reservations: suggested. Semiformal attire. Address: 100 Cloister Dr 31561 Location: Just over Sea Island Bridge Cswy; in The Cloister. Parking: valet only. [☰] [B] [D] CALL [&M] [◣]

TAVOLA   912/638-3611
▼▼▼▼ Italian. Casual Dining. $20-$40 AAA Inspector Notes: This rustic Italian eatery has upscale food and décor keeping with the beautiful Cloister resort, but with large tables and a bustling environment, the ambience that is more casual family meal than quiet romantic dinner. The Wagyu beef carpaccio and fresh made pastas are the standouts on the menu. Features: full bar, happy hour. Reservations: suggested. Address: 100 Cloister Dr 31561 Location: Just over Sea Island Bridge Cswy; in The Cloister. Parking: valet only. [☰] [D] CALL [&M]

SMYRNA (H-2) pop. 51,271, elev. 1,060'
• Hotels & Restaurants map & index p. 76, 82
• Part of Atlanta area — see map p. 44

About 10 miles northwest of Atlanta, Smyrna is considered part of the Atlanta metropolitan area but has a small town feel. The downtown area is a mixed-use space populated with townhomes, a library, a community center and green spaces. In the spring, gardens throughout the city flourish with lovely jonquil flowers, earning Smyrna the nickname Jonquil City.

BAYMONT INN & SUITES   (404)794-1600 61
▼▼ Hotel. $69-$121 Address: 5130 S Cobb Dr 30082 Location: I-285 exit 15, 0.3 mi w. Facility: 56 units. 2 stories (no elevator), interior corridors. Pool(s): heated indoor. Activities: hot tub. Guest Services: valet laundry.
[↑+] CALL [&M] [≈] [BIZ] [HS] [≈] [♨] [🖿] [▭]
/SOME UNITS [🐾]

COUNTRY INN & SUITES BY CARLSON   (404)564-1105 60
▼▼▼ Hotel. $90-$114 Address: 2175 Church Rd SE 30080 Location: I-285 exit 15, 0.3 mi w. Facility: 67 units. 4 stories, interior corridors. Terms: cancellation fee imposed, resort fee. Pool(s): heated indoor. Activities: exercise room. Guest Services: valet and coin laundry.
[↑+] CALL [&M] [≈] [BIZ] [HS] [≈] [✕] [♨] [🖿] [▭]

EXTENDED STAY AMERICA-ATLANTA-CUMBERLAND MALL
                                  (770)432-4000 58
▼▼ Extended Stay Motel. $75-$100 Address: 3103 Sports Ave 30080 Location: I-285 exit 20 westbound; exit 19 eastbound, just n to Spring Rd, then 0.3 mi w. Facility: 125 efficiencies. 2 stories (no elevator), exterior corridors. Terms: cancellation fee imposed. Guest Services: coin laundry.
[↑+] CALL [&M] [BIZ] [≈] [✕] [♨] [🖿] [▭] /SOME UNITS [🐾]

GALLERIA/MARIETTA COMFORT INN & SUITES
                                  (770)541-1499 55
▼▼▼ Hotel. $99-$214 Address: 2221 Corporate Plaza Pkwy S 30080 Location: I-75 exit 260, just w. Facility: 77 units. 2-3 stories, interior corridors. Pool(s): heated indoor. Activities: exercise room. Guest Services: valet and coin laundry.
[↑+] CALL [&M] [≈] [BIZ] [≈] [✕] [♨] [🖿] [▭]

(See maps & indexes p. 76, 82.)

HYATT PLACE ATLANTA/COBB GALLERIA
(770)384-0060 **59**

Hotel
$84-$179

HYATT PLACE

AAA Benefit: Members save 10%!

Address: 2876 Spring Hill Pkwy 30080 **Location:** I-285 exit 20 westbound; exit 19 eastbound, just n to Spring Rd, then just w. **Facility:** 123 units. 6 stories, interior corridors. **Terms:** cancellation fee imposed. **Pool(s):** outdoor. **Activities:** exercise room. **Guest Services:** valet laundry, area transportation. **Featured Amenity: full hot breakfast.**

RED ROOF INN-ATLANTA SMYRNA (770)952-6966 **56**

Motel
$55-$80

Address: 2200 Corporate Plaza 30080 **Location:** I-75 exit 260, just w to Corporate Plaza, then just s. **Facility:** 134 units. 2 stories (no elevator), exterior corridors. **Guest Services:** valet and coin laundry.

RESIDENCE INN BY MARRIOTT-ATLANTA CUMBERLAND
(770)433-8877 **57**

Extended Stay Hotel. $79-$206 **Address:** 2771 Cumberland Blvd 30080 **Location:** I-285 exit 20 westbound; exit 19 eastbound, just n to Spring Rd, 0.3 mi w to Cumberland Blvd, then just n. **Facility:** 130 kitchen units. 3 stories (no elevator), exterior corridors. **Pool(s):** outdoor. **Activities:** exercise room. **Guest Services:** valet and coin laundry.

AAA Benefit: Members save 5% or more!

WHERE TO EAT

HOUSE OF CHAN 770/955-9444 **93**
Chinese. Casual Dining. $9-$30 **AAA Inspector Notes:** Diners can feast on ample portions of well-prepared family recipes, including the popular bass and duck entrées. Hidden in a small plaza off a busy highway, the restaurant has a cozy and bustling dining room that is well tended by the fast, friendly staff. **Features:** beer & wine. **Address:** 2469 Cobb Pkwy SE 30080 **Location:** I-285 exit 20 westbound; exit 19 eastbound, 1 mi n on US 41 (Cobb Pkwy).

JACKS NEW YORKER DELI 404/799-8500
Sandwiches. Quick Serve. $6-$16 **AAA Inspector Notes:** This deli serves up a plethora of sandwich types and styles. The traditional Reuben is the most popular but others include the Times Square tenderloin, Peachtree pastrami and triple Linden club. Multiple styles of heroes, panini, subs and wedges are offered. Soups, salads and desserts also are available. **Features:** full bar. **Address:** 4691 S Atlanta Rd 30080 **Location:** I-285 exit 16, 0.4 mi e; in Vinings Court.

JIM 'N NICK'S BAR-B-Q 678/556-0011
Barbecue. Casual Dining. $8-$32 **AAA Inspector Notes:** Southern hospitality reigns at Jim 'N Nick's, where diners get neighborly treatment as they dig into huge portions of tasty lean sausage, fresh chili, juicy smoked beef and pork. A slice of sublime homemade pie ends the meal on a high note. **Features:** full bar. **Address:** 4574 S Cobb Dr 30080 **Location:** Jct S Cobb Dr and Cumberland Pkwy SE.

MINATO JAPANESE RESTAURANT 770/432-6012 **96**
Japanese. Casual Dining. $5-$34 **AAA Inspector Notes:** Enjoy udon noodles and tempura or relax and let a table side chef cook shrimp, chicken or beef hibachi style. The sushi here comes in large portions and is some of the best around. **Features:** beer & wine. **Address:** 2697 Spring Rd 30080 **Location:** I-285 exit 20 westbound; exit 19 eastbound, just n to Spring Rd, then just w.

MUSS & TURNER'S 770/434-1114 **98**
American. Casual Dining. $8-$24 **AAA Inspector Notes:** A deli by day and a bistro by night, this is a hugely popular neighborhood eatery. Some samples of sandwiches include the funky chicken, the insult to Philly and the no mama tuna salad. All sandwiches come with a choice of four pickle options. Dinner entrées include small charcuterie plates, grilled hanger steak and pheasant breast. The service is fast and informed. **Features:** full bar, patio dining, Sunday brunch. **Address:** 1675 Cumberland Pkwy, Suite 309 30080 **Location:** I-285 exit 16, 0.5 mi w; in Ivy Walk at Vinings.

OLD SOUTH BAR-B-Q 770/435-4215 **94**
Barbecue. Casual Dining. $6-$19 **AAA Inspector Notes:** Representing the tradition of Old South barbecue, this restaurant serves up some of the most delicious ribs in the area, as well as some mouth-watering barbecue pork and Brunswick stew. Top off the meal with a slice of homemade pie. The kitchen also accepts bulk orders for those wanting to take some barbecue to the next family gathering. **Address:** 601 Burbank Cir 30080 **Location:** I-75 exit 260, 3.7 mi w; corner of Windy Hill Rd and Burbank Cir.

ROY'S CHEESESTEAKS 404/799-7939 **99**
Sandwiches. Quick Serve. $3-$8 **AAA Inspector Notes:** This spot offers cheesesteaks just like the ones found in Philadelphia, made with bread transported from Amoroso's Baking Company in the City of Brotherly Love. Each cheesesteak comes with or without onions and a choice of American, provolone, mozzarella or Cheez Whiz. Diners also can find Italian hoagies, hamburgers (only after 2 pm), hot dogs, chicken tenders, entrée salads and hand-dipped ice cream. The milk shakes are made by hand and are delicious! **Features:** patio dining. **Address:** 2900 Highlands Pkwy SE 30082 **Location:** I-285 exit 15, 0.3 mi w; in Highlands Village.

SCALINI'S ITALIAN RESTAURANT 770/952-7222 **92**
Italian. Casual Dining. $13-$23 **AAA Inspector Notes:** Skillfully served pasta dishes bathed in excellent homemade sauces are highlights at the warm, family-oriented eatery. Worth a splurge are the delicious homemade desserts, including spumoni served with a coconut macaroon or the decadent chocolate mousse cake. **Features:** full bar. **Reservations:** suggested. **Address:** 2390 Cobb Pkwy SE 30080 **Location:** I-285 exit 20 westbound; exit 19 eastbound, 1 mi n on US 41 (Cobb Pkwy); in The Promenade.

SIAM SQUARE 770/333-1700 **89**
Thai. Casual Dining. $8-$19 **AAA Inspector Notes:** Gracious servers deliver well-prepared Thai selections, such as pad thai and panang curry. The atmosphere is relaxed yet classy. Make sure to ask the server about the heat level of the dish as some are extremely spicy! **Features:** beer & wine. **Address:** 1995 Windy Hill Rd 30080 **Location:** I-75 exit 260, 1 mi w; in Windy Hill West Shopping Center.

(See maps & indexes p. 76, 82.)

SOUTH CITY KITCHEN　　　　770/435-0700　(97)

♥♥ New Southern. Fine Dining. $11-$33 **AAA Inspector Notes:** In a relaxed and sophisticated ambience, this restaurant prepares contemporary Southern cuisine from fresh, traditional ingredients. Duck breast, Georgia mountain trout, catfish and shrimp and red mule grits are examples. The desserts, such as cheesecake-bread pudding and pecan pie, are must haves. Service is most knowledgeable and attentive. **Features:** full bar, patio dining, Sunday brunch. **Address:** 1675 Cumberland Pkwy SE 30080 **Location:** I-285 exit 16, 0.5 mi w; in Ivy Walk at Vinings. (D) CALL (Ⓜ)

THIS IS IT!　　　　　　770/435-3159　(95)

♥ Soul Food. Quick Serve. $6-$27 **AAA Inspector Notes:** Enjoy a great selection of items from the cafeteria line at this restaurant, including tilapia, ribs, pork, chicken and vegetables—any items found here can also be fried and brought to your table within five minutes. To-go items such as wings and seafood baskets are very popular along with chicken and pork barbecue sandwiches. **Address:** 2776 Cumberland Blvd 30080 **Location:** I-285 exit 19 eastbound; exit 20 westbound, just n to Spring Rd, 0.3 mi w to Cumberland Blvd, then just n. (L) (D)

THOMPSON BROTHERS BBQ　　770/818-9098　(91)

♥ Barbecue. Quick Serve. $6-$14 **AAA Inspector Notes:** This spot has been serving up tasty smoked barbecue to the Atlanta area for several years. Try the pork, chicken, ribs, beef brisket, ham, sausage or bologna as a sandwich, plate or platter. If it is too tough to decide then just create a combo of any two meats. Be sure to top it off with sweet or spicy sauce. Sides include baked beans, coleslaw, potato salad and macaroni and cheese. You can take any of the menu options home by the pound. **Features:** beer only. **Address:** 2445 Cobb Pkwy 30080 **Location:** I-285 exit 20 westbound; exit 19 eastbound, 1 mi n; in Cumberland Square North. (L) (D)

YAKITORI JINBEI　　　　770/818-9215　(90)

♥♥ Japanese. Casual Dining. $8-$23 **AAA Inspector Notes:** Guests visit this restaurant for an authentic Japanese dining experience and the house specialty yakitori. The sushi is excellent as are the ramen noodle bowls. **Features:** beer & wine. **Address:** 2421 Cobb Pkwy SE 30080 **Location:** I-285 exit 20 westbound; exit 19 eastbound, 1 mi n. (L) (D)

SNELLVILLE pop. 18,242

- **Hotels & Restaurants map & index p. 90**
- **Part of Atlanta area — see map p. 44**

LA QUINTA INN & SUITES SNELLVILLE-STONE MOUNTAIN
(770)736-4723　(41)

♥♥♥ Hotel. $101-$180 **Address:** 2971 Main St W 30078 **Location:** Jct US 78 and SR 124, 0.9 mi w. **Facility:** 58 units. 4 stories, interior corridors. **Pool(s):** heated indoor. **Activities:** exercise room. **Guest Services:** coin laundry.

(¶↑) CALL (Ⓜ) (🖭) (BIZ) (📶) (❌) (🛏) (🍽) (🖥)
/ SOME UNITS (🐾)

WHERE TO EAT

BONEFISH GRILL　　　　678/344-8945　(27)

♥♥♥ Seafood. Fine Dining. $10-$28 **AAA Inspector Notes:** Fish is the house specialty, and the menu and nightly specials offer a variety of choices. Well-prepared food is cooked to perfection. Service is casual in nature, and the staff is skilled and attentive. **Features:** full bar. **Address:** 1350 Scenic Hwy 124 30078 **Location:** Jct Webb Gin Rd. (D) CALL (Ⓜ)

SOCIAL CIRCLE (B-3) pop. 4,262, elev. 861'

WINERIES

- **Fox Vineyards and Winery,** I-20 exit 98, then 1 mi. s. to 225 SR 11S. **Hours:** Wed.-Sat. 10-6, Sun. 1-6. Closed Easter, Thanksgiving and Christmas. **Phone:** (770) 787-5402. (GT)

BLUE WILLOW INN RESTAURANT　　770/464-2131

♥♥ Southern. Casual Dining. $15-$24 **AAA Inspector Notes:** The cordial waitstaff at this Greek-Revival mansion with a beautiful fountain serves a traditional, home-cooked Southern buffet featuring fried chicken, roast beef, baked ham and many vegetables and salads as well as desserts. Wash down your meal with a specialty lemonade or tea made on the premises. **Reservations:** suggested. **Address:** 294 N Cherokee Rd 30025 **Location:** I-20 exit 98, 4 mi n on SR 11. (L) (D)

STATESBORO (D-5) pop. 28,422, elev. 258'

Statesboro was established in 1803, and a century later the town was shipping one-eighth of the world's supply of cotton. Today it remains a regional commercial and industrial center but also is a center for higher education. Founded in 1906, the pine-studded, gently rolling 630-acre campus of Georgia Southern University is home to 20,000 students seeking traditional 4-year, graduate and doctoral degrees. Founded in 1991, Ogeechee Technical College's focused curriculum gives approximately 3,220 students the opportunity to pursue career-oriented studies.

Statesboro Convention & Visitors Bureau: 222 S. Main St., P.O. Box 1516, Statesboro, GA 30459. **Phone:** (912) 489-1869 or (800) 568-3301.

BOTANIC GARDEN AT GEORGIA SOUTHERN UNIVERSITY, 1 mi. s. on SR 67 to 1505 Bland Ave., features 11 acres of nature trails, native flora and heritage gardens. The grounds also include the Rural Life Museum, housed in the restored Weathervane Barn, the Oak Grove one-room schoolhouse, the Heritage Pavilion and Bland Cottage, a restored 1920s homestead. Educational programs are offered by appointment. **Time:** Allow 30 minutes minimum. **Hours:** Gardens open Mon.-Fri. 9:30-7 (buildings close at 5:30), Sun. 1-4, during DST; Mon.-Fri. 9:30-5:30, Sun. 1-4, rest of year. Closed holidays and during academic holidays. **Cost:** Free. **Phone:** (912) 478-1149.

THE CENTER FOR WILDLIFE EDUCATION & THE LAMAR Q. BALL, JR. RAPTOR CENTER is on the campus of Georgia Southern University on Forest Dr. The center comprises almost 18 acres and showcases species of eagles, falcons, hawks, owls and vultures in natural habitats, in addition to a number of native waterfowl and wading birds. Indoor exhibits and wildlife shows present a variety of birds and reptiles. The 12-acre Wetland Preserve focuses on ornithology and water resource conservation.

Hours: Mon.-Fri. 9-5, Sat. 1-5, Sept.-May; Mon.-Fri. 9-5, rest of year. Wildlife program Mon.-Fri. at 3:30, year-round. Sat. reptile program at 2, raptor program at 3, Sept.-May. Closed major holidays. **Cost:** $2; $1 (ages 3-11, ages 55+ and military with ID). Annual passes (unlimited visits) $8; $6 (ages 3-11, ages 55+ and military with ID). Fees exclude special events. **Phone:** (912) 478-0831. (🏛)

GEORGIA SOUTHERN MUSEUM is in the Rosenwald Building on Southern Dr. on the grounds of Georgia Southern University, .5 mi. s. on US 301/25. This museum interprets the natural and cultural history of Georgia's coastal plain emphasizing the relationship between ancient and modern oceans. The main attraction is a 26-foot Mosasaur skeleton believed to be about 78 million years old. A replica of a 40 million-year-old whale skeleton is displayed. One exhibit showcases artifacts excavated from Camp Lawton, a Confederate Prisoner of War camp. An additional gallery presents a variety of temporary exhibits. **Time:** Allow 1 hour minimum. **Hours:** Tues.-Fri. 9-5, Sat.-Sun. 2-5. Closed major holidays. **Cost:** $2; free (ages 0-3 and to all last Sat. of the month). **Phone:** (912) 478-5444.

SPLASH IN THE BORO WATERPARK is at 1388 SR 24E (Main St.) within Mill Creek Park. After you get your fill of the winding and twisting slides, move on to the lazy river to rest up. The children's play pool is complete with a fort and a splash bucket that continuously overflows and spills. Test your balance on the lily pad obstacle course. Are you skilled enough to make it across before falling into the water? **Hours:** Mon.-Sat. 10-6 (also Thurs. and Sat. 6-8 p.m.), Sun. noon-6, mid-May to mid-Aug.; Sat. 10-6, Sun. noon-6, mid-Aug. to early Sept. **Cost:** $13.99 (over 48 inches tall), $10.99 (under 48 inches tall), $7 (ages 60+). **Phone:** (912) 489-3000.

DAYS INN STATESBORO   (912)681-7700
Motel. $69-$129 **Address:** 616 Fair Rd 30458 **Location:** Jct US 25/301 and SR 67, 0.6 mi se on SR 67. **Facility:** 81 units. 2 stories (no elevator), exterior corridors. **Pool(s):** outdoor. **Guest Services:** valet laundry.

HAMPTON INN STATESBORO   (912)489-8989
Hotel. $99-$264 **Address:** 350 Brampton Ave 30458 **Location:** Jct US 25/301 and SR 67, 0.6 mi se on SR 67 (Fair Rd). **Facility:** 90 units. 4 stories, interior corridors. **Terms:** 1-7 night minimum stay, cancellation fee imposed. **Pool(s):** outdoor. **Activities:** exercise room. **Guest Services:** valet and coin laundry.
AAA Benefit: Members save up to 10%!

HOLIDAY INN STATESBORO   (912)489-4545
Hotel. $79-$459 **Address:** 455 Commerce Dr 30461 **Location:** Jct US 80 and 301 Bypass/SR 73 Bypass, 0.5 mi s. **Facility:** 93 units. 4 stories, interior corridors. **Terms:** 30 day cancellation notice-fee imposed. **Pool(s):** heated outdoor. **Activities:** hot tub, exercise room. **Guest Services:** valet and coin laundry.

SPRINGHILL SUITES BY MARRIOTT STATESBORO UNIVERSITY AREA   (912)489-0000
Contemporary Hotel. $85-$134 **Address:** 105 Springhill Dr 30458 **Location:** Jct US 301 Bypass and SR 67, just s. **Facility:** 113 units. 3 stories, interior corridors. **Pool(s):** outdoor. **Activities:** exercise room. **Guest Services:** valet and coin laundry.
AAA Benefit: Members save 5% or more!

40 EAST GRILL   912/764-4040
Deli. Casual Dining. $8-$36 **AAA Inspector Notes:** Deli by day and fine dining by night, guests always can find something right at this casual downtown restaurant. The sandwich board offerings at lunch are plentiful and diverse with vegetarian, seafood, beef and chicken signature dishes, try the soup, salad and half-sandwich combo. At night the chef kicks it up a notch with full entrée offerings like pan-seared chicken or pork, duck, salmon and inventive pasta dishes. Suggested wine pairings always are available. **Features:** full bar, happy hour. **Address:** 40 E Main St 30458 **Location:** Center. **Parking:** street only.

BEAVER HOUSE RESTAURANT   912/764-2821
Regional Southern. Casual Dining. $8-$10 **AAA Inspector Notes:** Historic. This Southern-style restaurant is set in a circa 1911 mansion. Many items such as biscuits, salad dressings and desserts are made in-house. The restaurant is known for its boarding house family-style service. Complimentary seconds always are offered. **Features:** full bar, Sunday brunch. **Address:** 121 S Main St 30458 **Location:** On US 301/25, just s of center; downtown.

GNATS LANDING   912/489-8291
American. Casual Dining. $6-$18 **AAA Inspector Notes:** Located close to the college, this popular gathering spot can get busy in a snap. A wide variety of sandwiches include fried grouper, blackened flounder, chicken tarragon and pulled pork or choose shrimp, oysters and scallops prepared various ways. Be sure to leave some room for the blueberry crumble cake. **Features:** full bar, patio dining, happy hour. **Address:** 470 S Main St 30458 **Location:** Jct US 301/25 and SR 67, just s.

R J 'S SEAFOOD & STEAKS   912/489-8658
Seafood Steak. Casual Dining. $7-$22 **AAA Inspector Notes:** This popular, casual, buffet-style restaurant serves up made-to-order entrées while you fetch your soup and salad. The selections are broad—steak and plenty of seafood along with an extensive, inviting salad bar. A great end to the good meal is a slice of rich German chocolate cake. **Address:** 434 S Main St (US 301/25) 30458 **Location:** Jct US 25/301 and SR 67, just s.

STOCKBRIDGE (B-2) pop. 25,636, elev. 812'
• Hotels p. 284 • Restaurants p. 284
• Hotels & Restaurants map & index p. 94

PANOLA MOUNTAIN STATE PARK, 9 mi. e. on SR 138, then 4 mi. n. on SR 155, encompasses a 100-acre granite mountain that shelters plants and animals indigenous to the Piedmont region. The 1,635-acre park offers a 30-acre play area; a paved, 12-mile, multi-use nature trail; three 1-mile nature trails; two fishing lakes and an interpretive center with displays about the natural history of the area. Nature programs and guided hikes are offered from the visitor center. Fishing, biking and archery (bring your own gear) are available in the Alexander Lake area of the park. Self-guiding hikes are permitted on three trails, but due to conservation concerns, hikes up the mountain are always guided. Bicycle, kayak and paddleboard rentals are available.

Keep your focus safely

on the road when driving

(See map & index p. 94.)

Hours: Park open daily 7 a.m.-dusk. Nature center and park office open daily 8-5; closed Thanksgiving and Christmas. Guided hikes are available by advance reservation only. Phone for schedule and minimum participants required. **Cost:** $5 per private vehicle. Guided hikes $5. **Phone:** (770) 389-7801. 〔GT〕 ⬛ ⬛ ⬛ ⬛

COMFORT SUITES STOCKBRIDGE   (770)507-0444 **78**
▼▼▼ **Hotel.** $109-$169 **Address:** 3540 Cameron Pkwy 30281 **Location:** I-75 exit 228, just e; I-675 exit 1, just w. 4 stories, interior corridors. **Amenities:** safes. **Pool(s):** heated indoor. **Activities:** hot tub, exercise room. **Guest Services:** valet and coin laundry.

〔⫟⫠〕 CALL 〔&M〕 ⬛ 〔BIZ〕 〔HS〕 ⬛ ⬛ ⬛ ⬛ ⬛

HAMPTON INN-ATLANTA-STOCKBRIDGE
          (770)389-0065 **75**
▼▼▼ **Hotel.** $115-$160 **Address:** 7342 Hanover Pkwy N 30281 **Location:** I-75 exit 228, just e; I-675 exit 1, just w. **Facility:** 72 units. 3 stories, interior corridors. **Terms:** 1-7 night minimum stay, cancellation fee imposed. **Pool(s):** heated indoor. **Activities:** exercise room. **Guest Services:** valet and coin laundry.

AAA Benefit: Members save up to 10%!

〔⫟⫠〕 CALL 〔&M〕 ⬛ 〔BIZ〕 〔HS〕 ⬛ ⬛ ⬛ ⬛ ⬛

HOLIDAY INN HOTEL & SUITES   678/782-4000 **79**
▼▼▼ **Hotel.** Rates not provided. **Address:** 638 Hwy 138 W 30281 **Location:** I-75 exit 228, just e; I-675 exit 1, just w. **Facility:** 112 units. 5 stories, interior corridors. **Pool(s):** heated indoor. **Activities:** exercise room. **Guest Services:** valet and coin laundry.

〔⫟⫠〕 ⬛ ⬛ CALL 〔&M〕 ⬛ 〔BIZ〕 〔HS〕 ⬛ ⬛ ⬛ ⬛ ⬛

LA QUINTA INN & SUITES ATLANTA STOCKBRIDGE
          (770)506-9991 **76**

▼▼ ▼▼
Hotel
$86-$229

Address: 3581 Cameron Pkwy 30281 **Location:** I-75 exit 228, just e; I-675 exit 1, just w. **Facility:** 71 units. 4 stories, interior corridors. **Pool(s):** heated indoor. **Activities:** hot tub, exercise room. **Guest Services:** coin laundry. **Featured Amenity:** continental breakfast.

〔SAVE〕 〔⫟⫠〕 CALL 〔&M〕 ⬛ 〔BIZ〕 〔HS〕
⬛ ⬛ ⬛ ⬛ /SOME UNITS ⬛

QUALITY INN & SUITES   (770)507-7911 **74**

▼▼ ▼▼
Motel
$60-$99

Address: 7325 Pkwy N 30281 **Location:** I-675 exit 1, just e, then just n; I-75 exit 228, 1 mi e, then just n. **Facility:** 50 units. 2 stories (no elevator), exterior corridors. **Pool(s):** outdoor. **Guest Services:** coin laundry. **Featured Amenity:** full hot breakfast.

〔SAVE〕 〔⫟⫠〕 CALL 〔&M〕 ⬛ 〔BIZ〕 〔HS〕
⬛ ⬛ ⬛ ⬛ /SOME UNITS ⬛

RED ROOF INN ATLANTA/SOUTHEAST   (678)782-4100 **80**
▼▼ **Hotel.** $57-$127 **Address:** 637 Hwy 138 30281 **Location:** I-75 exit 228, just e; I-675 exit 1, just w. **Facility:** 64 units. 3 stories, interior corridors. **Pool(s):** outdoor. **Guest Services:** coin laundry.
〔⫟⫠〕 CALL 〔&M〕 ⬛ ⬛ ⬛ ⬛ /SOME UNITS ⬛ ⬛

SLEEP INN & SUITES   (770)474-3870 **77**
▼▼▼ **Hotel.** $61-$119 **Address:** 7423 Davidson Cir W 30281 **Location:** I-675 exit 1, just e, then just s; I-75 exit 228, 1 mi e, then just s. **Facility:** 73 units. 3 stories (no elevator), interior corridors. **Pool(s):** outdoor. **Activities:** exercise room. **Guest Services:** coin laundry.

〔⫟⫠〕 CALL 〔&M〕 ⬛ 〔BIZ〕 〔HS〕 ⬛ ⬛ ⬛ ⬛ ⬛
/SOME UNITS 〔S⤵〕

WHERE TO EAT

FRONTERA MEX-MEX GRILL   770/474-1540 **61**
▼▼ Tex-Mex. Casual Dining. $5-$17 **AAA Inspector Notes:** Cheery surroundings and traditional Tex-Mex food served quickly are the claims to fame at this grill. Chips and two salsas (one is smoked chipotle) precede the entrée. The outdoor seating area is a delightful place to eat during good weather. **Features:** full bar, patio dining. **Address:** 3607 SE Hwy 138 30281 **Location:** I-75 exit 228, just e; I-675 exit 1, just w. 〔L〕 〔D〕

KAZU JAPANESE & CHINESE RESTAURANT
          678/565-8881 **60**
▼▼ Asian. Casual Dining. $5-$28 **AAA Inspector Notes:** Enjoy a diverse menu of favorite Chinese and Japanese dishes at this cozy eatery. The simple décor puts the focus on the food—where it belongs. Try the artistic Love Boat which includes enough sushi for two in a decorative boat. **Features:** beer & wine. **Address:** 697 Davis Rd, Suite 1100 30281 **Location:** I-675 exit 1, just e on SR 138, 0.5 mi e on Henry Blvd; in Walmart Shopping Plaza.
〔L〕 〔D〕 CALL 〔&M〕

PAPI'S CUBAN & CARIBBEAN GRILL   770/506-9664
▼▼ Cuban. Casual Dining. $3-$15 **AAA Inspector Notes:** Take a quick culinary trip to the islands at this Cuban and Caribbean restaurant. The menu features many traditional favorites such as vaca frita, chicken fricassee, churrasco steak, plantains and coconut flan. The atmosphere is casual and appropriate for families. **Features:** full bar. **Address:** 1375 Rock Quarry Rd 30281 **Location:** I-75 exit 224 (Hudson Bridge Rd), 0.4 mi e on Hudson Bridge Rd, then just n. 〔L〕 〔D〕 CALL 〔&M〕

STONE MOUNTAIN (H-4) pop. 5,802, elev. 1,043'
- Hotels p. 286 • Restaurants p. 287
- Hotels & Restaurants map & index p. 82, 90, 94
- Part of Atlanta area — see map p. 44

STONE MOUNTAIN PARK is about 18 mi. e. of downtown Atlanta; take I-20 east to I-285 north, get off at exit 39B, then take US 78 e. about 8 mi. to exit 8. This major Atlanta-area tourist attraction has grown up around Stone Mountain, a massive, bowl-shaped granite formation that formed beneath the Earth's surface some 300 million years ago, eventually becoming exposed through a combination of weathering and the passage of untold centuries.

The 3,200-acre park includes more than a dozen attractions, historical and natural sights and expansive natural woodlands with hiking trails. *See Recreation Areas Chart.*

Summit Skyride, a high-speed Swiss cable car, will whisk you to the top of the mountain in minutes. It also provides an amazing up-close view of the iconic bas-relief sculpture carved into the sheer face of Stone Mountain. This memorial carving, 400 feet above ground level and measuring an impressive 90 by 190 feet, is a tribute to three Confederate leaders: Jefferson Davis, Robert E. Lee and Thomas "Stonewall" Jackson.

(See maps & indexes p. 82, 90, 94.)

Crossroads is a cluster of family-oriented attractions, restaurants, Memorial Hall Museum and shops where skilled crafters and artisans demonstrate their specialties. The Great Barn is filled with interactive games, super slides, climbing structures and other kid stuff. Crossroads' 4-D Theater offers "YOGI BEAR 4-D Adventure," where visitors can enjoy the antics of Yogi Bear and Boo-Boo.

Geyser Towers offers multiple levels of suspended rope bridges and net tunnels connected to towering platforms that overlook a gushing geyser. Also family-friendly is Sky Hike, an obstacle course replete with dangling ropes and suspended wooden bridges. Visitors can also freefall from three different towers onto airbags at The JUMP. Two golf courses and a miniature golf course also are available. The long-running "Lasershow Spectacular in Mountainvision" is an explosion of music, state-of-the-art special effects and fireworks that transforms the lawn at the base of the mountain into a natural amphitheater.

It is also a prime place to just enjoy the great outdoors. The walk-up trail to the top of Stone Mountain is an easy enough trek from lower slopes dotted with scrubby growths of loblolly pine up to a bare, rocky, windswept summit. On clear days the 360-degree vista from this viewpoint is spectacular. Or set out on the 5-mile Cherokee Trail that encircles the mountain, a serene hike with scenic nature trail detours.

There are also plenty of festivals to enjoy throughout the year including the ▼ Yellow Daisy Festival in mid-September, which features arts, crafts and flowers; the ▼ Stone Mountain Highland Games in mid-October, when festivalgoers don their family tartans and the sounds of bagpipes fill the air; and ▼ A Stone Mountain Christmas, early November through late December or early January, which features a 4-D holiday movie, train rides and visits from Santa.

Note: Height restrictions apply to some attractions. **Hours:** Park open daily 5 a.m.-midnight. Attraction schedules vary seasonally but are generally open daily 10:30-8, late May-early Aug. Closing times vary rest of year. "Lasershow Spectacular in Mountainvision" takes place evenings Memorial Day weekend-early Aug. (weather permitting), and Saturday nights in spring and fall. Attractions closed Christmas.

Cost: One-Day Adventure Pass $31.95; $28.95 (ages 55+ with ID); $25.95 (ages 3-11); $23.95 (military with ID). Summit Skyride round-trip ticket $10 (per person). One-way skyride ticket $6 (per person). Lasershow free with $15 vehicle entrance. **Parking:** One-day parking $15 per private vehicle; annual parking pass $40. **Phone:** (800) 401-2407.
🅰 🍴 🎡

The Carillon, in Stone Mountain Park at jct. John B. Gordon Dr. and Jefferson Davis Dr., is a 13-story spire rising from the lakeshore. This tower uses miniature bell-tone rods and amplification to create its 732 bell sounds. **Hours:** Taped concerts are presented Mon.-Fri. at noon and 4. Live concerts are given Sat. at noon and 4, Sun. at 1, 3 and 5. **Cost:** Free with $15 vehicle entrance. **Phone:** (800) 401-2407.

Historic Square is at jct. John B. Gordon Dr. and Jefferson Davis Dr., in Stone Mountain Park just e. of downtown Atlanta off I-285 exit 39B via US 78 exit 8. This self-guiding compound is a complex of 18th- and 19th-century houses and buildings relocated from throughout the state. The 19 buildings include the main house, overseer's house, slave cabins, blacksmith shop and a cookhouse, all furnished in period. Traditional craft and skills demonstrations are given. The Farmyard is home to such barnyard animals as goats, pigs and sheep. **Time:** Allow 1 hour minimum. **Hours:** Daily 11:20-8, late May-early Aug.; closing time varies rest of year. Closed Christmas. **Cost:** Included in the One-Day Adventure Pass. Individual ticket $12 (per person). **Phone:** (800) 401-2407.

Ride The Ducks in Stone Mountain Park at Crossroads. Visitors learn about the park's history in an entertaining way while seated in a covered amphibious vehicle called a Duck, which received its name from the World War II era DUKW. **Time:** Allow 30 minutes minimum. **Hours:** Daily 11-8, late May-early Aug.; closing time varies rest of year and is weather permitting. Closed Christmas. Phone ahead to confirm schedule. **Cost:** Tours are not included in the One-Day Adventure Pass but can be added for $10. Individual ticket $15. Ages 0-15 must be accompanied by an adult. Reservations are required. **Phone:** (800) 401-2407. GT

Snow Mountain is e. of downtown Atlanta off I-285 exit 39B via US 78, exit 8 in Stone Mountain Park. It offers visitors acres of snow fun. Snow Mountain Tube Runners allows riders to participate in snow tubing without prior experience. Avalanche Alley is a family tube adventure for multiple riders. The SnowZone consists of Igloo City, Snowman Valley, Snowball Shootin' Gallery and Little Angels. Snow Fire Point offers a reprieve from the cold and the opportunity to toast some marshmallows for s'mores. Children are required to be at least 42 inches in height to participate in Tube Runners and must be at least 36 inches in height to participate in Avalanche Alley.

Time: Allow 2 hours minimum. **Hours:** Select days 10-7, mid-Nov. to late Feb. Closed Christmas. **Cost:** Snow Mountain Pass (includes 2-hour access to tubing hill and all-day access to SnowZone) $28 (ages 3+). Phone ahead to confirm rates. Advance reservations for tubing hill access are required. **Phone:** (800) 401-2407.

Stone Mountain is off US 78 exit 8 in Stone Mountain Park and is encircled by Robert E. Lee Blvd. The park's namesake and focal point is a massive dome of granite 1,683 feet tall that rises some 825 feet above the surrounding region. It was

(See maps & indexes p. 82, 90, 94.)

created around 300 million years ago (at the same time the Appalachians were formed) when heat and friction resulting from the shifting of the earth's crust produced magma, or molten rock, that then slowly hardened. Buried for millions of years, the dome eventually became exposed through erosion and the passage of time.

Bowl-shaped rather than craggy, Stone Mountain is an unmistakable landmark. Its lower slopes are forested with scrubby loblolly pines and Georgia oaks, but the summit is bare, pocked with depressions that give it an eerie resemblance to a lunar landscape.

It's a relatively easy (i.e., not that steep), 1.3-mile trek to the top via a designated trail; on clear days the downtown Atlanta skyline is plainly visible, and sometimes even the distant Appalachians can be seen. Wear nonslip shoes and bring your camera. You can rest, refuel and enjoy the panoramic views at the Top of the Mountain snack bar before heading back down.

Carved into Stone Mountain's sheer north face is an enormous bas-relief sculpture of three major Civil War figures—Confederate president Jefferson Davis, Gen. Thomas "Stonewall" Jackson and Gen. Robert E. Lee. An amazing feat of engineering, it's the size of a city block but still looks small compared to the mountain's massive bulk. It was begun by Gutzon Borglum, who later went on to complete the carving at Mount Rushmore. It also took 57 years to finish, and that included a 36-year hiatus. The figures are illuminated at night, creating quite a stirring sight.

The hiking trail to the top of Stone Mountain begins near the Confederate Hall Historical & Environmental Education Center, at the junction of Robert E. Lee Boulevard and Memorial Drive.

The story behind this work of art is fascinating. The day-to-day labor was carried out by quarrymen who had to stand on open, wind-whipped scaffolding 33 stories above the ground. Roy Faulkner, the chief carver who finally brought the sculpture to completion, never had a formal art lesson but displayed a mastery of the thermo-jet torch, which enabled carvers to exact fine details while still blasting away huge amounts of rock. **Hours:** Park open daily 5 a.m.-midnight. **Cost:** One-day parking $15 per private vehicle; annual parking pass $40. **Phone:** (800) 401-2407.

Stone Mountain Scenic Railroad departs Robert E. Lee Blvd. and Old Hugh Howell Rd. in Stone Mountain Park and runs along a 5-mile route around Stone Mountain. During the excursion, a detailed history of the mountain is presented. A live show is presented in summer and during the Christmas season. **Time:** Allow 30 minutes minimum. **Hours:** Trips daily 11-8, late May-early Aug.; operating schedule varies rest of year. Closed Christmas. **Cost:** Fare included in the One-Day Adventure

Pass. Individual ticket $12 (per person). **Phone:** (800) 401-2407. GT

Summit Skyride leaves from Robert E. Lee Blvd. and John B. Gordon Dr. in Stone Mountain Park. This cable-car ride more than 825 feet to the top of Stone Mountain provides spectacular views of the mountain's carving and the countryside. **Time:** Allow 30 minutes minimum. **Hours:** Rides daily (weather permitting) 10:30-8, late May-early Aug.; departure of last car varies rest of year. Closed Christmas. **Cost:** Included in the One-Day Adventure Pass. Individual round-trip ticket $12 (per person). One-way ticket $7 (per person). **Phone:** (800) 401-2407.

ATLANTA EVERGREEN MARRIOTT CONFERENCE CENTER & RESORT   (770)879-9900   50

Resort Hotel
$121-$229

MARRIOTT

AAA Benefit:
Members save 5% or more!

Address: 4021 Lakeview Dr 30083 **Location:** US 78 exit 8; in Stone Mountain Park. **Facility:** Nestled in lush Stone Mountain Park, this resort caters to business functions, family gatherings and leisure travelers. This upscale hotel celebrates nature with style and class. 336 units, some two bedrooms. 5 stories, interior corridors. **Parking:** on-site and valet. **Terms:** check-in 4 pm. **Amenities:** safes. **Dining:** 3 restaurants. **Pool(s):** heated outdoor, heated indoor. **Activities:** hot tub, regulation golf, trails, spa. **Guest Services:** valet laundry.

COMFORT INN & SUITES AT STONE MOUNTAIN
(770)465-1888   48

Hotel. $70-$210 **Address:** 5355 Stone Mountain Hwy 30087 **Location:** US 78 exit 9. **Facility:** 57 units. 3 stories, interior corridors. **Pool(s):** heated indoor. **Guest Services:** valet and coin laundry.

COUNTRY INN & SUITES BY CARLSON   (770)465-6515   47

Hotel. $89-$149 **Address:** 1852 Rockbridge Rd 30087 **Location:** US 78 exit 9. **Facility:** 71 units. 3 stories, interior corridors. **Terms:** cancellation fee imposed. **Pool(s):** heated indoor. **Activities:** hot tub, exercise room. **Guest Services:** valet and coin laundry.

DAYS INN   (770)879-0800   46

Motel. $65-$107 **Address:** 2006 Glenn Club Dr 30087 **Location:** US 78 exit 9, 1.3 mi e of entrance to Stone Mountain Park. Located behind Krystal Restaurant. **Facility:** 81 units. 2 stories (no elevator), exterior corridors. **Terms:** cancellation fee imposed. **Pool(s):** outdoor. **Guest Services:** coin laundry.

HAMPTON INN STONE MOUNTAIN   (770)934-0004   87

Hotel. $109-$259 **Address:** 1737 Mountain Industrial Blvd 30083 **Location:** US 78 exit 4 (Mountain Industrial Blvd), just s. **Facility:** 112 units. 4 stories, interior corridors. **Terms:** 1-7 night minimum stay, cancellation fee imposed. **Pool(s):** outdoor. **Activities:** exercise room. **Guest Services:** valet and coin laundry.

AAA Benefit:
Members save up to 10%!

(See maps & indexes p. 82, 90, 94.)

HOLIDAY INN EXPRESS 770/465-8847 **45**
 Hotel. Rates not provided. **Address:** 1790 E Park Place Blvd 30087 **Location:** US 78 exit 9, 0.7 mi n. **Facility:** 60 units. 3 stories, interior corridors. **Pool(s):** outdoor. **Activities:** exercise room. **Guest Services:** valet and coin laundry.

QUALITY INN STONE MOUNTAIN (770)465-1022 **44**
 Motel $65-$149

Address: 1595 E Park Place Blvd 30087 **Location:** US 78 exit 9, 0.3 mi n. **Facility:** 60 units. 2 stories (no elevator), exterior corridors. **Amenities:** safes. **Pool(s):** outdoor. **Guest Services:** coin laundry. **Featured Amenity:** continental breakfast.

STONE MOUNTAIN INN (770)469-3311 **49**
 Motel $86-$249

AAA Benefit: Members save 5% or more!

 Address: 1058 Robert E Lee Blvd 30083 **Location:** US 78 exit 8; in Stone Mountain Park. **Facility:** 92 units. 2 stories (no elevator), interior/exterior corridors. **Terms:** check-in 4 pm, 3 day cancellation notice. **Pool(s):** outdoor. **Activities:** regulation golf, bicycles. **Guest Services:** complimentary and valet laundry. Affiliated with Marriott Hotels, Resorts and Suites.

ALWAYS FRESH NEIGHBORHOOD RESTAURANT & MARKET 678/380-4656 **30**
 American. Casual Dining. $6-$13 **AAA Inspector Notes:** This popular spot serves up daily lunch specials featuring meat and veggie plates that include baked chicken, barbecue pork, meatloaf, pot roast and beef tips. Georgia dogs, hamburgers, deli sandwiches, soups and salads are available as well. Dinner is served on weeknights but not on Saturday and Sunday; however, there is a favored lunch buffet on Sunday. The caramel pie is a revelation. A neighborhood market is on site. **Features:** Sunday brunch. **Address:** 5385 Five Forks Trickum Rd 30087 **Location:** US 78 exit 9, just n to Rockbridge Rd, then 1.5 mi w; in Mountain Park Plaza.
L D CALL

WEEYUMS PHILLY STYLE 770/322-0000 **31**
Sandwiches. Casual Dining. $3-$7 **AAA Inspector Notes:** This small, walk-in sandwich shop has been serving up authentic Philly cheesesteaks and delicious hoagies since 2000. The small restaurant has a waiting area but no dining room. If you are in a hurry call ahead to place your order. **Address:** 900 Main St 30083 **Location:** SR 155 SW, 3.4 mi e on Panola Rd, 8 mi w on Stone Mountain Lithonia Rd. **Parking:** on-site and street. L D CALL

Turn your road trip dreams into reality with the TripTik® Travel Planner

SUWANEE pop. 15,355
• Hotels & Restaurants map & index p. 90
• Part of Atlanta area — see map p. 44

COMFORT INN & SUITES (678)714-7707 **14**
 Hotel $100-$199

Address: 2945-A Lawrenceville Suwanee Rd 30024 **Location:** I-85 exit 111, just e. **Facility:** 65 units. 4 stories, interior corridors. **Pool(s):** heated indoor. **Activities:** exercise room. **Guest Services:** coin laundry. **Featured Amenity: full hot breakfast.**

COURTYARD BY MARRIOTT ATLANTA SUWANEE (770)831-7473 **15**
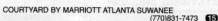 **Hotel.** $98-$183 **Address:** 310 Celebration Dr 30024 **Location:** I-85 exit 111, just e to Celebration Dr, then 0.3 mi s. **Facility:** 78 units. 3 stories, interior corridors. **Pool(s):** heated indoor. **Activities:** exercise room. **Guest Services:** valet and coin laundry.

AAA Benefit: Members save 5% or more!

QUALITY INN (770)945-1608 **13**
 Motel $70-$120

Address: 2945 Lawrenceville Suwanee Rd 30024 **Location:** I-85 exit 111, just e. **Facility:** 80 units. 2 stories (no elevator), exterior corridors. **Amenities:** safes. **Pool(s):** outdoor. **Guest Services:** valet and coin laundry. **Featured Amenity: full hot breakfast.**

CHEESEBURGER BOBBY'S 678/381-2022
Burgers. Quick Serve. $3-$6 **AAA Inspector Notes:** Nibble on hand-cut fries with your fresh, hand-patted burger, which you'll gussy up with onions, lettuce, tomatoes, pickles and other items on the condiment station. Other choices include hot dogs, chicken sandwiches and custard for dessert. Friendly servers tend the bright, fresh and clean dining room. **Address:** 3630 Peachtree Pkwy 30024 **Location:** Jct SR 141 and 120, 1.2 mi n. L D CALL

JIM 'N NICK'S BAR-B-Q 770/255-1717
Barbecue. Casual Dining. $8-$32 **AAA Inspector Notes:** Southern hospitality reigns at Jim 'N Nick's, where diners get neighborly treatment as they dig into huge portions of tasty lean sausage, fresh chili, juicy smoked beef and pork. A slice of sublime homemade pie ends the meal on a high note. **Features:** full bar. **Address:** 1103 Old Peachtree Rd 30024 **Location:** I-85 exit 109, just w. L D

TAQUERIA LOS HERMANOS 678/600-8322 **11**
Tex-Mex. Casual Dining. $4-$13 **AAA Inspector Notes:** Start a meal here with a cup of shrimp corn chowder and then choose an entrée from such choices as fajitas, grilled tilapia, enchiladas rancheros or one of many taco plates. Complimentary chips and salsa are offered. Be sure to try a tempting dessert such as the coconut flan. And do not forget the refreshing margaritas. **Features:** full bar. **Address:** 3245 Peachtree Pkwy 30024 **Location:** Jct Peachtree and Laurel Springs pkwys; in The Shops at Laurel Springs. L D CALL

SWAINSBORO   pop. 7,277

BEST WESTERN BRADFORD INN   (478)237-2400

Motel
$70-$99

AAA Benefit: Save 10% or more every day and earn 10% bonus points!

Address: 688 S Main St 30401 **Location:** I-16 exit 90 (US 1), 12.4 mi n. **Facility:** 50 units. 2 stories (no elevator), exterior corridors. **Pool(s):** outdoor. **Featured Amenity: continental breakfast.**

SYLVANIA   pop. 2,956

POP'S KITCHEN   912/564-2988

Comfort Food. Casual Dining. $6-$11 **AAA Inspector Notes:** You can saddle up to the buffet or opt for table service at this down-home restaurant staffed with eager-to-please servers. Choose from a good selection of favorites, from barbecue and meatloaf, to chicken, fish, burgers and a host of typical comfort accompaniments. **Address:** 109 Mims Rd 30467 **Location:** Jct US 301 business route and SR 21, 0.9 mi e; in Harvey's Shopping Center.

TALLULAH FALLS   (A-3) pop. 168, elev. 1,629'

Near the turn of the 20th century, Tallulah Falls was a resort area with scenery and a mountain climate that brought visitors from other parts of Georgia and neighboring states.

TALLULAH GORGE STATE PARK, within the city limits at 338 Jane Hurt Yarn Dr., offers 20 miles of trails including a 1.5-mile walking trail along the rim of Tallulah Gorge, a sheer-walled, 1,000-foot-deep crevice with waterfalls and lush vegetation. Overlooks at various points along the trail offer views of geologic formations as well as native flora and fauna. The Jane Hurt Yarn Interpretive Center offers presentations about history and safety. Entry to the gorge floor is by permit only, obtainable at the interpretive center; a limited number is available. *See Recreation Areas Chart.*

During the first three weekends in November and first two weekends in April, water is released into the gorge at 500-700 cubic feet per second creating class IV rapids for expert kayakers and boaters to enjoy. Water releases of 200 cubic feet per second are scheduled for the remaining April weekends through the weekend before Memorial Day and the three weekends following Labor Day and 8 days in October and early November. Phone for the exact water-release dates. Hiking and rock climbing are not permitted in the gorge on release days. **Hours:** Park open daily 8-dusk. Center open daily 8-5; closed Christmas. Beach area open daily 8-dusk, Memorial Day-Labor Day. **Cost:** Parking $5 per private vehicle. **Phone:** (706) 754-7981.

THOMASTON   pop. 9,170

DAYS INN   (706)648-9260

Hotel. $63-$85 **Address:** 1211 Hwy 19 N 30286 **Location:** 2.5 mi n of center. **Facility:** 42 units. 2 stories (no elevator), exterior corridors. **Pool(s):** outdoor.

QUALITY INN   (706)648-2232

Motel. $76-$99 **Address:** 1010 Hwy 19 N 30286 **Location:** Jct SR 74, 2.3 mi n. **Facility:** 57 units. 2 stories, exterior corridors. **Pool(s):** outdoor. **Activities:** exercise room. **Guest Services:** coin laundry.

WHERE TO EAT

AVIANOS ITALIAN RESTAURANT   706/646-3939

Italian. Casual Dining. $4-$15 **AAA Inspector Notes:** This family-friendly eatery offers up classic comfort foods featuring Italian and Greek cuisines. The gyro wrap is deliciously juicy while the homemade lasagna is perfection. Other popular offerings are the Italian steak sandwich, chicken parmigiana and fettuccine Alfredo. Save room for some homemade apple pie. **Address:** 1021 US 19 30286 **Location:** In Northcreek shopping center.

NORRIS'S FINE FOODS   706/647-8216

Southern. Casual Dining. $3-$15 **AAA Inspector Notes:** What this country eatery lacks in sophistication is made up with delicious down-home goodness! The menu is stocked with all your Southern favorites, such as fried chicken, roast beef and macaroni and cheese. Add to that a cool dish of chocolate mousse in a graham cracker crust topped with whipped cream or banana pudding with vanilla wafers and you have a scrumptious, hearty meal! **Address:** 695 Short E St 30286 **Location:** Just off SR 19; downtown. **Parking:** street only.

THOMASVILLE   (F-3) pop. 18,413, elev. 290'

Thomasville was spared most of the ravages of the Civil War. Afterward, railroad lines were repaired and Northerners soon were traveling south to enjoy the mild winter climate of the high pinelands; it was believed that the pine-scented air was of therapeutic value. By the 1880s Thomasville had become a popular winter resort with some of the country's finest hotels.

The winter residents brought money to this small town and left behind community improvements and a collection of shooting plantations, as they called their mansions. The Lapham-Patterson House, at 626 N. Dawson St., is a restored, asymmetrical 1885 Victorian home where each room is a different shape with none square. Built by prosperous merchant C.W. Lapham, the house featured a gas lighting system, indoor plumbing with hot and cold running water, modern closets, a cantilevered balcony and an unusual double-flue chimney with a walk-through stairway, all state of the art for the time. Phone (229) 226-7664.

Perhaps Thomasville's oldest resident is Big Oak, on the corner of E. Monroe and N. Crawford streets. Dating from the late 17th century, the tree is 68 feet high, with a trunk circumference of 26 feet and a limb spread of 165 feet.

For three days in late April, the ⬧ Rose Show and Festival includes a juried rose show, the Rose Parade on Broad Street, a street dance, museum tours and an arts and crafts fair. ⬧ Victorian Christmas Festival features jingle bells, twinkling lights, a live nativity, costumed carolers and dancers, carriage rides, jolly St. Nick and real snow in the Winter Wonderland.

Thomasville Visitors Center: 144 E. Jackson St., Thomasville, GA 31792. **Phone:** (229) 228-7977 or (866) 577-3600.

Self-guiding tours: Visitor guides that include details about walking/driving tours of Thomasville's historic districts are available at the visitor center.

BIRDSONG NATURE CENTER 2106 Meridian Rd., features a historic farmhouse with a large window perfect for observing the many bird species that are attracted to the surrounding gardens and pool. A seasonal (May through October) butterfly garden encourages visitors to spend time observing these vibrantly colorful insects. The Bluebird Trail houses nest boxes. Special events are offered.

Time: Allow 1 hour, 30 minutes minimum. **Hours:** Wed. and Fri.-Sat. 9-5, Sun. 1-5. Closed late Aug., Thanksgiving and Christmas. Phone ahead to confirm schedule. **Cost:** $5; $2.50 (ages 4-12). **Phone:** (229) 377-4408 or (800) 953-2473.

PEBBLE HILL PLANTATION is 5 mi. s. on US 319. The former winter retreat of the Hanna family of Cleveland, Pebble Hill is surrounded by extensive grounds. The lavish neoclassical main house is typical of late 19th- and early 20th-century homes built in the area by wealthy Northerners. Sporting-themed art, antiques, Audubon prints and Native American artifacts are displayed in the main house. Grounds highlights include gardens, redbrick outbuildings and the stable complex.

Hours: Grounds open Tues.-Sat. 10-5, Sun. noon-5. Guided house tours are offered daily on the half-hour and hour; last tour begins at 3:45. Closed Jan. 1, Thanksgiving, Christmas Eve and Christmas. **Cost:** Grounds $5; $2 (ages 2-12). Grounds and main house tour $15; $6 (ages 6-12). Ages 0-5 are not permitted in the main house. **Phone:** (229) 226-2344. GT

THOMAS COUNTY MUSEUM OF HISTORY is at 725 N. Dawson St. Museum exhibits depict the area's history and document the transformation of the county's antebellum cotton plantations into quail-hunting plantations. The museum consists of six historic buildings, including an 1870 log house, the 1896 Ewart bowling alley, the 1893 Metcalfe Courthouse and the 1910 Flowers Playhouse.

Time: Allow 1 hour, 30 minutes minimum. **Hours:** Mon.-Sat. 9-4, Sept. 1 to mid-Aug. Phone for guided tour availability. Closed Memorial Day, Labor Day and major holidays. **Cost:** Self-guiding tour $5; $1 (ages 0-17). Guided tour $8; $3 (ages 0-17). **Phone:** (229) 226-7664. GT

1884 PAXTON HOUSE INN 229/226-5197
▽▽▽ ▽▽▽ **Historic Bed & Breakfast.** Rates not provided. **Address:** 445 Remington Ave 31792 **Location:** Corner of S Hansell St; just e of downtown. Located in a historic residential area. **Facility:** You will be awed by this pristine Victorian mansion and the adjacent quaint cottages that are complemented with lush landscaping. Rooms are lavish and elegantly decorated with period design. 9 units, some two bedrooms and cottages. 2 stories (no elevator), interior/exterior corridors. **Terms:** off-site registration.
⬛ 📶 ☒ /SOME UNITS 🛏 🍴 🖥 📺

BEST WESTERN ROSE CITY CONFERENCE CENTER INN (229)226-9998

▽▽▽ ▽▽
Hotel
$119-$140

BW Best Western. **AAA Benefit:** Save 10% or more every day and earn 10% bonus points!

Address: 133 Liberty St 31757 **Location:** Jct US 19 S and 84 E. **Facility:** 69 units. 4 stories, interior corridors. *Bath:* shower only. **Pool(s):** heated indoor. **Activities:** sauna, exercise room. **Guest Services:** coin laundry.
SAVE ⬛ CALL 🄼 ⊇ BIZ HS 📶 ☒ 🍴 🖥 📺

HAMPTON INN THOMASVILLE (229)227-0040
▽▽ ▽▽ **Hotel.** $109-$134 **Address:** 1950 GA Hwy 122 31757 **Location:** Jct US 19/84 and SR 122/300. **Facility:** 67 units. 3 stories, interior corridors. **Terms:** 1-7 night minimum stay, cancellation fee imposed. **Pool(s):** outdoor. **Activities:** sauna, hot tub, exercise room. **Guest Services:** valet laundry.

AAA Benefit: Members save up to 10%!

⬛ CALL 🄼 ⊇ BIZ 📶 ☒ 🍴 🖥 📺

HOLIDAY INN EXPRESS HOTEL & SUITES 229/226-4666
▽▽▽ ▽ **Hotel.** Rates not provided. **Address:** 452 Liberty St 31757 **Location:** Jct US 19 S and 84 E. **Facility:** 81 units. 3 stories, interior corridors. **Pool(s):** heated indoor. **Activities:** exercise room. **Guest Services:** coin laundry.
⬛ CALL 🄼 ⊇ BIZ HS 📶 ☒ 🍴 🖥 📺

WHERE TO EAT

GEORGE & LOUIE'S FRESH SEAFOOD RESTAURANT 229/226-1218
▽ Seafood. Quick Serve. $7-$20 **AAA Inspector Notes:** Fresh seafood is offered in this wide open dining room with wood tables and stainless-steel chairs. Desserts are displayed under glass at the counter. The family-style seafood platter and Greek salad are the house specialties. **Features:** beer & wine, patio dining. **Address:** 217 Remington Ave 31792 **Location:** Downtown. L D

GRANDDADDY'S BARBEQUE 229/225-9500
▽ Barbecue. Casual Dining. $7-$15 **AAA Inspector Notes:** A variety of barbecue dishes are served in a simple, casual setting at this family-style, self-service restaurant. **Features:** patio dining. **Address:** 2128 Smith Ave 31792 **Location:** Jct US 19 and 84.
B L D 🛏

GRASSROOTS COFFEE SHOP 229/226-3388
▽ Coffee/Tea. Quick Serve. $3-$7 **AAA Inspector Notes:** These folks are serious about their coffee. They also offer some pretty scrumptious sandwiches and pastries during breakfast and lunch. The food is made fresh to order and the coffee is roasted in-house to ensure perfection. Relax in the trendy atmosphere, contemplate the beauty of the local art work and soak up the mellow tunes. **Address:** 118 S Broad St 31792 **Location:** Between Jackson St and Remington Ave; downtown. **Parking:** street only. B L

JONAH'S FISH & GRITS   229/226-0508

▼▼▼ Seafood. Casual Dining. $10-$24 **AAA Inspector Notes:** In trendy downtown is this quaint Victorian storefront on a brick paved street. Inside, a tree branch chandelier and a boat helm rising out of the ceiling give way to a Jonah and the whale theme. This family friendly restaurant serves up tasty recipes from the big blue and puts a Southern twist on it. Locals love the fresh and flaky fish paired with its renowned cheesy grits. The menu also comes equipped with fried green tomatoes, delicious mahi mahi and homemade hush puppies. **Features:** patio dining. **Address:** 109 E Jackson St 31792 **Location:** Between Broad and Crawford sts; downtown. **Parking:** on-site and street. L D CALL &M

LA FOGATA   229/228-9787

▼▼ Mexican. Casual Dining. $5-$18 **AAA Inspector Notes:** The gold and terra cotta colored stucco exterior of the Mission-style facade easily identifies what type of restaurant this is. Colorful walls feature delicately stenciled borders while lush plants add greenery throughout. The menu offers all of the standard selections which are authentically prepared. **Features:** full bar. **Address:** 14418 Hwy 19 S 31757 **Location:** Jct US 19 and 84, just n. L D

LIAM'S RESTAURANT   229/226-9944

▼▼▼ New American. Fine Dining. $10-$31 **AAA Inspector Notes:** A garland of cotton bolls and pine cones adorns the threshold of this cozy bistro. The friendly, welcoming service along with the rustic décor create a relaxed atmosphere but it is the interesting, weekly-changing menu of uncommon selections which brings the regulars back. This is a place where one can experience a culinary adventure if so desired. **Features:** full bar, patio dining, happy hour. **Address:** 113 E Jackson St 31792 **Location:** Between Broad and Crawford sts; downtown. **Parking:** on-site and street.

L D CALL &M

MOM & DAD'S ITALIAN RESTAURANT   229/226-6265

▼▼ Italian. Casual Dining. $9-$25 **AAA Inspector Notes:** *Classic.* Family owned for 27 years, this Italian, family-style restaurant is known for its delicious pasta dishes with various sauces. The Italian salad dressing is made fresh, in-house. Two specials you will want to try are sauteed grouper and chicken Florentine. **Features:** full bar. **Address:** 1800 Smith Ave 31792 **Location:** 2.5 mi e on US 84 E.

D

THE PLAZA RESTAURANT & LOUNGE   229/226-5153

▼▼▼ American. Fine Dining. $9-$38 **AAA Inspector Notes:** *Historic.* Established in 1916, this restaurant offers a variety of Greek, Italian and steakhouse favorites. Guests can enjoy the restaurant's long history, friendly service and romantic décor. The bacon-wrapped filet mignon and creme brûlée are especially delightful. **Features:** full bar, patio dining, Sunday brunch, happy hour. **Address:** 217 S Broad St 31792 **Location:** Corner of Smith Ave; downtown.

L D CALL &M

SONNY'S REAL PIT BAR-B-Q   229/558-9000

▼▼ Barbecue. Casual Dining. $8-$17 **AAA Inspector Notes:** Bearing the name after its founder, Floyd "Sonny" Tillman, this barbecue restaurant first opened its doors circa 1968 in Gainesville, Florida and has since spawned over 150 more throughout the Southeast. The menu is steeped in finger lickin' favorites such as ribs, pulled pork, beef brisket, burgers, catfish, shrimp and chargrilled chicken. Let's not forget about the fried okra, which is the perfect starter dish, and their homemade baked beans. **Features:** beer only. **Address:** 14293 US Hwy 19 S 31792 **Location:** 0.4 mi n of jct US 84 S. L D

THOMSON pop. 6,778

HAMPTON INN THOMSON   (706)595-5300

▼▼▼ Hotel. $99-$134 **Address:** 1702 Washington Rd 30824 **Location:** I-20 exit 172 (US 78), 0.6 mi s. **Facility:** 88 units. 4 stories, interior corridors. **Terms:** 1-7 night minimum stay, cancellation fee imposed. **Pool(s):** outdoor. **Activities:** exercise room. **Guest Services:** coin laundry.

| **AAA Benefit:** |
| Members save up to 10%! |

🍴➕ CALL &M 🛋 BIZ 📶 ✕ 📺

WHITE COLUMNS INN   (706)595-8000

▼▼◆ Motel. $70-$320 **Address:** 1890 Washington Rd 30824 **Location:** I-20 exit 172 (US 78), just s. **Facility:** 133 units, some efficiencies. 2 stories (no elevator), exterior corridors. **Parking:** winter plug-ins. **Pool(s):** outdoor. **Activities:** exercise room. **Guest Services:** coin laundry.

🖃 ▼ 🛋 BIZ 📶 🖪 🖼 📺

/ SOME UNITS 🅂 HS

TIFTON (E-3) pop. 16,350, elev. 370'

Tifton was founded in 1890 and named for Nelson Tift, Georgia representative to the U.S. Congress 1868-69. Pecans, peanuts, tomatoes and honey are important to the region's agricultural base.

Tifton-Tift County Chamber of Commerce: 100 Central Ave., P.O. Box 165, Tifton, GA 31793. **Phone:** (229) 382-6200.

GEORGIA MUSEUM OF AGRICULTURE AND HISTORIC VILLAGE is at Abraham Baldwin Agricultural College off I-75 exit 63B at 1392 Whiddon Mill Rd. This agriculture museum and outdoor living-history village re-creates rural life in the late 19th and early 20th centuries. Costumed interpreters at the exhibits offer insight into the daily activities of the era.

The 35 structures on the 95-acre site include the Tift House, a steam-powered sawmill, a cotton gin, farmhouses, blacksmith shop, 19th-century drugstore, Masonic hall, water-powered gristmill, newspaper office and a turpentine still with cooper's shed. Events include the Folk Life Festival in April, Independence Day Celebration, Victorian Village by Candlelight and North Pole Express in December. A steam train operates on Saturday.

Time: Allow 1 hour, 15 minutes minimum. **Hours:** Museum and historic site open Tues.-Sat. 9-4 (weather permitting). Closed Labor Day, Thanksgiving, day after Thanksgiving and during the university Christmas break. **Cost:** Admission Tues.-Fri. $7; $6 (ages 55+); $4 (ages 5-16); free (active and retired military with ID). Admission Sat. (includes train ride) $10; $8 (ages 55+); $5 (ages 5-16); free (active and retired military with ID). **Phone:** (229) 391-5205. 🍴

COMFORT INN & SUITES   (229)382-8250

▼▼▼ Hotel. $94-$190 **Address:** 320 S Virginia Ave 31794 **Location:** I-75 exit 62, just e. **Facility:** 93 units. 4 stories, interior corridors. **Pool(s):** outdoor. **Activities:** exercise room. **Guest Services:** valet and coin laundry.

🍴➕ CALL &M 🛋 BIZ HS 📶 ✕ 🖪 🖼 📺

COUNTRY INN & SUITES BY CARLSON   229/382-8100

▼▼▼ Hotel. Rates not provided. **Address:** 310 S Virginia Ave 31794 **Location:** I-75 exit 62, just e on US 82. **Facility:** 87 units. 4 stories, interior corridors. **Pool(s):** heated outdoor. **Activities:** hot tub, exercise room. **Guest Services:** valet and coin laundry.

🍴➕ 🛋 BIZ HS 📶 ✕ 🖪 🖼 📺

/ SOME UNITS 🅂

DAYS INN & SUITES (229)382-8505
▼▼ **Hotel.** $57-$80 **Address:** 1199 Hwy 82 W 31793 **Location:** I-75 exit 62, just sw. **Facility:** 80 units. 3 stories, interior corridors. **Guest Services:** coin laundry.

ECONO LODGE (229)382-0280
▼▼ **Motel.** $60-$130 **Address:** 1025 W 2nd St 31794 **Location:** I-75 exit 63A, just e. **Facility:** 77 units. 2 stories (no elevator), exterior corridors. **Pool(s):** outdoor. **Guest Services:** coin laundry.

FAIRFIELD INN & SUITES BY MARRIOTT TIFTON
(229)387-8288
▼▼▼ **Hotel.** $94-$139 **Address:** 806 W 7th St 31794 **Location:** I-75 exit 62, just e. **Facility:** 81 units. 3 stories, interior corridors. **Pool(s):** outdoor. **Activities:** exercise room. **Guest Services:** valet and coin laundry.

AAA Benefit: Members save 5% or more!

HILTON GARDEN INN (229)382-8484
▼▼▼ Hotel $109-$189

AAA Benefit: Members save up to 10%!

Address: 201 Boo Dr 31793 **Location:** I-75 exit 62, just sw on US 82 to McCormick Dr, then just se. **Facility:** 105 units. 4 stories, interior corridors. **Terms:** 1-7 night minimum stay, cancellation fee imposed. **Pool(s):** heated indoor. **Activities:** hot tub, exercise room. **Guest Services:** valet and coin laundry.

Hilton **Garden Inn** Tifton

Centrally located and close to everything Tifton has to offer.

HOLIDAY INN EXPRESS (229)382-3300
▼▼▼ **Hotel.** $118-$133 **Address:** 814 W 7th St 31794 **Location:** I-75 exit 62, just e on US 82. **Facility:** 90 units. 3 stories, interior corridors. **Terms:** cancellation fee imposed. **Pool(s):** heated indoor. **Activities:** exercise room. **Guest Services:** valet and coin laundry.

MICROTEL INN & SUITES BY WYNDHAM TIFTON
(229)387-0112
▼▼ **Hotel.** $51-$80 **Address:** 196 S Virginia Ave 31794 **Location:** I-75 exit 62, just e. **Facility:** 82 units. 3 stories, interior corridors. **Terms:** cancellation fee imposed. **Pool(s):** outdoor. **Activities:** exercise room. **Guest Services:** coin laundry.

WHERE TO EAT

THE BISTRO AT 219 229/382-7997
▼▼ American. Casual Dining. $5-$13 **AAA Inspector Notes:** Located in the heart of historic downtown, this casual café offers a variety of salads, wraps, burgers and wings. The fried pickles are a salty, crunchy way to start a meal or to share with friends. The fish tacos and build-your-own-burger options are also crowd favorites. Enjoy live music from local artists on the weekends. **Features:** full bar. **Address:** 219 Main St 31794 **Location:** In historic downtown. **Parking:** street only. B L D CALL M

CHARLES SEAFOOD RESTAURANT 229/382-9696
▼▼ Seafood. Casual Dining. $8-$17 **AAA Inspector Notes:** Since 1970, this bustling restaurant has served the community seafood at reasonable prices. An extensive variety of seafood and classic Southern side dishes are offered. Do not expect bells and whistles, just good home cooking. **Features:** beer & wine. **Address:** 701 W 7th St 31794 **Location:** I-75 exit 62, just e on US 82/319. L D

CHICAGO PIZZA & PASTA 229/382-4181
▼▼ Italian. Casual Dining. $3-$11 **AAA Inspector Notes:** This casual eatery won't win any beauty pageants, but the delicious comfort food makes it a local favorite. While my favorite dish is the Pizzaroli, the pizza, calzones and lasagna are all good. This family-owned restaurant has been serving pizza and pasta since 1974. **Address:** 401 Virginia Ave 31793 **Location:** I-75 exit 63B, just e on 8th St, then just n. L D

EL CAZADOR MEXICAN RESTAURANT 229/386-2126
▼▼ Mexican. Casual Dining. $5-$19 **AAA Inspector Notes:** This colorful, casual eatery offers friendly service and basic, flavorful Mexican fare. This place fills fast so get there early or wait. The steak rancheros is seasoned and portioned perfectly. **Features:** full bar, patio dining, happy hour. **Address:** 1021 W 2nd St 31794 **Location:** I-75 exit 63B, just e. L D

HOG-N-BONES 229/238-2491
▼ Barbecue. Quick Serve. $3-$7 **AAA Inspector Notes:** If you are looking for a casual, family-friendly restaurant that serves up yummy barbecue, then look no further. Step up to the counter to try pulled pork, smoked chicken or delicious chicken wings. For those that do not have time, visit the drive-through and take home a succulent "Boston Butt" for the whole family to enjoy. **Features:** beer only. **Address:** 2008 Hwy 82 W 31793 **Location:** I-75 exit 62, 2.2 mi w. B L D CALL M

MI LADY BAKERY 229/382-1955
▼ Breads/Pastries. Casual Dining. $2-$8 **AAA Inspector Notes:** Historic. Since 1959 this bakery has been serving delicious breads, pastries and sandwiches. With made-from-scratch creations this is a local favorite for carb nirvana. Fresh glazed donuts and hot coffee are a great start to any day. During lunch hour try the grilled chicken Hawaiian sandwich, the Mi-Lady Cuban, a healthy salad or the Philly cheese wrap. There always is room on my plate for the massive chocolate bon bon or filled croissant. If you come during a rush just be patient, it is worth the wait. **Address:** 275 Brumby Way 31794 **Location:** In historic downtown. B L CALL M

PIT STOP BAR-B-QUE & GRILL 229/387-0888
▼▼▼ Barbecue Casual Dining $8-$23
AAA Inspector Notes: Award-winning barbecue is not the only popular menu item with the patrons, the mouthwatering steaks and grilled fish are crowd-pleasers, too. The menu offers great selections at very affordable prices. **Features:** beer & wine. **Address:** 1112 W 8th St 31793 **Location:** I-75 exit 63B, just w. L D

TOCCOA (A-3) pop. 8,491, elev. 1,045'

A mountain community bounded by the Chattahoochee-Oconee National Forest (see place listing p. 155) and Lake Hartwell, Toccoa has both military and Native American connections. During World War II paratroopers trained at nearby Camp Toccoa and 1,740-foot-tall Currahee Mountain. Much earlier, the area was the center of the Cherokee Nation.

Toccoa is a popular vacation area and offers fishing, hunting, swimming, boating and water recreation. Toccoa Falls College offers guided campus tours; phone (888) 785-5624 to confirm tour schedule.

Traveler's Rest State Historic Site, 5 mi. e. off US 123 on Riverdale Rd., dates from 1815. Devereaux Jarrett, a Georgia planter and businessman, bought the dwelling in 1833 and expanded it not only to accommodate his family but also to serve as a stagecoach inn. The center of a thriving plantation, the structure became known as Traveler's Rest. At one time, it also was home to Mary Jarrett White, the first woman in Georgia to vote. The restored inn and plantation house is furnished in period and is open Saturday and Sunday 9-5. Phone (706) 886-2256.

Toccoa-Stephens County Chamber of Commerce: 160 N. Alexander St., P.O. Box 577, Toccoa, GA 30577. **Phone:** (706) 886-2132 or (877) 428-7724.

CURRAHEE MILITARY MUSEUM, 160 N. Alexander St., is focused on paratrooper regiments, including the Band of Brothers that trained at Camp Toccoa during World War II. Uniforms, medals, military equipment and personal correspondence are some of the items on display. **Hours:** Mon.-Sat. 10-4, Sun. 1-4. Closed Jan. 1, Easter, Thanksgiving, Christmas Eve, Christmas and Dec. 31. **Cost:** $10; $3 (students with ID). **Phone:** (706) 282-5055.

TOCCOA FALLS is 2 mi. n.e. on Alt. SR 17 on the campus of Toccoa Falls College, a short walk from the Gate Cottage. The 186-foot falls are one of the highest free-falling waterfalls east of the Mississippi River. Visitors have enjoyed this scenic spot since the early 1800s. Toccoa comes from a Cherokee word meaning "beautiful." Entrance is through the campus book store. **Hours:** Mon.-Sat. 10-5, Sun. 1-5. **Cost:** $2; $1 (ages 60+); free (ages 0-6, military with ID and Stephens County residents); $6 (family, four or more members). **Phone:** (706) 886-6831, ext. 5219.

TUCKER (H-4) pop. 27,581, elev. 1,125'
- Hotels & Restaurants map & index p. 82
- Part of Atlanta area — see map p. 44

Tucker was built up around the railroad that was constructed in 1892, and today it has a charming downtown area that is inviting to pedestrians who wish to peruse through the shops that line Main Street. The town is located 14 miles northeast of Atlanta and 5 mi. north of Stone Mountain.

COMFORT SUITES-NORTHLAKE (770)496-1070 84
Hotel. $90-$140 **Address:** 2060 Crescent Centre Blvd 30084 **Location:** I-285 exit 37, 0.5 mi se. **Facility:** 110 units. 6 stories, interior corridors. **Amenities:** safes. **Pool(s):** outdoor. **Activities:** exercise room. **Guest Services:** valet and coin laundry.

COURTYARD BY MARRIOTT-ATLANTA NORTHLAKE
(770)938-1200 83

Hotel
$77-$160

COURTYARD Marriott

AAA Benefit: Members save 5% or more!

Address: 4083 Lavista Rd 30084 **Location:** I-285 exit 37, 0.3 mi w. **Facility:** 128 units. 2 stories (no elevator), interior corridors. **Pool(s):** outdoor. **Activities:** hot tub, exercise room. **Guest Services:** valet and coin laundry, area transportation.

DOUBLETREE BY HILTON HOTEL ATLANTA-NORTHLAKE
770/938-1026 82

Hotel
Rates not provided

DOUBLETREE by Hilton

AAA Benefit: Members save 5% or more!

Address: 4156 Lavista Rd 30084 **Location:** I-285 exit 37, just w. **Facility:** 183 units. 5 stories, interior corridors. **Pool(s):** outdoor. **Activities:** exercise room. **Guest Services:** valet and coin laundry.

HAMPTON INN ATLANTA-NORTHLAKE (770)493-1966 78
Hotel. $104-$109 **Address:** 3400 Northlake Pkwy 30345 **Location:** I-285 exit 37, just w to Parklake Dr, then 0.5 mi n. Located in an office park area. **Facility:** 121 units. 5 stories, interior corridors. **Terms:** 1-7 night minimum stay, cancellation fee imposed. **Pool(s):** outdoor. **Activities:** exercise room. **Guest Services:** valet and coin laundry.

AAA Benefit: Members save up to 10%!

HOLIDAY INN ATLANTA NORTHLAKE 770/934-6000 80
Hotel. Rates not provided. **Address:** 2158 Ranchwood Dr NE 30345 **Location:** I-285 exit 37, 0.4 mi w to Ranchwood Dr, then just n. **Facility:** 129 units. 5 stories, interior corridors. **Amenities:** safes. **Pool(s):** outdoor. **Activities:** exercise room. **Guest Services:** valet and coin laundry.

QUALITY INN ATLANTA/NORTHLAKE
(770)491-7444 81

Motel
$75-$99

Address: 2155 Ranchwood Dr 30345 **Location:** I-285 exit 37, 0.4 mi w, then just n. **Facility:** 132 units. 3 stories, interior/exterior corridors. **Pool(s):** outdoor. **Guest Services:** valet and coin laundry. **Featured Amenity:** continental breakfast.

(See map & index p. 82.)

TOWNEPLACE SUITES BY MARRIOTT ATLANTA NORTHLAKE
(770)938-0408 **79**

WV WV **Extended Stay Hotel.** $94-$144 **Address:** 3300 Northlake Pkwy 30345 **Location:** I-285 exit 36 southbound, just w; exit 37 northbound, just w to Parklake Dr, 0.5 mi n, then just w. **Facility:** 97 kitchen units, some two bedrooms. 5 stories, interior corridors. **Pool(s):** outdoor. **Activities:** exercise room. **Guest Services:** valet and coin laundry.

AAA Benefit: Members save 5% or more!

ECO [I↑] CALL [⌖M] [⇆] [BIZ] [📶] [✕] [🛢] [🖨] [💻] / SOME UNITS [S▤] [HS]

WHERE TO EAT

BLUE RIBBON GRILL   770/491-1570 **121**

WV WV American. Casual Dining. $7-$20 **AAA Inspector Notes:** Families are welcomed at this popular restaurant, which is praised for its comfort foods. Savor the hot and tasty fried catfish filet plate or the meatloaf for a simple dining experience. Lunch specials always are popular and you can enjoy your favorite sporting event on one of many flat-screen TVs throughout the restaurant. **Features:** full bar, patio dining, Sunday brunch. **Address:** 4006 Lavista Rd 30084 **Location:** I-285 exit 37, 0.3 mi w. [L] [D]

FUJI YA & LUCKY KEY   770/270-9962 **122**

WV WV Asian. Casual Dining. $7-$33 **AAA Inspector Notes:** Patrons can order from the sushi bar, the menu or enjoy a hibachi-style meal all under one roof. Options vary from traditional chicken and pork offerings to items for the more adventurous, such as baby octopus salad. Other menu highlights include ginger lobster, tung ting duck and a variety of noodle bowls. The express boxes are popular at both lunch and dinner. **Features:** full bar, early bird specials. **Address:** 4135 Lavista Rd 30084 **Location:** I-285 exit 37, just w; in Northlake Square Shopping Center. [L] [D]

MATTHEWS CAFETERIA   770/239-2357 **120**

WV Comfort Food. Buffet Style. $5-$10 **AAA Inspector Notes:** This hugely popular place, featured on the Food Network, serves up three good country-style meals a day. The fried chicken and pork chops get rave reviews. Barbecue ribs, beef tips, country fried steak and pot roast are good options as well. A good selection of veggies also are available as are green salads and deviled eggs. Lemon pie and strawberry shortcake are some of the great desserts. **Address:** 2299 Main St 30084 **Location:** Downtown. [B] [L] [D]

NORTHLAKE THAI CUISINE   770/938-2223 **123**

WV WV WV Thai. Fine Dining. $9-$23 **AAA Inspector Notes:** This spot offers upscale service and creative Thai dishes such as spicy tofu soup, crisp honey-glazed prawns, Panang duck and curry laksa. **Features:** beer & wine. **Reservations:** suggested. **Address:** 3939 Lavista Rd 30084 **Location:** I-285 exit 37, 0.5 mi w to Montreal Rd, then just s. [L] [D]

TAQUERIA LOS HERMANOS   678/937-0660 **119**

WV WV Tex-Mex. Casual Dining. $3-$13 **AAA Inspector Notes:** Start your meal here with a cup of shrimp corn chowder and then move on to an entrée from such choices as fajitas, grilled tilapia, enchiladas rancheras or one of many taco plates available. Complimentary chips and salsa are available, of course, and you just might want to try a refreshing margarita. Save some room for a tempting dessert such as the coconut flan. **Features:** full bar. **Address:** 4418 Hugh Howell Rd, Suite B-3 30084 **Location:** Jct US 29, just e; downtown; in The Centre. [L] [D] [✎]

TUNNEL HILL (A-2) pop. 856, elev. 840'

WESTERN & ATLANTIC RAILROAD TUNNEL AND MUSEUM is at 215 Clisby Austin Rd. Displays relate the history of the town and historic 1850 railroad tunnel. The railroad tracks at the museum provide excellent opportunities for train viewing. Visitors

may take a golf cart tour of the tunnel. Civil War reenactments of the Battle of Tunnel Hill take place the first weekend after Labor Day. **Time:** Allow 30 minutes minimum. **Hours:** Mon.-Sat. 9-5 (also Fri.-Sat. 5-6, during DST). Closed Jan. 1, Thanksgiving, Christmas Eve and Christmas. **Cost:** $6; free (ages 0-4). **Phone:** (706) 876-1571. [GT]

TYBEE ISLAND (D-6) pop. 2,990, elev. 10'
• Restaurants p. 294

To visitors who flock to the island's 3 miles of sandy shoreline, Tybee means beach resort, but originally the name came from a Native American word for salt. The island's strategic location at the mouth of the Savannah River resulted in the construction of a lighthouse in the 1770s and a defensive fortification in the 1880s.

The laid-back community off the coast of Savannah offers a slightly slower pace than its more famous vacation neighbor, but the hospitality is the same. Several retail areas line US 80 as you drive into town. Shops like Gallery by the Sea, Seaside Sisters and Fish Art Gallerie are just three of many places that offer beach-themed gifts, handmade goods and unique art.

Tybee Island Regional Visitor Information Center: 802 1st St., P.O. Box 491, Tybee Island, GA 31328. **Phone:** (912) 786-5444 or (877) 344-3361.

TYBEE ISLAND MARINE SCIENCE CENTER, off the 14th Street parking lot at 1509 Strand Ave., provides visitors the opportunity to learn about coastal Georgia's marine environment. The Coastal Georgia Gallery features indigenous marine animals, a touch pool and exhibits about shells, sea turtles, jellyfish, sharks and whales. Organized activities include guided "Walks, Talks and Treks" walks and the Sea Camp Kid's Ocean Adventure.

Hours: Center open daily 10-5. Closed Jan. 1, Thanksgiving and Christmas. **Cost:** Gallery admission $5; free (ages 0-4). Guided activity walks $10; free (ages 0-4). **Phone:** (912) 786-5917 or (866) 557-9172. [GT]

TYBEE LIGHTHOUSE AND MUSEUM, off US 80E at the n. end of Tybee Island at 30 Meddin Dr., is thought to be the tallest and oldest lighthouse in Georgia. It was built in 1867 atop the lower 60 feet of the light, and all of the support buildings on the 5-acre site remain intact. They include a fully restored keeper's house, which is open for tours; a summer kitchen; and a second keeper's cottage where visitors can watch a video about the history of the light station.

The 178-step climb to the top of the lighthouse offers panoramic views of the ocean and Tybee Island. The museum, housed in one of the gun batteries of Fort Screven, has exhibits on the diverse cultural history of Tybee Island as well as a video about this turn-of-the-20th-century fortification.

A raised Tybee cottage that illustrates summer living on the island also can be visited.

Time: Allow 1 hour, 30 minutes minimum. **Hours:** Wed.-Mon. 9-5:30. Raised cottage open 11-3. Last ticket sold 1 hour before closing. Closed Jan. 1, Mar. 17, Thanksgiving and Christmas. **Cost:** $9; $7 (ages 6-17, ages 62+ and military with ID). **Phone:** (912) 786-5801.

COCO'S SUNSET GRILLE   912/786-7810

▼▼ Seafood Sandwiches. Casual Dining. $9-$28 **AAA Inspector Notes:** Located on Lazaretto Creek at the marina, diners can be assured of fresh seafood as well as beautiful sunsets over the marsh. Featured on the menu are delicious homemade crab cakes as an appetizer, sandwich or entrée, bourbon-glazed salmon smothered in a tasty sauce, blackened mahi mahi and shrimp any way. Nothing fancy here but the relaxed atmosphere and well-prepared food make the stop well worth the time. **Features:** full bar, patio dining, happy hour. **Address:** 1 Old US Hwy 80 31328 **Location:** On US 80, east side of Lazaretto Creek Bridge, just s. [L] [D]

THE CRAB SHACK   912/786-9857

▼▼ Seafood. Casual Dining. $6-$50 **AAA Inspector Notes:** This area legend, where the elite come to eat in their bare feet (so says the signage) is located at a former fish camp and is comprised of several fish shacks and wood decks sprawling along Tybee Creek. There is a collection of rescued parrots, a cat house for area feral cats, a baby alligator exhibit where guests can take part in feeding, and pirates, lots of pirates. Oh yeah, there is a restaurant as well—one that specializes in local shellfish and a few barbecue items. **Features:** full bar, patio dining, happy hour. **Address:** 40 Estill Hammock Rd 31328 **Location:** Jct US 80 and Lazaretto Creek Bridge, just e on US 80 to Catalina Dr, then just s, follow signs.

[L] [D]

SUNDAE CAFE AT TYBEE   912/786-7694

▼▼▼ American. Fine Dining. $11-$32 **AAA Inspector Notes:** Located in a former ice cream parlor, this spot now turns out gourmet meals in a casually upscale atmosphere. The refined menu covers the gamut from seafood, steaks and chops to distinctive pasta dishes. Specialties of the house include sweet potato-crusted grouper, bacon-wrapped and crab-stuffed local jumbo shrimp, jambalaya pasta, fire-roasted rib-eye and rack of lamb. Every night there are off-menu specialties. For those seeking something simpler, try the fried seafood platter. **Features:** full bar. **Reservations:** required, for dinner. **Address:** 304 First St 31328 **Location:** Between Jones and 2nd aves; on US 80. [L] [D]

UNION CITY pop. 19,456
• **Hotels & Restaurants map & index p. 94**
• **Part of Atlanta area — see map p. 44**

DAYS INN & SUITES   (770)969-4567   [83]

Hotel

$70-$95

Address: 6743 Shannon Pkwy 30291 **Location:** I-85 exit 64, 0.3 mi w, then just n. **Facility:** 58 units. 3 stories, interior corridors. **Pool(s):** outdoor. **Featured Amenity:** full hot breakfast.

MAGNUSON HOTEL ATLANTA SOUTH   (770)306-6067   [84]

▼▼ Motel. $50-$125 **Address:** 6840 Shannon Pkwy S 30291 **Location:** I-85 exit 64, 0.3 mi w to Shannon Pkwy, then just s. Opposite Shannon Southpark Mall. **Facility:** 73 units. 2 stories (no elevator), exterior corridors. **Pool(s):** outdoor. **Activities:** exercise room. **Guest Services:** coin laundry.

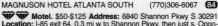

WHERE TO EAT

THE HISTORIC GREEN MANOR RESTAURANT
770/964-4343   [64]

▼▼ Southern. Casual Dining. $12-$19 **AAA Inspector Notes:** Historic. Step back into the days of yesteryear where Southern hospitality and traditional cuisine reign supreme. This buffet-style restaurant mixes residential charm and all-you-can-eat, homespun favorites for an experience that feels like coming home. Menu classics include fried chicken, smothered country-fried steak, collard greens and delicious banana pudding. **Features:** full bar, Sunday brunch. **Address:** 6400 Westbrook St 30291 **Location:** I-85 exit 66, 3 mi w to Westbrook St, then just s. [L]

VALDOSTA (F-3) pop. 54,518, elev. 215'
• **Restaurants p. 296**

Valdosta's history is linked with transportation growth and a strategic location in the path of early westward expansion. Originally called Troupville, the settlement was designated a county seat in 1837. When it became evident that Troupville would not be on a proposed 1860 railroad route from Savannah to Mobile, Ala., the townsite was moved to take advantage of the potential prosperity. Troupville citizens renamed the town Valdosta for the governor's home Val de Aosta, or "Vale of Beauty."

The city has six historic districts featuring Victorian-era commercial and residential buildings.

James H. Rainwater Conference Center and Tourism Authority: 1 Meeting Pl., Valdosta, GA 31601. **Phone:** (229) 245-0513 or (800) 569-8687.

Self-guiding tours: A brochure describing a driving tour of Valdosta's six historic districts can be obtained from the conference center and tourism authority and at the Lowndes County Historical Society and Museum.

Shopping: Factory outlet shops lure bargain hunters to the Lake Park Outlets Mall, I-75 exit 5. Anchor stores at the Valdosta Mall on SR 94W are Belk, JCPenney and Sears. Summit Pointe is located at Inner Perimeter and Country Club rds.

ANNETTE HOWELL TURNER CENTER FOR THE ARTS, 527 N. Patterson St., displays various types of art on a rotating basis. Four of the center's six galleries feature emerging and recognized local, national and international talent, with an emphasis on professional artists. Two galleries house permanent collections of East African art and European porcelain. **Time:** Allow 30 minutes minimum. **Hours:** Tues.-Thurs. 10-6, Fri.-Sat. 10-4. Closed Jan. 1, Martin Luther King Jr. Day, Good Friday, Memorial Day, July 4, Labor Day, Thanksgiving weekend, Christmas Eve, Christmas and Dec. 31. **Cost:** Free. **Phone:** (229) 247-2787.

BARBER HOUSE, 416 N. Ashley St., was built by one of the early bottlers and promoters of Coca-Cola. The restored 1915 neoclassical mansion is decorated with late 19th-century furnishings. A home until 1977, the structure now houses the chamber of commerce. **Time:** Allow 30 minutes minimum. **Hours:** Mon.-Fri. 8:30-5. Closed major holidays. **Cost:** Free. **Phone:** (229) 247-8100.

THE CRESCENT, 904 N. Patterson St., is a stately neoclassical mansion with a crescent-shaped tile and marble porch supported by 13 columns representing the 13 original Colonies. The 23-room 1898 house built by Sen. W.S. West is furnished in period. The house has a large ballroom and orchestra room, ornate woodwork, numerous fireplaces and a wide, curving stairway. An octagonal kindergarten schoolhouse, a chapel and eight gardens complete the complex. **Time:** Allow 30 minutes minimum. **Hours:** Mon.-Fri. 2-5. Closed major holidays. **Cost:** Donations. **Phone:** (229) 244-6747.

LOWNDES COUNTY HISTORICAL SOCIETY AND MUSEUM, 305 W. Central Ave., has photographs, documents and memorabilia reflecting the development of Valdosta and the surrounding area. Period clothing, antique handworks, and city directories dating from 1904 are displayed along with an exhibit about John Henry "Doc" Holliday, who lived in the area in his youth. Temporary exhibits and a genealogical library also are available. **Time:** Allow 1 hour minimum. **Hours:** Mon.-Fri. 10-5, Sat. 10-2. Closed major holidays. **Cost:** Donations. **Phone:** (229) 247-4780.

WILD ADVENTURES THEME PARK is off I-75 exit 13, then 4 mi. s. to 3766 Old Clyattville Rd. Offering more than 40 rides, including seven roller coasters, Wild Adventures also features animal exhibits, a petting zoo, shows and concerts by well-known entertainers. Access to Splash Island Water Park, featuring a dozen water attractions, is included in the Wild Adventures admission. A wave pool, more water slides, a lazy river and a wet play area complete the family fun. Go-carts and miniature golf are offered for an additional fee.

Hours: Park opens daily at 10, late May-July 31; closing time varies. Open weekends and select days, rest of year. Closed Jan.-Feb. and Nov., and Christmas Eve and Christmas with select days and holiday events. Phone ahead to confirm schedule. **Cost:** (includes next operating day free) $48; $43 (ages 3-9 and 55+). **Parking:** $10-$12. **Phone:** (229) 219-7080.

BEST WESTERN PLUS VALDOSTA HOTEL & SUITES (229)241-9221

Hotel
$89-$164

Best Western PLUS AAA Benefit: Save 10% or more every day and earn 10% bonus points!

Address: 4025 Northlake Dr 31602 **Location:** I-75 exit 22, just e on N Valdosta Rd (US 41). **Facility:** 87 units, some efficiencies. 4 stories, interior corridors. **Pool(s):** outdoor. **Activities:** hot tub, exercise room. **Guest Services:** valet and coin laundry.

COMFORT SUITES (229)249-8880
Hotel. $80-$209 **Address:** 1332 N St. Augustine Rd 31601 **Location:** I-75 exit 18; adjacent to interchange. **Facility:** 88 units. 4 stories, interior corridors. **Pool(s):** outdoor. **Activities:** exercise room. **Guest Services:** valet and coin laundry.

COUNTRY INN & SUITES BY CARLSON (229)245-1700
Hotel. $89-$149 **Address:** 1308 N St. Augustine Rd 31601 **Location:** Waterfront. I-75 exit 18, just se. **Facility:** 71 units. 5 stories, interior corridors. **Terms:** cancellation fee imposed. **Amenities:** safes. **Pool(s):** heated indoor. **Activities:** hot tub, exercise room. **Guest Services:** valet and coin laundry.

DAYS INN VALDOSTA/NEAR VALDOSTA MALL (229)244-7600
Hotel. $58-$80 **Address:** 1383 N St Augustine Rd 31602 **Location:** I-75 exit 18, just w off SR 94. **Facility:** 62 units. 3 stories, exterior corridors. **Pool(s):** outdoor. **Activities:** exercise room. **Guest Services:** valet and coin laundry.

DRURY INN & SUITES VALDOSTA (229)253-0023
Hotel. $79-$159 **Address:** 1327 N St. Augustine Rd 31601 **Location:** I-75 exit 18, just e. **Facility:** 180 units. 7 stories, interior corridors. **Terms:** cancellation fee imposed. **Pool(s):** outdoor, indoor. **Activities:** hot tub, exercise room. **Guest Services:** valet and coin laundry.

ECONO LODGE (229)671-1511

Hotel
$57-$100
Address: 3022 James Rd 31602 **Location:** I-75 exit 18, just nw. **Facility:** 65 units, some efficiencies. 3 stories, interior corridors. **Pool(s):** outdoor. **Guest Services:** valet laundry, area transportation.

FAIRFIELD INN & SUITES BY MARRIOTT VALDOSTA (229)242-1225
Hotel. $81-$137 **Address:** 2010 W Hill Ave 31601 **Location:** I-75 exit 16, just ne. **Facility:** 132 units. 5 stories, interior corridors. **Terms:** check-in 4 pm. **Amenities:** Some: safes. **Pool(s):** outdoor. **Activities:** exercise room. **Guest Services:** valet and coin laundry.
AAA Benefit: Members save 5% or more!

HAMPTON INN & SUITES VALDOSTA CONVENTION CENTER (229)241-1234
Hotel. $89-$169 **Address:** 2 Meeting Place Dr 31601 **Location:** I-75 exit 16, just ne to Norman Dr, then just n. Next to convention center. **Facility:** 184 units. 4 stories, interior corridors. **Terms:** 1-7 night minimum stay, cancellation fee imposed. **Pool(s):** outdoor. **Activities:** exercise room. **Guest Services:** valet and coin laundry.
AAA Benefit: Members save up to 10%!

HILTON GARDEN INN　　　　(229)219-1011

 Hotel. $104-$174 Address: 1702 Gornto Rd 31601 Location: I-75 exit 18, just se. Facility: 163 units. 7 stories, interior corridors. Terms: 1-7 night minimum stay, cancellation fee imposed. Pool(s): heated outdoor. Activities: exercise room. Guest Services: valet and coin laundry.

AAA Benefit: Members save up to 10%!

[icons]

HOLIDAY INN EXPRESS HOTEL & SUITES VALDOSTA WEST MALL AREA　　　　229/249-8900

Hotel. Rates not provided. Address: 1330 N St Augustine Rd 31601 Location: I-75 exit 18, just se. Facility: 95 units. 4 stories, interior corridors. Pool(s): heated outdoor. Activities: hot tub, exercise room. Guest Services: valet and coin laundry.

[icons]

HOLIDAY INN VALDOSTA CONFERENCE CENTER　　　　(229)244-1111

Hotel. $89-$169 Address: 1805 W Hill Ave 31601 Location: I-75 exit 16, 0.4 mi ne. Facility: 158 units. 5 stories, interior corridors. Pool(s): outdoor. Activities: hot tub, exercise room. Guest Services: valet and coin laundry.

[icons]

SLEEP INN & SUITES　　　　(229)671-1111

Hotel
$70-$170

Address: 3026 James Rd 31602 Location: I-75 exit 18, just nw. Facility: 71 units. 3 stories, interior corridors. Pool(s): outdoor. Activities: exercise room. Guest Services: coin laundry.

[icons]

SUPER 8 VALDOSTA MALL　　　　(229)244-8440

Hotel. Rates not provided. Address: 1389 N St. Augustine Rd 31602 Location: I-75 exit 18, just w off SR 94. Facility: 72 units. 3 stories, exterior corridors. Pool(s): outdoor. Activities: exercise room. Guest Services: valet and coin laundry.

[icons]

WHERE TO EAT

306 NORTH　　　　229/249-5333

American. Fine Dining. $7-$26 AAA Inspector Notes: This downtown eatery offers upscale dining in a sophisticated atmosphere. Quick but tasty lunches give way to fine dinners in the evenings, when the menu lists creative presentations made with a Southern twist. Among examples are mustard-crusted salmon with fried green tomatoes, buttermilk-fried wild Georgia shrimp and oysters with creamy cheddar grits, as well as steaks, chops and pasta. Features: full bar, patio dining, early bird specials, happy hour. Address: 306 N Patterson St 31601 Location: Jct US 84 and SR 31A, just n on SR 31A (Patterson St). Parking: on-site and street.

[icons]

AUSTIN'S CATTLE COMPANY　　　　229/259-9333

Steak. Casual Dining. $8-$25 AAA Inspector Notes: Celebrating the heyday of the cowboy, this restaurant is a must do for those with vivacious appetites. After a day of rustling the kids or traveling happy trails refuel with a hand-cut steak cooked to order. Seafood, burgers, sandwiches and salads also are available. With its rustic wood décor, display of wildlife, collection of antique hand tools and a wagon wheel chandelier, one half expects John Wayne to mosey in and say howdy partner. Features: full bar, happy hour. Address: 2101 W Hill Ave 31601 Location: I-75 exit 16, just w.

[icons]

THE BLEU CAFE　　　　229/244-2248

Pizza Sandwiches. Casual Dining. $7-$15 AAA Inspector Notes: This trendy café features contemporary décor, a full bar and live entertainment. The low lighting, dark wood tones and light rock playing in the background invite you to come in, chill out and have a philosophical conversation with your friends. The menu offers a generous selection of upscale tacos, pizzas and sandwiches with an urban twist. Features: full bar, patio dining, happy hour. Address: 125 N Patterson St 31601 Location: Between W Central and E Hill aves; downtown. Parking: street only. [icons]

BUBBA JAX CRAB SHACK　　　　229/469-4368

Seafood. Casual Dining. $9-$25 AAA Inspector Notes: The residential style building which houses this no frills seafood joint projects the expectations of dining at a friend's house. If crab legs are what you desire, be prepared for a messy and lengthy meal. The time and effort invested in cracking and peeling shells to satisfy your craving is well worth it. Features: beer only, patio dining. Address: 1700 W Hill Ave 31601 Location: I-75 exit 16, 0.7 mi ne on US 84/221. [icons]

CRYSTAL RIVER SEAFOOD　　　　229/249-9515

Seafood. Casual Dining. $8-$29 AAA Inspector Notes: Seafood choices are plentiful on the menu, and guests can pick a favorite or try something new. Flavors are good and portions ample. Features: beer & wine. Address: 958 N St Augustine Rd 31601 Location: I-75 exit 18, 0.6 mi w on SR 94; in shopping center. [icons]

GIULIO'S GREEK & ITALIAN RESTAURANT　　　　229/333-0929

Mediterranean. Casual Dining. $13-$30 AAA Inspector Notes: The stucco Mediterranean-style house where this café is situated perfectly reflects the cuisine style offered here. Feast on all the traditional Greek and Italian standards, seated in one of the various sized dining rooms or al fresco on the wide veranda. Although the décor inside is a hodgepodge of eclectic paraphernalia, the food is always scrumptious. Features: beer & wine, patio dining. Address: 105 E Ann St 31601 Location: Jct SR 31 (N Patterson St), just e. Parking: on-site and street. [icons]

MICHAEL'S DELI & SEAFOOD　　　　229/293-9905

Deli. Quick Serve. $4-$14 AAA Inspector Notes: This quick-serve deli offers subs on hoagie rolls, large salads, fried mushrooms, tilapia, flounder and catfish. Portions are large and prices are favorable for the value conscious. Address: 1307 N Ashley St 31602 Location: Downtown. [icons]

MOM & DAD'S ITALIAN RESTAURANT　　　　229/333-0848

Italian. Casual Dining. $7-$29 AAA Inspector Notes: Savor the delicious pasta dishes and various sauces served at this family-owned Italian restaurant which is attractively decorated with Italian landscapes and still-life murals exuding a Tuscan villa atmosphere. The homemade vinaigrette dressing bursts with flavor, as does the stuffed tortellini. On occasion, the pastry chef makes white chocolate ravioli, a very rich and delicious dessert. Features: full bar. Address: 4143 N Valdosta Rd 31602 Location: I-75 exit 22, 1.5 mi e. [icons]

SMOK'N PIG BBQ　　　　229/245-8227

Barbecue. Casual Dining. $6-$24 AAA Inspector Notes: In the mood for some barbecue, look no further than the first selection on the menu where diners can choose classic St. Louis spare ribs, or combo platters that include ribs, beef brisket and smoked chicken. Lovers of side items will be pleased with collard greens, macaroni and cheese, baked beans and corn bread. For those who are extra hungry there is a salad and dessert bar. Parking is plentiful and on most nights full. Features: beer & wine. Address: 4228 N Valdosta Rd 31602 Location: I-75 exit 22, 1.9 mi e. [icons]

SONNY'S REAL PIT BAR-B-Q　　　　229/241-8090

Barbecue. Casual Dining. $8-$17 AAA Inspector Notes: Bearing the name after its founder, Floyd "Sonny" Tillman, this barbecue restaurant first opened its doors circa 1968 in Gainesville, Florida and has since spawned over 150 more throughout the Southeast. The menu is steeped in finger lickin' favorites such as ribs, pulled pork, beef brisket, burgers, catfish, shrimp and chargrilled chicken. Let's not forget about the fried okra, which is the perfect starter dish, and their homemade baked beans. Features: beer only. Address: 1701 Norman Dr 31601 Location: I-75 exit 18, 0.6 mi e on St Augustine Rd, then just n. [icons]

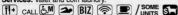

STEEL MAGNOLIAS   229/259-0010
WWWW Southern American. Fine Dining. $8-$28 **AAA Inspector Notes:** Looking like it just stepped out of the pages of Martha Stewart Living, the background of light country/rock, Southern chic décor and warm hospitality will put this place on the top of your love it list. Featuring a constantly evolving menu of fresh, modern dishes, do not miss the tomato bruschetta served in a mini cast iron skillet. Duck confit, Gayla grits, poached pear salad and banana crème brûlée are but a small sample of the culinary delights that await. **Features:** full bar, patio dining, happy hour. **Address:** 132 N Patterson St 31601 **Location:** Between W Central and E Hill aves; downtown. **Parking:** street only. [L] [D]

VIDALIA pop. 10,473

AMERICINN LODGE & SUITES   (912)537-2728

WWWWW
Hotel
$110-$150

Address: 155 Mose Coleman Dr 30474 **Location:** 3 mi e on US 280, just s. **Facility:** 54 units, some efficiencies. 3 stories, interior corridors. **Terms:** cancellation fee imposed. **Pool(s):** heated indoor. **Activities:** hot tub, trails, exercise room. **Guest Services:** coin laundry. **Featured Amenity: full hot breakfast.**

HAMPTON INN   (912)526-0235
WWWW Hotel. $104-$134 **Address:** 3303 E 1st St 30474 **Location:** 3.5 mi s on SR 15/29. **Facility:** 61 units. 3 stories, interior corridors. **Terms:** 1-7 night minimum stay, cancellation fee imposed. **Pool(s):** outdoor. **Activities:** exercise room. **Guest Services:** valet laundry.

AAA Benefit:
Members save up to 10%!

WHERE TO EAT

STEEPLECHASE GRILLE AND TAVERN   912/537-7900
WW WW American. Casual Dining. $7-$18 **AAA Inspector Notes:** Start with the spinach con queso or fried pickle chips but save room for delicious entrées such as freshly-baked quiche, filet mignon or chicken Havana. To wrap up the meal, any of the sweet temptations from the dessert tray will do the trick. The Italian lemon cream cake with raspberry sauce was delightful! **Features:** full bar. **Address:** 306 E 2nd St 30474 **Location:** Just off US 280; southwest of center.

[L] [D]

VILLA RICA pop. 13,956

COMFORT INN & SUITES   (678)941-3401
WWWW Hotel. $74-$139 **Address:** 132 Hwy 61 Connector 30180 **Location:** I-20 exit 24, just n. **Facility:** 59 units. 4 stories, interior corridors. **Pool(s):** heated indoor. **Activities:** exercise room. **Guest Services:** valet and coin laundry.

DAYS INN   (770)459-8888
WW WW Hotel. $53-$70 **Address:** 195 Hwy 61 Connector 30180 **Location:** I-20 exit 24, just n. **Facility:** 61 units. 3 stories, interior corridors. **Terms:** cancellation fee imposed. **Guest Services:** coin laundry.

ECONO LODGE-VILLA RICA INN   (770)459-6669
WW WW Motel. $65-$131 **Address:** 124 Hwy 61 Connector 30180 **Location:** I-20 exit 24, just n. **Facility:** 39 units. 2 stories (no elevator), exterior corridors. **Pool(s):** outdoor. **Guest Services:** coin laundry.

WHERE TO EAT

OLIVE TREE   770/456-6456
WWWW Mediterranean. Casual Dining. $7-$20 **AAA Inspector Notes:** Savor the combination of Greek and Italian fare here while gazing upon beautiful paintings and murals of sun-kissed countrysides. Enjoy traditional dishes of chicken Marsala, a premium gyro, veal Romano and shrimp Greco. The cheesecake will make diners want to exclaim opa, but please do not throw the plates. **Features:** full bar. **Address:** 150 Stone St, Suite A 30180 **Location:** Downtown. [L] [D] CALL [M]

TRADING POST CAFE   770/456-4221
WW WW American. Casual Dining. $7-$19 **AAA Inspector Notes:** Chicken and dressing, fried catfish and fried chicken, and steak and gravy are just some of the meat choices that go with a wide array of vegetable options here. Other menu staples include rib-eye steaks, burgers, sandwiches and pasta dishes. **Address:** 664 W Bankhead Hwy, Suite 2B 30180 **Location:** I-20 exit 24, 0.3 mi n; in Villa Rica Crossing. [B] [L] [D] CALL [M]

WARM SPRINGS (C-2) pop. 425, elev. 930'

The legendary curative powers of Warm Springs have lured the hopeful for centuries. Wounded Native American warriors gathered at the springs before Europeans colonized the New World. In the late 1700s the springs were discovered by yellow fever victims, and by 1832 Warm Springs had become a popular summer health resort. The resort survived the torch of Gen. William Tecumseh Sherman only to be reduced to ashes by a runaway bonfire in 1865. Rebuilt, Warm Springs flourished in the 1880s and 1890s and was incorporated in 1893.

After contracting polio, Franklin Delano Roosevelt visited the springs in 1924 hoping to improve his health. A few years later he established the Warm Springs Foundation for the care and treatment of fellow polio victims who could not afford such medical help.

Although Warm Springs' popularity as a resort waned after Roosevelt's death, restoration efforts have attracted visitors who come to browse through the crafts shops housed in former grocery and dime stores. Artisans can be seen at work in more than 30 stores, and musicians and cloggers perform on the stage of the old pavilion during events.

Meriwether Warm Springs Regional Visitor Information Center: 1 Broad St., Warm Springs, GA 31830. **Phone:** (706) 655-3322 or (800) 337-1927.

FDR'S LITTLE WHITE HOUSE STATE HISTORIC SITE is .2 mi. s. on US 27A at 401 Little White House Rd. Built by President Franklin Roosevelt in 1932, this National Historic Landmark was the site of his death on April 12, 1945. Many of FDR's visionary programs were conceived within the walls of this house. A guest house, servant's quarters, garage and walkway of state flags and stones also are on the grounds. One mile away is the Historic Pools Complex, where a small museum relates the story of the springs and the town.

A self-guiding tour brochure is available in English, French, Dutch, Spanish, German, Russian, Japanese, Chinese, Italian and Swedish. Guided tours are offered by advance reservation. **Time:** Allow 1 hour minimum. **Hours:** Daily 9-5. Last admission 15 minutes before closing. Guided tours Sat. at 9:30. Closed Jan. 1, Thanksgiving and Christmas. **Cost:** (includes site, memorial museum and pool museum) $12; $10 (ages 62+); $7 (ages 6-17). Sat. guided tour $20. Reservations required for guided tour. **Phone:** (706) 655-5870. [GT] [A]

Franklin D. Roosevelt Memorial Museum, part of FDR's Little White House State Historic Site, is .2 mi. s. on US 27A adjacent to Roosevelt's Little White House at 401 Little White House Rd. The 11,000-square-foot museum features exhibits about Roosevelt's life and political career. Visitors can see his parade stagecoach and hand-controlled 1938 Ford convertible and listen to radio recordings of the famous "Fireside Chats." A film narrated by Walter Cronkite shows footage of FDR visiting his Warm Springs neighbors. Roosevelt died after suffering a stroke while posing for a portrait; the "Unfinished Portrait" is displayed. An exhibit about Eleanor Roosevelt's life also is on display.

Hours: Daily 9-4:45. Last film begins at 4. Closed Jan. 1, Thanksgiving and Christmas. **Cost:** included with historic site admission. **Phone:** (706) 655-5870. [A]

WARM SPRINGS NATIONAL FISH HATCHERY, s. on SR 41 to 5308 Spring St., also is a wildlife and wetlands habitat area. The hatchery focuses its efforts on fish species native to the southeastern United States. Striped bass, lake sturgeon, alligator gar and freshwater mussels are among the marine life visitors will see. The hatchery features a public aquarium and two outdoor habitat pools, a display of carnivorous plants, a nature trail and an enclosed wetland area containing an American alligator. **Time:** Allow 30 minutes minimum. **Hours:** Daily 8-4; aquarium closed major holidays. **Cost:** Free. **Phone:** (706) 655-3382.

WARNER ROBINS (D-3) pop. 66,588, elev. 381'

MUSEUM OF AVIATION, 10 mi. e. of I-75 exit 144 to jct. SR 247 and Russell Pkwy., features more than 95 aircraft, missiles and cockpits and 200,000 square feet of indoor exhibits housed in four buildings. Aircraft displays include a B-1B bomber, F-4D MiG killer, U-2 spy plane, MiG-17, SR-71 Blackbird, F-15 Eagle, B-29, a Global Hawk, B-17 Flying Fortress, P-51 Mustang and a 60-foot cutaway replica of a B-17 bomber. Exhibits describe the World War II D-Day Invasion, CBI Hump pilots of World War II, Tuskegee Airmen, Gen. Robert L. Scott Jr. and the 14th Air Force Flying Tigers. The Georgia Aviation Hall of Fame recognizes commercial and military aviation greats from across the state. One hangar is devoted entirely to aircraft, vehicles and equipment used in Southeast Asia during the Vietnam War.

Comfortable walking shoes are advised. **Time:** Allow 3 hours minimum. **Hours:** Daily 9-5. Closed Jan. 1, Easter, Thanksgiving and Christmas. Closes Christmas Eve and Dec. 31 at 1. **Cost:** Free. **Phone:** (478) 926-6870. [¶] [A]

BAYMONT INN & SUITES WARNER ROBINS   (478)953-5522
◆◆ **Hotel.** $59-$89 **Address:** 2731 Watson Blvd 31093 **Location:** I-75 exit 146 (SR 247C), 4.1 mi e. **Facility:** 59 units. 2 stories (no elevator), exterior corridors. **Pool(s):** outdoor. **Activities:** exercise room. **Guest Services:** valet laundry.
[¶] [≈] [BIZ] [≈] [⊟] [⊜] [⊒] / SOME UNITS [⇲] [HS]

COMFORT INN & SUITES   (478)922-7555
◆◆ **Hotel.** $95-$119 **Address:** 95 Georgia Hwy 247 S 31088 **Location:** Jct SR 247C and US 129/SR 247, 1.6 mi s on US 129/SR 247. **Facility:** 77 units, some efficiencies. 1-2 stories, interior/exterior corridors. **Pool(s):** outdoor. **Activities:** exercise room. **Guest Services:** valet and coin laundry.
[¶] [≈] [BIZ] [≈] [✕] [⊟] [⊜] [⊒] / SOME UNITS [⇲]

COMFORT SUITES   (478)953-5240
◆◆ **Motel.** $99-$169 **Address:** 3101 Watson Blvd 31093 **Location:** I-75 exit 146 (SR 247C), 2.9 mi e. **Facility:** 64 units. 3 stories, interior corridors. **Pool(s):** indoor. **Activities:** hot tub, exercise room. **Guest Services:** valet and coin laundry.
[¶] [≈] [BIZ] [HS] [≈] [✕] [⊟] [⊜] [⊒]

COURTYARD BY MARRIOTT WARNER ROBINS
(478)602-6200

◆◆◆ Hotel $116-$183

COURTYARD *Marriott* **AAA Benefit:** Members save 5% or more!

Address: 589 Carl Vinson Pkwy 31088 **Location:** Jct SR 247 and Carl Vinson Pkwy. **Facility:** 106 units. 4 stories, interior corridors. **Pool(s):** heated indoor. **Activities:** hot tub, exercise room. **Guest Services:** valet and coin laundry.
[SAVE] [¶] CALL [⌖M] [≈] [BIZ] [HS]
[≈] [✕] [⊟] [⊒] / SOME UNITS [⊜]

DAYS INN & SUITES   (478)953-3800

◆◆ Hotel $69-$129

Address: 2739 Watson Blvd 31093 **Location:** I-75 exit 146 (SR 247C), 4.1 mi e. **Facility:** 47 units. 2 stories (no elevator), exterior corridors. **Terms:** 3 day cancellation notice. **Pool(s):** outdoor. **Activities:** exercise room. **Guest Services:** valet and coin laundry.
[SAVE] [¶] [≈] [BIZ] [≈] [⊟] [⊜]
[⊒] / SOME UNITS [⇲] [HS]

FAIRFIELD INN & SUITES BY MARRIOTT WARNER ROBINS
(478)953-4200
◆◆◆ **Hotel.** $102-$166 **Address:** 221 Margie Dr 31088 **Location:** I-75 exit 146 (SR 247C), 3.2 mi e, then just s. **Facility:** 74 units. 3 stories, interior corridors. **Pool(s):** heated indoor. **Activities:** hot tub, exercise room. **Guest Services:** valet and coin laundry.

AAA Benefit: Members save 5% or more!

[¶] CALL [⌖M] [≈] [BIZ] [HS] [≈] [✕] [⊟] [⊜] [⊒]

HAMPTON INN-WARNER ROBINS   (478)953-9443

▼▼◆▼ **Hotel.** $137-$161 **Address:** 4000 Watson Blvd 31093 **Location:** I-75 exit 146 (SR 247C), 2.8 mi e. **Facility:** 87 units. 3 stories, interior corridors. **Terms:** 1-7 night minimum stay, cancellation fee imposed. **Pool(s):** heated indoor. **Activities:** hot tub, exercise room. **Guest Services:** valet and coin laundry.

AAA Benefit: Members save up to 10%!

[ⅱ→] CALL [ⒶM] [🛒] [BIZ] [HS] [📶] [✕] [🍴] [🔒] [🖼] [💻]

HILTON GARDEN INN WARNER ROBINS   478/971-1550

▼▼◆▼ **Hotel.** Rates not provided. **Address:** 207 N Willie Lee Pkwy 31093 **Location:** I-75 exit 146 (SR 247C), 2.8 mi e, then just n. **Facility:** 90 units. 3 stories, interior corridors. **Pool(s):** heated indoor. **Activities:** hot tub, exercise room. **Guest Services:** valet and coin laundry.

AAA Benefit: Members save up to 10%!

[ⅱ] [🍽] CALL [ⒶM] [🛒] [BIZ] [HS] [📶] [✕] [🔒] [🖼] [💻]

LA QUINTA INN & SUITES   (478)333-6920

▼▼◆▼
Hotel
$91-$185

Address: 4080 Watson Blvd 31093 **Location:** I-75 exit 146 (SR 247C), 2.7 mi e. **Facility:** 76 units. 4 stories, interior corridors. **Pool(s):** heated indoor. **Activities:** hot tub, exercise room. **Guest Services:** valet and coin laundry. **Featured Amenity:** full hot breakfast.

[SAVE] [ⅱ→] [🛒] [BIZ] [HS] [📶] [✕]
[🔒] [🖼] [💻] / SOME UNITS [🐾]

WHERE TO EAT

EL BRONCO MEXICAN RESTAURANT   478/328-0344

▼▼◆▼ Mexican. Casual Dining. $6-$12 **AAA Inspector Notes:** The authentic ambiance of the dining room combined with the congenial staff and authentic dishes make this a delightful dining experience. Chicken enchiladas, chile relleno, carne asada, combination platters, fajitas and burritos highlight the menu. There are several vegetarian dishes, also. **Features:** full bar, patio dining. **Address:** 2067 Watson Blvd 31093 **Location:** I-75 exit 146 (SR 247C), 5.3 mi e. [L] [D]

FATZ   478/971-1090

▼▼◆▼ Regional American. Casual Dining. $8-$19 **AAA Inspector Notes:** Friendly staff and appealing country decor help set the tone for a relaxed and enjoyable dining experience. It's not unusual for guests to wait to be seated at the popular spot, which earns raves for its well-prepared variations on chicken, steak, ribs and pasta, as well as salads and sandwiches. The signature Southern-style peach cobbler served with vanilla ice cream and walnuts is scrumptious. **Features:** full bar. **Address:** 2715 Watson Blvd 31093 **Location:** I-75 exit 146 (SR 247C), 4.3 mi e.

[L] [D] CALL [ⒶM]

SONNY'S REAL PIT BAR-B-Q   478/929-3333

▼▼◆▼ Barbecue. Casual Dining. $8-$20 **AAA Inspector Notes:** Bearing the name after its founder, Floyd "Sonny" Tillman, this barbecue restaurant first opened its doors circa 1968 in Gainesville, Florida and has since spawned over 150 more throughout the Southeast. The menu is steeped in finger lickin' favorites such as ribs, pulled pork, beef brisket, burgers, catfish, shrimp and chargrilled chicken. Let's not forget about the fried okra, which is the perfect starter dish, and their homemade baked beans. **Features:** beer only. **Address:** 811 Russell Pkwy 31088 **Location:** Jct US 129/SR 247, 2 mi w. [L] [D]

SUSHI THAI RESTAURANT   478/923-0898

▼▼ ▼▼ Thai. Casual Dining. $9-$30 **AAA Inspector Notes:** Select from the traditional Thai menu or from the Japanese sushi menu. The sushi bar offers a large variety. The chef specialties include curry duck, spicy catfish and Thai royal duck roasted, fried and topped with secret sauce. **Features:** beer & wine. **Address:** 2624 Watson Blvd, Suite D 31093 **Location:** Just e of Carl Vinson Pkwy.

[L] [D]

WASHINGTON (B-4) pop. 4,134, elev. 630'

Washington was established and designated temporary capital of Georgia in 1780. The town has antebellum Greek Revival mansions as well as Colonial-style houses dating from the days following the Revolution; some are occupied by descendants of the original owners. Tree-shaded streets bear such patriotic names as Jefferson and Liberty.

The Battle of Kettle Creek, the decisive battle of the Revolutionary War in Georgia, was fought west of town in 1779. A granite marker at the southwest corner of the courthouse indicates the location of the meeting that dissolved the government of the Confederacy on May 4, 1865.

Washington-Wilkes Welcome Center: 22B West Square, P.O. Box 661, Washington, GA 30673. **Phone:** (706) 678-5111.

CALLAWAY PLANTATION is 5 mi. w. on US 78 at 2160 Lexington Rd., across from the airport. This restored plantation includes an 1869 manor house, a smokehouse, a cemetery and a one-room schoolhouse. A 1785 hewn-log house, once a settler's home, has displays of domestic and agricultural implements. A two-story Federal house dating from the 1790s and an 1869 red brick Greek Revival house are both furnished in period, reflecting the increasing wealth and comfort of successive generations of a pioneer family.

Mule Day-Southern Heritage Festival is held the second Sat. in Oct. **Hours:** Guided 1-hour tours are given Tues.-Sat. 10-5. Last tour begins 1 hour before closing. Closed major holidays. **Cost:** $7; $5 (ages 6-12); $3 (age 5). **Parking:** Overnight RV parking is available for a fee. **Phone:** (706) 678-7060. [GT] [📷]

ROBERT TOOMBS HOUSE STATE HISTORIC SITE, 216 E. Robert Toombs Ave./Bus. Rte. 78, is the former home of the Confederate Secretary of State who was instrumental in leading Georgia to secession and war. The state has carefully restored the structure to its condition at the time of Toombs' death in 1885. The antebellum house displays furnishings once owned by the Toombs family.

Hours: Site open Tues.-Sat. 9-5. Self-guiding house tours 10-4. Last tour begins at 4. Closed Jan. 1, Thanksgiving and Christmas. Phone ahead to confirm schedule. **Cost:** $5; $3 (ages 6-12); $1 (ages 3-5). **Phone:** (706) 678-2226. [📷]

WASHINGTON HISTORICAL MUSEUM is at 308 E. Robert Toombs Ave./Bus. Rte. 78. Built about 1835, this museum houses antique furnishings and Confederate relics, including Jefferson Davis' camp chest. Revolutionary War and Native American history exhibits also are on display. A turn-of-the-20th-century doctor's office is on the grounds. **Hours:** Tues.-Sat. 10-5. Last tour begins 45 minutes before closing. Closed major holidays. **Cost:** Self-guiding tour $5; $3 (ages 6-12). Guided tour $10; $3 (ages 6-12). **Phone:** (706) 678-2105. GT

WAYCROSS (E-5) pop. 14,649, elev. 135'

Known as the "crossing of the ways" in the mid- to late 19th century because of the intersection of several railroad lines, Waycross has maintained its railroad heritage. At Rice Yard, the largest classification facility in the country, freight cars are organized into trains to move shipments across the nation. Other industries in the area include lumber and related concerns, manufactured housing, tobacco and pecan farming, bee culture and the production of honey. The town is at the northern entrance to the Okefenokee National Wildlife Refuge *(see attraction listing p. 182).*

Waycross Tourism Bureau/Visitors Center: 417 Pendleton St., Waycross, GA 31501. **Phone:** (912) 287-2969.

Self-guiding tours: Walking tour maps of the historic district are available from the visitor center.

OBEDIAH'S OKEFENOK, US 82W to Gillmore St., then 8.5 mi. s. to 5115 Swamp Rd., offers a self-guiding tour, a 1,100-foot boardwalk through the Okefenokee Swamp, wildlife exhibits and an 1870s homestead containing various displays. **Time:** Allow 1 hour, 30 minutes minimum. **Hours:** Fri.-Sun. 10-5 (weather permitting). Closed major holidays. Phone ahead to confirm schedule. **Cost:** $6.50; $5.50 (ages 65+); $5 (ages 3-17). **Phone:** (912) 287-0090. 🏞

OKEFENOKEE HERITAGE CENTER, 2 mi. n.w. via US 1/23, then 4 blks. w. to 1460 N. Augusta Ave., has an art gallery that features permanent and changing exhibits about history and the arts along with an interactive exhibit about singer Gram Parsons. The museum includes a late 19th-century printshop, a restored 1912 steam locomotive, train cars, a railroad depot and a restored 1820s farmhouse.

Time: Allow 1 hour minimum. **Hours:** Tues.-Sat. 9-2. Closed major holidays. **Cost:** $7; $5 (ages 6-18); free (ages 0-5). **Phone:** (912) 285-4260.

OKEFENOKEE SWAMP PARK is 8 mi. s.e. on US 1/23, then 4.7 mi. s. on SR 177 to 5700 Okefenokee Swamp Park Rd. This 1,600-acre wildlife sanctuary on Cowhouse Island is the northern entrance to Okefenokee Swamp. The park features flower and seasonal butterfly gardens, a wilderness walkway

and several educational centers. The Swamp Creation Center has dioramas, charts and animated exhibits explaining the swamp's evolution. The Nature Center includes a bear observatory and snake exhibits. Outdoor museum displays at Pioneer Island pertain to the history of the swamp's early settlers. Alligators may be seen in their natural habitat spring through fall.

Live reptiles are featured in the "Eye on Nature" show. The Walt Kelly Studio honors the late cartoonist and his most famous creation, Pogo the Possum. Optional guided boat tours offer an up-close look at plants and wildlife. Visitors also can take a 1.5-mile railroad tour. The Okefenokee Swamp Park Light Show is offered during the holiday season.

Food is available daily mid-Mar. through July 31; Fri.-Sun., Aug.-Oct.; Sat.-Sun., in Nov. and days with light show in Dec.

Hours: Park open daily 9-5:30. Light show Fri.-Sun. 6-9 p.m. (also Mon.-Fri. during week of Christmas), Thanksgiving weekend-Dec. 31; park opens at 1 on days when light show is offered. Nature shows are presented seasonally; phone for schedule. Optional 45-minute guided boat tours depart daily (depending on water level and guide availability). Closed Jan. 1, Thanksgiving, Christmas Eve and Christmas; phone ahead to confirm holiday schedule. **Cost:** Park $17; $16 (ages 3-11, ages 62+ and active military with ID). Combination park admission and boat tours $27; $22 (ages 3-11). Inquire about boat tour refund policies. **Phone:** (912) 283-0583. GT 🍽 🏞

BAYMONT INN & SUITES WAYCROSS   (912)283-3800
▼▼ **Motel.** $59-$79 **Address:** 950 S City Blvd 31501 **Location:** Between US 1 and 82; east of city. **Facility:** 62 units. 2 stories (no elevator), exterior corridors. **Pool(s):** outdoor. **Activities:** exercise room.

BEST WESTERN PLUS BRADBURY INN & SUITES
(912)284-0095

▼▼▼▼
Hotel
$75-$150

BW Best Western PLUS | **AAA Benefit:** Save 10% or more every day and earn 10% bonus points!

Address: 2570 Memorial Dr 31503 **Location:** Jct US 1 and 82, 1.5 mi se on US 1 (Memorial Dr). **Facility:** 38 units. 2 stories, interior corridors. **Amenities:** safes. **Pool(s):** outdoor. **Guest Services:** coin laundry.

COMFORT SUITES   (912)548-0555
▼▼▼ **Hotel.** $82-$142 **Address:** 1922 Memorial Dr 31501 **Location:** Jct US 1 and 82, just se on US 1 (Memorial Dr). **Facility:** 77 units. 4 stories, interior corridors. **Pool(s):** heated indoor. **Activities:** hot tub, exercise room. **Guest Services:** valet and coin laundry.

HAMPTON INN (912)285-5515

▼▼▼ **Hotel.** $89-$139 **Address:** 1720 Brunswick Hwy (US 82) 31501 **Location:** Jct US 1 and 82, just e. Across from railway. **Facility:** 69 units. 3 stories, interior corridors. **Terms:** 1-7 night minimum stay, cancellation fee imposed. **Pool(s):** outdoor. **Activities:** exercise room. **Guest Services:** valet and coin laundry.

AAA Benefit: Members save up to 10%!

[Amenity icons]

HOLIDAY INN EXPRESS & SUITES 912/548-0720

▼▼▼ **Hotel.** Rates not provided. **Address:** 1761 Memorial Dr 31501 **Location:** Between US 1 and 82. **Facility:** 78 units. 4 stories, interior corridors. **Pool(s):** heated indoor. **Activities:** sauna, hot tub, exercise room. **Guest Services:** valet and coin laundry.

[Amenity icons]

WHERE TO EAT

CAVAGNAROS 912/285-4000

▼▼ American. Casual Dining. $6-$20 **AAA Inspector Notes:** On the corner of a busy intersection sits this one-story brick family-owned and -operated restaurant. The eclectic menu includes steaks, seafood, pasta and pizza, there is sure to be something for all tastes. Check out the dessert case on the way in where the fresh cakes and pies are displayed. **Features:** full bar, patio dining. **Address:** 1810 S Georgia Pkwy W 31501 **Location:** Jct US 84 and 1/82.

[L] [D] CALL [M]

FANCY Q SUSHI BAR & GRILL 912/548-1540

▼▼ Asian Sushi. Casual Dining. $5-$25 **AAA Inspector Notes:** From teriyaki, hibachi, tempura and of course, sushi, this casual joint has it all. A team of friendly staff members is at your service to ensure you enjoy your selections. Skilled chefs whip up colorful and artistic sushi and sashimi rolls with creative flair. **Features:** beer & wine. **Address:** 514 Mary St 31501 **Location:** Jct Tebeau St. **Parking:** street only. [L] [D] CALL [M]

RODEO MEXICAN RESTAURANT 912/285-9555

▼▼ Mexican. Casual Dining. $6-$16 **AAA Inspector Notes:** Zesty favorites such as fajitas, enchiladas, burritos and quesadillas bring guests in to indulge their cravings. This is a good place to meet up with friends over a margarita, and the sopaipillas make for a sweet ending to your meal. **Features:** full bar. **Address:** 2020 Memorial Dr 31501 **Location:** Jct US 1 and 82, just se on US 1 (Memorial Dr).

[L] [D] CALL [M]

WAYNESBORO pop. 5,766

EXECUTIVE INN 706/554-0806

▼▼▼ ▼▼
Hotel
Rates not provided

Address: 1224 N Liberty St 30830 **Location:** 0.8 mi n of downtown center on US 25. **Facility:** 38 units. 2 stories (no elevator), interior corridors. **Amenities:** safes. **Pool(s):** outdoor. **Featured Amenity:** continental breakfast.

[Amenity icons]

HAMPTON INN WAYNESBORO (706)558-4190

▼▼▼ ▼ **Hotel.** $109-$159 **Address:** 235 Peachtree St 30830 **Location:** 0.9 mi n of downtown center on US 25. **Facility:** 62 units. 3 stories, interior corridors. **Terms:** 1-7 night minimum stay, cancellation fee imposed. **Pool(s):** outdoor. **Activities:** exercise room. **Guest Services:** valet and coin laundry.

AAA Benefit: Members save up to 10%!

[Amenity icons]

QUALITY INN (706)437-0500

▼▼ **Motel.** $89 **Address:** 1436 N Liberty St 30830 **Location:** 0.9 mi n of downtown center on US 25. **Facility:** 42 units. 2 stories (no elevator), exterior corridors. **Pool(s):** outdoor. **Activities:** exercise room.

[Amenity icons]

WEST POINT (C-1) pop. 3,474, elev. 576'

Because of its strategic location on the Chattahoochee River at the Alabama state line, West Point was considered the key to the granary of the Tennessee Army during the Civil War. Word of Gen. Robert E. Lee's surrender was slow to reach the town, and the last battle east of the Mississippi River, the Battle of Fort Tyler, was fought a week after the war's official end.

Recovery after the war was ensured with the construction of two textile mills that eventually expanded into what is now WestPoint Home Inc., one of the world's largest textile manufacturing companies.

North of West Point is West Point Lake *(see Recreation Areas Chart)*, a 25,900-acre man-made site offering a variety of recreational pursuits. A visitor center, 4 miles north off US 29, contains dioramas, photographs and a video presentation describing the history of the region before, during and after construction of the dam that created the lake.

Greater Valley Area Chamber of Commerce: 2102 S. Broad Ave., P.O. Box 205, Lanett, AL 36863. **Phone:** (334) 642-1411.

Take Your **Imagination** to New Destinations

Use AAA Travel Guides online to explore the possibilities.

Go to AAA.com/travelguide today.

WINDER pop. 14,099

QUALITY INN   (770)868-5303

Hotel. $85-$149 **Address:** 177 W Athens St 30680 **Location:** Jct Broad St, 0.8 mi n; downtown. **Facility:** 42 units. 2 stories (no elevator), interior corridors. **Terms:** check-in 4 pm. **Pool(s):** outdoor. **Activities:** exercise room.

[TI+] CALL [&M] [≈] [BIZ] [≈] [🖥] [🖨] [▣] / [SOME UNITS] [S🔧]

WHERE TO EAT

FATZ   770/867-3344

Regional American. Casual Dining. $8-$19 **AAA Inspector Notes:** Friendly staff and appealing country decor help set the tone for a relaxed and enjoyable dining experience. It's not unusual for guests to wait to be seated at the popular spot, which earns raves for its well-prepared variations on chicken, steak, ribs and pasta, as well as salads and sandwiches. The signature Southern-style peach cobbler served with vanilla ice cream and walnuts is scrumptious. **Features:** full bar. **Address:** 442 Atlanta Hwy NW 30680 **Location:** On US 29 business route; just w of center.

[L] [D] CALL [&M]

WOODSTOCK pop. 23,896

COMFORT SUITES   (770)517-9650

Hotel. $94-$200 **Address:** 340 Parkway 575 30188 **Location:** I-575 exit 7, just e to Parkway 575, then just n. **Facility:** 59 units. 3 stories, interior corridors. **Pool(s):** outdoor. **Activities:** exercise room. **Guest Services:** valet and coin laundry.

[TI+] CALL [&M] [≈] [BIZ] [HS] [≈] [✕] [🖥] [🖨] [▣]

HAMPTON INN   (770)592-2323

Hotel. $104-$124 **Address:** 450 Parkway 575 30188 **Location:** I-575 exit 7, just e to Parkway 575, then just n. **Facility:** 60 units. 3 stories, interior corridors. **Terms:** 1-7 night minimum stay, cancellation fee imposed. **Pool(s):** outdoor. **Activities:** limited exercise equipment. **Guest Services:** valet and coin laundry.

> **AAA Benefit:**
> Members save up to 10%!

[TI+] CALL [&M] [≈] [BIZ] [HS] [≈] [✕] [🖥] [🖨] [▣]

Dream. Plan. Go.
Picture yourself on the ideal road trip.

TripTik® Travel Planner

AAA.com/ttp

MICROTEL INN & SUITES BY WYNDHAM WOODSTOCK/ATLANTA NORTH   (678)738-0001

Hotel. $59-$86 **Address:** 305 Molly Ln 30189 **Location:** I-575 exit 7, just w. **Facility:** 69 units. 3 stories, interior corridors. **Pool(s):** outdoor. **Activities:** exercise room. **Guest Services:** coin laundry.

[TI+] CALL [&M] [≈] [BIZ] [HS] [≈]
/ [SOME UNITS] [🖥] [🖨] [▣]

WHERE TO EAT

BUB-BA-Q   678/402-1662

Barbecue. Casual Dining. $5-$20 **AAA Inspector Notes:** Hearty Southern sides complement this simple eatery's slow-cooked barbecue. Begin with some fried pickles, burnt rib ends or potato skins and then gnaw on succulent ribs or savor flavorful chicken, pork or brisket. A variety of sandwiches and burgers also are available. Desserts vary from day to day. **Features:** beer only. **Address:** 10020 Hwy 92 30188 **Location:** I-575 exit 7, 0.5 mi e; in Woodstock Square. [L] [D]

BURGER INN   770/926-1308

Sandwiches. Quick Serve. $2-$8 **AAA Inspector Notes:** This no frills eatery has a simple country charm that makes you feel at home. The menu features a variety of classic comfort foods such as biscuits and gravy for breakfast and chili dogs and onion rings for lunch. Due to the value and popularity of this restaurant have patience during peak dining hours. **Features:** patio dining. **Address:** 9680 Main St 30188 **Location:** I-575 exit 7, 0.9 mi e to Main St (Canton Rd), then just s. [B] [L] [🖐]

CANYONS BURGER COMPANY   678/494-8868

Burgers. Quick Serve. $4-$8 **AAA Inspector Notes:** This casual, quick service restaurant is known for delicious burgers such as the Grand Canyon, Blue Bayou, Black Diamond and Red Smoke. All are hand patted and come with a plethora of topping options. If you want something lighter, try a Vine-Ripened salad with your choice of protein and dressing. Finish off the meal with a MoonPie or a rich, creamy shake. **Address:** 335 Chambers St 30188 **Location:** I-575 exit 8, 0.5 mi e; downtown. [L] [D] CALL [&M]

CENTURY HOUSE TAVERN   770/693-4552

New American. Fine Dining. $15-$23 **AAA Inspector Notes:** Fresh local and regional ingredients combined with creative preparation techniques make this eatery a hot spot. Begin with some meats and cheeses or such small bites as cashews with honey and chili. The blue crab salad is a good small plate and the Alaskan halibut is a cannot miss entrée. **Features:** full bar, patio dining. **Address:** 125 E Main St 30188 **Location:** I-575 exit 8, 0.5 mi e to Main St, then just s; downtown. **Parking:** on-site and valet.

[L] [D] CALL [&M] [🖐]

CORNER BISTRO   770/924-1202

Sandwiches. Quick Serve. $6-$11 **AAA Inspector Notes:** A wide selection of hot and cold sandwiches dominates the menu at this simple eatery. Also available are burgers, quesadillas, wraps, soups and salads as well as breakfast items. Expect to find the servers friendly and accommodating. **Features:** patio dining. **Address:** 2360 Towne Lake Pkwy 30189 **Location:** I-575 exit 8, 1.4 mi e to Towne Lake Pkwy, then just n; in Colonnade Shopping Center.

[L] [D] CALL [&M]

DONOVAN'S IRISH COBBLER   770/693-8763

Irish. Casual Dining. $5-$15 **AAA Inspector Notes:** This family-owned and -operated spot professes to be where Irish and central Illinois traditions meet the South. Traditional Irish favorites such as bangers, fish and chips and shepherd's pie share menu space with many types of burgers and sandwiches. This place is known for its shoes, a choice of meat served over a slice of Texas toast, piled high with fries and topped with cheese sauce. On the weekends, come for breakfast, and Saturday night means music is on the schedule. **Features:** full bar, patio dining, Sunday brunch, happy hour. **Address:** 1025 Rose Creek Dr, Suite 500 30189 **Location:** I-575 exit 8, 1.3 mi w to Towne Lake Pkwy, then 2.3 mi n.

[L] [D] [LATE] CALL [&M] [🖐]

EL RANCHERO 770/516-6616

▼▼ Tex-Mex. Casual Dining. $5-$18 **AAA Inspector Notes:** This neighborhood eatery is known for friendly service and a menu of standard Tex-Mex, including fajitas, tacos, burritos and enchiladas which all taste great with fresh salsas. **Features:** full bar. **Address:** 1025 Rose Creek Dr, Suite 180 30188 **Location:** I-575 exit 8, 1.3 mi w to Towne Lake Pkwy, then 2.3 mi n.

L D CALL M

FIRE STONE WOOD FIRED PIZZA & GRILL 770/926-6778

▼▼ American. Casual Dining. $10-$32 **AAA Inspector Notes:** The Italian influence is heavy here as calamari, antipasti and baked pasta grace the menu along many choices of wood-fired pizza. Smoked salmon, figs, barbecue and spicy lamb chorizo are just a few of the pie topping options. The grilled free-range chicken breast is a good entrée and the lamb meatballs are a tasty appetizer. **Features:** full bar, patio dining. **Address:** 120 Chambers St 30188 **Location:** I-575 exit 8, 0.5 mi e to Main St, then just s; downtown.

L D CALL M

FREIGHT KITCHEN & TAP 770/924-0144

▼▼ American. Casual Dining. $8-$25 **AAA Inspector Notes:** Situated in a converted railroad depot, this kitchen features different takes on traditional American cuisine. The homage to the pig is pork belly, tenderloin and sausage made on the premises. Other interesting items include Georgia wild shrimp and bone-in pork chops as well as a catch of the day and braise of the day. There also is a great selection of beer and bourbon. **Features:** full bar, patio dining, Sunday brunch. **Address:** 251 E Main St, Suite K 30188 **Location:** I-575 exit 8, 0.5 mi e; downtown.

L D CALL M

GUSTON'S GRILLE 770/485-6565

▼▼ American. Casual Dining. $8-$17 **AAA Inspector Notes:** This friendly neighborhood eatery serves up grilled rib-eyes, chicken pot pie, drunken pork and numerous appetizers, salads, soups, sandwiches and burgers as well as luscious desserts. A large bar lets patrons kick back and live music can be enjoyed on weekends. **Features:** full bar, patio dining, Sunday brunch, happy hour. **Address:** 12195 Hwy 92 30188 **Location:** I-575 exit 7, 3 mi e; in Centre at Woodstock Shopping Center.

L D CALL M

HOT DOG HEAVEN 770/591-5605

▼ Hot Dogs. Quick Serve. $3-$8 **AAA Inspector Notes:** The hot dogs are great here, especially the chili cheese slaw dog, but the hamburger is one of the best I have had anywhere and that is saying a lot. The owners serve up some good hospitality as well as other food favorites including the Chicago dog, Italian beef sandwich and Reuben. The decadent, homemade doughnuts should be outlawed. **Features:** patio dining. **Address:** 8558 Main St 30188 **Location:** I-575 exit 8, 0.5 mi e; downtown. **Parking:** street only.

L 🐾

ICE MARTINI BAR 770/672-6334

▼▼ Sushi Small Plates. Fine Dining. $5-$20 **AAA Inspector Notes:** The tuna carpaccio here is sublime, the shrimp crunchy salad is succulent and the sushi rolls are divine. Artful presentations only further enhance the dining experience. Cocktails are expertly created and the sleek, chic, contemporary ambience combines with the creative cuisine to make for a great night of food sampling. Do not miss the desserts with such selections as caramel apple with pumpkin cream cake or vanilla crème brûlée. **Features:** full bar. **Address:** 380 Chambers St 30188 **Location:** I-575 exit 8, 0.5 mi e; downtown. **Parking:** street only. D LATE CALL M

IPP'S PASTARIA & BAR 770/517-7305

▼▼ Italian. Casual Dining. $9-$16 **AAA Inspector Notes:** This family-style eatery meshes traditional Italian favorites with new twists on this style of cooking. Pizzas, such as pesto chicken and Greek, come with a choice of three crust types and the panini, calzones and stromboli are good bets as well. Popular pastas include fettuccine Bolognese, baked ziti and seafood cannelloni. All meals begin with free garlic rolls. **Features:** full bar. **Address:** 8496 Main St 30188 **Location:** I-575 exit 8, 0.5 mi e; downtown. L D CALL M

IZUMI ASIAN BISTRO 678/238-1899

▼▼ Asian. Casual Dining. $6-$22 **AAA Inspector Notes:** Warm, attentive service provides for an enjoyable experience at this stylish, contemporary eatery. Both Japanese and Thai cuisine—including curries, stir-fries, teriyaki and tempura—share space on the menu. A sushi bar offers an array of offerings. **Features:** beer & wine. **Address:** 2035 Towne Lake Pkwy, Suite 150 30189 **Location:** I-575 exit 8, 1 mi w. L D CALL M

J. CHRISTOPHER'S 770/592-5990

▼▼ Breakfast. Casual Dining. $5-$12 **AAA Inspector Notes:** Blueberry crunch cakes, strawberry waffles and eggs Christopher are some of the breakfast favorites found here along with such seasonal items as pumpkin pancakes. Many traditional breakfast standards are available also. Lunch goodies include the club house burger and the classic club sandwich. Waldorf salad and signature soups are popular choices. **Address:** 315 Chambers St 30188 **Location:** I-575 exit 8, 0.5 mi e; downtown. B L CALL M

J. D.'S BAR-B-QUE 678/445-7730

▼ Barbecue. Casual Dining. $6-$24 **AAA Inspector Notes:** This family restaurant prides itself on pit-cooked barbecue and Brunswick stew. The wings are a popular item as are the ribs, sandwiches and burgers. I had the rib sandwich, it comes bone-in or bone-out, and was tasty and satisfying. The barbecue brisket and chicken were tempting also. Homemade desserts round out the menu. **Address:** 6557 Bells Ferry Rd 30189 **Location:** Jct SR 92 and Bells Ferry Rd, 2.5 mi n. L D

JUMP KITCHEN & SPORTS SALOON 678/388-7717

▼▼ American. Casual Dining. $7-$17 **AAA Inspector Notes:** Fried alligator tail and lobster bisque are a couple of the creative items found here. Staples include tasty barbecue meatloaf, cedarplank salmon and cowboy rib-eye. The Marty Robbins and Blue Ridge are just two of the good burger selections and guests cannot go wrong with kitchen wings and nachos. Servers are attentive and friendly. **Features:** full bar, happy hour. **Address:** 1085 Buckhead Crossing 30189 **Location:** I-575 exit 8, 0.8 mi w to Buckhead Crossing, then just n. L D CALL M

KANI HOUSE 770/592-5264

▼▼ Japanese. Casual Dining. $7-$29 **AAA Inspector Notes:** A no-frills Asian decor defines the relaxed atmosphere. Hibachi dinners, tempura, teriyaki, noodles, sushi and combination platters make up the extensive menu. Lunch box specials are big favorites. **Features:** beer & wine. **Address:** 2455 Towne Lake Pkwy, Suite 110 30189 **Location:** I-575 exit 8, 1.3 mi w to Towne Lake Pkwy, then just n. L D CALL M

LA PARRILLA MEXICAN RESTAURANT 770/928-3606

▼▼ Mexican. Casual Dining. $6-$16 **AAA Inspector Notes:** This festive and colorful restaurant bustles with activity from patrons eager to eat its tacos, enchiladas, burritos and fajitas and to sip its yummy margaritas. **Features:** full bar, patio dining, happy hour. **Address:** 1065 Buckhead Crossing 30188 **Location:** I-575 exit 8, 0.8 mi w. L D CALL M

MAGNOLIA THOMAS RESTAURANT 678/445-5789

▼▼▼ New Southern. Fine Dining. $17-$30 **AAA Inspector Notes:** For a taste of creative contemporary Southern fare, try a fried green tomato appetizer, a tomato timbale salad and an entrée of magnolia buttermilk fried chicken, sautéed beef tenderloin, Pecan River trout or eggplant pancakes. Guests may have a hard time resisting the luscious desserts. Attentive, cordial servers circulate through this converted historic home. **Features:** beer & wine, Sunday brunch. **Address:** 108 Arnold Mill Rd 30188 **Location:** I-575 exit 8, 0.6 mi e; downtown. D CALL M

NEW BANGKOK CABIN 770/726-9357

▼▼ Thai. Casual Dining. $7-$15 **AAA Inspector Notes:** Contemporary Asian decor distinguishes this small dining room, where patrons try authentic Thai cuisine. Curry dishes as well as noodles and rice and vegetable dishes are the primary dining options as are lunch specials. The tom yum soup is good as is the shrimp salad which can be a meal unto itself. **Features:** beer & wine. **Address:** 2990 Eagle Dr, Unit 107 30189 **Location:** I-575 exit 8, 2 mi w; in Shoppes at Eagle's Landing. L D

PACIFIC SPICE   770/928-1899

Asian. Casual Dining. $6-$26 AAA Inspector Notes: Pacific Spice has made quite the splash since opening its doors a few years ago. You can choose from many contemporary preparations of Chinese and Thai food, such as glazed walnut mango prawns, Mandarin ribs, Beijing duck, the ever-popular pad thai and several curry dishes. Lunch specials always are popular as are the spring rolls and Thai soup preparations. **Features:** beer & wine. **Address:** 6234 Old Hwy 5, Suite D15 30188 **Location:** Jct Canton Hwy (Old Hwy 5) and E Cherokee Dr; in Village Shoppes of East Cherokee.
L D CALL M

PAPA P'S   770/592-3100

Mexican. Casual Dining. $6-$14 AAA Inspector Notes: Enjoy favorite Mexican dishes along with a side of Irish at this spot. I had the chicken mole which was quite tasty and standards such as fajitas, burritos, tacos, tamales and enchiladas also looked great. The Irish items make for an interesting menu with staples like Irish stew, shepherd's pie and fish and chips. Bread pudding and flan are a couple of the tempting desserts. **Features:** patio dining, Sunday brunch, happy hour. **Address:** 2295 Towne Lake Pkwy, Suite 160 30189 **Location:** I-575 exit 8, 1.3 mi w; in Kroger plaza.
L D CALL M

PURE TAQUERIA   770/952-7873

Mexican. Casual Dining. $10-$16 AAA Inspector Notes: Creative appetizers such as lump crab fritters and ceviche lead into standard main courses of tacos, enchiladas, burritos and quesadillas. You also can choose from a wide variety of salsas. Occasional live music cranks up an already vibrant, bustling atmosphere. **Features:** full bar, patio dining, Sunday brunch, happy hour. **Address:** 405 Chambers St 30188 **Location:** I-575 exit 8, 0.5 mi e; downtown. **Parking:** street only. L D

SAIGON CAFE   770/384-8599

Asian. Casual Dining. $8-$12 AAA Inspector Notes: Café patrons can choose from among steaming-hot noodle bowls and Thai favorites. The pho ga (chicken noodle soup) is my favorite here, and I always get an appetizer like the goi cuon (fresh spring rolls with shrimp and pork). The curry dishes are a good choice and include panang and rama. Both Thai and Vietnamese food make up the menu. **Features:** beer & wine. **Address:** 12195 Hwy 92, Suite 132 30188 **Location:** I-575 exit 7, 3 mi e; in Centre at Woodstock.
L D CALL M

TAKEYA JAPANESE RESTAURANT   678/445-5599

Japanese. Casual Dining. $9-$38 AAA Inspector Notes: A sushi bar with a great variety of fresh sushi and sashimi, and hibachi-style grilled meals are two dining options diners can find at this Japanese restaurant. Both are available at lunch and dinner. Bento boxes are good lunch specials as well. Enjoy the show that the hibachi chefs put on while preparing the meal. **Features:** beer & wine, early bird specials. **Address:** 6242 Old Hwy 5 30188 **Location:** Jct Canton Hwy (Old Hwy 5) and E Cherokee Dr; in Village Shoppes of East Cherokee. L D CALL M

TUSCANY ITALIAN RESTAURANT   678/453-0888

Northern Italian. Casual Dining. $11-$28 AAA Inspector Notes: The great hillside location and the delicious cuisine make this a popular spot for locals and out-of-towners alike. Lunch specials, including Tuscany panini are popular and dinner entrées include linguine Bolognese, scampi marinara, spaghetti frutti di mare and some great pizza selections. **Features:** beer & wine. **Address:** 250 Cinema View Way 30189 **Location:** I-575 exit 8, 1 mi w, follow signs to cinemas. L D CALL M

VINGENZO'S   770/924-9133

Regional Italian. Casual Dining. $10-$19 AAA Inspector Notes: Head out to the veranda to sip a cappuccino while dining on bistro-style Neapolitan cuisine. In addition to fresh pizza, made-in-house pasta and a selection of to-go market foods, there are some gluten-free items. **Features:** beer & wine, patio dining. **Reservations:** suggested. **Address:** 105 E Main St 30188 **Location:** I-575 exit 8, 0.5 mi e; downtown. D CALL M

WRENS pop. 2,187

THE DUTCH HOUSE RESTAURANT AND BAKERY   706/547-3261

Comfort Food. Buffet Style. $8-$22 AAA Inspector Notes: The family-friendly restaurant provides a rotating menu of blue-plate specials throughout the week, with fried chicken and roast beef in gravy mainstays appearing on the buffet line daily along with salads and a selection of hot vegetables and casseroles. What you'll really appreciate is the first decision you'll have to make when entering the line: Which dessert looks most tempting? Each is made fresh in the on-site bakery. Dinner service is offered Friday and Saturday. **Address:** 14455 Hwy 1 30833 **Location:** Jct US 1 and SR 88, 1.6 mi s. B L CALL M

YOUNG HARRIS pop. 899

BRASSTOWN VALLEY RESORT   706/379-9900

Resort Hotel. Rates not provided. **Address:** 6321 US Hwy 76 30582 **Location:** US 76 and US 76/SR 515. Located in a quiet area. **Facility:** Nestled in the quiet North Georgia mountains, this resort offers upscale designer furniture, panoramic mountain views and outdoor activities like fly fishing, golf and a new full-service spa. 134 units, some cottages. 5 stories, interior corridors. **Parking:** on-site and valet. **Terms:** check-in 4 pm. **Amenities:** safes. **Dining:** 2 restaurants. **Pool(s):** heated indoor. **Activities:** sauna, hot tub, steamroom, fishing, regulation golf, tennis, recreation programs, playground, game room, lawn sports, picnic facilities, trails, exercise room, spa. **Guest Services:** valet and coin laundry.

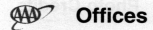 # Offices

Main office listings are shown in **BOLD TYPE** and toll-free member service numbers appear in *ITALIC TYPE*.
All are closed Saturdays, Sundays and holidays unless otherwise indicated.
The addresses, phone numbers and hours for any AAA/CAA office are subject to change.
The type of service provided is designated below the name of the city where the office is located:

✚ Auto travel services, including books and maps, and on-demand TripTik® routings.
● Auto travel services, including selected books and maps, and on-demand TripTik® routings.
■ Books/maps only, no marked maps or on-demand TripTik® routings.
▲ Travel Agency Services, cruise, tour, air, car and rail reservations; domestic and international hotel reservations; passport photo services; international and domestic travel guides and maps; travel money products; and International Driving Permits. In addition, assistance with travel related insurance products including trip cancellation, travel accident, lost luggage, trip delay and assistance products.
✪ Insurance services provided. If only this icon appears, only insurance services are provided at that office.
C Car Care Plus Facility provides car care services.
▣ Electric vehicle charging station on premises.

AAA NATIONAL OFFICE: 1000 AAA DRIVE, HEATHROW, FLORIDA 32746-5063, (407) 444-7000

GEORGIA

ATLANTA—AAA AUTO CLUB GROUP, 2161 LAVISTA RD NE, 30329. WEEKDAYS (M-F) 7:30-6:00, SAT 8:00-4:00. (404) 235-6754 C

ATLANTA—AAA AUTO CLUB GROUP, 2161 LAVISTA RD NE, 30329. WEEKDAYS (M-F) 8:30-6:00, SAT 10:00-4:00. (404) 633-9418 ✚ ▲ ✪

ATLANTA—AAA AUTO CLUB GROUP, 4410 ROSWELL RD, 30342. WEEKDAYS (M-F) 7:30-6:00, SAT 8:00-4:00. (404) 847-1070 C

ATLANTA—AAA AUTO CLUB GROUP, 4410 ROSWELL RD, 30342. WEEKDAYS (M-F) 8:30-6:00, SAT 10:00-4:00. (404) 843-4500 ✚ ▲ ✪

AUGUSTA—AAA AUTO CLUB GROUP, 3601 WALTON WAY EXT, 30909. WEEKDAYS (M-F) 9:00-6:00. (706) 738-6611 ✚ ▲ ✪

COLUMBUS—AAA AUTO CLUB GROUP, 5592 WHITESVILLE RD ST T, 31904. WEEKDAYS (M-F) 9:00-6:00. (706) 324-7121 ✚ ▲ ✪

JOHNS CREEK—AAA AUTO CLUB GROUP, 7150 MCGINNIS FERRY RD, 30024. WEEKDAYS (M-F) 7:30-6:00, SAT 8:00-4:00. (678) 417-0775 C

JOHNS CREEK—AAA AUTO CLUB GROUP, 7150 MCGINNIS FERRY RD, 30024. WEEKDAYS (M-F) 8:30-6:00, SAT 10:00-4:00. (678) 417-5578 ✚ ▲ ✪

MACON—AAA AUTO CLUB GROUP, 205 TOM HILL SR BLVD, 31210. WEEKDAYS (M-F) 8:30-5:30. (478) 471-0800 ✚ ▲ ✪

MARIETTA—AAA AUTO CLUB GROUP, 1197 JOHNSON FERRY RD, 30068. WEEKDAYS (M-F) 8:30-6:00, SAT 10:00-4:00. (770) 565-5700 ✚ ▲ ✪

MARIETTA—AAA AUTO CLUB GROUP, 1197 JOHNSON FERRY RD 100, 30068. WEEKDAYS (M-F) 7:30-6:00, SAT 8:00-4:00. (770) 565-5700 C

MARIETTA—AAA AUTO CLUB GROUP, 3445 GORDY PKWY, 30066. WEEKDAYS (M-F) 7:30-6:00, SAT 8:00-4:00. (770) 973-8126 C

MARIETTA—AAA AUTO CLUB GROUP, 3445 GORDY PKWY, 30066. WEEKDAYS (M-F) 8:30-6:00, SAT 10:00-4:00. (770) 973-2031 ✚ ▲ ✪

MORROW—AAA AUTO CLUB GROUP, 1500 MT ZION RD STE 205, 30260. WEEKDAYS (M-F) 9:00-6:00. (770) 961-8085 ✚ ▲ ✪

ROSWELL—AAA AUTO CLUB GROUP, 1035 MANSELL RD, 30076. WEEKDAYS (M-F) 7:30-6:00, SAT 8:00-4:00. (770) 518-3294 C

ROSWELL—AAA AUTO CLUB GROUP, 1035 MANSELL RD, 30076. WEEKDAYS (M-F) 8:30-6:00, SAT 10:00-4:00. (770) 518-3286 ✚ ▲ ✪

SAVANNAH—AAA AUTO CLUB GROUP, 712 MALL BLVD, 31406. WEEKDAYS (M-F) 9:00-6:00. (912) 352-8222 ✚ ▲ ✪

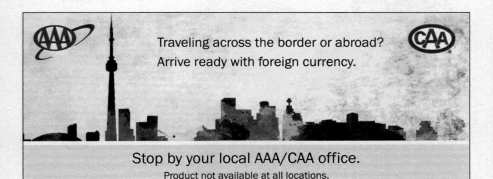

Photo Credits

Page numbers are in bold type. Picture credit abbreviations are as follows:
- (i) numeric sequence from top to bottom, left to right ▪ (AAA) AAA Travel library.

- (Cover) Centennial Olympic Park, Atlanta / © iStockphoto.com / Xavier Arnau

- **2** (i) © iStockphoto.com / Sean Pavone

- **2** (ii) © iStockphoto.com / Lisa Santore

- **2** (iii) © Durden Images / Shutterstock.com

- **2** (iv) © iStockphoto.com / aimintang

- **8** (i) © Durden Images / Shutterstock.com

- **8** (ii) © Rob Bixby / flickr

- **9** © Evilarry / Wikimedia Commons

- **10** (i) © Library of Congress / Wikimedia Commons

- **10** (ii) Courtesy of Wikimedia Commons

- **13** (i) © iStockphoto.com / Sean Pavone

- **13** (ii) © iStockphoto.com / mstroz

- **13** (iii) © iStockphoto.com / Lisa Santore

- **13** (iv) © AAA. Photo submitted by Jordan Krumbine

- **13** (v) © iStockphoto.com / nkuzmina

- **14** (i) © iStockphoto.com / aimintang

- **14** (ii) © Mark Goebel / flickr

- **14** (iii) © Clinton Steeds / flickr

- **14** (iv) © iStockphoto.com / Eneri LLC

- **43** © iStockphoto.com / Sean Pavone

- **46** © iStockphoto.com / Sterling Stevens

- **47** © DJLamar / Wikimedia Commons

- **48** © Ayleen Gaspar / flickr

- **49** © Lauren Holley / flickr

- **50** © Chris Yunker / flickr

- **51** Published with permission from AAA associate Diana Beyer

- **52** © iStockphoto.com / Bochkarev Photography

- **53** © Andre Jenny / Alamy Stock Photo

- **54** © iStockphoto.com / cyano66

- **58** © rasputin243 / Wikimedia Commons

- **63** © Daderot / Wikimedia Commons

Connect with #AAA and #CAA for the latest updates.

 AAA.com/Facebook
 AAA.com/Twitter
 AAA.com/Googleplus
 YouTube.com/AAA

CAA Social Media: CAA.ca/social

LET'S GET SOCIAL

GET YOUR DRIVE TRIP BACK ON TRACK

When a drive trip takes an unexpected turn, use the **MOBILE APP** or go **ONLINE** to quickly request roadside service.

- App GPS identifies your location

- Maps show the service vehicle en route to your location

- Status notifications keep you updated

AAA.com/mobile
CAA.ca/mobile

Planning a trip?

Reduce your risk of identity theft with these tips:

- Put mail on hold
- Leave important cards and documents behind
- Pay for purchases using a credit card
- Inform your bank and credit card company of your trip
- Don't post on social media sites while away

Before you go, contact us to learn about identity monitoring products available in your area.

Visit **AAA.com/IDtheft** or **CAA.ca**

Bring It Home

You always want the best for those you care about. Extend the same benefits you enjoy with a **AAA/CAA Associate Membership.** With roadside assistance, vacation planning, travel guides, exclusive savings, and much more, they can rely on AAA/CAA.

To purchase an Associate Membership, contact your local club office, visit **AAA.com** or **CAA.ca**, or call **800-Join-AAA** (564-6222).